SCHAUM'S OUTLINE OF

THEORY AND PROBLEMS

of

MATHEMATICS
for
ECONOMISTS

•

by

EDWARD T. DOWLING, Ph.D.

Chairman and Associate Professor
Department of Economics
Fordham University

SCHAUM'S OUTLINE SERIES

McGRAW-HILL BOOK COMPANY

New York   St. Louis   San Francisco   Auckland   Bogotá   Düsseldorf   Johannesburg
London   Madrid   Mexico   Montreal   New Delhi   Panama   Paris
São Paulo   Singapore   Sydney   Tokyo   Toronto

To my mother, May Finegan Dowling,
and to the memory of my father, Edward T. Dowling, M.D.

EDWARD T. DOWLING is Associate Professor of Economics at Fordham University, where he has been a member of the faculty since 1973. He served as Assistant Chairman of the Economics Department from 1975–1979 and was elected Chairman of the Department in 1979. His major areas of interest are economic development and mathematical economics. Dr. Dowling received his Ph.D. from Cornell University and has spent six years teaching and doing research in Southeast Asia. He has published articles in economic journals and is coauthor with Dominick Salvatore of *Schaum's Outline of Development Economics.* He is also a Jesuit priest, and a member of the Jesuit Community at Fordham.

Schaum's Outline of Theory and Problems of
MATHEMATICS FOR ECONOMISTS

3 4 5 6 7 8 9 10 11 12 13 14 15 16 17 18 19 20   SH   SH   8 5 4 3 2 1

Sponsoring Editor, Harriet Malkin
Editing Supervisor, Denise Schanck
Production Manager, Nick Monti

Library of Congress Cataloging in Publication Data

Dowling, Edward Thomas, 1938-
    Schaum's outline of mathematics for economists.

    (Schaum's outline series)
    Includes index.
    1. Mathematics—1961-   2. Economics, Mathe-
matical. I. Title.
QA37.2.D68   510'.2'433   79–22704
ISBN 0–07–017760–0

Preface

The importance of mathematics in the study of economics today requires that the student be familiar with a wide variety of mathematical concepts. *Mathematics for Economists* is designed to fill this need by presenting a thorough, easily understood introduction to differential and integral calculus, matrix algebra, linear programming, differential equations, and difference equations, with applications to economic problems. Since textbooks differ in the order in which differential calculus and linear algebra are presented, Chapters 10 and 11 on linear algebra have been designed for coverage after Chapter 2 if desired, with no loss in continuity.

The theory-and-solved-problem format of each chapter provides concise explanations illustrated by examples, plus numerous problems with fully worked-out solutions. The topics and related problems range in difficulty from simpler mathematical operations to sophisticated applications. No mathematical proficiency beyond the high-school level is assumed. This learning-by-doing pedagogy will enable students to progress at their own rate and adapt the book to their own needs.

Mathematics for Economists is intended primarily as a supplement for undergraduate and graduate students in economics and business. In addition, its comprehensive nature makes it appropriate for use by students of mathematics and the social sciences; it will also serve as a useful guide in preparing for the mathematical proficiency exams.

Mathematics for Economists is the newest title in the Schaum's Outline Series in Economics. The series includes *Microeconomic Theory*, *Macroeconomic Theory*, *Development Economics*, and *International Economics*, as well as the forthcoming *Principles of Economics*.

Because I could not have completed this book alone, I wish to express my deep gratitude to my colleague, Dr. Dominick Salvatore, for his continued support, interest, and availability; and to Sister Mary Immaculate Occhipinti, C.S.A.C., for her patience and diligence in typing the manuscript. I am grateful also to the graduate students at Fordham, especially Mary Acker, Edward Barbour, Evelyn Grossman, Rosemary Thomas, and Ann Waldron, for their helpful contributions throughout the development of the manuscript. Finally, I should like to thank the entire McGraw-Hill staff for their kind assistance.

EDWARD T. DOWLING

Contents

CONTENTS

CONTENTS

CONTENTS

Chapter 1

Terminology, Concepts, and Tools

1.1 CONSTANTS, VARIABLES, PARAMETERS, AND COEFFICIENTS

A typical supply equation takes the form

$$Q_s = -a + bP \tag{1.1}$$

where Q_s = quantity supplied and P = price. A *constant* is a quantity that does not change in a given problem. A *numerical constant* has the same value in all problems; a *symbolic constant* or *parameter*, such as a and b in (1.1), has the same value within a given problem but may assume other values in different problems. A *variable* ranges over a set of possible values within a given problem. In (1.1), Q_s and P are variables. Since the value of Q_s depends on P, Q_s is called the *dependent variable*, and P is called the *independent variable*. If there is a system of equations, the variables determined within the system are called *endogenous*; those determined outside the system are *exogenous*. A numerical or symbolic constant placed before a variable as a multiplier, such as b in (1.1), is called a *coefficient*.

Example 1. Given $C = 50 + 0.85Y$, where C = consumption and Y = income, C and Y are variables because Y can assume any positive value and C will change in the precise way set forth by the equation. 50 and 0.85 are numerical constants. C is the dependent variable and Y is the independent variable, because the value of C depends on Y; 0.85 is the coefficient of Y.

1.2 FUNCTIONS

A *function*, such as $y = f(x)$, expresses a relationship between two variables (x, y) such that for each value of x, there exists one and only one value of y, as illustrated in Example 2. The symbol $f(x)$ reads "f of x." y is called the *value* of the function; x is termed the *argument* of the function. x and y are also referred to as the *independent* and *dependent variables*, respectively. Functions can be expressed verbally, algebraically, or graphically (see Example 3).

Example 2. In Fig. 1-1(a), y is a function of x, $y = f(x)$, because for each value of x there exists one and only one value of y (e.g. for $x = 4$, $y = 2$). In Fig. 1-1(b), however, y is not a function of x, $y \neq f(x)$, because there is more than one value of y for a given value of x (e.g. for $x = 4$, $y = 2$ *and* 6).

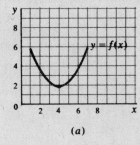

(a) (b)

Fig. 1-1

1

Example 3. Economists frequently refer to the relationship between consumption and income. Since consumption depends on income in a systematic way, consumption is said to be a function of income. The relationship is expressed algebraically as $C = f(Y)$. Note that the symbol $f(Y)$ means that C is a function of Y, and not f multiplied by Y. The graphic representation of this consumption function is shown in Fig. 1-2.

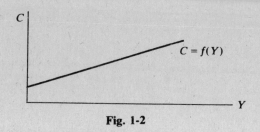

Fig. 1-2

Example 4. Other letters besides f can be used to denote a function. Instead of $y = f(x)$, one may use $y = g(x)$, $y = F(x)$, $y = G(x)$. If y and z are both functions of x, then different notation should be used for each, i.e. $y = f(x)$, $z = g(x)$. The Greek letters ϕ and ψ are also frequently used, as in $y = \phi(x)$ or $z = \psi(x)$. For greater economy and simplicity, economic textbooks frequently eliminate f and g and express functions simply as $y = y(x)$, $z = z(x)$, and $C = C(Y)$.

1.3 GENERAL VS. SPECIFIC FUNCTIONS

A *general function* enumerates the independent variables which influence the dependent variable, but does not enunciate the way in which they influence it. A *specific function* lists the arguments and the way in which they influence the dependent variable. See Example 5.

Example 5. Economists hold that the quantity of a good a consumer will buy depends on its price, the consumer's income, the price of related goods, and taste. This relationship can be expressed by the general function

$$Q_d = f(P, Y, P_r, T) \tag{1.2}$$

where Q_d = quantity demanded, P = price, Y = income, P_r = price of related goods, and T = taste. Equation (*1.2*) lists the arguments but leaves unspecified the way in which demand depends on price or how demand varies with income. The same relationship can be expressed by the specific function

$$Q_d = 250 - 5P + 0.03\,Y + 0.2\,P_r + 0.02\,T \tag{1.3}$$

which clearly enunciates the magnitude and direction of the influence of the independent variables on the dependent variable. Here, for instance, an increase of one unit in P will lead to a decrease of 5 units in Q_d. Parameters can also be used in specific functions. Thus,

$$Q_d = a - bP + cY + dP_r + eT \tag{1.4}$$

In contrast to (*1.2*), (*1.4*) specifies that none of the arguments are raised to a power higher than 1.

1.4 GRAPHS, SLOPES, AND INTERCEPTS

A function of one independent variable, $y = f(x)$, can easily be graphed in a two-dimensional space. The dependent variable y is graphed on the vertical axis; the independent variable x on the horizontal. The *slope* of a line measures the change (Δ) in the value of the variable on the vertical axis divided by the change in the value of the variable on the horizontal axis. Thus, the slope is equal to $\Delta y/\Delta x$. The *vertical intercept* is the point at which the graph crosses the vertical axis. It will be found when the independent variable x equals zero. A simple review of graphs is given in Solved Problems 1.11 and 1.12.

Example 6. The graph of the function $y = 16 - 4x$ is given in Fig. 1-3. The slope $= \Delta y/\Delta x = -4/1 = -4$. The vertical intercept is 16. [When $x = 0$, $y = 16 - 4(0) = 16$.]

The slope of a straight line is constant. A positive slope indicates an upward-sloping line; a negative slope, a downward-sloping line. (Remember that graphs, like the English language, always read from left to right.) Sometimes in economics, however, the direction of the change is taken for granted and only the magnitude of the change is of interest. In this case the *absolute value* of the slope is given (i.e. the value of the slope independent of the sign).

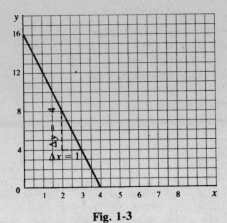

Fig. 1-3

Example 7. Graphs take different forms, depending on the function. Three functions frequently encountered in economics which involve a single independent variable are given below. Their corresponding graphs are shown in Fig. 1-4.

(1) Linear function: $y = a + bx$ No variable is raised to a power higher than 1.
(2) Quadratic function: $y = a + bx + cx^2$ Highest power to which a variable is raised is 2.
(3) Cubic function: $y = a + bx + cx^2 + dx^3$ Highest power to which a variable is raised is 3.

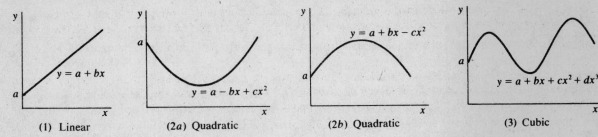

| (1) Linear | (2a) Quadratic | (2b) Quadratic | (3) Cubic |

Fig. 1-4

Points to note:

● The graph of a linear function will always be a straight line.

● The graph of a quadratic function with $c > 0$ is an upward-opening parabola; if $c < 0$, it is a downward-opening parabola.

● In all the functions, a gives the value of the vertical intercept.

● For linear functions, b gives the slope of the line. Check Example 6.

● Some of the parameters may at times be zero. For linear functions, a, but not b, may equal zero; for quadratic functions, a and b, but not c, may equal zero; for cubic functions, a, b, and c, but not d, may equal zero. If b and c in (3) equal zero, the cubic function reads $y = a + dx^3$.

1.5 INVERSE FUNCTIONS

Given a function $y = f(x)$, an *inverse function*, $x = f^{-1}(y)$ exists if each value of y yields a unique value of x. See Example 8.

Example 8. In traditional supply and demand analysis, $P = f(Q)$, with P graphed on the vertical axis and Q on the horizontal. In mathematically-oriented texts, $Q = F(P)$, with Q graphed on the vertical axis and P on the horizontal. To convert from one form of expression to the other, the inverse function is needed. Thus, if

$$Q_d = a - bP$$

then $bP = a - Q_d$ and $P = \dfrac{a - Q_d}{b} = \dfrac{a}{b} - \dfrac{Q_d}{b}$

See Solved Problems 1.10 and 2.3.

Example 9. Economic notation may also be confusing in another way. In mathematics y is typically used to designate the dependent variable. It is graphed on the vertical axis and the slope of the line is $\Delta y/\Delta x$. In economics, however, Y is generally used to designate income. In a typical consumption function such as $C = 25 + 0.75Y$, Y is the independent variable and will be graphed on the horizontal axis, as in Fig. 1-5. Here the slope of the line is $\Delta C/\Delta Y$ (i.e. the change in the dependent variable divided by the change in the independent variable). Be careful, therefore, to think in terms of dependent and independent variables, and not just symbols.

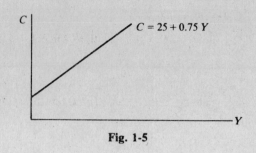

Fig. 1-5

Notice, too, that the consumption function is in the typical linear form $C = a + bY$, where $a = 25 =$ the vertical intercept and $b = 0.75 =$ the slope. Relating economics to math, a represents *autonomous consumption* since it indicates the level of consumption when $Y = 0$ and b equals the *marginal propensity to consume* (MPC), since it measures the change in consumption brought about by a unit change in income, $\Delta C/\Delta Y$.

1.6   SOLUTIONS

A single linear equation with a single unknown can be solved by moving the unknown variable to the left side of the equation and all the constants to the right. A single quadratic equation of the form, $ax^2 + bx + c = 0$, can be solved by factoring or by use of the quadratic formula

$$x_1, x_2 = \frac{-b \pm \sqrt{b^2 - 4ac}}{2a} \tag{1.5}$$

(Note that the traditional formula reverses the order of parameters and uses c instead of a for the vertical intercept, etc.)

Example 10. A typical profit function is $\pi = -Q^2 + 11Q - 24$, which from Fig. 1-4(2b) indicates that π will increase over a given range and then decrease. The breakeven point where $\pi = 0$ can be found with the quadratic formula where $a = -1$, $b = 11$, $c = -24$, and $x = Q$. Thus,

$$Q_1, Q_2 = \frac{-11 \pm \sqrt{(11)^2 - 4(-1)(-24)}}{2(-1)} = \frac{-11 \pm \sqrt{121 - 96}}{-2}$$

$$Q_1 = 3 \qquad Q_2 = 8$$

To solve a system of simultaneous equations, the equations must be (1) consistent (noncontradictory), (2) independent (not multiples of each other), and (3) there must be as many consistent and independent equations as variables. Such a system of simultaneous linear equations can be solved by the method of substitution or elimination (see Example 12). The method of determinants, discussed in Chapter 11, can also be used to solve such systems.

Example 11. The two equations below are an obvious example of inconsistency because $x + y$ cannot equal 6 and 10 at the same time.

$$x + y = 6 \qquad x + y = 10$$

The two equations below would not be independent, because the second equation is merely two times the first and so produces no new or independent information. The multiple relationship may not always be as obvious, however. See Problem 1.16.

$$2x + 3y = 13 \qquad 4x + 6y = 26$$

Example 12. The equilibrium conditions for two markets, butter and margarine, where P_b is the price of butter and P_m is the price of margarine, are given in (1.6) and (1.7) below.

$$8P_b - 3P_m = 7 \tag{1.6}$$

$$-P_b + 7P_m = 19 \tag{1.7}$$

The prices that will bring equilibrium to the model can be found by either the substitution or elimination method for solving simultaneous equations.

Substitution method

(1) Solve one of the equations for one variable in terms of the other.   Solving (*1.7*),

$$-P_b + 7P_m = 19$$
$$P_b = 7P_m - 19$$

(2) Substitute the value of that term in (*1.6*).

$$8P_b - 3P_m = 7$$
$$8(7P_m - 19) - 3P_m = 7$$
$$56P_m - 152 - 3P_m = 7$$
$$53P_m = 159 \qquad P_m = 3$$

(3) Substitute $P_m = 3$ in either (*1.6*) or (*1.7*) to find P_b.

$$8P_b - 3P_m = 7$$
$$8P_b - 3(3) = 7$$
$$8P_b = 16 \qquad P_b = 2$$

Elimination method

(1) Multiply (*1.7*) by the absolute value of the coefficient of P_b (or P_m) in (*1.6*) and (*1.6*) by the absolute value of the coefficient of P_b (or P_m) in (*1.7*).   If P_m is selected,

$$7(8P_b - 3P_m = 7) \qquad 56P_b - 21P_m = 49 \qquad\qquad (1.8)$$
$$3(-P_b + 7P_m = 19) \qquad -3P_b + 21P_m = 57 \qquad\qquad (1.9)$$

(2) Add or subtract (*1.8*) and (*1.9*), whichever is needed to eliminate the selected variable.   Adding here,

$$53P_b = 106 \qquad P_b = 2$$

(3) Substitute $P_b = 2$ in either (*1.6*) or (*1.7*) to find P_m, as in Step 3 above.

Solved Problems

FUNCTIONAL RELATIONSHIPS

1.1.   Given the two sets of equations

$$(1)\quad Q_d = a + bP \qquad (2)\quad S = -50 + 0.3Y$$
$$Q_s = c + dP \qquad\qquad I = 250 - 0.2i$$

where S = savings, I = investment, i = interest rate, and all the other variables are familiar, identify (*a*) the constants, as numerical and parametric; (*b*) the variables, as independent and dependent; and (*c*) the coefficients.

(*a*) In set (1), the constants are a, b, c, d; they are all parametric constants or parameters. In set (2), $-50, 0.3, 250$, and -0.2 are all numerical constants.

(*b*) In set (1), the variables are Q_d, Q_s, P, where Q_d and Q_s are dependent because their value is determined by P, and P is independent.   In set (2), S, Y, I, and i are variables; S and I are the dependent variables, Y and i are the independent variables.

(*c*) In set (1), b and d are coefficients, each being a multiplicative constant of the variable P.   In set (2), 0.3 and -0.2 are coefficients.

1.2.   (*a*) Define the term function.   (*b*) Which of the graphs in Fig. 1-6 does not represent y as a function of x?   Why?

(*a*) A function, $y = f(x)$,   indicates a relationship between y and x in which y depends on x and for each value of x there is a unique value for y.

(b) Figure 1-6(a) does not represent y as a function of x because for any given value of x, there is more than one value of y. For x_1, for example, there are three values of y: y_1, y_2, y_3. Figure 1-6(b), on the other hand, does indicate y is a function of x. For any given value of x, there is one and *only* one value of y. At x_2, $y = y_4$.

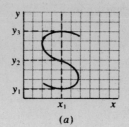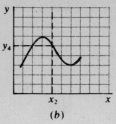

(a)   (b)

Fig. 1-6

1.3. Express each of the following statements in functional notation, giving first the general function, then the specific function. Practice the use of symbols other than $f(\ )$.

(a) The area (A) of a circle as a function of the radius (r).

(b) The perimeter (P) of a rectangle as a function of its length (l) and width (w).

(c) Total factor costs (TFC) as a function of the amount of labor (L) hired and the amount of capital (K) hired, when the price of labor is \$3 and the price of capital is \$5.

(d) Total revenue (TR) as a function of output (Q), when $P_Q = 5$.

(e) The daily wage bill (W) for labor (L) as a function of L, when $P_L = 42.50$ a day.

(a) $A = f(r)$, $A = \pi r^2$

(b) $P = g(l, w)$, $P = 2l + 2w$

(c) TFC $= \phi(K, L,)$, TFC $= 3L + 5K$

(d) TR $=$ TR(Q), TR $= 5Q$

(e) $W = W(L)$, $W = 42.50L$

1.4. A club agrees to serve 100 members at a price of \$15 each and any additional guests at a price of \$20 each. (a) Express the cost c of the banquet as a function of guests (G). (b) Identify the dependent and independent variables. (c) Draw the function as a graph.

(a) Since 100 members are coming at a cost of \$15 each, \$1500 is a fixed cost that will not vary with the number of guests invited. Costs will increase above \$1500 by \$20 for every guest invited. Thus, $c = 1500 + 20G$.

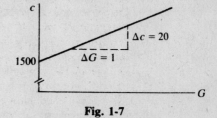

(b) c is the dependent variable since it depends on the number of guests invited. G is the independent variable because it is determined independently of the equation.

Fig. 1-7

(c) Since cost is the dependent variable, it is graphed on the vertical axis; the number of guests on the horizontal. The function is in the linear form of $y = a + bx$; 1500 is the vertical intercept and the slope is 20. See Fig. 1-7.

1.5. A firm's fixed costs (FC) are \$600 regardless of output; variable costs (VC) are \$5 per unit of output (Q). Total costs (TC) $=$ FC $+$ VC. The selling price of the good is \$10 per unit. State (a) the fixed cost function, (b) the variable cost function, (c) the total cost function, and (d) the total revenue function. (e) Find the breakeven point algebraically, and (f) graphically.

(a) Since the fixed cost is independent of output (Q), the fixed cost function is simply FC $= 600$.

(b) Variable costs are \$5 per unit of output, so VC $= 5Q$.

(c) Since TC $=$ FC $+$ VC, TC $= 600 + 5Q$.

(d) TR $= PQ$. Substituting $P = 10$, TR $= 10Q$.

(e) At the breakeven point, TR = TC.   Substituting from (c) and (d) above,

$$TR = TC$$
$$10Q = 600 + 5Q$$
$$5Q = 600 \qquad Q = 120 \qquad \text{the breakeven point}$$

(f) See Fig. 1-8.

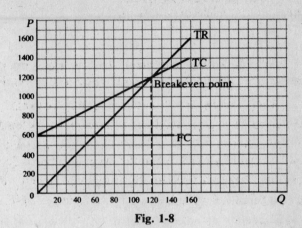

Fig. 1-8

1.6. From Table 1, (a) express savings (S) as a linear function of income. (b) Graph the function.

Table 1

Y	0	1000	2000	3000	4000
S	−400	−200	0	200	400

(a) As a linear function, the equation will take the form $S = a + bY$, where a is the vertical intercept and b is the slope. The vertical intercept is defined as the point where the independent variable (here Y) is zero. Hence, $a = -400$. In the savings function this point is also called *autonomous savings* since it represents a level of saving that takes place independent of income, or when income equals zero. The slope of the line (b) measures the change in the dependent variable (S) brought about by a change in the independent variable. Since saving increases by 200 for every 1000 increase in income, the slope $\Delta S/\Delta Y = \frac{200}{1000} = 0.2$. In economic terms, the slope $\Delta S/\Delta Y$ is also the *marginal propensity to save* (MPS), or the change in savings related to a unit change in income. The equation therefore reads

$$S = -400 + 0.2\,Y$$

(b) The function is graphed with savings (the dependent variable) on the vertical axis and income (the independent variable) on the horizontal. The graph may be plotted directly from the data in Table 1 or more simply by making use of the equation derived in (a). It will start at the vertical intercept (−400) and proceed upward at a rate (slope) of 0.2. See Fig. 1-9.

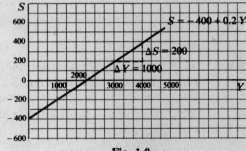

Fig. 1-9

1.7. Three separate economies are represented by the consumption functions (a) $C_1 = 1600 + 0.75\,Y$, (b) $C_2 = 750 + 0.9\,Y$, and (c) $C_3 = 1200 + 0.8\,Y$. Derive their respective savings functions.

(a) In a linear consumption function of the form $C = a + bY$, a = autonomous consumption and b = MPC (see Example 9). Here, therefore, 1600 is consumed independently of income. For this to be possible people must borrow 1600 or dissave that amount by dipping into their previous savings. Consequently, the level of autonomous saving is -1600. With $b = 0.75 =$ MPC, the MPS $= 0.25$ since MPC + MPS $= 1$. The savings function, therefore, is $S_1 = -1600 + 0.25Y$. This answer can also be found by using $S = Y - C$.

(b) $S_2 = -750 + 0.1Y$

(c) $S_3 = -1200 + 0.2Y$

1.8. Given $C = 25 + 0.6Yd$, $Yd = Y - T$, and $T = 5$, where Yd = disposable income and T = tax, express C as a function of Y, not Yd.

$$C = 25 + 0.6Yd$$

Substituting $Yd = Y - T$, $\qquad C = 25 + 0.6(Y - T)$

Substituting $T = 5$, $\qquad C = 25 + 0.6(Y - 5) = 25 + 0.6Y - 3 = 22 + 0.6Y$

1.9. Identify (a) $Y = f(C, I)$, (b) $Y = C_0 + bY + I_0$, and (c) $\pi = -Q^2 + 13Q - 42$ as a general or specific function. Explain.

Function (a) is general. It indicates a relationship between Y and C, I, but does not detail the precise way in which they are related.

Function (b) is specific, because it stipulates a linear relationship.

Function (c) is also specific. It is a quadratic function delineating the exact way in which Q influences π.

1.10. Find the inverse function for (a) $I = 130 + 0.25Y$ and (b) $Q_d = 75 - 15P$.

(a) Since I is a function of Y, the inverse function is found simply by making Y a function of I by solving for Y in terms of I. Thus,

$$I = 130 + 0.25Y$$
$$0.25Y = I - 130$$
$$Y = 4I - 520$$

(b) Similarly,

$$Q_d = 75 - 15P$$
$$15P = 75 - Q_d$$
$$P = 5 - \tfrac{1}{15}Q_d$$

GRAPHS

1.11. Graph the following equations and give the slopes and vertical intercepts:

(a) $3y - 6x = 3$ (b) $2y - \tfrac{2}{3}x = 6$ (c) $y + 5x - 20 = 0$ (d) $x + 2y - 4 = 0$

To graph an equation, first solve for one variable in terms of the other, usually the dependent in terms of the independent, or y in terms of x. Thus,

(a) $3y - 6x = 3$ (b) $2y - \tfrac{2}{3}x = 6$ (c) $y + 5x - 20 = 0$ (d) $x + 2y - 4 = 0$

$\quad\ 3y = 3 + 6x$ $\quad\ 2y = 6 + \tfrac{2}{3}x$ $\qquad y = 20 - 5x$ $\qquad y = 2 - \tfrac{1}{2}x$

$\quad\ \ y = 1 + 2x$ $\quad\ \ y = 3 + \tfrac{1}{3}x$

Then construct a schedule of the different combinations of points that fit the equation and plot the points. See Fig. 1-10. For a linear function you need only draw a straight line between any two points, or you can use your knowledge of a linear equation $y = a + bx$ to construct the line directly by starting from the vertical intercept a and proceeding with the proper slope b.

Equation (a):

$$\text{Slope} = \frac{\Delta y}{\Delta x} = \frac{+2}{+1} = +2$$

For every positive one unit change in x, y increases by 2.

$$\text{Vertical intercept} = 1$$

When $x = 0$, $y = 1 + 2(0) = 1$.

x	y
0	1
1	3
2	5
3	7
4	9
5	11

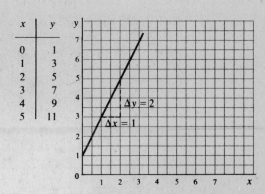

Fig. 1-10 (a)

Equation (b):

$$\text{Slope} = \frac{\Delta y}{\Delta x} = \frac{+1}{+3} = +\frac{1}{3}$$

For every positive one unit change in x, y increases by $\frac{1}{3}$.

$$\text{Vertical intercept} = 3$$

When $x = 0$, $y = 3 + \frac{1}{3}(0) = 3$.

x	y
0	3
1	$3\frac{1}{3}$
2	$3\frac{2}{3}$
3	4
4	$4\frac{1}{3}$
5	$4\frac{2}{3}$
6	5

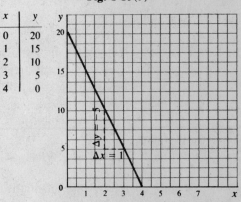

Fig. 1-10 (b)

Equation (c):

$$\text{Slope} = \frac{\Delta y}{\Delta x} = \frac{-5}{+1} = -5$$

For every positive one unit change in x, y decreases by 5.

$$\text{Vertical intercept} = 20$$

When $x = 0$, $y = 20 - 5(0) = 20$.

x	y
0	20
1	15
2	10
3	5
4	0

Fig. 1-10 (c)

Equation (d):

$$\text{Slope} = \frac{\Delta y}{\Delta x} = \frac{-1}{+2} = -\frac{1}{2}$$

For every positive one unit change in x, y falls by $\frac{1}{2}$.

$$\text{Vertical intercept} = 2$$

When $x = 0$, $y = 2 - \frac{1}{2}(0) = 2$.

x	y
0	2
1	$1\frac{1}{2}$
2	1
3	$\frac{1}{2}$
4	0

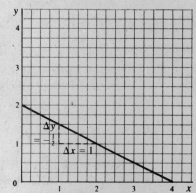

Fig. 1-10 (d)

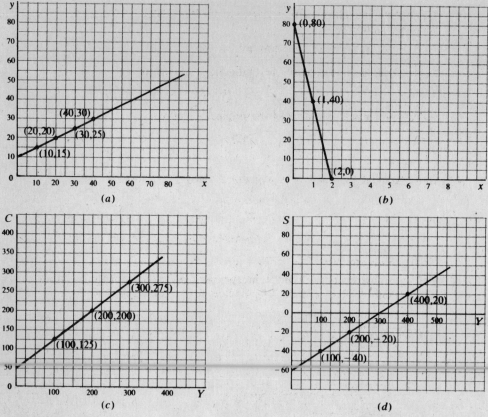

Fig. 1-11

1.12. Determine the slopes and vertical intercepts of the graphs shown in Fig. 1-11.

(a)   Slope $= \Delta y/\Delta x = +5/+10 = +1/2$.   For every positive one unit change in x, y increases by $\frac{1}{2}$.   Vertical intercept $= 10$.   When $x = 0$, $y = 10$.

(b)   Slope $= \Delta y/\Delta x = -40/1 = -40$.   For every positive one unit change in x, y decreases by 40.   Vertical intercept $= 80$.

(c)   Slope $= \Delta C/\Delta Y = +75/100 = +3/4 = 0.75$.   Vertical intercept $= 50$.

(d)   Slope $= \Delta S/\Delta Y = +20/100 = +1/5 = 0.2$.   Vertical intercept $= -60$.

1.13. Using your knowledge of math, give the equations for each of the graphs in Fig. 1-11.

(a) $y = 10 + \frac{1}{2}x$ (b) $y = 80 - 40x$ (c) $C = 50 + \frac{3}{4}Y$ (d) $S = -60 + \frac{1}{5}Y$

Note: Because these graphs are linear (straight-line) functions, they all conform to the general formula $y = a + bx$, where $a =$ the vertical intercept and $b =$ the slope.

1.14. What important economic information do Fig. 1-11(c) and (d) provide?

The vertical intercept in Fig. 1-11(c) indicates the level of autonomous consumption in society; the slope of the line ($\Delta C/\Delta Y$) represents society's MPC.   Similarly, the vertical intercept in Fig. 1-11(d) represents the level of autonomous saving while the slope indicates the MPS or $\Delta S/\Delta Y$.   This information can also be read directly from the equations in Problem 1.13 where a equals the autonomous levels of consumption or saving and b equals the MPC or MPS.

1.15. Solve the set of simultaneous equations given below (a) algebraically, using the elimination method, and (b) graphically.   (c) Classify the set as consistent or inconsistent, independent or dependent.

$$2x - 4y = -24 \qquad 9x - 3y = -3$$

(a) Using the elimination method discussed in Example 12, multiply the first equation by 3 and the second equation by 4.

$$3(2x - 4y = -24) \qquad 4(9x - 3y = -3) \qquad 6x - 12y = -72 \qquad 36x - 12y = -12$$

Subtract the second equation from the first, eliminating y.

$$-30x = -60 \qquad x = 2$$

Substitute $x = 2$ in either of the original equations.

$$2(2) - 4y = -24$$
$$-4y = -28 \qquad y = 7$$

(b) In a graphical approach, each equation is solved for y in terms of x:

$$2x - 4y = -24 \qquad\qquad 9x - 3y = -3$$
$$-4y = -24 - 2x \qquad\qquad -3y = -3 - 9x$$
$$y = 6 + \tfrac{1}{2}x \qquad\qquad y = 1 + 3x$$

The graph is shown in Fig. 1-12.

(c) The equations are consistent and independent, providing a unique solution $(x = 2, \ y = 7)$.   The single point of intersection in Fig. 1-12 confirms this conclusion.

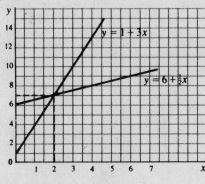

Fig. 1-12

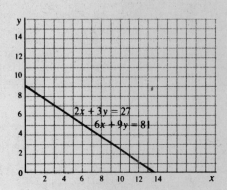

Fig. 1-13

1.16.   Redo Problem 1.15 in terms of the following set of equations:

$$2x + 3y = 27$$
$$6x + 9y = 81$$

(a) To eliminate x, multiply the first equation by 6 and the second by 2, or more simply, multiply the first equation by 3.   Thus,

$$3(2x + 3y = 27) \qquad 6x + 9y = 81$$

Since the two equations are now identical, it is obvious that one was merely a multiple of the other.   There is not enough information for a unique solution, because there is only one equation but two unknowns.

(b) Graphically, the two equations are solved for y in terms of x:

$$2x + 3y = 27 \qquad\qquad 6x + 9y = 81$$
$$3y = 27 - 2x \qquad\qquad 9y = 81 - 6x$$
$$y = 9 - \tfrac{2}{3}x \qquad\qquad y = 9 - \tfrac{2}{3}x$$

The graph appears in Fig. 1-13.

(c) Since any number of combinations for x and y will satisfy both equations, there is no unique solution.   The fact that the graphs of the two lines coincide, or are identical, is further evidence that the equations are consistent but dependent.

1.17. Redo Problem 1.15 in terms of the following set of equations. Use the substitution method in part (a).

$$2x - 4y = -8$$
$$6y - 3x = 24$$

(a) Using the substitution method, the first equation is solved for x in terms of y, as follows:

$$2x - 4y = -8$$
$$2x = -8 + 4y$$
$$x = 2y - 4$$

Substituting $x = 2y - 4$ into the second equation,

$$6y - 3x = 24$$
$$6y - 3(2y - 4) = 24$$
$$6y - 6y + 12 = 24$$
$$12 \neq 24$$

(b) Graphically, the results of the following computations are shown in Fig. 1-14.

$$2x - 4y = -8 \qquad\qquad 6y - 3x = 24$$
$$-4y = -8 - 2x \qquad\qquad 6y = 24 + 3x$$
$$y = 2 + \tfrac{1}{2}x \qquad\qquad y = 4 + \tfrac{1}{2}x$$

(c) The lack of a solution in part (a) indicates that these equations are inconsistent. Further, two lines that never intersect (such as two parallel lines) will not produce a unique solution and denote inconsistent equations.

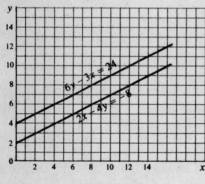

Fig. 1-14

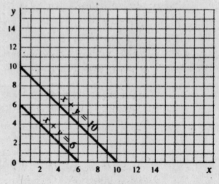

Fig. 1-15

1.18. Discuss the set of simultaneous equations given below.

$$x + y = 6$$
$$x + y = 10$$

It is immediately evident that the equations are inconsistent because $x + y$ cannot equal 6 and 10 at the same time. The graphs of the two equations (where $y = 6 - x$ and $y = 10 - x$) reveal parallel lines, and thus support this conclusion. See Fig. 1-15.

ALGEBRAIC SOLUTIONS

1.19. The demand for sugar is given by the function $Q_d = 30 - \tfrac{3}{5}P$. Find Q_d for (a) $P = 5$, (b) $P = 15$, and (c) $P = 25$.

(a) $Q_d = 30 - \tfrac{3}{5}(5) = 27$ (b) $Q_d = 30 - \tfrac{3}{5}(15) = 21$ (c) $Q_d = 30 - \tfrac{3}{5}(25) = 15$

1.20. Given the supply function $Q_s - 4P + 3 = 0$, find Q_s for (a) $P = 3$, (b) $P = 7$, and (c) $P = 12$.

(a) Rearranging terms, $Q_s = 4P - 3$. Thus, $Q_s = 4(3) - 3 = 9$.

(b) $Q_s = 4(7) - 3 = 25$ (c) $Q_s = 4(12) - 3 = 45$

1.21. Given $Q_d = 15 - \frac{1}{5}P$ and $Q_s = -1 + \frac{3}{5}P$, construct a schedule for Q_d and Q_s when $P = 5$, 10, 15, 20, 25. Circle the equilibrium price at which $Q_d = Q_s$.

P	5	10	15	20	25
Q_d	14	13	12	11	10
Q_s	2	5	8	11	14

1.22. Given $I = I_0 - bi$ where I_0 is autonomous investment and i is the interest rate. (a) If $I_0 = 100$ and $b = 250$, what is the level of investment when $i = 0.06, 0.07, 0.08$? (b) Find b if $I = 115$, $I_0 = 175$, and $i = 0.12$.

(a) $I_1 = 100 - 250(0.06) = 100 - 15 = 85$ (b) $I = I_0 - bi$

$I_2 = 100 - 250(0.07) = 100 - 17.50 = 82.50$ $115 = 175 - b(0.12)$

$I_3 = 100 - 250(0.08) = 100 - 20 = 80$ $-60 = -0.12b$

$b = 500$

1.23. The profit functions for two different firms are given by π_1 and π_2, respectively.

$$\pi_1 = -Q^2 + 17Q - 42 \qquad \pi_2 = -Q^2 + 16Q - 38$$

(a) At what level of output will the first firm earn zero profits?

(b) At what level of output will the second firm earn a profit of $25?

(a) If π_1 is equal to zero, $-Q^2 + 17Q - 42 = 0$. The function is then in the proper form to apply the quadratic formula (see Example 10), where $a = -1$, $b = 17$, $c = -42$. Thus,

$$Q_1, Q_2 = \frac{-17 \pm \sqrt{(17)^2 - 4(-1)(-42)}}{2(-1)} = \frac{-17 \pm \sqrt{121}}{-2} = 14, 3$$

(b) If π_2 is to equal 25, $-Q^2 + 16Q - 38 = 25$ and $-Q^2 + 16Q - 63 = 0$. Applying the quadratic formula with $a = -1$, $b = 16$, $c = -63$,

$$Q_1, Q_2 = \frac{-16 \pm \sqrt{(16)^2 - 4(-1)(-63)}}{2(-1)} = \frac{-16 \pm \sqrt{4}}{-2} = 9, 7$$

1.24. An electronics firm produces TVs (T) and stereos (S). The *transformation curve* (also called the *production-possibility curve*), representing the different combinations of each good the firm can produce while using all of its resources efficiently, is given by the equation $S^2 + 3S + 5T = 130$.

Find (a) the maximum number of stereos the firm can produce, (b) the maximum number of TVs, (c) the maximum number of stereos if 18 TVs are produced, and (d) the maximum number of TVs if 7 stereos are produced. (e) Draw a graph of the firm's transformation curve.

(a) The firm will maximize its stereo production at the point where $T = 0$, i.e. when no TVs are produced. Thus,

$$S^2 + 3S + 5(0) = 130$$

$$S^2 + 3S - 130 = 0$$

Applying the quadratic formula,

$$S_1, S_2 = \frac{-3 \pm \sqrt{(3)^2 - 4(1)(-130)}}{2(1)} = \frac{-3 \pm \sqrt{529}}{2} = \frac{-3 \pm 23}{2} = 10, -13$$

$S = 10$, since negative numbers have no meaning in a production-possibilities curve.

(b) Stereo production will equal zero when TV production is maximized.

$$S^2 + 3S + 5T = 130$$
$$0 + 0 + 5T = 130 \qquad T = 26$$

(c) When 18 TVs are produced,

$$S^2 + 3S + 5(18) = 130$$
$$S^2 + 3S - 40 = 0$$
$$S_1, S_2 = \frac{-3 \pm \sqrt{(3)^2 - 4(1)(-40)}}{2(1)} = \frac{-3 \pm \sqrt{169}}{2} = 5, -8$$
$$S = 5$$

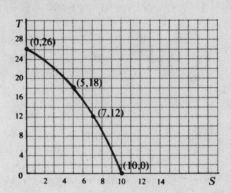

Fig. 1-16

(d) When stereo production equals 7,

$$S^2 + 3S + 5T = 130$$
$$(7)^2 + 3(7) + 5T = 130$$
$$5T = 60 \qquad T = 12$$

(e) The function is graphed by expressing T as a function of S.

$$5T = 130 - S^2 - 3S \qquad T = -\tfrac{1}{5}S^2 - \tfrac{3}{5}S + 26$$

Since it was determined in part (a) that $S = 10$ when $T = 0$, the horizontal intercept is 10. The vertical intercept was found in part (b), where $T = 26$ when $S = 0$. In parts (c) and (d) $T = 18$, $S = 5$, and $S = 7$, $T = 12$, respectively. The graph can be easily sketched using these four points. It will be a downward-opening parabola with only one side showing because S and T are restricted to positive values. See Fig. 1-16.

1.25. The transformation curve for a bakery is given by the function $B^2 + 2B + 4R - 168 = 0$ where B is bread and R is rolls. (a) What is the bakery's maximum capacity for rolls? For bread? (b) What combination will be produced if $B = 8$? If $B = 4$? If $R = 30$? (c) Draw the production-possibility curve.

(a) When total capacity is given to rolls, $B = 0$.

$$4R = 168 \qquad R = 42$$

If total capacity is given to bread, $R = 0$.

$$B^2 + 2B - 168 = 0$$

Applying the quadratic formula to the preceding equation, $B = 12$.

(b) If $B = 8$,
$$B^2 + 2B + 4R - 168 = 0$$
$$(8)^2 + 2(8) + 4R - 168 = 0$$
$$4R = 88 \qquad R = 22$$

If $B = 4$,
$$(4)^2 + 2(4) + 4R - 168 = 0$$
$$4R = 144 \qquad R = 36$$

If $R = 30$,
$$B^2 + 2B + 4(30) - 168 = 0$$
$$B^2 + 2B - 48 = 0$$

Use of the quadratic formula or simply factoring gives

$$(B + 8)(B - 6) = 0 \qquad B = -8 \qquad B = +6$$

Since negative values are unacceptable, $B = 6$.

(c) See Fig. 1-17.

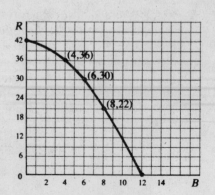

Fig. 1-17

Chapter 2

Economic Applications of Graphs and Equations

2.1 RELATIVE SCOPE OF GRAPHS AND EQUATIONS

Graphs are frequently used in economics when the problem at hand concerns the relationship between two variables or can be reduced to a problem of two variables. Such problems include supply and demand analysis, the income determination model, the marginal efficiency of investment, budget lines, and isocost curves. Equations are more versatile. They can be used as alternatives to graphs and can solve more complicated problems.

Example 1. An *isocost line* represents the different combinations of two inputs or factors of production that can be purchased with a given sum of money. The general formula is $P_K K + P_L L = E$, where K and L are capital and labor, P_K and P_L their respective prices, and E the amount allotted to expenditures. In isocost analysis the individual prices and the expenditure are initially held constant; only the different combinations of inputs are allowed to change. The function can then be graphed by expressing one variable in terms of the other. For example,

$$P_K K + P_L L = E$$
$$P_K K = E - P_L L$$
$$K = \frac{E - P_L L}{P_K}$$
$$= \frac{E}{P_K} - \left(\frac{P_L}{P_K}\right)L$$

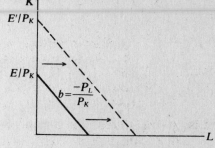

Fig. 2-1

This is the familiar linear function of the form $y = a + bx$, where $a = E/P_K =$ the vertical intercept and $b = -(P_L/P_K) =$ the slope. The graph is given by the solid line in Fig. 2-1.

From the equation and graph, the effects of a change in any one of the parameters are easily discernible. An increase in the expenditure from E to E' will increase the vertical intercept and cause the isocost line to shift out to the right (dashed line) parallel to the old line. The slope is unaffected because the slope depends on the relative prices $(-P_L/P_K)$ and prices are not affected by expenditure changes. A change in P_L will alter the slope of the line but leave the vertical intercept unchanged. A change in P_K will alter the slope and the vertical intercept. See Problems 2.6 and 2.7.

2.2 SUPPLY AND DEMAND ANALYSIS

Equilibrium in supply and demand analysis occurs when $Q_s = Q_d$. By equating the supply and demand functions, the equilibrium price and quantity can be determined.

Example 2. Given: $\qquad\qquad Q_s = -5 + 3P \qquad Q_d = 10 - 2P$

In equilibrium, $\qquad\qquad\qquad Q_s = Q_d$

Solving for P, $\qquad\qquad\qquad -5 + 3P = 10 - 2P$
$$5P = 15 \qquad P = 3$$

Substituting $P = 3$ in either of the equations,

$$Q_s = -5 + 3P = -5 + 3(3) = 4 = Q_d$$

15

2.3 INCOME DETERMINATION MODELS

Income determination models generally express the equilibrium level of income in a four-sector economy as

$$Y = C + I + G + (X - Z)$$

where Y = income, C = consumption, I = investment, G = government expenditures, X = exports, and Z = imports. By substituting the information supplied in the problem, it is an easy matter to solve for the equilibrium level of income. *Aggregating* (summing up) the variables on the right allows the equation to be graphed in two-dimensional space. See Problems 2.8 to 2.14.

Example 3. Assume a simple two-sector economy where $Y = C + I$, $C = C_0 + bY$, and $I = I_0$. Assume further that $C_0 = 85$, $b = 0.9$, and $I_0 = 55$. The equilibrium level of income can be calculated in terms of (1) the general parameters and (2) the specific values assigned to these parameters.

1. The *equilibrium equation* is

$$Y = C + I$$

Substituting for C and I,

$$Y = C_0 + bY + I_0$$

Solving for Y,

$$Y - bY = C_0 + I_0$$
$$(1 - b)Y = C_0 + I_0$$
$$Y = \frac{C_0 + I_0}{1 - b}$$

The solution in this form is called the reduced form. The *reduced form* (or *solution equation*) expresses the endogenous variable (here Y) as an explicit function of the exogenous variables (C_0, I_0) and the parameters (b).

2. The specific equilibrium level of income can be calculated by substituting the numerical values for the parameters in either the original equation (a) or the reduced form (b):

$$(a) \quad Y = C_0 + bY + I_0 = 85 + 0.9Y + 55$$
$$Y - 0.9Y = 140$$
$$0.1Y = 140$$
$$Y = 1400$$

$$(b) \quad Y = \frac{C_0 + I_0}{1 - b} = \frac{85 + 55}{1 - 0.9}$$
$$= \frac{140}{0.1} = 1400$$

The term $1/(1 - b)$ is called the *multiplier* in economics. It measures the multiple effect each dollar of autonomous spending has on the equilibrium level of income. Since $b = $ MPC in the income determination model, the multiplier $= 1/(1 - \text{MPC})$.

Note: Decimals may be converted to fractions for ease in working with the income determination model. For example, $0.1 = \frac{1}{10}$, $0.9 = \frac{9}{10}$, $0.5 = \frac{1}{2}$, $0.2 = \frac{1}{5}$, etc.

2.4 *IS-LM* ANALYSIS

The *IS schedule* is a locus of points representing all the different combinations of interest rates and income levels consistent with equilibrium in the goods (commodity) market. The *LM schedule* is a locus of points representing all the different combinations of interest rates and income levels consistent with equilibrium in the money market. *IS-LM analysis* seeks to find the level of income and the rate of interest at which both the commodity market and the money market will be in equilibrium. This can be accomplished with the techniques used for solving simultaneous equations. Unlike the simple income determination model in Section 2.3, *IS-LM* analysis deals explicitly with the interest rate and incorporates its effect into the model.

Example 4. The commodity market for a simple two-sector economy is in equilibrium when $Y = C + I$. The money market is in equilibrium when the supply of money (M_s) equals the demand for money (M_d), which in turn is composed of the transaction-precautionary demand for money (M_t) and the speculative demand for money (M_z). Assume a two-sector economy where $C = 48 + 0.8\,Y$, $I = 98 - 75i$, $M_s = 250$, $M_t = 0.3\,Y$, and $M_z = 52 - 150i$.

Commodity equilibrium (*IS*) exists when $Y = C + I$. Substituting into the equation,

$$Y = 48 + 0.8\,Y + 98 - 75i$$

$$Y - 0.8\,Y = 146 - 75i$$

$$0.2\,Y + 75i - 146 = 0 \tag{2.1}$$

Monetary equilibrium (*LM*) exists when $M_s = M_t + M_z$. Substituting into the equation,

$$250 = 0.3\,Y + 52 - 150i$$

$$0.3\,Y - 150i - 198 = 0 \tag{2.2}$$

A condition of simultaneous equilibrium in both markets can be found, then, by solving (2.1) and (2.2) simultaneously:

$$0.2\,Y + 75i - 146 = 0 \tag{2.1}$$

$$0.3\,Y - 150i - 198 = 0 \tag{2.2}$$

Multiply (2.1) by 2, add the result (2.3) to (2.2) to eliminate i, and solve for Y.

$$0.4\,Y + 150i - 292 = 0 \tag{2.3}$$

$$\underline{0.3\,Y - 150i - 198 = 0}$$

$$0.7\,Y - 490 = 0$$

$$Y = 700$$

Substitute $Y = 700$ in (2.1) or (2.2) to find i.

$$0.2\,Y + 75i - 146 = 0$$

$$0.2(700) + 75i - 146 = 0$$

$$140 + 75i - 146 = 0$$

$$75i = 6$$

$$i = \tfrac{6}{75} = 0.08$$

The commodity and money markets will be in simultaneous equilibrium when $Y = 700$ and $i = 0.08$. At that point $C = 48 + 0.8(700) = 608$, $I = 98 - 75(0.08) = 92$, $M_t = 0.3(700) = 210$, and $M_z = 52 - 150(0.08) = 40$. $C + I = 608 + 92 = 700$ and $M_t + M_z = 210 + 40 = 250 = M_s$.

Solved Problems

GRAPHS

2.1. A complete demand function is given by the equation

$$Q_d = -30P + 0.05\,Y + 2P_r + 4T$$

where P is the price of the good, Y is income, P_r is the price of a related good (here a substitute), and T is taste. Can the function be graphed?

Since the complete function contains five different variables, it cannot be graphed as is. In ordinary demand analysis, however, it is assumed that all the independent variables except price are held constant so that the effect of a change in price on the quantity demanded can be measured independently of the influence of other factors, or *ceteris paribus*. If the other variables (Y, P_r, T) are held constant, the function can be graphed.

2.2. (a) Draw the graph for the demand function in Problem 2.1, assuming $Y = 5000$, $P_r = 25$, and $T = 30$. (b) What does the typical demand function drawn in part (a) show? (c) What happens to the graph if the price of the good changes from 5 to 6? (d) What happens if any of the other variables change? For example, if income increases to 7400?

(a) By adding the new data to the equation in Problem 2.1, the function is easily graphable. See Fig. 2-2.

$$Q_d = -30P + 0.05 Y + 2P_r + 4T = -30P + 0.05(5000) + 2(25) + 4(30) = -30P + 420$$

(b) The demand function graphed in part (a) shows all the different quantities of the good that will be demanded at different prices, assuming a given level of income, taste, and prices of substitutes (here 5000, 30, 25) which are not allowed to change.

(c) If nothing changes but the price of the good, the graph remains exactly the same since the graph indicates the different quantities that will be demanded at all the possible prices. A simple change in the price of the good occasions a movement along the curve which is called a *change in quantity demanded*. When the price goes from 5 to 6, the quantity demanded falls from 270 [$420 - 30(5)$] to 240 [$420 - 30(6)$], a movement from A to B on the curve.

(d) If any of the other variables change, there will be a shift in the curve. This is called a *change in demand* because it results in a totally new demand function (and curve) in response to the changed conditions. If income increases to 7400, the new demand function becomes

$$Q_d = -30P + 0.05(7400) + 2(25) + 4(30) = -30P + 540$$

This is graphed as a dashed line in Fig. 2-2.

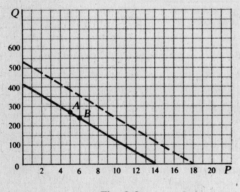

Fig. 2-2

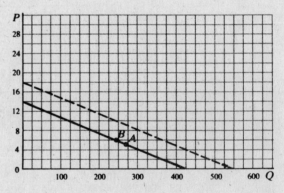

Fig. 2-3

2.3. In economics the independent variable (price) has traditionally been graphed on the vertical axis in supply and demand analysis and the dependent variable (quantity) has been graphed on the horizontal. (a) Graph the demand function in Problem 2.2 according to the traditional method. (b) Show what happens if the price goes from 5 to 6 and income increases to 7400.

(a) The function $Q_d = 420 - 30P$ is graphed according to traditional economic practice by means of the inverse function (see Section 1.5). Solving for P in terms of Q_d, $P = 14 - \frac{1}{30}Q_d$. The graph appears as a solid line in Fig. 2-3.

(b) If P goes from 5 to 6, Q_d falls from 270 to 240.

$$\begin{array}{ll} P = 14 - \frac{1}{30}Q_d & P = 14 - \frac{1}{30}Q_d \\ 5 = 14 - \frac{1}{30}Q_d & 6 = 14 - \frac{1}{30}Q_d \\ \frac{1}{30}Q_d = 9 & \frac{1}{30}Q_d = 8 \\ Q_d = 270 & Q_d = 240 \end{array}$$

The change is represented by a movement from A to B in Fig. 2-3.

If $Y = 7400$, as in Problem 2.2(d), $Q_d = 540 - 30P$. The inverse function is $P = 18 - \frac{1}{30}Q_d$ and is graphed as a dashed line in Fig. 2-3.

2.4.   (a) Graph the demand function

$$Q_d = -4P + 0.01\,Y - 5P_r + 10T$$

when $Y = 8000$, $P_r = 8$, and $T = 4$. (b) What type of good is the related good? (c) What happens if T increases to 8, indicating greater preference for the good? (d) Construct the graph along the traditional economic lines with P on the vertical axis and Q on the horizontal axis.

(a) $Q_d = -4P + 0.01(8000) - 5(8) + 10(4) = -4P + 80$

   This is graphed as a solid line in Fig. 2-4(a).

(b)   The related good has a negative coefficient. This means that a rise in the price of the related good will lead to a decrease in demand for the original good. The related good is, by definition, a complementary good.

(c)   If $T = 8$, indicating greater preference, there will be a totally new demand.

$$Q_d = -4P + 0.01(8000) - 5(8) + 10(8) = -4P + 120$$

   See the dashed line in Fig. 2-4(a).

(d)   Graphing P on the vertical calls for the inverse function. The inverse of $Q_d = 80 - 4P$ is $P = 20 - \frac{1}{4}Q_d$ and is graphed as a solid line in Fig. 2-4(b). The inverse of $Q_d = 120 - 4P$ is $P = 30 - \frac{1}{4}Q_d$. It is the dashed line in Fig. 2-4(b).

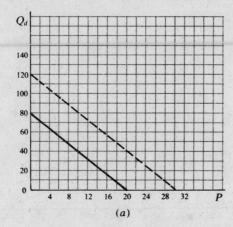 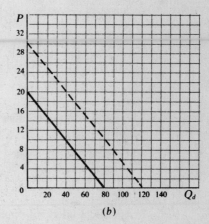

(a)   (b)

Fig. 2-4

2.5.   A supply function is given in the traditional economic form $P = -a + bQ$. Show what happens to the supply function if the government imposes a tax of T on every unit produced. Use a dashed line for the supply function with tax.

If the government imposes a per unit tax of T on producers, the effective price for producers becomes $P - T$. Thus the supply function must be altered to read

$$P - T = -a + bQ$$
$$P = -a + bQ + T$$

The addition of the constant T shifts the vertical intercept up by the amount of the tax, reducing the quantity supplied at any given price. See Fig. 2-5.

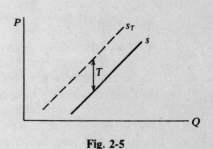

Fig. 2-5

2.6.   A person has \$120 to spend on two goods (X, Y) whose respective prices are \$3 and \$5. (a) Draw a *budget line* showing all the different combinations of the two goods that can be bought with the given budget (B). What happens to the original budget line, (b) if the budget falls by 25%? (c) If the price of X doubles? (d) If the price of Y falls to 4?

(a) The general function for a budget line is $\qquad P_X X + P_Y Y = B$

If $P_X = 3$, $P_Y = 5$, and $B = 120$, $\qquad 3X + 5Y = 120$

Solving for Y in terms of X in order to graph the function, $\qquad Y = 24 - \frac{3}{5}X$

The graph is given as a solid line in Fig. 2-6(a).

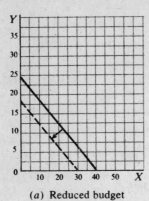
(a) Reduced budget

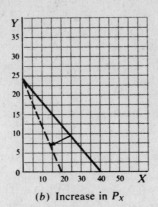
(b) Increase in P_X

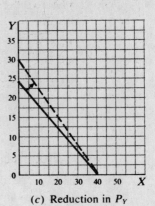
(c) Reduction in P_Y

Fig. 2-6

(b) If the budget falls by 25 percent, the new budget is 90 $[120 - \frac{1}{4}(120) = 90]$. The equation for the new budget line is

$$3X + 5Y = 90$$
$$Y = 18 - \frac{3}{5}X$$

The graph is a dashed line in Fig. 2-6(a). Lowering the budget causes the budget line to shift parallel to the left.

(c) If P_X doubles, the original equation becomes

$$6X + 5Y = 120$$
$$Y = 24 - \frac{6}{5}X$$

The vertical intercept remains the same, but the slope changes and becomes steeper. See the dashed line in Fig. 2-6(b). With a higher price for X, less X can be bought with the given budget.

(d) If P_Y now equals 4,

$$3X + 4Y = 120$$
$$Y = 30 - \frac{3}{4}X$$

With a change in P_Y, both the vertical intercept and the slope change. This is shown in Fig. 2-6 (c) by the dashed line.

2.7. Either coal (C) or gas (G) can be used in the production of steel. The cost of coal is 100, the cost of gas 500. Draw an isocost curve showing the different combinations of gas and coal that can be purchased (a) with an initial expenditure (E) of 10,000, (b) if expenditures increase by 50 percent, (c) if the price of gas is reduced by 20 percent, (d) if the price of coal rises by 25 percent. Always start from the original equation.

(a) $\qquad P_C C + P_G G = E$
$$100C + 500G = 10,000$$
$$C = 100 - 5G$$

The graph is a solid line in Fig. 2-7(a).

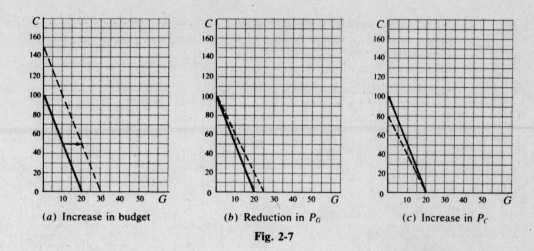

(a) Increase in budget   (b) Reduction in P_G (c) Increase in P_C

Fig. 2-7

(b) A 50 percent increase in expenditures makes the new outlay 15,000 [10,000 + 0.5(10,000)]. The new equation is

$$100C + 500G = 15,000$$
$$C = 150 - 5G$$

The graph is the dashed line in Fig. 2-7(a).

(c) If the price of gas is reduced by 20 percent, the new price is 400 [500 − 0.2(500)], and the new equation is

$$100C + 400G = 10,000$$
$$C = 100 - 4G$$

The graph is the dashed line in Fig. 2-7(b).

(d) A 25 percent rise in the price of coal makes the new price 125 [100 + 0.25(100)].

$$125C + 500G = 10,000$$
$$C = 80 - 4G$$

The graph appears as a dashed line in Fig. 2-7(c).

GRAPHS IN THE INCOME DETERMINATION MODEL

2.8. Given: $Y = C + I$, $C = 50 + 0.8Y$, and $I_0 = 50$. (a) Graph the consumption function. (b) Graph the aggregate demand function, $C + I_0$. (c) Find the equilibrium level of income from the graph.

(a) Since consumption is a function of income, it is graphed on the vertical axis; income is graphed on the horizontal. See Fig. 2-8. When other components of aggregate demand such as I, G, and $(X - Z)$ are added to the model, they are also graphed on the vertical axis. It is easily determined from the linear form of the consumption function that the vertical intercept is 50 and the slope of the line (the MPC or $\Delta C/\Delta Y$) is 0.8.

(b) Investment in the model is *autonomous investment*. This means investment is independent of income and does not change in response to changes in income. When considered by itself, the graph of a constant is a horizontal line; when added to a linear function, it causes a parallel shift in the original function by an amount equal to its value. In Fig. 2-8, autonomous investment causes the aggregate demand function to shift up by 50 parallel to the initial consumption function.

(c) To obtain the equilibrium level of income from a graph, a 45° dashed line is drawn from the origin. If the same scale of measurement is used on both axes, a 45° line has a slope of 1, meaning that as the line moves away from the origin, it moves up vertically (ΔY) by one unit for every unit it moves across horizontally (ΔX). Every point on the 45° line, therefore, has a horizontal coordinate (*abscissa*) exactly equal to its vertical coordinate (*ordinate*). Consequently, when the aggregate demand function intersects the 45° line, aggregate demand (as graphed on the vertical) will equal national income (as graphed on the horizontal).   From Fig. 2-8 it is clear that the equilibrium level of income is 500, since the aggregate demand function $(C + I)$ intersects the 45° line at 500.

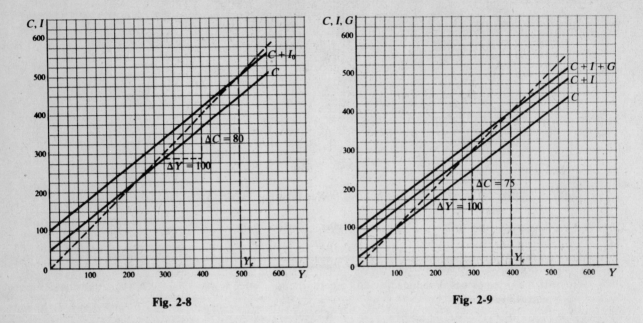

Fig. 2-8   Fig. 2-9

2.9. Given: $Y = C + I + G$, $C = 25 + 0.75\,Y$, $I = I_0 = 50$, and $G = G_0 = 25$.   (a) Graph the aggregate demand function and show its individual components.   (b) Find the equilibrium level of income.   (c) How can the aggregate demand function be graphed directly, without having to graph each of the component parts?

(a) See Fig. 2-9.

(b) Equilibrium income = 400.

(c) To graph the aggregate demand function directly, sum up the individual components,

$$\text{Agg. } D = C + I + G = 25 + 0.75\,Y + 50 + 25 = 100 + 0.75\,Y$$

The direct graphing of the aggregate demand function coincides exactly with the graph of the summation of the individual graphs of C, I, and G above.

2.10. Use a graph to show how the addition of a lump-sum tax (a tax independent of income) influences the parameters of the income determination model.   Graph the two systems individually, using a solid line for (1) and a dashed line for (2).

(1) $Y = C + I$	(2) $Y = C + I$	$Yd = Y - T$
$C = 100 + 0.6\,Y$	$C = 100 + 0.6\,Yd$	$T = 50$
$I_0 = 40$	$I_0 = 40$	

The first system of equations presents no problems; the second requires that C first be converted from a function of Yd to a function of Y.

(1) Agg. $D = C + I$ (2) Agg. $D = C + I$

$\qquad\qquad = 100 + 0.6\,Y + 40$ $\qquad\qquad\qquad = 100 + 0.6\,Yd + 40 = 140 + 0.6(Y - T)$

$\qquad\qquad = 140 + 0.6\,Y$ $\qquad\qquad\qquad\qquad = 140 + 0.6(Y - 50) = 110 + 0.6\,Y$

A lump-sum tax has a negative effect on the vertical intercept of the aggregate demand function equal to $-\text{MPC}(T)$.   Here $-0.6(50) = -30$.   The slope is not affected (note the parallel lines for the two graphs in Fig. 2-10).   Income falls from 350 to 275 as a result of the tax.   See Fig. 2-10.

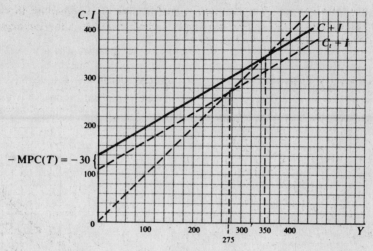

Fig. 2-10

2.11. Explain with the aid of a graph how the incorporation of a *proportional* tax (a tax depending on income) influences the parameters of the income determination model. Graph the model without the tax as a solid line and the model with the tax as a dashed line.

$$
\begin{array}{lll}
(1) \quad Y = C + I & (2) \quad Y = C + I & Yd = Y - T \\
\quad\quad C = 85 + 0.75\,Y & \quad\quad C = 85 + 0.75\,Yd & \quad T = 20 + 0.2\,Y \\
\quad\quad I_0 = 30 & \quad\quad I_0 = 30 &
\end{array}
$$

$$
\begin{aligned}
(1) \quad \text{Agg. } D &= C + I \\
&= 85 + 0.75\,Y + 30 \\
&= 115 + 0.75\,Y
\end{aligned}
$$

$$
\begin{aligned}
(2) \quad \text{Agg. } D &= C + I \\
&= 85 + 0.75\,Yd + 30 = 115 + 0.75(Y - T) \\
&= 115 + 0.75(Y - 20 - 0.2\,Y) \\
&= 115 + 0.75\,Y - 15 - 0.15\,Y = 100 + 0.6\,Y
\end{aligned}
$$

Incorporation of a proportional income tax into the model affects the slope of the line, or the MPC. In this case it lowers it from 0.75 to 0.6. The vertical intercept is also lowered because the tax structure includes a lump-sum tax of 20. Because of the tax structure, the equilibrium level of income falls from 460 to 250. See Fig. 2-11.

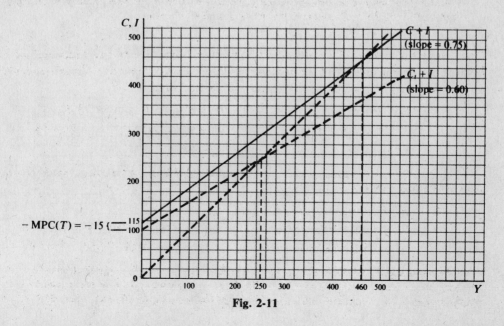

Fig. 2-11

2.12. (*a*) Graph the savings function $S = -100 + 0.25\,Y$. (*b*) Find the equilibrium level of income.

(*a*) Because saving is a function of income, S is graphed on the vertical axis and Y on the horizontal in Fig. 2-12. Since the vertical intercept is negative, the graph must be extended to include the fourth quadrant where the vertical coordinates are negative.

(*b*) In a simple income determination model where the only demand is consumption demand, the system will be in equilibrium when all that is produced is consumed, or when $S = 0$. At $S = 0$, the equilibrium level of income (Y_e) equals 400.

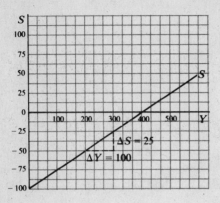

Fig. 2-12   Fig. 2-13

2.13. Given: $C = 50 + 0.6\,Y$ and $I_0 = 50$. Use the savings graph to find the equilibrium level of income.

If $C = 50 + 0.6\,Y$, $S = -50 + 0.4\,Y$. With investment in the model, equilibrium will be reached when $S = I$. In this model, therefore, $Y_e = 250$. See Fig. 2-13. (Note that investment is not added to the savings function. As a constant considered by itself, I_0 is merely a horizontal line.)

2.14. Find the graphical solution for the equilibrium level of income when $S = -70 + 0.25\,Yd$, $T = 20$, $I_0 = 40$, $G_0 = 30$, and $Yd = Y - T$.

In equilibrium, $S + T = I + G$. G, I, and T are all constants and present no problem but the savings function must be converted to a function of Y before graphing, as follows:

$$S = -70 + 0.25\,Yd = -70 + 0.25(Y - 20) = -75 + 0.25\,Y$$

In Fig. 2-14, $I + G = 40 + 30 = 70$, a horizontal line. The graph of

$$S + T = -75 + 0.25\,Y + 20 = -55 + 0.25\,Y$$

and the equilibrium level of income is 500.

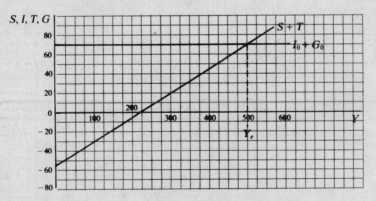

Fig. 2-14

EQUATIONS IN SUPPLY AND DEMAND ANALYSIS

2.15. Find the equilibrium price and quantity for the following markets:

$$(a) \quad Q_s = -20 + 3P \qquad (b) \quad Q_s = -45 + 8P$$
$$Q_d = 220 - 5P \qquad\qquad Q_d = 125 - 2P$$

$$(c) \quad Q_s + 32 - 7P = 0 \qquad (d) \quad 13P - Q_s = 27$$
$$Q_d - 128 + 9P = 0 \qquad\qquad Q_d + 4P - 24 = 0$$

Each of the markets will be in equilibrium when $Q_s = Q_d$.

(a)
$$Q_s = Q_d$$
$$-20 + 3P = 220 - 5P$$
$$8P = 240$$
$$P = 30$$
$$Q_s = -20 + 3P = -20 + 3(30)$$
$$Q_s = 70 = Q_d$$

(b)
$$Q_s = Q_d$$
$$-45 + 8P = 125 - 2P$$
$$10P = 170$$
$$P = 17$$
$$Q_d = 125 - 2P = 125 - 2(17)$$
$$Q_d = 91 = Q_s$$

(c)
$$Q_s = 7P - 32$$
$$Q_d = 128 - 9P$$
$$7P - 32 = 128 - 9P$$
$$16P = 160$$
$$P = 10$$
$$Q_s = 7P - 32 = 7(10) - 32$$
$$Q_s = 38 = Q_d$$

(d)
$$Q_s = -27 + 13P$$
$$Q_d = 24 - 4P$$
$$-27 + 13P = 24 - 4P$$
$$17P = 51$$
$$P = 3$$
$$Q_d = 24 - 4P = 24 - 4(3)$$
$$Q_d = 12 = Q_s$$

2.16. Given the following set of simultaneous equations for two related markets, beef (B) and pork (P), find the equilibrium conditions for each market, using the substitution method.

$$(1) \quad Q_{dB} = 82 - 3P_B + P_P \qquad (2) \quad Q_{dP} = 92 + 2P_B - 4P_P$$
$$Q_{sB} = -5 + 15P_B \qquad\qquad Q_{sP} = -6 + 32P_P$$

Equilibrium requires that $Q_s = Q_d$ in each market.

(1)
$$Q_{sB} = Q_{dB}$$
$$-5 + 15P_B = 82 - 3P_B + P_P$$
$$18P_B - P_P = 87$$

(2)
$$Q_{sP} = Q_{dP}$$
$$-6 + 32P_P = 92 + 2P_B - 4P_P$$
$$36P_P - 2P_B = 98$$

This reduces the problem to two equations and two unknowns:

$$18P_B - P_P = 87 \qquad\qquad (2.4)$$

$$-2P_B + 36P_P = 98 \qquad\qquad (2.5)$$

Solving for P_P in (2.4) gives

$$P_P = 18P_B - 87$$

Substituting the value of this term in (2.5) gives

$$-2P_B + 36(18P_B - 87) = 98 \qquad -2P_B + 648P_B - 3132 = 98$$
$$646P_B = 3230 \qquad\qquad P_B = 5$$

Substituting $P_B = 5$ in (2.5), or (2.4),

$$-2(5) + 36P_P = 98$$
$$36P_P = 108 \qquad P_P = 3$$

Finally, substituting the values for P_B and P_P in either the supply or the demand function for each market,

$$(1) \quad Q_{dB} = 82 - 3P_B + P_P = 82 - 3(5) + (3) \qquad (2) \quad Q_{dP} = 92 + 2P_B - 4P_P = 92 + 2(5) - 4(3)$$

$$Q_{dB} = 70 = Q_{sB} \qquad\qquad\qquad Q_{dP} = 90 = Q_{sP}$$

2.17. Find the equilibrium price and quantity for two complementary goods, slacks (S) and jackets (J), using the elimination method.

$$(1) \quad Q_{dS} = 410 - 5P_S - 2P_J \qquad (2) \quad Q_{dJ} = 295 - P_S - 3P_J$$

$$Q_{sS} = -60 + 3P_S \qquad\qquad Q_{sJ} = -120 + 2P_J$$

In equilibrium,

$$(1) \qquad\qquad Q_{dS} = Q_{sS} \qquad\qquad (2) \qquad\qquad Q_{dJ} = Q_{sJ}$$

$$410 - 5P_S - 2P_J = -60 + 3P_S \qquad 295 - P_S - 3P_J = -120 + 2P_J$$

$$470 - 8P_S - 2P_J = 0 \qquad\qquad 415 - P_S - 5P_J = 0$$

This leaves two equations

$$470 - 8P_S - 2P_J = 0 \tag{2.6}$$

$$415 - P_S - 5P_J = 0 \tag{2.7}$$

Multiplying (2.7) by 8 gives (2.8). Subtract (2.6) from (2.8) to eliminate P_S, and solve for P_J.

$$3320 - 8P_S - 40P_J = 0 \tag{2.8}$$

$$\underline{-(+470 - 8P_S - 2P_J = 0)}$$

$$2850 \qquad\quad - 38P_J = 0$$

$$P_J = 75$$

Substituting $P_J = 75$ in (2.6),

$$470 - 8P_S - 2(75) = 0$$

$$320 = 8P_S \qquad P_S = 40$$

Finally, substituting $P_J = 75$ and $P_S = 40$ into Q_d or Q_s for each market,

$$(1) \quad Q_{dS} = 410 - 5P_S - 2P_J = 410 - 5(40) - 2(75) \qquad (2) \quad Q_{dJ} = 295 - P_S - 3P_J = 295 - 40 - 3(75)$$

$$Q_{dS} = 60 = Q_{sS} \qquad\qquad\qquad Q_{dJ} = 30 = Q_{sJ}$$

2.18. Supply and demand conditions can also be expressed in quadratic form. Find the equilibrium price and quantity, given the demand function

$$P + Q^2 + 3Q - 20 = 0 \tag{2.9}$$

and the supply function

$$P - 3Q^2 + 10Q = 5 \tag{2.10}$$

Either the substitution method or the elimination method can be used, since this problem involves two equations and two unknowns. Using the substitution method, (2.10) is solved for P in terms of Q.

$$P - 3Q^2 + 10Q = 5$$

$$P = 3Q^2 - 10Q + 5$$

Substituting $P = 3Q^2 - 10Q + 5$ in (2.9),

$$(3Q^2 - 10Q + 5) + Q^2 + 3Q - 20 = 0$$

$$4Q^2 - 7Q - 15 = 0$$

Using the quadratic formula $Q_1, Q_2 = (-b \pm \sqrt{b^2 - 4ac})/2a$, where $a = 4$, $b = -7$, and $c = -15$, $Q_1 = 3$ and $Q_2 = -1.25$. Since neither price nor quantity can be negative, $Q = 3$. Substitute $Q = 3$ in (2.9) or (2.10) to find P.

$$P + (3)^2 + 3(3) - 20 = 0 \qquad P = 2$$

2.19. Use the elimination method to find the equilibrium price and quantity when the demand function is

$$3P + Q^2 + 5Q - 102 = 0 \tag{2.11}$$

and the supply function is

$$P - 2Q^2 + 3Q + 71 = 0 \tag{2.12}$$

Multiply (2.12) by 3 to get (2.13) and subtract it from (2.11) to eliminate P.

$$
\begin{aligned}
3P + \quad Q^2 + 5Q - 102 &= 0 \\
-(3P - 6Q^2 + 9Q + 213 &= 0) \\
\hline
7Q^2 - 4Q - 315 &= 0
\end{aligned} \tag{2.13}
$$

Use the quadratic formula (see Problem 2.18) to solve for Q, and substitute the result, $Q = 7$, in (2.12) or (2.11) to solve for P.

$$P - 2(7)^2 + 3(7) + 71 = 0 \qquad P = 6$$

2.20. Supply and demand analysis can also involve more than two markets. Find the equilibrium price and quantity for the three substitute goods below.

$$Q_{d1} = 23 - 5P_1 + P_2 + P_3 \qquad Q_{s1} = -8 + 6P_1$$
$$Q_{d2} = 15 + P_1 - 3P_2 + 2P_3 \qquad Q_{s2} = -11 + 3P_2$$
$$Q_{d3} = 19 + P_1 + 2P_2 - 4P_3 \qquad Q_{s3} = -5 + 3P_3$$

For equilibrium in each market,

$Q_{d1} = Q_{s1}$	$Q_{d2} = Q_{s2}$	$Q_{d3} = Q_{s3}$
$23 - 5P_1 + P_2 + P_3 = -8 + 6P_1$	$15 + P_1 - 3P_2 + 2P_3 = -11 + 3P_2$	$19 + P_1 + 2P_2 - 4P_3 = -5 + 3P_3$
$31 - 11P_1 + P_2 + P_3 = 0$	$26 + P_1 - 6P_2 + 2P_3 = 0$	$24 + P_1 + 2P_2 - 7P_3 = 0$

This leaves three equations with three unknowns:

$$31 - 11P_1 + P_2 + P_3 = 0 \tag{2.14}$$
$$26 + P_1 - 6P_2 + 2P_3 = 0 \tag{2.15}$$
$$24 + P_1 + 2P_2 - 7P_3 = 0 \tag{2.16}$$

Start by eliminating one of the variables (here P_2). Multiply (2.14) by 2 to get

$$62 - 22P_1 + 2P_2 + 2P_3 = 0$$

From this subtract (2.16).

$$
\begin{aligned}
62 - 22P_1 + 2P_2 + 2P_3 &= 0 \\
-(24 + \quad P_1 + 2P_2 - 7P_3) &= 0 \\
\hline
38 - 23P_1 \qquad\quad + 9P_3 &= 0
\end{aligned} \tag{2.17}
$$

Multiply (2.16) by 3.

$$72 + 3P_1 + 6P_2 - 21P_3 = 0$$

Add the result to (2.15).

$$
\begin{aligned}
26 + \quad P_1 - 6P_2 + \quad 2P_3 &= 0 \\
72 + 3P_1 + 6P_2 - 21P_3 &= 0 \\
\hline
98 + 4P_1 \qquad\quad - 19P_3 &= 0
\end{aligned} \tag{2.18}
$$

Now there are two equations, (2.17) and (2.18), and two unknowns. Multiply (2.17) by 19 and (2.18) by 9; then add to eliminate P_3.

$$
\begin{aligned}
722 - 437P_1 + 171P_3 &= 0 \\
882 + \quad 36P_1 - 171P_3 &= 0 \\
\hline
1604 - 401P_1 \qquad\quad &= 0 \\
P_1 &= 4
\end{aligned}
$$

Substitute $P_1 = 4$ in (2.18) to solve for P_3.

$$98 + 4(4) - 19P_3 = 0$$
$$19P_3 = 114 \quad P_3 = 6$$

Substitute $P_1 = 4$ and $P_3 = 6$ into (2.14), (2.15), or (2.16), to solve for P_2.

$$31 - 11(4) + P_2 + (6) = 0 \qquad P_2 = 7$$

EQUATIONS IN THE INCOME DETERMINATION MODEL

2.21. Given: $Y = C + I + G$, $C = C_0 + bY$, $I = I_0$, and $G = G_0$, where $C_0 = 135$, $b = 0.8$, $I_0 = 75$, and $G_0 = 30$. (a) Find the equation for the equilibrium level of income in the reduced form. (b) Solve for the equilibrium level of income (1) directly and (2) with the reduced form.

(a) From Section 2.3,
$$Y = C + I + G$$
$$= C_0 + bY + I_0 + G_0$$
$$Y - bY = C_0 + I_0 + G_0$$
$$(1 - b)Y = C_0 + I_0 + G_0$$
$$Y = \frac{C_0 + I_0 + G_0}{1 - b}$$

(b) (1) $Y = C + I + G = 135 + 0.8\,Y + 75 + 30$
$$Y - 0.8\,Y = 240$$
$$0.2\,Y = 240$$
$$Y = 1200$$

(2) $Y = \dfrac{C_0 + I_0 + G_0}{1 - b}$
$$= \frac{135 + 75 + 30}{1 - 0.8}$$
$$= 5(240) = 1200$$

2.22. Find the equilibrium level of income $Y = C + I$, when $C = 89 + 0.8\,Y$ and $I_0 = 24$.

$$Y = \frac{C_0 + I_0}{1 - b} = 5(89 + 24) = 565$$

From Problem 2.21, the value of the multiplier $[1/(1 - b)]$ is already known for cases when $b = 0.8$. Use of the reduced form to solve the equation in this instance is faster, therefore, although the other method is also correct.

2.23. (a) Find the reduced form of the following income determination model where investment is not autonomous but is a function of income. (b) Find the numerical value of the equilibrium level of income (Y_e). (c) Show what happens to the multiplier.

$$Y = C + I \qquad C = C_0 + bY \qquad I = I_0 + aY$$

where $C_0 = 65$, $I_0 = 70$, $b = 0.6$, and $a = 0.2$.

(a) $Y = C + I$
$$= C_0 + bY + I_0 + aY$$
$$Y - bY - aY = C_0 + I_0$$
$$(1 - b - a)Y = C_0 + I_0$$
$$Y = \frac{C_0 + I_0}{1 - b - a}$$

(b) $Y = C + I$
$$= 65 + 0.6\,Y + 70 + 0.2\,Y$$
$$Y - 0.6\,Y - 0.2\,Y = 65 + 70$$
$$0.2\,Y = 135$$
$$Y = 675$$

(c) When investment is a function of income, and no longer autonomous, the multiplier changes from $1/(1 - b)$ to $1/(1 - b - a)$. This increases the value of the multiplier because it reduces the denominator of the fraction and makes the quotient larger, as substitution of the values of the parameters in the problem shows:

$$\frac{1}{1 - b} = \frac{1}{1 - 0.6} = \frac{1}{0.4} = 2.5 \qquad \frac{1}{1 - b - a} = \frac{1}{1 - 0.6 - 0.2} = \frac{1}{0.2} = 5$$

2.24. Find (a) the reduced form, (b) the numerical value of Y_e, and (c) the effect on the multiplier when a lump-sum tax is added to the model and consumption becomes a function of disposable income (Yd).

$$Y = C + I \qquad C = C_0 + bYd \qquad I = I_0 \qquad Yd = Y - T$$

where $C_0 = 100$, $b = 0.6$, $I_0 = 40$, and $T = 50$.

(a)
$$Y = C + I = C_0 + bYd + I_0 = C_0 + b(Y - T) + I_0 = C_0 + bY - bT + I_0$$
$$Y - bY = C_0 + I_0 - bT$$
$$Y = \frac{C_0 + I_0 - bT}{1 - b}$$

(b)
$$Y = 100 + 0.6Yd + 40 = 140 + 0.6(Y - T) \qquad \text{or} \qquad Y = \frac{100 + 40 - 0.6(50)}{1 - 0.6} = \frac{110}{0.4}$$
$$= 140 + 0.6(Y - 50) = 140 + 0.6Y - 30$$
$$= 275$$
$$Y - 0.6Y = 110$$
$$0.4Y = 110$$
$$Y = 275$$

The graph of this function is given in Problem 2.10.

(c) As seen in part (a), incorporation of a lump-sum tax into the model leaves the multiplier at $1/(1 - b)$. Only the aggregate value of the exogenous variables is reduced by an amount equal to $-bT$. Incorporation of other autonomous variables such as G_0, X_0, or Z_0 will not affect the value of the multiplier either.

2.25. Find (a) the reduced form, (b) the numerical value of Y_e, and (c) the effect on the multiplier if a proportional income tax (t) is incorporated into the model.

$$Y = C + I \qquad C = C_0 + bYd \qquad T = T_0 + tY \qquad Yd = Y - T$$

where $I = I_0 = 30$, $C_0 = 85$, $b = 0.75$, $t = 0.2$, and $T_0 = 20$.

(a)
$$Y = C + I = C_0 + bYd + I_0$$
$$= C_0 + b(Y - T) + I_0 = C_0 + b(Y - T_0 - tY) + I_0$$
$$= C_0 + bY - bT_0 - btY + I_0$$
$$Y - bY + btY = C_0 + I_0 - bT_0$$
$$(1 - b + bt)Y = C_0 + I_0 - bT_0$$
$$Y = \frac{C_0 + I_0 - bT_0}{1 - b + bt}$$

(b) Once the reduced form is found, its use speeds the solution. But sometimes the reduced form is not available, making it necessary to be familiar with the other method.

$$Y = C + I = 85 + 0.75Yd + 30 = 115 + 0.75(Y - T)$$
$$= 115 + 0.75(Y - 20 - 0.2Y) = 115 + 0.75Y - 15 - 0.15Y$$
$$Y - 0.75Y + 0.15Y = 100$$
$$0.4Y = 100$$
$$Y = 250$$

The graph of this function is given in Problem 2.11.

(c) The multiplier is changed from $1/(1 - b)$ to $1/(1 - b + bt)$. This reduces the size of the multiplier because it makes the denominator larger and the fraction smaller:

$$\frac{1}{1 - b} = \frac{1}{1 - 0.75} = \frac{1}{0.25} = 4$$

$$\frac{1}{1 - b + bt} = \frac{1}{1 - 0.75 + 0.75(0.2)} = \frac{1}{1 - 0.75 + 0.15} = \frac{1}{0.4} = 2.5$$

2.26. If the foreign sector is added to the model and there is a positive marginal propensity to import (z), find (a) the reduced form, (b) the equilibrium level of income, and (c) the effect on the multiplier.

$$Y = C + I + G + (X - Z) \qquad C = C_0 + bY \qquad Z = Z_0 + zY$$

where $I = I_0 = 90$, $G = G_0 = 65$, $X = X_0 = 80$, $C_0 = 70$, $Z_0 = 40$, $b = 0.9$, and $z = 0.15$.

(a)
$$Y = C + I + G + (X - Z) = C_0 + bY + I_0 + G_0 + X_0 - Z_0 - zY$$
$$Y - bY + zY = C_0 + I_0 + G_0 + X_0 - Z_0$$
$$(1 - b + z)Y = C_0 + I_0 + G_0 + X_0 - Z_0$$
$$Y = \frac{C_0 + I_0 + G_0 + X_0 - Z_0}{1 - b + z}$$

(b) Using the reduced form above,

$$Y = \frac{70 + 90 + 65 + 80 - 40}{1 - 0.9 + 0.15} = \frac{265}{0.25} = 1060$$

(c) Introduction of the marginal propensity to import (z) into the model reduces the size of the multiplier. It makes the denominator larger and the fraction smaller:

$$\frac{1}{1 - b} = \frac{1}{1 - 0.9} = \frac{1}{0.1} = 10$$

$$\frac{1}{1 - b + z} = \frac{1}{1 - 0.9 + 0.15} = \frac{1}{0.25} = 4$$

2.27. Find the equilibrium level of income when $S = -70 + 0.25\,Yd$, $Yd = Y - T$, $I = I_0 = 40$, $G = G_0 = 30$, and $T = T_0 = 20$.

In equilibrium, leakages from the system ($S + T$) are balanced by injections into the system ($I + G$).

$$S + T = I + G$$
$$-70 + 0.25\,Yd + 20 = 40 + 30$$

But $Yd = Y - T$,

$$-70 + 0.25(Y - 20) + 20 = 40 + 30$$
$$-70 + 0.25\,Y - 5 + 20 = 70$$
$$0.25\,Y = 125$$
$$Y = 500$$

The graph for this problem is found in Problem 2.14.

IS-LM EQUATIONS

2.28. Given: $C = 102 + 0.7\,Y$, $I = 150 - 100i$, $M_s = 300$, $M_t = 0.25\,Y$, and $M_z = 124 - 200i$. Find (a) the equilibrium level of income and the equilibrium rate of interest, and (b) the level of C, I, M_t, and M_z when the economy is in equilibrium.

(a) Commodity market equilibrium (IS) exists where

$$Y = C + I$$
$$= 102 + 0.7\,Y + 150 - 100i$$
$$Y - 0.7\,Y = 252 - 100i$$
$$0.3\,Y + 100i - 252 = 0$$

Monetary equilibrium (LM) exists where

$$M_s = M_t + M_z$$
$$300 = 0.25\,Y + 124 - 200i$$
$$0.25\,Y - 200i - 176 = 0$$

Simultaneous equilibrium in both markets requires that

$$0.3\,Y + 100i - 252 = 0 \tag{2.19}$$
$$0.25\,Y - 200i - 176 = 0 \tag{2.20}$$

Multiply (2.19) by 2, and add the result to (2.20) to eliminate i:

$$0.6\,Y + 200i - 504 = 0$$
$$\underline{0.25\,Y - 200i - 176 = 0}$$
$$0.85\,Y \qquad\qquad = 680$$
$$Y = 800$$

Substitute $Y = 800$ in (2.19) or (2.20):

$$0.25\,Y - 200i - 176 = 0$$
$$0.25(800) - 200i - 176 = 0$$
$$-200i = -24$$
$$i = 0.12$$

(b)   At $Y = 800$ and $i = 0.12$,

$$C = 102 + 0.7(800) = 662 \qquad M_t = 0.25(800) = 200$$
$$I = 150 - 100(0.12) = 138 \qquad M_z = 124 - 200(0.12) = 100$$

and

$$C + I = Y \qquad\qquad M_t + M_z = M_s$$
$$662 + 138 = 800 \qquad\qquad 200 + 100 = 300$$

2.29.   If the money supply in Problem 2.28 increases by 17,   (a) what happens to the equilibrium level of income and interest rate?   (b) What are C, I, M_t, and M_z at the new equilibrium?

(a)   If the money supply (M_s) increases by 17, the LM equation becomes

$$M_s = M_t + M_z$$
$$317 = 0.25\,Y + 124 - 200i$$
$$0.25\,Y - 200i - 193 = 0 \tag{2.21}$$

The IS equation remains the same:

$$0.3\,Y + 100i - 252 = 0 \tag{2.19}$$

Multiply (2.19) by 2, and add the result to (2.21) to eliminate i.

$$0.25\,Y - 200i - 193 = 0$$
$$\underline{0.6\,Y + 200i - 504 = 0}$$
$$0.85\,Y \qquad\qquad = 697$$
$$Y = 820$$

Substitute $Y = 820$ in (2.19) or (2.21) to solve for i.

$$0.3(820) + 100i - 252 = 0$$
$$246 + 100i - 252 = 0$$
$$100i = 6$$
$$i = 0.06$$

An increase in the money supply, other things being equal, leads to an increase in the equilibrium level of income and a decrease in the interest rate.

(b) When $Y = 820$ and $i = 0.06$,

$$C = 102 + 0.7(820) = 676 \qquad M_t = 0.25(820) = 205$$
$$I = 150 - 100(0.06) = 144 \qquad M_z = 124 - 200(0.06) = 112$$

and

$$C + I = Y \qquad M_t + M_z = M_s$$
$$676 + 144 = 820 \qquad 205 + 112 = 317$$

2.30. Find (a) the equilibrium income level and interest rate, and (b) the levels of C, I, M_t, and M_z in equilibrium when

$$C = 89 + 0.6\,Y \qquad I = 120 - 150i \qquad M_s = 275 \qquad M_t = 0.1\,Y \qquad M_z = 240 - 250i$$

(a) For *IS*:

$$Y = 89 + 0.6\,Y + 120 - 150i$$
$$Y - 0.6\,Y = 209 - 150i$$
$$0.4\,Y + 150i - 209 = 0$$

For *LM*:

$$M_s = M_t + M_z$$
$$275 = 0.1\,Y + 240 - 250i$$
$$0.1\,Y - 250i - 35 = 0$$

In equilibrium,

$$0.4\,Y + 150i - 209 = 0 \qquad\qquad (2.22)$$
$$0.1\,Y - 250i - 35 = 0 \qquad\qquad (2.23)$$

Multiply (2.23) by 4, and subtract the result from (2.22) to eliminate Y.

$$0.4\,Y + 150i - 209 = 0$$
$$-(0.4\,Y - 1000i - 140 = 0)$$
$$\overline{\quad 1150i \qquad\quad = 69\quad}$$
$$i = 0.06$$

Substitute $i = 0.06$ in (2.22) or (2.23).

$$0.4\,Y + 150(0.06) - 209 = 0$$
$$0.4\,Y = 200$$
$$Y = 500$$

(b) At $Y = 500$ and $i = 0.06$,

$$C = 89 + 0.6(500) = 389 \qquad M_t = 0.1(500) = 50$$
$$I = 120 - 150(0.06) = 111 \qquad M_z = 240 - 250(0.06) = 225$$

and

$$C + I = Y \qquad M_t + M_z = M_s$$
$$389 + 111 = 500 \qquad 50 + 225 = 275$$

2.31. Show what happens to the equilibrium conditions in Problem 2.30 if autonomous investment drops to 97.

If $I_0 = 97$, the *IS* equation becomes

$$Y = 89 + 0.6\,Y + 97 - 150i$$
$$Y - 0.6\,Y = 186 - 150i$$
$$0.4\,Y + 150i - 186 = 0$$

The LM equation remains the same $(0.1\,Y - 250i - 35 = 0)$.   Thus, in equilibrium,

$$0.4\,Y + 150i - 186 = 0 \tag{2.24}$$

$$0.1\,Y - 250i - 35 = 0 \tag{2.23}$$

Multiply (2.23) by 4, and subtract the result from (2.24) to eliminate Y.

$$0.4\,Y + 150i - 186 = 0$$
$$\underline{-(0.4\,Y - 1000i - 140 = 0)}$$
$$1150i \qquad = 46$$
$$i = 0.04$$

Substitute $i = 0.04$ in (2.23) to find Y.

$$0.1\,Y - 250(0.04) - 35 = 0$$
$$0.1\,Y = 45$$
$$Y = 450$$

A fall in autonomous investment, *ceteris paribus*, will lead to a decrease in the equilibrium level of income and a drop in the interest rate.

    In part (b)

$$C = 89 + 0.6(450) = 359 \qquad M_t = 0.1(450) = 45$$
$$I = 97 - 150(0.04) = 91 \qquad M_z = 240 - 250(0.04) = 230$$

and

$$C + I = Y \qquad\qquad M_t + M_z = M_s$$
$$359 + 91 = 450 \qquad\qquad 45 + 230 = 275$$

Chapter 3

The Derivative and the Rules
of Differentiation

3.1 THE SLOPE OF A CURVILINEAR FUNCTION

The average rate of change ($\Delta y/\Delta x$) for a linear function is constant, and is equal to the slope. In contrast, the average rate of change for a curvilinear function varies with successive movements along the curve (see Fig. 3-1). Thus, the slope of a curvilinear function is not constant; it varies at different points on the curve. The slope of a curvilinear function at any given point is equal to the slope of a line drawn tangent to the curve at that point (see Fig. 3-2).

Example 1. In Fig. 3-1(a), the average rate of change ($\Delta y/\Delta x$) is constant. For every one unit change in x, $\Delta y/\Delta x$ is equal to $1\frac{1}{3}$. In Fig. 3-1(b), the average rate of change varies with each successive move along the curve. For the first unit change in x, the change in y is 2; for the second unit change in x, the change in y is 1; and for the third unit change in x, the change in y is $\frac{2}{3}$.

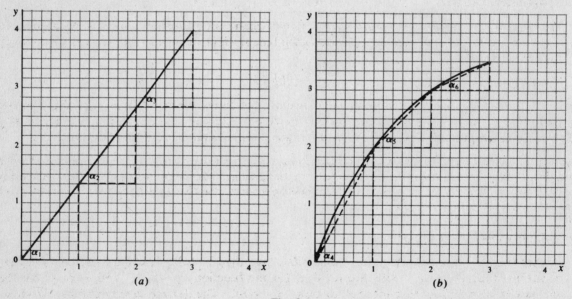

Fig. 3-1

The average rate of change can also be measured by the tangent of α. In trigonometry, the *tangent* of an angle is equal to the side opposite the angle divided by the side adjacent to the angle, here $\Delta y/\Delta x$. In Fig. 3-1(a), the tangent of α measures the actual rate of change of the function and hence the slope. In Fig. 3-1(b), the tangent of α only approximates the actual rate of change of the function as seen by the *chord* (the dashed line) connecting two points on the curve. This rough approximation will later be refined in the derivative. See Example 4.

Example 2. As a straight line, the tangent has a constant slope which measures the change in y for a change in x for each movement along the line, no matter how small. This includes the point at which the tangent just touches the curve. Thus, the slope of a tangent at a point equals the slope of the curve at that point.

34

In Fig. 3-2, three different tangents are drawn at points A, B, C on the curve. The slopes of these tangents provide the slope of the function at the given points. For visual purposes, Δy and Δx are drawn relatively large, but since the slope of a straight line is everywhere constant, it also provides a measure of the change in y associated with a change in x for the curvilinear function *at the given point.*

Example 3. Figure 3-2 also illustrates that the slope of a curvilinear function changes at different points along the curve. The slope of the tangent (and hence of the curvilinear function) at A is larger than the slope at B and the slope at B is larger than the slope at C. As a general rule, the steeper the tangent, the larger the absolute value of the slope of the curve at that point; the flatter the tangent, the smaller the absolute value of the slope at that point.

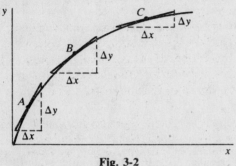 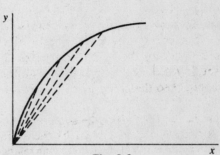

Fig. 3-2   **Fig. 3-3**

3.2 THE DERIVATIVE

The derivative measures the instantaneous rate of change of a function, i.e., how the dependent variable changes for a very small unit change in the independent variable. The formal terminology for the derivative is

$$\frac{dy}{dx} = \lim_{\Delta x \to 0} \frac{\Delta y}{\Delta x}$$

Here dy/dx is a combined expression which reads: the derivative of y with respect to x; it equals the limit of the ratio $\Delta y/\Delta x$ as Δx approaches zero. The derivative measures the slope of a function and is particularly helpful in measuring the slope of a curvilinear function.

Example 4. As seen in Fig. 3-3, the smaller the change in x, the more closely the chord approximates the function. The smaller the change in x, therefore, the closer the tangent of α comes to measuring the actual rate of change of the function. If Δx approaches zero, as in the derivative, the chord will be tangent to the curve and measure the actual slope (dy/dx) at that point.

3.3 DERIVATIVE NOTATION

The derivative can be expressed in forms other than dy/dx. Such notation includes both $f'(x)$ and f_x for the derivative of y with respect to x for the function $y = f(x)$, and y' or y_x for the derivative of y with respect to x for the function $y = y(x)$. The derivative may also be written as $\frac{d}{dx}y$ or $\frac{d}{dx}f(x)$.

Example 5. The derivative of $y = \phi(x)$ can be expressed as dy/dx, ϕ', ϕ_x, $\frac{d}{dx}y$, or $\frac{d}{dx}\phi(x)$. For the derivative of $y = F(x)$, dy/dx, F', F_x, $\frac{d}{dx}y$, or $\frac{d}{dx}F(x)$, are all equally correct. The derivative for $C = C(Y)$ is dC/dY and reads: the derivative of C with respect to Y. It can also be expressed as C', C_Y, $\frac{d}{dY}C$, or $\frac{d}{dY}C(Y)$. If $y = u(x) + v(x)$, or $u \cdot v$, or u/v, the derivative dy/dx can also be expressed $\frac{d}{dx}(u + v)$, $\frac{d}{dx}(u \cdot v)$, $\frac{d}{dx}(u/v)$. Thus, if $u = 3x^2$ and $v = 2x$, dy/dx in each instance could be expressed as $\frac{d}{dx}(3x^2 + 2x)$, $\frac{d}{dx}[3x^2(2x)]$, $\frac{d}{dx}(3x^2/2x)$. Sometimes, too, the derivative dy/dx for a function, $y = f(x)$, is also expressed simply as Dy.

3.4 RULES OF DIFFERENTIATION

Differentiation is the process of determining the derivative of a function, i.e., finding the change in y for a change in x when the change in $x(\Delta x)$ approaches zero. It involves nothing more complicated than applying a few basic formulas or rules to the function.   In explaining these rules, it is common to use auxiliary functions such as u and v, where u is an unspecified function of x, $u(x)$, and v is an unspecified function of x, $v(x)$.

(*a*)   *The Constant Function Rule.*   The derivative of a constant function, $y = k$, where k is any constant, is zero.

$$\text{Given} \quad y = k, \qquad\qquad \frac{dy}{dx} = 0$$

Example 6

$$\text{Given} \quad y = 5, \qquad\qquad \frac{dy}{dx} = 0$$

$$\text{Given} \quad y = -10, \qquad\qquad \frac{dy}{dx} = 0$$

Since y is constant, y will not change for any change in x. Hence $dy = 0$ and no matter what the change in x, $dy/dx = 0$.   See Problem 3.1.

(*b*)   *The Linear Function Rule.*   The derivative of a linear function, $y = a + bx$, is equal to b, the coefficient of x.

$$\text{Given} \quad y = a + bx, \qquad\qquad \frac{dy}{dx} = b$$

Example 7

$$\text{Given} \quad y = 2 + 3x, \qquad\qquad \frac{dy}{dx} = 3$$

$$\text{Given} \quad y = 5 - \tfrac{1}{4}x, \qquad\qquad \frac{dy}{dx} = -\frac{1}{4}$$

$$\text{Given} \quad y = 12x, \qquad\qquad \frac{dy}{dx} = 12$$

The derivative dy/dx measures the instantaneous rate of change of the function, the slope.   From Chapter 1, we know that the slope of a linear function is b, the coefficient of the independent variable, and that it is constant.

(*c*)   *The Power Function Rule.*   The derivative of a power function, $y = ax^p$, is equal to the exponent p times the coefficient a, multiplied by the variable x raised to the $(p - 1)$ power.

$$\text{Given} \quad y = ax^p, \qquad\qquad \frac{dy}{dx} = pax^{p-1}$$

Example 8

$$\text{Given} \quad y = 4x^3, \qquad\qquad \frac{dy}{dx} = 3(4)x^{3-1} = 12x^2$$

$$\text{Given} \quad y = 5x^2, \qquad\qquad \frac{dy}{dx} = 2(5)x^{2-1} = 10x$$

$$\text{Given} \quad y = x^4, \qquad\qquad \frac{dy}{dx} = 4(1)x^{4-1} = 4x^3 \qquad (\textit{Note:} \quad a = 1.)$$

(d)   *The Rule for Sums and Differences.*   The derivative of a sum, $y = u(x) + v(x)$,   is equal to the sum of the derivatives of the *individual* functions.   The derivative of a difference is equal to the difference of the derivatives of the *individual* functions.

Given $y = u(x) \pm v(x)$, $$\frac{dy}{dx} = \frac{du}{dx} \pm \frac{dv}{dx}$$

Example 9

Given $y = 12x^5 - 4x^4$, $$\frac{dy}{dx} = 60x^4 - 16x^3$$

Given $y = 9x^2 + 2x - 3$, $$\frac{dy}{dx} = 18x + 2$$

Note: To find the derivatives for the individual terms, apply whatever rule is appropriate.

(e)   *The Product Rule.*   The derivative of a product, $y = u(x) \cdot v(x)$,   is equal to the first function multiplied by the derivative of the second plus the second function multiplied by the derivative of the first.

Given $y = u(x) \cdot v(x)$, $$\frac{dy}{dx} = u\frac{dv}{dx} + v\frac{du}{dx}$$

(Remember to add exponents in multiplication.   For example, $3x^3 \cdot 4x^2 = 12x^5$,   not $12x^6$. A review of exponents is found in Chapter 7.)

Example 10.   Given $y = 3x^4(2x - 5)$, let $u = 3x^4$ and $v = (2x - 5)$.   Then $du/dx = 12x^3$ and $dv/dx = 2$. Substituting these values in the product rule formula,

$$\frac{dy}{dx} = 3x^4(2) + (2x - 5)(12x^3)$$

Simplifying the equation algebraically,

$$\frac{dy}{dx} = 6x^4 + 24x^4 - 60x^3 = 30x^4 - 60x^3$$

(f)   *The Quotient Rule.*   The derivative of a quotient, $y = u/v$,   is equal to the denominator times the derivative of the numerator, minus the numerator times the derivative of the denominator, all divided by the denominator squared.

Given $y = \dfrac{u(x)}{v(x)}$, $$\frac{dy}{dx} = \frac{v(du/dx) - u(dv/dx)}{v^2}$$

The order in the numerator of the formula for the derivative is important and cannot be reversed.   (Remember, too, to subtract exponents in division.   For example, $6x^6/3x^2 = 2x^4$, not $2x^3$.)

Example 11.   Given

$$y = \frac{5x^3}{4x + 3}$$

where $u = 5x^3$ and $v = 4x + 3$, $du/dx = 15x^2$ and $dv/dx = 4$.   Substituting these values in the quotient rule formula,

$$\frac{dy}{dx} = \frac{(4x + 3)(15x^2) - 5x^3(4)}{(4x + 3)^2}$$

Simplifying algebraically,

$$\frac{dy}{dx} = \frac{60x^3 + 45x^2 - 20x^3}{(4x + 3)^2} = \frac{40x^3 + 45x^2}{(4x + 3)^2}$$

(g) *The Rule for a Function of a Function.* The derivative (dy/dx) of a function of a function, $y = f(u)$, where $u = g(x)$, is equal to the derivative of the first function with respect to u times the derivative of the second function with respect to x. This is called the *chain rule*.

Given $y = f(u)$, $u = g(x)$, $$\frac{dy}{dx} = \frac{dy}{du}\frac{du}{dx}$$

Example 12. If $y = u^4$ and $u = 2x^2 + 3$, then $dy/du = 4u^3$, and $du/dx = 4x$. Substituting in the chain rule formula,

$$\frac{dy}{dx} = 4u^3(4x) = 16xu^3$$

But $u = 2x^2 + 3$, which when substituted above, gives

$$\frac{dy}{dx} = 16x(2x^2 + 3)^3$$

Similarly, if $y = (4x + 2)^3$, we can let $u = 4x + 2$, then $y = u^3$, $dy/du = 3u^2$, and $du/dx = 4$. Then using the chain rule,

$$\frac{dy}{dx} = 3u^2(4) = 12u^2$$

and substituting $u = 4x + 2$,

$$\frac{dy}{dx} = 12(4x + 2)^2$$

For more complicated functions, different combinations of the seven basic rules outlined above must be used. See Problems 3.17 to 3.24.

3.5 HIGHER-ORDER DERIVATIVES

The second-order derivative (d^2y/dx^2) measures the rate of change of the first derivative, just as the first derivative (dy/dx) measures the rate of change of the original or *primitive function*. The third-order derivative (d^3y/dx^3) measures the rate of change of the second derivative, etc. Higher-order derivatives are found simply by applying the rules of differentiation to the derivative of the previous order.

Example 13. Besides d^2y/dx^2, common notation for the second derivative includes $f''(x)$, y'', D^2y, f_{xx}; for the third-order derivative, d^3y/dx^3, D^3y, f'''; for the fourth-order derivative, d^4y/dx^4, D^4y, $f^{(4)}$; etc.

Higher-order derivatives are found by applying the rules of differentiation to lower-order derivatives. Thus, if $y = 2x^4 + 5x^3 + 3x^2$,

$$\frac{dy}{dx} = 8x^3 + 15x^2 + 6x \qquad \frac{d^3y}{dx^3} = 48x + 30 \qquad \frac{d^5y}{dx^5} = 0$$

$$\frac{d^2y}{dx^2} = 24x^2 + 30x + 6 \qquad \frac{d^4y}{dx^4} = 48$$

Solved Problems

SLOPES AND DERIVATIVES

3.1. Explain, with the aid of a graph, why the derivative of a constant is equal to zero. Assume $y = 6$. Explain why $dy/dx = 0$.

The function $y = 6$ as graphed in Fig. 3-4 is a horizontal line, indicating that y equals 6 no matter what value x assumes. Hence a small change in x, or any change in x, produces no change in y. If $dy = 0$ for any change in x, then dy/dx (the derivative) must also equal zero.

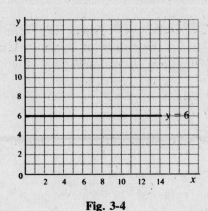

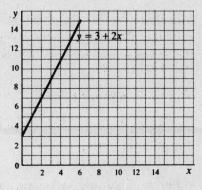

Fig. 3-4   **Fig. 3-5**

3.2. Using a graph, explain why the derivative of a linear function is constant and equal to the coefficient of x. Assume $y = 3 + 2x$.

Figure 3-5 shows graphically that for every one unit change in x, y increases by 2, or $\Delta y/\Delta x = 2$. Because this graph is a straight line, any change in x, no matter how small, will produce a change in y that is two times larger than itself. Thus, the derivative, dy/dx, will in this case equal 2 at any point along the line, and is therefore constant.

Since the derivative of a function gives the slope of a line, and since the slope of a linear function is given by the coefficient of the independent variable, the derivative of a linear function must always equal the coefficient of the independent variable. See Section 3.4, item (b).

3.3. For each of the curvilinear functions in Fig. 3-6, show at which of the given points the absolute value of the slope of the curve is greatest.

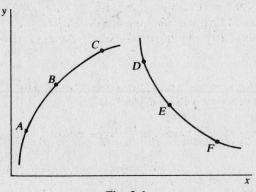

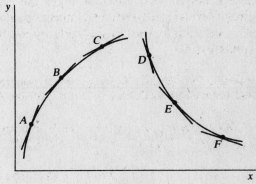

Fig. 3-6   **Fig. 3-7**

The slope of a curvilinear function at a given point is given by the slope of a line drawn tangent to the curve at that point. By drawing tangents to the curves at the different points (see Fig. 3-7), it is clear that the absolute value of the slope $|\Delta y/\Delta x|$ is greater at A than B, and greater at B than C. Using the symbol $>$ (meaning greater than),

$$\left|\frac{\Delta y}{\Delta x}\right|_A > \left|\frac{\Delta y}{\Delta x}\right|_B > \left|\frac{\Delta y}{\Delta x}\right|_C$$

Similarly, the absolute value of the slope at D is greater than at E, and greater at E than F. Or,

$$\left|\frac{\Delta y}{\Delta x}\right|_D > \left|\frac{\Delta y}{\Delta x}\right|_E > \left|\frac{\Delta y}{\Delta x}\right|_F$$

In graphs of similar dimensions, the relative size of the slope in terms of absolute value is always indicated by the relative steepness of the tangent.

3.4. Given $y = f(x) = 7x + 6$, use the different possible notations to express the derivative of the function.

The derivative of the given function can read:

$$\frac{dy}{dx} = 7 \qquad y_x = 7 \qquad Dy = 7 \qquad \frac{d}{dx}y = 7 \qquad f_x = 7$$

$$y' = 7 \qquad f' = 7 \qquad \frac{d}{dx}(7x + 6) = 7 \qquad \frac{d}{dx}f(x) = 7$$

3.5. For each of the following functions, find the value of the slope at $x = 2$ and $x = 5$. Familiarize yourself with the different notations.

(a) $y = 7x^2 + 3$

$$\frac{dy}{dx} = 14x$$

At $x = 2$, the slope $dy/dx = 14(2) = 28$. At $x = 5$, $dy/dx = 14(5) = 70$.

(b) $y = 2x^3 - 2x$

$$Dy = 6x^2 - 2$$

At $x = 2$, the slope $Dy = 6(2)^2 - 2 = 22$. At $x = 5$, $Dy = 6(5)^2 - 2 = 148$.

(c) $y = 30 + 6x$

$$y' = 6$$

At $x = 2$, the slope $y' = 6$. At $x = 5$, $y' = 6$.

(d) $y = -x^3 + 4x - 3$

$$y_x = -3x^2 + 4$$

At $x = 2$, the slope $y_x = -3(2)^2 + 4 = -8$. At $x = 5$, $y_x = -3(5)^2 + 4 = -71$.

SIMPLE DERIVATIVES

3.6. Differentiate each of the following functions. Practice the use of different notations for the derivative.

(a) $y = 17$

$$\frac{dy}{dx} = 0 \quad \text{(Constant Rule)}$$

(b) $y = 12$

$$\frac{d}{dx}y = 0$$

(c) $y = 5x + 12$

$$y' = 5 \quad \text{(Linear Function Rule)}$$

(d) $f(x) = 9x - 6$

$$f' = 9$$

(e) $y = 3x^2$

$$\frac{d}{dx}(3x^2) = 6x \quad \text{(Power Function Rule)}$$

(f) $f(x) = 4x^9$

$$f_x = 36x^8$$

(g) $y = 5x^3 - 7x^2 + 4x + 9$

$$\frac{dy}{dx} = 15x^2 - 14x + 4 \quad \text{(Sums and Differences Rule)}$$

(h) $y = 2x^6 + 7x^4 - 3x^3 - 12$

$$y' = 12x^5 + 28x^3 - 9x^2$$

3.7. Differentiate the following functions, using the rule for sums and differences:

(a) $z = -8t^5 - 5t^4 + 6t^3$ (b) $p = -3q^2 + 7q - 15$

$$\frac{dz}{dt} = -40t^4 - 20t^3 + 18t^2 \qquad\qquad \frac{dp}{dq} = -6q + 7$$

Note: Introduction of different variables does not change the concept of the derivative. Simply think in terms of the dependent and independent variable.

3.8. Find the following derivatives:

(a) $\dfrac{d}{du}(4u^7 - 3u^6)$ (b) $\dfrac{d}{ds}(9s^2 - 11s + 6)$

$$\frac{d}{du}(4u^7 - 3u^6) = 28u^6 - 18u^5 \qquad\qquad \frac{d}{ds}(9s^2 - 11s + 6) = 18s - 11$$

THE PRODUCT RULE

3.9. Given $y = 5x^4(3x - 7)$, (a) find the derivative directly, using the product rule. (b) Simplify the original function by multiplication and then find the derivative. (c) Compare the derivatives in parts (a) and (b).

(a) Given the formula for the product rule, $dy/dx = u(dv/dx) + v(du/dx)$, let $u = 5x^4$ and $v = 3x - 7$. Then $du/dx = 20x^3$ and $dv/dx = 3$. Substituting these values in the product rule formula,

$$\frac{dy}{dx} = 5x^4(3) + (3x - 7)(20x^3)$$

Simplifying algebraically,

$$\frac{dy}{dx} = 15x^4 + 60x^4 - 140x^3 = 75x^4 - 140x^3$$

(b) Simplifying the original function through multiplication,

$$y = 5x^4(3x - 7) = 15x^5 - 35x^4$$

Taking the derivative,

$$\frac{dy}{dx} = 75x^4 - 140x^3$$

(c) The derivatives found in parts (a) and (b) are identical. The derivative of a product can be found by either method, but as the functions grow more complicated, the power rule becomes more useful. Note that knowledge of an alternate method can be used to check answers.

3.10. Redo Problem 3.9, given $y = (x^8 + 8)(x^6 + 11)$.

(a) Let $u = x^8 + 8$ and $v = x^6 + 11$. Then $du/dx = 8x^7$ and $dv/dx = 6x^5$. Substituting these values in the product rule formula,

$$\frac{dy}{dx} = (x^8 + 8)(6x^5) + (x^6 + 11)(8x^7) = 6x^{13} + 48x^5 + 8x^{13} + 88x^7 = 14x^{13} + 88x^7 + 48x^5$$

(b) Simplifying first through multiplication,

$$y = (x^8 + 8)(x^6 + 11) = x^{14} + 11x^8 + 8x^6 + 88$$

Then,

$$\frac{dy}{dx} = 14x^{13} + 88x^7 + 48x^5$$

(c) The derivatives are, of course, identical.

3.11. Differentiate each of the following functions, using the product rule:

(a) $y = (4x^2 - 3)(2x^5)$

$$\frac{dy}{dx} = (4x^2 - 3)(10x^4) + 2x^5(8x) = 40x^6 - 30x^4 + 16x^6 = 56x^6 - 30x^4$$

(b) $y = 7x^9(3x^2 - 12)$

$$\frac{dy}{dx} = 7x^9(6x) + (3x^2 - 12)(63x^8) = 42x^{10} + 189x^{10} - 756x^8 = 231x^{10} - 756x^8$$

(c) $y = (2x^4 + 5)(3x^5 - 8)$

$$\frac{dy}{dx} = (2x^4 + 5)(15x^4) + (3x^5 - 8)(8x^3) = 30x^8 + 75x^4 + 24x^8 - 64x^3 = 54x^8 + 75x^4 - 64x^3$$

(d) $z = (3 - 12t^3)(5 + 4t^6)$

$$\frac{dz}{dt} = (3 - 12t^3)(24t^5) + (5 + 4t^6)(-36t^2) = 72t^5 - 288t^8 - 180t^2 - 144t^8 = -432t^8 + 72t^5 - 180t^2$$

THE QUOTIENT RULE

3.12. Given

$$y = \frac{10x^8 - 6x^7}{2x}$$

(a) find the derivative directly, using the quotient rule.   (b) Simplify the function by division and then take its derivative.   (c) Compare the results.

(a)   The formula for the quotient rule is

$$\frac{dy}{dx} = \frac{v(du/dx) - u(dv/dx)}{v^2}$$

where u = the numerator = $10x^8 - 6x^7$ and v = the denominator = $2x$.   Thus,

$$\frac{du}{dx} = 80x^7 - 42x^6 \quad \text{and} \quad \frac{dv}{dx} = 2$$

Substituting in the formula,

$$\frac{dy}{dx} = \frac{2x(80x^7 - 42x^6) - (10x^8 - 6x^7)(2)}{(2x)^2}$$

$$= \frac{160x^8 - 84x^7 - 20x^8 + 12x^7}{4x^2} = \frac{140x^8 - 72x^7}{4x^2} = 35x^6 - 18x^5$$

(b)   Simplifying the original function first by division,

$$y = \frac{10x^8 - 6x^7}{2x} = 5x^7 - 3x^6$$

$$\frac{dy}{dx} = 35x^6 - 18x^5$$

(c)   The derivatives are identical, as you might have expected.   The derivative can be found by either method, but more complicated functions will generally require the quotient rule.   See Problem 3.13(b)–(e).   The alternate method again provides a way of checking your answers, however.

3.13. Differentiate each of the following functions by means of the quotient rule:

(a)

$$y = \frac{3x^8 - 4x^7}{4x^3}$$

u = the   numerator = $3x^8 - 4x^7$; v = the   denominator = $4x^3$. Thus, $du/dx = 24x^7 - 28x^6$ and $dv/dx = 12x^2$. Substituting in the quotient formula,

$$\frac{dy}{dx} = \frac{4x^3(24x^7 - 28x^6) - (3x^8 - 4x^7)(12x^2)}{(4x^3)^2}$$

$$\frac{dy}{dx} = \frac{96x^{10} - 112x^9 - 36x^{10} + 48x^9}{16x^6}$$

$$= \frac{60x^{10} - 64x^9}{16x^6} = \frac{15}{4}x^4 - 4x^3$$

[For the denominator, remember to multiply exponents when they are raised to a power. For example $(x^2)^3 = x^6$.]

(b) $y = \dfrac{4x^5}{1 - 3x}$ $(x \neq \frac{1}{3})$

(*Note*:   The qualifying statement is added because if $x = \frac{1}{3}$,   the denominator would equal zero and the function would be undefined.)

$$\frac{dy}{dx} = \frac{(1 - 3x)(20x^4) - 4x^5(-3)}{(1 - 3x)^2} = \frac{20x^4 - 60x^5 + 12x^5}{(1 - 3x)^2} = \frac{20x^4 - 48x^5}{(1 - 3x)^2}$$

(c) $y = \dfrac{15x^2}{2x^2 + 7x - 3}$

$$\frac{dy}{dx} = \frac{(2x^2 + 7x - 3)(30x) - 15x^2(4x + 7)}{(2x^2 + 7x - 3)^2}$$

$$= \frac{60x^3 + 210x^2 - 90x - 60x^3 - 105x^2}{(2x^2 + 7x - 3)^2} = \frac{105x^2 - 90x}{(2x^2 + 7x - 3)^2}$$

(d) $y = \dfrac{6x - 7}{8x - 5}$ $(x \neq \frac{5}{8})$

$$\frac{dy}{dx} = \frac{(8x - 5)(6) - (6x - 7)(8)}{(8x - 5)^2} = \frac{48x - 30 - 48x + 56}{(8x - 5)^2} = \frac{26}{(8x - 5)^2}$$

(e) $y = \dfrac{5x^2 - 9x + 8}{x^2 + 1}$

$$\frac{dy}{dx} = \frac{(x^2 + 1)(10x - 9) - (5x^2 - 9x + 8)(2x)}{(x^2 + 1)^2}$$

$$= \frac{10x^3 - 9x^2 + 10x - 9 - 10x^3 + 18x^2 - 16x}{(x^2 + 1)^2} = \frac{9x^2 - 6x - 9}{(x^2 + 1)^2}$$

CHAIN RULE

3.14.   Given $y = u^6$ and $u = 3x^4 + 5$,   find dy/dx.

To find the derivative of a function of a function, the chain rule is necessary. According to the chain rule,

$$\frac{dy}{dx} = \frac{dy}{du}\frac{du}{dx}$$

Here $dy/du = 6u^5$, $du/dx = 12x^3$. Substituting these values in the formula,

$$\frac{dy}{dx} = 6u^5(12x^3) = 72x^3 u^5$$

But $u = 3x^4 + 5$. Therefore,

$$\frac{dy}{dx} = 72x^3(3x^4 + 5)^5$$

3.15. Given $y = (7x + 9)^2$, (a) use the chain rule to find the derivative directly, (b) square the function and find its derivative, and (c) compare the results.

(a) Letting $u = 7x + 9$, $y = u^2$, $du/dx = 7$, and $dy/du = 2u$. By the chain rule,

$$\frac{dy}{dx} = 2u(7) = 14u$$

But $u = 7x + 9$, so

$$\frac{dy}{dx} = 14(7x + 9) = 98x + 126$$

(b) Squaring the function first, we get

$$y = (7x + 9)^2 = 49x^2 + 126x + 81$$

$$\frac{d}{dx}(49x^2 + 126x + 81) = 98x + 126$$

(c) The derivatives are, of course, identical, and either method can be used. When a function is raised to a power higher than 2, however, such as in Problem 3.14, the chain rule greatly simplifies the task.

3.16. Use the chain rule to differentiate each of the following:

(a) $y = u^{20}$, $u = 7x - 4$

$$\frac{dy}{dx} = 20u^{19}(7) = 140u^{19}$$

But since $u = 7x - 4$,

$$\frac{dy}{dx} = 140(7x - 4)^{19}$$

(b) $y = u^4$, $u = -x^2 + 8x - 7$

$$\frac{dy}{dx} = 4u^3(-2x + 8) = (-8x + 32)u^3$$

But since $u = -x^2 + 8x - 7$,

$$\frac{dy}{dx} = (-8x + 32)(-x^2 + 8x - 7)^3$$

(c) $y = (5x - 7)^3$

When a polynomial is raised to a power higher than one, the chain rule is needed. Letting $u = 5x - 7$, then $y = u^3$, $dy/du = 3u^2$, and $du/dx = 5$. From the chain rule,

$$\frac{dy}{dx} = \frac{dy}{du}\frac{du}{dx}$$

Substituting the values above,

$$\frac{dy}{dx} = 3u^2(5) = 15u^2$$

But $u = 5x - 7$. Therefore,

$$\frac{dy}{dx} = 15(5x - 7)^2$$

(d) $y = (4x^2 - 1)^7$

Let $u = 4x^2 - 1$. Then $y = u^7$, $dy/du = 7u^6$, and $du/dx = 8x$. Substituting in the chain rule,

$$\frac{dy}{dx} = 7u^6(8x) = 56xu^6 = 56x(4x^2 - 1)^6$$

(e) $y = (x^2 + 3x - 1)^5$

Let $u = x^2 + 3x - 1$.   Then $y = u^5$, $dy/du = 5u^4$,   and $du/dx = 2x + 3$.   Substituting   in the chain rule,

$$\frac{dy}{dx} = 5u^4(2x + 3) = (10x + 15)u^4 = (10x + 15)(x^2 + 3x - 1)^4$$

COMBINATION OF RULES

3.17.   Given $y = 3x(2x - 1)/(3x - 2)$,   find the derivative.

Because the numerator of this quotient contains a product, the product rule must be used in conjunction with the quotient rule to find the derivative of this equation.   See Section 3.4, item (f).   From the quotient rule,

$$\frac{dy}{dx} = \frac{v(du/dx) - u(dv/dx)}{v^2}$$

where $u = 3x(2x - 1)$, $v = 3x - 2$,   and $dv/dx = 3$.   From the product rule,

$$\frac{du}{dx} = 3x(2) + (2x - 1)(3) = 12x - 3.$$

Thus,

$$\frac{dy}{dx} = \frac{(3x - 2)(12x - 3) - 3x(2x - 1)(3)}{(3x - 2)^2}$$

Simplifying algebraically,

$$\frac{dy}{dx} = \frac{36x^2 - 9x - 24x + 6 - 18x^2 + 9x}{(3x - 2)^2} = \frac{18x^2 - 24x + 6}{(3x - 2)^2}$$

3.18.   Given $y = (4x - 1)/[2x(5x + 2)]$,   find the derivative.

This case involves a quotient with a product in the denominator.   As in Problem 3.17, the product rule must be used in conjunction with the quotient rule.   Thus,

$$\frac{dy}{dx} = \frac{v(du/dx) - u(dv/dx)}{v^2}$$

where $u = 4x - 1$, $v = 2x(5x + 2)$,   and $du/dx = 4$.   From the product rule,

$$\frac{dv}{dx} = 2x(5) + (5x + 2)(2) = 20x + 4.$$

Substituting in the basic formula,

$$\frac{dy}{dx} = \frac{2x(5x + 2)(4) - (4x - 1)(20x + 4)}{[2x(5x + 2)]^2}$$

Simplifying algebraically,

$$\frac{dy}{dx} = \frac{40x^2 + 16x - 80x^2 - 16x + 20x + 4}{4x^2(5x + 2)^2} = \frac{-40x^2 + 20x + 4}{4x^2(5x + 2)^2}$$

3.19.   Given $y = 3x(4x - 5)^2$,   find the derivative.

This product requires the use of the product rule.   However, the chain rule is also needed to get the derivative of the second function $(4x - 5)^2$.   From the product rule,

$$\frac{dy}{dx} = u\frac{dv}{dx} + v\frac{du}{dx}$$

where $u = 3x$, $v = (4x - 5)^2$, and $du/dx = 3$. From the chain rule, $dv/dx = 2(4x - 5)(4)$. Substituting these values in the product formula,

$$\frac{dy}{dx} = 3x(8)(4x - 5) + (4x - 5)^2(3)$$

Simplifying algebraically,

$$\frac{dy}{dx} = 96x^2 - 120x + 3(16x^2 - 40x + 25) = 144x^2 - 240x + 75$$

3.20. Check Problem 3.19 by simplifying the function and then taking the derivative.

Simplifying $y = 3x(4x - 5)^2$ algebraically,

$$y = 3x(16x^2 - 40x + 25) = 48x^3 - 120x^2 + 75x$$

Thus, as in Problem 3.19,

$$\frac{d}{dx}(48x^3 - 120x^2 + 75x) = 144x^2 - 240x + 75$$

3.21. Given $y = 3x[(5x + 2)/(2x + 3)]$, find the derivative.

This product involves a quotient. Thus, in addition to the product rule, the quotient rule is needed to get the derivative of the second function required by the product rule. From the product rule,

$$\frac{dy}{dx} = u\frac{dv}{dx} + v\frac{du}{dx}$$

where $u = 3x$, $v = (5x + 2)/(2x + 3)$, and $du/dx = 3$. From the quotient rule,

$$\frac{dv}{dx} = \frac{(2x + 3)(5) - (5x + 2)(2)}{(2x + 3)^2} = \frac{11}{(2x + 3)^2}$$

Substituting in the product rule formula,

$$\frac{dy}{dx} = 3x\frac{11}{(2x + 3)^2} + \frac{5x + 2}{2x + 3}(3)$$

Simplifying algebraically,

$$\frac{dy}{dx} = \frac{33x}{(2x + 3)^2} + \frac{15x + 6}{2x + 3} = \frac{33x + (15x + 6)(2x + 3)}{(2x + 3)^2}$$

$$= \frac{30x^2 + 90x + 18}{(2x + 3)^2}$$

Note: This problem can also be treated as a quotient involving a product. Find the derivative using the quotient rule to check this answer on your own.

3.22. Given $y = (8x - 5)^2/(7x + 4)$, find y'.

This solution involves the quotient rule, plus the chain rule to obtain the derivative of the numerator required by the quotient rule. Thus, from the quotient rule,

$$\frac{dy}{dx} = \frac{v(du/dx) - u(dv/dx)}{v^2}$$

where $u = (8x - 5)^2$, $v = 7x + 4$, $dv/dx = 7$. From the chain rule, $du/dx = 2(8x - 5)(8) = 128x - 80$. Substituting these values in the quotient rule formula,

$$\frac{dy}{dx} = \frac{(7x + 4)(128x - 80) - (8x - 5)^2(7)}{(7x + 4)^2}$$

$$= \frac{896x^2 - 560x + 512x - 320 - 7(64x^2 - 80x + 25)}{(7x + 4)^2} = \frac{448x^2 + 512x - 495}{(7x + 4)^2}$$

3.23.   Given $y = [(3x + 4)/(2x + 5)]^2$,   find dy/dx.

This problem requires the chain rule and the quotient rule.   From the chain rule,

$$\frac{dy}{dx} = \frac{dy}{du}\frac{du}{dx}$$

Letting $u = (3x + 4)/(2x + 5)$,   then $y = u^2$ and $dy/du = 2u$.   From the quotient rule,

$$\frac{du}{dx} = \frac{(2x + 5)(3) - (3x + 4)(2)}{(2x + 5)^2} = \frac{7}{(2x + 5)^2}$$

Substituting in the chain rule formula,

$$\frac{dy}{dx} = 2u\frac{7}{(2x + 5)^2}$$

But $u = (3x + 4)/(2x + 5)$,   so

$$\frac{dy}{dx} = \frac{2(3x + 4)}{(2x + 5)}\frac{7}{(2x + 5)^2} = \frac{14(3x + 4)}{(2x + 5)^3} = \frac{42x + 56}{(2x + 5)^3}$$

3.24.   Differentiate each of the following, using whatever rules are necessary:

(*a*) $y = (5x - 1)(3x + 4)^3$

Using the product rule together with the chain rule,

$$\frac{dy}{dx} = (5x - 1)[3(3x + 4)^2(3)] + (3x + 4)^3(5)$$

Simplifying algebraically,

$$\frac{dy}{dx} = (5x - 1)(9)(3x + 4)^2 + 5(3x + 4)^3 = (45x - 9)(3x + 4)^2 + 5(3x + 4)^3$$

(*b*) $y = \frac{(9x^2 - 2)(7x + 3)}{5x}$

Using the quotient rule along with the product rule,

$$y' = \frac{5x[(9x^2 - 2)(7) + (7x + 3)(18x)] - (9x^2 - 2)(7x + 3)(5)}{(5x)^2}.$$

Simplifying algebraically,

$$y' = \frac{5x(63x^2 - 14 + 126x^2 + 54x) - 5(63x^3 + 27x^2 - 14x - 6)}{25x^2} = \frac{630x^3 + 135x^2 + 30}{25x^2}$$

(*c*) $y = \frac{15x + 23}{(3x + 1)^2}$

Using the quotient rule plus the chain rule,

$$y' = \frac{(3x + 1)^2(15) - (15x + 23)[2(3x + 1)(3)]}{(3x + 1)^4}$$

Simplifying algebraically,

$$y' = \frac{15(3x + 1)^2 - (15x + 23)(18x + 6)}{(3x + 1)^4} = \frac{-135x^2 - 414x - 123}{(3x + 1)^4}$$

(*d*) $y = (6x + 1)\frac{(4x)}{9x - 1}$

Using the product rule and the quotient rule,

$$Dy = (6x + 1)\left[\frac{(9x - 1)(4) - 4x(9)}{(9x - 1)^2}\right] + \frac{4x}{9x - 1}(6)$$

Simplifying algebraically,

$$Dy = \frac{(6x+1)(36x-4-36x)}{(9x-1)^2} + \frac{24x}{9x-1} = \frac{216x^2-48x-4}{(9x-1)^2}$$

Note: To check this answer, use the quotient rule involving a product.   See Problem 3.17.

(e) $y = \left(\dfrac{3x-1}{2x+5}\right)^3$

Using the chain rule and the quotient rule,

$$y' = 3\left(\frac{3x-1}{2x+5}\right)^2 \frac{(2x+5)(3)-(3x-1)(2)}{(2x+5)^2}$$

Simplifying algebraically,

$$y' = \frac{3(3x-1)^2}{(2x+5)^2} \frac{17}{(2x+5)^2} = \frac{51(3x-1)^2}{(2x+5)^4}$$

HIGHER-ORDER DERIVATIVES

3.25.   For each of the following functions, (1) find the second-order derivative and   (2) evaluate it at $x = 2$.   Practice the use of the different second-order notations.

(a) $y = 7x^3 + 5x^2 + 12$

    (1) $\dfrac{dy}{dx} = 21x^2 + 10x$ (2)   At $x = 2$, $d^2y/dx^2 = 42(2) + 10$

        $\dfrac{d^2y}{dx^2} = 42x + 10$ $= 94$

(b) $f(x) = x^6 + 3x^4 + x$

    (1) $f'(x) = 6x^5 + 12x^3 + 1$ (2)   At $x = 2$, $f''(x) = 30(2)^4 + 36(2)^2$

        $f''(x) = 30x^4 + 36x^2$ $= 624$

(c) $y = (2x+3)(8x^2-6)$

    (1) $Dy = (2x+3)(16x) + (8x^2-6)(2)$ (2)   At $x = 2$, $D^2y = 96(2) + 48$

           $= 32x^2 + 48x + 16x^2 - 12$ $= 240$

           $= 48x^2 + 48x - 12$

        $D^2y = 96x + 48$

(d) $f(x) = (x^4-3)(x^3-2)$

    (1) $f_x = (x^4-3)(3x^2) + (x^3-2)(4x^3)$ (2)   At $x = 2$, $f_{xx} = 42(2)^5 - 24(2)^2 - 18(2)$

          $= 3x^6 - 9x^2 + 4x^6 - 8x^3$ $= 1212$

          $= 7x^6 - 8x^3 - 9x^2$

        $f_{xx} = 42x^5 - 24x^2 - 18x$

(e) $y = \dfrac{5x}{1-3x}$

    (1) $y' = \dfrac{(1-3x)(5)-5x(-3)}{(1-3x)^2}$ (2)   At $x = 2$, $y'' = \dfrac{30-90(2)}{[1-3(2)]^4}$

          $= \dfrac{5-15x+15x}{(1-3x)^2} = \dfrac{5}{(1-3x)^2}$ $= \dfrac{-150}{(-5)^4}$

        $y'' = \dfrac{(1-3x^2)(0)-5[2(1-3x)(-3)]}{(1-3x)^4}$ $= -\dfrac{6}{25}$

          $= \dfrac{-5(-6+18x)}{(1-3x)^4} = \dfrac{30-90x}{(1-3x)^4}$

(f) $y = \dfrac{7x^2}{x-1}$

(1) $y' = \dfrac{(x-1)(14x) - 7x^2(1)}{(x-1)^2}$

$= \dfrac{14x^2 - 14x - 7x^2}{(x-1)^2} = \dfrac{7x^2 - 14x}{(x-1)^2}$

$y'' = \dfrac{(x-1)^2(14x-14) - (7x^2-14x)[2(x-1)(1)]}{(x-1)^4}$

$= \dfrac{(x^2-2x+1)(14x-14) - (7x^2-14x)(2x-2)}{(x-1)^4}$

$= \dfrac{14(x-1)}{(x-1)^4} = \dfrac{14}{(x-1)^3}$

(2) At $x = 2$, $y'' = \dfrac{14}{(2-1)^3}$

$= 14$

(g) $f(x) = (8x-4)^3$

(1) $f' = 3(8x-4)^2(8)$

$= 24(8x-4)^2$

$f'' = 2(24)(8x-4)(8)$

$= 384(8x-4)$

(2) At $x = 2$, $f'' = 384[8(2) - 4]$

$= 4608$

(h) $y = (5x^3 - 7x^2)^2$

(1) $Dy = 2(5x^3 - 7x^2)(15x^2 - 14x)$

$= 150x^5 - 350x^4 + 196x^3$

$D^2y = 750x^4 - 1400x^3 + 588x^2$

(2) At $x = 2$, $D^2y = 750(2)^4 - 1400(2)^3 + 588(2)^2$

$= 3152$

3.26. For each of the following functions, (1) investigate the successive derivatives and (2) evaluate them at $x = 3$.

(a) $y = x^3 + 3x^2 + 9x - 7$

(1) $y' = 3x^2 + 6x + 9$

$y'' = 6x + 6$

$y''' = 6$

$y^{(4)} = 0$

(2) At $x = 3$, $y' = 3(3)^2 + 6(3) + 9 = 54$

$y'' = 6(3) + 6 = 24$

$y''' = 6$

$y^{(4)} = 0$

(b) $y = (4x-7)(9x+2)$

(1) $y' = (4x-7)(9) + (9x+2)(4)$

$= 36x - 63 + 36x + 8 = 72x - 55$

$y'' = 72$

$y''' = 0$

(2) At $x = 3$, $y' = 72(3) - 55 = 161$

$y'' = 72$

$y''' = 0$

(c) $y = (5-x)^4$

(1) $Dy = 4(5-x)^3(-1) = -4(5-x)^3$

$D^2y = -12(5-x)^2(-1) = 12(5-x)^2$

$D^3y = 24(5-x)(-1)$

$= -24(5-x) = 24x - 120$

$D^4y = 24$

$D^5y = 0$

(2) At $x = 3$, $Dy = -4(5-3)^3 = -32$

$D^2y = 12(5-3)^2 = 48$

$D^3y = 24(3) - 120 = -48$

$D^4y = 24$

$D^5y = 0$

Chapter 4

Use of the Derivative in Economics

4.1 MARGINAL CONCEPTS

Marginal cost in economics is defined as the change in total cost incurred from the production of an additional unit. *Marginal revenue* is defined as the change in total revenue brought about by the sale of an extra good. Since total cost and total revenue are both functions of the level of output (Q), marginal cost and marginal revenue can each be expressed mathematically as derivatives of their respective total functions. Thus,

if $TC = TC(Q)$,   then $$MC = \frac{dTC}{dQ}$$

and if $TR = TR(Q)$,   then $$MR = \frac{dTR}{dQ}$$

In short, the marginal concept of any economic function can be expressed as the derivative of its total function.

Example 1.

1. If $TR = 75Q - 4Q^2$,   then $MR = dTR/dQ = 75 - 8Q$.
2. If $TC = Q^2 + 7Q + 23$,   then $MC = dTC/dQ = 2Q + 7$.

Example 2. Given the demand function $P = 30 - 2Q$,   the marginal revenue function can be found by first finding the total revenue function and then taking the derivative of that function with respect to Q. Thus,

$$TR = PQ = (30 - 2Q)Q = 30Q - 2Q^2$$

Then, $$MR = \frac{dTR}{dQ} = 30 - 4Q$$

If $Q = 4$, $MR = 30 - 4(4) = 14$;   if $Q = 5$, $MR = 30 - 4(5) = 10$.

4.2 MAXIMIZATION AND MINIMIZATION OF A FUNCTION

To be at a relative maximum or minimum, a function must be at a *plateau* (i.e. neither increasing nor decreasing at that point). If the function is neither increasing nor decreasing, the derivative of the function at that point must be zero. The first, and necessary, condition for a relative maximum or minimum, therefore, is that the first derivative be equal to zero. The second, and sufficient, condition is that the second derivative be negative for a relative maximum, and positive for a relative minimum. Thus,

for a relative maximum: $$\frac{dy}{dx} = 0 \qquad \frac{d^2y}{dx^2} < 0$$

and for a relative minimum: $$\frac{dy}{dx} = 0 \qquad \frac{d^2y}{dx^2} > 0$$

Example 3. The derivative measures the instantaneous rate of change of a function. At those points where the derivative is positive (as depicted by the positive slope of the tangents at A and E in Fig. 4-1), the function is increasing. At those points where the derivative is negative (as depicted by the negative slope of the tangents at C and F), the function is decreasing. At those points where the function is at a relative maximum or minimum (B and D), the slope is clearly equal to zero. This is a necessary condition for both a relative maximum and a relative minimum. To distinguish between them mathematically, the second derivative is necessary.

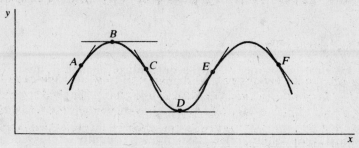

Fig. 4-1

Example 4. The second derivative measures the rate of change in the marginal function (as given by the first derivative). If the first derivative is zero, indicating a zero slope and hence a plateau in the function, while the second derivative is *negative*, it means that the function is moving *down* from the plateau and must have been at a *relative maximum*. If the first derivative is zero and the second derivative is *positive*, it means that the function is moving *upward* from a plateau and the plateau was a *relative minimum*. Keeping in mind that a positive second derivative in these circumstances $(++)$ means the curve is moving up from a plateau $(\cup)$ and a negative second derivative $(--)$ means the curve is moving down from a plateau $(\cap)$, a simple mnemonic to remember the rule is

(a) Minimum   (b) Maximum

A point at which the first derivative equals zero is called a *critical value*, a *stationary value*, or an *extreme value*. If the second derivative equals zero but the third derivative does not equal zero, then the critical value is neither a maximum nor a minimum, but an *inflection point* at which the function alters its rate of change. Point A in Fig. 4-4(a) is an inflection point.

Example 5. Given $TC = 31 + 24Q - 5.5Q^2 + \frac{1}{3}Q^3$, to find the relative minimum or maximum for a total cost function,

1. First find the critical values by taking the derivative of the function and setting it equal to zero.

$$\frac{dTC}{dQ} = 24 - 11Q + Q^2 = 0$$

$$(Q - 8)(Q - 3) = 0$$

The critical values are $\qquad Q = 8 \qquad Q = 3$

2. Take the second derivative to see if, at the critical values, the function is minimized or maximized.

$$\frac{d^2TC}{dQ^2} = -11 + 2Q$$

At $Q = 8$, $\qquad \frac{d^2TC}{dQ^2} = -11 + 2(8) = 5 > 0$

At $Q = 3$, $\qquad \frac{d^2TC}{dQ^2} = -11 + 2(3) = -5 < 0$

Thus, at $Q = 8$, TC is at a relative minimum and at $Q = 3$, TC is at a relative maximum.

3. Evaluate the original function at $Q = 8$ to find the relative minimum, and at $Q = 3$ to find the relative maximum.

At $Q = 8$, $TC = 31 + 24(8) - 5.5(8)^2 + \frac{1}{3}(8)^3 = 41.67$

At $Q = 3$, $TC = 31 + 24(3) - 5.5(3)^2 + \frac{1}{3}(3)^3 = 62.5$

4.3 PRICE ELASTICITY

In economics, *price elasticity* ϵ measures the percentage change in quantity associated with a percentage change in price. Mathematically,

$$\epsilon = \frac{dQ/Q}{dP/P}$$

For ease in mathematical computation, price elasticity is frequently expressed in the alternate form:

$$\epsilon = \frac{dQ/dP}{Q/P} = \frac{\text{marginal function}}{\text{average function}} \qquad \text{or} \qquad \epsilon = \frac{dQ}{dP}\frac{P}{Q}$$

There are price elasticities for both supply and demand. Either is said to be *elastic* if $|\epsilon| > 1$, *inelastic if* $|\epsilon| < 1$, and *unitary elastic* if $|\epsilon| = 1$.

Example 6. Given the demand function $Q_d = 650 - 5P - P^2$, where $P = 10$, the price elasticity of demand is determined as shown below.

Using the alternate form of the formula: $\epsilon = \frac{dQ}{dP}\frac{P}{Q}$

first take the derivative. $\frac{dQ}{dP} = -5 - 2P$

Then substitute the given price level ($P = 10$).

$$\frac{dQ}{dP} = -5 - 2(10) = -25$$

Next, find the level of output (Q) when $P = 10$.

$$Q = 650 - 5(10) - (10)^2 = 500$$

Substituting these values in the elasticity formula,

$$\epsilon = -25(\tfrac{10}{500}) = -0.5$$

(For the elasticity of the inverse of this type of function, with P as a function of Q along traditional economic lines, see Problem 4.25.)

Example 7. Since $\epsilon = (dQ/dP)/(Q/P) = $ marginal function/average function, the elasticity of supply and demand can be calculated visually as in Fig. 4-2 by estimating the marginal and average functions. The marginal function is estimated by the slope of the tangent to the curve; the average function is estimated by the slope of a straight line from the origin to the desired point on the curve.

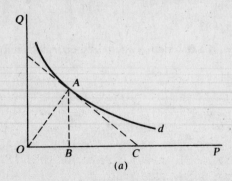 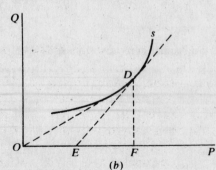

Fig. 4-2

For the demand function in Fig. 4-2(a):   The slope of the marginal function at A is $-AB/BC$.   The slope of the average function at A is AB/OB.   Therefore

$$\epsilon_d = \frac{-AB/BC}{AB/OB} = -\frac{AB}{BC}\frac{OB}{AB} = -\frac{OB}{BC}$$

For the supply function in Fig. 4-2(b):   The slope of the marginal function at D is DF/EF.   The slope of the average function at D is DF/OF.   Therefore

$$\epsilon_s = \frac{DF/EF}{DF/OF} = \frac{DF}{EF}\frac{OF}{DF} = \frac{OF}{EF}$$

When $Q = f(P)$, the price elasticity of demand $|\epsilon_d|$ at a particular point equals the horizontal distance of the point from the origin (OB) divided by the horizontal distance of the point from the point at which the tangent to the demand curve crosses the horizontal axis (BC).   The price elasticity of supply at a given point, when $Q = f(P)$, equals the horizontal distance of the point from the origin (OF) divided by the horizontal distance of the point from the point at which the tangent to the supply curve crosses the horizontal axis (EF).   For adaptation of these relationships when $P = f(Q)$ and measurement of elasticity of demand in terms of segments of the demand curve itself, see Problems 4.25–4.44.

Example 8.   Using the techniques from Example 7, the elasticity of demand and supply at the designated points in Fig. 4-3 are calculated below.

Elasticity of demand: *Elasticity of supply*:

At point A, $\epsilon_d = -\dfrac{OE}{EF} = -\dfrac{30}{50} = -0.6$ At point C, $\epsilon_s = \dfrac{OK}{IK} = \dfrac{70}{50} = 1.4$

At point B, $\epsilon_d = -\dfrac{OG}{GH} = -\dfrac{100}{60} = -1.67$ At point D, $\epsilon_s = \dfrac{OL}{JL} = \dfrac{120}{60} = 2$

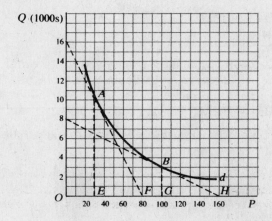
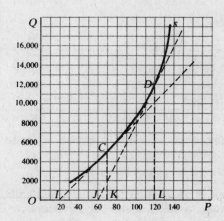

Fig. 4-3

4.4   RELATIONSHIP AMONG TOTAL, MARGINAL, AND AVERAGE CONCEPTS

The relationship among total, marginal, and average concepts is very important and is illustrated in Fig. 4-4.   Figure 4-4(a) represents a total product (TP) curve for input x, holding input y constant.   Figure 4-4(b) represents the marginal product (MP) and average product (AP) curves for x.   The marginal product curve in (b) is derived from the total product curve in (a).   Since MP_x is the change in TP associated with a change in x, MP_x equals the slope of the TP curve ($d\text{TP}/dx$), which can be estimated visually by the slopes of tangents at various points along the TP curve. Five characteristics of the relationship between TP and MP warrant attention:

TP	⇔	MP
1. The slope is positive from O to C.		1. MP is positive (above the x axis) from O to C.
2. The slope gets steeper from O to A, an inflection point.		2. MP increases from O to A and peaks at A.
3. The slope grows less steep (but remains positive) from A to C.		3. MP declines (though remains positive) from A to C.
4. The slope equals zero at C.		4. MP equals zero at C.
5. The slope is negative to the right of C.		5. MP is negative to the right of C.

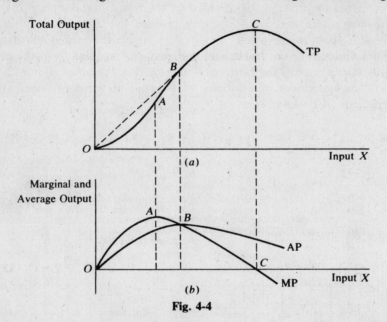

Fig. 4-4

Average product (AP) is total product divided by x. It is estimated from graph (a) by the slope of a straight line drawn from the origin to a point on the TP curve, as at B, since the slope of a line constructed in this way equals the value of the vertical coordinate divided by the value of the horizontal coordinate, or TP/x. Three characteristics of the AP curve should be noted.

1. The slope of a line from the origin to the TP curve gets steeper from O to B, where it is tangent to TP.		1. AP increases from O to B and reaches a maximum at B.
2. Since the line from the origin to the TP curve is tangent to the TP curve at B, it also equals the slope, or MP.		2. At B, AP = MP.
3. To the right of B, the slope of a line from the origin to the TP curve decreases, but still remains positive.		3. AP decreases after B, but remains positive (is above the x axis).

There is also an important relationship between marginal and average functions. In Fig. 4-4(b), note that the MP curve is above the AP curve (MP > AP) throughout the entire range in which the AP is increasing; MP = AP where the AP curve is at a maximum; and MP < AP when AP is falling. This is true of all marginal and average relationships.

Example 9. Suppose that the average height of a basketball team is 6 feet. If a new (marginal) member 7 feet tall joins, the average height of the team increases. If the marginal member is exactly 6 feet tall, the average height remains the same; if he is shorter than 6 feet, the average height declines.

Solved Problems

MARGINAL, AVERAGE, AND TOTAL CONCEPTS

4.1. Find (1) the marginal and (2) the average functions for each of the following total functions. Evaluate them at $Q = 3$ and $Q = 5$.

(a) $TC = 3Q^2 + 7Q + 12$

(1) $MC = \dfrac{dTC}{dQ} = 6Q + 7$ (2) $AC = \dfrac{TC}{Q} = 3Q + 7 + \dfrac{12}{Q}$

At $Q = 3$, $MC = 6(3) + 7 = 25$ At $Q = 3$, $AC = 3(3) + 7 + \frac{12}{3} = 20$

At $Q = 5$, $MC = 6(5) + 7 = 37$ At $Q = 5$, $AC = 3(5) + 7 \times \frac{12}{5} = 24.4$

Note: When finding the average function, be sure to divide the constant term by Q.

(b) $\pi = Q^2 - 13Q + 78$

(1) $\dfrac{d\pi}{dQ} = 2Q - 13$ (2) $A\pi = \dfrac{\pi}{Q} = Q - 13 + \dfrac{78}{Q}$

At $Q = 3$, $\dfrac{d\pi}{dQ} = 2(3) - 13 = -7$.   At $Q = 3$, $A\pi = 3 - 13 + \frac{78}{3} = 16$.

At $Q = 5$, $A\pi = 5 - 13 + \frac{78}{5} = 7.6$.

At $Q = 5$, $\dfrac{d\pi}{dQ} = 2(5) - 13 = -3$.

(c) $TR = 12Q - Q^2$

(1) $MR = \dfrac{dTR}{dQ} = 12 - 2Q$ (2) $AR = \dfrac{TR}{Q} = 12 - Q$

At $Q = 3$, $MR = 12 - 2(3) = 6$.   At $Q = 3$, $AR = 12 - 3 = 9$.

At $Q = 5$, $MR = 12 - 2(5) = 2$.   At $Q = 5$, $AR = 12 - 5 = 7$.

(d) $TC = 35 + 5Q - 2Q^2 + 2Q^3$

(1) $MC = \dfrac{dTC}{dQ} = 5 - 4Q + 6Q^2$ (2) $AC = \dfrac{TC}{Q} = \dfrac{35}{Q} + 5 - 2Q + 2Q^2$

At $Q = 3$, $MC = 5 - 4(3) + 6(3)^2 = 47$.   At $Q = 3$, $AC = \frac{35}{3} + 5 - 2(3) + 2(3)^2 = 28.67$.

At $Q = 5$, $MC = 5 - 4(5) + 6(5)^2 = 135$.   At $Q = 5$, $AC = \frac{35}{5} + 5 - 2(5) + 2(5)^2 = 52$.

4.2. Find the MR functions associated with each of the following supply functions. Evaluate them at $Q = 4$ and $Q = 10$.

(a) $P = Q^2 + 2Q + 1$

To find the MR function, given a simple supply (or demand) function, find the TR function and take its derivative with respect to Q.

$$TR = PQ = (Q^2 + 2Q + 1)Q = Q^3 + 2Q^2 + Q$$

$$MR = \frac{dTR}{dQ} = 3Q^2 + 4Q + 1$$

At $Q = 4$, $MR = 3(4)^2 + 4(4) + 1 = 65$. At $Q = 10$, $MR = 3(10)^2 + 4(10) + 1 = 341$.

(b) $P = Q^2 + 0.5Q + 3$

$$TR = PQ = (Q^2 + 0.5Q + 3)Q = Q^3 + 0.5Q^2 + 3Q$$

$$MR = 3Q^2 + Q + 3$$

At $Q = 4$, $MR = 3(4)^2 + 4 + 3 = 55$. At $Q = 10$, $MR = 3(10)^2 + 10 + 3 = 313$.

4.3. Find the MR functions associated with each of the following supply functions. Evaluate them at $Q = 4$ and $Q = 10$.

(a) $Q = -72 + 3P$

When the supply (or demand) function is expressed as $Q = f(P)$, first find the inverse function by solving for $P = f(Q)$ and then proceed as in Problem 4.2.

$$P = \tfrac{1}{3}Q + 24$$
$$\text{TR} = (\tfrac{1}{3}Q + 24)Q = \tfrac{1}{3}Q^2 + 24Q$$
$$\text{MR} = \frac{d\text{TR}}{dQ} = \tfrac{2}{3}Q + 24$$

At $Q = 4$, $\text{MR} = \tfrac{2}{3}(4) + 24 = 26\tfrac{2}{3}$. At $Q = 10$, $\text{MR} = \tfrac{2}{3}(10) + 24 = 30\tfrac{2}{3}$.

(b) $Q + 60 - 5P = 0$

$$P = 0.2Q + 12$$
$$\text{TR} = (0.2Q + 12)Q = 0.2Q^2 + 12Q$$
$$\text{MR} = \frac{d\text{TR}}{dQ} = 0.4Q + 12$$

At $Q = 4$, $\text{MR} = 0.4(4) + 12 = 13.6$. At $Q = 10$, $\text{MR} = 0.4(10) + 12 = 16$.

4.4. Find the MR functions for each of the following demand functions and evaluate them at $Q = 4$ and $Q = 10$.

(a) $Q = 36 - 2P$

$$P = 18 - 0.5Q$$
$$\text{TR} = (18 - 0.5Q)Q = 18Q - 0.5Q^2$$
$$\text{MR} = \frac{d\text{TR}}{dQ} = 18 - Q$$

At $Q = 4$, $\text{MR} = 18 - 4 = 14$.
At $Q = 10$, $\text{MR} = 18 - 10 = 8$.

(b) $44 - 4P - Q = 0$

$$P = 11 - 0.25Q$$
$$\text{TR} = (11 - 0.25Q)Q = 11Q - 0.25Q^2$$
$$\text{MR} = \frac{d\text{TR}}{dQ} = 11 - 0.5Q$$

At $Q = 4$, $\text{MR} = 11 - 0.5(4) = 9$.
At $Q = 10$, $\text{MR} = 11 - 0.5(10) = 6$.

4.5. For each of the following consumption functions, use the derivative to find the marginal propensity to consume, $\text{MPC} = dC/dY$.

(a) $C = C_0 + bY$

$$\text{MPC} = \frac{dC}{dY} = b$$

(b) $C = 1500 + 0.75Y$

$$\text{MPC} = \frac{dC}{dY} = 0.75$$

4.6. Given $C = 1200 + 0.8Yd$, where $Yd = Y - T$ and $T = 100$, use the derivative to find the MPC.

When $C = f(Yd)$, make $C = f(Y)$ before taking the derivative. Thus,

$$C = 1200 + 0.8(Y - 100) = 1120 + 0.8Y$$
$$\text{MPC} = \frac{dC}{dY} = 0.8$$

Note that the introduction of a lump-sum tax into the income determination model *does not* affect the value of the MPC (or the multiplier).

4.7. Given $C = 2000 + 0.9Yd$, where $Yd = Y - T$ and $T = 300 + 0.2Y$, use the derivative to find the MPC.

$$C = 2000 + 0.9(Y - 300 - 0.2Y) = 2000 + 0.9Y - 270 - 0.18Y = 1730 + 0.72Y$$
$$\text{MPC} = \frac{dC}{dY} = 0.72$$

The introduction of a proportional tax into the income determination model *does* affect the value of the MPC and hence of the multiplier.

4.8.   Find the marginal cost functions for each of the following average cost functions.

(a) $AC = 1.5Q + 4 + \dfrac{46}{Q}$

>   Given the average cost function, the marginal cost function is determined by first finding the total cost function and then taking its derivative, as follows:

$$TC = AC(Q) = \left(1.5Q + 4 + \frac{46}{Q}\right)Q = 1.5Q^2 + 4Q + 46$$

$$MC = \frac{dTC}{dQ} = 3Q + 4$$

(b) $AC = \dfrac{160}{Q} + 5 - 3Q + 2Q^2$

$$TC = \left(\frac{160}{Q} + 5 - 3Q + 2Q^2\right)Q = 160 + 5Q - 3Q^2 + 2Q^3$$

$$MC = \frac{dTC}{dQ} = 5 - 6Q + 6Q^2$$

(c) $AC - \dfrac{18}{Q} - 0.1 - 0.5Q = 0$

$$AC = \frac{18}{Q} + 0.1 + 0.5Q$$

$$TC = \left(\frac{18}{Q} + 0.1 + 0.5Q\right)Q = 18 + 0.1Q + 0.5Q^2$$

$$MC = \frac{dTC}{dQ} = 0.1 + Q$$

OPTIMIZING FUNCTIONS OF A SINGLE VARIABLE

4.9.   Maximize the following total revenue and total profit functions, as follows: (1) Take the first derivative and set it equal to zero to get the critical value(s),   (2) take the second derivative and evaluate it at the critical value(s) to see if the function is at a relative minimum or maximum, and   (3) evaluate the original function at the desired critical value.

(a) $TR = 32Q - Q^2$

>   (1) $\dfrac{dTR}{dQ} = 32 - 2Q = 0$
>
> $Q = 16$
>
>   (2) $\dfrac{d^2TR}{dQ^2} = \dfrac{d}{dQ}(32 - 2Q) = -2 < 0$
>
> $Q = 16$ gives a relative maximum.
>
>   (3) $TR = 32Q - Q^2 = 32(16) - (16)^2 = 256$

(b) $\pi = -Q^2 + 11Q - 24$

>   (1) $\dfrac{d\pi}{dQ} = -2Q + 11 = 0$
>
> $Q = 5.5$
>
>   (2) $\dfrac{d^2\pi}{dQ^2} = \dfrac{d}{dQ}(-2Q + 11) = -2 < 0$
>
> $Q = 5.5$ provides a relative maximum.
>
>   (3) $\pi = -Q^2 + 11Q - 24$
>
> $= -(5.5)^2 + 11(5.5) - 24 = 6.25$

(c) $\pi = -\frac{1}{3}Q^3 + 8Q^2 - 39Q - 50$

(1)
$$\frac{d\pi}{dQ} = -Q^2 + 16Q - 39 = 0$$
$$(-Q + 13)(Q - 3) = 0$$
$$Q = 13 \qquad Q = 3$$

(2)
$$\frac{d^2\pi}{dQ^2} = \frac{d}{dQ}(-Q^2 + 16Q - 39) = -2Q + 16$$

At $Q = 13$, $d^2\pi/dQ^2 = -2(13) + 16 = -10 < 0$. At $Q = 3$, $d^2\pi/dQ^2 = -2(3) + 16 = +10 > 0$.

Thus $Q = 13$ fulfills the second-order requirements for a maximum; $Q = 3$ is rejected because it provides a relative minimum.

(3) $\pi = -\frac{1}{3}Q^3 + 8Q^2 - 39Q - 50 = -\frac{1}{3}(13)^3 + 8(13)^2 - 39(13) - 50 = 62.67$

(d) $\pi = -Q^3 + 48Q^2 - 180Q - 800$

(1) $\dfrac{d\pi}{dQ} = -3Q^2 + 96Q - 180 = 0$ (2) $\dfrac{d^2\pi}{dQ^2} = \dfrac{d}{dQ}(-3Q^2 + 96Q - 180) = -6Q + 96$

$(-3Q + 6)(Q - 30) = 0$ At $Q = 2$, $d^2\pi/dQ^2 = -6(2) + 96 = 84 > 0$

$Q = 2 \qquad Q = 30$ At $Q = 30$, $d^2\pi/dQ^2 = -6(30) + 96 = -84 < 0$

$Q = 30$ provides a relative maximum

(3) $\pi = -Q^3 + 48Q^2 - 180Q - 800 = -27{,}000 + 43{,}200 - 5400 - 800 = 10{,}000$

4.10. Minimize the following cost functions, using the procedure detailed in Problem 4.9.

(a) $AC = 200 - 24Q + Q^2$

(1) $\dfrac{dAC}{dQ} = 2Q - 24 = 0$

$Q = 12$

(2) $\dfrac{d^2AC}{dQ^2} = \dfrac{d}{dQ}(2Q - 24) = 2 > 0$

$Q = 12$ gives a relative minimum

(3) $AC = 200 - 24(12) + (12)^2 = 56$

(b) $TC = \frac{1}{3}Q^3 - 4.5Q^2 + 14Q + 22$

(1) $MC = Q^2 - 9Q + 14 = 0$

$(Q - 7)(Q - 2) = 0$

$Q = 7 \qquad Q = 2$

(2) $\dfrac{d^2TC}{dQ^2} = \dfrac{d}{dQ}(Q^2 - 9Q + 14) = 2Q - 9$

At $Q = 7$, $d^2TC/dQ^2 = 2(7) - 9 = 5 > 0$.

At $Q = 2$, $d^2TC/dQ^2 = 2(2) - 9 = -5 < 0$.

$Q = 7$ gives a relative minimum.

(3) $TC = \frac{1}{3}(7)^3 - 4.5(7)^2 + 14(7) + 22 = 13.83$

(c) $TC = \frac{1}{3}Q^3 - 8.5Q^2 + 60Q + 27$

(1) $MC = Q^2 - 17Q + 60 = 0$

$(Q - 5)(Q - 12) = 0$

$Q = 5 \qquad Q = 12$

(2) $\dfrac{d^2\text{TC}}{dQ^2} = \dfrac{d}{dQ}(Q^2 - 17Q + 60) = 2Q - 17$

   At $Q = 5$, $d^2\text{TC}/dQ^2 = 2(5) - 17 = -7 < 0$.

   At $Q = 12$, $d^2\text{TC}/dQ^2 = 2(12) - 17 = +7 > 0$.

   $Q = 12$ gives a relative minimum.

(3) $\text{TC} = \frac{1}{3}(12)^3 - 8.5(12)^2 + 60(12) + 27 = 99$

4.11.   Given a firm's demand function $Q - 90 + 2P = 0$ and its average cost function

$$\text{AC} = Q^2 - 8Q + 57 + 2/Q$$

find the level of output which   (*a*) maximizes total revenue,   (*b*) minimizes marginal costs, and   (*c*) maximizes profits.

(*a*)   The demand function is $Q - 90 + 2P = 0$.   Therefore,

$$P = 45 - 0.5\,Q$$
$$\text{TR} = PQ = (45 - 0.5\,Q)Q = 45Q - 0.5\,Q^2 \qquad\qquad (4.1)$$

To maximize TR,

$$\frac{d\text{TR}}{dQ} = 45 - Q = 0 \qquad Q = 45$$

Testing the second-order conditions, $d^2\text{TR}/dQ^2 = -1 < 0$.   Therefore, at $Q = 45$,   TR is maximized.

(*b*)   From the average cost function $\text{AC} = Q^2 - 8Q + 57 + 2/Q$,

$$\text{TC} = \text{AC}(Q) = (Q^2 - 8Q + 57 + 2/Q)Q = Q^3 - 8Q^2 + 57Q + 2 \qquad\qquad (4.2)$$

$$\text{MC} = \frac{d\text{TC}}{dQ} = 3Q^2 - 16Q + 57$$

Marginal cost is minimized where

$$\frac{d\text{MC}}{dQ} = 6Q - 16 = 0 \qquad Q = 2\tfrac{2}{3}$$

Testing the second-order conditions, $d^2\text{MC}/dQ^2 = 6 > 0$.   Therefore, at $Q = 2\tfrac{2}{3}$,   MC is at a relative minimum.

(*c*) $$\pi = \text{TR} - \text{TC}$$

Substituting from (*4.1*) and (*4.2*),

$$\pi = 45Q - 0.5Q^2 - (Q^3 - 8Q^2 + 57Q + 2) = -Q^3 + 7.5Q^2 - 12Q - 2 \qquad\qquad (4.3)$$

Maximizing π,

$$\frac{d\pi}{dQ} = -3Q^2 + 15Q - 12 = 0$$

$$(-3Q + 3)(Q - 4) = 0$$
$$Q = 1 \qquad Q = 4$$

Testing the second-order conditions,

$$\frac{d^2\pi}{dQ^2} = -6Q + 15$$

At $Q = 1$, $d^2\pi/dQ^2 = -6(1) + 15 = 9 > 0$.

At $Q = 4$, $d^2\pi/dQ^2 = -6(4) + 15 = -9 < 0$.

Profits are maximized at $Q = 4$,   where from (*4.3*),

$$\pi = -(4)^3 + 7.5(4)^2 - 12(4) - 2 = 6$$

4.12.   A firm has the demand function $\ 22 - 0.5\,Q - P = 0\ $ and the average cost function

$$\text{AC} = \tfrac{1}{3}Q^2 - 8.5\,Q + 50 + 90/Q.$$

Find the level of output which maximizes   (a) total revenue and   (b) total profits.

(a)   With the demand function $\ 22 - 0.5\,Q - P = 0$,

$$P = 22 - 0.5\,Q$$
$$\text{TR} = (22 - 0.5\,Q)Q = 22Q - 0.5\,Q^2$$

TR is maximized when

$$\frac{d\text{TR}}{dQ} = 22 - Q = 0 \qquad Q = 22$$

Testing the second-order conditions, $\ d^2\text{TR}/dQ^2 = -1 < 0$.   Therefore, at $\ Q = 22$.   TR is maximized.

(b) $\pi = \text{TR} - \text{TC}$,   where $\text{TR} = 22Q - 0.5\,Q^2$.

$$\text{TC} = \text{AC}(Q) = \left(\frac{1}{3}Q^2 - 8.5\,Q + 50 + \frac{90}{Q}\right)Q = \frac{1}{3}Q^3 - 8.5\,Q^2 + 50Q + 90$$

Thus,

$$\pi = 22Q - 0.5\,Q^2 - (\tfrac{1}{3}Q^3 - 8.5\,Q^2 + 50Q + 90) = -\tfrac{1}{3}Q^3 + 8Q^2 - 28Q - 90$$

Maximizing π,

$$\frac{d\pi}{dQ} = -Q^2 + 16Q - 28 = 0$$
$$(-Q + 14)(Q - 2) = 0$$
$$Q = 14 \qquad Q = 2$$

Testing the second-order conditions,

$$\frac{d^2\pi}{dQ^2} = \frac{d}{dQ}(-Q^2 + 16Q - 28) = -2Q + 16$$

At $\ Q = 14$, $d^2\pi/dQ^2 = -2(14) + 16 = -12 < 0$.   At $\ Q = 2$, $d^2\pi/dQ^2 = -2(2) + 16 = 12 > 0$.

π is maximized at $Q = 14$,   where $\pi = -\tfrac{1}{3}(14)^3 + 8(14)^2 - 28(14) - 90 = 171.33$

4.13.   A producer has the possibility of discriminating between the domestic and foreign market for a product where the demand respectively is

$$Q_1 = 21 - 0.1\,P_1 \tag{4.4}$$
$$Q_2 = 50 - 0.4\,P_2 \tag{4.5}$$

Total cost $= 2000 + 10Q$ where $Q = Q_1 + Q_2$.   What price will the producer charge in order to maximize profits (a) with discrimination between markets? (b) without discrimination? (c) Compare the profit differential between discrimination and nondiscrimination.

(a)   To maximize profits under price discrimination, the producer will set prices so that   MC = MR in each market.   Thus, $\text{MC} = \text{MR}_1 = \text{MR}_2$.   With $\text{TC} = 2000 + 10Q$,

$$\text{MC} = \frac{d\text{TC}}{dQ} = 10$$

Hence MC will be the same at all levels of output.   In the domestic market,

$$Q_1 = 21 - 0.1\,P_1$$

Hence, $$P_1 = 210 - 10Q_1$$

$$TR_1 = (210 - 10Q_1)Q_1 = 210Q_1 - 10Q_1^2$$

and $$MR_1 = \frac{dTR_1}{dQ_1} = 210 - 20Q_1$$

When $MR_1 = MC$, $\qquad 210 - 20Q_1 = 10 \qquad Q_1 = 10$

When $Q_1 = 10$, $\qquad\qquad P_1 = 210 - 10(10) = 110$

In the foreign market,

$$Q_2 = 50 - 0.4P_2$$

Hence, $$P_2 = 125 - 2.5Q_2$$

$$TR_2 = (125 - 2.5Q_2)Q_2 = 125Q_2 - 2.5Q_2^2$$

Thus, $$MR_2 = \frac{dTR_2}{dQ_2} = 125 - 5Q_2$$

When $MR_2 = MC$,

$$125 - 5Q_2 = 10 \qquad Q_2 = 23$$

When $Q_2 = 23$,

$$P_2 = 125 - 2.5(23) = 67.5$$

The discriminating producer charges a lower price in the foreign market where the demand is relatively more elastic, and a higher price ($P_1 = 110$) in the domestic market where the demand is relatively less elastic.

(b) If the producer does not discriminate, $P_1 = P_2$ and the two demand functions (4.4) and (4.5) may simply be aggregated. Thus,

$$Q = Q_1 + Q_2 = 21 - 0.1P + 50 - 0.4P = 71 - 0.5P$$

Hence, $$P = 142 - 2Q$$

$$TR = (142 - 2Q)Q = 142Q - 2Q^2$$

and $$MR = \frac{dTR}{dQ} = 142 - 4Q$$

When $MR = MC$,

$$142 - 4Q = 10 \qquad Q = 33$$

When $Q = 33$,

$$P = 142 - 2(33) = 76$$

When no discrimination takes place, the price falls somewhere between the relatively high price of the domestic market and the relatively low price of the foreign market. Notice, however, that the quantity sold remains the same: $Q_1 = 10$, $Q_2 = 23$, $Q = 33$.

(c) With discrimination,

$$TR = TR_1 + TR_2 = P_1Q_1 + P_2Q_2 = 110(10) + 67.5(23) = 2652.50$$

$TC = 2000 + 10Q$, where $Q = Q_1 + Q_2$.

$$TC = 2000 + 10(10 + 23) = 2330$$

Thus, $$\pi = TR - TC = 2652.50 - 2330 = 322.50$$

Without discrimination,

$$TR = PQ = 76(33) = 2508$$

$TC = 2330$ since costs do not change with or without discrimination. Thus, $\pi = 2508 - 2330 = 178$. Profits are higher with discrimination (322.50) than without discrimination.

4.14. Faced with two distinct demand functions

$$Q_1 = 24 - 0.2 P_1 \qquad Q_2 = 10 - 0.05 P_2$$

where $TC = 35 + 40Q$, what price will the firm charge (a) with discrimination and (b) without discrimination?

(a) With $Q_1 = 24 - 0.2 P_1$,

$$P_1 = 120 - 5Q_1$$
$$TR_1 = (120 - 5Q_1)Q_1 = 120Q_1 - 5Q_1^2$$
$$MR_1 = 120 - 10Q_1$$

The firm will maximize profits where $MC = MR_1 = MR_2$.

$$TC = 35 + 40Q$$
$$MC = 40$$

When $MC = MR_1$,

$$40 = 120 - 10Q_1 \qquad Q_1 = 8$$

When $Q_1 = 8$,

$$P_1 = 120 - 5(8) = 80$$

In the second market, with $Q_2 = 10 - 0.05 P_2$,

$$P_2 = 200 - 20Q_2$$
$$TR_2 = (200 = -20Q_2)Q_2 = 200Q_2 - 20Q_2^2$$
$$MR_2 = 200 - 40Q_2$$

When $MC = MR_2$,

$$40 = 200 - 40Q_2 \qquad Q_2 = 4$$

When $Q_2 = 4$,

$$P_2 = 200 - 20(4) = 120$$

(b) If the producer does not discriminate, $P_1 = P_2 = P$ and the two demand functions can be combined, as follows:

$$Q = Q_1 + Q_2 = 24 - 0.2 P + 10 - 0.05 P = 34 - 0.25 P$$

Thus,

$$P = 136 - 4Q$$
$$TR = (136 - 4Q)Q = 136Q - 4Q^2$$
$$MR = 136 - 8Q$$

At the profit-maximizing level, $MC = MR$.

$$40 = 136 - 8Q \qquad Q = 12$$

At $Q = 12$,

$$P = 136 - 4(12) = 88$$

For more detailed treatment of price discrimination, see Problems 12.19–12.22.

4.15. Prove that total revenue is maximized for a linear demand function, $P = a - bQ$, at the point where $Q = a/2b$.

$$TR = PQ$$

For a typical linear demand function

$$TR = (a - bQ)Q = aQ - bQ^2$$

For TR to be at a maximum,

$$(1)\quad \frac{d\text{TR}}{dQ} = \text{MR} = a - 2bQ = 0 \qquad (2)\quad \frac{d^2\text{TR}}{dQ^2} = \frac{d}{dQ}(a - 2bQ) = -2b < 0$$

$$Q = \frac{a}{2b}$$

At $Q = a/2b$, the function is at a relative maximum. This provides an easy, shortcut method to determine the point of maximum revenue for typical linear demand functions.

4.16. Use the shortcut method derived in Problem 4.15 to determine the point at which total revenue will be maximized for each of the following linear demand functions. Check the answer to part (*a*).

(*a*) $P = 24 - 3Q$

A linear demand function will generate a total revenue function which will be maximized at the level of output (Q) equal to the vertical intercept (a) divided by two times the absolute value of the slope.

$$Q = \frac{a}{2b} = \frac{24}{2(3)} = 4$$

Checking,

$$P = 24 - 3Q$$
$$\text{TR} = PQ = (24 - 3Q)Q = 24Q - 3Q^2$$
$$\frac{d\text{TR}}{dQ} = 24 - 6Q = 0 \qquad Q = 4$$

Testing the second-order conditions, $d^2\text{TR}/dQ^2 = -6 < 0$.

(*b*) $P = 50 - 2.5Q$

TR is maximized at $\qquad Q = \dfrac{a}{2b} = \dfrac{50}{5} = 10$

(*c*) $P = 38 - 0.5Q$

TR is maximized at $\qquad Q = \dfrac{a}{2b} = \dfrac{38}{1} = 38$

4.17. Prove that marginal cost (MC) must equal marginal revenue (MR) at the profit-maximizing level of output.

$$\pi = \text{TR} - \text{TC}$$

To maximize π, $d\pi/dQ$ must equal zero.

$$\frac{d\pi}{dQ} = \frac{d\text{TR}}{dQ} - \frac{d\text{TC}}{dQ} = 0$$
$$\frac{d\text{TR}}{dQ} = \frac{d\text{TC}}{dQ}$$
$$\text{MR} = \text{MC} \qquad \text{Q.E.D.}$$

4.18. Use the $\text{MR} = \text{MC}$ condition derived in Problem 4.17 to find the critical values at which profit will be maximized when $\text{TR} = 45Q - 0.5Q^2$ and $\text{TC} = Q^3 - 39.5Q^2 + 120Q + 125$.

$$\text{MR} = \frac{d\text{TR}}{dQ} = 45 - Q$$
$$\text{MC} = \frac{d\text{TC}}{dQ} = 3Q^2 - 79Q + 120$$

At the profit-maximizing level of output,

$$45 - Q = 3Q^2 - 79Q + 120$$
$$-3Q^2 + 78Q - 75 = 0$$
$$(-3Q + 3)(Q - 25) = 0$$

The critical values are $Q = 1$, $Q = 25$.

The second-order conditions must then be tested. Check this answer with that to Problem 4.11(c).

4.19. Find the critical values for profit-maximization using $MC = MR$, when $TR = 22Q - 2Q^2$ and $TC = \frac{1}{3}Q^3 - 10Q^2 + 50Q + 45$.

$$MR = \frac{dTR}{dQ} = 22 - 4Q$$

$$MC = \frac{dTC}{dQ} = Q^2 - 20Q + 50$$

For profit maximization, $22 - 4Q = Q^2 - 20Q + 50$
$$-Q^2 + 16Q - 28 = 0$$
$$(-Q + 14)(Q - 2) = 0$$
$$Q = 14 \qquad Q = 2$$

GENERAL ELASTICITY

4.20. Find the price elasticity of demand for each of the following functions at $P = 3$ and $P = 5$.

(a) $Q = 75 - 5P$

$$\frac{dQ}{dP} = -5$$

and at $P = 3$, $Q = 75 - 5(3) = 60$. Substituting these values in the elasticity formula

$$\epsilon = \frac{dQ}{dP} \frac{P}{Q}$$

we get

$$\epsilon = -5(\tfrac{3}{60}) = -0.25$$

At $P = 5$, $Q = 75 - 5(5) = 50$. Substituting these values in the elasticity formula, where dQ/dP remains constant at -5,

$$\epsilon = -5(\tfrac{5}{50}) = -0.5$$

(b) $Q = 42 - 6P$

$$\frac{dQ}{dP} = -6$$

At $P = 3$, $Q = 42 - 6(3) = 24$.

$$\epsilon = -6(\tfrac{3}{24}) = -0.75$$

At $P = 5$, $Q = 42 - 6(5) = 12$.

$$\epsilon = -6(\tfrac{5}{12}) = -2.5$$

(c) $8Q + 2P = 56$

Since $Q = 7 - 0.25P$

$$\frac{dQ}{dP} = -0.25$$

At $P = 3$, $\quad Q = 7 - 0.25(3) = 6.25$.

$$\epsilon = -0.25\left(\frac{3}{6.25}\right) = -0.12$$

At $P = 5$, $\quad Q = 7 - 0.25(5) = 5.75$.

$$\epsilon = -0.25\left(\frac{5}{5.75}\right) = -\tfrac{5}{23} \cong -0.22$$

4.21. Find the price elasticity of supply for each of the following functions at $\quad P = 3$ and $P = 5$.

(a) $\quad Q = -2 + 0.8P$

$$\frac{dQ}{dP} = 0.8$$

At $P = 3$, $\quad Q = -2 + 0.8(3) = 0.4$.

$$\epsilon = 0.8\left(\frac{3}{0.4}\right) = 6$$

At $P = 5$, $\quad Q = -2 + 0.8(5) = 2$.

$$\epsilon = 0.8(\tfrac{5}{2}) = 2$$

(b) $\quad Q - 1.5P + 3 = 0$

$$Q = -3 + 1.5P$$

$$\frac{dQ}{dP} = 1.5$$

At $P = 3$, $\quad Q = -3 + 1.5(3) = 1.5$.

$$\epsilon = 1.5\left(\frac{3}{1.5}\right) = 3$$

At $P = 5$, $\quad Q = -3 + 1.5(5) = 4.5$

$$\epsilon = 1.5\left(\frac{5}{4.5}\right) = 1\tfrac{2}{3}$$

4.22. Find the elasticity of the following functions using marginal and average functions, and determine the price level at which the absolute value of the elasticity will be equal to or greater than one: $\quad |\epsilon| \geqslant 1$.

(a) $\quad Q = 120 - 4P$

As discussed in Section 4.3, the elasticity formula can be expressed as

$$\epsilon = \frac{dQ/dP}{Q/P} = \frac{\text{marginal function}}{\text{average function}}$$

or

$$\epsilon = \frac{dQ}{dP}\frac{P}{Q} = \text{marginal function} \left(\frac{1}{\text{average function}}\right)$$

With $\quad Q = 120 - 4P$,

$$\frac{dQ}{dP} = -4 = \text{marginal function}$$

and

$$\frac{Q}{P} = \frac{120 - 4P}{P} = \text{average function}$$

Substituting in the second formula above, and using the reciprocal of the average function,

$$\epsilon = -4\left(\frac{P}{120 - 4P}\right) = \frac{-P}{30 - P}$$

For $\quad |\epsilon| \geqslant 1$,

$$P \geqslant 30 - P$$
$$2P \geqslant 30$$
$$P \geqslant 15$$

(b) $\quad Q = 84 - 7P$

$$\frac{dQ}{dP} = -7$$

$$\frac{Q}{P} = \frac{84 - 7P}{P}$$

Substituting,

$$\epsilon = -7\left(\frac{P}{84-7P}\right) = \frac{-P}{12-P}$$

For $|\epsilon| \geqslant 1$,

$$P \geqslant 12 - P$$
$$P \geqslant 6$$

(c) $Q = 80 - 6P$

$$\frac{dQ}{dP} = -6$$
$$\frac{Q}{P} = \frac{80-6P}{P}$$

Substituting,

$$\epsilon = -6\left(\frac{P}{80-6P}\right) = \frac{-3P}{40-3P}$$

For $|\epsilon| \geqslant 1$,

$$3P \geqslant 40 - 3P$$
$$P \geqslant 6\tfrac{2}{3}$$

4.23.   The demand function $Q_1 = 50 - P_1$ intersects another linear demand function Q_2 at $P = 10$.   The elasticity of demand for Q_2 is six times larger than that of Q_1 at that point. Find the demand function for Q_2.

At $P = 10$, $Q_1 = 50 - 10 = 40$.   The derivative

$$\frac{d}{dP}(50 - P_1) = -1$$

Substituting these values in the elasticity formula,

$$\epsilon_1 = -1(\tfrac{10}{40}) = -0.25$$

The elasticity of Q_2 is six times larger at $P = 10$.   Therefore,

$$\epsilon_2 = 6(-0.25) = -1.5$$

Since the two functions intersect at $P = 10$, $Q = 40$,   the slope of Q_2 can be found by substituting the known values into the elasticity formula, as follows:

$$-1.5 = \frac{dQ}{dP}\left(\frac{10}{40}\right)$$

$$\frac{dQ}{dP} = -6$$

Thus, $Q_2 = a - 6P_2$

But $Q_2 = 40$ when $P = 10$, so

$$40 = a - 6(10)$$
$$a = 100$$

Therefore, $Q_2 = 100 - 6P_2$

4.24.   The demand function $Q_1 = 80 - 4P_1$ intersects Q_2 at $P = 5$.   If the elasticity of demand for Q_2 is one-fourth as large as that of Q_1 at that point, find Q_2, assuming it is also linear.

At $P = 5$, $Q_1 = 80 - 4(5) = 60$.

$$\frac{dQ_1}{dP} = -4$$

Thus,

$$\epsilon_1 = -4(\tfrac{5}{60}) = -\tfrac{1}{3}$$

But,

$$\epsilon_2 = \tfrac{1}{4}(-\tfrac{1}{3}) = -\tfrac{1}{12}$$

Since $\epsilon_2 = -\tfrac{1}{12}$ at $P = 5$ and $Q = 60$, substitute these values in the elasticity formula,

$$-\frac{1}{12} = \frac{dQ_2}{dP}\left(\frac{5}{60}\right)$$

$$\frac{dQ_2}{dP} = -1$$

Thus,

$$Q_2 = a - 1P_2$$

Substituting $Q = 60$ and $P = 5$,

$$60 = a - 1(5)$$

$$a = 65$$

Thus,

$$Q_2 = 65 - P_2$$

ELASTICITY OF DEMAND

4.25. How would you modify the elasticity formula in Section 4.3 if, as in typical economic textbooks, $P = f(Q)$?

Elasticity is generally defined as

$$\epsilon = \frac{dQ}{dP}\frac{P}{Q}$$

When a function is given as $P = f(Q)$, as is typical in economics, the derivative of the function will be dP/dQ. This is the reciprocal of the derivative in the elasticity formula:

$$\frac{dQ}{dP} = \frac{1}{dP/dQ}$$

To express the elasticity formula directly in terms of the original function when $P = f(Q)$, therefore, simply use the reciprocal:

$$\epsilon = \frac{1}{dP/dQ}\frac{P}{Q}$$

4.26. Using Fig. 4-5,

(a) Prove that in traditional economic graphs when $P = f(Q)$, price elasticity of a linear demand function $|\epsilon_d|$ is equal to the length of the bottom segment of the demand curve divided by the length of the top segment of the curve.

(b) Compare this to the case where $Q = f(P)$. Use absolute values.

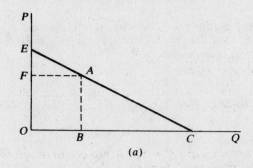
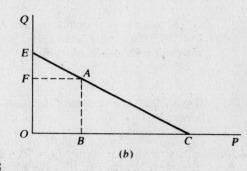

Fig. 4-5

(a) From Fig. 4-5(a), it can be proven that price elasticity at point $A = BC/OB$, as follows:

$$\epsilon_d = \frac{dQ}{dP}\frac{P}{Q}$$

When $P = f(Q)$ and the derivative (and hence the slope) of the function is measured by dP/dQ,

$$\epsilon_d = \frac{1}{dP/dQ}\frac{P}{Q}$$

For a linear function the slope is everywhere the same. Hence,

$$\frac{dP}{dQ} = \frac{\Delta P}{\Delta Q} = \frac{AB}{BC}$$

At point A, $P = AB$, $Q = OB$. Substituting these values in the elasticity formula above,

$$\epsilon_d = \frac{1}{AB/BC}\frac{AB}{OB} = \frac{BC}{AB}\frac{AB}{OB} = \frac{BC}{OB} \tag{4.6}$$

It can also be shown that $BC/OB = AC/EA$. Since ABC and EFA are similar right triangles, and since $FA = OB$, from the properties of similar right triangles, we can write

$$\frac{AC}{BC} = \frac{EA}{OB}$$

Multiplying each side by BC/EA,

$$\frac{AC}{EA} = \frac{BC}{OB} = \epsilon_d \qquad \text{Q.E.D.}$$

Elasticity of demand $|\epsilon_d|$, when $P = f(Q)$, equals the length of the bottom segment of the demand curve (AC) divided by the length of the top segment (EA).

(b)   If the mathematically correct, but less frequently encountered, $Q = f(P)$ is used, the axes are *reversed* and the elasticity equals the length of the *top* segment of the demand curve divided by the length of the *bottom* segment. Thus, with Fig. 4-5(b)

$$\epsilon_d = \frac{dQ}{dP}\frac{P}{Q} = \frac{AB}{BC}\frac{OB}{AB} = \frac{OB}{BC} \tag{4.7}$$

Using the properties of similar right triangles, and noting that $FA = OB$,

$$\frac{EA}{OB} = \frac{AC}{BC}$$

Multiplying both sides by OB/AC,

$$\frac{EA}{AC} = \frac{OB}{BC} = \epsilon_d$$

Elasticity of demand, when $Q = f(P)$, equals the length of the top segment of the demand curve (EA) divided by the bottom segment (AC). In this section, we will generally follow the traditional economic format, $P = f(Q)$.

4.27. Prove that price elasticity of demand is negative $(\epsilon_d < 0)$ for all negatively sloped demand curves.

All negatively sloped demand curves will have negative price elasticity, $\epsilon_d < 0$, since $dQ/dP = 1/(dP/dQ) < 0$ and P and Q must both be positive in all feasible regions. Frequently in economics, however, price elasticity is referred to in terms of absolute values.

4.28. Prove that for a linear demand function in the form $P = f(Q)$,

(a) $|\epsilon_d| = 1$ in the middle of the demand curve,

(b) $|\epsilon_d| > 1$ above the middle of the demand curve, and

(c) $|\epsilon_d| < 1$ below the middle of the demand curve.

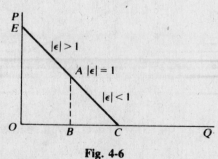

Fig. 4-6

Use Fig. 4-6 where A is in the middle of the demand curve.

(a) In Problem 4.26(a), it was demonstrated that elasticity of demand for a linear function is given by the length of the bottom segment of the demand curve divided by the length of the top segment. At point A, therefore,

$$\epsilon_d = \frac{AC}{EA}$$

Since $AC = EA$ on the graph, at point A, $\epsilon_d = 1$.

(b) For any point on the curve above A, hence to the left of A, $EA < AC$. With $EA < AC$, $\epsilon_d > 1$ for any point on the line above A.

(c) For any point on the curve below A, hence to the right of A, $EA > AC$. With $EA > AC$, $\epsilon_d < 1$ for any point on the line below A.

If $Q = f(P)$ and the axes are reversed [as in Problem 4.26(b)] $|\epsilon_d| < 1$ at the top portion of the curve and $|\epsilon_d| > 1$ on the bottom portion of the curve. Prove this.

4.29. Using another method, prove that, unlike the slope, the elasticity of a linear demand function ranges in absolute value from zero to infinity. Indicate the range on a graph where $P = f(Q)$.

$$\epsilon = \frac{1}{dP/dQ} \frac{P}{Q}$$

where $1/(dP/dQ)$ is the reciprocal of the slope of the linear function, which is everywhere constant and does not change. See Problem 4.25. ϵ changes, however, because the ratio P/Q changes with every movement along the curve.

In Fig. 4-7, for every movement to the left, P grows larger and Q grows smaller, causing the ratio P/Q to approach infinity as the vertical axis is approached. For every movement to the right, P grows smaller and Q larger, causing the ratio P/Q to approach zero as the horizontal axis is approached.

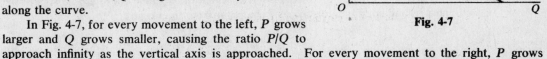

Fig. 4-7

If $Q = f(P)$ and the axes are reversed, ϵ approaches zero at the vertical axis and infinity at the horizontal axis. Prove this.

4.30. (a) Find the elasticity for the following inverse functions at $P = 2$ and $P = 3$: (1) $P = 4 - 0.2Q$ and (2) $Q = 20 - 5P$. (b) Graph the functions and indicate the estimated elasticities in order to show that the price elasticity of demand for both functions is the same and that only the relative positions on the curve differ.

(a) (1) $P = 4 - 0.2Q$

$$\frac{dP}{dQ} = -0.2$$

At $P = 2$, $2 = 4 - 0.2Q$

$Q = 10$

Thus,

$$\epsilon = \frac{1}{dP/dQ} \frac{P}{Q} = \frac{1}{-0.2}\left(\frac{2}{10}\right) = -1$$

At $P = 3$, $3 = 4 - 0.2Q$

$Q = 5$

$$\epsilon = \frac{1}{-0.2}\left(\frac{3}{5}\right) = -3$$

(2) $Q = 20 - 5P$

$$\frac{dQ}{dP} = -5$$

At $P = 2$, $Q = 20 - 5(2) = 10$.

Thus,

$$\epsilon = \frac{dQ}{dP}\frac{P}{Q} = -5\left(\frac{2}{10}\right) = -1$$

At $P = 3$, $Q = 20 - 5(3) = 5$

$$\epsilon = -5\left(\frac{3}{5}\right) = -3$$

(b) The graphs for each function are given in Fig. 4-8. While the elasticities are the same at any given price level and $|\epsilon| = 1$ always appears in the middle of the curve, Fig. 4-8 shows that $|\epsilon| > 1$ appears in the top segment of the curve when $P = f(Q)$ and in the bottom segment of the curve when $Q = f(P)$.

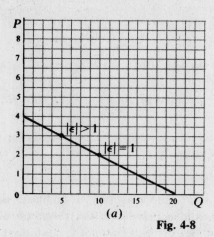
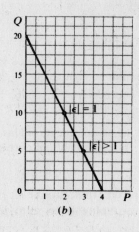

(a)   (b)

Fig. 4-8

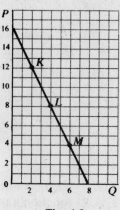

Fig. 4-9

4.31. Given the graph of the demand function in Fig. 4-9 for $P = 16 - 2Q$, (a) find the price elasticity graphically for points K, L, M, using the method demonstrated in Problem 4.26(a). (b) Check your answer for point K.

From (4.6) and Fig. 4-5, we know that price elasticity of demand at a particular point equals the horizontal distance of the point from the point at which the demand curve crosses the horizontal axis (BC) divided by the horizontal distance of the point from the origin (OB). Thus,

(a) At K,

$$|\epsilon| = \frac{8-2}{2-0} = \frac{6}{2} = 3$$

At L,

$$|\epsilon| = \frac{8-4}{4-0} = \frac{4}{4} = 1$$

At M,

$$|\epsilon| = \frac{8-6}{6-0} = \frac{2}{6} = \frac{1}{3}$$

(b) Checking K,

$$\epsilon = \frac{1}{dP/dQ} \frac{P}{Q}$$

With $P = 16 - 2Q$,

$$\frac{dP}{dQ} = -2$$

At K, $P = 12$, $Q = 2$. Thus,

$$\epsilon = \frac{1}{-2}\left(\frac{12}{2}\right) = -3$$

$$|\epsilon| = 3$$

4.32. Given the graph for $Q = 8 - 0.5P$, the inverse of the previous demand function, (a) find the price elasticity at points K, L, M in Fig. 4-10. (b) Check your answer for M.

From (4.7) and Fig. 4-5(b) in Problem 4.26, price elasticity of demand at a particular point equals the horizontal distance of the point from the origin (OB) divided by the horizontal distance of the point from the point where the demand curve crosses the horizontal axis (BC). Thus,

(a)   At K, $|\epsilon| = \dfrac{4-0}{16-4} = \dfrac{4}{12} = \dfrac{1}{3}$

     At L, $|\epsilon| = \dfrac{8-0}{16-8} = \dfrac{8}{8} = 1$

     At M, $|\epsilon| = \dfrac{12-0}{16-12} = \dfrac{12}{4} = 3$

(b)   Checking M, $\epsilon = \dfrac{dQ}{dP}\dfrac{P}{Q}$

     With $Q = 8 - 0.5P$,

$$\frac{dQ}{dP} = -0.5$$

At M, $P = 12$, $Q = 2$.

$$\epsilon = -0.5(\tfrac{12}{2}) = -3$$
$$|\epsilon| = 3$$

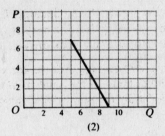

Fig. 4-10

4.33.   Given the linear demand functions in Fig. 4-11(a), is it accurate to say that   (1) is relatively elastic and   (2) is relatively inelastic, as is sometimes done in economics textbooks?

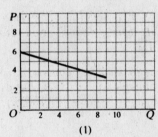   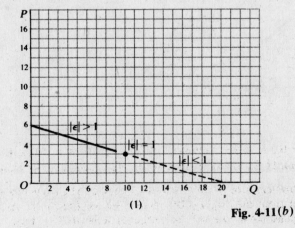

        (1)   (2)

Fig. 4-11(a)

    The answer requires a qualification. It is not accurate to refer to any linear function as relatively elastic or relatively inelastic. The elasticity of a linear demand function is different at every point along the curve and ranges from zero to infinity.   See Problems 4.28 and 4.29.

    It is accurate, however, to refer to a relatively elastic or inelastic *portion* of a linear demand function.   Thus, in Fig. 4-11(b) where the curves from (a) are extended, part (1) deals with the top segment of a linear function, where $|\epsilon| > 1$;   part (2) deals with the bottom segment of a linear function in which $|\epsilon| < 1$.

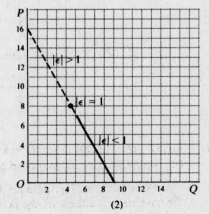

        (1)   **Fig. 4-11(b)**   (2)

4.34. Given Fig. 4-12, prove that for $P = f(Q)$, price elasticity of demand for a curvilinear function at point A equals the length of the bottom segment of the tangent to the curve at A divided by the top segment of the tangent.

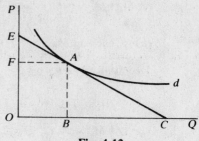

Fig. 4-12

From Fig. 4-12, it can be proven that elasticity at point $A = -BC/OB$, as follows:

$$\epsilon_d = \frac{1}{dP/dQ} \frac{P}{Q}$$

But the slope of the curvilinear function at A equals dP/dQ, which equals the slope of the tangent at A: $-AB/BC$. Thus,

$$\frac{dP}{dQ} = -\frac{AB}{BC}$$

At A, $P = AB$, $Q = OB$, so

$$\epsilon_d = \frac{1}{-AB/BC} \frac{AB}{OB} = -\frac{BC}{AB} \frac{AB}{OB} = -\frac{BC}{OB} \qquad (4.8)$$

It can also be shown that $-BC/OB = -AC/EA$. From the properties of similar right triangles,

$$\frac{AC}{BC} = \frac{EA}{OB}$$

Multiplying both sides by $-BC/EA$,

$$-\frac{AC}{EA} = -\frac{BC}{OB} = \epsilon_d \qquad \text{Q.E.D.}$$

[For $Q = f(P)$, see Example 7.]

4.35. Find the price elasticity of demand at points K, L, and M on the curvilinear demand function given in Fig. 4-13.

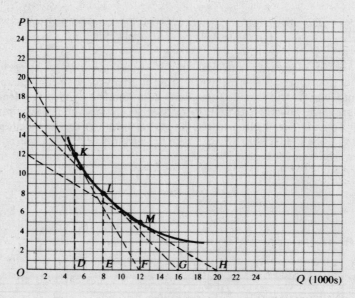

Fig. 4-13

Draw a tangent to the curve at the desired point. From (4.8), price elasticity of demand $|\epsilon_d|$ at a particular point equals the horizontal distance of the point from the point at which the tangent crosses the horizontal axis (BC) divided by the horizontal distance of the point from the origin (OB). Thus,

At K, $\epsilon = -\dfrac{DF}{OD} = -\dfrac{12{,}000 - 5000}{5000 - 0} = -\dfrac{7000}{5000} = -1.4$

At L, $\epsilon = -\dfrac{EG}{OE} = -\dfrac{16{,}000 - 8000}{8000 - 0} = -\dfrac{8000}{8000} = -1$

At M, $\epsilon = -\dfrac{FH}{OF} = -\dfrac{20{,}000 - 12{,}000}{12{,}000 - 0} = -\dfrac{8000}{12{,}000} = -0.67$

4.36. In terms of marginal and average concepts, find the price elasticity   (*a*) at point G in Fig. 4-14(*a*), and   (*b*) where $|\epsilon| = 1$ in Fig. 4-14(*b*).

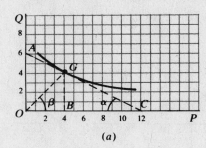
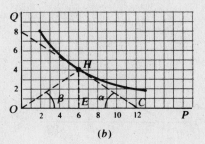

(*a*)   (*b*)

Fig. 4-14

(*a*) To get the marginal concept, dQ/dP, draw a tangent to the curve at G. The slope of the curve (and the tangent of α) equals the marginal function. To get the average function Q/P draw a straight line from the origin to G. The slope of OG (and the tangent of β) equals the average function. Since,

$$\epsilon = \frac{\text{marginal function}}{\text{average function}} = \frac{\text{tangent of } \alpha}{\text{tangent of } \beta} = \frac{-GB/BC}{GB/OB} = \frac{-OB}{BC} = \frac{-(4-0)}{12-4} = -\frac{1}{2}$$

(*b*) To find the point in Fig. 4-14(*b*) where $|\epsilon| = 1$,   simply find the point where the slope of the marginal function equals the slope of the average function, i.e. where $HE/EC = HE/OE$,   or where $OE = EC$,   or where tangent α = tangent β.

ELASTICITY OF SUPPLY

4.37. Using a graph prove that for a linear supply function, $P = f(Q)$,   price elasticity of supply at a given point equals the horizontal distance of that point from the point at which the supply curve intersects the horizontal axis divided by the horizontal distance of the given point from the origin.

It is shown below that in Fig. 4-15, price elasticity of supply at point $C = AB/OB$.

$$\epsilon_s = \frac{1}{dP/dQ}\frac{P}{Q}$$

Since the slope of a linear function is everywhere constant,

$$\text{Slope at } C = \frac{\Delta P}{\Delta Q} = \frac{dP}{dQ} = \frac{CB}{AB}$$

Here, $P = CB$ and $Q = OB$. Substituting   in   the   elasticity formula,

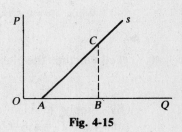

Fig. 4-15

$$\epsilon_s = \frac{1}{CB/AB}\frac{CB}{OB} = \frac{AB}{CB}\frac{CB}{OB} = \frac{AB}{OB} \qquad \text{Q.E.D.}$$

[For price elasticity of supply when $Q = f(P)$,   see Example 7.]

4.38. Prove that the price elasticity of supply is positive $(\epsilon_s > 0)$ for all positively sloped supply curves.

All positively sloped supply curves will have positive elasticity, $\epsilon_s > 0$, since $dQ/dP = 1/(dP/dQ) > 0$ and P and Q must be positive in all feasible regions.

4.39. Given Fig. 4-16, prove that for all positively-sloped linear supply curves,

(a) $\epsilon_s < 1$, if the supply curve intersects the horizontal axis (i.e. if the vertical intercept $a < 0$).

(b) $\epsilon_s > 1$, if the supply curve intersects the vertical axis (if $a > 0$).

(c) $\epsilon_s = 1$, if the supply curve originates from the origin (if $a = 0$).

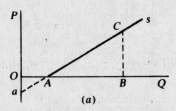
(a)
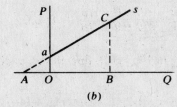
(b)
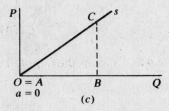
(c)

Fig. 4-16

(a) In Fig. 4-16(a),

$$\epsilon = \frac{AB}{OB}$$

Since $AB < OB$, $\epsilon < 1$.

When $a < 0$, the supply curve intersects the horizontal axis. AB will be less than OB, and $\epsilon_s < 1$.

(b) In Fig. 4-16(b) the graph is extended to A, a nonfeasible region, to provide the necessary measurement.

$$\epsilon = \frac{AB}{OB} > 1$$

When $a > 0$, the supply curve intersects the vertical axis. AB will be greater than OB and $\epsilon_s > 1$.

(c) In Fig. 4-16(c),

$$\epsilon = \frac{AB}{OB} = 1$$

When $a = 0$, the supply curve starts from the origin. $AB = OB$, and $\epsilon_s = 1$.

4.40. Tell whether the elasticity of supply,

$$\epsilon_s \gtreqless 1$$

by simply looking at the following supply functions: (a) $P = 3Q$, (b) $P = -2 + 5Q$, and (c) $P = 3 + 4Q$.

(a) $\epsilon_s = 1$. The vertical intercept $a = 0$, hence the function originates from the origin.

(b) $\epsilon_s < 1$. The function intersects the horizontal axis, since $a < 0$.

(c) $\epsilon_s > 1$. The function intersects the vertical axis, since $a > 0$.

4.41. Using a graph, prove that price elasticity of supply for a curvilinear function can be measured by drawing a tangent to the curve at the desired point and applying the rules of Problem 4.37 to the tangent.

It is shown below that in Fig. 4-17, the elasticity of supply at point $C = AB/OB$.

$$\epsilon_s = \frac{1}{dP/dQ} \frac{P}{Q}$$

But the slope of the curvilinear supply curve at $C = dP/dQ$, which equals the slope of the tangent at $C = CB/AB$. Thus,

$$\frac{dP}{dQ} = \frac{CB}{AB}$$

With $P = CB$ and $Q = OB$,

$$\epsilon_s = \frac{1}{CB/AB} \frac{CB}{OB} = \frac{AB}{CB} \frac{CB}{OB} = \frac{AB}{OB} \qquad \text{Q.E.D.}$$

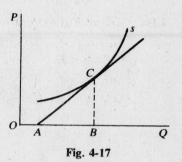

Fig. 4-17

4.42. Given the supply curve in Fig. 4-18, find the elasticity of supply at points A, B, and C.

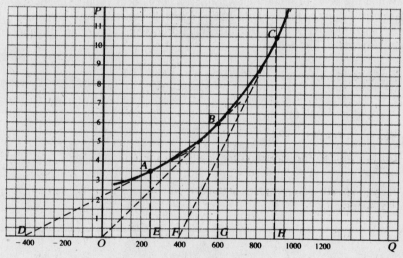

Fig. 4-18

At A, $\epsilon_s = \dfrac{DE}{OE} = \dfrac{250 - (-400)}{250 - 0} = \dfrac{650}{250} = 2.6$

At B, $\epsilon_s = \dfrac{OG}{OG} = \dfrac{600 - 0}{600 - 0} = \dfrac{600}{600} = 1$

At C, $\epsilon_s = \dfrac{FH}{OH} = \dfrac{900 - 400}{900 - 0} = \dfrac{500}{900} = 0.56$

4.43. Given Fig. 4-19 and using marginal and average functions, determine (a) whether at point B, $\epsilon_s \gtreqless 1$, and (b) the elasticity of supply at B. [Note that $Q = f(P)$.]

(a) $\epsilon_s = \dfrac{dQ/dP}{Q/P} = \dfrac{\text{marginal function}}{\text{average function}}$

The marginal function is given by the slope of the tangent to the supply curve at point B, or the tangent of α. The average function is given by the slope of a straight line from the origin to B, or the tangent of β. Since the marginal function is greater than the average function, $\alpha > \beta$, at B, $\epsilon_s > 1$.

(b)

$$\epsilon_s = \frac{\text{tangent of } \alpha}{\text{tangent of } \beta} = \frac{BC/AC}{BC/OC} = \frac{OC}{AC}$$

$$= \frac{8-0}{4-0} = 2$$

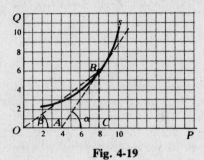

Fig. 4-19

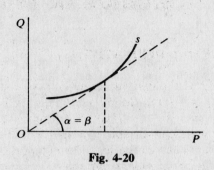

Fig. 4-20

4.44. How do you find the point of unitary elasticity on a curvilinear supply function? Assume $Q = f(P)$.

To find the point of unitary elasticity on a curvilinear supply function, construct a line from the origin that is tangent to the supply curve.   A line so constructed will represent both the marginal and average functions.   When the marginal function equals the average function, $\alpha = \beta$, and $\epsilon_s = 1$; this is illustrated in Fig. 4-20.

Chapter 5

Calculus of Multivariable Functions

5.1 PARTIAL DERIVATIVES

Study of the derivative in Chapter 4 was limited to functions of a single independent variable such as $y = f(x)$. Many economic activities, however, involve functions of more than one variable, such as $z = f(x,y)$. To measure the effect of a change in a single independent variable on the dependent variable in a multivariable function, the partial derivative is needed. The *partial derivative* measures the instantaneous rate of change of the dependent variable (z) with respect to one of the independent variables (x), when the other independent variable or variables (y) are assumed held constant. Partial derivatives are particularly important in *comparative statics*. Comparative static analysis examines the effects of changes in autonomous variables on equilibrium positions by assuming that other variables do not change.

The partial derivative of z with respect to x for the multivariable function $z = f(x,y)$, can be written $\partial z/\partial x$, z_x, f_x, or f_1. Partial differentiation follows the same rules as for ordinary differentiation, but treats all the other independent variables as constants.

Example 1. The partial derivatives for $z = 5x^3 + 3xy + 4y^2$ are found as follows:

1. When differentiating with respect to x, only those terms containing x are differentiated. Ignore $4y^2$, as if an additive constant, and treat the y in $3xy$ as a multiplicative constant. Thus,

$$\frac{\partial z}{\partial x} = z_x = 15x^2 + 3y$$

2. When differentiating with respect to y, only those terms containing y are differentiated. Ignore $5x^3$, as if an additive constant, and treat the x in $3xy$ as a multiplicative constant. Thus,

$$\frac{\partial z}{\partial y} = z_y = 3x + 8y$$

Example 2. To find the partial derivatives for $z = 3x^2y^3$:

1. When differentiating with respect to x, treat y^3 as a multiplicative constant, as follows:

$$\frac{\partial z}{\partial x} = z_x = 6xy^3$$

2. When differentiating with respect to y, treat x^2 as a multiplicative constant:

$$\frac{\partial z}{\partial y} = z_y = 9x^2y^2$$

Example 3. Partial differentiation follows all the rules of differentiation. See Section 3.4.

1. Given: $z = (3x + 5)(2x + 6y)$, by the product rule,

$$\frac{\partial z}{\partial x} = z_x = (3x + 5)(2) + (2x + 6y)(3) = 12x + 10 + 18y$$

and,

$$\frac{\partial z}{\partial y} = z_y = (3x + 5)(6) + (2x + 6y)(0) = 18x + 30$$

2. Given: $z = (6x + 7y)/(5x + 3y)$, by the quotient rule,

$$\frac{\partial z}{\partial x} = z_x = \frac{(5x+3y)(6)-(6x+7y)(5)}{(5x+3y)^2} = \frac{30x+18y-30x-35y}{(5x+3y)^2} = \frac{-17y}{(5x+3y)^2}$$

and,

$$\frac{\partial z}{\partial y} = z_y = \frac{(5x+3y)(7)-(6x+7y)(3)}{(5x+3y)^2} = \frac{35x+21y-18x-21y}{(5x+3y)^2} = \frac{17x}{(5x+3y)^2}$$

5.2 SECOND-ORDER PARTIAL DERIVATIVES

The second-order partial derivative f_{xx} indicates that the function has been differentiated partially with respect to x twice and that the other independent variable(s) have been held constant. Thus, f_{xx} gives the rate of change of the first-order partial derivative f_x with respect to x, while y remains constant. Other notations for the second-order partial derivative include z_{xx}, $\partial^2 z/\partial x^2$, and $\frac{\partial}{\partial x}\frac{(\partial z)}{(\partial x)}$. The case for f_{yy} is exactly parallel.

The first partial derivative f_x (or f_y) can also be differentiated with respect to y (or x). This gives rise to the *cross* (or *mixed*) *partial derivative*, f_{xy} (or f_{yx}). The cross partial derivative measures the instantaneous rate of change of one of the first-order partial derivatives with respect to the other variable. In short, f_{xy} indicates that the primitive function $z = f(x, y)$ has been partially differentiated with respect to x and that the resulting partial derivative has been partially differentiated with respect to y. Other notations for f_{xy} include z_{xy}, $\frac{\partial}{\partial y}\frac{(\partial z)}{(\partial x)}$, and $\frac{\partial^2 z}{\partial y \partial x}$. The cross partial derivatives for a given function will always be equal (i.e. $f_{xy} = f_{yx}$), if both cross partials are continuous. This is known as *Young's Theorem*.

Example 4. The first and second partial derivatives (including cross partials) for $z = 7x^3 + 9xy + 2y^5$ are taken as shown below.

$$\frac{\partial z}{\partial x} = z_x = 21x^2 + 9y \qquad \text{and} \qquad \frac{\partial z}{\partial y} = z_y = 9x + 10y^4$$

$$\frac{\partial^2 z}{\partial x^2} = z_{xx} = 42x \qquad\qquad\qquad \frac{\partial^2 z}{\partial y^2} = z_{yy} = 40y^3$$

$$\frac{\partial}{\partial y}\frac{(\partial z)}{(\partial x)} = \frac{\partial}{\partial y}(21x^2 + 9y) = z_{xy} = 9 \qquad\qquad \frac{\partial}{\partial x}\frac{(\partial z)}{(\partial y)} = \frac{\partial}{\partial x}(9x + 10y^4) = z_{yx} = 9$$

Example 5. In functions such as $z = 3xy^2$, it is important to note that $3xy^2 \neq (3xy)^2$. The first and second partial derivatives (including cross partials) would be

$$\frac{\partial z}{\partial x} = z_x = 3y^2 \qquad \text{and} \qquad \frac{\partial z}{\partial y} = z_y = 6xy$$

$$\frac{\partial^2 z}{\partial x^2} = z_{xx} = 0 \qquad\qquad\qquad \frac{\partial^2 z}{\partial y^2} = z_{yy} = 6x$$

$$\frac{\partial}{\partial y}\frac{(\partial z)}{(\partial x)} = \frac{\partial}{\partial y}(3y^2) = z_{xy} = 6y \qquad\qquad \frac{\partial}{\partial x}\frac{(\partial z)}{(\partial y)} = \frac{\partial}{\partial x}(6xy) = z_{yx} = 6y$$

5.3 DIFFERENTIALS

In Section 3.2, the derivative dy/dx was given as a single symbol denoting the limit of $\Delta y/\Delta x$ as $\Delta x \to 0$ as a limit. dy/dx may also be treated as a ratio of differentials in which dy is the differential of y and dx the differential of x. The *differential* of y measures the change in y resulting from a small change in x. Thus, if $y = 2x^2 + 5x + 4$, the derivative is

$$\frac{dy}{dx} = 4x + 5$$

and multiplying both sides by dx, the differential is

$$dy = (4x + 5)\, dx$$

Example 6

1. If $y = 4x^3 + 5x^2 - 7$,   then $dy/dx = 12x^2 + 10x$ and the differential is

$$dy = (12x^2 + 10x)\, dx$$

2. If $y = (2x - 5)^2$,   then $dy/dx = 2(2x - 5)(2) = 8x - 20$ and the differential is

$$dy = (8x - 20)\, dx$$

5.4   TOTAL AND PARTIAL DIFFERENTIALS

For a function of two or more variables, the *total differential* measures the change in the dependent variable brought about by a small change in each of the independent variables. Thus, if $z = f(x, y)$,   the total differential (dz) is expressed mathematically as

$$dz = z_x\, dx + z_y\, dy$$

where z_x and z_y are the partial derivatives of z with respect to x and y respectively, and dx and dy are small changes in x and y. The total differential can thus be found by taking the partial derivatives of the function with respect to each independent variable and substituting these values in the formula above.

Example 7.   The total differential is found as follows:

1. Given: $z = x^4 + 8xy + 3y^3$

$$z_x = 4x^3 + 8y \qquad z_y = 8x + 9y^2$$

which, when substituted in the total differential formula, gives

$$dz = (4x^3 + 8y)\, dx + (8x + 9y^2)\, dy$$

2. Given: $z = (x - y)/(x + 1)$

$$z_x = \frac{(x + 1)(1) - (x - y)(1)}{(x + 1)^2} = \frac{y + 1}{(x + 1)^2}$$

$$z_y = \frac{(x + 1)(-1) - (x - y)(0)}{(x + 1)^2} = \frac{-1(x + 1)}{(x + 1)^2} = \frac{-1}{x + 1}$$

The total differential is $dz = \dfrac{y + 1}{(x + 1)^2}\, dx - \left(\dfrac{1}{x + 1}\right) dy$

If one of the independent variables is held constant, e.g. $dy = 0$,   we then have a partial differential:

$$dz = z_x\, dx$$

A *partial differential* measures the change in the dependent variable of a multivariate function resulting from a small change in one of the independent variables and assumes the other independent variables are constant.   See Problem 5.13.

5.5   TOTAL DERIVATIVES

Given a case where $z = f(x, y)$ and $y = g(x)$, i.e. when x and y are not independent, a change in x will affect z directly through the function f and indirectly through the function g. This is illustrated in the channel map in Fig. 5-1. To measure the effect of a change in x on z when x and y are not

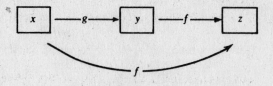

Fig. 5-1

independent, the total derivative must be found.   The *total derivative* measures the *direct* effect of x on z $(\partial z/\partial x)$ *plus* the *indirect* effect of x on z through $y\left(\dfrac{\partial z}{\partial y}\dfrac{dy}{dx}\right)$.   In brief, the total derivative is

$$\frac{dz}{dx} = z_x + z_y \frac{dy}{dx}$$

Example 8.   An alternate method of finding the total derivative is to take the total differential of z,

$$dz = z_x\, dx + z_y\, dy$$

and divide through by dx.   Thus,

$$\frac{dz}{dx} = z_x \frac{dx}{dx} + z_y \frac{dy}{dx}$$

Since $dx/dx = 1$,

$$\frac{dz}{dx} = z_x + z_y \frac{dy}{dx}$$

Example 9.   The total derivative can also be expanded to accommodate other links.   If $z = f(x, y)$ while $x = g(t)$ and $y = h(t)$,   then

$$\frac{dz}{dt} = z_x \frac{dx}{dt} + z_y \frac{dy}{dt}$$

Example 10.   Given:

$$z = f(x, y) = 6x^3 + 7y$$

where $y = g(x) = 4x^2 + 3x + 8$,   the total derivative (dz/dx) with respect to x is

$$\frac{dz}{dx} = z_x + z_y \frac{dy}{dx}$$

where $z_x = 18x^2$, $z_y = 7$, and $dy/dx = 8x + 3$.   Substituting above,

$$\frac{dz}{dx} = 18x^2 + 7(8x + 3) = 18x^2 + 56x + 21$$

To check the answer, substitute $y = 4x^2 + 3x + 8$ in the original function to make z a function of x alone and then take the derivative as follows:

$$z = 6x^3 + 7(4x^2 + 3x + 8) = 6x^3 + 28x^2 + 21x + 56$$

Thus,

$$\frac{dz}{dx} = 18x^2 + 56x + 21$$

Example 11.   Find the total derivative dz/dt, given

$$z = 8x^2 + 3y^2$$

where $x = 4t$ and $y = 5t$.   The total derivative with respect to t is

$$\frac{dz}{dt} = z_x \frac{dx}{dt} + z_y \frac{dy}{dt}$$

where $z_x = 16x$, $z_y = 6y$, $dx/dt = 4$, and $dy/dt = 5$.   Substituting above,

$$\frac{dz}{dt} = 16x(4) + 6y(5) = 64x + 30y$$

Then substituting $x = 4t$, $y = 5t$,   immediately above,

$$\frac{dz}{dt} = 64(4t) + 30(5t) = 406t$$

5.6 IMPLICIT AND INVERSE FUNCTION RULES

Functions of the form $y = f(x)$ express y explicitly in terms of x and are called *explicit functions*. Functions of the form $f(x,y) = 0$ do not express y explicitly in terms of x and are called *implicit functions*. If an implicit function $f(x,y) = 0$ exists, and $f_y \neq 0$ at the point around which the implicit function is defined, the total differential can be written $f_x\, dx + f_y\, dy = 0$.

Recalling that a derivative is a ratio of differentials, we can rearrange the terms to get the *implicit function rule*:

$$\frac{dy}{dx} = \frac{-f_x}{f_y}$$

Notice that the derivative dy/dx is the *negative* of the *reciprocal* of the corresponding partials.

$$\frac{dy}{dx} = \frac{-f_x}{f_y} = -\frac{1}{f_y/f_x}$$

If an inverse function exists (see Section 1.5), the *inverse function rule* states that the derivative of the inverse function is the reciprocal of the derivative of the original function. Thus, if $Q = f(P)$ is the original function, the derivative of the original function is dQ/dP, the derivative of the inverse function $[P = f(Q)]$ is dP/dQ, and

$$\frac{dP}{dQ} = \frac{1}{dQ/dP} \qquad \text{provided } \frac{dQ}{dP} \neq 0$$

Example 12. The derivative dy/dx for each of the following implicit functions is found as follows:

1. Given: $7x^2 - y = 0$. The derivative for an implicit function is

$$\frac{dy}{dx} = -\frac{f_x}{f_y}$$

where $f_x = 14x$ and $f_y = -1$. Thus,

$$\frac{dy}{dx} = -\frac{14x}{(-1)} = 14x$$

The derivative in this case can be easily checked by solving for y in terms of x and taking the derivative. Since

$$y = 7x^2 \qquad \frac{dy}{dx} = 14x$$

2. Given: $5x^2 + 8xy + 6y^2 = 0$.

$$\frac{dy}{dx} = -\frac{f_x}{f_y} = -\frac{10x + 8y}{8x + 12y}$$

Example 13. Find the derivative for the inverse of the following functions:

1. Given: $Q = 20 - 2P$,

$$\frac{dP}{dQ} = \frac{1}{dQ/dP}$$

where $dQ/dP = -2$. Thus,

$$\frac{dP}{dQ} = \frac{1}{-2} = -\frac{1}{2}$$

2. Given: $Q = 25 + 3P^3$,

$$\frac{dP}{dQ} = \frac{1}{dQ/dP} = \frac{1}{9P^2} \qquad (P \neq 0)$$

5.7 OPTIMIZATION OF A MULTIVARIABLE FUNCTION

In economics, for a typical multivariable function, such as $z = f(x,y)$ in Fig. 5-2, to be at a maximum or minimum:

1. The first-order partial derivatives must equal zero simultaneously, i.e. $z_x = z_y = 0$. This insures that at the given points the function is neither rising nor falling. These points are called *critical values*.

2. The second-order direct partials, when evaluated at the critical values, must both be positive for a minimum $(z_{xx}, z_{yy} > 0)$ and negative for a maximum $(z_{xx}, z_{yy} < 0)$. This insures that at the critical values the function is moving upwards in relation to the principal axes in the case of a minimum, and downwards in relation to the principal axes in the case of a maximum.

3. The product of the second-order direct partials evaluated at the critical values must exceed the value of the square of the cross partials, i.e. $z_{xx} z_{yy} > (z_{xy})^2$. This insures that the function is at an optimum when viewed from all directions, and not simply in relation to the principal axes.

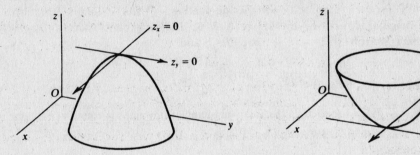

Fig. 5-2

Example 14. To determine the critical values and test to see if the function is at a minimum or maximum, given:

$$z = 6x^2 - 9x - 3xy - 7y + 5y^2$$

1. Take the first-order partials, set them equal to zero, and solve for x and y simultaneously.

$$z_x = 12x - 9 - 3y = 0$$
$$z_y = -3x - 7 + 10y = 0$$

Thus,

$$12x - 3y = 9$$
$$-3x + 10y = 7$$

which when solved simultaneously gives

$$\bar{x} = 1 \qquad \bar{y} = 1$$

2. Determine the signs of the second direct partials.

$$z_{xx} = 12 \qquad z_{yy} = 10$$

With $z_{xx}, z_{yy} > 0$, the function is at a minimum in relation to the two principal axes.

3. Find the mixed partials and test to see if $z_{xx} z_{yy} > (z_{xy})^2$.

$$z_{xy} = -3$$
$$z_{xx} z_{yy} > (z_{xy})^2$$
$$(12)(10) > (-3)^2$$
$$120 > 9$$

The function is at a minimum when $\bar{x} = \bar{y} = 1$.

Example 15. If $z_{xx}z_{yy} < (z_{xy})^2$ and the second-order condition is not fully satisfied, the function when evaluated at the critical values may be at an *inflection point* (see Problem 5.21) or a *saddle point*. If it is a saddle point, as illustrated in Fig. 5-3, the function will be at a maximum when viewed along one axis (here the y axis) and at a minimum when viewed along the other (here x). In the case of a saddle point, the second direct partials will assume different signs, and the third condition $z_{xx}z_{yy} > (z_{xy})^2$ will not be met. See Problem 5.22.

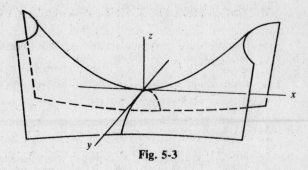

Fig. 5-3

5.8 CONSTRAINED OPTIMIZATION

Differential calculus can also be used to maximize or minimize a function subject to constraint. Given a function $f(x,y)$ subject to a constraint $g(x,y)$, a new function can be formed by setting the constraint equal to zero, multiplying it by λ (the Lagrangian multiplier), and adding the product to the original function. Thus,

$$F(x,y,\lambda) = f(x,y) + \lambda g(x,y)$$

Here $F(x,y,\lambda)$ is the *Lagrangian function*, $f(x,y)$ is the original or *objective function*, and $g(x,y)$ is the *constraining function*. Since the constraint is always set equal to zero, $\lambda g(x,y) = 0$ and the addition of the term does not change the value of the objective function. Critical values $\bar{x}$, $\bar{y}$, and $\bar{\lambda}$, at which the function is optimized, are found by setting the first-order partial derivatives equal to zero and solving simultaneously:

$$F_x = F_y = F_\lambda = 0$$

Second-order conditions differ from those of unconstrained optimization and are treated in Section 12.4.

Example 16. To optimize the function

$$z = 4x^2 + 3xy + 6y^2 \qquad (5.1)$$

subject to $x + y = 56$,

1. Set the constraint equal to zero,

$$x + y - 56 = 0$$

Multiply it by λ and add it to the objective function to form the Lagrangian function (Z).

$$Z = 4x^2 + 3xy + 6y^2 + \lambda(x + y - 56) \qquad (5.2)$$

2. Take the first-order partials, set them equal to zero, and solve simultaneously.

$$Z_x = 8x + 3y + \lambda = 0 \qquad (5.3)$$
$$Z_y = 3x + 12y + \lambda = 0 \qquad (5.4)$$
$$Z_\lambda = x + y - 56 = 0 \qquad (5.5)$$

Subtracting (5.4) from (5.3) gives

$$5x - 9y = 0 \qquad x = 1.8y$$

Substituting $x = 1.8y$ in (5.5) gives

$$1.8y + y = 56 \qquad \bar{y} = 20$$

From which, we find

$$\bar{x} = 36 \qquad \bar{\lambda} = -348$$

The function will be optimized at $\bar{x} = 36$, $\bar{y} = 20$, $\bar{\lambda} = -348$,   where from (5.2)

$$Z = 4(36)^2 + 3(36)(20) + 6(20)^2 + (-348)(36 + 20 - 56)$$
$$= 4(1296) + 3(720) + 6(400) - 348(0) = 9744$$

In Chapter 12, Example 5, it will be shown that Z is a minimum.   Notice that at the critical values, the Lagrangian function equals the objective function, $Z = z$.

5.9   THE LAGRANGIAN MULTIPLIER

The Lagrangian multiplier λ *approximates* the effect on the objective function of a one-unit change in the constant of the constraining function.   If λ is positive, for every one-unit increase (decrease) in the constant of the constraining function, the objective function will decrease (increase) by a value approximately equal to the value of λ.   If λ is negative, for every one-unit increase (decrease) in the constant of the constraining function, the objective function will increase (decrease) by a value approximately equal to the value of λ.

Example 17.   In Example 16, $\bar{x} = 36$, $\bar{y} = 20$, $\bar{\lambda} = -348$, and $\bar{Z} = 9744$.   With λ negative, a unit increase in the constant of the constraining function will lead to an increase in the objective function of approximately 348.   As proof, take the original objective function

$$z = 4x^2 + 3xy + 6y^2$$

and maximize it subject to a new constraint in which the value of the constant term is greater by one:

$$x + y = 57$$

Then the Lagrangian function becomes

$$Z = 4x^2 + 3xy + 6y^2 + \lambda(x + y - 57)$$

and

$$Z_x = 8x + 3y + \lambda = 0$$
$$Z_y = 3x + 12y + \lambda = 0$$
$$Z_\lambda = x + y - 57 = 0$$

which when solved simultaneously gives

$$\bar{x} = 36.64 \qquad \bar{y} = 20.36 \qquad \bar{\lambda} = -354.2$$

Substituting these values in the Lagrangian function gives the new constrained optimum of $\bar{Z} = 10,095$. Z is 351 larger than the old constrained optimum of 9744, while 351 is approximately equal to the 348 value of λ, the original Lagrangian multiplier.

Solved Problems

FIRST-ORDER PARTIAL DERIVATIVES

5.1.   Find the first-order partial derivatives for each of the following functions:

(a) $z = 8x^2 + 14xy + 5y^2$ (b) $z = 4x^3 + 2x^2y - 7y^5$

$\qquad z_x = 16x + 14y$ $\qquad z_x = 12x^2 + 4xy$

$\qquad z_y = 14x + 10y$ $\qquad z_y = 2x^2 - 35y^4$

(c) $z = 6w^3 + 4wx + 3x^2 - 7xy - 8y^2$ (d) $z = 2w^2 + 8wxy - x^2 + y^3$

$\qquad z_w = 18w^2 + 4x$ $\qquad z_w = 4w + 8xy$

$\qquad z_x = 4w + 6x - 7y$ $\qquad z_x = 8wy - 2x$

$\qquad z_y = -7x - 16y$ $\qquad z_y = 8wx + 3y^2$

5.2. Use the product rule to find the first-order partials for each of the following functions:

(a) $z = 3x^2(5x + 7y)$

$$z_x = 3x^2(5) + (5x + 7y)(6x)$$
$$= 45x^2 + 42xy$$
and $z_y = 3x^2(7) + (5x + 7y)(0)$
$$= 21x^2$$

(b) $z = (9x - 4y)(12x + 2y)$

$$z_x = (9x - 4y)(12) + (12x + 2y)(9)$$
$$= 108x - 48y + 108x + 18y = 216x - 30y$$
and $z_y = (9x - 4y)(2) + (12x + 2y)(-4)$
$$= 18x - 8y - 48x - 8y = -30x - 16y$$

(c) $z = (2x^2 + 6y)(5x - 3y^3)$

$$z_x = (2x^2 + 6y)(5) + (5x - 3y^3)(4x)$$
$$= 10x^2 + 30y + 20x^2 - 12xy^3$$
$$= 30x^2 + 30y - 12xy^3$$
and $z_y = (2x^2 + 6y)(-9y^2) + (5x - 3y^3)(6)$
$$= -18x^2y^2 - 54y^3 + 30x - 18y^3$$
$$= -72y^3 - 18x^2y^2 + 30x$$

(d) $z = (w - x - y)(3w + 2x - 4y)$

$$z_w = (w - x - y)(3) + (3w + 2x - 4y)(1)$$
$$= 6w - x - 7y$$
$$z_x = (w - x - y)(2) + (3w + 2x - 4y)(-1)$$
$$= -w - 4x + 2y$$
and $z_y = (w - x - y)(-4) + (3w + 2x - 4y)(-1)$
$$= -7w + 2x + 8y$$

5.3. Use the quotient rule to find the first-order partials of the following functions:

(a) $z = \dfrac{5x}{6x - 7y}$

$$z_x = \frac{(6x - 7y)(5) - (5x)(6)}{(6x - 7y)^2}$$
$$= \frac{-35y}{(6x - 7y)^2}$$
and $z_y = \dfrac{(6x - 7y)(0) - (5x)(-7)}{(6x - 7y)^2}$
$$= \frac{35x}{(6x - 7y)^2}$$

(b) $z = \dfrac{x + y}{3y}$

$$z_x = \frac{3y(1) - (x + y)(0)}{(3y)^2}$$
$$= \frac{1}{3y}$$
and $z_y = \dfrac{3y(1) - (x + y)(3)}{(3y)^2}$
$$= \frac{-3x}{(3y)^2} = \frac{-x}{3y^2}$$

(c) $z = \dfrac{4x - 9y}{5x + 2y}$

$$z_x = \frac{(5x + 2y)(4) - (4x - 9y)(5)}{(5x + 2y)^2}$$
$$= \frac{53y}{(5x + 2y)^2}$$
and $z_y = \dfrac{(5x + 2y)(-9) - (4x - 9y)(2)}{(5x + 2y)^2}$
$$= \frac{-53x}{(5x + 2y)^2}$$

(d) $z = \dfrac{x^2 - y^2}{3x + 2y}$

$$z_x = \frac{(3x + 2y)(2x) - (x^2 - y^2)(3)}{(3x + 2y)^2}$$
$$= \frac{3x^2 + 4xy + 3y^2}{(3x + 2y)^2}$$
and $z_y = \dfrac{(3x + 2y)(-2y) - (x^2 - y^2)(2)}{(3x + 2y)^2}$
$$= \frac{-2x^2 - 6xy - 2y^2}{(3x + 2y)^2}$$

5.4. Find the first-order partial derivatives for each of the following functions by using the chain rule:

(a) $z = (x + y)^2$

$$z_x = 2(x + y)(1)$$
$$= 2(x + y)$$
and $z_y = 2(x + y)(1)$
$$= 2(x + y)$$

(b) $z = (2x - 5y)^3$

$$z_x = 3(2x - 5y)^2(2)$$
$$= 6(2x - 5y)^2$$
and $z_y = 3(2x - 5y)^2(-5)$
$$= -15(2x - 5y)^2$$

(c) $z = (7x^2 + 4y^3)^5$

$$z_x = 5(7x^2 + 4y^3)^4(14x)$$
$$= 70x(7x^2 + 4y^3)^4$$

and $z_y = 5(7x^2 + 4y^3)^4(12y^2)$
$$= 60y^2(7x^2 + 4y^3)^4$$

(d) $z = (5w + 4x + 7y)^3$

$$z_w = 3(5w + 4x + 7y)^2(5)$$
$$= 15(5w + 4x + 7y)^2$$
$$z_x = 3(5w + 4x + 7y)^2(4)$$
$$= 12(5w + 4x + 7y)^2$$

and $z_y = 3(5w + 4x + 7y)^2(7)$
$$= 21(5w + 4x + 7y)^2$$

5.5.   Use whatever combination of rules is necessary to find the first-order partials for the following equation.

$$z = \frac{(5x^2 - 7y)(3x^2 + 8y)}{4x + 2y}$$

Using the quotient rule and product rule,

$$z_x = \frac{(4x + 2y)[(5x^2 - 7y)(6x) + (3x^2 + 8y)(10x)] - (5x^2 - 7y)(3x^2 + 8y)(4)}{(4x + 2y)^2}$$

$$= \frac{(4x + 2y)(30x^3 - 42xy + 30x^3 + 80xy) - (5x^2 - 7y)(12x^2 + 32y)}{(4x + 2y)^2}$$

$$= \frac{(4x + 2y)(60x^3 + 38xy) - (5x^2 - 7y)(12x^2 + 32y)}{(4x + 2y)^2}$$

and $z_y = \dfrac{(4x + 2y)[(5x^2 - 7y)(8) + (3x^2 + 8y)(-7)] - (5x^2 - 7y)(3x^2 + 8y)(2)}{(4x + 2y)^2}$

$$= \frac{(4x + 2y)(40x^2 - 56y - 21x^2 - 56y) - (5x^2 - 7y)(6x^2 + 16y)}{(4x + 2y)^2}$$

$$= \frac{(4x + 2y)(19x^2 - 112y) - (5x^2 - 7y)(6x^2 + 16y)}{(4x + 2y)^2}$$

5.6.   Redo Problem 5.5, given $z = (5x^2 - 4y)^2(2x + 7y^3)$.

Using the product rule and the chain rule, the first-order partials are

$$z_x = (5x^2 - 4y)^2(2) + (2x + 7y^3)[2(5x^2 - 4y)(10x)]$$
$$= 2(5x^2 - 4y)^2 + (2x + 7y^3)(100x^3 - 80xy)$$

and $z_y = (5x^2 - 4y)^2(21y^2) + (2x + 7y^3)[2(5x^2 - 4y)(-4)]$
$$= 21y^2(5x^2 - 4y)^2 + (2x + 7y^3)(-40x^2 + 32y)$$

5.7.   Redo Problem 5.5, given

$$z = \frac{(3x + 11y)^3}{2x + 6y}$$

Using the quotient and chain rule, the first-order partials are

$$z_x = \frac{(2x + 6y)[3(3x + 11y)^2(3)] - (3x + 11y)^3(2)}{(2x + 6y)^2}$$

$$= \frac{(18x + 54y)(3x + 11y)^2 - 2(3x + 11y)^3}{(2x + 6y)^2}$$

and $z_y = \dfrac{(2x + 6y)[3(3x + 11y)^2(11)] - (3x + 11y)^3(6)}{(2x + 6y)^2}$

$$= \frac{(66x + 198y)(3x + 11y)^2 - 6(3x + 11y)^3}{(2x + 6y)^2}$$

5.8.   Redo Problem 5.5, given

$$z = \left(\frac{8x + 7y}{5x + 2y}\right)^2$$

Using the chain rule and the quotient rule, the first-order partials are

$$z_x = 2\left(\frac{8x + 7y}{5x + 2y}\right)\left[\frac{(5x + 2y)(8) - (8x + 7y)(5)}{(5x + 2y)^2}\right]$$

$$= \frac{16x + 14y}{5x + 2y}\left[\frac{-19y}{(5x + 2y)^2}\right] = \frac{-(266y^2 + 304xy)}{(5x + 2y)^3}$$

and

$$z_y = 2\left(\frac{8x + 7y}{5x + 2y}\right)\left[\frac{(5x + 2y)(7) - (8x + 7y)(2)}{(5x + 2y)^2}\right]$$

$$= \frac{16x + 14y}{5x + 2y}\left[\frac{19x}{(5x + 2y)^2}\right] = \frac{304x^2 + 266xy}{(5x + 2y)^3}$$

SECOND-ORDER PARTIAL DERIVATIVES

5.9.   Find the second-order direct partial derivatives z_{xx} and z_{yy} for each of the following functions:

(a) $z = x^2 + 2xy + y^2$

$$z_x = 2x + 2y \qquad z_y = 2x + 2y$$
$$z_{xx} = 2 \qquad\qquad z_{yy} = 2$$

(b) $z = x^3 - 9xy - 3y^3$

$$z_x = 3x^2 - 9y \qquad z_y = -9x - 9y^2$$
$$z_{xx} = 6x \qquad\qquad z_{yy} = -18y$$

(c) $z = 2xy^4 + 7x^3y$

$$z_x = 2y^4 + 21x^2y \qquad z_y = 8xy^3 + 7x^3$$
$$z_{xx} = 42xy \qquad\qquad z_{yy} = 24xy^2$$

(d) $z = x^4 + x^3y^2 - 3xy^3 - 2y^3$

$$z_x = 4x^3 + 3x^2y^2 - 3y^3 \qquad z_y = 2x^3y - 9xy^2 - 6y^2$$
$$z_{xx} = 12x^2 + 6xy^2 \qquad\qquad z_{yy} = 2x^3 - 18xy - 12y$$

(e) $z = (12x - 7y)^2$

$$z_x = 2(12x - 7y)(12) \qquad z_y = 2(12x - 7y)(-7)$$
$$= 288x - 168y \qquad\qquad = -168x + 98y$$
$$z_{xx} = 288 \qquad\qquad z_{yy} = 98$$

(f) $z = (7x + 3y)^3$

$$z_x = 3(7x + 3y)^2(7) \qquad z_y = 3(7x + 3y)^2(3)$$
$$= 21(7x + 3y)^2 \qquad\qquad = 9(7x + 3y)^2$$
$$z_{xx} = 42(7x + 3y)(7) \qquad z_{yy} = 18(7x + 3y)(3)$$
$$= 2058x + 882y \qquad\qquad = 378x + 162y$$

(g) $z = (x^2 + 2y)^4$

$$z_x = 4(x^2 + 2y)^3(2x) = 8x(x^2 + 2y)^3 \qquad\qquad z_y = 4(x^2 + 2y)^3(2) = 8(x^2 + 2y)^3$$
$$*z_{xx} = 8x[3(x^2 + 2y)^2(2x)] + (x^2 + 2y)^3(8) \qquad z_{yy} = 24(x^2 + 2y)^2(2) = 48(x^2 + 2y)^2$$
$$= 48x^2(x^2 + 2y)^2 + 8(x^2 + 2y)^3$$

*By the product rule.

5.10. Find the cross partial derivatives z_{xy} and z_{yx} for each of the following functions:

(a) $z = 3x^2 + 12xy + 5y^2$

$$z_x = 6x + 12y \qquad z_y = 12x + 10y$$
$$z_{xy} = 12 \qquad z_{yx} = 12$$

(b) $z = x^3 - xy - 2y^3$

$$z_x = 3x^2 - y \qquad z_y = -x - 6y^2$$
$$z_{xy} = -1 \qquad z_{yx} = -1$$

(c) $z = 8x^2y - 11xy^3$

$$z_x = 16xy - 11y^3 \qquad z_y = 8x^2 - 33xy^2$$
$$z_{xy} = 16x - 33y^2 \qquad z_{yx} = 16x - 33y^2$$

(d) $z = (8x - 4y)^5$

$$z_x = 5(8x - 4y)^4(8) \qquad z_y = 5(8x - 4y)^4(-4)$$
$$= 40(8x - 4y)^4 \qquad = -20(8x - 4y)^4$$
$$z_{xy} = 160(8x - 4y)^3(-4) \qquad z_{yx} = -80(8x - 4y)^3(8)$$
$$= -640(8x - 4y)^3 \qquad = -640(8x - 4y)^3$$

In items (a) through (d) above, notice how, in accord with Young's Theorem, $z_{xy} = z_{yx}$, no matter which first partial is taken initially.

DIFFERENTIALS

5.11. Find the differential, dy, for each of the following functions:

(a) $y = 7x^3 - 5x^2 + 6x - 3$

$$\frac{dy}{dx} = 21x^2 - 10x + 6$$

Thus, $dy = (21x^2 - 10x + 6)\, dx$

(b) $y = (4x + 3)(3x - 8)$

$$\frac{dy}{dx} = (4x + 3)(3) + (3x - 8)(4) = 24x - 23$$

Thus, $dy = (24x - 23)\, dx$

(c) $y = \dfrac{9x - 4}{5x}$

$$\frac{dy}{dx} = \frac{5x(9) - (9x - 4)(5)}{(5x)^2} = \frac{20}{25x^2}$$
$$dy = \frac{4}{5x^2}\, dx$$

(d) $y = (11x + 9)^3$

$$\frac{dy}{dx} = 3(11x + 9)^2(11)$$
$$dy = 33(11x + 9)^2\, dx$$

5.12. Find the total differential, $dz = z_x\, dx + z_y\, dy$ for each of the following functions:

(a) $z = 5x^3 - 12xy - 6y^5$

$$z_x = 15x^2 - 12y \qquad z_y = -12x - 30y^4$$
$$dz = (15x^2 - 12y)\, dx - (12x + 30y^4)\, dy$$

(b) $z = 7x^2 y^3$

$$z_x = 14xy^3 \qquad z_y = 21x^2 y^2$$
$$dz = 14xy^3 \, dx + 21x^2 y^2 \, dy$$

(c) $z = 3x^2 (8x - 7y)$

$$z_x = 3x^2(8) + (8x - 7y)(6x) \qquad z_y = 3x^2(-7) + (8x - 7y)(0)$$
$$dz = (72x^2 - 42xy) \, dx - 21x^2 \, dy$$

(d) $z = (5x^2 + 7y)(2x - 4y^3)$

$$z_x = (5x^2 + 7y)(2) + (2x - 4y^3)(10x) \qquad z_y = (5x^2 + 7y)(-12y^2) + (2x - 4y^3)(7)$$
$$dz = (30x^2 - 40xy^3 + 14y) \, dx - (112y^3 + 60x^2 y^2 - 14x) \, dy$$

(e) $z = \dfrac{9y^3}{x - y}$

$$z_x = \frac{(x - y)(0) - 9y^3(1)}{(x - y)^2} \qquad z_y = \frac{(x - y)(27y^2) - 9y^3(-1)}{(x - y)^2}$$
$$dz = \frac{-9y^3}{(x - y)^2} \, dx + \frac{27xy^2 - 18y^3}{(x - y)^2} \, dy$$

(f) $z = (x - 3y)^3$

$$z_x = 3(x - 3y)^2(1) \qquad z_y = 3(x - 3y)^2(-3)$$
$$dz = 3(x - 3y)^2 \, dx - 9(x - 3y)^2 \, dy$$

5.13. Find the partial differential for a small change in x for each of the functions given in Problem 5.12 assuming $dy = 0$.

(a) $dz = (15x^2 - 12y) \, dx$ (b) $dz = 14xy^3 \, dx$ (c) $dz = (72x^2 - 42xy) \, dx$

(d) $dz = (30x^2 - 40xy^3 + 14y) \, dx$ (e) $dz = \dfrac{-9y^3}{(x - y)^2} \, dx$ (f) $dz = 3(x - 3y)^2 \, dx$

TOTAL DERIVATIVES

5.14. Find the total derivative, dz/dx, for each of the following functions:

(a) $z = 6x^2 + 15xy + 3y^2$, where $y = 7x^2$.

$$\frac{dz}{dx} = z_x + z_y \frac{dy}{dx}$$
$$= (12x + 15y) + (15x + 6y)(14x)$$
$$= 210x^2 + 84xy + 12x + 15y$$

(b) $z = (13x - 18y)^2$, where $y = x + 6$.

$$\frac{dz}{dx} = z_x + z_y \frac{dy}{dx}$$
$$= 26(13x - 18y) - 36(13x - 18y)(1)$$
$$= -10(13x - 18y)$$

(c) $z = \dfrac{9x - 7y}{2x + 5y}$, where $y = 3x - 4$.

$$\frac{dz}{dx} = z_x + z_y \frac{dy}{dx}$$
$$= \frac{59y}{(2x + 5y)^2} - \left[\frac{59x}{(2x + 5y)^2}\right](3) = \frac{59(y - 3x)}{(2x + 5y)^2}$$

(d) $z = 8x - 12y$,   where $y = (x + 1)/x^2$.

$$\frac{dz}{dx} = z_x + z_y \frac{dy}{dx}$$

$$= 8 - \frac{12(-x^2 - 2x)}{x^4}$$

$$= 8 + \frac{12(x + 2)}{x^3}$$

5.15. Find the total derivative, dz/dw, for each of the following functions:

(a) $z = 7x^2 + 4y^2$,   where $x = 5w$ and $y = 4w$.

$$\frac{dz}{dw} = z_x \frac{dx}{dw} + z_y \frac{dy}{dw} = 14x(5) + 8y(4) = 70x + 32y$$

(b) $z = 10x^2 - 6xy - 12y^2$,   where $x = 2w$ and $y = 3w$.

$$\frac{dz}{dw} = z_x \frac{dx}{dw} + z_y \frac{dy}{dw} = (20x - 6y)(2) + (-6x - 24y)(3) = 22x - 84y$$

IMPLICIT AND INVERSE FUNCTION RULES

5.16. Find the derivatives, dy/dx and dx/dy, for each of the following implicit functions:

(a) $y - 6x + 7 = 0$

$$\frac{dy}{dx} = \frac{-f_x}{f_y} = \frac{-(-6)}{1} = 6 \qquad \frac{dx}{dy} = \frac{-f_y}{f_x} = \frac{-(1)}{-6} = \frac{1}{6}$$

(b) $3y - 12x + 17 = 0$

$$\frac{dy}{dx} = \frac{-f_x}{f_y} = \frac{-(-12)}{3} = 4 \qquad \frac{dx}{dy} = \frac{-f_y}{f_x} = \frac{-(3)}{-12} = \frac{1}{4}$$

(c) $x^2 + 6x - 13 - y = 0$

$$\frac{dy}{dx} = \frac{-f_x}{f_y} = \frac{-(2x + 6)}{-1} = 2x + 6 \qquad \frac{dx}{dy} = \frac{-f_y}{f_x} = \frac{-(-1)}{2x + 6} = \frac{1}{2x + 6} \qquad (x \neq -3)$$

Notice that in each of the above cases, one derivative is the inverse of the other.

5.17. Use the implicit function rule to find dy/dx, and, where applicable, dy/dz.

(a) $f(x, y) = 3x^2 + 2xy + 4y^3$

$$\frac{dy}{dx} = \frac{-f_x}{f_y} = -\frac{6x + 2y}{12y^2 + 2x}$$

(b) $f(x, y) = 12x^5 - 2y$

$$\frac{dy}{dx} = \frac{-f_x}{f_y} = \frac{-60x^4}{-2} = 30x^4$$

(c) $f(x, y) = 7x^2 + 2xy^2 + 9y^4$

$$\frac{dy}{dx} = \frac{-f_x}{f_y} = -\frac{14x + 2y^2}{36y^3 + 4xy}$$

(d) $f(x, y) = 6x^3 - 5y$

$$\frac{dy}{dx} = \frac{-f_x}{f_y} = -\frac{18x^2}{-5} = 3.6x^2$$

(e) $f(x, y, z) = x^2y^3 + z^2 + xyz$

$$\frac{dy}{dx} = \frac{-f_x}{f_y} = -\frac{2xy^3 + yz}{3x^2y^2 + xz}$$

$$\frac{dy}{dz} = \frac{-f_z}{f_y} = -\frac{2z + xy}{3x^2y^2 + xz}$$

(f) $f(x, y, z) = x^3z^2 + y^3 + 4xyz$

$$\frac{dy}{dx} = \frac{-f_x}{f_y} = -\frac{3x^2z^2 + 4yz}{3y^2 + 4xz}$$

$$\frac{dy}{dz} = \frac{-f_z}{f_y} = -\frac{2x^3z + 4xy}{3y^2 + 4xz}$$

5.18.   Find the derivative for the inverse function, dP/dQ.

(a) $Q = 210 - 3P$

$$\frac{dP}{dQ} = \frac{1}{dQ/dP} = -\frac{1}{3}$$

(b) $Q = 35 - 0.25P$

$$\frac{dP}{dQ} = \frac{1}{-0.25} = -4$$

(c) $Q = 14 + P^2$

$$\frac{dP}{dQ} = \frac{1}{2P} \quad (P \neq 0)$$

(d) $Q = P^3 + 2P^2 + 7P$

$$\frac{dP}{dQ} = \frac{1}{3P^2 + 4P + 7}$$

OPTIMIZATION OF MULTIVARIATE FUNCTIONS

5.19.   Given the function $z = 3x^2 + 2y^2 - xy - 4x - 7y + 12$ (a) find the extreme values, (b) determine whether the function is at a maximum, minimum, inflection point, or saddle point, and   (c) evaluate it at the critical values.

(a)   Take the first-order partial derivatives, set them equal to zero, and solve simultaneously.

$$z_x = 6x - y - 4 = 0 \qquad z_y = 4y - x - 7 = 0$$

When solved simultaneously, $\bar{x} = 1$ and $\bar{y} = 2$.

(b)   Take the second-order direct partials and check their sign.

$$z_{xx} = 6 \qquad z_{yy} = 4$$

With both second-order direct partials positive, the function is at a minimum along the principal axes.

Finally, find the cross partials and test to see if the product of the second-order direct partials is greater than the square of the cross partials.

$$z_{xy} = -1 = z_{yx}$$

Thus,
$$z_{xx}z_{yy} > (z_{xy})^2$$
$$(6)(4) > (-1)^2$$

and the function is at a minimum when viewed from all directions.

(c)   When evaluated at the critical values,

$$z = 3(1)^2 + 2(2)^2 - (1)(2) - 4(1) - 7(2) + 12 = 3$$

5.20.   Redo Problem 5.19, given $z = 60x + 34y - 4xy - 6x^2 - 3y^2 + 5$.

(a)   Take the first partials and set them equal to zero.

$$z_x = 60 - 4y - 12x = 0 \qquad z_y = 34 - 4x - 6y = 0$$

When solved simultaneously, $\bar{x} = 4$ and $\bar{y} = 3$.

(b)   Take the second-order direct partials.

$$z_{xx} = -12 \qquad z_{yy} = -6$$

With both second partials negative, the function is at a maximum along the principal axes.

Taking the cross partials and applying the test,

$$z_{xy} = -4 = z_{yx}$$

Thus,

$$z_{xx}z_{yy} > (z_{xy})^2$$
$$(-12)(-6) > (-4)^2$$

and the function is maximized from all directions.

(c) $z = 60(4) + 34(3) - 4(4)(3) - 6(4)^2 - 3(3)^2 + 5 = 176$

5.21.   Redo Problem 5.19, given $z = 8x - 2x^2 + 12xy - 12y^2 + 6y$.

(a)   Take the first partials and set them equal to zero.

$$z_x = 8 - 4x + 12y = 0 \qquad z_y = 12x - 24y + 6 = 0$$

When solved simultaneously, $\bar{x} = -5.5$ and $\bar{y} = -2.5$.

(b)   Take the second direct partials.

$$z_{xx} = -4 \qquad z_{yy} = -24$$

With both second partials negative, the function is maximized along the principal axes. Taking the mixed partials and applying the test,

$$z_{xy} = 12 = z_{yx}$$

Here,

$$z_{xx}z_{yy} \not> (z_{xy})^2$$
$$(-4)(-24) < (12)^2$$

Consequently, the function is *not* maximized in all directions.   Whenever the two second-order direct partials are of the same sign, but $z_{xx}z_{yy} < (z_{xy})^2$,   the function is at an inflection point.

(c) $z = 8(-5.5) - 2(-5.5)^2 + 12(-5.5)(-2.5) - 12(-2.5)^2 + 6(-2.5) = -29.5$

5.22.   Redo Problem 5.19, given $z = 5x^2 - 30x + 4xy - 3y^2 + 7y$.

(a)   The first-order conditions are

$$z_x = 10x - 30 + 4y = 0 \qquad z_y = 4x - 6y + 7 = 0$$

When solved simultaneously, $\bar{x} = 2$ and $\bar{y} = 2.5$.

(b)   Testing the second-order condition, where $z_{xx} = 10$, $z_{yy} = -6$, and $z_{xy} = 4$,   reveals that the direct second partials are of opposite signs and the product of the second partials is less than the square of the cross partial.

$$(10)(-6) < (4)^2$$

Consequently, when evaluated at the critical values, the function is neither at a maximum nor a minimum, but at a *saddle point*.

(c) $z = 5(2)^2 - 30(2) + 4(2)(2.5) - 3(2.5)^2 + 7(2.5) = -21.25$

5.23.   Given: $z = 9x - 3x^2 + 6xy - 8y^2 + 12y$,   (a) find the extreme values,   (b) determine whether the function is at a maximum, minimum, inflection point, or saddle point, and   (c) evaluate it at the critical values.

(a)   The first-order condition is

$$z_x = 9 - 6x + 6y = 0 \qquad z_y = 6x - 16y + 12 = 0$$

When solved simultaneously, $\bar{x} = 3.6$ and $\bar{y} = 2.1$.

(b)   Take all the second partials and apply the test.

$$z_{xx} = -6 \qquad z_{yy} = -16 \qquad z_{xy} = 6$$

Since both second direct partials are negative and the product of the direct partials is greater than the square of the cross partials, $(-6)(-16) > (6)^2$, the function is maximized at $\bar{x} = 3.6$, $\bar{y} = 2.1$.

(c) $z = 9(3.6) - 3(3.6)^2 + 6(3.6)(2.1) - 8(2.1)^2 + 12(2.1) = 28.8$

5.24. Redo Problem 5.23, given $z = 48y - 3x^2 - 6xy - 2y^2 + 72x$.

(a) $z_x = -6x - 6y + 72 = 0$ $z_y = 48 - 6x - 4y = 0$

When solved simultaneously, $\bar{x} = 0$ and $\bar{y} = 12$.

(b)   The second order partials are

$$z_{xx} = -6 \qquad z_{yy} = -4 \qquad z_{xy} = -6$$

Both second direct partials are negative, indicating that the function is at a maximum along the principal axes, but $z_{xx}z_{yy} \not> (z_{xy})^2$. Thus, the function is at an inflection point when evaluated at $\bar{x} = 0$, $\bar{y} = 12$.

(c) $z = 48(12) - 3(0)^2 - 6(0)(12) - 2(12)^2 + 72(0) = 288$

5.25. Redo Problem 5.23, given $z = 120x - 2.25x^2 - 4xy - 2.4y^2 + 200y$.

(a) $z_x = 120 - 4.5x - 4y = 0$ $z_y = -4x - 4.8y + 200 = 0$

Thus, $\bar{x} = -40$ and $\bar{y} = 75$.

(b)   The second partials are

$$z_{xx} = -4.5 \qquad z_{yy} = -4.8 \qquad z_{xy} = -4$$

With the second partials both negative, and $(-4.5)(-4.8) > (-4)^2$, the function is maximized at $\bar{x} = -40$, $\bar{y} = 75$.

(c) $z = 120(-40) - 2.25(-40)^2 - 4(-40)(75) - 2.4(75)^2 + 200(75) = 5100$

OPTIMIZING CUBIC FUNCTIONS

5.26. Given: $z = 3x^3 + 3y^3 - 9xy$. Determine the critical values at which this cubic function is maximized or minimized. Note that with a cubic function, the extreme points, $\bar{x}$ and $\bar{y}$, may assume two values, each of which must be tested for the second-order condition.

The first-order condition is

$$z_x = 9x^2 - 9y = 0 \tag{5.6}$$
$$z_y = 9y^2 - 9x = 0 \tag{5.7}$$

From (5.6), $9y = 9x^2 \qquad y = x^2$

Substituting $y = x^2$ in (5.7),

$$9(x^2)^2 - 9x = 0$$
$$9x^4 - 9x = 0$$
$$9x(x^3 - 1) = 0$$

For a product, such as $9x(x^3 - 1)$, to equal zero, at least one of the terms must equal zero. Therefore, either

$$9x = 0 \qquad \text{or} \qquad x^3 - 1 = 0$$
$$\bar{x} = 0 \qquad\qquad\qquad x^3 = 1$$
$$\bar{x} = 1$$

Substituting these values in (5.6), when $\bar{x} = 0$, $\bar{y} = 0$, and when $\bar{x} = 1$, $\bar{y} = 1$.
Testing the second-order condition,

$$z_{xx} = 18x \qquad z_{yy} = 18y \qquad z_{xy} = -9$$

When evaluated at $\bar{x} = 0$ and $\bar{y} = 0$,

$$z_{xx} = 18(0) = 0 \qquad z_{yy} = 18(0) = 0 \qquad z_{xy} = -9$$

Since $z_{xx}z_{yy} < (z_{xy})^2$ when evaluated at $\bar{x} = 0$, $\bar{y} = 0$, the function cannot be at a maximum or a minimum at these critical values. When evaluated at $\bar{x} = 1$ and $\bar{y} = 1$,

$$z_{xx} = 18 \qquad z_{yy} = 18 \qquad z_{xy} = -9$$

With both second partials positive and $(18)(18) > (-9)^2$, the function is minimized at $\bar{x} = 1$, $\bar{y} = 1$. At that point,

$$z = 3(1)^3 + 3(1)^3 - 9(1)(1) = -3$$

5.27. Given: $z = 4x^3 + 6xy - x^2 + 3y^2 + 12$. Determine the critical values at which this function is maximized or minimized.

The first-order conditions are

$$z_x = 12x^2 + 6y - 2x = 0 \tag{5.8}$$
$$z_y = 6x + 6y = 0 \tag{5.9}$$

From (5.9), $y = -x$. Substituting in (5.8),

$$12x^2 + 6(-x) - 2x = 0$$
$$12x^2 - 8x = 0$$
$$x(12x - 8) = 0$$

Thus, $\bar{x} = 0$ or $12x - 8 = 0$
$$\bar{x} = \tfrac{2}{3}$$

Substituting these values in (5.9), if $\bar{x} = 0$, $\bar{y} = 0$, and if $\bar{x} = \tfrac{2}{3}$, $\bar{y} = -\tfrac{2}{3}$. Taking the second partials,

$$z_{xx} = 24x - 2 \qquad z_{yy} = 6 \qquad z_{xy} = 6$$

When evaluated at $\bar{x} = 0$, $\bar{y} = 0$,

$$z_{xx} = -2 \qquad z_{yy} = 6 \qquad z_{xy} = 6$$

Since $(-2)(6) < (6)^2$, the function is not optimized at $\bar{x} = 0$, $\bar{y} = 0$.
When evaluated at $\bar{x} = \tfrac{2}{3}$, $\bar{y} = -\tfrac{2}{3}$,

$$z_{xx} = 14 \qquad z_{yy} = 6 \qquad z_{xy} = 6$$

With both second partials positive and $(14)(6) > (6)^2$, the function is minimized at these critical values, and

$$z = 4(\tfrac{2}{3})^3 + 6(\tfrac{2}{3})(-\tfrac{2}{3}) - (\tfrac{2}{3})^2 + 3(-\tfrac{2}{3})^2 + 12 = 11\tfrac{11}{27}$$

5.28. Redo Problem 5.27, given $z = y^3 + 8xy - 5y^2 + 4x^2 + 13$.

$$z_x = 8y + 8x = 0 \qquad z_y = 3y^2 + 8x - 10y = 0$$

When solved simultaneously, $\bar{x} = 0$ and $\bar{y} = 0$ and $\bar{x} = -6$ and $\bar{y} = 6$. The second partials are

$$z_{xx} = 8 \qquad z_{yy} = 6y - 10 \qquad z_{xy} = 8$$

When evaluated at $\bar{x} = 0$, $\bar{y} = 0$,

$$z_{xx} = 8 \qquad z_{yy} = -10 \qquad z_{xy} = 8$$

Since $(8)(-10) < (8)^2$, the function is not optimized at $\bar{x} = 0$, $\bar{y} = 0$. When evaluated at $\bar{x} = -6$, $\bar{y} = 6$,

$$z_{xx} = 8 \qquad z_{yy} = 26 \qquad z_{xy} = 8$$

With $z_{xx}z_{yy} > 0$, and $(8)(26) > (8)^2$, the function is indeed minimized, and

$$z = (6)^3 + 8(-6)(6) - 5(6)^2 + 4(-6)^2 + 13 = -95$$

CONSTRAINED OPTIMIZATION

5.29. (a) Find the critical values at which the following function will be optimized subject to the given constraints, and   (b) estimate the effect on the value of the objective function from a one-unit change in the constant of the constraint.

$$\text{Given:} \quad z = 4x^2 - 2xy + 6y^2, \quad \text{subject to} \quad x + y = 72$$

(a) Set the constraint equal to zero, multiply it by λ, and add the result to the objective function, thus forming the Lagrangian expression

$$Z = 4x^2 - 2xy + 6y^2 + \lambda(x + y - 72)$$

The first-order conditions are

$$Z_x = 8x - 2y + \lambda = 0 \tag{5.10}$$
$$Z_y = -2x + 12y + \lambda = 0 \tag{5.11}$$
$$Z_\lambda = x + y - 72 = 0 \tag{5.12}$$

Subtracting (5.11) from (5.10) gives

$$10x - 14y = 0 \qquad x = 1.4y$$

Substituting $x = 1.4y$ in (5.12),

$$1.4y + y = 72 \qquad \bar{y} = 30$$

Substituting $\bar{y} = 30$ in the previous equations, the critical values are

$$\bar{x} = 42 \qquad \bar{y} = 30 \qquad \bar{\lambda} = -276$$

Thus,

$$Z = 4(42)^2 - 2(42)(30) + 6(30)^2 - 276(40 + 32 - 72) = 9936$$

(b) With λ negative, a one-unit increase in the constant of the constraint will lead to an increase of approximately 276 in the value of the objective function, and $Z \cong 10,212$.

5.30. Redo Problem 5.29, given

$$z = 26x - 3x^2 + 5xy - 6y^2 + 12y$$

subject to $3x + y = 170$.

(a) The Lagrangian expression is

$$Z = 26x - 3x^2 + 5xy - 6y^2 + 12y + \lambda(3x + y - 170)$$

Thus,

$$Z_x = 26 - 6x + 5y + 3\lambda = 0 \tag{5.13}$$
$$Z_y = 5x - 12y + 12 + \lambda = 0 \tag{5.14}$$
$$Z_\lambda = 3x + y - 170 = 0 \tag{5.15}$$

Multiplying (5.14) by 3 and subtracting from (5.13) gives

$$-21x + 41y = 10 \tag{5.16}$$

Multiplying (5.15) by 7 and adding to (5.16) gives

$$48y = 1200 \qquad \bar{y} = 25$$

Substituting $\bar{y} = 25$ in the previous equations gives the critical values,

$$\bar{x} = 48\tfrac{1}{3} \qquad \bar{y} = 25 \qquad \bar{\lambda} = 46\tfrac{1}{3}$$

Thus, $Z = -3159.54$.

(b) With λ positive, an increase of one unit in the constraint will lead to a decrease of approximately 46.33 in the value of the objective function. Thus, $Z \cong -3205.86$.

5.31. Redo Problem 5.29, given $z = 6x^2 - 8xy + 3y^2$, subject to $x + 0.5y = 68$.

(a)
$$Z = 6x^2 - 8xy + 3y^2 + \lambda(x + 0.5y - 68)$$
$$Z_x = 12x - 8y + \lambda = 0$$
$$Z_y = -8x + 6y + 0.5\lambda = 0$$
$$Z_\lambda = x + 0.5y - 68 = 0$$

When solved simultaneously, $\bar{x} = 40$, $\bar{y} = 56$, $\bar{\lambda} = -32$, and $Z = 1088$.

(b) Since $\lambda = -32$, $Z \cong 1120$.

5.32. In Problem 5.29 it was estimated that, if the constant in the constraint was increased by one unit, the constrained optimum would increase by approximately 276 from 9936 to 10,212. Check the accuracy of the estimate by optimizing the original function $z = 4x^2 - 2xy + 6y^2$ subject to the new constraint $x + y = 73$.

The Lagrangian function is $Z = 4x^2 - 2xy + 6y^2 + \lambda(x + y - 73)$

$$Z_x = 8x - 2y + \lambda = 0$$
$$Z_y = -2x + 12y + \lambda = 0$$
$$Z_\lambda = x + y - 73 = 0$$

Simultaneous solution gives $\bar{x} = 42.58$, $\bar{y} = 30.42$, and $\bar{\lambda} = -279.8$. Thus, $Z = 10,213.9$, compared to the 10,212 estimate from the original λ.

5.33. Constraints can also be used simply to insure that the two independent variables will always be in constant proportion, e.g. $x = 3y$. In this case measuring the effect of λ has no economic significance since a one-unit increase in the constant of the constraint would alter the constant proportion between the independent variables. With this in mind, optimize the following functions subject to the constant proportion constraint.

(a) $z = 4x^2 - 3x + 5xy - 8y + 2y^2$, subject to $x = 2y$.

With $x - 2y = 0$, the Lagrangian function is
$$Z = 4x^2 - 3x + 5xy - 8y + 2y^2 + \lambda(x - 2y)$$
$$Z_x = 8x - 3 + 5y + \lambda = 0$$
$$Z_y = 5x - 8 + 4y - 2\lambda = 0$$
$$Z_\lambda = x - 2y = 0$$

When solved simultaneously, $\bar{x} = 0.5$, $\bar{y} = 0.25$, and $\bar{\lambda} = -2.25$. Thus, $Z = -1.75$.

(b) $z = -5x^2 + 7x + 10xy + 9y - 2y^2$, subject to $y = 5x$.

The Lagrangian function is $Z = -5x^2 + 7x + 10xy + 9y - 2y^2 + \lambda(5x - y)$

$$Z_x = -10x + 7 + 10y + 5\lambda = 0$$
$$Z_y = 10x + 9 - 4y - \lambda = 0$$
$$Z_\lambda = 5x - y = 0$$

Solving simultaneously, $\bar{x} = 5.2$, $\bar{y} = 26$, and $\bar{\lambda} = -43$. Thus, $Z = 135.2$.

Chapter 6

Calculus of Multivariable Functions in Economics

6.1 MARGINAL PRODUCTIVITY

The marginal physical product of capital (MPP_K) is defined as the change in output brought about by a small change in capital when all the other factors of production are held constant. Given a production function such as

$$Q = 36KL - 2K^2 - 3L^2$$

the MPP_K is measured by taking the partial derivative $\partial Q/\partial K$. Thus,

$$MPP_K = \frac{\partial Q}{\partial K} = 36L - 4K$$

Similarly, for labor, $MPP_L = \partial Q/\partial L = 36K - 6L$.

6.2 INCOME DETERMINATION MULTIPLIERS

The partial derivative can also be used to derive the various multipliers of an income determination model. Given

$$Y = C + I + G + (X - Z)$$

where
$$C = C_0 + bY \qquad G = G_0 \qquad Z = Z_0$$
$$I = I_0 + aY \qquad X = X_0$$

it was shown in Problem 2.23 that the equilibrium level of income is

$$\bar{Y} = \frac{1}{1 - b - a}(C_0 + I_0 + G_0 + X_0 - Z_0) \tag{6.1}$$

Taking the partial derivative of (6.1) with respect to any of the variables or parameters gives the multiplier for that variable or parameter. Thus, the government multiplier is given by

$$\frac{\partial \bar{Y}}{\partial G_0} = \frac{1}{1 - b - a}$$

The import multiplier is given by

$$\frac{\partial \bar{Y}}{\partial Z_0} = -\frac{1}{1 - b - a}$$

And the multiplier for a change in the marginal propensity to invest is given by $\partial \bar{Y}/\partial a$, where, by means of the quotient rule,

$$\frac{\partial \bar{Y}}{\partial a} = \frac{(1 - b - a)(0) - (C_0 + I_0 + G_0 + X_0 - Z_0)(-1)}{(1 - b - a)^2} = \frac{C_0 + I_0 + G_0 + X_0 - Z_0}{(1 - b - a)^2}$$

This can alternately be expressed as

$$\frac{\partial \bar{Y}}{\partial a} = \frac{1}{1-b-a}(C_0 + I_0 + G_0 + X_0 - Z_0)\left(\frac{1}{1-b-a}\right)$$

which from (6.1) reduces to

$$\frac{\partial \bar{Y}}{\partial a} = \frac{\bar{Y}}{1-b-a}$$

6.3   PARTIAL ELASTICITIES

Income elasticity of demand (ϵ_Y) measures the percentage change in the demand for a good resulting from a percentage change in income, when all other variables are held constant. *Cross elasticity of demand* (ϵ_c) measures the relative responsiveness of the demand for one product to changes in the price of another, when all other variables are held constant.   Given the demand function

$$Q_1 = a - bP_1 + cP_2 + dY$$

where Y = income and P_2 = the price of a substitute good,   the income elasticity of demand is

$$\epsilon_Y = \frac{\partial Q_1}{\partial Y}\left(\frac{Y}{Q_1}\right) = \frac{\partial Q_1}{Q_1} \div \frac{\partial Y}{Y}$$

and the cross elasticity of demand is

$$\epsilon_c = \frac{\partial Q_1}{\partial P_2}\left(\frac{P_2}{Q_1}\right) = \frac{\partial Q_1}{Q_1} \div \frac{\partial P_2}{P_2}$$

Since a multivariate function has more than one elasticity, the various elasticities are called *partial elasticities*.

Example 1.   Given the demand for beef,

$$Q_b = 4850 - 5P_b + 1.5P_p + 0.1Y \tag{6.2}$$

with $Y = 10,000$, $P_b = 200$, and the price of pork, $P_p = 100$.   The calculations for   (1) the income elasticity and   (2) the cross elasticity of demand for beef are given below.

(1)
$$\epsilon_Y = \frac{\partial Q_b}{Q_b} \div \frac{\partial Y}{Y} = \frac{\partial Q_b}{\partial Y}\left(\frac{Y}{Q_b}\right) \tag{6.3}$$

From (6.2),
$$\frac{\partial Q_b}{\partial Y} = 0.1$$

and
$$Q_b = 4850 - 5(200) + 1.5(100) + 0.1(10,000) = 5000 \tag{6.4}$$

Substituting in (6.3), $\epsilon_Y = 0.1(10,000/5000) = 0.2$.

With $\epsilon_Y < 1$,   the good is income inelastic.   For any given percentage increase in national income, demand for the good will increase less than proportionately.   Hence the relative market share of the good will decline as the economy expands.   Since the income elasticity of demand suggests the growth potential of a market, the growth potential in this case is limited.

(2)
$$\epsilon_c = \frac{\partial Q_b}{Q_b} \div \frac{\partial P_p}{P_p} = \frac{\partial Q_b}{\partial P_p}\left(\frac{P_p}{Q_b}\right)$$

From (6.2), $\partial Q_b/\partial P_p = 1.5$;   from (6.4), $Q_b = 5000$.   Thus,

$$\epsilon_c = 1.5\left(\frac{100}{5000}\right) = 0.03$$

For *substitute goods,* such as beef and pork, $\partial Q_1/\partial P_2 > 0$ and the cross elasticity will be positive.   For *complementary goods,* $\partial Q_1/\partial P_2 < 0$ and the cross elasticity will be negative.   If $\partial Q_1/\partial P_2 = 0$,   the goods are unrelated.

Example 2.   Continuing with Example 1, the percentage change in the demand for beef resulting from a 10 percent increase in the price of pork is estimated as follows:

$$\epsilon_c = \frac{\partial Q_b}{Q_b} \div \frac{\partial P_p}{P_p}$$

Rearranging terms and substituting the known parameters,

$$\frac{\partial Q_b}{Q_b} = \epsilon_c \frac{\partial P_p}{P_p} = (0.03)(0.10) = 0.003$$

The percentage change in the demand for beef ($\partial Q_b / Q_b$) will be 0.3 percent.

6.4   INCREMENTAL CHANGES

Frequently in economics we want to measure the effect on the dependent variable (costs, revenue, profit) of a change in the independent variable (labor hired, capital used, items sold).   If the change is a relatively small one, the differential will measure the effect.   Thus, if $z = f(x,y)$, the effect on z of a small change in x is given by the partial differential

$$dz = z_x \, dx$$

The effect of larger changes can be approximated by multiplying the partial derivative by the proposed change.   Thus,

$$\Delta z \cong z_x \Delta x$$

If the original function $z = f(x,y)$ is linear,

$$\frac{dz}{dx} = \frac{\Delta z}{\Delta x}$$

and the effect of the change will be measured exactly:

$$\Delta z = z_x \, \Delta x$$

Example 3.   A firm's costs are related to its output of two goods x and y.   The functional relationship is

$$TC = x^2 - 0.5xy + y^2$$

The additional cost of a slight increment in output x will be given by the differential

$$dTC = (2x - 0.5y) \, dx$$

The costs of larger increments can be approximated by multiplying the partial derivative with respect to x by the change in x.   Mathematically,

$$\Delta TC \cong \frac{\partial TC}{\partial x} \Delta x \tag{6.5}$$

Since $\partial TC / \partial x = $ the marginal cost (MC_x) of x,   we can also write (6.5) as

$$\Delta TC \cong MC_x \, \Delta x$$

If initially $x = 100$, $y = 60$, and $\Delta x = 3$, then

$$\Delta TC \cong [2(100) - 0.5(60)](3) \cong 510$$

Example 4.   Assume in Section 6.2 that $b = 0.7$, $a = 0.1$, and $Y = 1200$.   The differential can then be used to calculate the effect of an increase in any of the independent variables.   Given the partial derivative

$$\frac{\partial \bar{Y}}{\partial G_0} = \frac{1}{1 - b - a}$$

the partial differential is

$$d\bar{Y} = \frac{1}{1 - b - a} dG_0$$

In a linear model such as this, where the slope is everywhere constant,

$$\frac{\partial \bar{Y}}{\partial G_0} = \frac{\Delta \bar{Y}}{\Delta G_0}$$

Hence

$$\Delta \bar{Y} = \frac{1}{1 - b - a} \Delta G_0$$

If the government increases expenditures by \$100,

$$\Delta \bar{Y} = \frac{1}{1 - 0.7 - 0.1}(100) = 500$$

6.5 MAXIMIZATION AND MINIMIZATION OF MULTIVARIABLE FUNCTIONS IN ECONOMICS

Food processors frequently sell different grades of the same product: quality, standard, economy; some, too, sell part of their output under their own brand name and part under the brand name of a large chain store. Clothing manufacturers and designers frequently have a top brand and cheaper imitations for discount department stores. Maximizing profits or minimizing costs under these conditions involves functions of more than one variable. Thus, the basic rules for optimization of multivariate functions (see Section 5.7) are required.

Example 5.   A firm producing two goods x and y has the profit function

$$\pi = 64x - 2x^2 + 4xy - 4y^2 + 32y - 14$$

To find the profit-maximizing level of output for each of the two goods and test to be sure profits are maximized:

1.   Take the first-order partial derivatives, set them equal to zero, and solve for x and y simultaneously.

$$\pi_x = 64 - 4x + 4y = 0 \tag{6.6}$$

$$\pi_y = 4x - 8y + 32 = 0 \tag{6.7}$$

When solved simultaneously, $\bar{x} = 40$ and $\bar{y} = 24$.

2.   Take the second-order direct partial derivatives since both must be negative for the function to be at a maximum.   From (6.6) and (6.7),

$$\pi_{xx} = -4 \qquad \pi_{yy} = -8$$

3.   Take the cross partials to make sure $\pi_{xx}\pi_{yy} > (\pi_{xy})^2$. From (6.6) and (6.7), $\pi_{xy} = 4 = \pi_{yx}$.   Thus,

$$\pi_{xx}\pi_{yy} > (\pi_{xy})^2$$

$$(-4)(-8) > (4)^2$$

$$32 > 16$$

Profits are indeed maximized at $\bar{x} = 40$ and $\bar{y} = 24$.   At that point, $\pi = 1650$.

Example 6.   In monopolistic competition producers must determine the price that will maximize their profit.   Assume that a producer offers two different brands of a product, for which the demand functions are

$$Q_1 = 14 - 0.25 P_1 \tag{6.8}$$

$$Q_2 = 24 - 0.5 P_2 \tag{6.9}$$

and the joint cost function is

$$TC = Q_1^2 + 5Q_1Q_2 + Q_2^2 \tag{6.10}$$

The profit-maximizing level of output, the price that should be charged for each brand, and the profits are determined as follows:

First, establish the profit function (π) in terms of Q_1 and Q_2.   Since $\pi = $ total revenue (TR) minus total cost (TC)   and the total revenue for the firm is $P_1Q_1 + P_2Q_2$,   the firm's profit is

$$\pi = P_1Q_1 + P_2Q_2 - TC$$

Substituting from (6.10),

$$\pi = P_1 Q_1 + P_2 Q_2 - (Q_1^2 + 5Q_1 Q_2 + Q_2^2) \tag{6.11}$$

Next find the inverse functions of (6.8) and (6.9) by solving for P in terms of Q. Thus, from (6.8),

$$P_1 = 56 - 4Q_1 \tag{6.12}$$

and from (6.9), $\qquad\qquad\qquad P_2 = 48 - 2Q_2 \tag{6.13}$

Substituting in (6.11),

$$\pi = (56 - 4Q_1)Q_1 + (48 - 2Q_2)Q_2 - Q_1^2 - 5Q_1 Q_2 - Q_2^2$$
$$= 56Q_1 - 5Q_1^2 + 48Q_2 - 3Q_2^2 - 5Q_1 Q_2 \tag{6.14}$$

Then maximize (6.14) by the familiar rules:

$$\pi_1 = 56 - 10Q_1 - 5Q_2 = 0 \qquad \pi_2 = 48 - 6Q_2 - 5Q_1 = 0$$

which, when solved simultaneously, gives $\bar{Q}_1 = 2.75$ and $\bar{Q}_2 = 5.7$.

Take the second derivatives to be sure π is maximized:

$$\pi_{11} = -10 \qquad \pi_{22} = -6 \qquad \pi_{12} = -5 = \pi_{21}$$

With both second direct partials negative and $\pi_{11}\pi_{22} > (\pi_{12})^2$, the function is maximized at the critical values.

Finally, substitute $\bar{Q}_1 = 2.75$ and $\bar{Q}_2 = 5.7$ in (6.12) and (6.13), respectively, to find the profit-maximizing price.

$$P_1 = 56 - 4(2.75) = 45 \qquad P_2 = 48 - 2(5.7) = 36.6$$

Prices should be set at \$45 for brand 1 and \$36.60 for brand 2, leading to sales of 2.75 of brand 1 and 5.7 of brand 2. From (6.11) or (6.14), maximum profit is

$$\pi = 45(2.75) + 36.6(5.7) - (2.75)^2 - 5(2.75)(5.7) - (5.7)^2 = 213.94$$

6.6 MAXIMIZATION AND MINIMIZATION OF ECONOMIC FUNCTIONS UNDER CONSTRAINT

Solutions to economic problems frequently have to be found under constraints (e.g. maximizing utility subject to a budget constraint, or minimizing costs subject to some such minimal requirement of output as a production quota). Use of the Lagrangian function (see Section 5.8) greatly facilitates this task.

Example 7. Find the critical values for minimizing the costs of a firm producing two goods, x and y, when the total cost function is $c = 8x^2 - xy + 12y^2$ and the firm is bound by contract to produce a minimum combination of goods totaling 42, i.e. subject to the constraint, $x + y = 42$.

Set the constraint equal to zero, multiply it by λ, and form the Lagrangian function,

$$C = 8x^2 - xy + 12y^2 + \lambda(x + y - 42)$$

Take the first-order partials,

$$C_x = 16x - y + \lambda = 0$$
$$C_y = -x + 24y + \lambda = 0$$
$$C_\lambda = x + y - 42 = 0$$

Solving simultaneously, $\bar{x} = 25$, $\bar{y} = 17$, and $\bar{\lambda} = -383$. With $\bar{\lambda} = -383$, a one-unit increase in the constraint or production quota will lead to an increase in cost of approximately \$383. For second-order conditions, see Section 12.4 and Problem 12.32(a).

6.7 INEQUALITY CONSTRAINTS

Several economic studies have suggested that large corporations maximize not profits, but rather sales revenue subject to some minimally acceptable level of profit. Given a function $f(x,y)$ subject to a constraint $g(x,y) \geqq 0$, the Lagrange multiplier method can be adapted to handle such inequalities. Simply assume the constraint is an equality, i.e. $g(x,y) = 0$, and solve with the familiar Lagrange method (see Section 5.8). Then apply these simple rules:

I.   For maximization subject to $g(x,y) \geqslant 0$.
  1. If $\lambda > 0$, the constraint is functioning as a real limitation, and the desired constrained optimum has been determined.
  2. If $\lambda \leqslant 0$, the constraint is not a limitation. Ignore the equality constraint previously imposed and maximize the objective function by itself.

II. For maximization subject to $g(x,y) \leqslant 0$.
  1. If $\lambda > 0$, the constraint is not a limitation. Maximize the objective function independently of the constraint.
  2. If $\lambda \leqslant 0$, the constraint is operative and the desired constrained optimum has been found.

III. For minimization subject to $g(x,y) \geqslant 0$.
  1. If $\lambda > 0$, the constraint is not a limitation. Ignore the constraint and minimize the objective function.
  2. If $\lambda \leqslant 0$, the constraint is limiting the objective function and the constrained minimum has been found.

IV. For minimization subject to $g(x,y) \leqslant 0$.
  1. If $\lambda > 0$, the constraint is operative and the constrained minimum is found.
  2. If $\lambda \leqslant 0$, the constraint is not a limitation. Minimize the objective function by itself.

Example 8.   Given: $\pi = 64x - 2x^2 + 4xy - 4y^2 + 32y - 14$, subject to $x + y \leqslant 50$.

To maximize this function, assume the constraint is $x + y = 50$ and form the Lagrange expression

$$\Pi = 64x - 2x^2 + 4xy - 4y^2 + 32y - 14 + \lambda(x + y - 50)$$

Then,
$$\Pi_x = 64 - 4x + 4y + \lambda = 0$$
$$\Pi_y = 4x - 8y + 32 + \lambda = 0$$
$$\Pi_\lambda = x + y - 50 = 0$$

from which $\bar{x} = 31.6$, $\bar{y} = 18.4$, $\bar{\lambda} = -11.2$, and $\pi = 1571.6$.

With λ negative when maximizing subject to $g(x,y) \leqslant 0$, the constraint is a limitation and the desired constrained maximum has been found. $\pi = 1571.6$ compared with $\pi = 1650$ for the unconstrained optimum of this function as presented in Example 5.

Example 9.   If the function given in Example 8 were subject to the constraint $x + y \leqslant 79$, it would be maximized as follows:

First, assume $x + y = 79$. Then, the Lagrangian function is

$$\Pi = 64x - 2x^2 + 4xy - 4y^2 + 32y - 14 + \lambda(x + y - 79)$$

and
$$\Pi_x = 64 - 4x + 4y + \lambda = 0$$
$$\Pi_y = 4x - 8y + 32 + \lambda = 0$$
$$\Pi_\lambda = x + y - 79 = 0$$

Hence, $\bar{x} = 49$, $\bar{y} = 30$, $\bar{\lambda} = 12$, and $\pi = 1560$.

With λ positive, the constraint is not a limitation. Maximum profits will be found by optimizing the objective function independently of the constraint. Unconstrained maximization in Example 5 led to $\pi = 1650$. Constrained optimization here leads to $\pi = 1560$.

Solved Problems

MARGINAL CONCEPTS

6.1. Find the marginal physical productivity of the different inputs or factors of production for each of the following production functions (Q).

(a) $Q = 6x^2 + 3xy + 2y^2$

$$\text{MPP}_x = \frac{\partial Q}{\partial x} = 12x + 3y$$

$$\text{MPP}_y = \frac{\partial Q}{\partial y} = 3x + 4y$$

(b) $Q = 0.5K^2 - 2KL + L^2$

$$\text{MPP}_K = K - 2L$$

$$\text{MPP}_L = 2L - 2K$$

(c) $Q = 20 + 8x + 3x^2 - 0.25x^3 + 5y + 2y^2 - 0.5y^3$

$$\text{MPP}_x = 8 + 6x - 0.75x^2$$

$$\text{MPP}_y = 5 + 4y - 1.5y^2$$

(d) $Q = x^2 + 2xy + 3y^2 + 1.5yz + 0.2z^2$

$$\text{MPP}_x = 2x + 2y$$

$$\text{MPP}_y = 2x + 6y + 1.5z$$

$$\text{MPP}_z = 1.5y + 0.4z$$

6.2. (a) Assume $\bar{y} = 4$ in Problem 6.1(a) and find the MPP$_x$ for $x = 5$ and $x = 8$. (b) If the marginal revenue at $\bar{x} = 5$, $\bar{y} = 4$ is \$3, compute the marginal revenue product for the fifth unit of x.

(a) $\text{MPP}_x = 12x + 3y$

At $x = 5$, $\bar{y} = 4$, $\text{MPP}_x = 12(5) + 3(4) = 72$.

At $x = 8$, $\bar{y} = 4$, $\text{MPP}_x = 12(8) + 3(4) = 108$.

(b) $\text{MRP}_x = \text{MPP}_x(\text{MR})$

At $\bar{x} = 5$, $\bar{y} = 4$, $\text{MRP}_x = (72)(3) = 216$.

6.3. (a) Find the marginal cost of a firm's different products when the total cost function is $c = 3x^2 + 7x + 1.5xy + 6y + 2y^2$. (b) Determine the marginal cost of x, when $x = 5$, $\bar{y} = 3$.

(a)

$$\text{MC}_x = 6x + 7 + 1.5y$$

$$\text{MC}_y = 1.5x + 6 + 4y$$

(b) The marginal cost of x, when $x = 5$ and y is held constant at 3, is

$$\text{MC}_x = 6(5) + 7 + 1.5(3) = 41.5$$

INCOME DETERMINATION MULTIPLIERS

6.4. Given a three-sector income determination model in which

$$Y = C + I_0 + G_0 \qquad Yd = Y - T \qquad C_0, I_0, G_0, T_0 > 0 \qquad 0 < b, t < 1$$

$$C = C_0 + bYd \qquad T = T_0 + tY$$

determine the magnitude and direction of a change in (a) government spending, (b) lump-sum taxation, and (c) the tax rate on the equilibrium level of income. In short, calculate the *government multiplier*, the *autonomous tax multiplier*, and the *tax-rate multiplier*.

To find the different multipliers, first solve for the equilibrium level of income, as follows:

$$Y = C_0 + bY - bT_0 - btY + I_0 + G_0$$

$$\bar{Y} = \frac{1}{1 - b + bt}(C_0 - bT_0 + I_0 + G_0) \tag{6.15}$$

Then take the appropriate partial derivatives.

(a)
$$\frac{\partial \bar{Y}}{\partial G_0} = \frac{1}{1 - b + bt}$$

Since $0 < b < 1$, $\partial \bar{Y}/\partial G_0 > 0$. A one-unit increase in government spending will increase the equilibrium level of income by $1/(1 - b + bt)$.

(b)
$$\frac{\partial \bar{Y}}{\partial T_0} = \frac{-b}{1 - b + bt} < 0$$

A one-unit increase in autonomous taxation will cause national income to fall by $b/(1 - b + bt)$.

(c) Since t appears in the denominator in (6.15), the quotient rule is necessary.

$$\frac{\partial \bar{Y}}{\partial t} = \frac{(1 - b + bt)(0) - (C_0 - bT_0 + I_0 + G_0)(b)}{(1 - b + bt)^2}$$

$$= \frac{-b(C_0 - bT_0 + I_0 + G_0)}{(1 - b + bt)^2} = \frac{-b}{1 - b + bt}\left(\frac{C_0 - bT_0 + I_0 + G_0}{1 - b + bt}\right)$$

Thus, from (6.15),
$$\frac{\partial \bar{Y}}{\partial t} = \frac{-b\bar{Y}}{1 - b + bt} < 0$$

A one-unit increase in the tax rate will cause national income to fall by an amount equal to the tax rate multiplier.

6.5. Given a simple model

$$Y = C_0 + I_0 + G_0 \qquad Yd = Y - T$$
$$C = C_0 + bYd \qquad\qquad T = T_0$$

where taxation does *not* depend on income, calculate the effect on the equilibrium level of income of a one-unit change in government expenditure exactly offset by a one-unit change in taxation. That is, calculate the balanced-budget multiplier for an economy in which there is only autonomous taxation.

$$Y = C_0 + b(Y - T_0) + I_0 + G_0$$
$$\bar{Y} = \frac{1}{1 - b}(C_0 - bT_0 + I_0 + G_0)$$

Thus, the government multiplier is

$$\frac{\partial \bar{Y}}{\partial G_0} = \frac{1}{1 - b} \tag{6.16}$$

and the tax multiplier is

$$\frac{\partial \bar{Y}}{\partial T_0} = \frac{-b}{1 - b} \tag{6.17}$$

The balanced-budget effect of a one-unit increase in government spending matched by a one-unit increase in taxation is the sum of (6.16) and (6.17). Therefore,

$$\Delta \bar{Y} = \frac{1}{1 - b} + \left(\frac{-b}{1 - b}\right) = \frac{1}{1 - b} - \frac{b}{1 - b} = \frac{1 - b}{1 - b} = 1$$

A change in government expenditure matched by an equal change in government taxation will have a *positive* effect on the equilibrium level of income exactly equal to the change in government expenditure and taxation. The multiplier in this case is $+1$.

6.6. Given

$$Y = C + I_0 + G_0 \qquad Yd = Y - T$$
$$C = C_0 + bYd \qquad\qquad T = T_0 + tY$$

where taxation is now a function of income, demonstrate the effect on the equilibrium level of income of a one-unit change in government expenditure offset by a one-unit change in *autonomous* taxation (T_0). That is, demonstrate the effect of the *balanced-budget multiplier* in an economy in which taxes are a positive function of income.

From (6.15), $\bar{Y} = [1/(1 - b + bt)](C_0 - bT_0 + I_0 + G_0)$.   Thus,

$$\frac{\partial \bar{Y}}{\partial G_0} = \frac{1}{1 - b + bt} \qquad (6.18)$$

and

$$\frac{\partial \bar{Y}}{\partial T_0} = \frac{-b}{1 - b + bt} \qquad (6.19)$$

The combined effect on $\bar{Y}$ of a one-unit increase in government spending and an equal increase in autonomous taxation is the sum of (6.18) and (6.19).   Thus,

$$\Delta \bar{Y} = \frac{1}{1 - b + bt} + \left(\frac{-b}{1 - b + bt}\right) = \frac{1 - b}{1 - b + bt}$$

which is positive but less than 1 because $(1 - b) < (1 - b + bt)$.   A change in government expenditures equaled by a change in autonomous taxes, when taxes are positively related to income in the model, will have a positive effect on the equilibrium level of income, but the effect is smaller than the initial change in government expenditure.   Here the multiplier is less than 1 because the total change in taxes $(\Delta T = \Delta T_0 + t \Delta Y)$ is greater than the change in G_0.

6.7.   Given
$$Y = C + I_0 + G_0 + X_0 - Z \qquad\qquad T = T_0 + tY$$
$$C = C_0 + bYd \qquad\qquad\qquad Z = Z_0 + zYd$$

where all the independent variables are positive and $0 < b, z, t < 1$.   Determine the effect on the equilibrium level of income of a change in (a) exports, (b) autonomous imports, and (c) autonomous taxation.   In short, find the *export*, *autonomous import*, and *autonomous taxation multipliers*.   [Note that $Z = f(Yd)$.]

From the equilibrium level of income,

$$Y = C_0 + b(Y - T_0 - tY) + I_0 + G_0 + X_0 - Z_0 - z(Y - T_0 - tY)$$

$$\bar{Y} = \frac{1}{1 - b + bt + z - zt}(C_0 - bT_0 + I_0 + G_0 + X_0 - Z_0 + zT_0)$$

(a)
$$\frac{\partial \bar{Y}}{\partial X_0} = \frac{1}{1 - b + bt + z - zt} > 0$$

because $0 < b, z < 1$.   A one-unit increase in exports will have a positive effect on $\bar{Y}$, which is given by the multiplier.

(b)
$$\frac{\partial \bar{Y}}{\partial Z_0} = \frac{-1}{1 - b + bt + z - zt} < 0$$

An increase in autonomous imports will lead to a decrease in $\bar{Y}$.

(c)
$$\frac{\partial \bar{Y}}{\partial T_0} = \frac{z - b}{1 - b + bt + z - zt} < 0$$

because a country's marginal propensity to import (z) is usually smaller than its marginal propensity to consume (b).   With $z < b$, $z - b < 0$.   An increase in autonomous taxes will lead to a decrease in national income, as in (6.19), but the presence of z in the numerator has a mitigating effect on the decrease in income.   When there is a positive marginal propensity to import, increased taxes will reduce cash outflows for imports and thus reduce the negative effect of increased taxes on the equilibrium level of income.

6.8.   Determine the effect on $\bar{Y}$ of a change in the marginal propensity to import (z) in Problem 6.7.

$$\frac{\partial \bar{Y}}{\partial z} = \frac{(1 - b + bt + z - zt)(T_0) - (C_0 - bT_0 + I_0 + G_0 + X_0 - Z_0 + zT_0)(1 - t)}{(1 - b + bt + z - zt)^2}$$

$$= \frac{T_0}{1 - b + bt + z - zt} - \frac{\bar{Y}(1 - t)}{1 - b + bt + z - zt}$$

$$= \frac{-[\bar{Y} - (T_0 + t\bar{Y})]}{1 - b + bt + z - zt} = \frac{-\bar{Y}d}{1 - b + bt + z - zt} < 0$$

6.9.

$$Y = C + I_0 + G_0 \qquad Yd = Y - T \qquad C_0 = 100 \qquad I_0 = 90 \qquad b = 0.75$$

$$C = C_0 + bYd \qquad T = T_0 + tY \qquad G_0 = 330 \qquad T_0 = 240 \qquad t = 0.20$$

(a) What is the equilibrium level of income ($\bar{Y}$)? What is the effect on $\bar{Y}$ of a \$50 increase in (b) government spending and (c) autonomous taxation (T_0)?

(a) From (6.15),

$$\bar{Y} = \frac{1}{1 - b + bt}(C_0 - bT_0 + I_0 + G_0)$$

$$= \frac{1}{1 - 0.75 + 0.75(0.20)}[100 - 0.75(240) + 90 + 330]$$

$$= \frac{1}{0.40}(100 - 180 + 90 + 330) = 2.5(340) = 850$$

(b) If government increases spending by 50,

$$\Delta \bar{Y} = \frac{\partial \bar{Y}}{\partial G_0} \Delta G_0 = \frac{1}{1 - b + bt}(50) = 2.5(50) = 125$$

(c) If autonomous taxation (T_0) increases by 50,

$$\Delta \bar{Y} = \frac{\partial \bar{Y}}{\partial T_0} \Delta T_0 = \frac{-b}{1 - b + bt}(50) = \frac{-0.75}{1 - 0.75 + 0.75(0.20)}(50) = -1.875(50) = -93.75$$

6.10. If the full-employment level of income (Y_{fe}) in Problem 6.9(a) is 1000 and the government wishes to achieve it, by how much should it change (a) government spending or (b) autonomous taxation?

(a) The desired increase in economic activity is the difference between the full-employment level of income (1000) and the present level (850). Thus, the desired $\Delta \bar{Y} = 150$. Substituting in the formula from Problem 6.9(b),

$$\Delta \bar{Y} = \frac{\partial \bar{Y}}{\partial G_0} \Delta G_0$$

$$150 = 2.5 \,\Delta G_0 \qquad \Delta G_0 = 60$$

Increased government expenditure of 60 will increase $\bar{Y}$ by 150.

(b) If the government wishes to alter autonomous taxes to achieve full employment, from Problem 6.9(c),

$$\Delta \bar{Y} = \frac{\partial \bar{Y}}{\partial T_0} \Delta T_0$$

$$150 = -1.875 \,\Delta T_0 \qquad \Delta T_0 = -80$$

The government should cut autonomous taxes by 80.

6.11. Explain the effect on the government deficit (a) if policy a in Problem 6.10 is adopted. (b) If policy b is adopted instead.

(a) The government's financial condition is given by the difference between receipts (T) and expenditures (G). At the initial 850 level of income,

$$T = 240 + 0.2(850) = 410 \qquad G_0 = 330 \qquad T - G_0 = 410 - 330 = 80$$

The government has a surplus of 80.

  If the government increases spending by 60, expenditures rise by 60. But tax revenues also increase as a result of the increase in income. With $\Delta \bar{Y} = 150$, $\Delta T = 0.2(150) = 30$. With expenditures rising by 60 and receipts increasing by 30, the net cost to the government of stimulating the economy to full employment is only \$30. At the new $\bar{Y} = 1000$,

$$T = 240 + 0.2(1000) = 440 \qquad G_0 = 330 + 60 = 390 \qquad T - G_0 = 440 - 390 = 50$$

The government surplus is reduced to \$50 from the previous \$80 surplus.

(b) If the government reduces T_0 by 80, tax revenue falls initially by 80. But the $150 stimulatory effect on income has a positive effect on total tax collections, since $\Delta T = 0.2(150) = 30$. Thus, the net cost of reducing autonomous taxation to stimulate the economy to full employment is $50. The government surplus is reduced to $30:

$$T = 160 + 0.2(1000) = 360 \qquad G_0 = 330 \qquad T - G_0 = 360 - 330 = 30$$

6.12. (a) If the proportional tax in Problem 6.9 is increased by 10 percent, what is the effect on $\bar{Y}$? (b) If the government wants to alter the original marginal tax rate of 20 percent to achieve $Y_{fe} = 1000$, by how much should it change t?

(a) If the proportional tax is increased by 10 percent,

$$\Delta t = 0.10(0.20) = 0.02$$

The resulting change in income is

$$\Delta \bar{Y} = \frac{\partial \bar{Y}}{\partial t} \Delta t$$

Substituting from Problem 6.4(c),

$$\Delta \bar{Y} \cong \frac{-b\bar{Y}}{1 - b + bt}(0.02)$$

Since a change in one of the parameters, unlike a change in one of the independent variables, will alter the value of the multiplier, the multiplier will only approximate the effect of the change.

$$\Delta \bar{Y} \cong \frac{-0.75(850)}{0.4}(0.02) = -31.88$$

(b) The government wants to raise $\bar{Y}$ by 150. Substituting $\Delta \bar{Y} = 150$ in the equation above,

$$150 \cong \frac{-0.75(850)}{0.4} \Delta t$$

$$\Delta t \cong -0.09$$

The tax rate should be reduced by approximately 0.09. The new tax rate should be around 11 percent ($0.20 - 0.09 = 0.11$).

6.13. Given

$$Y = C + I_0 + G_0 + X_0 - Z \qquad T = T_0 + tY$$
$$C = C_0 + bYd \qquad Z = Z_0 + zYd$$

with

$$b = 0.9 \qquad t = 0.2 \qquad C_0 = 125$$
$$X_0 = 150 \qquad Z_0 = 55 \qquad I_0 = 92.5$$
$$z = 0.15 \qquad T_0 = 150 \qquad G_0 = 600$$

Calculate (a) the equilibrium level of income, (b) the effect on $\bar{Y}$ of an increase of 60 in autonomous exports (X_0), and (c) the effect on $\bar{Y}$ of an increase of 30 in autonomous imports (Z_0).

(a) From Problem 6.7,

$$\bar{Y} = \frac{1}{1 - b + bt + z - zt}(C_0 - bT_0 + I_0 + G_0 + X_0 - Z_0 + zT_0)$$

$$= \frac{1}{1 - 0.9 + 0.9(0.2) + 0.15 - 0.15(0.2)}[125 - 0.9(150) + 92.5 + 600 + 150 - 55 + 22.5]$$

$$= 2.5(800) = 2000$$

(b)
$$\Delta \bar{Y} = \frac{\partial \bar{Y}}{\partial X_0}\Delta X_0 = \frac{1}{1 - b + bt + z - zt}(60) = 2.5(60) = 150$$

(c)
$$\Delta \bar{Y} = \frac{\partial \bar{Y}}{\partial Z_0}\Delta Z_0 = \frac{-1}{1 - b + bt + z - zt}(30) = -2.5(30) = -75$$

6.14. If the full-employment level of income in Problem 6.13 is 2075, (a) by how much should the government increase expenditures to achieve it? (b) By how much should it cut autonomous taxes to have the same effect?

(a) The effect of government spending on national income is

$$\Delta \bar{Y} = \frac{\partial \bar{Y}}{\partial G_0} \Delta G_0$$

substituting $\Delta \bar{Y} = 75$,

$$75 = \frac{1}{1 - b + bt + z - zt} \Delta G_0 = 2.5 \, \Delta G_0 \qquad \Delta G_0 = 30$$

(b) $$\Delta \bar{Y} = \frac{\partial \bar{Y}}{\partial T_0} \Delta T_0$$

$$75 = \frac{z - b}{1 - b + bt + z - zt} \Delta T_0 = -1.875 \, \Delta T_0 \qquad \Delta T_0 = -40$$

The government should cut autonomous taxation by 40.

6.15. Calculate the effect on the government deficit if the government in Problem 6.14 achieves full employment through (a) increased expenditure or (b) a tax cut.

(a) If the government increases expenditures by 30, the government deficit increases initially by 30. However, income is stimulated by 75. With $\Delta \bar{Y} = 75$, $\Delta T = 0.2(75) = 15$. Tax revenue increases by 15. Thus the net cost to the government from this policy and the effect on the deficit is \$15 $(30 - 15 = 15)$.

(b) If the government cuts autonomous taxation by 40, tax revenues fall initially by 40. But income increases by 75, causing tax revenues to increase by 15. Thus the net cost to the government of this policy is 25 $(40 - 15 = 25)$ and the government deficit worsens by 25.

6.16. Calculate the effect on the balance of payments (B/P) from (a) government spending and (b) the tax reduction in Problem 6.14.

(a) Since $B/P = X - Z$, substituting from Problem 6.13,

$$B/P = X_0 - (Z_0 + zYd) = X_0 - Z_0 - zY + zT_0 + ztY \qquad (6.20)$$

With an increase of 30 in government spending, $\Delta \bar{Y} = 75$. Since Y is the only variable on the right-hand side of (6.20) to change,

$$\Delta(B/P) = -z(75) + zt(75)$$

Substituting $z = 0.15$, $zt = 0.03$, $\Delta(B/P) = -9$.

(b) When the government cuts autonomous taxes by 40, $\Delta \bar{Y} = 75$. Adjusting (6.20),

$$\Delta(B/P) = -z(75) + z(-40) + zt(75) = -15$$

The reduction in taxes leads to a greater increase in disposable income than the increased government spending, resulting in a higher level of imports and a more serious balance of payments deficit.

6.17. Estimate the effect on $\bar{Y}$ of a one-percentage-point decrease in the marginal propensity to import from Problem 6.13.

$$\Delta \bar{Y} \cong \frac{\partial \bar{Y}}{\partial z} \Delta z$$

Substituting from Problem 6.8,

$$\Delta \bar{Y} = \frac{-\bar{Y}d}{1 - b + bt + z - zt} \Delta Z$$

where $$\bar{Y}d = \bar{Y} - T_0 - t\bar{Y} = 2000 - 150 - 0.2(2000) = 1450$$

Thus, $$\Delta \bar{Y} = \frac{-1450}{0.4}(-0.01) = +36.25$$

MORE COMPARATIVE STATICS

6.18.   Given the traditional functions for

Supply: $P = -g + hQ$ $(g, h > 0)$ (6.21)

and Demand: $P = u - vQ$ $(u, v > 0)$ (6.22)

(a) find the equilibrium price ($\bar{P}$). (b) Show how a small change in each of the four parameters will affect the equilibrium price, and graph the changes using the traditional economic format.

(a)   To find $\bar{P}$, set $s = d$, and solve for the equilibrium level of output ($\bar{Q}$). Then set $\bar{Q}$ into either (6.21) or (6.22) and solve for $\bar{P}$, as follows:

$$-g + hQ = u - vQ$$
$$hQ + vQ = g + u$$
$$\bar{Q} = \frac{g + u}{h + v} \tag{6.23}$$

Substituting (6.23) in (6.21),

$$\bar{P} = -g + h\left(\frac{g + u}{h + v}\right) = -g + \frac{gh + hu}{h + v}$$
$$= \frac{-gh - gv + gh + hu}{h + v} = \frac{hu - gv}{h + v}$$

(b)   To find the effect on $\bar{P}$ of a small change in any of the different parameters, simply take the appropriate partial derivative. Thus,

(1)
$$\frac{\partial \bar{P}}{\partial g} = \frac{(h + v)(-v) - (hu - gv)(0)}{(h + v)^2} = \frac{-v}{h + v}$$

Since all the parameters are positive, the negative sign in the numerator makes $\partial P/\partial g < 0$. As seen in Fig. 6-1(a), with exaggerated dimensions, an increase in g in (6.21) makes $-g$ smaller and lowers the vertical intercept. This shifts the supply curve to the right (s_2), parallel to s_1, and lowers the equilibrium price to P_2.

(2)
$$\frac{\partial \bar{P}}{\partial h} = \frac{(h + v)(u) - (hu - gv)(1)}{(h + v)^2} = \frac{v(g + u)}{(h + v)^2} > 0$$

An increase in h in (6.21) makes the slope of the supply curve steeper and causes the equilibrium price level to rise. See Fig. 6-1(b).

(3)
$$\frac{\partial \bar{P}}{\partial u} = \frac{(h + v)(h) - (hu - gv)(0)}{(h + v)^2} = \frac{h}{h + v} > 0$$

An increase in u in (6.22) will raise the vertical intercept of the demand function and cause the curve to shift to the right parallel to d_1. This causes $\bar{P}$ to rise. See Fig. 6-1(c).

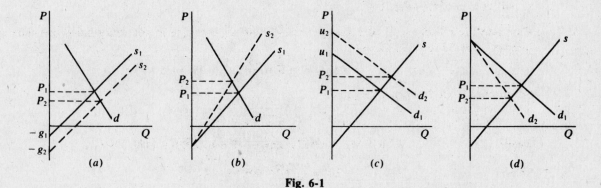

Fig. 6-1

(4)
$$\frac{\partial \bar{P}}{\partial v} = \frac{(h+v)(-g)-(hu-gv)(1)}{(h+v)^2} = \frac{-h(g+u)}{(h+v)^2} < 0$$

An increase in v in (6.22) makes the absolute value of the slope of the demand curve greater, causing it to become steeper and shift to the left. Equilibrium price falls to P_2. See Fig. 6-1(d).

6.19. Assuming the public wishes to hold a constant amount of coin and currency ($\bar{C}$) and time deposits ($\overline{TD}$), the formula for the money supply (M_s) can be written

$$M_s = \bar{C} - \frac{r_t \overline{TD}}{r_d} + \frac{R}{r_d}$$

where R = reserves and r_t and r_d = the reserve requirement for time deposits and demand deposits respectively. (a) What is the effect on the money supply of a change in reserves? (b) If $r_d = 0.25$ and reserves increase by 15 million, what is the change in the money supply?

(a) $\quad \dfrac{\partial M_s}{\partial R} = \dfrac{1}{r_d}$ $\qquad$ (b) $\quad \Delta M_s = \dfrac{\partial M_s}{\partial R} \Delta R = \dfrac{1}{0.25}(15) = 60$

6.20. (a) Determine the effect on the money supply when the Fed changes the reserve requirement on demand deposits. (b) If $R = 20$ million, $\overline{TD} = 2$ million, and $r_t = 0.15$, estimate the effect on the money supply of a change in r_d from 0.25 to 0.2. (c) Check your answer to part (b).

(a) Since r_d is in the denominator of the money equation, a simple trick is to take the partial derivative with respect to $1/r_d$. Thus,

$$\frac{\partial M_s}{\partial (1/r_d)} = R - r_t \overline{TD}$$

(b)
$$\Delta M_s = (R - r_t \overline{TD}) \Delta \frac{1}{r_d}$$

where $\Delta(1/r_d) = 1/0.2 - 1/0.25 = 1$. Thus,

$$\Delta M_s = [20 - 0.15(2)](1) = 19.7$$

(c) Assume $\bar{C} = 5$ million. Substituting in the money equation (see Problem 6.19),

$$M_{s_1} = 5 - \frac{0.15(2)}{0.25} + \frac{20}{0.25} = 83.8$$

$$M_{s_2} = 5 - \frac{0.15(2)}{0.2} + \frac{20}{0.2} = 103.5$$

$$M_{s_2} - M_{s_1} = 19.7 \qquad \text{Compare.}$$

6.21. Refer to Problems 6.19–6.20. (a) Determine the effect on M_s of a change in r_t. (b) Estimate the effect on M_s if r_t is increased from 0.15 to 0.2, assuming $r_d = 0.25$. (c) Check your answer.

(a)
$$\frac{\partial M_s}{\partial r_t} = -\frac{\overline{TD}}{r_d}$$

(b)
$$\Delta M_s = \frac{-\overline{TD}}{r_d} \Delta r_t = \frac{-2}{0.25}(0.05) = -0.4$$

(c)
$$M_{s_1} = 5 - \frac{0.15(2)}{0.25} + \frac{20}{0.25} = 83.8$$

$$M_{s_2} = 5 - \frac{0.2(2)}{0.25} + \frac{20}{0.25} = 83.4$$

$$M_{s_2} - M_{s_1} = -0.4 \qquad \text{Compare.}$$

PARTIAL ELASTICITIES

6.22.   Given $Q = 700 - 2P + 0.02\,Y$,   where $P = 25$ and $Y = 5000$.   Find   (*a*) the price elasticity of demand and · (*b*) the income elasticity of demand.

(*a*)
$$\epsilon_d = \frac{\partial Q}{\partial P}\left(\frac{P}{Q}\right)$$

where $\partial Q/\partial P = -2$ and $Q = 700 - 2(25) + 0.02(5000) = 750$.   Thus,

$$\epsilon_d = -2\left(\frac{25}{750}\right) = -0.067$$

(*b*).
$$\epsilon_Y = \frac{\partial Q}{\partial Y}\left(\frac{Y}{Q}\right) = 0.02\left(\frac{5000}{750}\right) = 0.133$$

6.23.   Given $Q = 400 - 8P + 0.05\,Y$,   where $P = 15$ and $Y = 12{,}000$.   Find   (*a*) the   income elasticity of demand and   (*b*) the growth potential of the product, if income is expanding by 5 percent a year.   (*c*) Comment on the growth potential of the product.

(*a*) $Q = 400 - 8(15) + 0.05(12{,}000) = 880$ and $\partial Q/\partial Y = 0.05$.   Thus,

$$\epsilon_Y = \frac{\partial Q}{\partial Y}\left(\frac{Y}{Q}\right) = 0.05\left(\frac{12{,}000}{880}\right) = 0.68$$

(*b*)
$$\epsilon_Y = \frac{\partial Q}{Q} \div \frac{\partial Y}{Y}$$

Rearranging terms and substituting the known parameters,

$$\frac{\partial Q}{Q} = \epsilon_Y \frac{\partial Y}{Y} = 0.68(0.05) = 0.034$$

The demand for the good will increase by 3.4 percent.

(*c*)   Since $0 < \epsilon_Y < 1$,   it can be expected that demand for the good will increase with national income, but the increase will be less than proportionate.   Thus, while demand grows absolutely, the relative market share of the good will decline in an expanding economy.   If $\epsilon_Y > 1$,   the demand for the product would grow faster than the rate of expansion in the economy, and increase its relative market share.   And if $\epsilon_Y < 0$,   demand for the good would decline as income increases.

6.24.   Given $Q_1 = 100 - P_1 + 0.75\,P_2 - 0.25\,P_3 + 0.0075\,Y$.   At $P_1 = 10$, $P_2 = 20$, $P_3 = 40$,   and $Y = 10{,}000$, $Q_1 = 170$.   Find the different cross elasticities of demand.

$$\epsilon_{12} = \frac{\partial Q_1}{\partial P_2}\left(\frac{P_2}{Q_1}\right) = 0.75\left(\frac{20}{170}\right) = 0.088$$

$$\epsilon_{13} = \frac{\partial Q_1}{\partial P_3}\left(\frac{P_3}{Q_1}\right) = -0.25\left(\frac{40}{170}\right) = -0.059$$

6.25.   Given $Q_1 = 50 - 4P_1 - 3P_2 + 2P_3 + 0.001\,Y$.   At $P_1 = 5$, $P_2 = 7$, $P_3 = 3$,   and $Y = 11{,}000$, $Q_1 = 26$.   (*a*) Use cross elasticities to determine the relationship between good 1 and the other two goods.   (*b*) Determine the effect on Q_1 of a 10 percent price increase for each of the other goods individually.

(*a*) $\qquad\qquad \epsilon_{12} = -3(\tfrac{7}{26}) = -0.81 \qquad \epsilon_{13} = 2(\tfrac{3}{26}) = 0.23$

With ϵ_{12} negative, goods 1 and 2 are complements.   An increase in P_2 will lead to a decrease in Q_1.   With ϵ_{13} positive, goods 1 and 3 are substitutes.   An increase in P_3 will increase Q_1.

(b)
$$\epsilon_{12} = \frac{\partial Q_1}{Q_1} \div \frac{\partial P_2}{P_2}$$

Rearranging terms and substituting the known parameters,

$$\frac{\partial Q_1}{Q_1} = \epsilon_{12} \frac{\partial P_2}{P_2} = -0.81(0.10) = -0.081$$

If P_2 increases by 10 percent, Q_1 decreases by 8.1 percent.

$$\epsilon_{13} = \frac{\partial Q_1}{Q_1} \div \frac{\partial P_3}{P_3}$$

$$\frac{\partial Q_1}{Q_1} = \epsilon_{13} \frac{\partial P_3}{P_3} = 0.23(0.10) = 0.023$$

If P_3 increases by 10 percent, Q_1 increases by 2.3 percent.

OPTIMIZING ECONOMIC FUNCTIONS

6.26. Given the total cost (c) function $c = 8x^2 + 6y^2 - 2xy - 40x - 42y + 180$ for a firm producing two goods, x and y, (a) minimize costs, (b) test the second-order condition, and (c) evaluate the function at the critical values.

(a)
$$c_x = 16x - 2y - 40 = 0 \qquad c_y = 12y - 2x - 42 = 0$$

Solving simultaneously, $\bar{x} = 3$ and $\bar{y} = 4$.

(b) Taking the second partials,

$$c_{xx} = 16 \qquad c_{yy} = 12 \qquad c_{xy} = -2$$

With the second direct partials both positive, and the product of the direct partials greater than the square of the mixed partials, $(16)(12) > (-2)^2$,   total cost is minimized at $\bar{x} = 3$ and $\bar{y} = 4$.

(c)
$$c = 8(3)^2 + 6(4)^2 - 2(3)(4) - 40(3) - 42(4) + 180 = 36$$

6.27. Given the profit (π) function $\pi = 160x - 3x^2 - 2xy - 2y^2 + 120y - 18$ for a firm producing two goods, x and y, (a) maximize profits, (b) test the second-order condition, and (c) evaluate the function at the critical values.

(a)
$$\pi_x = 160 - 6x - 2y = 0 \qquad \pi_y = -2x - 4y + 120 = 0$$

When solved simultaneously, $\bar{x} = 20$ and $\bar{y} = 20$.

(b) Taking the second partials,

$$\pi_{xx} = -6 \qquad \pi_{yy} = -4 \qquad \pi_{xy} = -2$$

With both direct second partials negative, and $\pi_{xx}\pi_{yy} > (\pi_{xy})^2$, π is maximized at $\bar{x} = \bar{y} = 20$.

(c)
$$\pi = 2782$$

6.28. Redo Problem 6.26, given $c = 5x^2 - 50x - 3xy + 6y^2 - 22y + 240$.

(a)
$$c_x = 10x - 50 - 3y = 0 \qquad c_y = -3x + 12y - 22 = 0$$

Solved simultaneously, $\bar{x} = 6$ and $\bar{y} = 3\frac{1}{3}$.

(b) The second partials are

$$c_{xx} = 10 \qquad c_{yy} = 12 \qquad c_{xy} = -3$$

With $c_{xx}, c_{yy} > 0$ and $c_{xx}c_{yy} > (c_{xy})^2$,   costs are minimized at $\bar{x} = 6$, and $\bar{y} = 3\frac{1}{3}$.

(c)
$$c = 53.33$$

6.29. Redo Problem 6.27, given $\pi = 25x - x^2 - xy - 2y^2 + 30y - 28$.

(a) $\pi_x = 25 - 2x - y = 0 \qquad \pi_y = -x - 4y + 30 = 0$

Thus, $\bar{x} = 10$ and $\bar{y} = 5$.

(b) $\pi_{xx} = -2 \qquad \pi_{yy} = -4 \qquad \pi_{xy} = -1$

With π_{xx} and π_{yy} both negative and $\pi_{xx}\pi_{yy} > (\pi_{xy})^2$, π is maximized.

(c) $\pi = 172$

6.30. A monopolist sells two products, x and y, for which the demand is

$$x = 25 - 0.5P_x \tag{6.24}$$

$$y = 30 - P_y \tag{6.25}$$

and the combined cost function is

$$c = x^2 + 2xy + y^2 + 20 \tag{6.26}$$

Find   (a) the profit-maximizing level of output for each product,   (b) the profit-maximizing price for each product, and   (c) the maximum profit.

(a)   Since $\pi = TR_x + TR_y - TC$,   in this case,

$$\pi = P_x x + P_y y - c \tag{6.27}$$

From (6.24) and (6.25),

$$P_x = 50 - 2x \tag{6.28}$$

$$P_y = 30 - y \tag{6.29}$$

Substituting in (6.27),

$$\pi = (50 - 2x)x + (30 - y)y - (x^2 + 2xy + y^2 + 20)$$
$$= 50x - 3x^2 + 30y - 2y^2 - 2xy - 20 \tag{6.30}$$

The first-order condition for maximizing (6.30) is

$$\pi_x = 50 - 6x - 2y = 0 \qquad \pi_y = 30 - 4y - 2x = 0$$

Solving simultaneously, $\bar{x} = 7$ and $\bar{y} = 4$. Testing the second-order condition, $\pi_{xx} = -6$, $\pi_{yy} = -4$, and $\pi_{xy} = -2$. With both direct partials negative and $\pi_{xx}\pi_{yy} > (\pi_{xy})^2$, π is maximized.

(b) Substituting $\bar{x} = 7$, $\bar{y} = 4$ in (6.28) and (6.29),

$$P_x = 50 - 2(7) = 36 \qquad P_y = 30 - 4 = 26$$

(c) Substituting $\bar{x} = 7$, $\bar{y} = 4$ in (6.30), $\pi = 215$.

6.31. Find the profit-maximizing level of   (a) output,   (b) price, and   (c) profit for a monopolist with the demand functions

$$x = 50 - 0.5P_x \tag{6.31}$$

$$y = 76 - P_y \tag{6.32}$$

and the total cost function $c = 3x^2 + 2xy + 2y^2 + 55$.

(a) From (6.31) and (6.32),

$$P_x = 100 - 2x \tag{6.33}$$

$$P_y = 76 - y \tag{6.34}$$

Substituting in $\pi = P_x x + P_y y - c$,

$$\pi = (100 - 2x)x + (76 - y)y - (3x^2 + 2xy + 2y^2 + 55)$$
$$= 100x - 5x^2 + 76y - 3y^2 - 2xy - 55 \tag{6.35}$$

Maximizing (6.35),

$$\pi_x = 100 - 10x - 2y = 0 \qquad \pi_y = 76 - 6y - 2x = 0$$

Thus, $\bar{x} = 8$ and $\bar{y} = 10$. Checking the second-order condition, $\pi_{xx} = -10$, $\pi_{yy} = -6$, and $\pi_{xy} = -2$. Since $\pi_{xx}, \pi_{yy} < 0$ and $\pi_{xx}\pi_{yy} > (\pi_{xy})^2$, π is maximized at the critical values.

(b) Substituting $\bar{x} = 8$, $\bar{y} = 10$ in (6.33) and (6.34),

$$P_x = 100 - 2(8) = 84 \qquad P_y = 76 - 10 = 66$$

(c) From (6.35), $\pi = 725$.

6.32. Find the profit-maximizing level of (a) output, (b) price, and (c) profit for the monopolistic producer with the demand functions,

$$Q_1 = 49\tfrac{1}{3} - \tfrac{2}{3}P_1 \tag{6.36}$$

$$Q_2 = 36 - \tfrac{1}{2}P_2 \tag{6.37}$$

and the joint cost function $c = Q_1^2 + 2Q_1Q_2 + Q_2^2 + 120$.

(a) From (6.36) and (6.37),

$$P_1 = 74 - 1.5Q_1 \tag{6.38}$$

$$P_2 = 72 - 2Q_2 \tag{6.39}$$

Substituting in $\pi = P_1Q_1 + P_2Q_2 - c$,

$$\pi = (74 - 1.5Q_1)Q_1 + (72 - 2Q_2)Q_2 - (Q_1^2 + 2Q_1Q_2 + Q_2^2 + 120)$$
$$= 74Q_1 - 2.5Q_1^2 + 72Q_2 - 3Q_2^2 - 2Q_1Q_2 - 120 \tag{6.40}$$

The first-order condition for maximizing (6.40) is

$$\pi_1 = 74 - 5Q_1 - 2Q_2 = 0 \qquad \pi_2 = 72 - 6Q_2 - 2Q_1 = 0$$

Thus, $\bar{Q}_1 = 11.54$ and $\bar{Q}_2 = 8.15$. Testing the second-order condition, $\pi_{11} = -5$, $\pi_{22} = -6$, and $\pi_{12} = -2$. Thus, $\pi_{11}, \pi_{22} < 0$; $\pi_{11}\pi_{22} > (\pi_{12})^2$, and π is maximized.

(b) Substituting the critical values in (6.38) and (6.39),

$$P_1 = 74 - 1.5(11.54) = 56.69 \qquad P_2 = 72 - 2(8.15) = 55.70$$

(c) $$\pi = 600.46$$

6.33. Find the profit-maximizing level of (a) output, (b) price, and (c) profit, when

$$Q_1 = 5200 - 10P_1 \tag{6.41}$$

$$Q_2 = 8200 - 20P_2 \tag{6.42}$$

and $$c = 0.1Q_1^2 + 0.1Q_1Q_2 + 0.2Q_2^2 + 325$$

(a) From (6.41) and (6.42),
$$P_1 = 520 - 0.1Q_1 \tag{6.43}$$

$$P_2 = 410 - 0.05Q_2 \tag{6.44}$$

Thus, $$\pi = (520 - 0.1Q_1)Q_1 + (410 - 0.05Q_2)Q_2 - (0.1Q_1^2 + 0.1Q_1Q_2 + 0.2Q_2^2 + 325)$$
$$= 520Q_1 - 0.2Q_1^2 + 410Q_2 - 0.25Q_2^2 - 0.1Q_1Q_2 - 325 \tag{6.45}$$

Maximizing (6.45),

$$\pi_1 = 520 - 0.4Q_1 - 0.1Q_2 = 0 \qquad \pi_2 = 410 - 0.5Q_2 - 0.1Q_1 = 0$$

Thus, $\bar{Q}_1 = 1152.63$ and $\bar{Q}_2 = 589.47$. Checking the second-order condition, $\pi_{11} = -0.4$, $\pi_{22} = -0.5$, and $\pi_{12} = -0.1 = \pi_{21}$. Since $\pi_{11}, \pi_{22} < 0$ and $\pi_{11}\pi_{22} > (\pi_{12})^2$, π is maximized at $\bar{Q}_1 = 1152.63$ and $\bar{Q}_2 = 589.47$.

(b) Substituting in (6.43) and (6.44),

$$P_1 = 520 - 0.1(1152.63) = 404.74 \qquad P_2 = 410 - 0.05(589.47) = 380.53$$

(c)
$$\pi = 420{,}201.32$$

CONSTRAINED OPTIMIZATION IN ECONOMICS

6.34. (a) What combination of goods x and y should a firm produce to minimize costs when the joint cost function is $c = 6x^2 + 10y^2 - xy + 30$ and the firm has a production quota of $x + y = 34$? (b) Estimate the effect on costs if the production quota is reduced by one unit.

(a) Form a new function by setting the constraint equal to zero, multiplying it by λ, and adding it to the original or objective function. Thus,

$$C = 6x^2 + 10y^2 - xy + 30 + \lambda(x + y - 34)$$
$$C_x = 12x - y + \lambda = 0$$
$$C_y = 20y - x + \lambda = 0$$
$$C_\lambda = x + y - 34 = 0$$

Solving simultaneously, $\bar{x} = 21$, $\bar{y} = 13$, and $\bar{\lambda} = -239$. Thus, $C = 4093$. Second-order conditions are discussed in Section 12.5.

(b) With λ negative, a decrease in the constant of the constraint (the production quota) will lead to a cost reduction of approximately 239.

6.35. (a) What output mix should a profit-maximizing firm produce when its total profit function is $\pi = 80x - 2x^2 - xy - 3y^2 + 100y$ and its maximum output capacity is $x + y = 12$? (b) Estimate the effect on profits if output capacity is expanded by one unit.

(a)
$$\Pi = 80x - 2x^2 - xy - 3y^2 + 100y + \lambda(x + y - 12)$$
$$\Pi_x = 80 - 4x - y + \lambda = 0$$
$$\Pi_y = -x - 6y + 100 + \lambda = 0$$
$$\Pi_\lambda = x + y - 12 = 0$$

When solved simultaneously, $\bar{x} = 5$, $\bar{y} = 7$, and $\bar{\lambda} = -53$. Thus, $\pi = 868$.

(b) With $\bar{\lambda} = -53$, an increase in output capacity should lead to increased profits of approximately 53.

6.36. A rancher faces the profit function

$$\pi = 110x - 3x^2 - 2xy - 2y^2 + 140y$$

where x = sides of beef and y = hides. Since there are two sides of beef for every hide, it follows that output must be in the proportion

$$\frac{x}{2} = y \qquad x = 2y$$

At what level of output will the rancher maximize profits?

$$\Pi = 110x - 3x^2 - 2xy - 2y^2 + 140y + \lambda(x - 2y)$$
$$\Pi_x = 110 - 6x - 2y + \lambda = 0$$
$$\Pi_y = -2x - 4y + 140 - 2\lambda = 0$$
$$\Pi_\lambda = x - 2y = 0$$

Solving simultaneously, $\bar{x} = 20$, $\bar{y} = 10$, $\bar{\lambda} = 30$, and $\pi = 1800$.

6.37. (a) Minimize costs for a firm with the cost function $c = 5x^2 + 2xy + 3y^2 + 800$ subject to the production quota $x + y = 39$. (b) Estimate additional costs if the production quota is increased to 40.

(a)
$$C = 5x^2 + 2xy + 3y^2 + 800 + \lambda(x + y - 39)$$
$$C_x = 10x + 2y + \lambda = 0$$
$$C_y = 2x + 6y + \lambda = 0$$
$$C_\lambda = x + y - 39 = 0$$

When solved simultaneously, $\bar{x} = 13$, $\bar{y} = 26$, $\bar{\lambda} = -182$, and $C = 4349$.

(b) Since $\bar{\lambda} = -182$, an increased production quota will lead to additional costs of approximately 182.

6.38. A monopolistic firm has the following demand functions for each of its products x and y:

$$x = 72 - 0.5 P_x \qquad (6.46)$$
$$y = 120 - P_y \qquad (6.47)$$

The combined cost function is $c = x^2 + xy + y^2 + 35$ and maximum joint production is 40. Thus, $x + y = 40$. Find the profit-maximizing level of (a) output, (b) price, and (c) profit.

(a) From (6.46) and (6.47),

$$P_x = 144 - 2x \qquad (6.48)$$
$$P_y = 120 - y \qquad (6.49)$$

Thus, $\pi = (144 - 2x)x + (120 - y)y - (x^2 + xy + y^2 + 35) = 144x - 3x^2 - xy - 2y^2 + 120y - 35$

Incorporating the constraint,

$$\Pi = 144x - 3x^2 - xy - 2y^2 + 120y - 35 + \lambda(x + y - 40)$$

Thus,
$$\Pi_x = 144 - 6x - y + \lambda = 0$$
$$\Pi_y = -x - 4y + 120 + \lambda = 0$$
$$\Pi_\lambda = x + y - 40 = 0$$

and, $\bar{x} = 18$, $\bar{y} = 22$, and $\bar{\lambda} = -14$.

(b) Substituting in (6.48) and (6.49),

$$P_x = 144 - 2(18) = 108 \qquad P_y = 120 - 22 = 98$$

(c)
$$\pi = 2861$$

6.39. A manufacturer of parts for the tricycle industry sells three tires (x) for every frame (y). Thus,

$$\frac{x}{3} = y \qquad x = 3y$$

If the demand is

$$x = 63 - 0.25 P_x \qquad (6.50)$$
$$y = 60 - \tfrac{1}{3}P_y \qquad (6.51)$$

and costs are

$$c = x^2 + xy + y^2 + 190$$

find the profit-maximizing level of (a) output, (b) price, and (c) profit.

(a) From (6.50) and (6.51),

$$P_x = 252 - 4x \tag{6.52}$$

$$P_y = 180 - 3y \tag{6.53}$$

Thus, $\pi = (252 - 4x)x + (180 - 3y)y - (x^2 + xy + y^2 + 190) = 252x - 5x^2 - xy + 180y - 190 - 4y^2$

Forming a new, constrained function,

$$\Pi = 252x - 5x^2 - xy - 4y^2 + 180y - 190 + \lambda(x - 3y)$$

Hence, $\Pi_x = 252 - 10x - y + \lambda = 0$ $\Pi_y = -x - 8y + 180 - 3\lambda = 0$ $\Pi_\lambda = x - 3y = 0$

and $\bar{x} = 27$, $\bar{y} = 9$, and $\bar{\lambda} = 27$.

(b) From (6.52) and (6.53), $P_x = 144$ and $P_y = 153$.

(c) $\pi = 4022$

6.40. Problem 4.13 dealt with the profit-maximizing level of output for a firm producing a single product that is sold in two distinct markets when it does and does not discriminate.   The functions given were

$$Q_1 = 21 - 0.1 P_1 \tag{6.54}$$

$$Q_2 = 50 - 0.4 P_2 \tag{6.55}$$

$$c = 2000 + 10Q \quad \text{where} \quad Q = Q_1 + Q_2 \tag{6.56}$$

Use multivariable calculus to check your solution to Problem 4.13.

From (6.54), (6.55), and (6.56),

$$P_1 = 210 - 10Q_1 \tag{6.57}$$

$$P_2 = 125 - 2.5Q_2 \tag{6.58}$$

$$c = 2000 + 10Q_1 + 10Q_2$$

With discrimination $P_1 \neq P_2$ since different prices are charged in different markets, and therefore

$$\pi = (210 - 10Q_1)Q_1 + (125 - 2.5Q_2)Q_2 - (2000 + 10Q_1 + 10Q_2) = 200Q_1 - 10Q_1^2 + 115Q_2 - 2.5Q_2^2 - 2000$$

Taking the first partials,

$$\pi_1 = 200 - 20Q_1 = 0 \qquad \pi_2 = 115 - 5Q_2 = 0$$

Thus, $\bar{Q}_1 = 10$ and $\bar{Q}_2 = 23$.   Substituting in (6.57) and (6.58), $\bar{P}_1 = 110$ and $\bar{P}_2 = 67.5$.   Compare.
  If there is no discrimination, the same price must be charged in both markets.   Hence $P_1 = P_2$.
Substituting from (6.57) and (6.58),

$$210 - 10Q_1 = 125 - 2.5 Q_2$$

$$2.5 Q_2 - 10Q_1 = -85$$

Taking this as a constraint and forming a new function,

$$\Pi = 200Q_1 - 10Q_1^2 + 115Q_2 - 2.5 Q_2^2 - 2000 + \lambda(2.5Q_2 - 10Q_1 + 85)$$

Thus, $\Pi_1 = 200 - 20Q_1 - 10\lambda = 0$ $\Pi_2 = 115 - 5Q_2 + 2.5\lambda = 0$ $\Pi_\lambda = 2.5Q_2 - 10Q_1 + 85 = 0$

and $\bar{Q}_1 = 13.4$, $\bar{Q}_2 = 19.6$, and $\bar{\lambda} = -6.8$.   Substituting in (6.57) and (6.58),

$$P_1 = 210 - 10(13.4) = 76$$

$$P_2 = 125 - 2.5(19.6) = 76$$

$$Q = 13.4 + 19.6 = 33 \qquad \text{Compare.}$$

6.41. Check your answers to Problem 4.14, given

$$Q_1 = 24 - 0.2 P_1 \qquad Q_2 = 10 - 0.05 P_2$$

$$c = 35 + 40Q \quad \text{where} \quad Q = Q_1 + Q_2$$

From the information given,

$$P_1 = 120 - 5Q_1 \tag{6.59}$$

$$P_2 = 200 - 20Q_2 \tag{6.60}$$

$$c = 35 + 40Q_1 + 40Q_2$$

With price discrimination,

$$\pi = (120 - 5Q_1)Q_1 + (200 - 20Q_2)Q_2 - (35 + 40Q_1 + 40Q_2) = 80Q_1 - 5Q_1^2 + 160Q_2 - 20Q_2^2 - 35$$

Thus, $\pi_1 = 80 - 10Q_1 = 0$ $\pi_2 = 160 - 40Q_2 = 0$

and $\bar{Q}_1 = 8$, $\bar{Q}_2 = 4$, $P_1 = 80$, and $P_2 = 120$.   Compare.

If there is no price discrimination, $P_1 = P_2$. Substituting from (6.59) and (6.60),

$$120 - 5Q_1 = 200 - 20Q_2$$

$$20Q_2 - 5Q_1 = 80 \tag{6.61}$$

Forming a new function with (6.61) as a constraint,

$$\Pi = 80Q_1 - 5Q_1^2 + 160Q_2 - 20Q_2^2 - 35 + \lambda(20Q_2 - 5Q_1 - 80)$$

Thus, $\Pi_1 = 80 - 10Q_1 - 5\lambda = 0$ $\Pi_2 = 160 - 40Q_2 + 20\lambda = 0$ $\Pi_\lambda = 20Q_2 - 5Q_1 - 80 = 0$

and $\bar{Q}_1 = 6.4$, $\bar{Q}_2 = 5.6$, and $\bar{\lambda} = 3.2$. Substituting in (6.59) and (6.60),

$$P_1 = 120 - 5(6.4) = 88$$

$$P_2 = 200 - 20(5.6) = 88$$

$$Q = 6.4 + 5.6 = 12 \qquad \text{Compare.}$$

6.42.   (a) Maximize utility $u = Q_1 Q_2$,   when $P_1 = 1$, $P_2 = 4$, and one's budget, $B = 120$.
        (b) Estimate the effect of a one-unit increase in the budget.

(a)   The budget constraint is $Q_1 + 4Q_2 = 120$. Forming a new function to incorporate the constraint,

$$U = Q_1 Q_2 + \lambda(Q_1 + 4Q_2 - 120)$$

Thus, $U_1 = Q_2 + \lambda = 0$ $U_2 = Q_1 + 4\lambda = 0$ $U_\lambda = Q_1 + 4Q_2 - 120 = 0$

and $\bar{Q}_1 = 60$, $\bar{Q}_2 = 15$, and $\bar{\lambda} = -15$.

(b)   With λ negative, a one dollar increase in the budget will lead to an increase in the utility function of approximately 15. Thus, the marginal utility of money (or income) at $\bar{Q}_1 = 60$ and $\bar{Q}_2 = 15$ is approximately 15.

6.43.   (a) Maximize utility $u = Q_1 Q_2$,   subject to $P_1 = 10$, $P_2 = 2$, and $B = 240$.   (b) What is the marginal utility of money?

(a)   Form the Lagrangian function $U = Q_1 Q_2 + \lambda(10Q_1 + 2Q_2 - 240)$.

$$U_1 = Q_2 + 10\lambda = 0 \qquad U_2 = Q_1 + 2\lambda = 0 \qquad U_\lambda = 10Q_1 + 2Q_2 - 240 = 0$$

Thus, $\bar{Q}_1 = 12$, $\bar{Q}_2 = 60$, and $\bar{\lambda} = -6$.

(b)   The marginal utility of money at $\bar{Q}_1 = 12$ and $\bar{Q}_2 = 60$ is approximately 6.

6.44.   Maximize utility $u = Q_1 Q_2 + Q_1 + 2Q_2$,   subject to $P_1 = 2$, $P_2 = 5$, and $B = 51$.

Form the Lagrangian function $U = Q_1 Q_2 + Q_1 + 2Q_2 + \lambda(2Q_1 + 5Q_2 - 51)$.

$$U_1 = Q_2 + 1 + 2\lambda = 0 \qquad U_2 = Q_1 + 2 + 5\lambda = 0 \qquad U_\lambda = 2Q_1 + 5Q_2 - 51 = 0$$

Thus, $\bar{Q}_1 = 13$, $\bar{Q}_2 = 5$, and $\bar{\lambda} = -3$.

6.45. Maximize utility $u = xy + 3x + y$,   subject to $P_x = 8$, $P_y = 12$, and $B = 212$.

The Lagrangian function is $U = xy + 3x + y + \lambda(8x + 12y - 212)$.

$$U_x = y + 3 + 8\lambda = 0 \qquad U_y = x + 1 + 12\lambda = 0 \qquad U_\lambda = 8x + 12y - 212 = 0$$

Thus, $\bar{x} = 15$, $\bar{y} = 7\frac{2}{3}$, and $\bar{\lambda} = -1\frac{1}{3}$.

INEQUALITY CONSTRAINTS

6.46. Minimize the total cost function $c = 8x^2 + 6y^2 - 2xy - 40x - 42y + 180$ subject to the production quota $x + y \geq 12$.

Assuming initially that $x + y = 12$,   the new function incorporating the constraint is

$$C = 8x^2 + 6y^2 - 2xy - 40x - 42y + 180 + \lambda(x + y - 12)$$

Thus, $C_x = 16x - 2y - 40 + \lambda = 0 \qquad C_y = -2x + 12y - 42 + \lambda = 0 \qquad C_\lambda = x + y - 12 = 0$

and $\bar{x} = 5.19$, $\bar{y} = 6.81$, $\bar{\lambda} = -29.4$, and $C = 109.44$.

According to rule III in Section 6.7, when minimizing subject to $g(x,y) \geq 0$,   if $\bar{\lambda} \leq 0$,   the constraint is a limitation and the desired constrained minimum has been found. If there were no constraint, costs would be minimized at $\bar{x} = 3$ and $\bar{y} = 4$,   where $c = 36$ (see Problem 6.26).

6.47. Minimize the function given in Problem 6.46 subject to $x + y \geq 5$.

In this case, the Lagrangian function is

$$C = 8x^2 + 6y^2 - 2xy - 40x - 42y + 180 + \lambda(x + y - 5)$$

and $C_x = 16x - 2y - 40 + \lambda = 0 \qquad C_y = 12y - 2x - 42 + \lambda = 0 \qquad C_\lambda = x + y - 5 = 0$

Thus, $\bar{x} = 2.125$, $\bar{y} = 2.875$, $\bar{\lambda} = 11.75$, and $C = 47.76$.

With $\bar{\lambda} > 0$,   the constraint is not a limitation. By minimizing the objective function without the equality constraint, the desired minimum will be found. From Problem 6.26, at $\bar{x} = 3$, $\bar{y} = 4$, $c = 36$,   which satisfies $x + y \geq 5$.

6.48. Maximize a firm's profit function $\pi = 160x - 3x^2 - 2xy - 2y^2 + 120y - 18$ given the fact that the firm's joint output cannot exceed 35, i.e. $x + y \leq 35$.

The Lagrangian function is

$$\Pi = 160x - 3x^2 - 2xy - 2y^2 + 120y - 18 + \lambda(x + y - 35)$$

$$\Pi_x = 160 - 6x - 2y + \lambda = 0 \qquad \Pi_y = -2x - 4y + 120 + \lambda = 0 \qquad \Pi_\lambda = x + y - 35 = 0$$

Thus, $\bar{x} = 18.33$, $\bar{y} = 16.67$, $\bar{\lambda} = -16.67$, and $\pi = 2740.34$.

When maximizing subject to $g(x,y) \leq 0$,   if $\bar{\lambda} < 0$,   the constraint is a limitation and the constrained maximum has been found. From Problem 6.27, unconstrained profits are $\pi = 2782$ at $\bar{x} = 20$ and $\bar{y} = 20$.

6.49. Maximize the function in Problem 6.48 subject to $x + y \leq 50$.

Form the Lagrangian function $\Pi = 160x - 3x^2 - 2xy - 2y^2 + 120y - 18 + \lambda(x + y - 50)$.

$$\Pi_x = 160 - 6x - 2y + \lambda = 0 \qquad \Pi_y = -2x - 4y + 120 + \lambda = 0 \qquad \Pi_\lambda = x + y - 50 = 0$$

Thus, $\bar{x} = 23.33$, $\bar{y} = 26.67$, $\bar{\lambda} = 33.33$, and $\pi = 2615.33$.

With $\bar{\lambda} > 0$,   the constraint is not a limitation. Ignore the imposed equality constraint and simply maximize the objective function.

Chapter 7

A Review of Logarithms and Exponents

7.1 POWER FUNCTIONS

A power function is a function of the form $y = x^a$ where $y =$ the dependent variable, $x =$ the independent variable, and $a =$ a constant exponent. By definition, $x^0 = 1$, as does any number raised to the zero power. A number or variable without an exponent is always assumed raised to the first power, i.e. $x = x^1$, $8 = 8^1$.

The most important rules for power functions are:

(1) $x^a(x^c) = x^{a+c}$

(2) $(x^a)^c = x^{ac}$

(3) $(xz)^a = x^a(z^a)$

(4) $\left(\dfrac{x}{z}\right)^c = \dfrac{x^c}{z^c}$

(5) $\dfrac{1}{x^a} = x^{-a}$

(6) $\dfrac{x^a}{x^c} = x^{a-c}$

(7) $\sqrt{x} = x^{1/2}$

(8) $\sqrt[a]{x} = x^{1/a}$

(9) $\sqrt[c]{x^a} = x^{a/c}$

Example 1. The power function rules are illustrated below.

(1) $x^3(x^5) = x^{3+5} = x^8$

(2) $(x^4)^3 = x^{4(3)} = x^{12}$

(3) $(xz)^5 = x^5(z^5)$

(4) $\left(\dfrac{x}{z}\right)^3 = \dfrac{x^3}{z^3}$

(5) $\dfrac{1}{x^2} = x^{-2}$

(6) $\dfrac{x^6}{x^2} = x^{6-2} = x^4$

(7) $\sqrt[3]{x} = x^{1/3}$

(8) $\sqrt[5]{x^3} = x^{3/5}$

(9) $\sqrt{x^5} = x^{5/2}$

(10) $\dfrac{1}{\sqrt{x}} = \dfrac{1}{x^{1/2}} = x^{-1/2}$

7.2 EXPONENTIAL FUNCTIONS

An exponential function is a function composed of a constant base a and a variable exponent x: $y = a^x$, where a is greater than zero and not equal to one. Exponential functions depict constant rates of *discrete growth*, i.e., growth that takes place at such discrete intervals as at the end of the year or at the end of the quarter. Exponential functions are frequently used in problems of interest compounding, discounting, and depreciation. For many economic problems, the base and exponent are multiplied by constants, giving $y = ba^{cx}$. Exponential functions follow the same basic rules as do power functions (see Section 7.1).

Example 2

1. The future value (S) of a present sum (P) when compounded annually at interest rate (i) for time period (t) is given by the exponential function,

$$S = P(1 + i)^t$$

where $(1 + i)$ is the base, t is the variable exponent, and P is a constant multiplying the base. If $P = \$100$, $i = 0.10$, and $t = 2$,

$$S = 100(1 + 0.10)^2 = \$121$$

2. For problems of depreciation or decay, the growth is negative. Thus, the value of a \$100,000 machine depreciated by 25 percent a year after one year is given by the exponential function,

$$S = 100,000(1 - 0.25)^1$$

where $(1 - 0.25)$ is the base, 1 is the exponent, and 100,000 is a constant multiplying the base. Thus,

$$S = 100,000(0.75) = 75,000$$

7.3 NATURAL EXPONENTIAL FUNCTIONS

A natural exponential function has as its base the natural base e, $y = e^n$, where $e = \lim_{n \to \infty} [1 + (1/n)]^n = 2.718281828$. Natural exponential functions describe constant rates of *continuous growth*, i.e., growth that takes place constantly rather than at discrete intervals. In economics, natural exponential functions are used to express such things as population growth rates and the rate of weight gain for cattle in feed pens.

Example 3. Unlike ordinary interest compounding, population grows continuously and not merely at the end of the year. A population of 1,000,000 growing at 3 percent a year can be expressed by the natural exponential function

$$P = 1,000,000e^{0.03t}$$

After two years, when $t = 2$,

$$P = 1,000,000e^{0.03(2)}$$

From Appendix III under $x = 0.06$,

$$P = 1,000,000(1.0618) = 1,061,800$$

For any function expressed in the form $P = e^{rt}$, r will always give the continuous rate of growth. A negative r suggests negative growth rates, as in depreciation.

The following rules of natural exponents are important:

(1) $e^0 = 1$ (4) $(e^a)^b = e^{ab}$

(2) $e^1 = e = 2.71828$

(3) $e^a(e^b) = e^{a+b}$ (5) $\dfrac{e^a}{e^b} = e^{a-b}$

7.4 LOGARITHMIC FUNCTIONS

A logarithm is the power to which a given base must be raised to obtain a particular number. Common logarithms use a base of 10 and are written $\log_{10}$ or, simply, log. Since $10^2 = 100$, 2 is the common log of 100. Thus,

$$\log_{10} 10 \quad = 1 \quad \text{since} \quad 10^1 = 10$$
$$\log_{10} 100 \quad = 2 \quad \text{since} \quad 10^2 = 100$$
$$\log_{10} 1000 = 3 \quad \text{since} \quad 10^3 = 1000$$

Similarly, for any exponential function $y = a^x$, where a is the base and x the exponent,

$$\log_a y = x$$

which can be read, x is the power to which a must be raised in order to obtain y.

Example 4. For numbers that are even powers of the base, logs are easily calculated.

$$\log_{10} 1 \quad = 0 \quad \text{since} \quad 10^0 = 1 \qquad\qquad \log_4 16 = 2 \quad \text{since} \quad 4^2 = 16$$

$$\log_{10} 0.1 \quad = -1 \quad \text{since} \quad 10^{-1} = \frac{1}{10} = 0.1 \qquad \log_3 27 = 3 \quad \text{since} \quad 3^3 = 27$$

$$\log_5 125 = 3 \quad \text{since} \quad 5^3 = 125$$

$$\log_{10} 0.01 = -2 \quad \text{since} \quad 10^{-2} = \frac{1}{10^2} = 0.01 \qquad \log_2 32 = 5 \quad \text{since} \quad 2^5 = 32$$

7.5 LOG FORMATION

To find the log of a number which is not an even power of base 10, e.g. 521, first express it in scientific notation, $N = a(10)^x$, where $1 < a < 10$. Thus $521 = 5.21(10)^2$. The power to which 10 is raised is the first part of the logarithm, called the *characteristic*. The second part of the logarithm is called the *mantissa* and is found in Appendix I. Ignore any decimal point in the number and read down Appendix I to 52 and across to 1. The mantissa for 521 is 0.7168, since all mantissas in the table are assumed preceded by a decimal point. Thus,

$$\log_{10} 521 = 2.7168$$

Similarly,

$$\log_{10} 5.21 = 0.7168$$
$$\log_{10} 52.1 = 1.7168$$
$$\log_{10} 5210 = 3.7168$$

The four-place table is precise to four significant figures. All answers derived from four-place logs, therefore, should be rounded to four places.

Example 5.   To find the log of 0.307, first express 0.307 in scientific notation:

$$0.307 = 3.07(10)^{-1}$$

The characteristic is thus $\bar{1}$ or $9 - 10$. With logs a negative sign is always placed above the characteristic and not before it. [A negative sign before a characteristic has a different meaning. See Example 8, item (5)]. Next, ignore the decimal point in the number and read down Appendix I to 30 and across to 7. The mantissa of $307 = .4871$. Thus,

log 0.307	$= \bar{1}.4871$	or	9.4871–10	or	0.4871–1
log 0.0307	$= \bar{2}.4871$	or	8.4871–10	or	0.4871–2
log 0.00307	$= \bar{3}.4871$	or	7.4871–10	or	0.4871–3

Similarly,

7.6 INTERPOLATION

To find the log of a number with more than three digits, interpolation is necessary. The log of 2536, for instance, will be somewhere between the log for 2530 and 2540. Since the difference between 2536 and 2530 $(2536 - 2530 = 6)$ is 60 percent of the difference between 2530 and 2540 $(2540 - 2530 = 10)$, the log for 2536 will equal the log for 2530 plus 60 percent of the difference between the log for 2530 and 2540. Thus,

$$\log 2536 = \log 2530 + 0.6(\log 2540 - \log 2530)$$
$$= 3.4031 + 0.6(3.4048 - 3.4031) = 3.4031 + 0.0010 = 3.4041$$

For interpolation of antilogs, see Example 7, item (3). For interpolation of exponential functions, see Problem 7.16(*a*).

Example 6.   The log of 0.7342 will be between the log for 0.7340 and 0.7350. Since the difference between 0.7342 and 0.7340 is 20 percent of the difference between 0.7340 and 0.7350,

$$\log 0.7342 = \log 0.7340 + 0.2(\log 0.7350 - \log 0.7340) = \bar{1}.8657 + 0.2(\bar{1}.8663 - \bar{1}.8657) = \bar{1}.8657 + 0.0001 = \bar{1}.8658$$

7.7 ANTILOGARITHMS

Finding an antilogarithm is the reverse process of finding a logarithm. To find the antilog of 3.9253, look up the number corresponding to the mantissa 0.9253 in Appendix I. Set that number in scientific notation, using the characteristic (here, 3) as the exponent of 10. Since the number corresponding to 0.9253 is 842,

$$\text{antilog } 3.9253 = 8.42(10)^3 = 8420$$

Example 7

1. The antilog of $\bar{2}.6243$ is found as follows:

    The number corresponding to the mantissa 0.6243 is 421.   Setting it in scientific notation and using the characteristic as the exponent of 10,

$$\text{antilog } \bar{2}.6243 = 4.21(10)^{-2} = 0.0421$$

2. The antilog of 4.7966 is found as follows:

    The number corresponding to the mantissa 0.7966 is 626.   Setting it in scientific notation and using the characteristic as the exponent of 10,

$$\text{antilog } 4.7966 = 6.26(10)^{4} = 62,600$$

3. The antilog of 1.3310 is found as follows:

    Since the mantissa 0.3310 is not found directly in Appendix I, interpolation is necessary.   The mantissa 0.3310 lies between the mantissas 0.3304 and 0.3324.   Hence the antilog of 1.3310 will lie between the antilog of 1.3304 and the antilog of 1.3324.   Since the difference between 1.3310 and 1.3304 is 30 percent of the difference between 1.3304 and 1.3324,

$$\text{antilog } 1.3310 = \text{antilog } 1.3304 + 0.3(\text{antilog } 1.3324 - \text{antilog } 1.3304)$$
$$= 21.4 + 0.3(21.5 - 21.4) = 21.4 + 0.03 = 21.43$$

7.8 RULES OF LOGARITHMS

Logarithms can be used to simplify complicated calculations involving numbers >0.   To multiply two numbers, add their logarithms; to divide two numbers, subtract their logarithms; to raise a number to a power, multiply its log by that power; to find the nth root of a number, divide its log by n.   In short, the rules for logs are

$$(1) \quad \log(xy) = \log x + \log y \qquad (3) \quad \log x^a = a \log x$$

$$(2) \quad \log\left(\frac{x}{y}\right) = \log x - \log y \qquad (4) \quad \log(\sqrt[a]{x}) = \frac{\log x}{a}$$

Example 8.   Logs are used to solve each of the following equations:

(1) $y = 950 \times 80$.

$$\log y = \log 950 + \log 80$$
$$= 2.9777 + 1.9031 = 4.8808$$

Then taking the antilog,

$$y = \text{antilog } 4.8808 = 76,000$$

(2) $y = 8400/240$.

$$\log y = \log 8400 - \log 240$$
$$= 3.9243 - 2.3802 = 1.5441$$
$$y = \text{antilog } 1.5441 = 35$$

(3) $y = 8^3$.

$$\log y = 3 \log 8$$
$$= 3(0.9031) = 2.7093$$
$$y = \text{antilog } 2.7093 = 512$$

(4) $y = \sqrt[3]{343}$.

$$\log y = \frac{\log 343}{3} = \frac{2.5353}{3} = 0.8451$$
$$y = \text{antilog } 0.8451 = 7$$

(5) $y = \frac{30}{50}$.

$$\log y = \log 30 - \log 50 = 1.4771 - 1.6990 = -0.2219$$

As a result of the calculations the log for equation (5) is negative.   Since all mantissas in Appendix I are positive, to find the antilog we must first add and then subtract the smallest integer that will make the log positive.   Adding and subtracting the same value (here 1) does not change the value of the expression.   Thus, $\log y = -0.2219 = 0.7781 - 1$,   since $-0.2219 + 1.0000 = 0.7781$.   Consequently, $y = \text{antilog }(-0.2219) = \text{antilog }(0.7781 - 1) = 6.00(10)^{-1} = 0.60$.   (Whenever calculations lead to a negative common log, add and subtract the smallest integer needed to make the mantissa positive before taking the antilog.)

7.9 NATURAL LOGARITHMS

Logarithms to the natural base e are called natural or Naperian logarithms and are written $\log_e$ or, more simply, ln. Since natural logs are based on 2.71828 and not 10, their formation is more complex. Appendix II gives both characteristic and mantissa for numbers ranging from 0.000 to 999. For numbers not given explicitly in Appendix II, first express them in scientific notation. Then to raise them to a multiple of 10, *add* the natural log of 10, 2.30259; to raise them to a multiple of 100, *add* 2 ln 10, 2(2.30259); etc. Because the natural log of 10 = 2.302585093, use of 2.30259 may produce slight discrepancies due to rounding. Natural logs follow all the rules set forth in Section 7.8. Unlike common logs, natural logs for positive numbers less than one will be preceded by a negative sign.

Example 9. To find the natural log of a number from 0 to 999, simply look it up in Appendix II. If the characteristic is not mentioned explicitly, it is the same as at the start of the series of entries:

$$\ln 0.521 = -0.65201$$
$$\ln 5.21 = 1.65058$$
$$\ln 521 = 6.25575$$

ln 52.1 is not given explicitly in Appendix II. Since $52.1 = 5.21(10)^1$,

$$\ln 52.1 = \ln 5.21 + \ln 10 = 1.65058 + 2.30259 \cong 3.95317$$

Similarly, $\qquad \ln 5210 = \ln 5.21 + 3 \ln 10 = 1.65058 + 3(2.30259) \cong 8.55835$

Interpolation can also be used for ln 52.1.

$$\ln 52.1 = \ln 52 + 0.1(\ln 53 - \ln 52) = 3.95124 + 0.1(3.97029 - 3.95124) \cong 3.95315$$

Example 10. For numbers with more than three significant digits, such as 190.2, interpolate. Since the difference between 190.2 and 190 is 20 percent of the difference between 190 and 191,

$$\ln 190.2 = \ln 190 + 0.2(\ln 191 - \ln 190)$$
$$= 5.24702 + 0.2(5.25227 - 5.24702) = 5.24702 + (0.00105) = 5.24807$$

Example 11. Provided n is a real number, the natural log of any expression e^n is n. $\ln e^3 = 3$ since e must be raised to the third power to get e^3. Similarly,

$$\ln e^2 = 2$$
$$\ln e = 1 \quad \text{since} \quad e^1 = e$$
$$\ln 1 = 0 \quad \text{since} \quad e^0 = 1$$

$$\ln \frac{1}{e} = -1 \quad \text{since} \quad e^{-1} = \frac{1}{e}$$
$$\ln 2.71828 = 1 \quad \text{since} \quad e = 2.71828$$
$$\ln e^x = x$$

7.10 LOGARITHMIC SOLUTIONS OF EXPONENTIAL FUNCTIONS

Logarithms are particularly helpful in solving problems involving exponential functions. For exponential functions to a common base, use common logs; for exponential functions to a natural base, use natural logs.

Example 12

1. Given $y = 150(1.04)^{2x}$, where $x = 3$. To find y, first substitute $x = 3$, so that $y = 150(1.04)^6$. Then take the common log of both sides, as follows:

$$\log y = \log 150 + 6 \log (1.04) = 2.1761 + 6(0.0170) = 2.2781$$

Finally, take the antilog through interpolation:

$$y = \text{antilog } 2.2781 \cong 189.70$$

2. Given $262 = 200e^{0.1x}$. To solve for an exponent (here x), take the log of both sides of the equation. Since this is a natural exponential function, take the natural log.

$$\ln 262 = \ln 200 + 0.1x$$

because $\ln e^{0.1x} = 0.1x$. Then, from the natural logs in Appendix II,

$$5.56834 = 5.29832 + 0.1x$$
$$x = 2.7$$

7.11 RELATIONSHIP BETWEEN LOGARITHMIC AND EXPONENTIAL FUNCTIONS

Log functions are inverse functions of certain exponential functions. As such, it is an easy matter to express a log function as an exponential function, or certain exponential functions as log functions. Since $\log_a y = x$ can be read x is the power to which a must be raised to get y, $y = a^x$. Conversely, given $y = a^x$, the log of y to base a must equal x, i.e., $\log_a y = x$.

Example 13. The relationship between logarithmic and exponential functions is illustrated below.

If $\log_{10} y = 2x$, then $y = 10^{2x}$	If $y = a^{3x}$, then $\log_a y = 3x$
If $\log_a y = xz$, then $y = a^{xz}$	If $y = 10^{6x}$, then $\log_{10} y = 6x$
If $\ln y = 5t$, then $y = e^{5t}$	If $y = e^{t+1}$, then $\ln y = t + 1$

Solved Problems

RULES OF EXPONENTS

7.1. Simplify each of the following power functions, using the laws of exponents.

(a) $y = x^5(x^7)$
$$y = x^{5+7} = x^{12}$$

(b) $y = \dfrac{x^2}{x^5}$
$$y = x^{2-5} = x^{-3} = \frac{1}{x^3}$$

(c) $y = x\sqrt{x}$
$$y = x(x^{1/2}) = x^{1+(1/2)} = x^{3/2}$$

(d) $y = x\sqrt[3]{x^4}$
$$y = x(x^{4/3}) = x^{1+(4/3)} = x^{7/3}$$

(e) $y = (x^2)^4$
$$y = x^{2(4)} = x^8$$

(f) $y = 2x^2(x^6)^3$
$$y = 2x^2(x^{6(3)}) = 2x^2(x^{18}) = 2x^{2+18} = 2x^{20}$$

7.2. Using the laws of exponents, simplify the power function $y = (2/3)^3$.

$$y = \frac{2^3}{3^3} = \frac{8}{27}$$

Note that $(2/3)^3 \neq 2/3$, since exponents to different bases do not cancel.

7.3. Simplify each of the following exponential functions.

(a) $y = a^{4x}(a^{3x})$
$$y = a^{4x+3x} = a^{7x}$$

(b) $y = \dfrac{a^{6x}}{a^{4x}}$
$$y = a^{6x-4x} = a^{2x}$$

   (c) $y = e^{2x}(e^{3x})$ (d) $y = e^2(e^t)$

            $y = e^{2x+3x} = e^{5x}$ $y = e^{2+t} = e^{t+2}$

   (e) $y = e^3(e^5)$ (f) $y = (e^t)^2$

            $y = e^{3+5} = e^8$ $y = e^{2t}$

   (g) $y = \dfrac{e^{t+1}}{e^t}$ (h) $y = \dfrac{e(e^t)}{e^{t+1}}$

            $y = e^{t+1-t} = e^1 = e$ $y = e^{t+1-(t+1)} = e^0 = 1$

7.4.   Determine the log for each of the following:

   (a) $\log_4 64$ (b) $\log_5 625$

            $\log_4 64 = 3$ since $(4)^3 = 64$ $\log_5 625 = 4$ since $(5)^4 = 625$

   (c) $\log_{10} 1000$ (d) $\log_{10} 0.01$

            $\log_{10} 1000 = 3$ since $(10)^3 = 1000$ $\log_{10} 0.01 = \bar{2}$ since $(10)^{-2} = 0.01$

   (e) $\log_2 32$ (f) $\log_{12} 144$

            $\log_2 32 = 5$ since $(2)^5 = 32$ $\log_{12} 144 = 2$ since $(12)^2 = 144$

USE OF TABLES

7.5.   Using Appendix I of Common Logs, determine the value of each of the following:

   (a)   log 26.9

        In scientific notation, $26.9 = 2.69 \times 10^1$.   Ignoring the decimal point, the mantissa for 269 = 0.4298.   Then using the exponent of 10 as the characteristic,   log 26.9 = 1.4298.

   (b)   log 11,400

        $11{,}400 = 1.14 \times 10^4$.   Thus,   log 11,400 = 4.0569.

   (c)   log 5.48

        $5.48 = 5.48 \times 10^0$.   Thus,   log 5.48 = 0.7388.

   (d)   log 0.764

        $0.764 = 7.64 \times 10^{-1}$.   Thus,   log 0.764 = $\bar{1}.8831$, or 0.8831 − 1, or 9.8831 − 10.

   (e)   log 0.006

        $0.006 = 6.00 \times 10^{-3}$.   Thus,   log 0.006 = $\bar{3}.7782$, or 0.7782 − 3, or 7.7782 − 10.

   (f)   log 0.089

        $0.089 = 8.90 \times 10^{-2}$.   Thus,   log 0.089 = $\bar{2}.9494$, or 0.9494 − 2, or 8.9494 − 10.

7.6.   Using Appendix I, find the value of each of the following logs:

   (a)   log 32.87

        Since the mantissa of a number with more than three digits is not found explicitly in Appendix I, interpolation is necessary.   The log of 32.87 will lie somewhere between the log of 32.80 and 32.90.   Since the difference between 32.87 and 32.80 is 70 percent of the difference between 32.80 and 32.90,

$$\log 32.87 = \log 32.80 + 0.7(\log 32.90 - \log 32.80)$$
$$= 1.5159 + 0.7(1.5172 - 1.5159) = 1.5159 + 0.0009 = 1.5168$$

(b)   log 796.3

$$\log 796.3 = \log 796.0 + 0.3(\log 797.0 - \log 976.0)$$
$$= 2.9009 + 0.3(2.9015 - 2.9009) = 2.9009 + 0.0002 = 2.9011$$

7.7.   Use Appendix I to find the following antilogs:

(a)   antilog 3.7752

The number under which the mantissa 0.7752 is listed is 596. Setting this number in scientific notation and using the given characteristic 3 as the exponent of 10, $5.96 \times 10^3 = 5960$. Thus, antilog 3.7752 = 5960.

(b)   antilog 0.3874

0.3874 is the mantissa for 244. Thus, antilog $0.3874 = 2.44 \times 10^0 = 2.44$.

(c)   antilog 2.5855

0.5855 is the mantissa for 385. Hence, antilog $2.5855 = 3.85 \times 10^2 = 385$.

(d)   antilog $\bar{1}.9643$

0.9643 is the mantissa for 921. Thus, antilog $\bar{1}.9643 = 9.21 \times 10^{-1} = 0.921$.

(e)   antilog 7.5933−10

0.5933 is the mantissa for 392. The characteristic $7 - 10 = \bar{3}$. Thus,

$$\text{antilog } 7.5933 - 10 = 3.92 \times 10^{-3} = 0.00392 \cong 0.0039$$

(f)   antilog 0.8494−2

0.8494 is the mantissa for 707. The characteristic is −2. Thus,

$$\text{antilog } 0.8494 - 2 = 7.07 \times 10^{-2} = 0.0707$$

7.8.   Calculate the value of each of the following antilogs, using Appendix I:

(a)   antilog −1.2314

Whenever a negative sign precedes a common log, the log is negative. Since Appendix I is set up in terms of positive mantissas, add and subtract the smallest integer that will make the log positive. Adding and subtracting the same integer does not change the value of the antilog. Thus,

$$
\begin{array}{ll}
2.0000 & -2 \\
-1.2314 & \\
\hline
.7686 & -2 \\
\end{array}
$$

Then find the value of the antilog. Since 0.7686 is the mantissa for 587,   antilog $(-1.2314) =$ antilog $(0.7686 - 2) = 5.87 \times 10^{-2} = 0.0587$. See Problem 7.17(c) and (d).

(b)   antilog (−3.6882)

Again the log is negative. Thus,

$$
\begin{array}{ll}
4.0000 & -4 \\
-3.6882 & \\
\hline
.3118 & -4 \\
\end{array}
$$

0.3118 is the mantissa for 205. Hence,

$$\text{antilog } (-3.6882) = \text{antilog } (0.3118 - 4) = 2.05 \times 10^{-4} = 0.000205 \cong 0.0002$$

7.9.   Use Appendix II to determine the value of each of the following natural logs:

(a)   ln 8.42

The entry under 8.42 reads simply .13061.   It is assumed that the characteristic at the beginning of the line or paragraph is continued throughout.   Thus,

$$\ln 8.42 = 2.13061$$

(b)   ln 4.53

$$\ln 4.53 = 1.51072$$

(c)   ln 2.72

The asterisk in Appendix II before .00063 indicates the characteristic in the series has changed and the appropriate characteristic will be found at the beginning of the next line.   Here the characteristic changes from zero to one.   Thus,

$$\ln 2.72 = 1.00063$$

7.10.   Redo Problem 7.9 for each of the following logs:

(a)   ln 0.137   (b)   ln 263

$$\ln 0.137 = -1.98777$$ $$\ln 263 = 5.57215$$

(c)   ln 32   (d)   ln 77

$$\ln 32 = 3.46574$$ $$\ln 77 = 4.34381$$

7.11.   Find the value of each of the following natural logs:

(a)   ln 43.1

ln 43.1 is not given explicitly in Appendix II.   Using scientific notation and then converting to natural logs,

$$43.1 = 4.31 \times 10^1$$

Thus, $$\ln 43.1 = \ln 4.31 + \ln 10$$
$$= 1.46094 + 2.30259 \cong 3.76353$$

ln 43.1 can also be found by interpolation since $\ln 43.1 = \ln 43 + 0.1(\ln 44 - \ln 43)$.   See Problem 7.12.

(b)   ln 29.4

$29.4 = 2.94 \times 10^1$.   Thus,

$$\ln 29.4 = \ln 2.94 + \ln 10 = 1.07841 + 2.30259 \cong 3.38100$$

(c)   ln 1250

$1250 = 1.25 \times 10^3$.   Thus,

$$\ln 1250 = \ln 1.25 + 3 \ln 10 = 0.22314 + 3(2.30259) \cong 7.13091$$

(d)   ln 47,900

$$\ln 47,900 = \ln 4.79 + 4 \ln 10 = 1.56653 + 4(2.30259) \cong 10.77689$$

7.12.   Find the value of each of the following natural logs:

(a)   ln 442.5

Since Appendix II does not cover four-digit numbers explicitly, interpolation is necessary. The difference between 442.5 and 442.0 is 50 percent of the difference between 442 and 443. Therefore,

$$\ln 442.5 = \ln 442 + 0.5(\ln 443 - \ln 442)$$
$$= 6.09131 + 0.5(6.09357 - 6.09131) = 6.09131 + 0.00113 = 6.09244$$

(b)   ln 7.656

$$ln\ 7.656 = ln\ 7.65 + 0.6(ln\ 7.66 - ln\ 7.65)$$
$$= 2.03471 + 0.6(2.03601 - 2.03471) = 2.03471 + 0.00078 = 2.03549$$

7.13.   Use Appendix II to find the following antilogs:

(a)   antilog$_e$ 5.40268

The number in Appendix II for which the natural log is 5.40268 is 222. Thus, antilog$_e$ 5.40268 = 222.

(b)   antilog$_e$ 1.92425

$$antilog_e\ 1.92425 = 6.85$$

(c)   antilog$_e$ (−2.33304)

$$antilog_e\ (-2.33304) = 0.097$$

(d)   antilog$_e$ (−0.14503)

$$antilog_e\ (-0.14503) = 0.865$$

7.14.   Find the value of each of the following antilogs:

(a)   antilog$_e$ 6.30335

The antilog$_e$ 6.30335 is not given explicitly in Appendix II.   It lies somewhere between the antilogs for 546 and 547.   Since the difference between 6.30335 and 6.30262 is 40 percent of the difference between 6.30262 and 6.30445,

$$antilog_e\ 6.30335 = antilog_e\ 6.30262 + 0.4(antilog_e\ 6.30445 - antilog_e\ 6.30262)$$
$$= 546 + 0.4(547 - 546) = 546.4$$

(b)   antilog$_e$ 1.81238

$$antilog_e\ 1.81238 = antilog_e\ 1.81156 + 0.5(antilog_e\ 1.81319 - antilog_e\ 1.81156)$$
$$= 6.12 + 0.5(6.13 - 6.12) = 6.125$$

(c)   antilog$_e$ 8.44033

Appendix II does not go higher than a characteristic of 6.   Therefore subtract the largest multiple of ln 10 that will still leave the antilog positive.   This will give the antilog$_e$ of the number in scientific notation form.   Thus,

$$
\begin{array}{r}
8.44033 \\
-6.90777 = 3\ ln\ 10 \\
\hline
1.53256
\end{array}
$$

Antilog$_e$ 1.53256 = 4.63.   Since subtracting 3 ln 10 is equivalent to dividing by 1000,

$$antilog_e\ 8.44033 = 4.63 \times 10^3 = 4630$$

(d)   antilog$_e$ 10.14250

Subtracting the largest multiple of ln 10,

$$
\begin{array}{r}
10.14250 \\
-9.21034 = 4\ ln\ 10 \\
\hline
.93216
\end{array}
$$

Antilog$_e$ 0.93216 = 2.54.   Since subtracting 4 ln 10 is equivalent to dividing by 10,000,

$$antilog_e\ 10.14250 = 2.54 \times 10^4 = 25,400$$

7.15. Use Appendix III to determine the value of each of the following natural exponential functions:

(a) $y = e^x$, when $x = 0.07$

$$y = e^{0.07} = 1.0725$$

(b) $y = e^{3x}$, when $x = 0.04$

$$y = e^{3(0.04)} = e^{0.12} = 1.1275$$

(c) $y = 100e^{0.5x}$, when $x = 0.16$

$$y = 100e^{0.5(0.16)} = 100e^{0.08} = 108.33$$

(d) $y = e^{2x+3}$, when $x = 0.3$

$$y = e^{0.6+3} = e^{3.6} = 36.60$$

(e) $y = 1000e^{-0.25}$

$$y = 1000(0.778801) = 778.801$$

(f) $y = e^{-5x}$, when $x = 0.02$

$$y = e^{-0.1} = 0.904837$$

(g) $y = (e^x)^2$, when $x = 0.03$

$$y = e^{2x} = e^{0.06} = 1.0618$$

(h) $y = e^{x^2}$, when $x = 0.9$

$$y = e^{0.81} = 2.2479$$

(i) $y = 100e^{x^2}$, when $x = -0.8$

$$y = 100e^{0.64} = 189.65$$

7.16. Redo Problem 7.15 for each of the following:

(a) $y = e^{0.175}$

By interpolation from Appendix III,

$$y = e^{0.17} + 0.5(e^{0.18} - e^{0.17})$$
$$= 1.1853 + 0.5(1.1972 - 1.1853) = 1.1853 + 0.0059 = 1.1912$$

(b) $y = e^{0.65738}$

$$y = e^{0.65} + 0.738(e^{0.66} - e^{0.65})$$
$$= 1.9155 + 0.738(1.9348 - 1.9155)$$
$$= 1.9155 + 0.0142 = 1.9297$$

(c) $y = e^{2.64529}$

$$y = e^{2.6} + 0.45(e^{2.7} - e^{2.6})$$
$$= 13.46 + 0.45(14.88 - 13.46)$$
$$= 13.46 + 0.64 = 14.10$$

LOGARITHMIC SOLUTIONS OF EQUATIONS

7.17. Use common logs to solve each of the following equations:

(a) $y = 625(0.8)$

$$\log y = \log 625 + \log 0.8$$
$$= 2.7959 + 0.9031 - 1 = 3.6990 - 1 = 2.6990$$
$$y = \text{antilog } 2.6990 = 500$$

(b) $y = \dfrac{130}{0.25}$

$$\log y = \log 130 - \log 0.25$$
$$= 2.1139 - (.3979 - 1) = 1.7160 + 1 = 2.7160$$
$$y = \text{antilog } 2.7160 = 520$$

(c) $y = \dfrac{40}{100}$

$$\log y = \log 40 - \log 100$$
$$= 1.6021 - 2 = -0.3979$$

Adding and subtracting 1 before taking the antilog, $\log y = 0.6021 - 1$. Thus,

$$y = \text{antilog } (-0.3979) = \text{antilog } (0.6021 - 1) = 4.00 \times 10^{-1} = 0.40$$

(d) $y = \dfrac{36}{5000}$

$$\log y = \log 36 - \log 5000$$
$$= 1.5563 - 3.6990 = -2.1427$$

Adding and subtracting 3 before taking the antilog,

$$y = \text{antilog}\,(-2.1427) = \text{antilog}\,(0.8573 - 3) = 7.20 \times 10^{-3} = 0.0072$$

(e) $y = (1.06)^{10}$

$$\log y = 10 \log 1.06 = 10(0.0253) = 0.2530$$
$$y = \text{antilog}\,0.2530 = 1.79$$

(f) $y = 1024^{0.20}$

$$\log y = 0.20 \log 1024$$

where by interpolation,

$$\log 1024 = \log 1020 + 0.4(\log 1030 - \log 1020)$$
$$= 3.0086 + 0.4(3.0128 - 3.0086) = 3.0103$$

Thus, $\log y = 0.20(3.0103) = 0.6021$

$$y = \text{antilog}\,0.6021 = 4$$

(g) $y = \sqrt[5]{1024}$

$y = 1024^{1/5} = 1024^{0.20} = 4$, as found in part (f). Both problems are the same because taking the fifth root is the same thing as raising to the $\frac{1}{5}$ or 0.2 power. In one case the log of 1024 is divided by 5; in the second it is multiplied by 0.20.

7.18.   Use natural logs to solve each of the following equations:

(a) $y = 300(0.58)$

$$\ln y = \ln 300 + \ln 0.58 = 5.70378 + (-0.54473)$$

For positive numbers smaller than 1, natural logs are negative and are treated algebraically as negative numbers. Thus,

$$\ln y = 5.15905$$
$$y = \text{antilog}_e\,5.15905 = 174$$

(b) $y = \dfrac{150}{750}$

$$\ln y = \ln 150 - \ln 750 = 5.01064 - 6.62007 = -1.60943$$
$$y = \text{antilog}_e\,(-1.60943) = 0.20$$

(c) $y = \sqrt[3]{729}$

$$\ln y = \tfrac{1}{3} \ln 729 = \tfrac{1}{3}(6.59167) = 2.19722$$
$$y = \text{antilog}_e\,2.19722 = 9$$

(d) $y = 9200(0.015)$

$$\ln y = \ln 9200 + \ln 0.015$$

where $\ln 9200 = \ln 9.2 + 3 \ln 10 = 2.21920 + 3(2.30259) = 9.12697$. Thus,

$$\ln y = 9.12697 + (-4.19971) = 4.92726$$
$$y = \text{antilog}_e\,4.92726 = 138$$

(e) $y = \dfrac{712}{16}$

$$\ln y = \ln 712 - \ln 16 = 6.56808 - 2.77259 = 3.79549$$
$$y = \text{antilog}_e\ 3.79549$$

Since 3.79549 is not listed explicitly in Appendix II, interpolate or subtract the largest multiple of $\ln 10$ that will leave the antilog$_e$ positive. Using the second method, $3.79549 - 2.30259 = 1.49290$.   Antilog$_e$ $1.49290 = 4.45$.   Thus,   antilog$_e$ $3.79549 = 4.45 \times 10^1 = 44.5$.

INVERSE FUNCTION RELATIONSHIPS

7.19.   Express the following log functions as exponential functions, recalling that log functions are inverse functions of certain exponential functions:

(a) $\log_{10} 25 = 1.3979$

The above log indicates that 1.3979 is the power to which 10 must be raised to get 25. Therefore, the inverse exponential function is

$$10^{1.3979} = 25$$

(b) $\log_{10} 1000 = 3$ (c) $\log_a y = 6x$ (d) $\log_6 36 = 2$

   $10^3 = 1000$ $y = a^{6x}$ $6^2 = 36$

(e) $\ln y = 2t + 1$

$y = e^{2t+1}$,   since $2t + 1$ is the power to which e must be raised to get y.

(f) $\ln 1.6 = 0.47000$ (g) $\ln 24 = 3.17805$ (h) $\ln y = 3x$

   $e^{0.47000} = 1.6$ $e^{3.17805} = 24$ $y = e^{3x}$

7.20.   Express the following exponential functions as logs:

(a) $y = 2^{7x}$

$\log_2 y = 7x$,   which reads $7x$ is the power to which 2 must be raised to get y.

(b) $y = a^{x^{3/4}}$ (c) $y = e^{t-2}$ (d) $y = e^{(1/2)t}$

   $\log_a y = x^{3/4}$ $\ln y = t - 2$ $\ln y = \tfrac{1}{2}t$

(e) $y = e^{3.61092}$ (f) $49 = e^{3.89182}$ (g) $112 = e^{4.71850}$

   $\ln y = 3.61092$ $\ln 49 = 3.89182$ $\ln 112 = 4.71850$

7.21.   Simplify each of the following, using the rules for logs:

(a) $\ln (Pe^3)$ (b) $\ln (ce^t)$

   $\ln (Pe^3) = \ln P + 3 \ln e$ $\ln (ce^t) = \ln c + t \ln e$
   $\qquad\quad = \ln P + 3(1) = \ln P + 3$ $\qquad\quad = \ln c + t$

(c) $\ln \dfrac{a}{e^3}$ (d) $\ln \dfrac{e^2}{e^6}$

   $\ln \dfrac{a}{e^3} = \ln a - 3 \ln e$ $\ln \dfrac{e^2}{e^6} = 2 \ln e - 6 \ln e$
   $\qquad\quad = \ln a - 3$ $\qquad\quad = 2 - 6 = -4$

(e) $\ln x^3$

$$\ln x^3 = 3 \ln x$$

(f) $\ln e^{10}$

$$\ln e^{10} = 10$$

(g) $\ln (xy^3)$

$$\ln (xy^3) = \ln x + 3 \ln y$$

(h) $\ln (x^2 e^t)$

$$\ln (x^2 e^t) = 2 \ln x + t$$

(i) $\ln \left(\dfrac{ce^2}{d} \right)$

(j) $\ln \left(\dfrac{a}{e^5} \right)$

$$\ln \left(\frac{ce^2}{d} \right) = \ln c + 2 \ln e - \ln d$$
$$= \ln c - \ln d + 2$$

$$\ln \left(\frac{a}{e^5} \right) = \ln a - 5 \ln e$$
$$= \ln a - 5$$

7.22.   Solve each of the following equations for x in terms of y:

(a) $\log_a x = y^3$

$$x = a^{y^3}$$

(b) $\log_a x = \log_a 3 + \log_a y$

$$x = 3y \quad \text{since addition in logs = multiplication in algebra.}$$

(c) $\ln x = 3y$

$$x = e^{3y}$$

(d) $\ln x = \log_a y$

$$x = e^{\log_a y}$$

(e) $\log_a x = \ln y$

$$x = a^{\ln y}$$

(f) $y = ge^{hx}$

To solve for x when x is an exponent in a natural exponential function, take the natural log of both sides and solve algebraically, as follows:

$$\ln y = \ln g + hx \ln e = \ln g + hx$$

$$x = \frac{\ln y - \ln g}{h}$$

(g) $y = ae^{x+1}$

$$\ln y = \ln a + (x + 1) \ln e = \ln a + x + 1$$
$$x = \ln y - \ln a - 1$$

(h) $y = p(1 + i)^x$

When x is an exponent in an exponential function with a base other than e, take the common log of both sides and solve algebraically.

$$\log y = \log p + x \log (1 + i)$$

$$x = \frac{\log y - \log p}{\log (1 + i)}$$

Chapter 8

Exponential, Logarithmic, and Power Functions in Economics

8.1 INTEREST COMPOUNDING

A given principal (P) compounded annually at an interest rate (i) for a given number of years (t) will have a value (S) at the end of that time given by the exponential function

$$S = P(1+i)^t$$

If compounded m times a year for t years,

$$S = P\left(1 + \frac{i}{m}\right)^{mt}$$

If compounded continuously at 100 percent interest for one year,

$$S = P \lim_{m \to \infty}\left(1 + \frac{1}{m}\right)^m = P(2.71828) = Pe$$

For interest rates r other than 100 percent and time periods t other than one year,

$$S = Pe^{rt}$$

For negative growth rates, such as depreciation or deflation, the same formulas apply, but i and r are negative.

Example 1. To find the value of \$100 at 10 percent interest for two years compounded:

1. Annually, $S = P(1+i)^t$.

$$S = 100(1 + 0.10)^2 = 121$$

2. Semiannually, where $m = 2$ and $t = 2$, $S = P[1 + (i/m)]^{mt}$.

$$S = 100\left(1 + \frac{0.10}{2}\right)^{2(2)} = 100(1 + 0.05)^4$$

Using logs to solve for S,

$$\log S = \log 100 + 4 \log 1.05 = 2 + 4(0.0212) = 2.0848$$

and $$S = \text{antilog } 2.0848 \cong 121.6$$

3. Continuously, $S = Pe^{rt}$.

$$S = 100e^{0.10(2)} = 100e^{0.2}$$

From Appendix III,

$$S = 100(1.2214) = 122.14$$

8.2 EFFECTIVE VS. NOMINAL RATES OF INTEREST

As seen in Example 1, a given principal set out at the same *nominal rate of interest* will earn different *effective rates of interest* which depend on the type of compounding. When compounded annually for two years, \$100 will be worth \$121; when compounded semiannually, $S = \$121.60$; when compounded continuously, $S = \$122.14$.

To find the effective annual rate of interest (i_e) for multiple compounding:

$$P(1 + i_e)^t = P \left(1 + \frac{i}{m}\right)^{mt}$$

Dividing by P and taking the tth root of each side,

$$1 + i_e = \left(1 + \frac{i}{m}\right)^m$$

$$i_e = \left(1 + \frac{i}{m}\right)^m - 1$$

To find the effective annual rate of interest for continuous compounding:

$$(1 + i_e) = e^r$$

$$i_e = e^r - 1$$

Example 2.   Finding the effective annual rate of interest for a nominal interest rate of 10 percent when compounded for two years (1) semiannually and (2) continuously is illustrated below.

1.   Semiannually, $\qquad\qquad i_e = \left(1 + \dfrac{i}{m}\right)^m - 1 = (1.05)^2 - 1$

Using logs for $(1.05)^2$, $\log (1.05)^2 = 2 \log 1.05 = 2(0.0212) = 0.0424$.   Thus,

$$(1.05)^2 = \text{antilog } 0.0424 = 1.1025$$

Substituting,

$$i_e = 1.1025 - 1 = 0.1025 = 10.25\%$$

2.   Continuously, $\qquad\qquad i_e = e^r - 1 = e^{0.10} - 1$

From Appendix III, $\qquad\qquad i_e = 1.1052 - 1 = 0.1052 = 10.52\%$

8.3   DISCOUNTING

A sum of money to be received in the future is not worth as much as an equivalent amount of money in the present, because the money on hand can be loaned out at interest to grow to an even larger sum by the end of the year.   If present market conditions will enable a person to earn 8 percent interest compounded annually, $100 will grow to $108 by the end of the year. $108 one year from now, therefore, is equivalently worth (has a *present value* of) only $100 today.

Discounting is the process of determining the present value (P) of a future sum of money (S).   If under annual compounding,

$$S = P(1 + i)^t$$

then

$$P = \frac{S}{(1 + i)^t} = S(1 + i)^{-t}$$

Similarly, under multiple compoundings, $P = S[1 + (i/m)]^{-mt}$ and under continuous compounding, $P = Se^{-rt}$.   When finding the present value, the interest rate is called the *rate of discount*.

Example 3.   The present value of a five-year bond with a face value of $1000 and no coupons is calculated below.   It is assumed that comparable opportunities offer interest rates of 9 percent under annual compounding.

$$P = S(1 + i)^{-t} = 1000(1 + 0.09)^{-5}$$

$$\log P = \log 1000 + (-5 \log 1.09) = 3 - 5(0.0374) = 2.8130$$

$$P = \text{antilog } 2.8130 \cong 650.1$$

Thus, a bond promising to pay $1000 five years from now is worth approximately $650.10 today since $650.10 at 9 percent will grow to approximately $1000.00 in five years.

8.4   DISCOUNTING A FUTURE STREAM OF INCOME

Investment in plant or equipment normally returns a stream of income over a period of years. The present value of a stream of future income is the summation of each component discounted to its present value. If each component (S) is equal, and interest is compounded annually, the discounting formula is

$$P = S\left(\frac{1}{i}\right)\left[1 - \frac{1}{(1+i)^t}\right]$$

Example 4. The present value of $100 annually for eight years when the rate of discount in society is 6 percent is determined as follows:

$$P = S\left(\frac{1}{i}\right)\left[1 - \frac{1}{(1+i)^t}\right] = 100\left(\frac{1}{0.06}\right)\left[1 - \frac{1}{(1.06)^8}\right]$$

Using logs for $1/(1.06)^8$,

$$P = 100\left(\frac{1}{0.06}\right)(1 - 0.627) = 621.7$$

Example 5. A firm can determine how much it should be willing to pay for a machine that will raise net revenues by $1000 a year for ten years, with no scrap value, when the rate of discount is 2 percent, by using the formula illustrated in Example 4. In this case,

$$P = 1000\left(\frac{1}{0.02}\right)\left[1 - \frac{1}{(1.02)^{10}}\right]$$

Using logs for $1/(1.02)^{10}$, $$P = 1000\left(\frac{1}{0.02}\right)(1 - 0.82) = 9000$$

8.5   CONVERSION FACTOR FOR DISCRETE AND CONTINUOUS GROWTH

Sections 7.2 and 7.3 distinguished between discrete and continuous growth. Discrete growth is given by $S = P(1 + i/m)^{mt}$; continuous growth is given by $S = Pe^{rt}$. The exponential function $S = P(1 + i/m)^{mt}$ can be converted into a natural exponential function, expressed in terms of continuous growth. To do this, set the two expressions equal to each other and solve for r, as follows:

$$P\left(1 + \frac{i}{m}\right)^{mt} = Pe^{rt}$$

By canceling P's,

$$\left(1 + \frac{i}{m}\right)^{mt} = e^{rt}$$

Taking the natural log of each side,

$$\ln\left(1 + \frac{i}{m}\right)^{mt} = \ln e^{rt}$$

$$mt \ln\left(1 + \frac{i}{m}\right) = rt$$

Dividing both sides by t,

$$r = m \ln\left(1 + \frac{i}{m}\right)$$

Thus, $$S = P\left(1 + \frac{i}{m}\right)^{mt} = Pe^{m \ln(1 + i/m)t}$$

Example 6.   A natural exponential function can be used to determine the value of $100 at 10 percent interest compounded semiannually for two years, as shown below.

$$S = Pe^{rt}$$

where $r = m \ln (1 + i/m)$.   Thus,

$$r = 2 \ln \left(1 + \frac{0.10}{2}\right) = 2 \ln 1.05 = 2(0.04879) = 0.09758$$

Substituting above,

$$S = 100e^{(0.09758)2} = 100e^{0.19516}$$

Because $e^{0.19516}$ is not found explicitly in Appendix III, interpolation is necessary.   The difference between 0.19516 and 0.19 is 51.6 percent of the difference between 0.20 and 0.19, therefore

$$e^{0.19516} = e^{0.19} + 0.516(e^{0.20} - e^{0.19}) = 1.2092 + 0.516(1.2214 - 1.2092) = 1.2092 + 0.0063 = 1.2155$$

Thus, $S = 100(1.2155) = 121.55$,   which, when rounded to four places, is 121.6, as found in Example 1.

Note that with natural exponential functions, the continuous growth is given by r in Pe^{rt}.   Thus, the continuous growth rate of $100 at 10 percent interest compounded semiannually is 0.09758, or 9.758 percent a year.   That is to say, 9.758 percent interest at continuous compounding is equivalent to 10 percent interest when compounded semiannually.

Example 7.   A firm with current annual sales of $100,000 projects a 12 percent growth in sales annually.   Its projected sales in five years are calculated below in terms of an *ordinary exponential function*.

$$S = 100,000(1 + 0.12)^5$$

Thus, $\log S = \log 100,000 + 5 \log 1.12 = 5 + 5(0.0492) = 5.2460$

$$S = \text{antilog } 5.2460 = 176,200$$

Example 8.   The sales projections specified in Example 7 are recalculated below, using a natural exponential function where $r = m \ln (1 + i/m)$ and $m = 1$.

$$r = \ln 1.12 = 0.11333$$

Thus, $S = 100,000e^{0.11333(5)} = 100,000(1.762) = 176,200$

8.6   ESTIMATING GROWTH RATES FROM DATA POINTS

Given two sets of data for a function—sales, costs, profits—growing consistently over time, annual growth rates can be measured and a natural exponential function established through a system of simultaneous equations.   The two sets of data points can each be expressed in terms of $S = Pe^{rt}$.   For example, if sales volume equals 4.36 million in year 1 and 6.87 million in year 4, substitution in the general formula gives

$$4.36 = Pe^{r(1)}$$
$$6.87 = Pe^{r(4)}$$

where dollar values are expressed in millions.   With two equations and two unknowns, a solution can be found.   Taking the natural logs of each equation,

$$\ln 4.36 = \ln P + r$$
$$\ln 6.87 = \ln P + 4r$$

Substituting from Appendix II,

$$1.47247 = \ln P + r \qquad\qquad (8.1)$$
$$1.92716 = \ln P + 4r \qquad\qquad (8.2)$$

Subtracting (8.2) from (8.1) to eliminate $\ln P$,

$$-0.45469 = -3r \qquad r = 0.15156$$

Substituting $r = 0.15156$ in (8.1) or (8.2),

$$1.47247 = \ln P + 0.15156 \qquad \ln P = 1.32091$$

Thus, $$P = \text{antilog}_e\, 1.32091 \cong 3.746$$

and $$S = 3.746e^{0.15156t}$$

The rate of continuous growth per year, therefore, is 15.156 percent. To find the rate of discrete growth (i), recall that

$$r = m \ln \left(1 + \frac{i}{m}\right)$$

Thus, for annual compounding, with $m = 1$,

$$0.15156 = \ln(1 + i)$$

$$1 + i = \text{antilog}_e\, 0.15156 \cong 1.164$$

$$i = 1.164 - 1 = 0.164 \qquad \text{or} \qquad 16.4\%$$

Example 9. Using the data given above, an exponential function for growth in terms of $S = P(1 + i)^t$ can also be established.

Substituting the data in the general formula,

$$4.36 = P(1 + i)^1 \tag{8.3}$$

$$6.87 = P(1 + i)^4 \tag{8.4}$$

Taking the common log of both equations,

$$\log 4.36 = \log P + 1 \log(1 + i)$$

$$\log 6.87 = \log P + 4 \log(1 + i)$$

Substituting from Appendix I,

$$0.6395 = \log P + \log(1 + i) \tag{8.5}$$

$$0.8370 = \log P + 4 \log(1 + i) \tag{8.6}$$

Subtracting (8.6) from (8.5),

$$-0.1975 = -3 \log(1 + i) \qquad \log(1 + i) = 0.0658$$

$$1 + i = \text{antilog}\, 0.0658 \cong 1.164$$

$$i = 1.164 - 1 = 0.164 = 16.4\%$$

Then substituting $i = 0.164$ in (8.3),

$$4.36 = P(1 + 0.164) \qquad P = 3.746$$

Thus, $$S = 3.746(1 + 0.164)^t$$

8.7 HOMOGENEOUS PRODUCTION FUNCTIONS

A production function is said to be homogeneous if, when each input factor is multiplied by a positive real constant k, the constant can be completely factored out. If the exponent of the factor is one, the function is homogeneous of degree one; if the exponent of the factor is greater than one, the function is homogeneous of degree greater than one; and if the exponent of the factor is less than one, the function is homogeneous of degree less than one. Mathematically, a function $z = f(x,y)$ is homogeneous of degree n, if for all positive real values of k, $f(kx,ky) = k^n f(x,y)$.

Example 10.   The degree of homogeneity of a function is illustrated below.

1. $z = 8x + 9y$ is homogeneous of degree one because

$$f(kx,ky) = 8kx + 9ky = k(8x + 9y)$$

2. $z = x^2 + xy + y^2$ is homogeneous of degree two because

$$f(kx,ky) = (kx)^2 + (kx)(ky) + (ky)^2 = k^2(x^2 + xy + y^2)$$

3. $z = x^{0.3}y^{0.4}$ is homogeneous of degree less than one because

$$f(kx,ky) = (kx)^{0.3}(ky)^{0.4} = k^{0.3+0.4}(x^{0.3}y^{0.4}) = k^{0.7}(x^{0.3}y^{0.4})$$

4. $z = 2x/y$ is homogeneous of degree zero because

$$f(kx,ky) = \frac{2kx}{ky} = 1\left(\frac{2x}{y}\right) \qquad \text{since } \frac{k}{k} = k^\circ = 1$$

5. $z = x^3 + 2xy + y^3$ is not homogeneous because k cannot be completely factored out:

$$f(kx,ky) = (kx)^3 + 2(kx)(ky) + (ky)^3$$
$$= k^3x^3 + 2k^2xy + k^3y^3 = k^2(kx^3 + 2xy + ky^3)$$

8.8   RETURNS TO SCALE

A production function exhibits *constant returns to scale* if, when all inputs are increased by a given proportion k, output increases by the same proportion.   If output increases by a proportion greater than k, there are *increasing returns to scale*; and if output increases by a proportion smaller than k, there are *diminishing returns to scale*.   In other words, if the production function is homogeneous of degree greater than, equal to, or less than one, returns to scale are increasing, constant, or diminishing.

Example 11.   A *Cobb-Douglas production function* takes the form

$$Q = AK^\alpha L^\beta$$

in which A is a positive constant, K and L are inputs of capital and labor, respectively, and α and β are positive fractions less than one.   In a *strict* Cobb-Douglas production function $\alpha + \beta = 1$;   in a *generalized* Cobb-Douglas production function $\alpha + \beta$ may be $\gtreqless 1$.   In either case, the degree of homogeneity and the returns to scale can be read immediately from the sum of the exponents:

$$f(kK,kL) = A(kK)^\alpha(kL)^\beta = Ak^\alpha K^\alpha k^\beta L^\beta$$
$$= k^{\alpha+\beta}(AK^\alpha L^\beta) = k^{\alpha+\beta}(Q)$$

Thus, if

$\alpha + \beta = 1$,   returns to scale are constant.

$\alpha + \beta > 1$,   returns to scale are increasing.

$\alpha + \beta < 1$,   returns to scale are diminishing.

Note that for all strict Cobb-Douglas functions, returns to scale are constant.

Example 12.   Given: the production functions (1) $Q = 120K^{0.7}L^{0.8}$ and (2) $Q = 250K^{0.2}L^{0.7}$.
The returns to scale in (1) are *increasing* because $0.7 + 0.8 = 1.5 > 1$.   The returns to scale in (2) are *diminishing* because $0.2 + 0.7 = 0.9 < 1$.

Example 13.   Given: $Q = 1000K^{0.4}L^{0.5}$,   where $K = 80$ and $L = 220$.   Using logs to find Q:

$$Q = 1000(80)^{0.4}(220)^{0.5}$$
$$\log Q = \log 1000 + 0.4 \log 80 + 0.5 \log 220$$
$$= 3 + 0.4(1.9031) + 0.5(2.3424) = 4.9324$$
$$Q = \text{antilog } 4.9324 = 85,580$$

Solved Problems

COMPOUNDING INTEREST

8.1. Given a principal of $1000 at 6 percent for three years, use logs to find the future value (S) when the principal is compounded (a) annually, (b) semiannually, and (c) quarterly. Remember that since four-place logs are only accurate to four places, all answers should be rounded to four places.

(a)
$$S = P(1 + i)^t = 1000(1 + 0.06)^3$$
$$\log S = \log 1000 + 3 \log 1.06 = 3 + 3(0.0253) = 3.0759$$
$$S = \text{antilog } 3.0759 \cong 1191$$

(b)
$$S = P\left(1 + \frac{i}{m}\right)^{mt} = 1000\left(1 + \frac{0.06}{2}\right)^{2(3)} = 1000(1.03)^6$$
$$\log S = \log 1000 + 6 \log 1.03 = 3 + 6(0.0128) = 3.0768$$
$$S = \text{antilog } 3.0768 \cong 1194$$

(c)
$$S = 1000\left(1 + \frac{0.06}{4}\right)^{4(3)} = 1000(1.015)^{12}$$
$$\log S = \log 1000 + 12 \log 1.015 = 3 + 12(0.0065) = 3.0780$$
$$S = \text{antilog } 3.0780 \cong 1197$$

8.2. Redo Problem 8.1, given a principal of $100 at 8 percent for five years.

(a)
$$S = 100(1.08)^5$$
$$\log S = \log 100 + 5 \log 1.08 = 2 + 5(0.0334) = 2.1670$$
$$S = \text{antilog } 2.1670 \cong 146.9$$

(b)
$$S = 100\left(1 + \frac{0.08}{2}\right)^{2(5)} = 100(1.04)^{10}$$
$$\log S = \log 100 + 10 \log 1.04 = 2 + 10(0.0170) = 2.1700$$
$$S = \text{antilog } 2.1700 \cong 147.9$$

(c)
$$S = 100\left(1 + \frac{0.08}{4}\right)^{4(5)} = 100(1.02)^{20}$$
$$\log S = \log 100 + 20 \log 1.02 = 2 + 20(0.0086) = 2.1720$$
$$S = \text{antilog } 2.1720 \cong 148.6$$

8.3. Redo Problem 8.1, given a principal of $1250 at 12 percent for four years.

(a) $S = 1250(1.12)^4$

$\log S = 3.0969 + 4(0.0492) = 3.2937$

$S = \text{antilog } 3.2937 \cong 1966$

(c) $S = 1250(1.03)^{16}$

$\log S = 3.0969 + 16(0.0128) = 3.3017$

$S = \text{antilog } 3.3017 \cong 2003$

(b) $S = 1250(1.06)^8$

$\log S = 3.0969 + 8(0.0253) = 3.2993$

$S = \text{antilog } 3.2993 \cong 1992$

8.4. Use logs to find the future value for a principal of $100 at 5 percent for six years when compounded (a) annually and (b) continually.

(a) $S = 100(1.05)^6$

$\log S = 2 + 6(0.0212) = 2.1272$

$S = \text{antilog } 2.1272 \cong 134$

(b) $S = Pe^{rt} = 100e^{0.05(6)} = 100e^{0.3}$

From Appendix III, $S = 100(1.3499) = 134.99$

8.5.	Redo Problem 8.4, given a principal of $150 at 7 percent for four years.

(a)	$S = 150(1.07)^4$ 	(b)	$S = 150e^{0.07(4)} = 150e^{0.28}$

$\log S = 2.1761 + 4(0.0294) = 2.2937$ 	$S = 150(1.3231) = 198.47$

$S = \text{antilog } 2.2937 \cong 196.6$

8.6.	From Problem 8.5, use natural logs to find (a)	$S = 150e^{0.28}$	and (b)	$S = 100e^{0.3}$.

(a)	$\ln S = \ln 150 + 0.28 = 5.01064 + 0.28 = 5.29064$	(b)	$\ln S = \ln 100 + 0.3 = 4.60517 + 0.3 = 4.90517$

$S = \text{antilog}_e 5.29064 \cong 198.47$ 	$S = \text{antilog}_e 4.90517 \cong 134.99$

8.7.	Find the effective annual interest rate on $100 at 6 percent compounded	(a)	semiannually and	(b)	continuously.

(a)	From Section 8.2, 	$i_e = \left(1 + \dfrac{i}{m}\right)^m - 1 = (1.03)^2 - 1$

where	$\log (1.03)^2 = 2 \log 1.03 = 2(0.0128) = 0.0256;$	$(1.03)^2 = \text{antilog } 0.0256 = 1.061.$

Thus, 	$i_e = 1.061 - 1 = 0.061 = 6.1\%$

(b)	From Section 8.2, 	$i_e = e^r - 1 = e^{0.06} - 1$

From Appendix III,	$i_e = 1.0618 - 1 = 0.0618 = 6.18\%.$

8.8.	Calculate the rate of effective annual interest on $1000 at 12 percent compounded	(a) quarterly and	(b) continuously.

(a)	$i_e = \left(1 + \dfrac{i}{m}\right)^m - 1 = (1.03)^4 - 1$

where	$\log (1.03)^4 = 4 \log 1.03 = 4(0.0128) = 0.0512;$	$(1.03)^4 = \text{antilog } 0.0512 = 1.125.$

Thus, 	$i_e = 1.125 - 1 = 0.125 = 12.5\%$

(b)	$i_e = e^r - 1 = e^{0.12} - 1$

$= 1.1275 - 1 = 0.1275 = 12.75\%$

TIMING

8.9.	Determine the interest rate needed to have money double in ten years under annual compounding.

$$S = P(1 + i)^t$$

If money doubles,	$S = 2P.$	Thus,	$2P = P(1 + i)^{10}.$

Dividing by P, and taking the 10th root of each side,

$$2 = (1 + i)^{10} \qquad (1 + i) = \sqrt[10]{2}$$

Using natural logs for five place accuracy,

$$\ln (1 + i) = \tfrac{1}{10} \ln 2 = \tfrac{1}{10}(0.69315) = 0.06932$$

Thus, 	$1 + i = \text{antilog}_e 0.06932 = 1.0718$

$i = 1.0718 - 1 = 0.0718 = 7.18\%$

8.10. Determine the interest rate needed to have money double in six years when compounded semiannually.

$$S = P \left(1 + \frac{i}{m}\right)^{mt}$$

$$2P = P \left(1 + \frac{i}{2}\right)^{2(6)}$$

$$2 = 1(1 + 0.5\,i)^{12}$$

$$1 + 0.5\,i = \sqrt[12]{2}$$

$$\ln(1 + 0.5\,i) = \tfrac{1}{12}(\ln 2) = \tfrac{1}{12}(0.69315) = 0.05776$$

$$1 + 0.5\,i = \text{antilog}_e\, 0.05776 = 1.0595$$

$$0.5\,i = 0.0595 \qquad i = 0.119 = 11.9\%$$

8.11. What interest rate is needed to have money treble in ten years when compounded quarterly?

$$S = P \left(1 + \frac{i}{4}\right)^{4(10)}$$

If money trebles,

$$3P = P \left(1 + \frac{i}{4}\right)^{40}$$

$$3 = (1 + 0.25\,i)^{40}$$

$$(1 + 0.25\,i) = \sqrt[40]{3}$$

$$\ln(1 + 0.25\,i) = \tfrac{1}{40}\ln 3 = \tfrac{1}{40}(1.09861) = 0.02747$$

$$1 + 0.25\,i = \text{antilog}_e\, 0.02747 = 1.0279$$

$$0.25\,i = 0.0279 \qquad i = 0.1116 = 11.16\%$$

8.12. At what interest rate will money treble if compounded continuously for eight years?

$$S = Pe^{rt}$$

$$3P = Pe^{r(8)}$$

$$\ln 3 = \ln e^{8r}$$

$$1.09861 = 8r \qquad r = 0.1373 = 13.73\%$$

8.13. At what interest rate will money quintuple if compounded continuously for 25 years?

$$S = Pe^{rt}$$

$$5 = e^{25r}$$

$$\ln 5 = 25r$$

$$1.60944 = 25r \qquad r = 0.0644 = 6.44\%$$

8.14. How long will it take money to double at 12 percent interest under annual compounding? Round answers to two decimal places.

$$S = P(1 + i)^t \qquad 2 = (1 + 0.12)^t$$

$$\ln 2 = t \ln 1.12 \qquad 0.69315 = 0.11333\,t$$

$$t \cong 6.12 \text{ years}$$

8.15. How long will it take money to increase to $2\frac{1}{2}$ times its present value when compounded semiannually at 8 percent?

$$S = P\left(1+\frac{0.08}{2}\right)^{2t} \qquad 2.5 = (1.04)^{2t}$$

$$\ln 2.5 = 2t\ln 1.04 \qquad 0.91629 = 2(0.03922)t$$

$$t \cong 11.68 \text{ years}$$

8.16. How long will it take money to double at 5 percent interest when compounded quarterly?

$$S = P\left(1+\frac{0.05}{4}\right)^{4t} \qquad 2 = (1.0125)^{4t}$$

$$\ln 2 = 4t\ln 1.0125 \qquad 0.69315 = 4(0.01242)t$$

$$t \cong 13.95 \text{ years}$$

8.17. How long will it take money (*a*) to quadruple when compounded continuously at 9 percent? (*b*) To treble at 12 percent?

(*a*) $S = Pe^{rt}$ $\qquad 4 = e^{0.09t}$

$\ln 4 = 0.09t \qquad 1.38629 = 0.09t$

$t \cong 15.4 \text{ years}$

(*b*) $S = Pe^{rt}$ $\qquad 3 = e^{0.12t}$

$\ln 3 = 0.12t \qquad 1.09861 = 0.12t$

$t \cong 9.16 \text{ years}$

DISCOUNTING

8.18. Find the present value of $750 to be paid four years from now when the prevailing interest rate is 10 percent, if interest is compounded (*a*) annually and (*b*) semiannually.

(*a*) $P = S(1+i)^{-t} = 750(1.10)^{-4}$

$\log P = 2.8751 - 4(0.0414) = 2.7095$

$P = \text{antilog } 2.7095 = 512.3$

(*b*) $P = S\left(1+\dfrac{i}{m}\right)^{-mt} = 750(1.05)^{-8}$

$\log P = 2.8751 - 8(0.0212) = 2.7055$

$P = \text{antilog } 2.7055 = 507.6$

8.19. Redo Problem 8.18, for $600 to be paid seven years hence at a prevailing interest rate of 4 percent.

(*a*) $P = 600(1.04)^{-7}$

$\log P = 2.7782 - 7(0.0170) = 2.6592$

$P = \text{antilog } 2.6592 = 456.2$

(*b*) $P = 600(1.02)^{-14}$

$\log P = 2.7782 - 14(0.0086) = 2.6578$

$P = \text{antilog } 2.6578 = 454.8$

8.20. Find the present value of $500 in three years at 8 percent, when interest is compounded (*a*) annually and (*b*) continuously.

(*a*) $P = 500(1.08)^{-3}$

$\log P = 2.6990 - 3(0.0334) = 2.5988$

$P = \text{antilog } 2.5988 = 397.0$

(*b*) $P = Se^{-rt} = 500e^{-0.08(3)} = 500e^{-0.24}$

$P = 500(0.786628) = 393.31$

8.21. Redo Problem 8.20, for $120 in five years at 9 percent.

(*a*) $P = 120(1.09)^{-5}$

$\log P = 2.0792 - 5(0.0374) = 1.8922$

$P = \text{antilog } 1.8922 = 78.02$

(*b*) $P = 120e^{-0.09(5)} = 120e^{-0.45}$

$= 120(0.637628) = 76.52$

8.22.   Use natural logs to solve Problem 8.21(b).

$$P = 120e^{-0.45}$$
$$\ln P = \ln 120 + (-0.45) = 4.78749 - 0.45 = 4.33749$$
$$P = \text{antilog}_e\, 4.33749 = 76.52$$

DISCOUNTING A FUTURE STREAM

8.23.   Find the present value of $1000 to be received each year for four years when the rate of discount is 4 percent compounded annually.

$$P = S\left(\frac{1}{i}\right)\left[1 - \frac{1}{(1+i)^t}\right] = 1000\left(\frac{1}{0.04}\right)\left[1 - \frac{1}{(1.04)^4}\right]$$

where $\log[1/(1.04)^4] = \log 1 - 4\log 1.04 = 0 - 4(0.0170) = -0.0680 = 0.9320 - 1$.

Thus, $$\frac{1}{(1.04)^4} = \text{antilog}\,(0.9320 - 1) = 0.855$$

Substituting above, $$P = 1000\left(\frac{1}{0.04}\right)(1 - 0.855) = 25{,}000(0.145) = 3625$$

8.24.   How much should a firm be willing to pay for a machine that will provide net savings of $600 a year for eight years, with no scrap value, when the discount rate is 12 percent?

$$P = 600\left(\frac{1}{0.12}\right)\left[1 - \frac{1}{(1.12)^8}\right]$$

where $$\log\frac{1}{(1.12)^8} = \log 1 - 8\log 1.12$$
$$= 0 - 8(0.0492) = -0.3936 = 0.6064 - 1$$

and $$\frac{1}{(1.12)^8} = \text{antilog}\,(0.6064 - 1) = 0.404$$

Substituting above, $$P = 600\left(\frac{1}{0.12}\right)(1 - 0.404) = 2980$$

8.25.   A firm buys a machine for $6500. It expects an annual 10 percent rate of return over the machine's eleven-year life span. Calculate the projected net savings each year from the machine.

$$6500 = S\left(\frac{1}{0.10}\right)\left[1 - \frac{1}{(1.10)^{11}}\right]$$

where $$\log\frac{1}{(1.10)^{11}} = 1 - 11(0.0414) = -0.4554 = 0.5446 - 1$$

and $$\frac{1}{(1.10)^{11}} = \text{antilog}\,(0.5446 - 1) = 0.35$$

Substituting above, $$6500 = S\left(\frac{1}{0.10}\right)(1 - 0.35) \qquad S = \$1000$$

EXPONENTIAL GROWTH FUNCTIONS

8.26.   A firm with sales of 150,000 a year expects to grow by 8 percent a year. Determine the expected level of sales in six years.

$$S = 150{,}000(1.08)^6$$
$$\log S = \log 150{,}000 + 6\log 1.08 = 5.1761 + 6(0.0334) = 5.3765$$
$$S = \text{antilog}\, 5.3765 = 237{,}900$$

8.27. Profits are projected to rise by 9 percent a year over the decade. With current profits of 240,000, what will the level of profits be at the end of the decade?

$$\pi = 240,000(1.09)^{10}$$
$$\log \pi = \log 240,000 + 10 \log 1.09 = 5.3802 + 10(0.0374) = 5.7542$$
$$\pi = \text{antilog } 5.7542 = 567,900$$

8.28. The cost of food has been increasing by 3.6 percent a year. What can a family with current food expenditures of $200 a month be expected to pay for food each month in five years?

$$F = 200(1.036)^5$$
$$\log F = 2.3010 + 5(0.0153) = 2.3775$$
$$F = 238.5$$

8.29. If the cost of living had continued to increase by 12.5 percent a year from a base of 100 in 1973, what would the cost-of-living index be in 1980?

$$C = 100(1.125)^7$$
$$\log C = 2 + 7(0.0512) = 2.3584$$
$$C = 228.3$$

8.30. A discount clothing store reduces prices by 10 percent each day until the goods are sold. What will a $175 suit sell for in five days?

$$P = 175(1 - 0.10)^5 = 175(0.9)^5$$
$$\log P = 2.2430 + 5(0.9542 - 1) = 2.2430 + 4.7710 - 5 = 2.0140$$
$$P = \text{antilog } 2.0140 = \$103.30$$

8.31. A new car depreciates in value by 3 percent a month for the first year. What is the book value of a $6000 car at the end of the first year?

$$B = 6000(0.97)^{12}$$
$$\log B = 3.7782 + 11.8416 - 12 = 3.6198$$
$$B = \text{antilog } 3.6198 = \$4167$$

8.32. If the dollar depreciates at 2.6 percent a year, what will a dollar be worth in real terms 25 years from now?

$$D = 1.00(0.974)^{25}$$
$$\log D = 0 + 25(0.9886 - 1) = -0.2850 = 0.7150 - 1$$
$$D = \text{antilog } 0.7150 - 1 = 0.519 \quad \text{or} \quad 51.9\cent$$

8.33. The cost of an average hospital stay was $500 at the end of 1969. The average cost in 1979 was $1500. What was the annual rate of increase?

$$1500 = 500(1 + i)^{10}$$
$$3 = (1 + i)^{10}$$
$$1 + i = \sqrt[10]{3}$$
$$\log (1 + i) = \tfrac{1}{10}(0.4771) = 0.0477$$
$$1 + i = 1.116 \qquad i = 11.6\%$$

8.34.   A five-year development plan calls for boosting investment from 2.6 million a year to 4.2 million.   What average annual increase in investment is needed each year?

$$4.2 = 2.6(1 + i)^5$$
$$1.615 = (1 + i)^5$$
$$1 + i = \sqrt[5]{1.615}$$
$$\log(1 + i) = \tfrac{1}{5}(0.2082) = 0.0416$$
$$1 + i = \text{antilog } 0.0416 = 1.10 \qquad i = 0.10 = 10\%$$

8.35.   A developing country wishes to increase savings from a present level of 5.6 million to 12 million.   How long will it take if they can increase savings by 15 percent a year.

$$12 = 5.6(1.15)^t$$
$$\log 12 = \log 5.6 + t \log 1.15$$
$$1.0792 = 0.7482 + 0.607 t$$
$$t = 5.45 \text{ years}$$

8.36.   Population in many third world countries is growing at 3.2 percent.   Calculate the population 20 years from now for a country with 1,000,000 people.

Since population increases continually over time, a natural exponential function is needed.

$$P = 1,000,000e^{0.032(20)} = 1,000,000e^{0.64}$$
$$= 1,000,000(1.8965) = 1,896,500$$

8.37.   If the country in Problem 8.36 reduces its population increase to 2.4 percent, what will the population be in 20 years?

$$P = 1,000,000e^{0.024(20)} = 1,000,000e^{0.48}$$
$$= 1,000,000(1.6161) = 1,616,100$$

8.38.   If world population grows at 2.6 percent, how long will it take to double?

$$2 = e^{0.026t}$$
$$\ln 2 = 0.026t$$
$$0.69315 = 0.026t \qquad t = 26.66 \text{ years}$$

8.39.   If arable land in the Sahel is eroding by 3.5 percent a year because of climatic conditions, how much of the present arable land (A) will be left in 12 years?

$$P = Ae^{-0.035(12)} = Ae^{-0.42}$$
$$= 0.657047 A \quad \text{or} \quad 66\%$$

CONVERTING EXPONENTIAL FUNCTIONS

8.40.   Find the future value of a principal of $2000 compounded semiannually at 12 percent for three years, using   (a) an exponential function and   (b) the equivalent natural exponential function.

(a)
$$S = P \left(1 + \frac{i}{m}\right)^{mt} = 2000 \left(1 + \frac{0.12}{2}\right)^{2(3)} = 2000(1.06)^6$$
$$\log S = 3.3010 + 6(0.0253) = 3.4528$$
$$S = 2837$$

(b) $$S = Pe^{rt}$$

where $r = m \ln (1 + i/m) = 2 \ln 1.06 = 2(0.05827) = 0.11654$.

Thus, $$S = 2000e^{0.11654(3)} = 2000e^{0.34962}$$
$$= 2000(1.4185) = 2837$$

8.41. Redo Problem 8.40 for a principal of \$600 compounded annually at 9 percent for five years.

(a) $$S = 600(1.09)^5$$
$$\log S = 2.7782 + 5(0.0374) = 2.9652$$
$$S = 923$$

(b) $S = Pe^{rt}$,   where $r = \ln 1.09 = 0.08618$.   Thus,

$$S = 600e^{0.08618(5)} = 600e^{0.4309}$$
$$= 600(1.5386) = 923$$

8.42. Redo Problem 8.40 for a principal of \$1800 compounded quarterly at 8 percent interest for $2\frac{1}{2}$ years.

(a) $S = 1800(1.02)^{10}$ (b) $r = 4 \ln 1.02 = 4(0.01980) = 0.07920$

$\log S = 3.2553 + 10(0.0086) = 3.3413$ $S = 1800e^{0.07920(2.5)} = 1800e^{0.19800}$

$S = 2194$ $= 1800(1.21896) = 2194.1$

8.43. Find the equivalent form under annual discrete compounding for $S = Pe^{0.07696\,t}$.

$$r = m \ln \left(1 + \frac{i}{m}\right)$$

Since compounding is annual, $m = 1$

$$0.07696 = \ln (1 + i)$$
$$1 + i = \text{antilog}_e \, 0.07696 = 1.08$$
$$i = 0.08$$

Thus, $$S = P(1.08)^t$$

8.44. Find the equivalent form under semiannual discrete compounding for $Pe^{0.09758\,t}$.

$$r = 2 \ln (1 + 0.5\,i)$$
$$0.09758 = 2 \ln (1 + 0.5\,i)$$
$$1 + 0.5\,i = \text{antilog}_e \, 0.04879 = 1.05$$
$$0.5\,i = 0.05 \qquad i = 0.10$$

Thus, $$S = P(1.05)^{2t}$$

8.45. Find the equivalent form for $S = Pe^{0.15688\,t}$ under quarterly compounding.

$$r = 4 \ln (1 + 0.25\,i)$$
$$\tfrac{1}{4}(0.15688) = \ln (1 + 0.25\,i)$$
$$1 + 0.25\,i = \text{antilog}_e \, 0.03922 = 1.04$$
$$i = 0.16$$
$$S = P(1.04)^{4t}$$

ESTABLISHING EXPONENTIAL FUNCTIONS FROM DATA

8.46.   A firm's sales grew from \$1000 to \$1500 from year one to year six.   Express sales as an exponential function of time and determine the nominal rate of growth.

Substituting the data in the general formula $S = P(1+i)^t$,

$$1000 = P(1+i)^1 \tag{8.7}$$
$$1500 = P(1+i)^6 \tag{8.8}$$

Taking logs, $3 = \log P + \log(1+i)$ (8.9)

$$3.1761 = \log P + 6\log(1+i) \tag{8.10}$$

Subtracting (8.10) from (8.9), $-0.1761 = -5\log(1+i)$

$$\log(1+i) = 0.0352$$
$$1+i = 1.085 \qquad i = 8.5\%$$

Substituting in (8.7), $1000 = P(1.085) \qquad P = 921.66$

Thus, the exponential function is $S = 921.66(1.085)^t$ and the nominal growth rate is 8.5 percent.

8.47.   Average attendance at a new coliseum has increased from 22,000 in the second full year of operation to 40,000 in the sixth.   Express attendance (A) as an exponential function and determine the rate of growth.

$$22,000 = P(1+i)^2 \tag{8.11}$$
$$40,000 = P(1+i)^6$$

Using logs, $4.3424 = \log P + 2\log(1+i)$

$$4.6021 = \log P + 6\log(1+i)$$

Subtracting, $0.2597 = 4\log(1+i)$

$$\log(1+i) = 0.0649$$
$$i = 0.161$$

Substituting in (8.11), $22,000 = P(1.161)^2 \qquad P = 16,321$

Thus, $A = 16,321(1.161)^t$ and $i = 0.161$.

HOMOGENEITY AND RETURNS TO SCALE

8.48.   Determine the level of homogeneity and returns to scale for each of the following production functions:

(a) $Q = x^2 + 6xy + 7y^2$

Q is homogeneous of degree two and returns to scale are increasing because

$$f(kx,ky) = (kx)^2 + 6(kx)(ky) + 7(ky)^2 = k^2(x^2 + 6xy + 7y^2)$$

(b) $Q = x^3 - xy^2 + 3y^3 + x^2y$

Q is homogeneous of degree three and returns to scale are increasing because

$$f(kx,ky) = (kx)^3 - (kx)(ky)^2 + 3(ky)^3 + (kx)^2(ky) = k^3(x^3 - xy^2 + 3y^3 + x^2y)$$

(c) $Q = \dfrac{3x^2}{5y^2}$

Q is homogeneous of degree zero and returns to scale are decreasing because

$$f(kx,ky) = \frac{3(kx)^2}{5(ky)^2} = \frac{3x^2}{5y^2} \qquad \text{and} \qquad k^0 = 1$$

Chapter 9

Differentiation of Exponential, Logarithmic, and Power Functions

9.1 THE POWER FUNCTION RULE

The derivative of a power function $y = x^a$ is

$$\frac{dy}{dx} = ax^{a-1}$$

Example 1. Taking the derivative of a power function is illustrated below.

(1) Given $y = x^{1/4}$,

$$\frac{dy}{dx} = \frac{1}{4}x^{(1/4)-1} = \frac{1}{4}x^{-3/4}$$

(2) Given $y = x^{-3}$,

$$\frac{dy}{dx} = -3x^{-3-1} = -3x^{-4}$$

9.2 THE RULE FOR NATURAL EXPONENTIAL FUNCTIONS

The derivative of the natural exponential function $y = e^u$, where u is a function of x, is

$$\frac{dy}{dx} = e^u \frac{du}{dx} \tag{9.1}$$

In short, the derivative of a natural exponential function is equal to the original natural exponential function times the derivative of the exponent.

Example 2. Natural exponential functions are differentiated as follows:

1. To find the derivative of $y = e^{x^2}$, first set u equal to the exponent. In this case $u = x^2$; therefore, $du/dx = 2x$. Substituting in *(9.1)*,

$$\frac{dy}{dx} = e^{x^2}(2x) = 2xe^{x^2}$$

2. Given $y = e^x$, where $u = x$, then $du/dx = 1$. The derivative is

$$\frac{dy}{dx} = e^x(1) = e^x$$

Example 3. The slope of a function at a given point is given by the derivative of the function evaluated at the given point. Thus, to evaluate the slope of $y = 1.25e^{4x}$ at $x = 0.5$, first take the derivative:

$$\frac{dy}{dx} = 1.25e^{4x}(4) = 5e^{4x}$$

Then, evaluating at $x = 0.5$,

$$\frac{dy}{dx} = 5e^{4(0.5)} = 5e^2$$

From Appendix III,

$$\frac{dy}{dx} = 5(7.389) = 36.95$$

149

9.3   THE EXPONENTIAL FUNCTION RULE (FOR BASE a)

The derivative of the exponential function $y = a^u$,   where u is a function of x, is

$$\frac{dy}{dx} = a^u \frac{du}{dx} (\ln a) \tag{9.2}$$

It is simply the original function times the derivative of the exponent times the natural log of the base.

Example 4.   The exponential function rule for taking the derivative is demonstrated in the three cases below:

1.   Given $y = a^{1-2x}$.   Since $u = 1 - 2x$,   then $du/dx = -2$.   Substituting in (9.2), the derivative is

$$\frac{dy}{dx} = a^{1-2x}(-2) \ln a = -2a^{1-2x} \ln a$$

2.   Given $y = a^x$.   Letting $u = x$, $du/dx = 1$,   and

$$\frac{dy}{dx} = a^x(1) \ln a = a^x \ln a$$

a may also assume a numerical value.   See Problem 9.7, parts (c) through (g).

3.   Given $y = x^2 a^{3x}$.   Since the function is the product of x^2 and a^{3x}, the product rule must be used.

$$y' = x^2[a^{3x}(3) \ln a] + a^{3x}(2x)$$
$$= xa^{3x}(3x \ln a + 2)$$

9.4.   THE RULE FOR NATURAL LOGARITHMIC FUNCTIONS

The derivative of the natural log function $y = \ln u$,   where u is a function of x, is

$$\frac{dy}{dx} = \frac{1}{u} \frac{du}{dx} \tag{9.3}$$

Example 5.   Finding the derivative of a natural logarithmic function is illustrated below:

1.   Given $y = \ln 6x^2$.   Letting $u = 6x^2$,   then $du/dx = 12x$.   Substituting in (9.3),

$$\frac{dy}{dx} = \frac{1}{6x^2}(12x) = \frac{2}{x}$$

2.   Given $y = \ln x$.   Letting $u = x$, $du/dx = 1$, and

$$\frac{dy}{dx} = \frac{1}{x}(1) = \frac{1}{x}$$

3.   Given $y = \ln(x^2 + 6x + 2)$.   The derivative is

$$\frac{dy}{dx} = \frac{1}{x^2 + 6x + 2}(2x + 6) = \frac{2x + 6}{x^2 + 6x + 2}$$

Evaluating the slope of this function at $x = 4$,

$$\frac{dy}{dx} = \frac{14}{42} = \frac{1}{3}$$

9.5.   THE LOGARITHMIC FUNCTION RULE

The derivative of the logarithmic function $y = \log_a u$,   where u is a function of x, is

$$\frac{dy}{dx} = \frac{1}{u} \frac{du}{dx} \log_a e \qquad \text{or} \qquad \frac{dy}{dx} = \frac{1}{u} \frac{du}{dx} \frac{1}{\ln a}$$

since $\log_a e = 1/\ln a$.

Example 6.   Derivatives of logarithmic functions are found as shown below:

1. Given $y = \log_a (2x^2 + 1)$.   Letting $u = 2x^2 + 1$, $du/dx = 4x$.   The derivative in this case is either

$$\frac{dy}{dx} = \frac{1}{2x^2 + 1}(4x)\log_a e = \frac{4x}{2x^2 + 1}\log_a e$$

or

$$\frac{dy}{dx} = \frac{4x}{(2x^2 + 1)\ln a}$$

2. Given $y = \log_a x$.   Letting $u = x$, $du/dx = 1$, and

$$\frac{dy}{dx} = \frac{1}{x}(1)\log_a e = \frac{\log_a e}{x}$$

or

$$\frac{dy}{dx} = \frac{1}{x \ln a}$$

9.6   HIGHER DERIVATIVES

Higher derivatives are found by taking the derivative of the previous derivative.

Example 7.   Finding the first and second derivatives of a function is illustrated below:

1. Given $y = e^{5x}$.   The first and second derivatives are

$$\frac{dy}{dx} = e^{5x}(5) = 5e^{5x}$$

$$\frac{d^2y}{dx^2} = 5e^{5x}(5) = 25e^{5x}$$

2. Given $y = a^x$.   The first derivative is

$$\frac{dy}{dx} = a^x(1)\ln a = a^x \ln a$$

where $\ln a$ is a constant.   Thus, the second derivative is

$$\frac{d^2y}{dx^2} = a^x(\ln a)(1)(\ln a) = a^x(\ln a)^2 = a^x \ln^2 a$$

3. Given $y = \ln 2x$.   The first derivative is

$$\frac{dy}{dx} = \frac{1}{2x}(2) = \frac{1}{x} \quad \text{or} \quad x^{-1}$$

By the simple power function rule,

$$\frac{d^2y}{dx^2} = -x^{-2} \quad \text{or} \quad -\frac{1}{x^2}$$

4. Given $y = \log_a 3x$.   The first derivative is

$$\frac{dy}{dx} = \frac{1}{3x}(3)\frac{1}{\ln a} = \frac{1}{x \ln a}$$

By the quotient rule, where $\ln a$ is a constant, the second derivative is

$$\frac{d^2y}{dx^2} = \frac{x \ln a(0) - 1 \ln a}{(x \ln a)^2} = \frac{-\ln a}{x^2 \ln^2 a} = -\frac{1}{x^2 \ln a}$$

9.7   PARTIAL DERIVATIVES

Partial derivatives are found by differentiating the function with respect to one variable, while keeping the other independent variables constant.

Example 8.   Finding all the first and second partial derivatives for a function is illustrated below:

1. Given $z = e^{(3x+2y)}$.   The first and second partials are

$$z_x = e^{(3x+2y)}(3) = 3e^{(3x+2y)} \qquad z_y = e^{(3x+2y)}(2) = 2e^{(3x+2y)}$$

$$z_{xx} = 3e^{(3x+2y)}(3) = 9e^{(3x+2y)} \qquad z_{yy} = 2e^{(3x+2y)}(2) = 4e^{(3x+2y)}$$

$$z_{xy} = 6e^{(3x+2y)} = z_{yx}$$

2. Given $z = x^{0.6}y^{0.8}$.   The partial derivatives are

$$z_x = 0.6x^{-0.4}y^{0.8} \qquad z_y = 0.8x^{0.6}y^{-0.2}$$

$$z_{xx} = -0.24x^{-1.4}y^{0.8} \qquad z_{yy} = -0.16x^{0.6}y^{-1.2}$$

$$z_{xy} = 0.48x^{-0.4}y^{-0.2} = z_{yx}$$

9.8   OPTIMIZATION OF EXPONENTIAL AND LOGARITHMIC FUNCTIONS

Exponential and logarithmic functions follow the general rules for optimization presented in Sections 4.2 and 5.7.

Example 9.   The procedure for finding critical values and determining whether exponential and logarithmic functions are maximized or minimized is illustrated below:

1. Given $y = 2xe^{4x}$.   Using the product rule, and setting the derivative equal to zero,

$$\frac{dy}{dx} = 2x(4e^{4x}) + 2(e^{4x}) = 0$$

$$= 2e^{4x}(4x + 1) = 0$$

For the derivative to equal zero, either $2e^{4x} = 0$ or $4x + 1 = 0$.   Since $2e^{4x} \neq 0$ for any value of x,

$$4x + 1 = 0 \qquad \bar{x} = -\tfrac{1}{4}$$

Testing the second-order condition,

$$\frac{d^2y}{dx^2} = 2e^{4x}(4) + (4x + 1)(2e^{4x})(4) = 8e^{4x}(4x + 2)$$

Evaluated at the critical value, $\bar{x} = -\tfrac{1}{4}$, $d^2y/dx^2 = 8e^{-1}(-1+2) = 8/e > 0$.   The function is thus at a minimum, since the second derivative is positive.

2. Given $y = \ln(x^2 - 6x + 10)$.   By the natural log rule,

$$\frac{dy}{dx} = \frac{2x - 6}{x^2 - 6x + 10} = 0$$

Multiplying both sides by the denominator, $x^2 - 6x + 10$,

$$2x - 6 = 0, \qquad \bar{x} = 3$$

Using the simple quotient rule for the second derivative,

$$\frac{d^2y}{dx^2} = \frac{(x^2 - 6x + 10)(2) - (2x - 6)(2x - 6)}{(x^2 - 6x + 10)^2}$$

Evaluating the second derivative at $\bar{x} = 3$, $d^2y/dx^2 = 2 > 0$.   The function is minimized.

3. Given $z = e^{(x^2 - 2x + y^2 - 6y)}$.

$$z_x = (2x - 2)e^{(x^2 - 2x + y^2 - 6y)} = 0 \qquad z_y = (2y - 6)e^{(x^2 - 2x + y^2 - 6y)} = 0$$

Since $e^{(x^2 - 2x + y^2 - 6y)} \neq 0$ for any value of x or y,

$$2x - 2 = 0 \qquad 2y - 6 = 0$$

$$\bar{x} = 1 \qquad \bar{y} = 3$$

Testing the second-order conditions, using the product rule,

$$z_{xx} = (2x - 2)(2x - 2)e^{(x^2 - 2x + y^2 - 6y)} + e^{(x^2 - 2x + y^2 - 6y)}(2) \qquad z_{yy} = (2y - 6)(2y - 6)e^{(x^2 - 2x + y^2 - 6y)} + e^{(x^2 - 2x + y^2 - 6y)}(2)$$

When evaluated at $\bar{x} = 1$, $\bar{y} = 3$,

$$z_{xx} = 0 + 2e^{-10} > 0 \qquad z_{yy} = 0 + 2e^{-10} > 0$$

since e to any power is positive.   Then testing the mixed partials,

$$z_{xy} = (2x - 2)(2y - 6)e^{(x^2 - 2x + y^2 - 6y)} = z_{yx}$$

Evaluated at $\bar{x} = 1$, $\bar{y} = 3$, $z_{xy} = 0 = z_{yx}$. Thus, the function is at a minimum at $\bar{x} = 1$ and $\bar{y} = 3$ since z_{xx} and $z_{yy} > 0$ and $z_{xx}z_{yy} > (z_{xy})^2$.

9.9   ALTERNATIVE MEASURES OF GROWTH

Growth (G) of a function $y = f(t)$ is defined as

$$G = \frac{dy/dt}{y} = \frac{f'(t)}{f(t)} = \frac{y'}{y}$$

From Section 9.4 this is exactly equivalent to the derivative of ln y.   The growth of a function, therefore, can be measured   (1) by dividing the derivative of the function by the function itself or   (2) by taking the natural log of the function and then simply differentiating the natural log function.   This latter method is sometimes helpful with more complicated functions.

Example 10.   Finding the growth rate of $V = Pe^{rt}$, where P is a constant, is illustrated below using the two methods outlined above.

1.   Using the first method, $\qquad\qquad\qquad\qquad G = \dfrac{V'}{V}$

where $V' = Pe^{rt}(r) = rPe^{rt}$.   Thus,

$$G = \frac{rPe^{rt}}{Pe^{rt}} = r$$

2.   For the second method, take the natural log of the function, as follows:

$$\ln V = \ln P + rt$$

Then simply take the derivative of the natural log function:

$$G = \frac{d}{dt}(\ln V) = 0 + r = r$$

9.10   OPTIMAL TIMING

Exponential functions are used to express the value of goods that appreciate or depreciate over time.   Such goods include wine, cheese, and land.   Since a dollar in the future is worth less than a dollar today, their future value must be discounted to a present value.   Investors and speculators seek to maximize the present value of their assets.

Example 11.   The value of cheese that improves with age is given by $V = 1400(1.25)^{\sqrt{t}}$.   If the cost of capital under continuous compounding is 9 percent a year and there is no storage cost for aging the cheese in company caves, how long should the company store the cheese?

The company wants to maximize the present value of the cheese: $P = Ve^{-rt}$.   Substituting the given value of V and r, $P = 1400(1.25)^{\sqrt{t}}e^{-0.09t}$.   Taking the natural log,

$$\ln P = \ln 1400 + t^{1/2}\ln 1.25 - 0.09t$$

Then taking the derivative and setting it equal to zero to maximize P,

$$\frac{1}{P}\frac{dP}{dt} = 0 + \tfrac{1}{2}\ln(1.25)t^{-1/2} - 0.09 = 0$$

$$\frac{dP}{dt} = P[\tfrac{1}{2}\ln(1.25)t^{-1/2} - 0.09] = 0$$

Since $P \neq 0$,

$$\tfrac{1}{2} \ln (1.25) t^{-1/2} - 0.09 = 0$$

$$t^{-1/2} = \frac{0.18}{\ln 1.25}$$

$$t = \left[\frac{\ln 1.25}{0.18} \right]^2 = \left[\frac{0.22314}{0.18} \right]^2 = 1.54 \text{ years}$$

Testing the second-order condition, by the product rule since $P = f(t)$,

$$\frac{d^2 P}{dt^2} = P[-\tfrac{1}{4} \ln 1.25 \, t^{-3/2}] + [\tfrac{1}{2} \ln (1.25) t^{-1/2} - 0.09] \frac{dP}{dt}$$

Since $dP/dt = 0$ at the critical point,

$$\frac{d^2 P}{dt^2} = P[-\tfrac{1}{4} \ln (1.25) t^{-3/2}] = -P(0.05579 \, t^{-3/2})$$

With P, $t > 0$, $d^2 P/dt^2 < 0$ and the function is at a maximum.

9.11   CONSTRAINED OPTIMIZATION OF A GENERALIZED COBB–DOUGLAS FUNCTION

Given a production function $q = K^{0.4} L^{0.5}$ subject to a budget constraint of \$108 when $P_K = 3$ and $P_L = 4$,   the Lagrange function for optimization is

$$Q = K^{0.4} L^{0.5} + \lambda (3K + 4L - 108)$$

First-order conditions for maximization are

$$Q_K = 0.4 K^{-0.6} L^{0.5} + 3\lambda = 0 \tag{9.4}$$

$$Q_L = 0.5 K^{0.4} L^{-0.5} + 4\lambda = 0 \tag{9.5}$$

$$Q_\lambda = 3K + 4L - 108 = 0 \tag{9.6}$$

Solving simultaneously,

from (9.4),

$$-\lambda = 0.133 K^{-0.6} L^{0.5} \tag{9.7}$$

from (9.5),

$$-\lambda = 0.125 K^{0.4} L^{-0.5} \tag{9.8}$$

Equating (9.7) and (9.8),

$$0.133 K^{-0.6} L^{0.5} = 0.125 K^{0.4} L^{-0.5} \tag{9.9}$$

Multiplying both sides by $K^{0.6} L^{0.5}$, which from Section 7.1 is equivalent to adding exponents,

$$0.133 L = 0.125 K \qquad L = 0.9398 K$$

Substituting in (9.6),

$$3K + 4(0.9398)K = 108 \qquad \bar{K} = 16$$

Substituting $\bar{K} = 16$ in (9.6), $\bar{L} = 15$.

Second-order conditions for constrained optimization are treated in Section 12.4.   Second-order conditions for this particular problem are found in Example 6 in Chapter 12.   [A general rule for solving (9.9) in terms of L is to multiply both sides of the equation by K to the power that will make K on the left-hand side equal to K^0 or 1, and L on the left-hand side by L to the power that will leave L^1 or L.   This will automatically leave K^1 and L^0 on the other side of the equation.]

For a constant elasticity of substitution (CES) production function, see Problems 9.51 to 9.62.

Solved Problems

DIFFERENTIATION OF POWER FUNCTIONS

9.1. Use the power function rule to differentiate each of the following functions:

(a) $y = 6x^{-3} - 7x^{-2} + 4x^{-1}$

$y' = -18x^{-4} + 14x^{-3} - 4x^{-2}$

(b) $y = 3x^{1/4} - 5x^{1/2} + 4x^{3/2}$

$y' = \frac{3}{4}x^{-3/4} - 2.5x^{-1/2} + 6x^{1/2}$

9.2. Redo Problem 9.1, given

$$y = \frac{12}{x^{1/3}} - \frac{9}{x^{2/3}} + \frac{15}{x^{4/3}}$$

Converting to negative exponents before taking the derivative, $y = 12x^{-1/3} - 9x^{-2/3} + 15x^{-4/3}$. Thus,

$$y' = -4x^{-4/3} + 6x^{-5/3} - 20x^{-7/3} = \frac{-4}{x^{4/3}} + \frac{6}{x^{5/3}} - \frac{20}{x^{7/3}}$$

9.3. Redo Problem 9.1, given

$$y = \frac{3x + 1}{x^3}$$

Converting the quotient to a product and then using the product rule,

$y = (3x + 1)x^{-3}$

$y' = (3x + 1)(-3x^{-4}) + x^{-3}(3) = -9x^{-3} - 3x^{-4} + 3x^{-3} = -3x^{-4} - 6x^{-3}$

Thus by use of negative exponents, the derivative of a quotient can be found with the product rule.

9.4. Redo Problem 9.1, given $y = (6x)^3$.

Since the parentheses indicate that $6x$ is cubed and not merely x, the chain rule is necessary.

$$y' = 3(6x)^2(6) = 18(6x)^2 = 648x^2$$

9.5. Differentiate each of the following functions using the power function rule:

(a) $y = \sqrt{14x}$

$y = (14x)^{1/2}$ $y' = \frac{1}{2}(14x)^{-1/2}(14) = 7(14x)^{-1/2} = \frac{7}{\sqrt{14x}}$

(b) $y = \sqrt{2x^3}$

$y = (2x^3)^{1/2} \neq 2x^{3/2}$ $y' = \frac{1}{2}(2x^3)^{-1/2}(6x^2) = \frac{3x^2}{\sqrt{2x^3}} = \frac{3x^2}{x\sqrt{2x}} = \frac{3x}{\sqrt{2x}}$

(c) $y = \sqrt[3]{6x^2}$

$y = (6x^2)^{1/3}$ $y' = \frac{1}{3}(6x^2)^{-2/3}(12x) = \frac{4x}{(6x^2)^{2/3}} = \frac{4x}{\sqrt[3]{36x^4}} = \frac{4}{\sqrt[3]{36x}}$

(d) $y = \frac{1}{\sqrt{7x}}$

$y = (7x)^{-1/2}$ $y' = -\frac{1}{2}(7x)^{-3/2}(7) = \frac{-7}{2\sqrt{(7x)^3}} = \frac{-7}{2(7x)\sqrt{7x}} = \frac{-1}{2x\sqrt{7x}}$

DERIVATIVES OF NATURAL EXPONENTIAL FUNCTIONS

9.6. Differentiate each of the following natural exponential functions according to the rule $d/dx(e^u) = e^u \, du/dx$.

(a) $y = e^{2x}$

Letting $u = 2x$, then $du/dx = 2$, and $y' = e^{2x}(2) = 2e^{2x}$

(b) $y = e^{(-1/3)x}$

$u = -\frac{1}{3}x$, $du/dx = -\frac{1}{3}$, and $y' = e^{-(1/3)x}(-\frac{1}{3}) = -\frac{1}{3}e^{(-1/3)x}$

(c) $y = e^{x^3}$

$y' = e^{x^3}(3x^2) = 3x^2 e^{x^3}$

(d) $y = 3e^{x^2}$

$y' = 3e^{x^2}(2x) = 6xe^{x^2}$

(e) $y = e^{2x+1}$

$y' = e^{2x+1}(2) = 2e^{2x+1}$

(f) $y = e^{1-4x}$

$y' = -4e^{1-4x}$

(g) $y = 5e^{1-x^2}$

$y' = -10xe^{1-x^2}$

(h) $y = 2xe^x$

By the product rule,

$y' = 2x(e^x) + e^x(2) = 2e^x(x+1)$

(i) $y = 3xe^{2x}$

$y' = 3x(2e^{2x}) + e^{2x}(3) = 3e^{2x}(2x+1)$

(j) $y = x^2 e^{5x}$

$y' = x^2(5e^{5x}) + e^{5x}(2x) = xe^{5x}(5x+2)$

(k) $y = \dfrac{e^{5x} - 1}{e^{5x} + 1}$

By the quotient rule,

$$y' = \frac{(e^{5x} + 1)(5e^{5x}) - (e^{5x} - 1)(5e^{5x})}{(e^{5x} + 1)^2} = \frac{10e^{5x}}{(e^{5x} + 1)^2}$$

(l) $y = \dfrac{e^{2x} + 1}{e^{2x} - 1}$

$$y' = \frac{(e^{2x} - 1)(2e^{2x}) - (e^{2x} + 1)(2e^{2x})}{(e^{2x} - 1)^2} = \frac{-4e^{2x}}{(e^{2x} - 1)^2}$$

DIFFERENTIATION OF EXPONENTIAL FUNCTIONS WITH BASE OTHER THAN e

9.7. Differentiate each of the following exponential functions according to the rule $d/dx(a^u) = a^u \, (du/dx)(\ln a)$.

(a) $y = a^{2x}$

Letting $u = 2x$, then $du/dx = 2$, and

$$y' = a^{2x}(2) \ln a = 2a^{2x} \ln a$$

(b) $y = a^{5x^2}$

$$y' = a^{5x^2}(10x) \ln a = 10xa^{5x^2} \ln a$$

(c) $y = 4^{2x+7}$

$$y' = 4^{2x+7}(2) \ln 4 = 2(4)^{2x+7} \ln 4$$

From Appendix II, $y' = 2(1.38629)(4)^{2x+7} = 2.77258(4)^{2x+7}$

(d) $y = 2^x$

$$y' = 2^x(1) \ln 2 = 2^x \ln 2 = 0.69315(2)^x$$

(e) $y = 7^{x^2}$

$$y' = 7^{x^2}(2x) \ln 7 = 2x(7)^{x^2} \ln 7 = 2x(7)^{x^2}(1.94591) = 3.89182x(7)^{x^2}$$

(f) $y = x^3 2^x$

By the product rule, recalling that x^3 is a power function and 2^x is an exponential function,

$$y' = x^3[2^x(1) \ln 2] + 2^x(3x^2) = x^2 2^x(x \ln 2 + 3)$$

(g) $y = x^2 2^{5x}$

$$y' = x^2[2^{5x}(5) \ln 2] + 2^{5x}(2x) = x2^{5x}(5x \ln 2 + 2)$$

DERIVATIVES OF NATURAL LOG FUNCTIONS

9.8. Differentiate each of the following natural log functions according to the rule $d/dx(\ln u) = (1/u) \, du/dx$.

(a) $y = \ln 2x^3$

Letting $u = 2x^3$, then $du/dx = 6x^2$, and

$$y' = \frac{1}{2x^3}(6x^2) = \frac{3}{x}$$

(b) $y = \ln 7x^2$

$$y' = \frac{1}{7x^2}(14x) = \frac{2}{x}$$

(c) $y = \ln(1+x)$

$$y' = \frac{1}{1+x}$$

(d) $y = \ln(4x+7)$

$$y' = \frac{1}{4x+7}(4) = \frac{4}{4x+7}$$

(e) $y = \ln 6x$

$$y' = \frac{1}{6x}(6) = \frac{1}{x}$$

(f) $y = 6 \ln x$

$$y' = 6\left(\frac{1}{x}\right) = \frac{6}{x}$$

Notice how a multiplicative constant within the log expression in part (e) drops out in differentiation, whereas a multiplicative constant outside the log expression in part (f) remains.

9.9. Redo Problem 9.8 for each of the following functions:

(a) $y = \ln^2 x = (\ln x)^2$

By the chain rule,

$$y' = 2 \ln x \frac{d}{dx}(\ln x) = 2 \ln x \left(\frac{1}{x}\right) = \frac{2 \ln x}{x}$$

(b) $y = \ln^2 8x = (\ln 8x)^2$

$$y' = 2 \ln 8x \left(\frac{1}{8x}\right)(8) = \frac{2 \ln 8x}{x}$$

(c) $y = \ln^2(3x+1) = [\ln(3x+1)]^2$

$$y' = 2 \ln(3x+1)\left(\frac{1}{3x+1}\right)(3) = \frac{6 \ln(3x+1)}{3x+1}$$

(d) $y = \ln^2(5x+6)$

$$y' = 2 \ln(5x+6)\left(\frac{1}{5x+6}\right)(5) = \frac{10 \ln(5x+6)}{5x+6}$$

(e) $y = \ln^3(4x+13)$

$$y' = 3[\ln(4x+13)]^2\left(\frac{1}{4x+13}\right)(4) = 3 \ln^2(4x+13)\left(\frac{4}{4x+13}\right) = \frac{12}{4x+13} \ln^2(4x+13)$$

(f) $y = \ln(x+5)^2 \neq [\ln(x+5)]^2$

Letting $u = (x+5)^2$, then $du/dx = 2(x+5)$, and

$$y' = \frac{1}{(x+5)^2}[2(x+5)] = \frac{2}{x+5}$$

(g) $y = \ln (x - 8)^2$

$$y' = \frac{1}{(x-8)^2}[2(x-8)] = \frac{2}{x-8}$$

(h) $y = 3 \ln (1 + x)^2$

$$y' = 3\left[\frac{1}{(1+x)^2}\right][2(1+x)] = \frac{6}{1+x}$$

9.10.   Use the laws of logarithms in Section 7.8 to simplify the differentiation of each of the following natural log functions:

(a) $y = \ln (x + 5)^2$

From the rules for logs, $\ln (x + 5)^2 = 2 \ln (x + 5)$.   Thus, as in Problem 9.9(f),

$$y' = 2\left(\frac{1}{x+5}\right)(1) = \frac{2}{x+5}$$

(b) $y = \ln (2x + 7)^2$

$$y = 2 \ln (2x + 7)$$
$$y' = 2\left(\frac{1}{2x+7}\right)(2) = \frac{4}{2x+7}$$

(c) $y = \ln [(3x + 7)(4x + 2)]$

$$y = \ln (3x + 7) + \ln (4x + 2)$$
$$y' = \frac{3}{3x+7} + \frac{4}{4x+2}$$

(d) $y = \ln [5x^2(3x^3 - 7)]$

$$y = \ln 5x^2 + \ln (3x^3 - 7)$$
$$y' = \frac{10x}{5x^2} + \frac{9x^2}{3x^3-7}$$
$$= \frac{2}{x} + \frac{9x^2}{3x^3-7}$$

(e) $y = \ln \left(\frac{3x^2}{x^2-1}\right)$

$$y = \ln 3x^2 - \ln (x^2 - 1)$$
$$y' = \frac{2}{x} - \frac{2x}{x^2-1}$$

(f) $y = \ln \left[\frac{x^3}{(2x+5)^2}\right]$

$$y = \ln x^3 - \ln (2x + 5)^2$$
$$y' = \frac{1}{x^3}(3x^2) - 2\left(\frac{1}{2x+5}\right)(2)$$
$$= \frac{3}{x} - \frac{4}{2x+5}$$

(g) $y = \ln \sqrt{\frac{2x^2+3}{x^2+9}}$

$$y = \tfrac{1}{2}[\ln (2x^2 + 3) - \ln (x^2 + 9)]$$
$$y' = \frac{1}{2}\left(\frac{4x}{2x^2+3} - \frac{2x}{x^2+9}\right)$$
$$= \frac{2x}{2x^2+3} - \frac{x}{x^2+9}$$

9.11.   Use whatever combinations of rules are necessary to differentiate each of the following functions:

(a) $y = x^2 \ln x^3$

By the product rule,

$$y' = x^2 \left(\frac{1}{x^3}\right)(3x^2) + \ln x^3(2x) = 3x + 2x \ln x^3 = 3x + 6x \ln x = 3x(1 + 2 \ln x)$$

(b) $y = x^3 \ln x^2$

$$y' = x^3 \left(\frac{1}{x^2}\right)(2x) + \ln x^2(3x^2) = 2x^2 + 6x^2 \ln x = 2x^2(1 + 3 \ln x)$$

(c) $y = e^x \ln x$

By the product rule,

$$y' = e^x \left(\frac{1}{x}\right) + (\ln x)(e^x) = e^x \left(\frac{1}{x} + \ln x\right)$$

(d) $y = e^{-2x} \ln 2x$

$$y' = e^{-2x} \left(\frac{1}{2x}\right)(2) + \ln 2x(-2e^{-2x}) = e^{-2x}\left(\frac{1}{x} - 2\ln 2x\right)$$

(e) $y = \ln e^{3x+2}$

$$y' = \frac{1}{e^{3x+2}}(3e^{3x+2}) = 3$$

Since $\ln e^{3x+2} = 3x + 2$, $d/dx(\ln e^{3x+2}) = d/dx(3x+2) = 3$.

(f) $y = e^{\ln x}$

$$y' = e^{\ln x}\left(\frac{1}{x}\right) = x\left(\frac{1}{x}\right) = 1$$

Since $e^{\ln x} = x$.

(g) $y = e^{\ln(2x+1)}$

$$y' = e^{\ln(2x+1)}\left(\frac{1}{2x+1}\right)(2) = 2$$

Since $e^{\ln(2x+1)} = 2x + 1$

(h) $y = e^{x \ln x}$

$$y' = e^{x \ln x}\frac{d}{dx}(x \ln x)$$

Then using the product rule for $d/dx(x \ln x)$,

$$y' = e^{x \ln x}\left[x\left(\frac{1}{x}\right) + (\ln x)(1)\right] = e^{x \ln x}(1 + \ln x)$$

(i) $y = e^{x^2 \ln 3x}$

$$y' = e^{x^2 \ln 3x}\left[x^2\left(\frac{1}{3x}\right)(3) + \ln 3x(2x)\right]$$

$$= e^{x^2 \ln 3x}(x + 2x \ln 3x) = xe^{x^2 \ln 3x}(1 + 2\ln 3x)$$

DERIVATIVES OF LOG FUNCTIONS WITH BASES OTHER THAN e

9.12.   Differentiate each of the following log functions according to the rule

$$\frac{d}{dx}\log_a u = \frac{1}{u}\frac{du}{dx}\left(\frac{1}{\ln a}\right) = \frac{1}{u}\frac{du}{dx}(\log_a e)$$

(a) $y = \log_a(4x^2 - 3)$

$$y' = \frac{1}{4x^2 - 3}(8x)\left(\frac{1}{\ln a}\right)$$

$$= \frac{8x}{(4x^2 - 3)\ln a}$$

(b) $y = \log_4 9x^3$

$$y' = \frac{1}{9x^3}(27x^2)\left(\frac{1}{\ln 4}\right)$$

$$= \frac{3}{x \ln 4}$$

(c) $y = \log_2(8 - x)$

$$y' = \frac{1}{(8-x)}(-1)\left(\frac{1}{\ln 2}\right)$$

$$= -\frac{1}{(8-x)\ln 2}$$

(d) $y = x^3 \log_6 x$

By the product rule,

$$y' = x^3\left[\frac{1}{x}(1)\left(\frac{1}{\ln 6}\right)\right] + \log_6 x(3x^2)$$

$$= \frac{x^2}{\ln 6} + 3x^2 \log_6 x$$

(e) $y = \log_a \sqrt{x^2 - 7}$

From the law of logs, $y = \frac{1}{2}\log_a(x^2 - 7)$.   Thus,

$$y' = \frac{1}{2}\left[\frac{1}{x^2 - 7}(2x)\left(\frac{1}{\ln a}\right)\right] = \frac{x}{(x^2 - 7)\ln a}$$

SLOPES OF EXPONENTIAL AND LOGARITHMIC FUNCTIONS

9.13. Evaluate the slope of each of the following functions at the point indicated.

(a) $y = 3e^{0.2x}$, at $x = 5$.

$$y' = 0.6e^{0.2x}$$

At $x = 5$, $y' = 0.6e^{0.2(5)} = 0.6(2.71828) = 1.63097$.

(b) $y = 2e^{-1.5x}$, at $x = 4$.

$$y' = -3e^{-1.5x}$$

At $x = 4$, $y' = -3e^{-1.5(4)} = -3e^{-6}$. From Appendix III, $y' = -3(0.0025) = -0.0075$.

(c) $y = \ln(x^2 + 8x + 4)$, at $x = 2$.

$$y' = \frac{2x + 8}{x^2 + 8x + 4}$$

At $x = 2$, $y' = \frac{12}{24} = 0.5$.

(d) $y = \ln^2(x + 4)$, at $x = 6$.

$$y' = [2\ln(x+4)]\left(\frac{1}{x+4}\right)(1) = \frac{2\ln(x+4)}{x+4}$$

At $x = 6$,

$$y' = \frac{2\ln 10}{10} = \frac{2(2.30259)}{10} = 0.46052$$

SECOND DERIVATIVES

9.14. Find the first and second derivatives of each of the following functions:

(a) $y = 6x^{1/2} + 2x^{1/3} + 8x^{3/2}$

$y' = 3x^{-1/2} + \frac{2}{3}x^{-2/3} + 12x^{1/2}$

$y'' = -\frac{3}{2}x^{-3/2} - \frac{4}{9}x^{-5/3} + 6x^{-1/2}$

(b) $y = 24x^{-1/4} - 18x^{-2/3} + 12x^{-5/4}$

$y' = -6x^{-5/4} + 12x^{-5/3} - 15x^{-9/4}$

$y'' = 7.5x^{-9/4} - 20x^{-8/3} + 33.75x^{-13/4}$

(c) $y = e^{3x}$

$y' = 3e^{3x}$

$y'' = 9e^{3x}$

(d) $y = e^{-(1/2)x}$

$y' = -\frac{1}{2}e^{-(1/2)x}$

$y'' = \frac{1}{4}e^{-(1/2)x}$

(e) $y = 3e^{5x+1}$

$y' = 15e^{5x+1}$

$y'' = 75e^{5x+1}$

(f) $y = 2xe^x$

By the product rule,

$y' = 2x(e^x) + e^x(2) = 2e^x(x + 1)$

$y'' = 2e^x(1) + (x + 1)(2e^x) = 2e^x(x + 2)$

(g) $y = \ln 2x^5$

$y' = \frac{1}{2x^5}(10x^4) = \frac{5}{x} = 5x^{-1}$

$y'' = -5x^{-2} = \frac{-5}{x^2}$

(h) $y = 4\ln x$

$y' = 4\left(\frac{1}{x}\right)(1) = \frac{4}{x} = 4x^{-1}$

$y'' = -4x^{-2}$

9.15. Take the first and second derivatives of each of the following functions:

(a) $y = a^{3x}$

$$y' = a^{3x}(3)\ln a = 3a^{3x}\ln a$$

where $\ln a = $ a constant. Thus,

$$y'' = (3a^{3x}\ln a)(3)\ln a = 9a^{3x}(\ln a)^2$$

(b) $y = a^{5x+1}$

$$y' = a^{5x+1}(5) \ln a = 5a^{5x+1} \ln a$$
$$y'' = (5a^{5x+1} \ln a)(5) \ln a = 25a^{5x+1}(\ln a)^2$$

(c) $y = \log_a 5x$

$$y' = \frac{1}{5x}(5)\frac{1}{\ln a} = \frac{1}{x \ln a} = (x \ln a)^{-1}$$

Using the chain rule,

$$y'' = -1(x \ln a)^{-2} \ln a = \frac{-\ln a}{x^2 \ln^2 a} = -\frac{1}{x^2 \ln a}$$

(d) $y = \log_3 6x$

$$y' = \frac{1}{6x}(6)\left(\frac{1}{\ln 3}\right) = \frac{1}{x \ln 3} = (x \ln 3)^{-1}$$

$$y'' = -1(x \ln 3)^{-2}(\ln 3) = \frac{-\ln 3}{x^2 \ln^2 3} = -\frac{1}{x^2 \ln 3}$$

(e) $y = 3xe^x$

By the product rule,

$$y' = 3x(e^x) + e^x(3) = 3e^x(x + 1)$$
$$y'' = 3e^x(1) + (x + 1)(3e^x) = 3e^x(x + 2)$$

(f) $y = \dfrac{4x}{3 \ln x}$

By the quotient rule,

$$y' = \frac{(3 \ln x)(4) - 4x(3)(1/x)}{9 \ln^2 x} = \frac{12 \ln x - 12}{9 \ln^2 x} = \frac{12(\ln x - 1)}{9 \ln^2 x}$$

$$y'' = \frac{(9 \ln^2 x)[12(1/x)] - 12(\ln x - 1)\{[9(2) \ln x](1/x)\}}{81 \ln^4 x} = \frac{(108/x)(\ln^2 x) - (216/x)(\ln x - 1)(\ln x)}{81 \ln^4 x}$$

$$= \frac{4 \ln x - 8(\ln x - 1)}{3x \ln^3 x} = \frac{-4 \ln x + 8}{3x \ln^3 x} = \frac{4(2 - \ln x)}{3x \ln^3 x}$$

PARTIAL DERIVATIVES

9.16. Find all the first and second partial derivatives for each of the following functions:

(a) $u = x^{0.6}y^{0.3}$

$$u_x = 0.6x^{-0.4}y^{0.3} \qquad u_y = 0.3x^{0.6}y^{-0.7}$$
$$u_{xx} = -0.24x^{-1.4}y^{0.3} \qquad u_{yy} = -0.21x^{0.6}y^{-1.7}$$
$$u_{xy} = 0.18x^{-0.4}y^{-0.7} = u_{yx}$$

(b) $q = x^{0.9}y^{0.1}$

$$q_x = 0.9x^{-0.1}y^{0.1} \qquad q_y = 0.1x^{0.9}y^{-0.9}$$
$$q_{xx} = -0.09x^{-1.1}y^{0.1} \qquad q_{yy} = -0.09x^{0.9}y^{-1.9}$$
$$q_{xy} = 0.09x^{-0.1}y^{-0.9} = q_{yx}$$

(c) $z = e^{x^2+y^2}$

$$z_x = 2xe^{x^2+y^2} \qquad z_y = 2ye^{x^2+y^2}$$

By the product rule,

$$z_{xx} = 2x(2xe^{x^2+y^2}) + e^{x^2+y^2}(2) \qquad z_{yy} = 2y(2ye^{x^2+y^2}) + e^{x^2+y^2}(2)$$
$$= 2e^{x^2+y^2}(2x^2 + 1) \qquad\qquad = 2e^{x^2+y^2}(2y^2 + 1)$$
$$z_{xy} = 4xye^{x^2+y^2} = z_{yx}$$

(d) $z = e^{2x^2+3y}$

$$z_x = 4xe^{2x^2+3y} \qquad\qquad z_y = 3e^{2x^2+3y}$$
$$z_{xx} = 4x(4xe^{2x^2+3y}) + e^{2x^2+3y}(4) \qquad z_{yy} = 9e^{2x^2+3y}$$
$$= 4e^{2x^2+3y}(4x^2 + 1)$$
$$z_{xy} = 12xe^{2x^2+3y} = z_{yx}$$

(e) $z = a^{2x+3y}$

$$z_x = a^{2x+3y}(2)\ln a \qquad\qquad z_y = a^{2x+3y}(3)\ln a$$
$$= 2a^{2x+3y}\ln a \qquad\qquad = 3a^{2x+3y}\ln a$$
$$z_{xx} = 2a^{2x+3y}\ln a\,(2)(\ln a) \qquad z_{yy} = 3a^{2x+3y}\ln a\,(3)(\ln a)$$
$$= 4a^{2x+3y}\ln^2 a \qquad\qquad = 9a^{2x+3y}\ln^2 a$$
$$z_{xy} = 6a^{2x+3y}\ln^2 a = z_{yx}$$

(f) $z = 4^{3x+5y}$

$$z_x = 4^{3x+5y}(3)\ln 4 \qquad\qquad z_y = 4^{3x+5y}(5)\ln 4$$
$$= 3(4)^{3x+5y}\ln 4 \qquad\qquad = 5(4)^{3x+5y}\ln 4$$
$$z_{xx} = 3(4)^{3x+5y}\ln 4\,(3)(\ln 4) \qquad z_{yy} = 5(4)^{3x+5y}\ln 4\,(5)(\ln 4)$$
$$= 9(4)^{3x+5y}\ln^2 4 \qquad\qquad = 25(4)^{3x+5y}\ln^2 4$$
$$z_{xy} = 15(4)^{3x+5y}\ln^2 4 = z_{yx}$$

(g) $z = \ln(7x + 2y)$

$$z_x = \frac{7}{7x+2y} \qquad z_y = \frac{2}{7x+2y}$$

By the quotient rule,

$$z_{xx} = \frac{(7x+2y)(0)-7(7)}{(7x+2y)^2} = \frac{-49}{(7x+2y)^2} \qquad z_{yy} = \frac{(7x+2y)(0)-2(2)}{(7x+2y)^2} = \frac{-4}{(7x+2y)^2}$$
$$z_{xy} = \frac{-14}{(7x+2y)^2} = z_{yx}$$

(h) $z = \ln(x^2 + 4y^2)$

$$z_x = \frac{2x}{x^2+4y^2} \qquad z_y = \frac{8y}{x^2+4y^2}$$
$$z_{xx} = \frac{(x^2+4y^2)(2)-2x(2x)}{(x^2+4y^2)^2} = \frac{8y^2-2x^2}{(x^2+4y^2)^2} \qquad z_{yy} = \frac{(x^2+4y^2)(8)-8y(8y)}{(x^2+4y^2)^2} = \frac{8x^2-32y^2}{(x^2+4y^2)^2}$$
$$z_{xy} = \frac{-16xy}{(x^2+4y^2)^2} = z_{yx}$$

(i) $z = \log_a(x - 2y)$

$$z_x = \frac{1}{(x-2y)\ln a} \qquad\qquad z_y = \frac{-2}{(x-2y)\ln a}$$
$$z_{xx} = \frac{-1\ln a}{(x-2y)^2\ln^2 a} = \frac{-1}{(x-2y)^2\ln a} \qquad z_{yy} = \frac{-4\ln a}{(x-2y)^2\ln^2 a} = \frac{-4}{(x-2y)^2\ln a}$$
$$z_{xy} = \frac{2}{(x-2y)^2\ln a} = z_{yx}$$

(j) $z = \log_a(3x^2 + y^2)$

$$z_x = \frac{6x}{(3x^2+y^2)\ln a} \qquad\qquad z_y = \frac{2y}{(3x^2+y^2)\ln a}$$
$$z_{xx} = \frac{(3x^2+y^2)\ln a\,(6)-6x(6x\ln a)}{(3x^2+y^2)^2\ln^2 a} \qquad z_{yy} = \frac{(3x^2+y^2)\ln a\,(2)-2y(2y\ln a)}{(3x^2+y^2)^2\ln^2 a}$$
$$= \frac{6y^2-18x^2}{(3x^2+y^2)^2\ln a} \qquad\qquad = \frac{6x^2-2y^2}{(3x^2+y^2)^2\ln a}$$
$$z_{xy} = \frac{-12xy}{(3x^2+y^2)^2\ln a} = z_{yx}$$

OPTIMIZATION OF EXPONENTIAL AND LOGARITHMIC FUNCTIONS

9.17. Given $y = 4xe^{3x}$ (a) find the critical values and   (b) determine whether the function is maximized or minimized.

(a) By the product rule,

$$y' = 4x(3e^{3x}) + e^{3x}(4) = 0$$
$$4e^{3x}(3x + 1) = 0$$

Since there is no value of x for which $4e^{3x} = 0$,   or for which $e^x = 0$,

$$3x + 1 = 0 \qquad \bar{x} = -\tfrac{1}{3}$$

(b) $$y'' = 4e^{3x}(3) + (3x + 1)(12e^{3x}) = 12e^{3x}(3x + 2)$$

At $\bar{x} = -\tfrac{1}{3}$, $y'' = 12e^{-1}(1)$.   From Appendix III, $y'' = 12(0.36787) > 0$.   The function is minimized.

9.18. Redo Problem 9.17, given $y = 5xe^{-0.2x}$.

(a) $$y' = 5x(-0.2e^{-0.2x}) + e^{-0.2x}(5) = 0$$
$$5e^{-0.2x}(1 - 0.2x) = 0$$

Since $5e^{-0.2x} \neq 0$, $(1 - 0.2x) = 0$ $\bar{x} = 5$

(b) $$y'' = 5e^{-0.2x}(-0.2) + (1 - 0.2x)(-1e^{-0.2x}) = e^{-0.2x}(0.2x - 2)$$

At $\bar{x} = 5$, $y'' = e^{-1}(1 - 2)$.   From Appendix III, $y'' = (0.36787)(-1) < 0$.   The function is at a maximum.

9.19. Redo Problem 9.17, given $y = \ln(x^2 - 8x + 20)$.

(a) $$y' = \frac{2x - 8}{x^2 - 8x + 20} = 0$$

Multiplying both sides by $(x^2 - 8x + 20)$, $2x - 8 = 0$ and $\bar{x} = 4$.

(b) $$y'' = \frac{(x^2 - 8x + 20)(2) - (2x - 8)(2x - 8)}{(x^2 - 8x + 20)^2}$$

At $\bar{x} = 4$, $y'' = \tfrac{8}{16} > 0$.   The function is at a minimum.

9.20. Redo Problem 9.17, given $y = \ln(2x^2 - 20x + 5)$.

(a) $$y' = \frac{4x - 20}{2x^2 - 20x + 5} = 0$$
$$4x - 20 = 0 \qquad \bar{x} = 5$$

(b) $$y'' = \frac{(2x^2 - 20x + 5)(4) - (4x - 20)(4x - 20)}{(2x^2 - 20x + 5)^2}$$

At $\bar{x} = 5$, $y'' = -180/2025 < 0$.   The function is at a maximum.

9.21. Given the function $z = \ln(2x^2 - 12x + y^2 - 10y)$,   (a) find the critical values and   (b) indicate whether the function is at a maximum or minimum.

(a) $$z_x = \frac{4x - 12}{2x^2 - 12x + y^2 - 10y} = 0 \qquad z_y = \frac{2y - 10}{2x^2 - 12x + y^2 - 10y} = 0$$
$$4x - 12 = 0 \qquad \bar{x} = 3 \qquad\qquad 2y - 10 = 0 \qquad \bar{y} = 5$$

(b)
$$z_{xx} = \frac{(2x^2 - 12x + y^2 - 10y)(4) - (4x - 12)(4x - 12)}{(2x^2 - 12x + y^2 - 10y)^2}$$

$$z_{yy} = \frac{(2x^2 - 12x + y^2 - 10y)(2) - (2y - 10)(2y - 10)}{(2x^2 - 12x + y^2 - 10y)^2}$$

Evaluated at $\bar{x} = 3$, $\bar{y} = 5$,

$$z_{xx} = \frac{(-43)(4) - 0}{(-43)^2} = \frac{-172}{1849} < 0 \qquad z_{yy} = \frac{(-43)(2) - 0}{(-43)^2} = \frac{-86}{1849} < 0$$

$$z_{xy} = \frac{-(4x - 12)(2y - 10)}{(2x^2 - 12x + y^2 - 10y)^2} = z_{yx}$$

At $\bar{x} = 3$, $\bar{y} = 5$, $z_{xy} = 0 = z_{yx}$. With $z_{xx}, z_{yy} < 0$ and $z_{xx}z_{yy} > (z_{xy})^2$, the function is at a maximum.

9.22.   Redo Problem 9.21, given $z = \ln(x^2 - 4x + 3y^2 - 6y)$.

(a)
$$z_x = \frac{2x - 4}{x^2 - 4x + 3y^2 - 6y} = 0 \qquad z_y = \frac{6y - 6}{x^2 - 4x + 3y^2 - 6y} = 0$$

$$2x - 4 = 0 \qquad \bar{x} = 2 \qquad 6y - 6 = 0 \qquad \bar{y} = 1$$

(b)
$$z_{xx} = \frac{(x^2 - 4x + 3y^2 - 6y)(2) - (2x - 4)(2x - 4)}{(x^2 - 4x + 3y^2 - 6y)^2}$$

$$z_{yy} = \frac{(x^2 - 4x + 3y^2 - 6y)(6) - (6y - 6)(6y - 6)}{(x^2 - 4x + 3y^2 - 6y)^2}$$

At $\bar{x} = 2$, $\bar{y} = 1$,

$$z_{xx} = \frac{(-7)(2) - 0}{(-7)^2} = -\frac{14}{49} < 0 \qquad z_{yy} = \frac{(-7)(6) - 0}{(-7)^2} = -\frac{42}{49} < 0$$

$$z_{xy} = \frac{-(2x - 4)(6y - 6)}{(x^2 - 4x + 3y^2 - 6y)^2} = z_{yx}$$

At $\bar{x} = 2$, $\bar{y} = 1$, $z_{xy} = 0 = z_{yx}$. With $z_{xx}, z_{yy} < 0$ and $z_{xx}z_{yy} > (z_{xy})^2$, the function is at a maximum.

9.23.   Redo Problem 9.21, given $z = e^{(3x^2 - 6x + y^2 - 8y)}$.

(a)
$$z_x = (6x - 6)e^{(3x^2 - 6x + y^2 - 8y)} = 0 \qquad z_y = (2y - 8)e^{(x^2 - 6x + y^2 - 8y)} = 0$$

$$6x - 6 = 0 \qquad \bar{x} = 1 \qquad 2y - 8 = 0 \qquad \bar{y} = 4$$

(b) Using the product rule,

$$z_{xx} = (6x - 6)(6x - 6)e^{(3x^2 - 6x + y^2 - 8y)} + e^{(3x^2 - 6x + y^2 - 8y)}(6)$$

$$z_{yy} = (2y - 8)(2y - 8)e^{(3x^2 - 6x + y^2 - 8y)} + e^{(3x^2 - 6x + y^2 - 8y)}(2)$$

Evaluated at $\bar{x} = 1$, $\bar{y} = 4$,

$$z_{xx} = 0 + 6e^{-19} > 0 \qquad z_{yy} = 0 + 2e^{-19} > 0$$

Then testing the cross partials,

$$z_{xy} = (6x - 6)(2y - 8)e^{(3x^2 - 6x + y^2 - 8y)} = z_{yx}$$

At $\bar{x} = 1$, $\bar{y} = 4$, $z_{xy} = 0 = z_{yx}$. The function is at a minimum since $z_{xx}, z_{yy} > 0$ and $z_{xx}z_{yy} > (z_{xy})^2$.

9.24.   Given $z = e^{(2x^2 - 12x - 2xy + y^2 - 4y)}$,   redo Problem 9.21.

(a)
$$z_x = (4x - 12 - 2y)e^{(2x^2 - 12x - 2xy + y^2 - 4y)} = 0$$

$$4x - 2y - 12 = 0 \qquad\qquad\qquad (9.10)$$

$$z_y = (-2x + 2y - 4)e^{(2x^2 - 12x - 2xy + y^2 - 4y)} = 0$$

$$-2x + 2y - 4 = 0 \tag{9.11}$$

Solving (9.10) and (9.11) simultaneously, $\bar{x} = 8$, $\bar{y} = 10$.

(b)
$$z_{xx} = (4x - 12 - 2y)(4x - 12 - 2y)e^{(2x^2 - 12x - 2xy + y^2 - 4y)} + e^{(2x^2 - 12x - 2xy + y^2 - 4y)}(4)$$

$$z_{yy} = (-2x + 2y - 4)(-2x + 2y - 4)e^{(2x^2 - 12x - 2xy + y^2 - 4y)} + e^{(2x^2 - 12x - 2xy + y^2 - 4y)}(2)$$

Evaluated at $\bar{x} = 8$, $\bar{y} = 10$,

$$z_{xx} = 0 + 4e^{-68} > 0 \qquad z_{yy} = 0 + 2e^{-68} > 0$$

Testing the mixed partials, by the product rule,

$$z_{xy} = (4x - 12 - 2y)(-2x + 2y - 4)e^{(2x^2 - 12x - 2xy + y^2 - 4y)} + e^{(2x^2 - 12x - 2xy + y^2 - 4y)}(-2) = z_{yx}$$

Evaluated at $\bar{x} = 8$, $\bar{y} = 10$, $z_{xy} = 0 - 2e^{-68} = z_{yx}$. Since $z_{xx}, z_{yy} > 0$ and $z_{xx}z_{yy} > (z_{xy})^2$,   the function is at a minimum.

9.25.   Given the demand function

$$P = 8.25\,e^{-0.02Q} \tag{9.12}$$

(a) determine the quantity and price at which total revenue will be maximized and   (b) test the second-order condition.

(a)
$$TR = PQ = (8.25\,e^{-0.02Q})Q$$

By the product rule,

$$\frac{dTR}{dQ} = (8.25\,e^{-0.02Q})(1) + Q(-0.02)(8.25\,e^{-0.02Q}) = 0$$

$$(8.25\,e^{-0.02Q})(1 - 0.02\,Q) = 0$$

Since $(8.25\,e^{-0.02Q}) \neq 0$ for any value of Q, $1 - 0.02\,Q = 0$; $\bar{q} = 50$.
   Substituting $\bar{Q} = 50$ in (9.12), $P = 8.25\,e^{-0.02(50)} = 8.25\,e^{-1}$. From   Appendix III, $P = 8.25(0.36787) = 3.03$.

(b)   By the product rule,

$$\frac{d^2TR}{dQ^2} = (8.25\,e^{-0.02Q})(-0.02) + (1 - 0.02\,Q)(-0.02)(8.25\,e^{-0.02Q}) = (-0.02)(8.25\,e^{-0.02Q})(2 - 0.02\,Q)$$

Evaluated   at $\bar{Q} = 50$, $d^2TR/dQ^2 = (-0.02)(8.25\,e^{-1})(1) = -0.165(0.36787) < 0$.   TR   is   at   a maximum.

9.26.   (a) Find the price and quantity that will maximize total revenue, given the demand function $P = 12.50\,e^{-0.005Q}$.   (b) Check the second-order condition.

(a)
$$TR = (12.50\,e^{-0.005Q})Q$$

$$\frac{dTR}{dQ} = (12.50\,e^{-0.005Q})(1) + Q(-0.005)(12.50\,e^{-0.005Q})$$

$$= (12.50\,e^{-0.005Q})(1 - 0.005\,Q) = 0$$

$$1 - 0.005\,Q = 0 \qquad \bar{Q} = 200$$

Thus,
$$P = 12.50\,e^{-0.005(200)} = 12.50\,e^{-1} = 12.50(0.36787) = 4.60$$

(b)
$$\frac{d^2TR}{dQ^2} = (12.50\,e^{-0.005Q})(-0.005) + (1 - 0.005\,Q)(-0.005)(12.50\,e^{-0.005Q})$$

$$= (-0.005)(12.50\,e^{-0.005Q})(2 - 0.005\,Q)$$

Evaluated at $\bar{Q} = 200$, $d^2TR/dQ^2 = (-0.005)(12.50\,e^{-1})(1) = -0.0625(0.36787) < 0$.   The function is maximized.

PARTIAL DERIVATIVES AND DIFFERENTIALS

9.27. Given $Q = 10K^{0.4}L^{0.6}$, (a) find the marginal productivity of capital and labor and (b) determine the effect on output of an additional unit of capital and labor at $K = 8$, $L = 20$.

(a) $\text{MP}_K = \dfrac{\partial Q}{\partial K} = 0.4(10)K^{-0.6}L^{0.6} = 4K^{-0.6}L^{0.6}$ $\text{MP}_L = \dfrac{\partial Q}{\partial L} = 0.6(10)K^{0.4}L^{-0.4} = 6K^{0.4}L^{-0.4}$

(b) $\Delta Q \cong (\partial Q/\partial K)\Delta K$. For a one-unit change in K, at $K = 8$, $L = 20$, $\Delta Q \cong 4K^{-0.6}L^{0.6} = 4(8)^{-0.6}(20)^{0.6}$. Using logs,

$$\log \Delta Q \cong \log 4 - 0.6 \log 8 + 0.6 \log 20 = 0.6021 - 0.6(0.9031) + 0.6(1.3010) = 0.8408$$

$$\Delta Q \cong \text{antilog } 0.8408 = 6.93$$

For a one-unit change in L, $\Delta Q \cong 6K^{0.4}L^{-0.4}$.

$$\log \Delta Q \cong \log 6 + 0.4 \log 8 - 0.4 \log 20 = 0.7782 + 0.4(0.9031) - 0.4(1.3010) = 0.6190$$

$$\Delta Q \cong \text{antilog } 0.6190 = 4.16$$

9.28. Redo Problem 9.27, given $Q = 12K^{0.3}L^{0.5}$ at $K = 10$, $L = 15$.

(a) $\text{MP}_K = 3.6 K^{-0.7}L^{0.5}$ $\text{MP}_L = 6K^{0.3}L^{-0.5}$

(b)   For a one-unit change in K, at $K = 10$, $L = 15$, $\Delta Q \cong 3.6 K^{-0.7}L^{0.5}$.

$$\log \Delta Q \cong 0.5563 - 0.7(1) + 0.5(1.1761) = 0.4444$$

$$\Delta Q \cong \text{antilog } 0.4444 = 2.78$$

For a one-unit change in L, $\Delta Q \cong 6K^{0.3}L^{-0.5}$.

$$\log \Delta Q \cong 0.7782 + 0.3(1) - 0.5(1.1761) = 0.4901$$

$$\Delta Q \cong \text{antilog } 0.4901 = 3.09$$

9.29. Given $Q = 4\sqrt{KL}$, find (a) MP_K and MP_L, and (b) determine the effect on Q of a one-unit change in K and L, when $K = 50$ and $L = 600$.

(a) $Q = 4\sqrt{KL} = 4(KL)^{1/2}$. By the chain rule,

$$\text{MP}_K = Q_K = 2(KL)^{-1/2}(L) = \frac{2L}{\sqrt{KL}}   \qquad \text{MP}_L = Q_L = 2(KL)^{-1/2}(K) = \frac{2K}{\sqrt{KL}}$$

(b)   For a one-unit change in K, at $K = 50$, $L = 600$, $\Delta Q \cong 2[50(600)]^{-1/2}(600)$.

$$\log \Delta Q \cong \log 2 - \tfrac{1}{2}(\log 50 + \log 600) + \log 600$$

$$\cong 0.3010 - \tfrac{1}{2}(1.6990 + 2.7782) + 2.7782 = 0.8406$$

$$\Delta Q \cong \text{antilog } 0.8406 = 6.93$$

For a one-unit change in L, $\Delta Q \cong 2[50(600)]^{-1/2}(50)$.

$$\log \Delta Q \cong \log 2 - \tfrac{1}{2}(\log 50 + \log 600) + \log 50$$

$$\cong 0.3010 - \tfrac{1}{2}(1.6990 + 2.7782) + 1.6990 = -0.2386$$

$$\Delta Q = \text{antilog } (-0.2386) = \text{antilog } (0.7614 - 1) = 0.58$$

9.30. Redo Problem 9.29, given $Q = 2\sqrt{KL}$, where $K = 100$ and $L = 1000$.

(a) $$Q = 2(KL)^{1/2}$$

$$\text{MP}_K = (KL)^{-1/2}(L) = \frac{L}{\sqrt{KL}}   \qquad \text{MP}_K = (KL)^{-1/2}(K) = \frac{K}{\sqrt{KL}}$$

(b) For a one-unit change in K, at $K = 100$, $L = 1000$, $\Delta Q \cong [100(1000)]^{-1/2}(1000)$.

$$\log \Delta Q \cong -\tfrac{1}{2}(2 + 3) + 3 = 0.5$$

$$\Delta Q \cong \text{antilog } 0.5 = 3.16$$

For a one-unit change in L, $\Delta Q \cong [100(1000)]^{-1/2}(100)$.

$$\log \Delta Q \cong -\tfrac{1}{2}(2 + 3) + 2 = -0.5$$

$$\Delta Q \cong \text{antilog } (-0.5) = \text{antilog } (0.5 - 1) = 0.316$$

9.31. A company's sales (s) have been found to depend on price (P), advertising (A), and the number of field representatives (r) it maintains.

$$s = (12{,}000 - 900P)A^{1/2}r^{1/2}$$

Find the change in sales associated with (a) hiring another field representative, (b) an extra \$1 of advertising, (c) a \$0.10 reduction in price, at $P = \$6$, $r = 49$, and $A = \$8100$.

(a) $$\Delta s \cong \frac{\partial s}{\partial r} \Delta r = \tfrac{1}{2}(12{,}000 - 900P)A^{1/2}r^{-1/2}\Delta r$$

$$= \tfrac{1}{2}[12{,}000 - 900(6)](8100)^{1/2}(49)^{-1/2}(1) = \tfrac{1}{2}(6600)(90)(\tfrac{1}{7}) = 42{,}429$$

(b) $$\Delta s \cong \frac{\partial s}{\partial A} \Delta A = \tfrac{1}{2}(12{,}000 - 900P)A^{-1/2}r^{1/2}\Delta A = \tfrac{1}{2}(6600)(\tfrac{1}{90})(7)(1) = 256.67$$

(c) $$\Delta s \cong \frac{\partial s}{\partial P} \Delta P = -900A^{1/2}r^{1/2}\Delta P = -900(90)(7)(-0.10) = 56{,}700$$

9.32. Given the sales function for a firm similar to the one in Problem 9.31: $s = (15{,}000 - 1000P)A^{2/3}r^{1/4}$, estimate the change in sales from (a) hiring an extra field representative, (b) a \$1 increase in advertising, and (c) a \$0.01 reduction in price, when $P = 4$, $A = \$6000$, and $r = 24$.

(a) $$\Delta s \cong \tfrac{1}{4}(15{,}000 - 1000P)A^{2/3}r^{-3/4}\Delta r$$

$$\cong \tfrac{1}{4}(11{,}000)(6000)^{2/3}(24)^{-3/4}(1)$$

$$\log \Delta s \cong \log \tfrac{1}{4} + \log (11{,}000) + \tfrac{2}{3}\log 6000 - \tfrac{3}{4}\log 24$$

$$\cong 0.3979 - 1 + 4.0414 + \tfrac{2}{3}(3.7782) - \tfrac{3}{4}(1.3802) = 4.9230$$

$$\Delta s \cong \text{antilog } 4.9230 \cong 83{,}760$$

(b) $$\Delta s \cong \tfrac{2}{3}(15{,}000 - 1000P)A^{-1/3}r^{1/4}\Delta A$$

$$\cong \tfrac{2}{3}(11{,}000)(6000)^{-1/3}(24)^{1/4}(1)$$

$$\log \Delta s \cong 0.8239 - 1 + 4.0414 - \tfrac{1}{3}(3.7782) + \tfrac{1}{4}(1.3802) = 2.9510$$

$$\Delta s \cong \text{antilog } 2.9510 = 893$$

(c) $$\Delta s \cong -1000A^{2/3}r^{1/4}\Delta P$$

$$\cong -1000(6000)^{2/3}(24)^{1/4}(-0.01) = 10(6000)^{2/3}(24)^{1/4}$$

$$\log \Delta s \cong 1 + \tfrac{2}{3}(3.7782) + \tfrac{1}{4}(1.3802) = 3.8639$$

$$\Delta s \cong \text{antilog } 3.8639 = 7310$$

OPTIMAL TIMING

9.33. Cut glass currently worth \$100 is appreciating in value according to the formula

$$V = 100e^{\sqrt{t}} = 100e^{t^{1/2}}$$

How long should the cut glass be kept to maximize its present value if under continuous compounding (a) $r = 0.08$ and (b) $r = 0.12$?

(a)   The present value (P) is $P = Ve^{-rt}$.   Substituting for V and r,

$$P = 100e^{\sqrt{t}}e^{-0.08t} = 100e^{\sqrt{t}-0.08t}$$

Converting to natural logs, $\ln P = \ln 100 + \ln e^{\sqrt{t}-0.08t} = \ln 100 + t^{1/2} - 0.08t$.   Taking the derivative, setting it equal to zero, and recalling that $\ln 100$ is a constant,

$$\frac{d}{dt}(\ln P) = \frac{1}{P}\frac{dP}{dt} = \tfrac{1}{2}t^{-1/2} - 0.08$$

$$\frac{dP}{dt} = P(\tfrac{1}{2}t^{-1/2} - 0.08) = 0 \qquad\qquad (9.13)$$

Since $P \neq 0$,

$$\tfrac{1}{2}t^{-1/2} = 0.08$$

$$t^{-1/2} = 0.16$$

$$t = (0.16)^{-2} = \frac{1}{0.0256} = 39.06$$

Testing the second-order condition, and using the product rule since $P = f(t)$,

$$\frac{d^2P}{dt^2} = P(-\tfrac{1}{4}t^{-3/2}) + (\tfrac{1}{2}t^{-1/2} - 0.08)\frac{dP}{dt}$$

Since $dP/dt = 0$ at the critical value,

$$\frac{d^2P}{dt^2} = \frac{-P}{4\sqrt{t^3}}$$

which is negative, since P and t must both be positive.   Thus, $t = 39.06$ maximizes the function.

(b)   If $r = 0.12$,   substituting 0.12 for 0.08 in (9.13) above,

$$\frac{dP}{dt} = P(\tfrac{1}{2}t^{-1/2} - 0.12) = 0$$

$$\tfrac{1}{2}t^{-1/2} = 0.12$$

$$t = (0.24)^{-2} = \frac{1}{0.0576} = 17.36$$

The second-order condition is unchanged.   Note that the higher the rate of discount r, the shorter the period of storage.

9.34.   Land bought for speculation is increasing in value according to the formula

$$V = 1000e^{\sqrt[3]{t}}$$

The discount rate under continuous compounding is 0.09.   How long should the land be held to maximize the present value?

$$P = 1000e^{\sqrt[3]{t}}e^{-0.09t} = 1000e^{\sqrt[3]{t}-0.09t}$$

Converting to natural logs, $\ln P = \ln 1000 + t^{1/3} - 0.09t$

Taking the derivative, $\dfrac{d}{dt}(\ln P) = \dfrac{1}{P}\dfrac{dP}{dt} = \dfrac{1}{3}t^{-2/3} - 0.09 = 0$

$$\frac{dP}{dt} = P(\tfrac{1}{3}t^{-2/3} - 0.09) = 0$$

$$\tfrac{1}{3}t^{-2/3} = 0.09 \qquad\qquad t = 0.27^{-3/2}$$

Using natural logs to solve for t,

$$\ln t = -\tfrac{3}{2}\ln 0.27 = -\tfrac{3}{2}(-1.30933) = 1.96400$$

$$t = \text{antilog}_e\, 1.96400 = 7.13 \text{ years}$$

The second-order condition, recalling $dP/dt = 0$ at the critical value, is

$$\frac{d^2P}{dt^2} = P(-\tfrac{2}{9}t^{-5/3}) + (\tfrac{1}{3}t^{-2/3} - 0.09)\frac{dP}{dt} = -\frac{2P}{9\sqrt[3]{t^5}} < 0$$

9.35. The art collection of a recently deceased painter has an estimated value of

$$V = 200{,}000(1.25)^{\sqrt[3]{t^2}}$$

How long should the executor of the estate hold on to the collection before putting it up for sale if the discount rate under continuous compounding is 6 percent?

Substituting the value of V in $P = Ve^{-rt}$,

$$P = 200{,}000(1.25)^{t^{2/3}}e^{-0.06t}$$

$$\ln P = \ln 200{,}000 + t^{2/3}\ln 1.25 - 0.06t$$

$$\frac{d}{dt}(\ln P) = \frac{1}{P}\frac{dP}{dt} = \frac{2}{3}\ln(1.25)t^{-1/3} - 0.06 = 0$$

$$\frac{dP}{dt} = P[\tfrac{2}{3}\ln(1.25)t^{-1/3} - 0.06] = 0$$

$$t^{-1/3} = \frac{3(0.06)}{2\ln 1.25} \qquad t = \left[\frac{0.18}{2(0.22314)}\right]^{-3} = (0.403)^{-3}$$

Using natural logs to solve for t,

$$\ln t = -3\ln 0.403 = -3(-0.90882) = 2.72646$$

$$t = \text{antilog}_e\, 2.72646 = 15.3 \text{ years}$$

9.36. The estimated value of a diamond bought for investment purposes is

$$V = 250{,}000(1.75)^{\sqrt[4]{t}}$$

If the discount rate under continuous compounding is 7 percent, how long should the diamond be held?

$$P = 250{,}000(1.75)^{t^{1/4}}e^{-0.07t}$$

$$\ln P = \ln 250{,}000 + t^{1/4}\ln(1.75) - 0.07t$$

$$\frac{d}{dt}(\ln P) = \frac{1}{P}\frac{dP}{dt} = \tfrac{1}{4}\ln(1.75)t^{-3/4} - 0.07 = 0$$

$$\frac{dP}{dt} = P[\tfrac{1}{4}\ln(1.75)t^{-3/4} - 0.07] = 0$$

$$\tfrac{1}{4}\ln(1.75)t^{-3/4} - 0.07 = 0 \qquad t = \left[\frac{0.28}{\ln 1.75}\right]^{-4/3} = (0.50)^{-4/3}$$

Using natural logs, $\ln t = -\tfrac{4}{3}\ln 0.50 = -\tfrac{4}{3}(-0.69315) = 0.92420$

$$t = \text{antilog}_e\, 0.92420 = 2.52 \text{ years}$$

CONSTRAINED OPTIMIZATION

9.37. Given a production function $q = K^{0.3}L^{0.5}$ subject to the constraint $6K + 2L = 384$, find the maximum output subject to the constraint.

$$Q = K^{0.3}L^{0.5} + \lambda(6K + 2L - 384)$$

$$Q_K = 0.3K^{-0.7}L^{0.5} + 6\lambda = 0 \qquad \lambda = -0.05K^{-0.7}L^{0.5}$$

$$Q_L = 0.5K^{0.3}L^{-0.5} + 2\lambda = 0 \qquad \lambda = -0.25K^{0.3}L^{-0.5}$$

$$Q_\lambda = 6K + 2L - 384 = 0$$

Equating λ's, $-0.05K^{-0.7}L^{0.5} = -0.25K^{0.3}L^{-0.5}$

Multiplying both sides by $K^{0.7}L^{0.5}$,

$$0.05L = 0.25K \qquad L = 5K$$

Substituting in the budget constraint, $\bar{K} = 24$ and $\bar{L} = 120$.
Second-order conditions are tested in Problem 12.32(b).

9.38. Given the production function $q = 10K^{0.7}L^{0.1}$ where $P_K = 28$ and $P_L = 10$, find the maximum output possible with an expenditure of \$4000.

$$Q = 10K^{0.7}L^{0.1} + \lambda(28K + 10L - 4000)$$

$$Q_K = 7K^{-0.3}L^{0.1} + 28\lambda = 0 \qquad \lambda = -0.25K^{-0.3}L^{0.1}$$

$$Q_L = 1K^{0.7}L^{-0.9} + 10\lambda = 0 \qquad \lambda = -0.1K^{0.7}L^{-0.9}$$

$$Q_\lambda = 28K + 10L - 4000 = 0$$

Equating λ's,
$$-0.25K^{-0.3}L^{0.1} = -0.1K^{0.7}L^{-0.9}$$

$$0.25L = 0.1K \qquad K = 2.5L$$

Substituting in the budget constraint, $\bar{L} = 50$ and $\bar{K} = 125$.
See Problem 12.32(c) for the second-order condition.

9.39. Maximize utility $u = x^{0.6}y^{0.25}$ subject to the budget constraint $8x + 5y = 680$.

$$U = x^{0.6}y^{0.25} + \lambda(8x + 5y - 680)$$

$$U_x = 0.6x^{-0.4}y^{0.25} + 8\lambda = 0 \qquad \lambda = -0.075x^{-0.4}y^{0.25}$$

$$U_y = 0.25x^{0.6}y^{-0.75} + 5\lambda = 0 \qquad \lambda = -0.05x^{0.6}y^{-0.75}$$

$$U_\lambda = 8x + 5y - 680 = 0$$

Equating λ's,
$$-0.075x^{-0.4}y^{0.25} = -0.05x^{0.6}y^{-0.75}$$

$$0.075y = 0.05x \qquad y = \tfrac{2}{3}x$$

Substituting in the budget constraint, $\bar{x} = 60$ and $\bar{y} = 40$.

9.40. Maximize $u = x^{0.8}y^{0.2}$ subject to $5x + 3y = 75$.

$$U = x^{0.8}y^{0.2} + \lambda(5x + 3y - 75)$$

$$U_x = 0.8x^{-0.2}y^{0.2} + 5\lambda = 0 \qquad \lambda = -0.16x^{-0.2}y^{0.2}$$

$$U_y = 0.2x^{0.8}y^{-0.8} + 3\lambda = 0 \qquad \lambda = -0.067x^{0.8}y^{-0.8}$$

$$U_\lambda = 5x + 3y - 75 = 0$$

Equating λ's,
$$-0.16x^{-0.2}y^{0.2} = -0.067x^{0.8}y^{-0.8}$$

$$0.16y = 0.067x \qquad y = 0.41875$$

Substituting in the budget constraint, $\bar{x} = 12$ and $\bar{y} = 5$.

GROWTH

9.41. The price of agricultural goods is going up by 4 percent each year; the quantity by 2 percent. What is the annual rate of growth of revenue (R) derived from the agricultural sector?

Converting the revenue formula $R = PQ$ to natural logs,

$$\ln R = \ln P + \ln Q$$

The derivative of the natural log function equals the instantaneous rate of growth (G) of the function (see Section 9.9). Thus,

$$G = \frac{d}{dt}(\ln R) = \frac{d}{dt}(\ln P) + \frac{d}{dt}(\ln Q)$$

But,
$$\frac{d}{dt}(\ln P) = \text{growth of } P = 4\% \qquad \frac{d}{dt}(\ln Q) = \text{growth of } Q = 2\%$$

Thus,
$$G = \frac{d}{dt}(\ln R) = 0.04 + 0.02 = 0.06$$

The rate of growth of a function involving a product is the sum of the rates of growth of the individual components.

9.42. A firm experiences a 10 percent increase in the use of inputs at a time when input costs are rising by 3 percent.   What is the rate of increase in total input costs?

$$C = PQ$$
$$\ln C = \ln P + \ln Q$$
$$G = \frac{d}{dt}(\ln C) = \frac{d}{dt}(\ln P) + \frac{d}{dt}(\ln Q) = 0.03 + 0.10 = 0.13$$

9.43. Employment opportunities (E) are increasing by 4 percent a year, population (P) by 2.5 percent.   What is the rate of growth of per capita employment (PCE)?

$$PCE = \frac{E}{P}$$
$$\ln PCE = \ln E - \ln P$$

Taking the derivative to find the growth rate,

$$G = \frac{d}{dt}(\ln PCE) = \frac{d}{dt}(\ln E) - \frac{d}{dt}(\ln P) = 0.04 - 0.025 = 0.015 = 1.5\%$$

The rate of growth of a function involving a quotient is the difference between the rate of growth of the numerator and denominator.

9.44. National income (Y) is increasing by 1.5 percent a year; population (P) by 2.5 percent a year.   What is the rate of growth of per capita income (PCY)?

$$PCY = \frac{Y}{P}$$
$$\ln PCY = \ln Y - \ln P$$
$$G = \frac{d}{dt}(\ln PCY) = \frac{d}{dt}(\ln Y) - \frac{d}{dt}(\ln P) = 0.015 - 0.025 = -0.01 = -1\%$$

Per capita income is falling by 1 percent a year.

9.45. A country exports two goods, copper (c) and bananas (b), where earnings in terms of million dollars are

$$c = c(t_0) = 4 \qquad b = b(t_0) = 1$$

If c grows by 10 percent and b by 20 percent, what is the rate of growth of export earnings (E)?

$$E = c + b$$
$$\ln E = \ln(c + b)$$
$$G = \frac{d}{dt}(\ln E) = \frac{d}{dt}\ln(c + b)$$

From the rules of derivatives in Section 9.4,

$$G_E = \frac{1}{c + b}[c'(t) + b'(t)] \tag{9.14}$$

From Section 9.9,

$$G_c = \frac{c'(t)}{c(t)} \qquad G_b = \frac{b'(t)}{b(t)}$$

Thus, $\qquad\qquad c'(t) = G_c\, c(t) \qquad b'(t) = G_b\, b(t)$

Substituting in (9.14), $\qquad G_E = \frac{1}{c + b}[G_c\, c(t) + G_b\, b(t)]$

Rearranging terms,
$$G_E = \frac{c(t)}{c+b} G_c + \frac{b(t)}{c+b} G_b$$

Then substituting the given values,

$$G_E = \frac{4}{4+1}(0.10) + \frac{1}{4+1}(0.20) = \tfrac{4}{5}(0.10) + \tfrac{1}{5}(0.20) = 0.12 \quad \text{or} \quad 12\%$$

The growth rate of a function involving the sum of other functions is the sum of the weighted average of the growth of the other functions.

9.46.   A company derives 70 percent of its revenue from bathing suits; 20 percent from bathing caps, and 10 percent from bathing slippers. If revenues from bathing suits increase by 15 percent, from caps 5 percent, and from slippers 4 percent, what is the rate of growth of total revenue?

$$G_R = 0.70(0.15) + 0.20(0.05) + 0.10(0.04) = 0.105 + 0.01 + 0.004 = 0.119 \quad \text{or} \quad 11.9\%$$

PROOFS

9.47.   Given the utility function $u = Ax^a y^b$, subject to the constraint $P_x x + P_y y = B$, prove that at the point of constrained utility maximization, the ratio of prices (P_y/P_x) must equal the ratio of marginal utilities $(\text{MU}_y/\text{MU}_x)$.

$$U = Ax^a y^b + \lambda(P_x x + P_y y - B)$$
$$U_x = aAx^{a-1}y^b + \lambda P_x = 0 \tag{9.15}$$
$$U_y = bAx^a y^{b-1} + \lambda P_y = 0 \tag{9.16}$$
$$U_\lambda = P_x x + P_y y - B = 0$$

where in (9.15) $aAx^{a-1}y^b = u_x = \text{MU}_x$, and in (9.16) $bAx^a y^{b-1} = u_y = \text{MU}_y$. Solving for $\bar{\lambda}$,

from (9.15),
$$\bar{\lambda} = \frac{-aAx^{a-1}y^b}{P_x} = -\frac{\text{MU}_x}{P_x}$$

from (9.16),
$$\bar{\lambda} = \frac{-bAx^a y^{b-1}}{P_y} = -\frac{\text{MU}_y}{P_y}$$

Equating $\bar{\lambda}$'s,
$$-\frac{\text{MU}_x}{P_x} = -\frac{\text{MU}_y}{P_y} \qquad \frac{P_y}{P_x} = \frac{\text{MU}_y}{\text{MU}_x} \qquad \text{Q.E.D.}$$

9.48.   Given a generalized Cobb–Douglas production function $q = AK^\alpha L^\beta$ subject to a budget constraint $P_K K + P_L L = B$, prove that for constrained optimization the least-cost input combination is

$$\frac{\bar{L}}{\bar{K}} = \frac{\beta P_K}{\alpha P_L}$$

The Lagrangian function is
$$Q = AK^\alpha L^\beta + \lambda(P_K K + P_L L - B)$$

The first-order conditions are
$$Q_K = \alpha AK^{\alpha-1}L^\beta + \lambda P_K = 0 \tag{9.17}$$
$$Q_L = \beta AK^\alpha L^{\beta-1} + \lambda P_L = 0 \tag{9.18}$$
$$Q_\lambda = P_K K + P_L L - B = 0 \tag{9.19}$$

From (9.17) and (9.18),
$$\frac{-\alpha AK^{\alpha-1}L^\beta}{P_K} = \lambda = -\frac{\beta AK^\alpha L^{\beta-1}}{P_L}$$

Canceling the mutual negative signs and rearranging terms,

$$\frac{\alpha A K^{\alpha-1} L^{\beta}}{\beta A K^{\alpha} L^{\beta-1}} = \frac{P_K}{P_L}$$

where $K^{\alpha-1} = K^{\alpha}/K$ and $1/L^{\beta-1} = L/L^{\beta}$.

Thus,
$$\frac{\alpha L}{\beta K} = \frac{P_K}{P_L}$$

$$\frac{\bar{L}}{\bar{K}} = \frac{\beta P_K}{\alpha P_L} \qquad \text{Q.E.D.} \qquad\qquad (9.20)$$

9.49. Equation (9.20) gives the least-cost input combination for a generalized Cobb–Douglas production function. The *elasticity of substitution* σ is defined as the relative change in the least-cost input combination $(\bar{L}/\bar{K})$ brought about by a relative change in the input-price ratio (P_K/P_L).

$$\sigma = \frac{\dfrac{d(\bar{L}/\bar{K})}{\bar{L}/\bar{K}}}{\dfrac{d(P_K/P_L)}{P_K/P_L}} = \frac{\dfrac{d(\bar{L}/\bar{K})}{d(P_K/P_L)}}{\dfrac{\bar{L}/\bar{K}}{P_K/P_L}} \qquad\qquad (9.21)$$

where $0 \leq \sigma \leq \infty$. If $\sigma = 0$, there is no substitutability and the two inputs are complements that must be used together in fixed proportions. If $\sigma = \infty$, the two goods are perfect substitutes.

Prove that the elasticity of any generalized Cobb–Douglas function is unitary, i.e. $\sigma = 1$.

Since α and β are constants in (9.20) and P_K and P_L are independent variables, $(\bar{L}/\bar{K})$ can be considered a function of (P_K/P_L). Hence $\sigma =$ the marginal function divided by the average function, as seen in the second ratio of (9.21). Finding the marginal function of (9.20),

$$\frac{d(\bar{L}/\bar{K})}{d(P_K/P_L)} = \frac{\beta}{\alpha}$$

Dividing both sides of (9.20) by P_K/P_L, the average function is

$$\frac{\bar{L}/\bar{K}}{P_K/P_L} = \frac{\beta}{\alpha}$$

Hence,
$$\sigma = \frac{\dfrac{d(L/K)}{d(P_K/P_L)}}{\dfrac{\bar{L}/\bar{K}}{P_K/P_L}} = \frac{\beta/\alpha}{\beta/\alpha} = 1 \qquad \text{Q.E.D.}$$

9.50. Use the least-cost input combination for a Cobb–Douglas function given in (9.20) to check the answer to the problem in Section 9.11, where $q = K^{0.4}L^{0.5}$, $P_K = 3$, and $P_L = 4$.

Since $\alpha = 0.4$, $\beta = 0.5$, from (9.20),

$$\frac{\bar{L}}{\bar{K}} = \frac{0.5(3)}{0.4(4)} = \frac{1.5}{1.6}$$

Labor and capital must be used in the ratio of 15/16. See Section 9.11.

9.51. A *constant elasticity of substitution* (CES) production function is one in which the elasticity of substitution σ is constant but not necessarily equal to one. The equation for a CES production function is

$$Q = A[\alpha K^{-\beta} + (1-\alpha)L^{-\beta}]^{-1/\beta} \qquad\qquad (9.22)$$

where $A > 0$, $0 < \alpha < 1$, and $\beta > -1$. Keeping in mind that the ratio of prices must equal the ratio of marginal products for optimization (see Problem 9.47), (a) prove that the elasticity of substitution is constant and (b) demonstrate the range that σ may assume.

(a) First-order conditions require that

$$\frac{\partial Q/\partial L}{\partial Q/\partial K} = \frac{P_L}{P_K} \tag{9.23}$$

Using the chain rule to take the first-order partials of (9.22),

$$\frac{\partial Q}{\partial L} = -\frac{1}{\beta} A[\alpha K^{-\beta} + (1-\alpha)L^{-\beta}]^{-(1/\beta)-1}(-\beta)(1-\alpha)L^{-\beta-1}$$

Canceling $(-\beta)$s, rearranging $(1-\alpha)$, and adding the exponents $-(1/\beta) - 1$,

$$\frac{\partial Q}{\partial L} = (1-\alpha)A[\alpha K^{-\beta} + (1-\alpha)L^{-\beta}]^{-(1+\beta)/\beta}L^{-(1+\beta)}$$

Substituting $A^{1+\beta}/A^\beta = A$ for A,

$$\frac{\partial Q}{\partial L} = (1-\alpha)\frac{A^{1+\beta}}{A^\beta}[\alpha K^{-\beta} + (1-\alpha)L^{-\beta}]^{-(1+\beta)/\beta}L^{-(1+\beta)}$$

From (9.22), $A^{1+\beta}[\alpha K^{-\beta} + (1-\alpha)L^{-\beta}]^{-(1+\beta)/\beta} = Q^{1+\beta}$ and $L^{-(1+\beta)} = 1/L^{1+\beta}$. Thus,

$$\frac{\partial Q}{\partial L} = \frac{1-\alpha}{A^\beta}\left(\frac{Q}{L}\right)^{1+\beta} \tag{9.24}$$

Similarly,

$$\frac{\partial Q}{\partial K} = \frac{\alpha}{A^\beta}\left(\frac{Q}{K}\right)^{1+\beta} \tag{9.25}$$

Substituting (9.24) and (9.25) in (9.23), which leads to the cancellation of A^β and Q,

$$\frac{1-\alpha}{\alpha}\left(\frac{K}{L}\right)^{1+\beta} = \frac{P_L}{P_K}$$

$$\left(\frac{K}{L}\right)^{1+\beta} = \frac{\alpha}{1-\alpha}\left(\frac{P_L}{P_K}\right)$$

$$\frac{\bar{K}}{\bar{L}} = \left(\frac{\alpha}{1-\alpha}\right)^{1/(1+\beta)}\left(\frac{P_L}{P_K}\right)^{1/(1+\beta)} \tag{9.26}$$

Since α and β are constants, by considering $(\bar{K}/\bar{L})$ a function of (P_L/P_K), as in Problem 9.49, we can find the elasticity of substitution as the ratio of the marginal and average functions. Simplifying first by letting

$$h = \left(\frac{\alpha}{1-\alpha}\right)^{1/(1+\beta)}$$

$$\frac{\bar{K}}{\bar{L}} = h\left(\frac{P_L}{P_K}\right)^{1/(1+\beta)} \tag{9.27}$$

The marginal function is

$$\frac{d(\bar{K}/\bar{L})}{d(P_L/P_K)} = \frac{h}{1+\beta}\left(\frac{P_L}{P_K}\right)^{1/(1+\beta)-1} \tag{9.28}$$

and the average function is

$$\frac{\bar{K}/\bar{L}}{P_L/P_K} = \frac{h(P_L/P_K)^{1/(1+\beta)}}{P_L/P_K} = h\left(\frac{P_L}{P_K}\right)^{1/(1+\beta)-1} \tag{9.29}$$

By dividing the marginal function in (9.28) by the average function in (9.29), the elasticity of substitution is $\sigma = 1/(1+\beta)$ which is constant, since β is a given parameter.

(b) If $-1 < \beta < 0$, $\sigma > 1$. If $\beta = 0$, $\sigma = 1$. If $0 < \beta < \infty$, $\sigma < 1$.

9.52. Prove that the CES production function is homogeneous of degree one.

From (9.22), $Q = A[\alpha K^{-\beta} + (1 - \alpha)L^{-\beta}]^{-1/\beta}$

Multiplying inputs K and L by k, from Section 8.7,

$$f(kK,kL) = A[\alpha(kK)^{-\beta} + (1 - \alpha)(kL)^{-\beta}]^{-1/\beta}$$
$$= A\{k^{-\beta}[\alpha K^{-\beta} + (1 - \alpha)L^{-\beta}]\}^{-1/\beta}$$
$$= A(k^{-\beta})^{-1/\beta}[\alpha K^{-\beta} + (1 - \alpha)L^{-\beta}]^{-1/\beta}$$
$$= kA[\alpha K^{-\beta} + (1 - \alpha)L^{-\beta}]^{-1/\beta} = kQ   \text{Q.E.D.}$$

9.53. Find the elasticity of substitution for the CES production function, $Q = 75(0.3 K^{-0.4} + 0.7 L^{-0.4})^{-2.5}$.

$$\sigma = \frac{1}{1 + \beta}$$

where $\beta = 0.4$. Thus, $\sigma = 1/(1 + 0.4) = 0.71$.

9.54. Optimize the CES production function $q = 75(0.3 K^{-0.4} + 0.7 L^{-0.4})^{-2.5}$ subject to the constraint $4K + 3L = 120$.

$$Q = 75(0.3 K^{-0.4} + 0.7 L^{-0.4})^{-2.5} + \lambda(4K + 3L - 120)$$

By the chain rule,

$$Q_K = -187.5(0.3 K^{-0.4} + 0.7 L^{-0.4})^{-3.5}(-0.12 K^{-1.4}) + 4\lambda$$
$$= 22.5 K^{-1.4}(0.3 K^{-0.4} + 0.7 L^{-0.4})^{-3.5} + 4\lambda = 0 \tag{9.30}$$
$$Q_L = -187.5(0.3 K^{-0.4} + 0.7 L^{-0.4})^{-3.5}(-0.28 L^{-1.4}) + 3\lambda$$
$$= 52.5 L^{-1.4}(0.3 K^{-0.4} + 0.7 L^{-0.4})^{-3.5} + 3\lambda = 0 \tag{9.31}$$
$$Q_\lambda = 4K + 3L - 120 = 0 \tag{9.32}$$

Solving for λ and equating λ's in (9.30) and (9.31),

$$-5.625 K^{-1.4} = -17.5 L^{-1.4}$$
$$K^{-1.4} = 3.11 L^{-1.4}$$
$$K = (3.11)^{-1/1.4}L = (3.11)^{-0.71}L$$
$$K = 0.45 L$$

Substituting in (9.32),

$$4(0.45 L) + 3L = 120   \bar{L} = 25$$

Thus, $K = 11.25$.

9.55. Use the optional $\bar{K}/\bar{L}$ ratio in (9.26) to check the answer to Problem 9.54.

From (9.26), $$\frac{\bar{K}}{\bar{L}} = \left(\frac{\alpha}{1 - \alpha} \frac{P_L}{P_K}\right)^{1/(1+\beta)}$$

Substituting $\alpha = 0.3$, $1 - \alpha = 0.7$, and $\beta = 0.4$,

$$\frac{\bar{K}}{\bar{L}} = \left(\frac{0.3}{0.7} \frac{3}{4}\right)^{1/1.4} = \left(\frac{0.9}{2.8}\right)^{0.71} = (0.32)^{0.71} \cong 0.45$$

With $\bar{K} = 11.25$ and $\bar{L} = 25$, $\bar{K}/\bar{L} = 11.25/25 = 0.45$.

9.56. Optimize the CES production function $q = 80(0.4 K^{-0.25} + 0.6 L^{-0.25})^{-4}$ subject to the constraint $5K + 2L = 150$.

$$Q = 80(0.4 K^{-0.25} + 0.6 L^{-0.25})^{-4} + \lambda(5K + 2L - 150)$$

$$Q_K = -320(0.4 K^{-0.25} + 0.6 L^{-0.25})^{-5}(-0.1 K^{-1.25}) + 5\lambda$$

$$= 32K^{-1.25}(0.4 K^{-0.25} + 0.6 L^{-0.25})^{-5} + 5\lambda = 0 \tag{9.33}$$

$$Q_L = -320(0.4 K^{-0.25} + 0.6 L^{-0.25})^{-5}(-0.15 L^{-1.25}) + 2\lambda$$

$$= 48L^{-1.25}(0.4 K^{-0.25} + 0.6 L^{-0.25})^{-5} + 2\lambda = 0 \tag{9.34}$$

$$Q_\lambda = 5K + 2L - 150 = 0 \tag{9.35}$$

Solving for and equating λ's in (9.33) and (9.34),

$$-6.4 K^{-1.25} = -24L^{-1.25}$$

$$K^{-1.25} = 3.75 L^{-1.25}$$

$$K = (3.75)^{-1/1.25} L = (3.75)^{-0.8} L \qquad K = 0.35 L$$

Substituting in (9.35),

$$5(0.35 L) + 2L = 150 \qquad \bar{L} = 40$$

Thus, $\bar{K} = 14$.

9.57. Use (9.26) to check the answer to Problem 9.56.

Substituting $\alpha = 0.4$, $1 - \alpha = 0.6$, and $\beta = 0.25$ in (9.26),

$$\frac{\bar{K}}{\bar{L}} = \left(\frac{0.4}{0.6}\frac{2}{5}\right)^{1/1.25} = \left(\frac{0.8}{3}\right)^{0.8} \cong 0.35$$

Substituting $\bar{K} = 14$ and $\bar{L} = 40$, $\frac{14}{40} = 0.35$.

9.58. Find the elasticity of substitution in Problem 9.56.

$$\sigma = \frac{1}{1+\beta} = \frac{1}{1+0.25} = 0.8$$

9.59. Given the CES production function $q = 100(0.2 K^{0.5} + 0.8 L^{0.5})^2$ subject to the constraint $10K + 4L = 4100$. Find (a) the critical values, and (b) the elasticity of substitution. (c) Check your answer to part (a).

(a)
$$Q = 100(0.2 K^{0.5} + 0.8 L^{0.5})^2 + \lambda(10K + 4L - 4100)$$

$$Q_K = 200(0.2 K^{0.5} + 0.8 L^{0.5})(0.1 K^{-0.5}) + 10\lambda$$

$$= 20K^{-0.5}(0.2 K^{0.5} + 0.8 L^{0.5}) + 10\lambda = 0 \tag{9.36}$$

$$Q_L = 200(0.2 K^{0.5} + 0.8 L^{0.5})(0.4 L^{-0.5}) + 4\lambda$$

$$= 80L^{-0.5}(0.2 K^{0.5} + 0.8 L^{0.5}) + 4\lambda = 0 \tag{9.37}$$

$$Q_\lambda = 10K + 4L - 4100 = 0 \tag{9.38}$$

Solving for and equating λ's in (9.36) and (9.37),

$$-2K^{-0.5} = -20L^{-0.5} \qquad K^{-0.5} = 10L^{-0.5}$$

$$K = (10)^{-1/0.5} L = (10)^{-2} L = 0.01 L$$

Substituting in (9.38), $10(0.01 L) + 4L = 4100$, $\bar{L} = 1000$, and $\bar{K} = 10$.

(b)
$$\sigma = \frac{1}{1+\beta} = \frac{1}{1-0.5} = 2$$

(c)   With $\alpha = 0.2$, $1 - \alpha = 0.8$, and $\beta = -0.5$,

$$\frac{\bar{K}}{\bar{L}} = \left(\frac{0.2}{0.8}\frac{4}{10}\right)^{1/(1-0.5)} = \left(\frac{0.8}{8}\right)^2 = (0.1)^2 = 0.01$$

Substituting $\bar{K} = 10$ and $\bar{L} = 1000$, $\frac{10}{1000} = 0.01$.

9.60.   (a) Use the elasticity of substitution found in Problem 9.58 to estimate the effect on the least-cost $(\bar{K}/\bar{L})$ ratio in Problem 9.56 if P_L increases by 25 percent.   (b) Check your answer by substituting the new P_L in (9.26).

(a)   The elasticity of substitution measures the relative change in the $(\bar{K}/\bar{L})$ ratio brought about by a relative change in the price ratio (P_L/P_K).   If P_L increases by 25 percent, $P_L = 1.25(2) = 2.5$. Thus, $P_L/P_K = 2.5/5 = 0.5$ vs. $\frac{2}{5} = 0.4$ in Problem 9.56.

The percentage increase in the price ratio, therefore, is $(0.5 - 0.4)/0.4 = 0.25$.   With the elasticity of substitution $= 0.8$ from Problem 9.58, the expected percentage change in the $(\bar{K}/\bar{L})$ ratio is

$$\frac{\Delta(\bar{K}/\bar{L})}{\bar{K}/\bar{L}} \cong 0.8(0.25) = 0.2 \qquad \text{or} \qquad 20\%$$

With $(\bar{K}/\bar{L})_1 = 0.35$, $(\bar{K}/\bar{L})_2 \cong 1.2(0.35) \cong 0.42$.

(b)   Substituting $P_L = 2.5$ in (9.26)

$$\frac{\bar{K}}{\bar{L}} = \left(\frac{0.4}{0.6}\frac{2.5}{5}\right)^{0.8} = \left(\frac{1}{3}\right)^{0.8} \cong 0.42$$

9.61.   (a) Use the elasticity of substitution to estimate the new $(\bar{K}/\bar{L})$ ratio, if the price of capital decreases by 20 percent.   Assume the initial data of Problem 9.56.   (b) Check your answer.

(a)   If P_K decreases by 20 percent, $P_K = 0.8(5) = 4$.   Thus, $P_L/P_K = \frac{2}{4} = 0.5$ which is a 25 percent increase in the (P_L/P_K) ratio, as seen above.   Therefore,

$$\frac{\Delta(\bar{K}/\bar{L})}{\bar{K}/\bar{L}} = 0.8(0.25) = 0.2 \qquad \text{or} \qquad 20\%$$

and $(\bar{K}/\bar{L})_2 \cong 1.2(0.35) = 0.42$.

(b)   Substituting $P_K = 4$ in (9.26),

$$\frac{\bar{K}}{\bar{L}} = \left(\frac{0.4}{0.6}\frac{2}{4}\right)^{0.8} = \left(\frac{0.8}{2.4}\right)^{0.8} = 0.42$$

9.62.   (a) If the price of labor decreases by 10 percent in Problem 9.59, use the elasticity of substitution to estimate the effect on the least-cost $(\bar{K}/\bar{L})$ ratio.   (b) Check your answer.

(a)   If P_L decreases by 10 percent, $P_L = 0.9(4) = 3.6$,   and the (P_L/P_K) ratio also decreases by 10 percent.   With a 10 percent decrease in (P_L/P_K) and an elasticity of substitution $= 2$,

$$\frac{\Delta(\bar{K}/\bar{L})}{\bar{K}/\bar{L}} \cong 2(-0.10) = -0.20 \qquad \text{or} \qquad -20\%$$

With the old $\bar{K}/\bar{L} = 0.01$, $(\bar{K}/\bar{L})_2 \cong (1 - 0.2)(0.01) = 0.8(0.01) = 0.008$.

(b)   Substituting $P_L = 3.6$ in (9.26),

$$\frac{\bar{K}}{\bar{L}} = \left(\frac{0.2}{0.8}\frac{3.6}{10}\right)^2 = \left(\frac{0.72}{8}\right)^2 = (0.09)^2 = 0.0081$$

Chapter 10

The Fundamentals of
Matrix or Linear Algebra

10.1 THE ROLE OF MATRIX ALGEBRA

Matrix algebra (1) permits expression of a complicated system of equations in a succinct, simplified way, (2) provides a shorthand method to determine whether a solution exists before it is attempted, and (3) furnishes the means of solving the equation system. Matrix algebra, however, can be applied *only* to systems of linear equations. Since many economic relationships can be approximated by linear equations and others can be converted to linear relationships, this limitation generally presents no serious problem.

Example 1. For a company with several different outlets selling several different products, a matrix provides a concise way of keeping track of stock.

Outlet	Skis	Poles	Bindings	Outfits
1	120	110	90	150
2	200	180	210	110
3	175	190	160	80
4	140	170	180	140

By reading across a row of the matrix, the firm can determine the level of stock in any one of its outlets. By reading down a column of the matrix, the firm can determine the stock of any one line of its products.

Example 2. A nonlinear function, such as a generalized Cobb–Douglas production function

$$Q = AK^\alpha L^\beta$$

can easily be converted to a linear function by taking the logarithm of each side, as follows:

$$\log Q = \log A + \alpha \log K + \beta \log L$$

In similar fashion, exponential functions and other power functions can easily be converted to linear functions, and then handled by matrix algebra.

10.2 DEFINITIONS AND TERMS

A *matrix* is a rectangular array of numbers, parameters, or variables, each of which has a carefully ordered place within the matrix. The numbers (parameters, or variables) are referred to as *elements* of the matrix. The numbers in a horizontal line are called *rows*; the numbers in a vertical line are called *columns*. The number of rows (m) and columns (n) define the *dimensions* of the matrix ($m \times n$), which is read m by n. The row number always precedes the column number. In a *square matrix*, the number of rows equals the number of columns (i.e. $m = n$). If the matrix is composed of a single column, such that its dimensions are $m \times 1$, it is a *column vector*; if a matrix is a single row, with dimensions $1 \times n$, it is a *row vector*. A matrix which converts the rows of A into columns and the columns of A into rows is called the *transpose* of A and is designated by A' (or A^T).

Example 3.   Given

$$A = \begin{bmatrix} a_{11} & a_{12} & a_{13} \\ a_{21} & a_{22} & a_{23} \\ a_{31} & a_{32} & a_{33} \end{bmatrix}_{(3\times3)} \qquad B = \begin{bmatrix} 3 & 9 & 8 \\ 4 & 2 & 7 \end{bmatrix}_{(2\times3)} \qquad C = \begin{bmatrix} 7 \\ 4 \\ 5 \end{bmatrix}_{(3\times1)} \qquad D = [3 \quad 0 \quad 1]_{(1\times3)}$$

A is a general matrix composed of $3 \times 3 = 9$ elements, arranged in 3 rows and 3 columns.   It is thus a square matrix.   Note that no punctuation separates the elements of a matrix.   The elements all have double subscripts; the first identifies the row in which the element appears and the second identifies the column.   Positioning is precise within a matrix.   Thus, a_{23} is the element which appears in the second row, third column; a_{32} is the element which appears in the third row, second column.   Since row always precedes column in matrix notation, it might be helpful to think of the subscripts in terms of RC or some other mnemonic device.

B is a 2×3 matrix.   Its b_{12} element is 9, its b_{21} element is 4. C is a column vector with dimensions (3×1). D is a row vector with dimensions (1×3).

The transpose of A is

$$A' = \begin{bmatrix} a_{11} & a_{21} & a_{31} \\ a_{12} & a_{22} & a_{32} \\ a_{13} & a_{23} & a_{33} \end{bmatrix}$$

and the transpose of C is

$$C' = [7 \quad 4 \quad 5]$$

10.3   ADDITION AND SUBTRACTION OF MATRICES

Addition (and subtraction) of two matrices $A + B$ (or $A - B$) requires that the matrices be of equal dimensions.   Each element of one matrix is then added to (subtracted from) the corresponding element of the other matrix.   Thus, a_{11} in A will be added to (subtracted from) b_{11} in B; a_{12} to b_{12}, etc.

Example 4.   The sum $A + B$ is calculated below, given matrices A and B:

$$A = \begin{bmatrix} 8 & 9 & 7 \\ 3 & 6 & 2 \\ 4 & 5 & 10 \end{bmatrix}_{(3\times3)} \quad B = \begin{bmatrix} 1 & 3 & 6 \\ 5 & 2 & 4 \\ 7 & 9 & 2 \end{bmatrix}_{(3\times3)} \quad A + B = \begin{bmatrix} 8+1 & 9+3 & 7+6 \\ 3+5 & 6+2 & 2+4 \\ 4+7 & 5+9 & 10+2 \end{bmatrix}_{(3\times3)} = \begin{bmatrix} 9 & 12 & 13 \\ 8 & 8 & 6 \\ 11 & 14 & 12 \end{bmatrix}_{(3\times3)}$$

The difference $C - D$, given matrices C and D, is found as follows:

$$C = \begin{bmatrix} 4 & 9 \\ 2 & 6 \end{bmatrix}_{(2\times2)} \qquad D = \begin{bmatrix} 1 & 7 \\ 5 & 4 \end{bmatrix}_{(2\times2)} \qquad C - D = \begin{bmatrix} 4-1 & 9-7 \\ 2-5 & 6-4 \end{bmatrix}_{(2\times2)} = \begin{bmatrix} 3 & 2 \\ -3 & 2 \end{bmatrix}_{(2\times2)}$$

Example 5.   Suppose that deliveries D are made to the outlets of the firm in Example 1.   What is the new level of stock?

$$D = \begin{bmatrix} 40 & 20 & 50 & 10 \\ 25 & 30 & 10 & 60 \\ 15 & 0 & 40 & 70 \\ 60 & 40 & 10 & 50 \end{bmatrix}$$

To find the new level of stock, label the initial matrix S, and solve for $S + D$.   Adding the corresponding elements of each matrix,

$$S + D = \begin{bmatrix} 120+40 & 110+20 & 90+50 & 150+10 \\ 200+25 & 180+30 & 210+10 & 110+60 \\ 175+15 & 190+0 & 160+40 & 80+70 \\ 140+60 & 170+40 & 180+10 & 140+50 \end{bmatrix} = \begin{bmatrix} 160 & 130 & 140 & 160 \\ 225 & 210 & 220 & 170 \\ 190 & 190 & 200 & 150 \\ 200 & 210 & 190 & 190 \end{bmatrix}$$

10.4   SCALAR MULTIPLICATION

In matrix algebra, a simple number such as 12, -2, 0.07, is called a *scalar*. Multiplication of a matrix by a number or scalar involves multiplication of every element of the matrix by the number. The process is called *scalar multiplication* because it scales the matrix up or down according to the size of the number.

Example 6. The result of scalar multiplication kA, given $k = 8$ and

$$A = \begin{bmatrix} 6 & 9 \\ 2 & 7 \\ 8 & 4 \end{bmatrix}_{(3 \times 2)}$$

is shown below.

$$kA = \begin{bmatrix} 8(6) & 8(9) \\ 8(2) & 8(7) \\ 8(8) & 8(4) \end{bmatrix}_{(3 \times 2)} = \begin{bmatrix} 48 & 72 \\ 16 & 56 \\ 64 & 32 \end{bmatrix}_{(3 \times 2)}$$

10.5   VECTOR MULTIPLICATION

Multiplication of a row vector (A) by a column vector (B) requires as a precondition that each vector have precisely the same number of elements. The product is then found by multiplying the individual elements of the row vector by their corresponding elements in the column vector, and summing up the products:

$$AB = (a_{11} \times b_{11}) + (a_{12} \times b_{21}) + (a_{13} \times b_{31}) \qquad \text{etc.}$$

The product of row-column multiplication will thus be a single number or scalar. Row-column vector multiplication is of paramount importance. It serves as the basis for all matrix multiplication.

Example 7. The product AB of the row vector A and the column vector B, given

$$A = \begin{bmatrix} 4 & 7 & 2 & 9 \end{bmatrix}_{(1 \times 4)} \qquad B = \begin{bmatrix} 12 \\ 1 \\ 5 \\ 6 \end{bmatrix}_{(4 \times 1)}$$

is calculated as follows.

$$AB = 4(12) + 7(1) + 2(5) + 9(6) = 48 + 7 + 10 + 54 = 119$$

The product of the following vectors:

$$C = \begin{bmatrix} 3 & 6 & 8 \end{bmatrix}_{(1 \times 3)} \qquad D = \begin{bmatrix} 2 \\ 4 \\ 5 \end{bmatrix}_{(3 \times 1)}$$

is $CD = (3 \times 2) + (6 \times 4) + (8 \times 5) = 6 + 24 + 40 = 70$.

Note that since each set of vectors above has the same number of elements, multiplication is possible.

Reversing the order of multiplication in either of the above and having column-row vector multiplication $(BA$ or $DC)$ will give a totally different answer. See Problem 10.36.

10.6   MULTIPLICATION OF MATRICES

Multiplication of two matrices with dimensions $(m \times n)_1$ and $(m \times n)_2$ requires that the matrices be *conformable*, i.e. that $n_1 = m_2$, or the number of columns in 1, the *lead matrix*, equals the number of rows in 2, the *lag matrix*. Each row vector in the lead matrix is then multiplied by each column vector of the lag matrix, according to the rules for multiplying row and column vectors discussed in Section 10.5. The row-column products are then used as elements in the formation of the product matrix, such that each element c_{ij} of the product matrix C is a scalar derived from the multiplication of the *i*th row of the lead matrix and the *j*th column of the lag matrix. The row-column products are called *inner products*.

Example 8. Given

$$A = \begin{bmatrix} 3 & 6 & 7 \\ 12 & 9 & 11 \end{bmatrix}_{(2\times3)} \qquad B = \begin{bmatrix} 6 & 12 \\ 5 & 10 \\ 13 & 2 \end{bmatrix}_{(3\times2)} \qquad C = \begin{bmatrix} 1 & 7 & 8 \\ 2 & 4 & 3 \end{bmatrix}_{(2\times3)}$$

A shorthand test for conformability, which should be applied before undertaking any matrix multiplication, is to place the two sets of dimensions in the order in which the matrices are to be multiplied, then mentally circle the last number of the first set and the first number of the second set. If they are equal, the two matrices will be conformable for multiplication in the given order, and the numbers outside the circle will provide, in proper order, the dimensions of the resulting product matrix. Thus, for AB,

$$(2 \times \textcircled{3}) = (\textcircled{3} \times 2)$$
$$(2 \times 2)$$

The matrices are conformable and the dimensions of the product matrix AB will be (2×2). When two matrices such as AB are conformable, AB is said to be *defined*.
For BC,

$$(3 \times \textcircled{2}) = (\textcircled{2} \times 3)$$
$$(3 \times 3)$$

The matrices are conformable and the dimensions of the product matrix BC will be (3×3).
For AC,

$$(2 \times \textcircled{3}) \neq (\textcircled{2} \times 3)$$

A and C are not conformable for multiplication. Thus, AC is not defined.

Example 9. Having determined the conformability of AB in Example 8, the product of the two matrices can be found. First, multiply the first row of the lead matrix by the first column of the lag matrix to find the first element d_{11} of the product matrix D. Then multiply the first row of the lead matrix by the second column of the lag matrix to get d_{12}. Since there are no more columns left in the lag matrix, move to the second row of the lead matrix. Multiply the second row of the lead matrix by the first column of the lag matrix to get d_{21}. Finally, multiply the second row of the lead matrix by the second column of the lag matrix to get d_{22}. Thus,

$$AB = D = \begin{bmatrix} 3(6)+6(5)+7(13) & 3(12)+6(10)+7(2) \\ 12(6)+9(5)+11(13) & 12(12)+9(10)+11(2) \end{bmatrix}_{(2\times2)} = \begin{bmatrix} 139 & 110 \\ 260 & 256 \end{bmatrix}_{(2\times2)}$$

The product of BC is calculated below, using the same method:

$$BC = E = \begin{bmatrix} 6(1)+12(2) & 6(7)+12(4) & 6(8)+12(3) \\ 5(1)+10(2) & 5(7)+10(4) & 5(8)+10(3) \\ 13(1)+2(2) & 13(7)+2(4) & 13(8)+2(3) \end{bmatrix}_{(3\times3)} = \begin{bmatrix} 30 & 90 & 84 \\ 25 & 75 & 70 \\ 17 & 99 & 110 \end{bmatrix}_{(3\times3)}$$

Example 10. Referring to Example 1, suppose that the price of skis is $200, poles $50, bindings $100, and outfits $150. To find the value ($V$) of the stock in the different outlets, express the prices as a column vector (P), and multiply S by P:

$$V = SP = \begin{bmatrix} 120 & 110 & 90 & 150 \\ 200 & 180 & 210 & 110 \\ 175 & 190 & 160 & 80 \\ 140 & 170 & 180 & 140 \end{bmatrix}_{(4\times4)} \begin{bmatrix} 200 \\ 50 \\ 100 \\ 150 \end{bmatrix}_{(4\times1)}$$

The matrices are conformable and the product matrix will be 4×1 since

$$(4 \times 4) = (4 \times 1)$$
$$(4 \times 1)$$

Thus,

$$V = \begin{bmatrix} 120(200) + 110(50) + 90(100) + 150(150) \\ 200(200) + 180(50) + 210(100) + 110(150) \\ 175(200) + 190(50) + 160(100) + 80(150) \\ 140(200) + 170(50) + 180(100) + 140(150) \end{bmatrix}_{(4 \times 1)} = \begin{bmatrix} 61,000 \\ 86,500 \\ 72,500 \\ 75,500 \end{bmatrix}_{(4 \times 1)}$$

10.7 COMMUTATIVE, ASSOCIATIVE, AND DISTRIBUTIVE LAWS IN MATRIX ALGEBRA

Matrix addition is commutative (i.e. $A + B = B + A$) since matrix addition merely involves the summing of corresponding elements of two matrices, and the order in which the addition takes place is inconsequential. For the same reason, matrix addition is also associative, $(A + B) + C = A + (B + C)$. The same is true of matrix subtraction. Since matrix subtraction $A - B$ can be converted to matrix addition $A + (-B)$, matrix subtraction is also commutative and associative.

Matrix multiplication, with few exceptions, is not commutative (i.e. $AB \neq BA$). Scalar multiplication, however, is commutative (i.e. $kA = Ak$). If three or more matrices are conformable, i.e. $X_{(a \times b)}$, $Y_{(c \times d)}$, $Z_{(e \times f)}$, where $b = c$ and $d = e$, the associative law will apply as long as the matrices are multiplied in the order of conformability. Thus $(XY)Z = X(YZ)$. Subject to these same conditions, matrix multiplication is also distributive: $A(B + C) = AB + AC$.

Example 11. Given

$$A = \begin{bmatrix} 4 & 11 \\ 17 & 6 \end{bmatrix} \qquad B = \begin{bmatrix} 3 & 7 \\ 6 & 2 \end{bmatrix}$$

To prove that matrix addition and subtraction are commutative, prove that (1) $A + B = B + A$, and (2) $A - B = -B + A$. The calculations are shown below.

(1) $$A + B = \begin{bmatrix} 4+3 & 11+7 \\ 17+6 & 6+2 \end{bmatrix} = \begin{bmatrix} 7 & 18 \\ 23 & 8 \end{bmatrix} = B + A = \begin{bmatrix} 3+4 & 7+11 \\ 6+17 & 2+6 \end{bmatrix} = \begin{bmatrix} 7 & 18 \\ 23 & 8 \end{bmatrix}$$

(2) $$A - B = \begin{bmatrix} 4-3 & 11-7 \\ 17-6 & 6-2 \end{bmatrix} = \begin{bmatrix} 1 & 4 \\ 11 & 4 \end{bmatrix} = -B + A = \begin{bmatrix} -3+4 & -7+11 \\ -6+17 & -2+6 \end{bmatrix} = \begin{bmatrix} 1 & 4 \\ 11 & 4 \end{bmatrix}$$

Example 12. Given

$$A = \begin{bmatrix} 3 & 6 & 7 \\ 12 & 9 & 11 \end{bmatrix}_{(2 \times 3)} \qquad B = \begin{bmatrix} 6 & 12 \\ 5 & 10 \\ 13 & 2 \end{bmatrix}_{(3 \times 2)}$$

It can be proven that matrix multiplication is not commutative, by proving $AB \neq BA$, as follows:

AB is conformable. $(2 \times 3) = (3 \times 2)$, AB will be 2×2

$$AB = \begin{bmatrix} 3(6) + 6(5) + 7(13) & 3(12) + 6(10) + 7(2) \\ 12(6) + 9(5) + 11(13) & 12(12) + 9(10) + 11(2) \end{bmatrix}_{(2 \times 2)} = \begin{bmatrix} 139 & 110 \\ 260 & 256 \end{bmatrix}_{(2 \times 2)}$$

BA is conformable. $(3 \times 2) = (2 \times 3)$ BA will be 3×3

$$BA = \begin{bmatrix} 6(3) + 12(12) & 6(6) + 12(9) & 6(7) + 12(11) \\ 5(3) + 10(12) & 5(6) + 10(9) & 5(7) + 10(11) \\ 13(3) + 2(12) & 13(6) + 2(9) & 13(7) + 2(11) \end{bmatrix}_{(3 \times 3)} = \begin{bmatrix} 162 & 144 & 174 \\ 135 & 120 & 145 \\ 63 & 96 & 113 \end{bmatrix}_{(3 \times 3)}$$

Hence $AB \neq BA$. Frequently matrices will not even be conformable in two directions.

Example 13.   Given

$$A = \begin{bmatrix} 7 & 5 \\ 1 & 3 \\ 8 & 6 \end{bmatrix}_{(3\times 2)} \qquad B = \begin{bmatrix} 4 & 9 & 10 \\ 2 & 6 & 5 \end{bmatrix}_{(2\times 3)} \qquad C = \begin{bmatrix} 2 \\ 6 \\ 7 \end{bmatrix}_{(3\times 1)}$$

To prove that matrix multiplication is associative, i.e. $(AB)C = A(BC)$, the calculations are as follows:

$$AB = \begin{bmatrix} 7(4)+5(2) & 7(9)+5(6) & 7(10)+5(5) \\ 1(4)+3(2) & 1(9)+3(6) & 1(10)+3(5) \\ 8(4)+6(2) & 8(9)+6(6) & 8(10)+6(5) \end{bmatrix}_{(3\times 3)} = \begin{bmatrix} 38 & 93 & 95 \\ 10 & 27 & 25 \\ 44 & 108 & 110 \end{bmatrix}_{(3\times 3)}$$

$$(AB)C = \begin{bmatrix} 38 & 93 & 95 \\ 10 & 27 & 25 \\ 44 & 108 & 110 \end{bmatrix}_{(3\times 3)} \begin{bmatrix} 2 \\ 6 \\ 7 \end{bmatrix}_{(3\times 1)} = \begin{bmatrix} 38(2)+ 93(6)+ 95(7) \\ 10(2)+ 27(6)+ 25(7) \\ 44(2)+108(6)+110(7) \end{bmatrix}_{(3\times 1)} = \begin{bmatrix} 1299 \\ 357 \\ 1506 \end{bmatrix}_{(3\times 1)}$$

$$BC = \begin{bmatrix} 4(2)+9(6)+10(7) \\ 2(2)+6(6)+ 5(7) \end{bmatrix}_{(2\times 1)} = \begin{bmatrix} 132 \\ 75 \end{bmatrix}_{(2\times 1)}$$

$$A(BC) = \begin{bmatrix} 7 & 5 \\ 1 & 3 \\ 8 & 6 \end{bmatrix}_{(3\times 2)} \begin{bmatrix} 132 \\ 75 \end{bmatrix}_{(2\times 1)} = \begin{bmatrix} 7(132)+5(75) \\ 1(132)+3(75) \\ 8(132)+6(75) \end{bmatrix}_{(3\times 1)} = \begin{bmatrix} 1299 \\ 357 \\ 1506 \end{bmatrix}_{(3\times 1)} \qquad \text{Q.E.D.}$$

10.8   IDENTITY AND NULL MATRICES

An identity matrix I is a square matrix which has 1 for every element on the principal diagonal from left to right and zero everywhere else.   See Example 14.   When a subscript is used, as in I_n, n denotes the dimensions of the matrix $(n \times n)$.   The identity matrix is similar to the number 1 in algebra since multiplication of a matrix by an identity matrix leaves the original matrix unchanged (i.e. $AI = IA = A$).   Multiplication of an identity matrix by itself leaves the identity matrix unchanged: $I \times I = (I)^2 = I$.   Any matrix for which $A = A'$ is a *symmetric matrix*.   A symmetric matrix for which $A \times A = A$, is an *idempotent matrix*.   The identity matrix is symmetric and idempotent.

A *null matrix* is composed of all zeros and can be of any dimensions; it is not necessarily square.   Addition or subtraction of the null matrix leaves the original matrix unchanged; multiplication by a null matrix produces a null matrix.

Example 14.   Given

$$A = \begin{bmatrix} 7 & 10 & 14 \\ 9 & 2 & 6 \\ 1 & 3 & 7 \end{bmatrix} \qquad B = \begin{bmatrix} 5 & 12 \\ 20 & 4 \end{bmatrix} \qquad N = \begin{bmatrix} 0 & 0 \\ 0 & 0 \end{bmatrix} \qquad I = \begin{bmatrix} 1 & 0 & 0 \\ 0 & 1 & 0 \\ 0 & 0 & 1 \end{bmatrix}$$

it is possible to prove that   (1) multiplication by an identity matrix leaves the original matrix unchanged, i.e. $AI = A$, (2) multiplication by a null matrix produces a null matrix, i.e. $BN = N$, and   (3) addition or subtraction of a null matrix leaves the original matrix unchanged, i.e. $B + N = B$.   The calculations are shown below.

$$(1) \qquad AI = \begin{bmatrix} 7 & 10 & 14 \\ 9 & 2 & 6 \\ 1 & 3 & 7 \end{bmatrix} \begin{bmatrix} 1 & 0 & 0 \\ 0 & 1 & 0 \\ 0 & 0 & 1 \end{bmatrix} = \begin{bmatrix} 7(1)+10(0)+14(0) & 7(0)+10(1)+14(0) & 7(0)+10(0)+14(1) \\ 9(1)+ 2(0)+ 6(0) & 9(0)+ 2(1)+ 6(0) & 9(0)+ 2(0)+ 6(1) \\ 1(1)+ 3(0)+ 7(0) & 1(0)+ 3(1)+ 7(0) & 1(0)+ 3(0)+ 7(1) \end{bmatrix}$$

$$AI = \begin{bmatrix} 7 & 10 & 14 \\ 9 & 2 & 6 \\ 1 & 3 & 7 \end{bmatrix} \qquad \text{Q.E.D.}$$

(2)
$$BN = \begin{bmatrix} 5(0) + 12(0) & 5(0) + 12(0) \\ 20(0) + 4(0) & 20(0) + 4(0) \end{bmatrix} = \begin{bmatrix} 0 & 0 \\ 0 & 0 \end{bmatrix} \quad \text{Q.E.D.}$$

(3)
$$B + N = \begin{bmatrix} 5+0 & 12+0 \\ 20+0 & 4+0 \end{bmatrix} = \begin{bmatrix} 5 & 12 \\ 20 & 4 \end{bmatrix} \quad \text{Q.E.D.}$$

10.9 MATRIX EXPRESSION OF A SET OF LINEAR EQUATIONS

Matrix algebra permits the concise expression of a system of linear equations. As a simple illustration, note that the system of linear equations

$$7x_1 + 3x_2 = 45$$
$$4x_1 + 5x_2 = 29$$

can be expressed in matrix form

$$AX = B$$

where
$$A = \begin{bmatrix} 7 & 3 \\ 4 & 5 \end{bmatrix} \qquad X = \begin{bmatrix} x_1 \\ x_2 \end{bmatrix} \qquad \text{and} \qquad B = \begin{bmatrix} 45 \\ 29 \end{bmatrix}$$

A is the *coefficient matrix*, X is the *solution vector*, and B is the *vector of constant terms*. X and B will always be column vectors.

Example 15.   To prove that $AX = B$ accurately represents the given system of equations in Section 10.9, find the product AX.   Multiplication is possible since AX is conformable, and the product matrix will be 2×1.

$$\underbrace{(2 \times 2) \quad = \quad (2 \times 1)}_{(2 \times 1)}$$

Thus,
$$AX = \begin{bmatrix} 7 & 3 \\ 4 & 5 \end{bmatrix} \begin{bmatrix} x_1 \\ x_2 \end{bmatrix} = \begin{bmatrix} 7x_1 + 3x_2 \\ 4x_1 + 5x_2 \end{bmatrix}_{(2 \times 1)}$$

and
$$AX = B: \quad \begin{bmatrix} 7x_1 + 3x_2 \\ 4x_1 + 5x_2 \end{bmatrix} = \begin{bmatrix} 45 \\ 29 \end{bmatrix} \quad \text{Q.E.D.}$$

Here, despite appearances, AX is a (2×1) column vector since each row is composed of a single element which cannot be simplified further through addition.

Example 16.   Given
$$8w + 12x - 7y + 2z = 139$$
$$3w - 13x + 4y + 9z = 242$$

To express this system of equations in matrix notation, mentally reverse the order of matrix multiplication:

$$\begin{bmatrix} 8 & 12 & -7 & 2 \\ 3 & -13 & 4 & 9 \end{bmatrix}_{(2 \times 4)} \begin{bmatrix} w \\ x \\ y \\ z \end{bmatrix}_{(4 \times 1)} = \begin{bmatrix} 139 \\ 242 \end{bmatrix}_{(2 \times 1)}$$

Then, letting $A =$ the matrix of coefficients, $W =$ the column vector of variables,   and $B =$ the column vector of constants,   the given system of equations can be expressed in matrix form

$$A_{(2 \times 4)} W_{(4 \times 1)} = B_{(2 \times 1)}$$

10.10 ROW OPERATIONS

Row operations means the application of simple algebraic operations to the rows of a matrix. With no change in the linear relationship, the three basic row operations allow   (1) any two rows of a matrix to be interchanged, (2) any row or rows to be multiplied by a constant, provided the constant does not equal zero, and (3) any multiple of a row to be added to or subtracted from any other row.

Example 17. Row operations, which should be familiar from algebra, are illustrated below, given

$$5x + 2y = 16$$
$$8x + 4y = 28$$

Without any change in the linear relationship, one may

1. Interchange the two rows:

$$8x + 4y = 28$$
$$5x + 2y = 16$$

2. Multiply any row by a constant, here $8x + 4y = 28$ by $\frac{1}{4}$, leaving

$$2x + \ y = 7$$
$$5x + 2y = 16$$

3. Subtract a multiple of one row from another, here $2(2x + y = 7)$ from $5x + 2y = 16$, leaving

$$5x + 2y = 16$$
$$\underline{-4x - 2y = -14}$$
$$x \qquad = 2$$

10.11 AUGMENTED MATRIX

Given a system of equations in matrix form $AX = B$, the augmented matrix $A \mid B$ is the coefficient matrix A with the column vector of constants B set along side it, separated by a line or bar. Thus, for the system of equations in Section 10.9,

$$A \mid B = \begin{bmatrix} 7 & 3 & \mid & 45 \\ 4 & 5 & \mid & 29 \end{bmatrix}$$

Augmented matrices are used as a means of solving a system of linear equations.

Example 18. The augmented matrix $A \mid B$ for

$$4x_1 + 5x_2 + 7x_3 = 42$$
$$2x_1 + 3x_2 + 8x_3 = 40$$
$$6x_1 + 4x_2 + \ x_3 = 18$$

is

$$A \mid B = \begin{bmatrix} 4 & 5 & 7 & \mid & 42 \\ 2 & 3 & 8 & \mid & 40 \\ 6 & 4 & 1 & \mid & 18 \end{bmatrix}$$

10.12 GAUSSIAN METHOD OF SOLVING LINEAR EQUATIONS

To use the Gaussian elimination method of solving linear equations simply express the system of equations as an augmented matrix and apply repeated row operations to the augmented matrix until the coefficient matrix A is reduced to an identity matrix. The solution to the system of equations can then be read from the remaining elements in the column vector B (see Example 19). To transform the coefficient matrix into an identity matrix, work along the principal axis. First obtain a 1 in the a_{11} position of the coefficient matrix; then use row operations to obtain zeros everywhere else in the first column. Next obtain a 1 in the a_{22} position and use row operations to get zeros everywhere else in the column. Continue getting 1s along the principal diagonal and then clearing the column until the identity matrix is completed.

Example 19. The Gaussian elimination method is used below to solve for x_1 and x_2 in the system of equations

$$2x_1 + 12x_2 = 40$$
$$8x_1 + 4x_2 = 28$$

First express the equations in an augmented matrix,

$$A \mid B = \begin{bmatrix} 2 & 12 & \mid & 40 \\ 8 & 4 & \mid & 28 \end{bmatrix}$$

Then,

1a. Multiply the first row by $\frac{1}{2}$ to obtain 1 in the a_{11} position.

$$\begin{bmatrix} 1 & 6 & \mid & 20 \\ 8 & 4 & \mid & 28 \end{bmatrix}$$

1b. Subtract 8 times the first row from the second row to clear the first column.

$$\begin{bmatrix} 1 & 6 & \mid & 20 \\ 0 & -44 & \mid & -132 \end{bmatrix}$$

2a. Multiply the second row by $(-\frac{1}{44})$ to obtain 1 in a_{22}.

$$\begin{bmatrix} 1 & 6 & \mid & 20 \\ 0 & 1 & \mid & 3 \end{bmatrix}$$

2b. Subtract 6 times the second row from the first row to clear the second column.

$$\begin{bmatrix} 1 & 0 & \mid & 2 \\ 0 & 1 & \mid & 3 \end{bmatrix}$$

The solution is $x_1 = 2$, $x_2 = 3$ since

$$\begin{bmatrix} 1 & 0 \\ 0 & 1 \end{bmatrix} \begin{bmatrix} x_1 \\ x_2 \end{bmatrix} = \begin{bmatrix} 2 \\ 3 \end{bmatrix}$$
$$x_1 + 0 = 2$$
$$0 + x_2 = 3$$

Solved Problems

MATRIX FORMAT

10.1. (a) Give the dimensions of each of the following matrices.   (b) Give their transposes and indicate the new dimensions.

$$A = \begin{bmatrix} 6 & 7 & 9 \\ 2 & 8 & 4 \end{bmatrix} \qquad B = \begin{bmatrix} 12 & 9 & 2 & 6 \\ 7 & 5 & 8 & 3 \\ 9 & 1 & 0 & 4 \end{bmatrix} \qquad C = \begin{bmatrix} 12 \\ 19 \\ 25 \end{bmatrix}$$

$$D = \begin{bmatrix} 2 & 1 \\ 7 & 8 \\ 3 & 0 \\ 9 & 5 \end{bmatrix} \qquad E = [10 \ 2 \ 9 \ 6 \ 8 \ 1] \qquad F = \begin{bmatrix} 1 & 2 & 5 \\ 5 & 9 & 3 \\ 6 & 7 & 6 \\ 3 & 8 & 9 \end{bmatrix}$$

(a) Recalling that dimensions are always listed row by column or RC, $A = (2 \times 3)$, $B = (3 \times 4)$, $C = (3 \times 1)$, $D = (4 \times 2)$, $E = (1 \times 6)$, and $F = (4 \times 3)$. C is also called a column vector; E, a row vector.

(b) The transpose of A converts the rows of A into columns and the columns of A into rows.

$$A' = \begin{bmatrix} 6 & 2 \\ 7 & 8 \\ 9 & 4 \end{bmatrix}_{(3 \times 2)} \qquad B' = \begin{bmatrix} 12 & 7 & 9 \\ 9 & 5 & 1 \\ 2 & 8 & 0 \\ 6 & 3 & 4 \end{bmatrix}_{(4 \times 3)} \qquad C' = [12 \quad 19 \quad 25]_{(1 \times 3)}$$

$$D' = \begin{bmatrix} 2 & 7 & 3 & 9 \\ 1 & 8 & 0 & 5 \end{bmatrix}_{(2 \times 4)} \qquad E' = \begin{bmatrix} 10 \\ 2 \\ 9 \\ 6 \\ 8 \\ 1 \end{bmatrix}_{(6 \times 1)} \qquad F' = \begin{bmatrix} 1 & 5 & 6 & 3 \\ 2 & 9 & 7 & 8 \\ 5 & 3 & 6 & 9 \end{bmatrix}_{(3 \times 4)}$$

10.2. Given $a_{21} = 4$, $a_{32} = 5$, $a_{13} = 3$, $a_{23} = 6$, $a_{12} = 10$, and $a_{31} = -5$, use your knowledge of subscripts to complete the following matrix:

$$A = \begin{bmatrix} 6 & \_ & \_ \\ \_ & 7 & \_ \\ \_ & \_ & 9 \end{bmatrix}$$

Since the subscripts are always given in row-column order, $a_{21} = 4$ means that 4 is located in the second row, first column; $a_{32} = 5$ means that 5 appears in the third row, second column, etc. Thus,

$$A = \begin{bmatrix} 6 & 10 & 3 \\ 4 & 7 & 6 \\ -5 & 5 & 9 \end{bmatrix}$$

10.3. A firm with five retail stores has 10 TV's (t), 15 stereos (s), 9 tape decks (d), and 12 recorders (r) in store 1; $20t$, $14s$, $8d$, and $5r$ in store 2; $16t$, $8s$, $15d$, and $6r$ in store 3; $25t$, $15s$, $7d$, and $16r$ in store 4; and $5t$, $12s$, $20d$, and $18s$ in store 5.   Express present inventory in matrix form.

Retail store	t	s	d	r
1	10	15	9	12
2	20	14	8	5
3	16	8	15	6
4	25	15	7	16
5	5	12	20	18

MATRIX ADDITION AND SUBTRACTION

10.4. Find the sums $A + B$ of the following matrices:

(a) $A = \begin{bmatrix} 8 & 9 \\ 12 & 7 \end{bmatrix}$, $B = \begin{bmatrix} 13 & 4 \\ 2 & 6 \end{bmatrix}$

$$A + B = \begin{bmatrix} 8+13 & 9+4 \\ 12+2 & 7+6 \end{bmatrix} = \begin{bmatrix} 21 & 13 \\ 14 & 13 \end{bmatrix}$$

(b) $A = \begin{bmatrix} 7 & -10 \\ -8 & 2 \end{bmatrix}$, $B = \begin{bmatrix} -8 & 4 \\ 12 & -6 \end{bmatrix}$

$$A + B = \begin{bmatrix} 7+(-8) & -10+4 \\ -8+12 & 2+(-6) \end{bmatrix} = \begin{bmatrix} -1 & -6 \\ 4 & -4 \end{bmatrix}$$

(c) $A = [12 \quad 16 \quad 2 \quad 7 \quad 8]$, $B = [0 \quad 1 \quad 9 \quad 5 \quad 6]$

$A + B = [12 \quad 17 \quad 11 \quad 12 \quad 14]$

(d) $A = \begin{bmatrix} 9 & 4 \\ 2 & 7 \\ 3 & 5 \\ 8 & 6 \end{bmatrix}$, $B = \begin{bmatrix} 1 & 3 \\ 6 & 5 \\ 2 & 8 \\ 9 & 2 \end{bmatrix}$

$A + B = \begin{bmatrix} 10 & 7 \\ 8 & 12 \\ 5 & 13 \\ 17 & 8 \end{bmatrix}$

10.5.   Redo Problem 10.4, given

$$A = \begin{bmatrix} 0 & 1 & -6 & 2 \\ -3 & 5 & 8 & 7 \\ 2 & 9 & -1 & 6 \end{bmatrix} \qquad B = \begin{bmatrix} 7 & 2 & 12 & 6 & 5 \\ 4 & 3 & 8 & 10 & 6 \\ 1 & 0 & 5 & 11 & 9 \end{bmatrix}$$

A and B are not conformable for addition because they are not of equal dimensions; $A = (3 \times 4)$, $B = (3 \times 5)$.

10.6.   The parent company in Problem 10.3 sends out deliveries (D) to its stores:

$$D = \begin{bmatrix} 4 & 3 & 5 & 2 \\ 0 & 9 & 6 & 1 \\ 5 & 7 & 2 & 6 \\ 12 & 2 & 4 & 8 \\ 9 & 6 & 3 & 5 \end{bmatrix}$$

What is the new level of stock?

$$I_2 = I_1 + D = \begin{bmatrix} 10 & 15 & 9 & 12 \\ 20 & 14 & 8 & 5 \\ 16 & 8 & 15 & 6 \\ 25 & 15 & 7 & 16 \\ 5 & 12 & 20 & 18 \end{bmatrix} + \begin{bmatrix} 4 & 3 & 5 & 2 \\ 0 & 9 & 6 & 1 \\ 5 & 7 & 2 & 6 \\ 12 & 2 & 4 & 8 \\ 9 & 6 & 3 & 5 \end{bmatrix} = \begin{bmatrix} 14 & 18 & 14 & 14 \\ 20 & 23 & 14 & 6 \\ 21 & 15 & 17 & 12 \\ 37 & 17 & 11 & 24 \\ 14 & 18 & 23 & 23 \end{bmatrix}$$

10.7.   Find the differences $A - B$ for each of the following.

(a) $A = \begin{bmatrix} 3 & 7 & 11 \\ 12 & 9 & 2 \end{bmatrix}$, $B = \begin{bmatrix} 6 & 8 & 1 \\ 9 & 5 & 8 \end{bmatrix}$

$A - B = \begin{bmatrix} 3-6 & 7-8 & 11-1 \\ 12-9 & 9-5 & 2-8 \end{bmatrix} = \begin{bmatrix} -3 & -1 & 10 \\ 3 & 4 & -6 \end{bmatrix}$

(b) $A = \begin{bmatrix} 16 \\ 2 \\ 15 \\ 9 \end{bmatrix}$, $B = \begin{bmatrix} 7 \\ 11 \\ 3 \\ 8 \end{bmatrix}$

$A - B = \begin{bmatrix} 16 - 7 \\ 2 - 11 \\ 15 - 3 \\ 9 - 8 \end{bmatrix} = \begin{bmatrix} 9 \\ -9 \\ 12 \\ 1 \end{bmatrix}$

(c) $A = \begin{bmatrix} 13 & -5 & 8 \\ 4 & 9 & 1 \\ 10 & 6 & -2 \end{bmatrix}$, $B = \begin{bmatrix} 14 & 2 & -5 \\ 9 & 6 & 8 \\ -3 & 13 & 11 \end{bmatrix}$

$$A - B = \begin{bmatrix} -1 & -7 & 13 \\ -5 & 3 & -7 \\ 13 & -7 & -13 \end{bmatrix}$$

10.8.   A monthly report (R) on sales for the company in Problem 10.6 indicates

$$R = \begin{bmatrix} 8 & 12 & 6 & 9 \\ 10 & 11 & 8 & 3 \\ 15 & 6 & 9 & 7 \\ 21 & 14 & 5 & 18 \\ 6 & 11 & 13 & 9 \end{bmatrix}$$

What is the inventory left at the end of the month?

$$I_2 - R = \begin{bmatrix} 14 & 18 & 14 & 14 \\ 20 & 23 & 14 & 6 \\ 21 & 15 & 17 & 12 \\ 37 & 17 & 11 & 24 \\ 14 & 18 & 23 & 23 \end{bmatrix} - \begin{bmatrix} 8 & 12 & 6 & 9 \\ 10 & 11 & 8 & 3 \\ 15 & 6 & 9 & 7 \\ 21 & 14 & 5 & 18 \\ 6 & 11 & 13 & 9 \end{bmatrix} = \begin{bmatrix} 6 & 6 & 8 & 5 \\ 10 & 12 & 6 & 3 \\ 6 & 9 & 8 & 5 \\ 16 & 3 & 6 & 6 \\ 8 & 7 & 10 & 14 \end{bmatrix}$$

CONFORMABILITY

10.9.   Given

$$A = \begin{bmatrix} 7 & 2 & 6 \\ 5 & 4 & 8 \\ 3 & 1 & 9 \end{bmatrix}, \qquad B = \begin{bmatrix} 6 & 2 \\ 5 & 0 \end{bmatrix} \qquad C = \begin{bmatrix} 11 \\ 4 \\ 13 \end{bmatrix}$$

$$D = \begin{bmatrix} 14 \\ 4 \end{bmatrix} \qquad E = \begin{bmatrix} 8 & 1 & 10 \end{bmatrix} \qquad F = \begin{bmatrix} 13 & 3 \end{bmatrix}$$

Determine for each of the following whether the products are defined, i.e. conformable for multiplication. If so, indicate the dimensions of the product matrix. (a) AC, (b) BD, (c) EC, (d) DF, (e) CA, (f) DE, (g) DB, (h) CF, (i) EF.

(a)   The dimensions of AC, in the order of multiplication, are $(3 \times 3) = (3 \times 1)$. AC is defined since the numbers within the dotted circle indicate that the number of columns in A equals the number of rows in C. The numbers outside the circle indicate that the product matrix will be a (3×1).

(b)   The dimensions of BD are $(2 \times 2) = (2 \times 1)$. BD is defined; the product matrix will be (2×1).

(c)   The dimensions of EC are $(1 \times 3) = (3 \times 1)$. EC is defined; the product matrix will be (1×1), or a scalar.

(d)   The dimensions of DF are $(2 \times 1) = (1 \times 2)$. DF is defined; the product matrix will be (2×2).

(e)   The dimensions of CA are $(3 \times 1) \neq (3 \times 3)$. CA is undefined. The matrices are not conformable for multiplication in that order. [Note that AC in part (a) is defined. This illustrates that matrix multiplication is not commutative: $AC \neq CA$.]

(f)   The dimensions of DE are $(2 \times 1) = (1 \times 3)$. DE is defined; the product matrix will be (2×3).

(g)   The dimensions of DB are $(2 \times 1) \neq (2 \times 2)$. The matrices are not conformable for multiplication. DB is not defined.

(*h*)   The dimensions of *CF* are   (3 × 1) = (1 × 2).   The matrices are conformable; the product matrix will be (3 × 2).

(*i*)   The dimensions of *EF* are   (1 × 3) ≠ (1 × 2).   The matrices are not conformable.   *EF* is not defined.

SCALAR AND VECTOR MULTIPLICATION

10.10.   Determine *Ak*, given

$$A = \begin{bmatrix} 3 & 2 \\ 9 & 5 \\ 6 & 7 \end{bmatrix} \qquad k = 4$$

k is a scalar, and scalar multiplication is possible with a matrix of any dimension.   Hence the product is defined.

$$Ak = \begin{bmatrix} 3(4) & 2(4) \\ 9(4) & 5(4) \\ 6(4) & 7(4) \end{bmatrix} = \begin{bmatrix} 12 & 8 \\ 36 & 20 \\ 24 & 28 \end{bmatrix}$$

10.11.   Find *kA*, given

$$k = -2 \qquad A = \begin{bmatrix} 7 & -3 & 2 \\ -5 & 6 & 8 \\ 2 & -7 & -9 \end{bmatrix}$$

$$kA = \begin{bmatrix} -2(7) & -2(-3) & -2(2) \\ -2(-5) & -2(6) & -2(8) \\ -2(2) & -2(-7) & -2(-9) \end{bmatrix} = \begin{bmatrix} -14 & 6 & -4 \\ 10 & -12 & -16 \\ -4 & 14 & 18 \end{bmatrix}$$

10.12.   A clothing store discounts all its slacks, jackets, and suits by 20 percent at the end of the year.   If V_1 is the value of stock in its three branches prior to the discount, find the value V_2 after the discount, when

$$V_1 = \begin{bmatrix} 5,000 & 4,500 & 6,000 \\ 10,000 & 12,000 & 7,500 \\ 8,000 & 9,000 & 11,000 \end{bmatrix}$$

A 20 percent reduction means that the clothing is selling for 80 percent of its original value.   Hence $V_2 = 0.8 V_1$, and

$$V_2 = 0.8 \begin{bmatrix} 5,000 & 4,500 & 6,000 \\ 10,000 & 12,000 & 7,500 \\ 8,000 & 9,000 & 11,000 \end{bmatrix} = \begin{bmatrix} 4000 & 3600 & 4800 \\ 8000 & 9600 & 6000 \\ 6400 & 7200 & 8800 \end{bmatrix}$$

10.13.   Find *AB*, given

$$A = \begin{bmatrix} 9 & 11 & 3 \end{bmatrix} \qquad B = \begin{bmatrix} 2 \\ 6 \\ 7 \end{bmatrix}$$

AB is defined   (1 × 3) = (3 × 1);   the product will be a scalar, derived by multiplying each element of the row vector by its corresponding element in the column vector and then summing the products.

$$AB = 9(2) + 11(6) + 3(7) = 18 + 66 + 21 = 105$$

10.14. Find AB, given

$$A = [12 \quad -5 \quad 6 \quad 11] \qquad B = \begin{bmatrix} 3 \\ 2 \\ -8 \\ 6 \end{bmatrix}$$

AB is defined; $(1 \times 4) = (4 \times 1)$.

$$AB = 12(3) + (-5)(2) + 6(-8) + 11(6) = 44$$

10.15. Find AB, given

$$A = [9 \quad 6 \quad 2 \quad 0 \quad -5] \qquad B = \begin{bmatrix} 2 \\ 13 \\ 5 \\ 8 \\ 1 \end{bmatrix}$$

AB is defined; $(1 + 5) = (5 \times 1)$.

$$AB = 9(2) + 6(13) + 2(5) + 0(8) + (-5)(1) = 101$$

10.16. Find AB, given

$$A = [12 \quad 9 \quad 2 \quad 4] \qquad B = \begin{bmatrix} 6 \\ 1 \\ 2 \end{bmatrix}$$

AB is undefined; $(1 \times 4) \neq (3 \times 1)$.   Multiplication is not possible.

10.17. If the price of a TV is \$300, the price of a stereo is \$250, the price of a tape deck is \$175, and the price of a recorder is \$125, use vectors to determine the value of stock for outlet 2 in Problem 10.3.

The value of stock is $V = QP$. The physical volume of stock in outlet 2 in vector form is $Q = [20 \quad 14 \quad 8 \quad 5]$. The price vector P can be written

$$P = \begin{bmatrix} 300 \\ 250 \\ 175 \\ 125 \end{bmatrix}$$

QP is defined; $(1 \times 4) = (4 \times 1)$. Thus

$$V = QP$$
$$= 20(300) + 14(250) + 8(175) + 5(125) = 11{,}525$$

10.18. Redo Problem 10.17 for outlet 5 in Problem 10.3.

$Q = [5 \quad 12 \quad 20 \quad 18]$, P remains the same. QP is defined. Thus,

$$V = 5(300) + 12(250) + 20(175) + 18(125) = 10{,}250$$

MATRIX MULTIPLICATION

10.19. Determine whether AB is defined, indicate what the dimensions of the product matrix will be, and find the product matrix AB, given

$$A = \begin{bmatrix} 12 & 14 \\ 20 & 5 \end{bmatrix} \qquad B = \begin{bmatrix} 3 & 9 \\ 0 & 2 \end{bmatrix}$$

AB is defined; $(2 \times 2) = (2 \times 2)$; the product matrix will be (2×2). Matrix multiplication is nothing but a series of row-column vector multiplications in which the a_{11} element of the product matrix is determined by the product of the first row of the lead matrix and the first column of the lag matrix; the a_{12} element of the product matrix is determined by the product of the first row of the lead matrix and the second column of the lag matrix; the a_{ij} element of the product matrix is determined by the product of the ith row of the lead matrix and the jth column of the lag matrix, etc. Thus,

$$AB = \begin{bmatrix} 12(3) + 14(0) & 12(9) + 14(2) \\ 20(3) + 5(0) & 20(9) + 5(2) \end{bmatrix} = \begin{bmatrix} 36 & 136 \\ 60 & 190 \end{bmatrix}$$

10.20. Redo Problem 10.19, given

$$A = \begin{bmatrix} 4 & 7 \\ 9 & 1 \end{bmatrix} \qquad B = \begin{bmatrix} 3 & 8 & 5 \\ 2 & 6 & 7 \end{bmatrix}$$

AB is defined; $(2 \times 2) = (2 \times 3)$; the product matrix will be (2×3).

$$AB = \begin{bmatrix} 4(3) + 7(2) & 4(8) + 7(6) & 4(5) + 7(7) \\ 9(3) + 1(2) & 9(8) + 1(6) & 9(5) + 1(7) \end{bmatrix} = \begin{bmatrix} 26 & 74 & 69 \\ 29 & 78 & 52 \end{bmatrix}$$

10.21. Redo Problem 10.19, given

$$A = \begin{bmatrix} 3 & 1 \\ 8 & 2 \end{bmatrix} \qquad B = \begin{bmatrix} 2 & 9 \\ 4 & 6 \\ 7 & 5 \end{bmatrix}$$

AB is not defined; $(2 \times 2) \neq (3 \times 2)$. The matrices cannot be multiplied because they are not conformable in the given order. The number of columns (2) in A does not equal the number of rows (3) in B.

10.22. Redo Problem 10.19 for BA in Problem 10.21.

BA is defined; $(3 \times 2) = (2 \times 2)$; the product matrix will be (3×2).

$$BA = \begin{bmatrix} 2 & 9 \\ 4 & 6 \\ 7 & 5 \end{bmatrix} \begin{bmatrix} 3 & 1 \\ 8 & 2 \end{bmatrix} = \begin{bmatrix} 2(3) + 9(8) & 2(1) + 9(2) \\ 4(3) + 6(8) & 4(1) + 6(2) \\ 7(3) + 5(8) & 7(1) + 5(2) \end{bmatrix} = \begin{bmatrix} 78 & 20 \\ 60 & 16 \\ 61 & 17 \end{bmatrix}$$

10.23. Redo Problem 10.19 for AB' for Problem 10.21, where B' is the transpose of B:

$$B' = \begin{bmatrix} 2 & 4 & 7 \\ 9 & 6 & 5 \end{bmatrix}$$

AB' is defined; $(2 \times 2) = (2 \times 3)$; the product will be a (2×3) matrix.

$$AB' = \begin{bmatrix} 3 & 1 \\ 8 & 2 \end{bmatrix} \begin{bmatrix} 2 & 4 & 7 \\ 9 & 6 & 5 \end{bmatrix} = \begin{bmatrix} 3(2) + 1(9) & 3(4) + 1(6) & 3(7) + 1(5) \\ 8(2) + 2(9) & 8(4) + 2(6) & 8(7) + 2(5) \end{bmatrix} = \begin{bmatrix} 15 & 18 & 26 \\ 34 & 44 & 66 \end{bmatrix}$$

(Note from Problems 10.21–10.23 that $AB \neq BA \neq AB'$. The noncommutative aspects of matrix multiplication are treated in Problems 10.36–10.41.)

10.24. Redo Problem 10.19, given

$$A = \begin{bmatrix} 7 & 11 \\ 2 & 9 \\ 10 & 6 \end{bmatrix} \qquad B = \begin{bmatrix} 12 & 4 & 5 \\ 3 & 6 & 1 \end{bmatrix}$$

AB is defined; (3×2) $=$ (2×3).   The product matrix will be (3×3).

$$AB = \begin{bmatrix} 7(12)+11(3) & 7(4)+11(6) & 7(5)+11(1) \\ 2(12)+9(3) & 2(4)+9(6) & 2(5)+9(1) \\ 10(12)+6(3) & 10(4)+6(6) & 10(5)+6(1) \end{bmatrix} = \begin{bmatrix} 117 & 94 & 46 \\ 51 & 62 & 19 \\ 138 & 76 & 56 \end{bmatrix}$$

10.25.   Redo Problem 10.19, given

$$A = \begin{bmatrix} 6 & 2 & 5 \\ 7 & 9 & 4 \end{bmatrix} \qquad B = \begin{bmatrix} 10 & 1 \\ 11 & 3 \\ 2 & 9 \end{bmatrix}$$

AB is defined; (2×3) $=$ (3×2).   The product matrix will be (2×2).

$$AB = \begin{bmatrix} 6(10)+2(11)+5(2) & 6(1)+2(3)+5(9) \\ 7(10)+9(11)+4(2) & 7(1)+9(3)+4(9) \end{bmatrix} = \begin{bmatrix} 92 & 57 \\ 177 & 70 \end{bmatrix}$$

10.26.   Redo Problem 10.19, given

$$A = \begin{bmatrix} 2 & 3 & 5 \end{bmatrix} \qquad B = \begin{bmatrix} 7 & 1 & 6 \\ 5 & 2 & 4 \\ 9 & 2 & 7 \end{bmatrix}$$

AB is defined; (1×3) $=$ (3×3).   The product matrix will be (1×3).

$$AB = \begin{bmatrix} 2(7)+3(5)+5(9) & 2(1)+3(2)+5(2) & 2(6)+3(4)+5(7) \end{bmatrix} = \begin{bmatrix} 74 & 18 & 59 \end{bmatrix}$$

10.27.   Redo Problem 10.19, given

$$A = \begin{bmatrix} 5 \\ 1 \\ 10 \end{bmatrix} \qquad B = \begin{bmatrix} 3 & 9 & 4 \\ 2 & 1 & 8 \\ 5 & 6 & 1 \end{bmatrix}$$

AB is not defined; (3×1) $\neq$ (3×3).   Multiplication is impossible in the given order.

10.28.   Find BA from Problem 10.27.

BA is defined; (3×3) $=$ (3×1).   The product matrix will be (3×1).

$$BA = \begin{bmatrix} 3 & 9 & 4 \\ 2 & 1 & 8 \\ 5 & 6 & 1 \end{bmatrix}\begin{bmatrix} 5 \\ 1 \\ 10 \end{bmatrix} = \begin{bmatrix} 3(5)+9(1)+4(10) \\ 2(5)+1(1)+8(10) \\ 5(5)+6(1)+1(10) \end{bmatrix} = \begin{bmatrix} 64 \\ 91 \\ 41 \end{bmatrix}$$

10.29.   Redo Problem 10.19, given

$$A = \begin{bmatrix} 2 & 1 & 5 \\ 3 & 2 & 6 \\ 1 & 4 & 3 \end{bmatrix} \qquad B = \begin{bmatrix} 10 & 1 & 2 \\ 5 & 3 & 6 \\ 2 & 1 & 2 \end{bmatrix}$$

AB is defined; (3×3) $=$ (3×3).   The product matrix will be (3×3).

$$AB = \begin{bmatrix} 2(10)+1(5)+5(2) & 2(1)+1(3)+5(1) & 2(2)+1(6)+5(2) \\ 3(10)+2(5)+6(2) & 3(1)+2(3)+6(1) & 3(2)+2(6)+6(2) \\ 1(10)+4(5)+3(2) & 1(1)+4(3)+3(1) & 1(2)+4(6)+3(2) \end{bmatrix} = \begin{bmatrix} 35 & 10 & 20 \\ 52 & 15 & 30 \\ 36 & 16 & 32 \end{bmatrix}$$

10.30.   Redo Problem 10.19, given

$$A = \begin{bmatrix} 3 \\ 1 \\ 4 \\ 5 \end{bmatrix} \qquad B = [2 \quad 6 \quad 5 \quad 3]$$

AB is defined; $(4 \times 1) = (1 \times 4)$.   The product matrix will be (4×4).

$$AB = \begin{bmatrix} 3(2) & 3(6) & 3(5) & 3(3) \\ 1(2) & 1(6) & 1(5) & 1(3) \\ 4(2) & 4(6) & 4(5) & 4(3) \\ 5(2) & 5(6) & 5(5) & 5(3) \end{bmatrix} = \begin{bmatrix} 6 & 18 & 15 & 9 \\ 2 & 6 & 5 & 3 \\ 8 & 24 & 20 & 12 \\ 10 & 30 & 25 & 15 \end{bmatrix}$$

10.31.   Find AB when

$$A = [3 \quad 9 \quad 8 \quad 7] \qquad B = \begin{bmatrix} 2 \\ 5 \\ 3 \end{bmatrix}$$

AB is undefined and cannot be multiplied as given; $(1 \times 4) \neq (3 \times 1)$.

10.32.   Find BA from Problem 10.31.

BA is defined; $(3 \times 1) = (1 \times 4)$.   The product matrix will be (3×4).

$$BA = \begin{bmatrix} 2 \\ 5 \\ 3 \end{bmatrix} [3 \quad 9 \quad 8 \quad 7] = \begin{bmatrix} 2(3) & 2(9) & 2(8) & 2(7) \\ 5(3) & 5(9) & 5(8) & 5(7) \\ 3(3) & 3(9) & 3(8) & 3(7) \end{bmatrix} = \begin{bmatrix} 6 & 18 & 16 & 14 \\ 15 & 45 & 40 & 35 \\ 9 & 27 & 24 & 21 \end{bmatrix}$$

10.33.   Use the inventory matrix for the company in Problem 10.3 and the price vector from Problem 10.17 to determine the value of inventory in all five of the company's outlets.

$V = QP$. QP is defined; $(5 \times 4) = (4 \times 1)$; V will be (5×1).

$$V = \begin{bmatrix} 10 & 15 & 9 & 12 \\ 20 & 14 & 8 & 5 \\ 16 & 8 & 15 & 6 \\ 25 & 15 & 7 & 16 \\ 5 & 12 & 20 & 18 \end{bmatrix} \begin{bmatrix} 300 \\ 250 \\ 175 \\ 125 \end{bmatrix} = \begin{bmatrix} 10(300) + 15(250) + 9(175) + 12(125) \\ 20(300) + 14(250) + 8(175) + 5(125) \\ 16(300) + 8(250) + 15(175) + 6(125) \\ 25(300) + 15(250) + 7(175) + 16(125) \\ 5(300) + 12(250) + 20(175) + 18(125) \end{bmatrix} = \begin{bmatrix} 9{,}825 \\ 11{,}525 \\ 10{,}175 \\ 14{,}475 \\ 10{,}250 \end{bmatrix}$$

THE COMMUTATIVE LAW AND MATRIX OPERATIONS

10.34.   To illustrate the commutative or noncommutative aspects of matrix operations (i.e. $A \pm B = B \pm A$,   but in general, $AB \neq BA$), find (a) $A + B$ and   (b) $B + A$, given

$$A = \begin{bmatrix} 7 & 3 & 2 \\ 1 & 4 & 6 \\ 2 & 5 & 4 \end{bmatrix} \qquad B = \begin{bmatrix} 2 & 0 & 5 \\ 3 & 4 & 1 \\ 7 & 9 & 6 \end{bmatrix}$$

$$(a) \; A + B = \begin{bmatrix} 7+2 & 3+0 & 2+5 \\ 1+3 & 4+4 & 6+1 \\ 2+7 & 5+9 & 4+6 \end{bmatrix} = \begin{bmatrix} 9 & 3 & 7 \\ 4 & 8 & 7 \\ 9 & 14 & 10 \end{bmatrix} \qquad (b) \; B + A = \begin{bmatrix} 2+7 & 0+3 & 5+2 \\ 3+1 & 4+4 & 1+6 \\ 7+2 & 9+5 & 6+4 \end{bmatrix} = \begin{bmatrix} 9 & 3 & 7 \\ 4 & 8 & 7 \\ 9 & 14 & 10 \end{bmatrix}$$

$A + B = B + A$.   This illustrates that the commutative law does apply to matrix addition.

Problems 10.35–10.42 illustrate the application of the commutative law to other matrix operations.

10.35. Find (a) $A - B$ and (b) $-B + A$, given

$$A = \begin{bmatrix} 5 & 3 \\ 4 & 9 \\ 10 & 8 \\ 6 & 12 \end{bmatrix} \qquad B = \begin{bmatrix} 3 & 13 \\ 7 & 9 \\ 2 & 1 \\ 8 & 6 \end{bmatrix}$$

(a) $A - B = \begin{bmatrix} 5-3 & 3-13 \\ 4-7 & 9-9 \\ 10-2 & 8-1 \\ 6-8 & 12-6 \end{bmatrix} = \begin{bmatrix} 2 & -10 \\ -3 & 0 \\ 8 & 7 \\ -2 & 6 \end{bmatrix}$ (b) $-B + A = \begin{bmatrix} -3+5 & -13+3 \\ -7+4 & -9+9 \\ -2+10 & -1+8 \\ -8+6 & -6+12 \end{bmatrix} = \begin{bmatrix} 2 & -10 \\ -3 & 0 \\ 8 & 7 \\ -2 & 6 \end{bmatrix}$

$A - B = -B + A$.   This illustrates that matrix subtraction is commutative.

10.36. Find (a) AB and (b) BA, given

$$A = \begin{bmatrix} 4 & 12 & 9 & 6 \end{bmatrix} \qquad B = \begin{bmatrix} 13 \\ 5 \\ -2 \\ 7 \end{bmatrix}$$

Check for conformability first and indicate the dimensions of the product matrix.

(a) AB is defined; $(1 \times 4) = (4 \times 1)$.   The product will be a (1×1) matrix or scalar.

$$AB = [4(13) + 12(5) + 9(-2) + 6(7)] = 136$$

(b) BA is also defined; $(4 \times 1) = (1 \times 4)$;   the product will be a (4×4) matrix.

$$BA = \begin{bmatrix} 13(4) & 13(12) & 13(9) & 13(6) \\ 5(4) & 5(12) & 5(9) & 5(6) \\ -2(4) & -2(12) & -2(9) & -2(6) \\ 7(4) & 7(12) & 7(9) & 7(6) \end{bmatrix} = \begin{bmatrix} 52 & 156 & 117 & 78 \\ 20 & 60 & 45 & 30 \\ -8 & -24 & -18 & -12 \\ 28 & 84 & 63 & 42 \end{bmatrix}$$

$AB \neq BA$.   This illustrates the noncommutative aspect of matrix multiplication.   Products generally differ in dimensions and elements if the order of multiplication is reversed.

10.37. Find (a) AB and (b) BA, given

$$A = \begin{bmatrix} 7 & 4 \\ 6 & 2 \\ 1 & 8 \end{bmatrix} \qquad B = \begin{bmatrix} -3 & 9 & 1 \\ 2 & 12 & 7 \end{bmatrix}$$

(a) AB is defined; $(3 \times 2) = (2 \times 3)$;   the product will be (3×3).

$$AB = \begin{bmatrix} 7(-3)+4(2) & 7(9)+4(12) & 7(1)+4(7) \\ 6(-3)+2(2) & 6(9)+2(12) & 6(1)+2(7) \\ 1(-3)+8(2) & 1(9)+8(12) & 1(1)+8(7) \end{bmatrix} = \begin{bmatrix} -13 & 111 & 35 \\ -14 & 78 & 20 \\ 13 & 105 & 57 \end{bmatrix}$$

(b) BA is also defined; $(2 \times 3) = (3 \times 2)$; the product will be (2×2).

$$BA = \begin{bmatrix} -3(7)+ 9(6)+1(1) & -3(4)+ 9(2)+1(8) \\ 2(7)+12(6)+7(1) & 2(4)+12(2)+7(8) \end{bmatrix} = \begin{bmatrix} 34 & 14 \\ 93 & 88 \end{bmatrix}$$

$AB \neq BA$. Matrix multiplication is not commutative. Here the products again differ in dimensions and elements.

10.38.   Find   (a) AB and   (b) BA, given

$$A = \begin{bmatrix} 4 & 9 & 8 \\ 7 & 6 & 2 \\ 1 & 5 & 3 \end{bmatrix} \qquad B = \begin{bmatrix} 1 & 2 & 0 \\ 5 & 3 & 1 \\ 0 & 2 & 4 \end{bmatrix}$$

(a)   AB is defined; $(3 \times 3) = (3 \times 3)$;   the product will be (3×3).

$$AB = \begin{bmatrix} 4(1)+9(5)+8(0) & 4(2)+9(3)+8(2) & 4(0)+9(1)+8(4) \\ 7(1)+6(5)+2(0) & 7(2)+6(3)+2(2) & 7(0)+6(1)+2(4) \\ 1(1)+5(5)+3(0) & 1(2)+5(3)+3(2) & 1(0)+5(1)+3(4) \end{bmatrix} = \begin{bmatrix} 49 & 51 & 41 \\ 37 & 36 & 14 \\ 26 & 23 & 17 \end{bmatrix}$$

(b)   BA is also defined and will result in a (3×3) matrix.

$$BA = \begin{bmatrix} 1(4)+2(7)+0(1) & 1(9)+2(6)+0(5) & 1(8)+2(2)+0(3) \\ 5(4)+3(7)+1(1) & 5(9)+3(6)+1(5) & 5(8)+3(2)+1(3) \\ 0(4)+2(7)+4(1) & 0(9)+2(6)+4(5) & 0(8)+2(2)+4(3) \end{bmatrix} = \begin{bmatrix} 18 & 21 & 12 \\ 42 & 68 & 49 \\ 18 & 32 & 16 \end{bmatrix}$$

$AB \neq BA$.   The dimensions are the same but the elements differ.

10.39.   Find   (a) AB and   (b) BA, given

$$A = \begin{bmatrix} 7 & 5 & 2 & 6 \\ 1 & 3 & 9 & 4 \end{bmatrix} \qquad B = \begin{bmatrix} 1 \\ 0 \\ -1 \\ 3 \end{bmatrix}$$

(a)   AB is defined; $(2 \times 4) = (4 \times 1)$;   the product will be (2×1).

$$AB = \begin{bmatrix} 7(1)+5(0)+2(-1)+6(3) \\ 1(1)+3(0)+9(-1)+4(3) \end{bmatrix} = \begin{bmatrix} 23 \\ 4 \end{bmatrix}$$

(b)   BA is not defined; $(4 \times 1) \neq (2 \times 4)$.   Multiplication is impossible.   This is but another way in which matrix multiplication is noncommutative.

10.40.   Find   (a) AB and   (b) BA, given

$$A = \begin{bmatrix} 11 & 14 \\ 2 & 6 \end{bmatrix} \qquad B = \begin{bmatrix} 7 & 6 \\ 4 & 5 \\ 1 & 3 \end{bmatrix}$$

(a)   AB is not defined; $(2 \times 2) \neq (3 \times 2)$ and so cannot be multiplied.

(b)   BA is defined; $(3 \times 2) = (2 \times 2)$ and will produce a (3×2) matrix.

$$BA = \begin{bmatrix} 7(11)+6(2) & 7(14)+6(6) \\ 4(11)+5(2) & 4(14)+5(6) \\ 1(11)+3(2) & 1(14)+3(6) \end{bmatrix} = \begin{bmatrix} 89 & 134 \\ 54 & 86 \\ 17 & 32 \end{bmatrix}$$

$BA \neq AB$,   because AB does not exist.

10.41.   Find   (a) AB and   (b) BA, given

$$A = \begin{bmatrix} -2 \\ 4 \\ 7 \end{bmatrix} \qquad B = \begin{bmatrix} 3 & 6 & -2 \end{bmatrix}$$

(a) AB is defined; $(3 \times 1) = (1 \times 3)$;   the product will be a (3×3) matrix.

$$AB = \begin{bmatrix} -2(3) & -2(6) & -2(-2) \\ 4(3) & 4(6) & 4(-2) \\ 7(3) & 7(6) & 7(-2) \end{bmatrix} = \begin{bmatrix} -6 & -12 & 4 \\ 12 & 24 & -8 \\ 21 & 42 & -14 \end{bmatrix}$$

(b) BA is also defined; $(1 \times 3) = (3 \times 1)$,   producing a (1×1) matrix or scalar.

$$BA = [3(-2) + 6(4) + (-2)(7)] = 4$$

Since matrix multiplication is not commutative, reversing the order of multiplication can lead to widely different answers. AB results in a (3×3) matrix, BA results in a scalar.

10.42.   Find   (a) AB and   (b) BA, for a case where B is an identity matrix, given

$$A = \begin{bmatrix} 23 & 6 & 14 \\ 18 & 12 & 9 \\ 24 & 2 & 6 \end{bmatrix} \qquad B = \begin{bmatrix} 1 & 0 & 0 \\ 0 & 1 & 0 \\ 0 & 0 & 1 \end{bmatrix}$$

(a) AB is defined; $(3 \times 3) = (3 \times 3)$.   The product matrix will also be (3×3).

$$AB = \begin{bmatrix} 23(1)+ 6(0)+14(0) & 23(0)+ 6(1)+14(0) & 23(0)+ 6(0)+14(1) \\ 18(1)+12(0)+ 9(0) & 18(0)+12(1)+ 9(0) & 18(0)+12(0)+ 9(1) \\ 24(1)+ 2(0)+ 6(0) & 24(0)+ 2(1)+ 6(0) & 24(0)+ 2(0)+ 6(1) \end{bmatrix} = \begin{bmatrix} 23 & 6 & 14 \\ 18 & 12 & 9 \\ 24 & 2 & 6 \end{bmatrix}$$

(b) BA is also defined; $(3 \times 3) = (3 \times 3)$.   The product matrix will also be (3×3).

$$BA = \begin{bmatrix} 1(23)+0(18)+0(24) & 1(6)+0(12)+0(2) & 1(14)+0(9)+0(6) \\ 0(23)+1(18)+0(24) & 0(6)+1(12)+0(2) & 0(14)+1(9)+0(6) \\ 0(23)+0(18)+1(24) & 0(6)+0(12)+1(2) & 0(14)+0(9)+1(6) \end{bmatrix} = \begin{bmatrix} 23 & 6 & 14 \\ 18 & 12 & 9 \\ 24 & 2 & 6 \end{bmatrix}$$

Here $AB = BA$.   Premultiplication or postmultiplication by an identity matrix gives the original matrix.   Thus in the case of an identity matrix, matrix multiplication is commutative. This will also be true of a matrix and its inverse.   See Section 11.7.

ASSOCIATIVE AND DISTRIBUTIVE LAWS

10.43.   To illustrate whether the associative and distributive laws apply to matrix operations [i.e. $(A + B) + C = A + (B + C)$, $(AB)C = A(BC)$, and $A(B + C) = AB + AC$,   subject to the conditions in Section 10.7], find   (a) $(A + B) + C$ and   (b) $A + (B + C)$, given

$$A = \begin{bmatrix} 6 & 2 & 7 \\ 9 & 5 & 3 \end{bmatrix} \qquad B = \begin{bmatrix} 9 & 1 & 3 \\ 4 & 2 & 6 \end{bmatrix} \qquad C = \begin{bmatrix} 7 & 5 & 1 \\ 10 & 3 & 8 \end{bmatrix}$$

(a)
$$A + B = \begin{bmatrix} 6+9 & 2+1 & 7+3 \\ 9+4 & 5+2 & 3+6 \end{bmatrix} = \begin{bmatrix} 15 & 3 & 10 \\ 13 & 7 & 9 \end{bmatrix}$$

$$(A + B) + C = \begin{bmatrix} 15+ 7 & 3+5 & 10+1 \\ 13+10 & 7+3 & 9+8 \end{bmatrix} = \begin{bmatrix} 22 & 8 & 11 \\ 23 & 10 & 17 \end{bmatrix}$$

(b)
$$B + C = \begin{bmatrix} 9+ 7 & 1+5 & 3+1 \\ 4+10 & 2+3 & 6+8 \end{bmatrix} = \begin{bmatrix} 16 & 6 & 4 \\ 14 & 5 & 14 \end{bmatrix}$$

$$A + (B + C) = \begin{bmatrix} 6+16 & 2+6 & 7+ 4 \\ 9+14 & 5+5 & 3+14 \end{bmatrix} = \begin{bmatrix} 22 & 8 & 11 \\ 23 & 10 & 17 \end{bmatrix}$$

Thus, $(A + B) + C = A + (B + C)$.   This illustrates that matrix addition is associative.   Other aspects of these laws are demonstrated in Problems 10.44–10.47.

10.44. Find (a) $(A - B) + C$ and (b) $A + (-B + C)$, given

$$A = \begin{bmatrix} 7 \\ 6 \\ 12 \end{bmatrix} \qquad B = \begin{bmatrix} 3 \\ 8 \\ 5 \end{bmatrix} \qquad C = \begin{bmatrix} 13 \\ 2 \\ 6 \end{bmatrix}$$

(a) $A - B = \begin{bmatrix} 7-3 \\ 6-8 \\ 12-5 \end{bmatrix} = \begin{bmatrix} 4 \\ -2 \\ 7 \end{bmatrix}$ (b) $-B + C = \begin{bmatrix} -3+13 \\ -8+2 \\ -5+6 \end{bmatrix} = \begin{bmatrix} 10 \\ -6 \\ 1 \end{bmatrix}$

$(A - B) + C = \begin{bmatrix} 4+13 \\ -2+2 \\ 7+6 \end{bmatrix} = \begin{bmatrix} 17 \\ 0 \\ 13 \end{bmatrix}$ $A + (-B + C) = \begin{bmatrix} 7+10 \\ 6+(-6) \\ 12+1 \end{bmatrix} = \begin{bmatrix} 17 \\ 0 \\ 13 \end{bmatrix}$

Matrix subtraction is also associative.

10.45. Find (a) $(AB)C$ and (b) $A(BC)$, given

$$A = [7 \quad 1 \quad 5] \qquad B = \begin{bmatrix} 6 & 5 \\ 2 & 4 \\ 3 & 8 \end{bmatrix} \qquad C = \begin{bmatrix} 9 & 4 \\ 3 & 10 \end{bmatrix}$$

(a) AB is defined; $(1 \times 3) = (3 \times 2)$, producing a (1×2) matrix.

$$AB = [7(6) + 1(2) + 5(3) \quad 7(5) + 1(4) + 5(8)] = [59 \quad 79]$$

$(AB)C$ is defined; $(1 \times 2) = (2 \times 2)$, leaving a (1×2) matrix.

$$(AB)C = [59(9) + 79(3) \quad 59(4) + 79(10)] = [768 \quad 1026]$$

(b) BC is defined; $(3 \times 2) = (2 \times 2)$, creating a (3×2) matrix.

$$BC = \begin{bmatrix} 6(9) + 5(3) & 6(4) + 5(10) \\ 2(9) + 4(3) & 2(4) + 4(10) \\ 3(9) + 8(3) & 3(4) + 8(10) \end{bmatrix} = \begin{bmatrix} 69 & 74 \\ 30 & 48 \\ 51 & 92 \end{bmatrix}$$

$A(BC)$ is also defined; $(1 \times 3) = (3 \times 2)$, producing a (1×2) matrix.

$$A(BC) = [7(69) + 1(30) + 5(51) \quad 7(74) + 1(48) + 5(92)] = [768 \quad 1026]$$

Matrix multiplication is associative, provided the proper order of multiplication is maintained.

10.46. Find (a) $A(B + C)$ and (b) $AB + AC$, given

$$A = [4 \quad 7 \quad 2] \qquad B = \begin{bmatrix} 6 \\ 5 \\ 1 \end{bmatrix} \qquad C = \begin{bmatrix} 9 \\ 5 \\ 8 \end{bmatrix}$$

(a) $B + C = \begin{bmatrix} 6+9 \\ 5+5 \\ 1+8 \end{bmatrix} = \begin{bmatrix} 15 \\ 10 \\ 9 \end{bmatrix}$

$A(B + C)$ is defined; $(1 \times 3) = (3 \times 1)$. The product matrix will be (1×1).

$$A(B + C) = [4(15) + 7(10) + 2(9)] = 148$$

(b) AB is defined; $(1 \times 3) = (3 \times 1)$, producing a (1×1) matrix.

$$AB = [4(6) + 7(5) + 2(1)] = 61$$

AC is defined; $(1 \times 3) = (3 \times 1)$, also producing a (1×1) matrix.

$$AC = [4(9) + 7(5) + 2(8)] = 87$$

Thus, $AB + AC = 61 + 87 = 148$. This illustrates the distributive law of matrix multiplication.

10.47. A hamburger chain sells 1000 hamburgers, 600 cheeseburgers, and 1200 milk shakes in a week. The price of a hamburger is 45¢, a cheeseburger 60¢, and a milk shake 50¢. The cost to the chain of a hamburger is 38¢, a cheeseburger 42¢, and a milk shake 32¢. Find the firm's profit for the week, using (a) total concepts and (b) per-unit analysis to prove that matrix multiplication is distributive.

(a) The quantity of goods sold (Q), the selling price of the goods (P), and the cost of goods (C) can all be represented in matrix form:

$$Q = \begin{bmatrix} 1000 \\ 600 \\ 1200 \end{bmatrix} \qquad P = \begin{bmatrix} 0.45 \\ 0.60 \\ 0.50 \end{bmatrix} \qquad C = \begin{bmatrix} 0.38 \\ 0.42 \\ 0.32 \end{bmatrix}$$

Total revenue (TR) is

$$TR = PQ = \begin{bmatrix} 0.45 \\ 0.60 \\ 0.50 \end{bmatrix} \begin{bmatrix} 1000 \\ 600 \\ 1200 \end{bmatrix}$$

which is not defined as given. Taking the transpose of P or Q will render the vectors conformable for multiplication. Note that the order of multiplication is all important. Row-vector multiplication ($P'Q$ or $Q'P$) will produce the scalar required; vector-row multiplication (PQ' or QP') will produce a (3×3) matrix that has no economic meaning. Thus, taking the transpose of P and premultiplying, we get

$$TR = P'Q = [0.45 \quad 0.60 \quad 0.50] \begin{bmatrix} 1000 \\ 600 \\ 1200 \end{bmatrix}$$

where $P'Q$ is defined; $(1 \times 3) = (3 \times 1)$, producing a (1×1) matrix or scalar.

$$TR = [0.45(1000) + 0.60(600) + 0.50(1200)] = 1410$$

Similarly, total cost (TC) is $TC = C'Q$:

$$TC = [0.38 \quad 0.42 \quad 0.32] \begin{bmatrix} 1000 \\ 600 \\ 1200 \end{bmatrix} = [0.38(1000) + 0.42(600) + 0.32(1200)] = 1016$$

Profits, therefore, are

$$\Pi = TR - TC = 1410 - 1016 = 394$$

(b) Using per-unit analysis, the per-unit profit (U) is

$$U = P - C = \begin{bmatrix} 0.45 \\ 0.60 \\ 0.50 \end{bmatrix} - \begin{bmatrix} 0.38 \\ 0.42 \\ 0.32 \end{bmatrix} = \begin{bmatrix} 0.07 \\ 0.18 \\ 0.18 \end{bmatrix}$$

Total profit (Π) is per-unit profit times the number of items sold.

$$\Pi = UQ = \begin{bmatrix} 0.07 \\ 0.18 \\ 0.18 \end{bmatrix} \begin{bmatrix} 1000 \\ 600 \\ 1200 \end{bmatrix}$$

which is undefined. Taking the transpose of U,

$$\Pi = U'P = [0.07 \quad 0.18 \quad 0.18] \begin{bmatrix} 1000 \\ 600 \\ 1200 \end{bmatrix}$$

$$= [0.07(1000) + 0.18(600) + 0.18(1200)] = 394 \qquad \text{Q.E.D.}$$

10.48. Crazy Teddie's sells 700 LP's, 400 tapes, and 200 stereos each week. The selling price of LP's is $4, tapes $6, and stereos $150. The cost to the shop is $3.25 for an LP, $4.75 for a tape, and $125 for a stereo. Find weekly profits by using (a) total and (b) per-unit concepts.

(a)
$$Q = \begin{bmatrix} 700 \\ 400 \\ 200 \end{bmatrix} \qquad P = \begin{bmatrix} 4 \\ 6 \\ 150 \end{bmatrix} \qquad C = \begin{bmatrix} 3.25 \\ 4.75 \\ 125.00 \end{bmatrix}$$

$$TR = P'Q = \begin{bmatrix} 4 & 6 & 150 \end{bmatrix} \begin{bmatrix} 700 \\ 400 \\ 200 \end{bmatrix} = [4(700) + 6(400) + 150(200)] = 35,200$$

$$TC = C'Q = \begin{bmatrix} 3.25 & 4.75 & 125 \end{bmatrix} \begin{bmatrix} 700 \\ 400 \\ 200 \end{bmatrix} = [3.25(700) + 4.75(400) + 125(200)] = 29,175$$

$$\Pi = TR - TC = 35,200 - 29,175 = 6025$$

(b) Per-unit profit (U) is

$$U = P - C = \begin{bmatrix} 4 \\ 6 \\ 150 \end{bmatrix} - \begin{bmatrix} 3.25 \\ 4.75 \\ 125.00 \end{bmatrix} = \begin{bmatrix} 0.75 \\ 1.25 \\ 25.00 \end{bmatrix}$$

Total profit Π is

$$\Pi = U'Q = \begin{bmatrix} 0.75 & 1.25 & 25 \end{bmatrix} \begin{bmatrix} 700 \\ 400 \\ 200 \end{bmatrix} = [0.75(700) + 1.25(400) + 25(200)] = 6025$$

UNIQUE PROPERTIES OF MATRICES

10.49. Given
$$A = \begin{bmatrix} 6 & -12 \\ -3 & 6 \end{bmatrix} \qquad B = \begin{bmatrix} 12 & 6 \\ 6 & 3 \end{bmatrix}$$

(a) Find AB. (b) Why is the product unique?

(a)
$$AB = \begin{bmatrix} 6(12) - 12(6) & 6(6) - 12(3) \\ -3(12) + 6(6) & -3(6) + 6(3) \end{bmatrix} = \begin{bmatrix} 0 & 0 \\ 0 & 0 \end{bmatrix}$$

(b) The product AB is unique to matrix algebra in that, unlike ordinary algebra in which the product of two nonzero numbers can never equal zero, the product of two non-null matrices may produce a null matrix. The reason for this is that the two original matrices are singular. A *singular matrix* is one in which a row or column is a multiple of another row or column (see Section 11.1). In this problem, row_1 of A is (-2) times row_2, and column_2 is (-2) times column_1. In B, row_1 is 2 times row_2, and column_1 is 2 times column_2. Thus, in matrix algebra, multiplication involving singular matrices may, but need not, produce a null matrix as a solution. See Problem 10.50.

10.50. (a) Find AB and (b) comment on the solution, given

$$A = \begin{bmatrix} 6 & 12 \\ 3 & 6 \end{bmatrix} \qquad B = \begin{bmatrix} 12 & 6 \\ 6 & 3 \end{bmatrix}$$

(a)
$$AB = \begin{bmatrix} 6(12) + 12(6) & 6(6) + 12(3) \\ 3(12) + 6(6) & 3(6) + 6(3) \end{bmatrix} = \begin{bmatrix} 144 & 72 \\ 72 & 36 \end{bmatrix}$$

(b) While both A and B are singular, they do not produce a null matrix. The product AB, however, is also singular.

10.51. Given

$$A = \begin{bmatrix} 4 & 8 \\ 1 & 2 \end{bmatrix} \qquad B = \begin{bmatrix} 2 & 1 \\ 2 & 2 \end{bmatrix} \qquad C = \begin{bmatrix} -2 & 1 \\ 4 & 2 \end{bmatrix}$$

(a) Find AB and AC. (b) Comment on the unusual property of the solutions.

(a)
$$AB = \begin{bmatrix} 4(2) + 8(2) & 4(1) + 8(2) \\ 1(2) + 2(2) & 1(1) + 2(2) \end{bmatrix} = \begin{bmatrix} 24 & 20 \\ 6 & 5 \end{bmatrix}$$

$$AC = \begin{bmatrix} 4(-2) + 8(4) & 4(1) + 8(2) \\ 1(-2) + 2(4) & 1(1) + 2(2) \end{bmatrix} = \begin{bmatrix} 24 & 20 \\ 6 & 5 \end{bmatrix}$$

(b) $AB = AC$, even though $B \neq C$. Unlike algebra where multiplication of one number by two different numbers cannot give the same product, in matrix algebra multiplication of one matrix by two different matrices may, but need not, produce identical matrices. In this case, A is a singular matrix.

GAUSSIAN METHOD OF SOLVING MATRIX EQUATIONS

10.52. Express the following system of linear equations in (a) matrix form and (b) an augmented matrix, letting A = the coefficient matrix, X = the column vector of variables, and B = the column vector of parameters.

$$7x_1 + 8x_2 = 120$$
$$6x_1 + 9x_2 = 98$$

(a)
$$AX = B$$
$$\begin{bmatrix} 7 & 8 \\ 6 & 9 \end{bmatrix} \begin{bmatrix} x_1 \\ x_2 \end{bmatrix} = \begin{bmatrix} 120 \\ 98 \end{bmatrix}$$

(b)
$$A \mid B = \begin{bmatrix} 7 & 8 & \vert & 120 \\ 6 & 9 & \vert & 98 \end{bmatrix}$$

10.53. Redo Problem 10.52, given

$$4x_1 + 2x_2 + 9x_3 = 149$$
$$2x_1 + 8x_2 + 7x_3 = 204$$
$$5x_1 + 6x_2 + 3x_3 = 168$$

(a)
$$AX = B$$
$$\begin{bmatrix} 4 & 2 & 9 \\ 2 & 8 & 7 \\ 5 & 6 & 3 \end{bmatrix} \begin{bmatrix} x_1 \\ x_2 \\ x_3 \end{bmatrix} = \begin{bmatrix} 149 \\ 204 \\ 168 \end{bmatrix}$$

(b)
$$A \mid B = \begin{bmatrix} 4 & 2 & 9 & \vert & 149 \\ 2 & 8 & 7 & \vert & 204 \\ 5 & 6 & 3 & \vert & 168 \end{bmatrix}$$

10.54. Use the Gaussian elimination method to solve the following system of linear equations:

$$3x_1 + 6x_2 = 60$$
$$5x_1 + 4x_2 = 52$$

First, express the system of equations in augmented matrix form.

$$\begin{bmatrix} 3 & 6 & \vert & 60 \\ 5 & 4 & \vert & 52 \end{bmatrix}$$

Then apply row operations to convert the coefficient matrix on the left to an identity matrix. The simplest way to do this is to get 1 as the first element on the principal diagonal and clear column$_1$, then get 1 as the second element on the principal diagonal and clear column$_2$, etc., as follows:

1a. Multiply row$_1$ by $\frac{1}{3}$:

$$\begin{bmatrix} 1 & 2 & | & 20 \\ 5 & 4 & | & 52 \end{bmatrix}$$

1b. Subtract 5 times row$_1$ from row$_2$:

$$\begin{bmatrix} 1 & 2 & | & 20 \\ 0 & -6 & | & -48 \end{bmatrix}$$

2a. Multiply row$_2$ by $(-\frac{1}{6})$:

$$\begin{bmatrix} 1 & 2 & | & 20 \\ 0 & 1 & | & 8 \end{bmatrix}$$

2b. Finally, subtract 2 times row$_2$ from row$_1$:

$$\begin{bmatrix} 1 & 0 & | & 4 \\ 0 & 1 & | & 8 \end{bmatrix}$$

Thus, $x_1 = 4$ and $x_2 = 8$, since

$$\begin{bmatrix} 1 & 0 \\ 0 & 1 \end{bmatrix}\begin{bmatrix} x_1 \\ x_2 \end{bmatrix} = \begin{bmatrix} 4 \\ 8 \end{bmatrix}$$

10.55. Redo Problem 10.54, given

$$2x_1 + 8x_2 = 34$$
$$4x_1 + 12x_2 = 56$$

The augmented matrix is

$$\begin{bmatrix} 2 & 8 & | & 34 \\ 4 & 12 & | & 56 \end{bmatrix}$$

1a. Multiply row$_1$ by $\frac{1}{2}$:

$$\begin{bmatrix} 1 & 4 & | & 17 \\ 4 & 12 & | & 56 \end{bmatrix}$$

1b. Subtract 4 times row$_1$ from row$_2$:

$$\begin{bmatrix} 1 & 4 & | & 17 \\ 0 & -4 & | & -12 \end{bmatrix}$$

2a. Multiply row$_2$ by $-\frac{1}{4}$:

$$\begin{bmatrix} 1 & 4 & | & 17 \\ 0 & 1 & | & 3 \end{bmatrix}$$

2b. Subtract 4 times row$_2$ from row$_1$:

$$\begin{bmatrix} 1 & 0 & | & 5 \\ 0 & 1 & | & 3 \end{bmatrix}$$

Thus, $x_1 = 5$ and $x_2 = 3$.

10.56. Redo Problem 10.54, given

$$4x_1 + 10x_2 = 30$$
$$6x_1 + 25x_2 = 67$$

The augmented matrix is

$$\begin{bmatrix} 4 & 10 & | & 30 \\ 6 & 25 & | & 67 \end{bmatrix}$$

1a. Multiply row$_1$ by $\frac{1}{4}$:

$$\begin{bmatrix} 1 & 2.5 & | & 7.5 \\ 6 & 25 & | & 67 \end{bmatrix}$$

1b. Subtract 6 times row$_1$ from row$_2$:

$$\begin{bmatrix} 1 & 2.5 & | & 7.5 \\ 0 & 10 & | & 22 \end{bmatrix}$$

2a. Multiply row$_2$ by $\frac{1}{10}$:

$$\begin{bmatrix} 1 & 2.5 & | & 7.5 \\ 0 & 1 & | & 2.2 \end{bmatrix}$$

2b. Subtract 2.5 times row$_2$ from row$_1$:

$$\begin{bmatrix} 1 & 0 & | & 2 \\ 0 & 1 & | & 2.2 \end{bmatrix}$$

Thus, $x_1 = 2$ and $x_2 = 2.2$.

10.57. Redo Problem 10.54, given

$$3x_1 + 7x_2 = 67$$
$$2x_1 + 9x_2 = 75$$

The augmented matrix is

$$\begin{bmatrix} 3 & 7 & | & 67 \\ 2 & 9 & | & 75 \end{bmatrix}$$

1a. Multiply row$_1$ by $\frac{1}{3}$:

$$\begin{bmatrix} 1 & \frac{7}{3} & | & \frac{67}{3} \\ 2 & 9 & | & 75 \end{bmatrix}$$

1b. Subtract 2 times row$_1$ from row$_2$:

$$\begin{bmatrix} 1 & \frac{7}{3} & | & \frac{67}{3} \\ 0 & \frac{13}{3} & | & \frac{91}{3} \end{bmatrix}$$

2a. Multiply row$_2$ by $\frac{3}{13}$:

$$\begin{bmatrix} 1 & \frac{7}{3} & | & \frac{67}{3} \\ 0 & 1 & | & 7 \end{bmatrix}$$

2b. Subtract $\frac{7}{3}$ times row$_2$ from row$_1$,

$$\begin{bmatrix} 1 & 0 & | & 6 \\ 0 & 1 & | & 7 \end{bmatrix}$$

Thus, $x_1 = 6$ and $x_2 = 7$.

10.58. Solve the following system of linear equations using the Gaussian elimination method:

$$3x_1 + 2x_2 + 6x_3 = 24$$
$$2x_1 + 4x_2 + 3x_3 = 23$$
$$5x_1 + 3x_2 + 4x_3 = 33$$

The augmented matrix is

$$\begin{bmatrix} 3 & 2 & 6 & | & 24 \\ 2 & 4 & 3 & | & 23 \\ 5 & 3 & 4 & | & 33 \end{bmatrix}$$

1a. Multiply row$_1$ by $\frac{1}{3}$:

$$\begin{bmatrix} 1 & \frac{2}{3} & 2 & | & 8 \\ 2 & 4 & 3 & | & 23 \\ 5 & 3 & 4 & | & 33 \end{bmatrix}$$

1b. Subtract 2 times row$_1$ from row$_2$ and 5 times row$_1$ from row$_3$:

$$\begin{bmatrix} 1 & \frac{2}{3} & 2 & | & 8 \\ 0 & \frac{8}{3} & -1 & | & 7 \\ 0 & -\frac{1}{3} & -6 & | & -7 \end{bmatrix}$$

2a. Multiply row$_2$ by $\frac{3}{8}$:

$$\begin{bmatrix} 1 & \frac{2}{3} & 2 & | & 8 \\ 0 & 1 & -\frac{3}{8} & | & \frac{21}{8} \\ 0 & -\frac{1}{3} & -6 & | & -7 \end{bmatrix}$$

2b. Subtract $\frac{2}{3}$ times row$_2$ from row$_1$ and add $\frac{1}{3}$ times row$_2$ to row$_3$:

$$\begin{bmatrix} 1 & 0 & \frac{9}{4} & | & \frac{25}{4} \\ 0 & 1 & -\frac{3}{8} & | & \frac{21}{8} \\ 0 & 0 & -\frac{49}{8} & | & -\frac{49}{8} \end{bmatrix}$$

3a. Multiply row$_3$ by $-\frac{8}{49}$:

$$\begin{bmatrix} 1 & 0 & \frac{9}{4} & \bigm| & \frac{25}{4} \\ 0 & 1 & -\frac{3}{8} & \bigm| & \frac{21}{8} \\ 0 & 0 & 1 & \bigm| & 1 \end{bmatrix}$$

3b. Subtract $\frac{9}{4}$ times row$_3$ from row$_1$ and add $\frac{3}{8}$ times row$_3$ to row$_2$:

$$\begin{bmatrix} 1 & 0 & 0 & \bigm| & 4 \\ 0 & 1 & 0 & \bigm| & 3 \\ 0 & 0 & 1 & \bigm| & 1 \end{bmatrix}$$

Thus, $x_1 = 4$, $x_2 = 3$, and $x_3 = 1$.

10.59. Redo Problem 10.58, given

$$6x_1 + 2x_2 + 5x_3 = 73$$
$$7x_1 - 3x_2 + x_3 = -1$$
$$4x_1 + 8x_2 - 9x_3 = -9$$

The augmented matrix in this case is

$$\begin{bmatrix} 6 & 2 & 5 & \bigm| & 73 \\ 7 & -3 & 1 & \bigm| & -1 \\ 4 & 8 & -9 & \bigm| & -9 \end{bmatrix}$$

1a. Multiply row$_1$ by $\frac{1}{6}$:

$$\begin{bmatrix} 1 & \frac{1}{3} & \frac{5}{6} & \bigm| & \frac{73}{6} \\ 7 & -3 & 1 & \bigm| & -1 \\ 4 & 8 & -9 & \bigm| & -9 \end{bmatrix}$$

1b. Subtract 7 times row$_1$ from row$_2$ and subtract 4 times row$_1$ from row$_3$:

$$\begin{bmatrix} 1 & \frac{1}{3} & \frac{5}{6} & \bigm| & \frac{73}{6} \\ 0 & -\frac{16}{3} & -\frac{29}{6} & \bigm| & -\frac{517}{6} \\ 0 & \frac{20}{3} & -\frac{74}{6} & \bigm| & -\frac{173}{3} \end{bmatrix}$$

2a. Multiply row$_2$ by $-\frac{3}{16}$:

$$\begin{bmatrix} 1 & \frac{1}{3} & \frac{5}{6} & \bigm| & \frac{73}{6} \\ 0 & 1 & \frac{29}{32} & \bigm| & \frac{517}{32} \\ 0 & \frac{20}{3} & -\frac{74}{6} & \bigm| & -\frac{173}{3} \end{bmatrix}$$

2b. Subtract $\frac{1}{3}$ times row$_2$ from row$_1$ and subtract $\frac{20}{3}$ times row$_2$ from row$_3$:

$$\begin{bmatrix} 1 & 0 & \frac{51}{96} & \bigm| & \frac{651}{96} \\ 0 & 1 & \frac{29}{32} & \bigm| & \frac{517}{32} \\ 0 & 0 & -\frac{441}{24} & \bigm| & -\frac{3969}{24} \end{bmatrix}$$

3a. Multiply row$_3$ by $-\frac{24}{441}$:

$$\begin{bmatrix} 1 & 0 & \frac{51}{96} & \bigm| & \frac{651}{96} \\ 0 & 1 & \frac{29}{32} & \bigm| & \frac{517}{32} \\ 0 & 0 & 1 & \bigm| & 9 \end{bmatrix}$$

3b. Subtract $\frac{51}{96}$ times row$_3$ from row$_1$ and subtract $\frac{29}{32}$ times row$_3$ from row$_2$:

$$\begin{bmatrix} 1 & 0 & 0 & \bigm| & 2 \\ 0 & 1 & 0 & \bigm| & 8 \\ 0 & 0 & 1 & \bigm| & 9 \end{bmatrix}$$

Thus, $x_1 = 2$, $x_2 = 8$, and $x_3 = 9$.

Chapter 11

Matrix Inversion

11.1 DETERMINANTS AND NONSINGULARITY

The determinant $|A|$ of a (2×2) matrix is called a *second-order determinant*, and is derived by taking the product of the two elements on the principal diagonal and subtracting from it the product of the two elements off the principal diagonal. Thus, given a general (2×2) matrix,

$$A = \begin{bmatrix} a_{11} & a_{12} \\ a_{21} & a_{22} \end{bmatrix}$$

the determinant, $|A| = a_{11}a_{22} - a_{21}a_{12}$.

The determinant is a single number or scalar and is found only in square matrices. If the determinant of a matrix is nonzero, the matrix is nonsingular (i.e. not linearly dependent). A *singular matrix*, for which $|A| = 0$, is one in which at least one row or column is a multiple of another row or column.

Example 1. Determinants are calculated as follows, given

$$A = \begin{bmatrix} 6 & 4 \\ 7 & 9 \end{bmatrix} \qquad B = \begin{bmatrix} 4 & 6 \\ 6 & 9 \end{bmatrix}$$

From the rules stated above,

$$|A| = 6(9) - 7(4) = 26$$

Since $|A| \neq 0$, the matrix is nonsingular, i.e. it is linearly independent. On the other hand,

$$|B| = 4(9) - 6(6) = 0$$

Since $|B| = 0$, B is singular or linearly dependent. Closer examination shows that row_2 and $column_2$ are 1.5 times row_1 and $column_1$ respectively.

11.2 HIGHER-ORDER DETERMINANTS

The determinant of a (3×3) matrix

$$A = \begin{bmatrix} a_{11} & a_{12} & a_{13} \\ a_{21} & a_{22} & a_{23} \\ a_{31} & a_{32} & a_{33} \end{bmatrix}$$

is called a *third-order determinant* and is the summation of three products. To derive the three products,

1. Take the first element of the first row, a_{11}, and mentally delete the row and column in which it appears. See (a) below. Then multiply a_{11} by the determinant of the remaining elements.

2. Take the second element of the first row, a_{12}, and mentally delete the row and column in which it appears. See (b) below. Then multiply a_{12} by (-1) times the determinant of the remaining elements.

3. Take the third element of the first row, a_{13}, and mentally delete the row and column in which it appears. See (c) below. Then multiply a_{13} by the determinant of the remaining elements.

$$\begin{bmatrix} a_{11} & a_{12} & a_{13} \\ a_{21} & a_{22} & a_{23} \\ a_{31} & a_{32} & a_{33} \end{bmatrix} \qquad \begin{bmatrix} a_{11} & a_{12} & a_{13} \\ a_{21} & a_{22} & a_{23} \\ a_{31} & a_{32} & a_{33} \end{bmatrix} \qquad \begin{bmatrix} a_{11} & a_{12} & a_{13} \\ a_{21} & a_{22} & a_{23} \\ a_{31} & a_{32} & a_{33} \end{bmatrix}$$

$$(a) \qquad\qquad\qquad (b) \qquad\qquad\qquad (c)$$

Thus, the calculations for the determinant are as follows:

$$|A| = a_{11}\begin{vmatrix} a_{22} & a_{23} \\ a_{32} & a_{33} \end{vmatrix} + a_{12}(-1)\begin{vmatrix} a_{21} & a_{23} \\ a_{31} & a_{33} \end{vmatrix} + a_{13}\begin{vmatrix} a_{21} & a_{22} \\ a_{31} & a_{32} \end{vmatrix} \qquad (11.1)$$

$$= a_{11}(a_{22}a_{33} - a_{32}a_{23}) - a_{12}(a_{21}a_{33} - a_{31}a_{23}) + a_{13}(a_{21}a_{32} - a_{31}a_{22}) = \text{a scalar}$$

Example 2. Given

$$A = \begin{bmatrix} 8 & 3 & 2 \\ 6 & 4 & 7 \\ 5 & 1 & 3 \end{bmatrix}$$

the determinant, $|A|$, is calculated as follows:

$$|A| = 8\begin{vmatrix} 4 & 7 \\ 1 & 3 \end{vmatrix} + 3(-1)\begin{vmatrix} 6 & 7 \\ 5 & 3 \end{vmatrix} + 2\begin{vmatrix} 6 & 4 \\ 5 & 1 \end{vmatrix}$$

$$= 8[4(3) - 1(7)] - 3[6(3) - 5(7)] + 2[6(1) - 5(4)]$$

$$= 8(5) - 3(-17) + 2(-14) = 63$$

Since $|A| \neq 0$, A is nonsingular.

11.3   MINORS AND COFACTORS

The elements of a matrix remaining after the deletion process described in Section 11.2 form a subdeterminant of the matrix called a *minor*. Thus, a *minor* $|M_{ij}|$ is the determinant of the submatrix formed by deleting the ith row and jth column of the matrix. Using the matrix from Section 11.2,

$$|M_{11}| = \begin{vmatrix} a_{22} & a_{23} \\ a_{32} & a_{33} \end{vmatrix} \qquad |M_{12}| = \begin{vmatrix} a_{21} & a_{23} \\ a_{31} & a_{33} \end{vmatrix} \qquad |M_{13}| = \begin{vmatrix} a_{21} & a_{22} \\ a_{31} & a_{32} \end{vmatrix}$$

where $|M_{11}|$ is the minor of a_{11}; $|M_{12}|$, the minor of a_{12}; and $|M_{13}|$, the minor of a_{13}. Thus, the determinant in (11.1) can be written

$$|A| = a_{11}|M_{11}| + a_{12}(-1)|M_{12}| + a_{13}|M_{13}| \qquad (11.2)$$

A minor coupled with a prescribed sign is called a *cofactor*, $|C_{ij}|$. The rule for the sign of the cofactor is

$$|C_{ij}| = (-1)^{i+j}|M_{ij}|$$

Thus if the sum of the subscripts is an even number, $|C_{ij}| = |M_{ij}|$, since (-1) raised to an even power is positive. If $i + j$ is equal to an odd number, $|C_{ij}| = -|M_{ij}|$, since (-1) raised to an odd power is negative.

Example 3.   The cofactors,   (1) $|C_{11}|$,   (2) $|C_{12}|$, and   (3) $|C_{13}|$,   for the matrix in Section 11.2 are found as follows:

(1) $$|C_{11}| = (-1)^{1+1}|M_{11}|$$

Since $(-1)^{1+1} = (-1)^2 = 1$,

$$|C_{11}| = |M_{11}| = \begin{vmatrix} a_{22} & a_{23} \\ a_{32} & a_{33} \end{vmatrix}$$

(2) $\qquad |C_{12}| = (-1)^{1+2}|M_{12}|$

Since $(-1)^{1+2} = (-1)^3 = -1$,

$$|C_{12}| = -|M_{12}| = -\begin{vmatrix} a_{21} & a_{23} \\ a_{31} & a_{33} \end{vmatrix}$$

(3) $\qquad |C_{13}| = (-1)^{1+3}|M_{13}|$

Since $(-1)^{1+3} = (-1)^4 = 1$,

$$|C_{13}| = |M_{13}| = \begin{vmatrix} a_{21} & a_{22} \\ a_{31} & a_{32} \end{vmatrix}$$

11.4 LAPLACE EXPANSION

Laplace expansion is a method for evaluating determinants in terms of cofactors. It thus simplifies matters by permitting higher-order determinants to be established in terms of lower-order determinants. Laplace expansion of a third-order determinant can be expressed as

$$|A| = a_{11}|C_{11}| + a_{12}|C_{12}| + a_{13}|C_{13}| \qquad (11.3)$$

where $|C_{ij}|$ is a cofactor based on a second-order determinant. Here, unlike (11.1) and (11.2), a_{12} is not explicitly multiplied by (-1), since by the rule of cofactors, $|C_{12}|$ will automatically be multiplied by (-1).

Laplace expansion also allows evaluation of a determinant along any row or column. Selection of a row or column with more zeros than others simplifies evaluation of the determinant by eliminating terms.

Example 4.   Given

$$A = \begin{bmatrix} 12 & 7 & 0 \\ 5 & 8 & 3 \\ 6 & 7 & 0 \end{bmatrix}$$

the determinant is found by Laplace expansion along the third column, as demonstrated below:

$$|A| = a_{13}|C_{13}| + a_{23}|C_{23}| + a_{33}|C_{33}|$$

Since a_{13} and $a_{33} = 0$,

$$|A| = a_{23}|C_{23}| \qquad (11.4)$$

Deleting row_2 and column_3 to find $|C_{23}|$,

$$|C_{23}| = (-1)^{2+3} \begin{vmatrix} 12 & 7 \\ 6 & 7 \end{vmatrix}$$

$$= (-1)[12(7) - 6(7)] = -42$$

Then substituting in (11.4) where $a_{23} = 3$, $\quad |A| = 3(-42) = -126$.

The accuracy of this answer can be readily checked by expanding along the first row and solving for $|A|$.

Example 5.   Laplace expansion for a fourth-order determinant is

$$|A| = a_{11}|C_{11}| + a_{12}|C_{12}| + a_{13}|C_{13}| + a_{14}|C_{14}|$$

where the cofactors are third-order subdeterminants which in turn can be reduced to second-order subdeterminants, as above. Fifth-order determinants and higher are treated in similar fashion. See Problem 11.30(d)–(f).

11.5. PROPERTIES OF A DETERMINANT

The following seven properties of determinants provide the ways in which a matrix can be manipulated to simplify its elements or reduce part of them to zero, before evaluating a determinant:

1. Adding or subtracting any nonzero multiple of one row (or column) from another row (or column) will have no effect on the determinant.

2. Interchanging any two rows or columns of a matrix will change the sign, but not the absolute value, of the determinant.

3. Multiplying the elements of any row or column by a constant will cause the determinant to be multiplied by the constant.

4. The determinant of a *triangular matrix*, i.e. a matrix with zero elements everywhere above *or* below the principal diagonal, is equal to the product of the elements on the principal diagonal.

5. The determinant of a matrix equals the determinant of its transpose: $|A| = |A'|$.

6. If all the elements of any row or column are zero, the determinant is zero.

7. If two rows or columns are identical or proportional, i.e. linearly dependent, the determinant is zero.

These properties and their use in matrix manipulation are treated in Problems 11.3–11.21.

11.6 COFACTOR AND ADJOINT MATRICES

A *cofactor matrix* is a matrix in which every element a_{ij} is replaced with its cofactor $|C_{ij}|$. An *adjoint matrix* is the transpose of a cofactor matrix. Thus,

$$C = \begin{bmatrix} |C_{11}| & |C_{12}| & |C_{13}| \\ |C_{21}| & |C_{22}| & |C_{23}| \\ |C_{31}| & |C_{32}| & |C_{33}| \end{bmatrix} \qquad \text{Adj } A = C' = \begin{bmatrix} |C_{11}| & |C_{21}| & |C_{31}| \\ |C_{12}| & |C_{22}| & |C_{32}| \\ |C_{13}| & |C_{23}| & |C_{33}| \end{bmatrix}$$

Example 6.   The cofactor matrix C and the adjoint matrix Adj A are found below, given

$$A = \begin{bmatrix} 2 & 3 & 1 \\ 4 & 1 & 2 \\ 5 & 3 & 4 \end{bmatrix}$$

Replacing the elements a_{ij} with their cofactors $|C_{ij}|$ according to the laws of cofactors,

$$C = \begin{bmatrix} \begin{vmatrix} 1 & 2 \\ 3 & 4 \end{vmatrix} & -\begin{vmatrix} 4 & 2 \\ 5 & 4 \end{vmatrix} & \begin{vmatrix} 4 & 1 \\ 5 & 3 \end{vmatrix} \\ -\begin{vmatrix} 3 & 1 \\ 3 & 4 \end{vmatrix} & \begin{vmatrix} 2 & 1 \\ 5 & 4 \end{vmatrix} & -\begin{vmatrix} 2 & 3 \\ 5 & 3 \end{vmatrix} \\ \begin{vmatrix} 3 & 1 \\ 1 & 2 \end{vmatrix} & -\begin{vmatrix} 2 & 1 \\ 4 & 2 \end{vmatrix} & \begin{vmatrix} 2 & 3 \\ 4 & 1 \end{vmatrix} \end{bmatrix} = \begin{bmatrix} -2 & -6 & 7 \\ -9 & 3 & 9 \\ 5 & 0 & -10 \end{bmatrix}$$

The adjoint matrix Adj A is the transpose of C,

$$\text{Adj } A = C' = \begin{bmatrix} -2 & -9 & 5 \\ -6 & 3 & 0 \\ 7 & 9 & -10 \end{bmatrix}$$

11.7 INVERSE MATRICES

An *inverse matrix* A^{-1}, which can only be found for a square, nonsingular matrix A, is a unique matrix satisfying the relationship,

$$AA^{-1} = I = A^{-1}A$$

Multiplying a matrix by its inverse reduces it to an identity matrix. Thus, the inverse matrix in linear algebra performs much the same function as the reciprocal in ordinary algebra. The formula for deriving the inverse is

$$A^{-1} = \frac{1}{|A|} \text{ Adj } A$$

Example 7.   To find the inverse for $\qquad A = \begin{bmatrix} 4 & 1 & -5 \\ -2 & 3 & 1 \\ 3 & -1 & 4 \end{bmatrix}$

1. Check that it is a square matrix, here 3×3, since only square matrices can have inverses.

2. Evaluate the determinant to be sure $|A| \neq 0$, since only nonsingular matrices can have inverses.

$$|A| = 4[3(4) - (-1)(1)] - 1[(-2)(4) - 3(1)] + (-5)[(-2)(-1) - 3(3)]$$
$$= 52 + 11 + 35 = 98 \neq 0$$

3. Find the cofactor matrix of A,

$$C = \begin{bmatrix} \begin{vmatrix} 3 & 1 \\ -1 & 4 \end{vmatrix} & -\begin{vmatrix} -2 & 1 \\ 3 & 4 \end{vmatrix} & \begin{vmatrix} -2 & 3 \\ 3 & -1 \end{vmatrix} \\ -\begin{vmatrix} 1 & -5 \\ -1 & 4 \end{vmatrix} & \begin{vmatrix} 4 & -5 \\ 3 & 4 \end{vmatrix} & -\begin{vmatrix} 4 & 1 \\ 3 & -1 \end{vmatrix} \\ \begin{vmatrix} 1 & -5 \\ 3 & 1 \end{vmatrix} & -\begin{vmatrix} 4 & -5 \\ -2 & 1 \end{vmatrix} & \begin{vmatrix} 4 & 1 \\ -2 & 3 \end{vmatrix} \end{bmatrix} = \begin{bmatrix} 13 & 11 & -7 \\ 1 & 31 & 7 \\ 16 & 6 & 14 \end{bmatrix}$$

Then transpose the cofactor matrix to get the adjoint matrix.

$$\text{Adj } A = C' = \begin{bmatrix} 13 & 1 & 16 \\ 11 & 31 & 6 \\ -7 & 7 & 14 \end{bmatrix}$$

4. Multiply the adjoint matrix by $1/|A| = \frac{1}{98}$ to get A^{-1}.

$$A^{-1} = \frac{1}{98} \begin{bmatrix} 13 & 1 & 16 \\ 11 & 31 & 6 \\ -7 & 7 & 14 \end{bmatrix} = \begin{bmatrix} \frac{13}{98} & \frac{1}{98} & \frac{16}{98} \\ \frac{11}{98} & \frac{31}{98} & \frac{6}{98} \\ -\frac{1}{14} & \frac{1}{14} & \frac{1}{7} \end{bmatrix}$$

5. To check your answer, multiply AA^{-1} or $A^{-1}A$. Both products will equal I if the answer is correct. An inverse is checked in Problem 11.31(a).

11.8 SOLVING MATRIX EQUATIONS WITH THE INVERSE

An inverse matrix can be used to solve matrix equations. If

$$A_{(n \times n)} X_{(n \times 1)} = B_{(n \times 1)}$$

and the inverse A^{-1} exists, multiplication of both sides of the equation by A^{-1}, following the laws of conformability, gives

$$A^{-1}_{(n \times n)} A_{(n \times n)} X_{(n \times 1)} = A^{-1}_{(n \times n)} B_{(n \times 1)}$$

From Section 11.7, $A^{-1}A = I$.   Thus,

$$I_{(n \times n)} X_{(n \times 1)} = A^{-1}_{(n \times n)} B_{(n \times 1)}$$

From Section 10.8, $IX = X$.   Therefore,

$$X_{(n \times 1)} = (A^{-1}B)_{(n \times 1)}$$

The solution of the equation is given by the product of the inverse of the coefficient matrix A^{-1} and the column vector of constants B.

Example 8.   Matrix equations and the inverse are used below to solve for x_1, x_2, and x_3, given

$$4x_1 + x_2 - 5x_3 = 8$$
$$-2x_1 + 3x_2 + x_3 = 12$$
$$3x_1 - x_2 + 4x_3 = 5$$

First, express the system of equations in matrix form,

$$AX = B$$

$$\begin{bmatrix} 4 & 1 & -5 \\ -2 & 3 & 1 \\ 3 & -1 & 4 \end{bmatrix} \begin{bmatrix} x_1 \\ x_2 \\ x_3 \end{bmatrix} = \begin{bmatrix} 8 \\ 12 \\ 5 \end{bmatrix}$$

From Section 11.8,

$$X = A^{-1}B$$

Since A^{-1} has already been found in Example 7,

$$X = \begin{bmatrix} \frac{13}{98} & \frac{1}{98} & \frac{16}{98} \\ \frac{11}{98} & \frac{31}{98} & \frac{6}{98} \\ -\frac{1}{14} & \frac{1}{14} & \frac{1}{7} \end{bmatrix} \begin{bmatrix} 8 \\ 12 \\ 5 \end{bmatrix} = \begin{bmatrix} \frac{104}{98} + \frac{12}{98} + \frac{80}{98} \\ \frac{88}{98} + \frac{372}{98} + \frac{30}{98} \\ -\frac{8}{14} + \frac{12}{14} + \frac{5}{7} \end{bmatrix} = \begin{bmatrix} \frac{196}{98} \\ \frac{490}{98} \\ \frac{14}{14} \end{bmatrix} = \begin{bmatrix} 2 \\ 5 \\ 1 \end{bmatrix}$$

Thus, $x_1 = 2$, $x_2 = 5$, and $x_3 = 1$.

11.9 CRAMER'S RULE FOR MATRIX SOLUTIONS

Cramer's rule provides a simplified method of solving a system of linear equations through the use of determinants.   Cramer's rule states

$$x_i = \frac{|A_i|}{|A|}$$

where x_i is the ith unknown variable in a series of equations, $|A|$ is the determinant of the coefficient matrix, and $|A_i|$ is the determinant of a special matrix formed from the original coefficient matrix by replacing the column of coefficients of x_i with the column vector of constants.   See Example 9.   Proof for Cramer's rule is given in Problem 11.44.

Example 9.   Cramer's rule is used below to solve the system of equations

$$6x_1 + 5x_2 = 49$$
$$3x_1 + 4x_2 = 32$$

1.   Express the equations in matrix form.

$$AX = B$$

$$\begin{bmatrix} 6 & 5 \\ 3 & 4 \end{bmatrix} \begin{bmatrix} x_1 \\ x_2 \end{bmatrix} = \begin{bmatrix} 49 \\ 32 \end{bmatrix}$$

2.   Find the determinant of A.

$$|A| = 6(4) - 3(5) = 9$$

3.   Then to solve for x_1, replace column$_1$, the coefficients of x_1, with the vector of constants B, forming a new matrix A_1.

$$A_1 = \begin{bmatrix} 49 & 5 \\ 32 & 4 \end{bmatrix}$$

Find the determinant of A_1,

$$|A_1| = 49(4) - 32(5) = 36$$

and use the formula for Cramer's rule,

$$x_1 = \frac{|A_1|}{|A|} = \frac{36}{9} = 4$$

4.   To solve for x_2, replace column$_2$, the coefficients of x_2, from the original matrix, with the column vector of constants B, forming a new matrix A_2.

$$A_2 = \begin{bmatrix} 6 & 49 \\ 3 & 32 \end{bmatrix}$$

Take the determinant,

$$|A_2| = 6(32) - 3(49) = 45$$

and use the formula,

$$x_2 = \frac{|A_2|}{|A|} = \frac{45}{9} = 5$$

For a system of three linear equations, see Problem 11.41(b)–(e).

11.10   THE GAUSSIAN METHOD OF INVERTING A MATRIX

The Gaussian method can also be used to invert a matrix.   Simply set up an augmented matrix with the identity matrix on the right.   Then apply row operations until the coefficient matrix on the left is reduced to an identity matrix.   At that point, the matrix on the right will be the inverse.

The rationale behind this method can be seen in a few mathematical steps.   Start with the augmented matrix, $A \,|\, I$, and multiply both sides by the inverse A^{-1}, $AA^{-1} \,|\, IA^{-1}$.   From Sections 11.7 and 10.8, this reduces to $I \,|\, A^{-1}$ where the identity matrix is now on the left and the inverse is on the right.

Example 10.   To use the Gaussian elimination method to find the inverse for

$$A = \begin{bmatrix} 4 & 1 & -5 \\ -2 & 3 & 1 \\ 3 & -1 & 4 \end{bmatrix}$$

set up the augmented matrix with the identity matrix on the right, as follows:

$$\left[\begin{array}{ccc|ccc} 4 & 1 & -5 & 1 & 0 & 0 \\ -2 & 3 & 1 & 0 & 1 & 0 \\ 3 & -1 & 4 & 0 & 0 & 1 \end{array} \right]$$

Then reduce the coefficient matrix on the left to an identity matrix by applying the row operations outlined in Section 10.12.

1a.   Multiply row$_1$ by $\frac{1}{4}$,

$$\left[\begin{array}{ccc|ccc} 1 & \frac{1}{4} & -\frac{5}{4} & \frac{1}{4} & 0 & 0 \\ -2 & 3 & 1 & 0 & 1 & 0 \\ 3 & -1 & 4 & 0 & 0 & 1 \end{array} \right]$$

1b.   Add 2 times row$_1$ to row$_2$ and subtract 3 times row$_1$ from row$_3$,

$$\left[\begin{array}{ccc|ccc} 1 & \frac{1}{4} & -\frac{5}{4} & \frac{1}{4} & 0 & 0 \\ 0 & \frac{7}{2} & -\frac{3}{2} & \frac{1}{2} & 1 & 0 \\ 0 & -\frac{7}{4} & \frac{31}{4} & -\frac{3}{4} & 0 & 1 \end{array} \right]$$

2a.   Multiply row$_2$ by $\frac{2}{7}$,

$$\left[\begin{array}{ccc|ccc} 1 & \frac{1}{4} & -\frac{5}{4} & \frac{1}{4} & 0 & 0 \\ 0 & 1 & -\frac{3}{7} & \frac{1}{7} & \frac{2}{7} & 0 \\ 0 & -\frac{7}{4} & \frac{31}{4} & -\frac{3}{4} & 0 & 1 \end{array} \right]$$

2b.   Subtract $\frac{1}{4}$ row$_2$ from row$_1$ and add $\frac{7}{4}$ row$_2$ to row$_3$,

$$\left[\begin{array}{ccc|ccc} 1 & 0 & -\frac{8}{7} & \frac{3}{14} & -\frac{1}{14} & 0 \\ 0 & 1 & -\frac{3}{7} & \frac{1}{7} & \frac{2}{7} & 0 \\ 0 & 0 & 7 & -\frac{1}{2} & \frac{1}{2} & 1 \end{array} \right]$$

3a. Multiply row$_3$ by $\frac{1}{7}$,

$$\begin{bmatrix} 1 & 0 & -\frac{8}{7} \\ 0 & 1 & -\frac{3}{7} \\ 0 & 0 & 1 \end{bmatrix} \begin{matrix} \frac{3}{14} & -\frac{1}{14} & 0 \\ \frac{1}{7} & \frac{2}{7} & 0 \\ -\frac{1}{14} & \frac{1}{14} & \frac{1}{7} \end{matrix}$$

3b. Add $\frac{8}{7}$ row$_3$ to row$_1$, and $\frac{3}{7}$ row$_3$ to row$_2$,

$$\begin{bmatrix} 1 & 0 & 0 \\ 0 & 1 & 0 \\ 0 & 0 & 1 \end{bmatrix} \begin{matrix} \frac{13}{98} & \frac{1}{98} & \frac{8}{49} \\ \frac{11}{98} & \frac{31}{98} & \frac{3}{49} \\ -\frac{1}{14} & \frac{1}{14} & \frac{1}{7} \end{matrix}$$

Thus,

$$A^{-1} = \begin{bmatrix} \frac{13}{98} & \frac{1}{98} & \frac{8}{49} \\ \frac{11}{98} & \frac{31}{98} & \frac{3}{49} \\ -\frac{1}{14} & \frac{1}{14} & \frac{1}{7} \end{bmatrix}$$

as found in Example 7 using the adjoint matrix.

Solved Problems

DETERMINANTS

11.1. Find the determinant $|A|$ for each of the following matrices.

(a) $A = \begin{bmatrix} 9 & 13 \\ 15 & 18 \end{bmatrix}$

$$|A| = 9(18) - 15(13) = -33$$

(b) $A = \begin{bmatrix} 40 & -10 \\ 25 & -5 \end{bmatrix}$

$$|A| = 40(-5) - 25(-10) = 50$$

(c) $A = \begin{bmatrix} 7 & 6 \\ 9 & 5 \\ 2 & 12 \end{bmatrix}$

The determinant does not exist because A is a (3×2) matrix and only a square matrix can have a determinant.

11.2. Redo Problem 11.1 for each of the following. Notice how the presence of zeros simplifies evaluating a determinant.

(a) $A = \begin{bmatrix} 3 & 6 & 5 \\ 2 & 1 & 8 \\ 7 & 9 & 1 \end{bmatrix}$

$$|A| = 3\begin{vmatrix} 1 & 8 \\ 9 & 1 \end{vmatrix} - 6\begin{vmatrix} 2 & 8 \\ 7 & 1 \end{vmatrix} + 5\begin{vmatrix} 2 & 1 \\ 7 & 9 \end{vmatrix}$$
$$= 3[1(1) - 9(8)] - 6[2(1) - 7(8)] + 5[2(9) - 7(1)]$$
$$= 3(-71) - 6(-54) + 5(11) = 166$$

(b) $A = \begin{bmatrix} 12 & 0 & 3 \\ 9 & 2 & 5 \\ 4 & 6 & 1 \end{bmatrix}$

$$|A| = 12\begin{vmatrix} 2 & 5 \\ 6 & 1 \end{vmatrix} - 0\begin{vmatrix} 9 & 5 \\ 4 & 1 \end{vmatrix} + 3\begin{vmatrix} 9 & 2 \\ 4 & 6 \end{vmatrix}$$
$$= 12(2 - 30) - 0 + 3(54 - 8) = -198$$

$$(c) \quad A = \begin{bmatrix} 0 & 6 & 0 \\ 3 & 5 & 2 \\ 7 & 6 & 9 \end{bmatrix}$$

$$|A| = 0 \begin{vmatrix} 5 & 2 \\ 6 & 9 \end{vmatrix} - 6 \begin{vmatrix} 3 & 2 \\ 7 & 9 \end{vmatrix} + 0 \begin{vmatrix} 3 & 5 \\ 7 & 6 \end{vmatrix}$$

$$= 0 - 6(27 - 14) + 0 = -78$$

PROPERTIES OF DETERMINANTS

11.3. Given

$$A = \begin{bmatrix} 2 & 5 & 1 \\ 3 & 2 & 4 \\ 1 & 4 & 2 \end{bmatrix}$$

Compare (a) the determinant of A and (b) the determinant of the transpose of A. (c) Specify which property of determinants the comparison illustrates.

(a)

$$|A| = 2(4 - 16) - 5(6 - 4) + 1(12 - 2) = -24$$

(b)

$$A' = \begin{bmatrix} 2 & 3 & 1 \\ 5 & 2 & 4 \\ 1 & 4 & 2 \end{bmatrix}$$

$$|A'| = 2(4 - 16) - 3(10 - 4) + 1(20 - 2) = -24$$

(c) This illustrates that the determinant of a matrix equals the determinant of its transpose. See Section 11.5.

11.4. Compare (a) the determinant of A and (b) the determinant of A', given

$$A = \begin{bmatrix} a_{11} & a_{12} \\ a_{21} & a_{22} \end{bmatrix}$$

(a) $\quad |A| = a_{11}a_{22} - a_{21}a_{12}$ (b) $\quad A' = \begin{bmatrix} a_{11} & a_{21} \\ a_{12} & a_{22} \end{bmatrix}$ $|A'| = a_{11}a_{22} - a_{12}a_{21}$

11.5. Given

$$A = \begin{bmatrix} 1 & 4 & 2 \\ 3 & 5 & 4 \\ 2 & 3 & 2 \end{bmatrix}$$

(a) Find the determinant of A. (b) Form a new matrix B by interchanging row$_1$ and row$_2$ of A, and find the determinant of B. (c) Compare determinants and specify which property of determinants is illustrated.

(a)

$$|A| = 1(10 - 12) - 4(6 - 8) + 2(9 - 10) = 4$$

(b)

$$B = \begin{bmatrix} 3 & 5 & 4 \\ 1 & 4 & 2 \\ 2 & 3 & 2 \end{bmatrix}$$

$$|B| = 3(8 - 6) - 5(2 - 4) + 4(3 - 8) = -4$$

(c) $|B| = -|A|$. Interchanging any two rows or columns will affect the sign of the determinant, but not the absolute value of the determinant.

11.6. (a) Interchange column$_1$ and column$_3$ of A in Problem 11.5, forming a new matrix C, and (b) find the determinant of C.

(a)
$$C = \begin{bmatrix} 2 & 4 & 1 \\ 4 & 5 & 3 \\ 2 & 3 & 2 \end{bmatrix}$$

(b)
$$|C| = 2(10 - 9) - 4(8 - 6) + 1(12 - 10) = -4$$

11.7. Given
$$W = \begin{bmatrix} w & x \\ y & z \end{bmatrix}$$

(a) Find the determinant of W. (b) Interchange row$_1$ and row$_2$ of W, forming a new matrix Y, and compare the determinant of Y with that of W.

(a)
$$|W| = wz - yx$$

(b)
$$Y = \begin{bmatrix} y & z \\ w & x \end{bmatrix} \qquad |Y| = yx - wz = -(wz - yx)$$

11.8. Given
$$A = \begin{bmatrix} 3 & 5 & 7 \\ 2 & 1 & 4 \\ 4 & 2 & 3 \end{bmatrix}$$

(a) Find the determinant of A. (b) Form a new matrix B by multiplying the first row of A by 2, and find the determinant of B. (c) Compare determinants and indicate which property of determinants this illustrates.

(a)
$$|A| = 3(3 - 8) - 5(6 - 16) + 7(4 - 4) = 35$$

(b)
$$B = \begin{bmatrix} 6 & 10 & 14 \\ 2 & 1 & 4 \\ 4 & 2 & 3 \end{bmatrix} \qquad |B| = 6(3 - 8) - 10(6 - 16) + 14(4 - 4) = 70$$

(c) $|B| = 2|A|$. Multiplying a single row or column of a matrix by a scalar will cause the value of the determinant to be multiplied by the scalar. Here doubling row$_1$ doubles the determinant.

11.9. Given
$$A = \begin{bmatrix} 2 & 5 & 8 \\ 3 & 10 & 1 \\ 1 & 15 & 4 \end{bmatrix}$$

(a) Find $|A|$. (b) Form a new matrix B by multiplying column$_2$ by $\frac{1}{5}$ and find $|B|$. (c) Compare determinants.

(a)
$$|A| = 2(40 - 15) - 5(12 - 1) + 8(45 - 10) = 275$$

(b) Recalling that multiplying by $\frac{1}{5}$ is the same thing as dividing by or factoring out 5,

$$B = \begin{bmatrix} 2 & 1 & 8 \\ 3 & 2 & 1 \\ 1 & 3 & 4 \end{bmatrix} \qquad |B| = 2(8 - 3) - 1(12 - 1) + 8(9 - 2) = 55$$

(c)
$$|B| = \tfrac{1}{5}|A|$$

11.10. Given
$$A = \begin{bmatrix} a_{11} & a_{12} \\ a_{21} & a_{22} \end{bmatrix} \qquad B = \begin{bmatrix} a_{11} & ka_{12} \\ a_{21} & ka_{22} \end{bmatrix}$$

Compare (a) the determinant of A and (b) the determinant of B.

(a) $|A| = a_{11}a_{22} - a_{21}a_{12}$

(b) $|B| = a_{11}ka_{22} - a_{21}ka_{12} = k(a_{11}a_{22}) - k(a_{21}a_{12})$
$$= k(a_{11}a_{22} - a_{21}a_{12}) = k|A|$$

11.11.   Given

$$A = \begin{bmatrix} 5 & 1 & 4 \\ 3 & 2 & 5 \\ 4 & 1 & 6 \end{bmatrix}$$

(a) Find $|A|$.   (b) Subtract 5 times column$_2$ from column$_1$ forming a new matrix B, and find $|B|$.   (c) Compare determinants and indicate which property of determinants is illustrated.

(a) $|A| = 5(12-5) - 1(18-20) + 4(3-8) = 17$

(b) $B = \begin{bmatrix} 0 & 1 & 4 \\ -7 & 2 & 5 \\ -1 & 1 & 6 \end{bmatrix}$ $|B| = 0 - 1(-42+5) + 4(-7+2) = 17$

(c) $|B| = |A|$.   Addition or subtraction of a nonzero multiple of any row or column to or from another row or column does not change the value of the determinant.

11.12.   (a) Subtract row$_3$ from row$_1$ in A of Problem 11.11, forming a new matrix C, and   (b) find $|C|$.

(a) $C = \begin{bmatrix} 1 & 0 & -2 \\ 3 & 2 & 5 \\ 4 & 1 & 6 \end{bmatrix}$

(b) $|C| = 1(12-5) - 0 + (-2)(3-8) = 17$

11.13.   Given the *upper-triangular matrix*,

$$A = \begin{bmatrix} -3 & 0 & 0 \\ 2 & -5 & 0 \\ 6 & 1 & 4 \end{bmatrix}$$

which has zero elements everywhere above the principal diagonal,   (a) find $|A|$.   (b) Find the product of the elements along the principal diagonal and   (c) specify which property of determinants this illustrates.

(a) $|A| = -3(-20-0) - 0 + 0 = 60$

(b)   Multiplying the elements along the principal diagonal, $(-3)(-5)(4) = 60$.

(c)   The determinant of a triangular matrix is equal to the product of the elements along the principal diagonal.

11.14.   Given the *lower-triangular matrix*,

$$A = \begin{bmatrix} 2 & -5 & -1 \\ 0 & 3 & 6 \\ 0 & 0 & -7 \end{bmatrix}$$

which has zero elements everywhere below the principal diagonal,   (a) find $|A|$ and   (b) the product of the diagonal elements.

(a) $|A| = 2(-21-0) - (-5)(0-0) - 1(0-0) = -42$

(b) $2(3)(-7) = -42$

11.15.   Given

$$A = \begin{bmatrix} 12 & 16 & 13 \\ 0 & 0 & 0 \\ -15 & 20 & -9 \end{bmatrix}$$

(a) Find $|A|$.   (b) What property of determinants is illustrated?

(a) $|A| = 12(0-0) - 16(0-0) + 13(0-0) = 0$

(b) If all the elements of a row or column equal zero, the determinant will equal zero.   With all the elements of row$_2$ in A equal to zero, the matrix is, in effect, a (2×3) matrix, not a (3×3) matrix.   Only square matrices have determinants.

MATRIX SIMPLIFICATION PRIOR TO DETERMINANT EVALUATION

11.16. Using the information from Problems 11.3–11.15, simplify the following matrices, where possible, before finding the determinant.   Start by factoring and remember to compensate for any factoring when finding a determinant.

(a) $A = \begin{bmatrix} -4 & 7 & 6 \\ 24 & -60 & 36 \\ 3 & -1 & 5 \end{bmatrix}$

Row$_2$ can be factored by 12.   Thus,

$$|A| = 12 \begin{vmatrix} -4 & 7 & 6 \\ 2 & -5 & 3 \\ 3 & -1 & 5 \end{vmatrix}$$

$$= 12[-4(-25+3) - 7(10-9) + 6(-2+15)] = 12(159) = 1908$$

(b) $A = \begin{bmatrix} 10 & 52 & 7 \\ 12 & 78 & 5 \\ 4 & 65 & 11 \end{bmatrix}$

Factoring out 13 from column$_2$,

$$|A| = 13 \begin{vmatrix} 10 & 4 & 7 \\ 12 & 6 & 5 \\ 4 & 5 & 11 \end{vmatrix}$$

Then factoring out 2 from column$_1$,

$$|A| = 13(2) \begin{vmatrix} 5 & 4 & 7 \\ 6 & 6 & 5 \\ 2 & 5 & 11 \end{vmatrix}$$

$$= 26[5(66-25) - 4(66-10) + 7(30-12)] = 26(107) = 2782$$

(c) $A = \begin{bmatrix} 24 & 16 & 20 \\ 18 & 4 & 5 \\ 6 & 7 & 15 \end{bmatrix}$

Row$_1$ can be factored by 4.

$$|A| = 4 \begin{vmatrix} 6 & 4 & 5 \\ 18 & 4 & 5 \\ 6 & 7 & 15 \end{vmatrix}$$

Column$_1$ can be factored by 6, and column$_3$ can be factored by 5.

$$|A| = 4(6)(5) \begin{vmatrix} 1 & 4 & 1 \\ 3 & 4 & 1 \\ 1 & 7 & 3 \end{vmatrix}$$

$$= 120[1(12-7) - 4(9-1) + 1(21-4)] = 120(-10) = -1200$$

11.17. Simplify the following matrices by adding or subtracting nonzero multiples of rows or columns, and then find the determinant.

(a)
$$A = \begin{bmatrix} 3 & 3 & 6 \\ 4 & 2 & 4 \\ 9 & 5 & 1 \end{bmatrix}$$

Subtracting column$_2$ from column$_1$ will leave zero as the a_{11} element. Thus,

$$A = \begin{bmatrix} 0 & 3 & 6 \\ 2 & 2 & 4 \\ 4 & 5 & 1 \end{bmatrix}$$

Subtracting 2 times column$_2$ from column$_3$ will leave zero in the a_{13} position.

$$A = \begin{bmatrix} 0 & 3 & 0 \\ 2 & 2 & 0 \\ 4 & 5 & -9 \end{bmatrix}$$

Thus, $|A| = 0 - 3(-18 - 0) + 0 = 54$

(b)
$$A = \begin{bmatrix} 28 & 34 & 2 \\ 23 & 45 & 3 \\ 19 & 41 & 1 \end{bmatrix}$$

Subtracting 14 times column$_3$ from column$_1$ will leave zero in the a_{11} position.

$$A = \begin{bmatrix} 0 & 34 & 2 \\ -19 & 45 & 3 \\ 5 & 41 & 1 \end{bmatrix}$$

Subtracting 17 times column$_3$ from column$_2$ will leave zero in the a_{12} position.

$$A = \begin{bmatrix} 0 & 0 & 2 \\ -19 & -6 & 3 \\ 5 & 24 & 1 \end{bmatrix}$$

Thus, $|A| = 2(-456 + 30) = -852$

11.18. Check your answer to Problem 11.17(b), without simplifying the matrix.

$$|A| = 28(45 - 123) - 34(23 - 57) + 2(943 - 855) = -2184 + 1156 + 176 = -852$$

11.19. Given
$$A = \begin{bmatrix} 4 & 36 & 28 \\ 5 & 35 & 55 \\ 3 & 23 & 18 \end{bmatrix}$$

(a) Reduce A to an upper-triangular matrix and find $|A|$. (b) Check your answer.

(a) Subtract 9 times column$_1$ from column$_2$ and 7 times column$_1$ from column$_3$.

$$A = \begin{bmatrix} 4 & 0 & 0 \\ 5 & -10 & 20 \\ 3 & -4 & -3 \end{bmatrix}$$

Then add 2 times column$_2$ to column$_3$.

$$A = \begin{bmatrix} 4 & 0 & 0 \\ 5 & -10 & 0 \\ 3 & -4 & -11 \end{bmatrix}$$

Thus, $|A| = 4(-10)(-11) = 440$.

(b) $|A| = 4(630 - 1265) - 36(90 - 165) + 28(115 - 105) = -2540 + 2700 + 280 = 440$

11.20. Given

$$A = \begin{bmatrix} 71 & -26 & 5 \\ 58 & 32 & 6 \\ 63 & -45 & 3 \end{bmatrix}$$

Reduce A to a lower-triangular matrix and find $|A|$.

Subtract 21 times column$_3$ from column$_1$ and add 15 times column$_3$ to column$_2$.

$$A = \begin{bmatrix} -34 & 49 & 5 \\ -68 & 122 & 6 \\ 0 & 0 & 3 \end{bmatrix}$$

Then, subtract 2 times row$_1$ from row$_2$.

$$A = \begin{bmatrix} -34 & 49 & 5 \\ 0 & 24 & -4 \\ 0 & 0 & 3 \end{bmatrix}$$

$$|A| = (-34)(24)(3) = -2448$$

11.21. Given

$$A = \begin{bmatrix} 126 & 42 & 63 \\ 108 & 56 & 49 \\ 96 & 60 & 74 \end{bmatrix}$$

Reduce A to an upper-triangular matrix and find $|A|$.

Subtract $\frac{1}{3}$ column$_1$ from column$_2$ and $\frac{1}{2}$ column$_1$ from column$_3$.

$$A = \begin{bmatrix} 126 & 0 & 0 \\ 108 & 20 & -5 \\ 96 & 28 & 26 \end{bmatrix}$$

Then add $\frac{1}{4}$ column$_2$ to column$_3$.

$$A = \begin{bmatrix} 126 & 0 & 0 \\ 108 & 20 & 0 \\ 96 & 28 & 33 \end{bmatrix}$$

$$|A| = 126(20)(33) = 83{,}160$$

SINGULAR AND NONSINGULAR MATRICES

11.22. Use determinants to determine whether a unique solution exists for each of the following systems of equations:

(a) $12x_1 + 7x_2 = 147$

$15x_1 + 19x_2 = 168$

To determine whether a unique solution exists, find the coefficient matrix A and take the determinant $|A|$. If $|A| \neq 0$, the matrix is nonsingular and a unique solution exists. If $|A| = 0$, the matrix is singular and there is no unique solution. Thus,

$$A = \begin{bmatrix} 12 & 7 \\ 15 & 19 \end{bmatrix}$$

$$|A| = 12(19) - 15(7) = 123$$

Since $|A| \neq 0$, A is nonsingular and a unique solution exists.

(b) $2x_1 + 3x_2 = 27$

$6x_1 + 9x_2 = 81$

$$A = \begin{bmatrix} 2 & 3 \\ 6 & 9 \end{bmatrix} \qquad |A| = 2(9) - 6(3) = 0$$

There is no unique solution. The equations are linearly dependent, as is illustrated graphically in Problem 1.15(b).

(c) $72x_1 - 54x_2 = 216$

$64x_1 - 48x_2 = 192$

$$A = \begin{bmatrix} 72 & -54 \\ 64 & -48 \end{bmatrix} \qquad |A| = 72(-48) - 64(-54) = -3456 + 3456 = 0$$

A unique solution does not exist because the equations are linearly dependent. Closer inspection reveals the second equation is $\frac{8}{9}$ times the first equation.

(d) $4x_1 + 3x_2 + 5x_3 = 27$

$x_1 + 6x_2 + 2x_3 = 19$

$3x_1 + x_2 + 3x_3 = 15$

$$A = \begin{bmatrix} 4 & 3 & 5 \\ 1 & 6 & 2 \\ 3 & 1 & 3 \end{bmatrix} \qquad |A| = 4(18 - 2) - 3(3 - 6) + 5(1 - 18) = -12$$

A unique solution exists.

(e) $4x_1 + 2x_2 + 6x_3 = 28$

$3x_1 + x_2 + 2x_3 = 20$

$10x_1 + 5x_2 + 15x_3 = 70$

$$A = \begin{bmatrix} 4 & 2 & 6 \\ 3 & 1 & 2 \\ 10 & 5 & 15 \end{bmatrix} \qquad |A| = 4(15 - 10) - 2(45 - 20) + 6(15 - 10) = 0$$

There is no unique solution because the equations are linearly dependent. Closer examination reveals the third equation is 2.5 times the first equation.

(f) $56x_1 + 47x_2 + 8x_3 = 365$

$84x_1 - 39x_2 + 12x_3 = 249$

$28x_1 - 81x_2 + 4x_3 = 168$

$$A = \begin{bmatrix} 56 & 47 & 8 \\ 84 & -39 & 12 \\ 28 & -81 & 4 \end{bmatrix}$$

Factoring out 28 from column$_1$ and 4 from column$_3$ before taking the determinant,

$$|A| = 28(4) \begin{vmatrix} 2 & 47 & 2 \\ 3 & -39 & 3 \\ 1 & -81 & 1 \end{vmatrix}$$

The linear dependence between column$_1$ and column$_3$ is now evident. The determinant will therefore be zero and no unique solution exists.

$$|A| = 112[2(-39 + 243) - 47(0) + 2(-243 + 39)] = 112(0) = 0$$

MINORS AND COFACTORS

11.23. Find (a) the minor $|M_{ij}|$ and (b) the cofactor $|C_{ij}|$ for each of the elements in the first row, given

$$A = \begin{bmatrix} a_{11} & a_{12} \\ a_{21} & a_{22} \end{bmatrix}$$

(a) To find the minor of a_{11}, mentally delete the row and column in which it appears. The remaining element is the minor. Thus, $|M_{11}| = a_{22}$. Similarly, $|M_{12}| = a_{21}$.

(b) From the rule of cofactors,

$$|C_{11}| = (-1)^{1+1}|M_{11}| = +1(a_{22}) = a_{22}$$
$$|C_{12}| = (-1)^{1+2}|M_{12}| = -1(a_{21}) = -a_{21}$$

11.24. Find (a) the minors and (b) the cofactors for the elements of the second row, given

$$A = \begin{bmatrix} 13 & 17 \\ 19 & 15 \end{bmatrix}$$

(a) $$|M_{21}| = 17 \qquad |M_{22}| = 13$$

(b) $$|C_{21}| = (-1)^{2+1}|M_{21}| = -1(17) = -17$$
$$|C_{22}| = (-1)^{2+2}|M_{22}| = +1(13) = 13$$

11.25. Find (a) the minors and (b) the cofactors for the elements of the second column, given

$$A = \begin{bmatrix} 6 & 7 \\ 12 & 9 \end{bmatrix}$$

(a) $$|M_{12}| = 12 \qquad |M_{22}| = 6$$

(b) $$|C_{12}| = (-1)^{1+2}|M_{12}| = -12$$
$$|C_{22}| = (-1)^{2+2}|M_{22}| = 6$$

11.26. Find (a) the minors and (b) the cofactors for the elements of the first row, given

$$A = \begin{bmatrix} 5 & 2 & -4 \\ 6 & -3 & 7 \\ 1 & 2 & 4 \end{bmatrix}$$

(a) Deleting row_1 and column_1,

$$|M_{11}| = \begin{vmatrix} -3 & 7 \\ 2 & 4 \end{vmatrix} = -26$$

Similarly, $$|M_{12}| = \begin{vmatrix} 6 & 7 \\ 1 & 4 \end{vmatrix} = 17$$

$$|M_{13}| = \begin{vmatrix} 6 & -3 \\ 1 & 2 \end{vmatrix} = 15$$

(b) $$|C_{11}| = (-1)^2|M_{11}| = -26$$
$$|C_{12}| = (-1)^3|M_{12}| = -17$$
$$|C_{13}| = (-1)^4|M_{13}| = 15$$

11.27. Find (a) the minors and (b) the cofactors for the elements of the third row, given

$$A = \begin{bmatrix} 9 & 11 & 4 \\ 3 & 2 & 7 \\ 6 & 10 & 4 \end{bmatrix}$$

(a) Deleting row_3 and column_1,

$$|M_{31}| = \begin{vmatrix} 11 & 4 \\ 2 & 7 \end{vmatrix} = 69$$

Similarly,

$$|M_{32}| = \begin{vmatrix} 9 & 4 \\ 3 & 7 \end{vmatrix} = 51$$

$$|M_{33}| = \begin{vmatrix} 9 & 11 \\ 3 & 2 \end{vmatrix} = -15$$

(b)

$$|C_{31}| = (-1)^4 |M_{31}| = 69$$
$$|C_{32}| = (-1)^5 |M_{32}| = -51$$
$$|C_{33}| = (-1)^6 |M_{33}| = -15$$

11.28. Find (a) the minors and (b) the cofactors for the elements in the second column, given

$$A = \begin{bmatrix} 13 & 6 & 11 \\ 12 & 9 & 4 \\ 7 & 10 & 2 \end{bmatrix}$$

(a)

$$|M_{12}| = \begin{vmatrix} 12 & 4 \\ 7 & 2 \end{vmatrix} = -4$$

$$|M_{22}| = \begin{vmatrix} 13 & 11 \\ 7 & 2 \end{vmatrix} = -51$$

$$|M_{32}| = \begin{vmatrix} 13 & 11 \\ 12 & 4 \end{vmatrix} = -80$$

(b)

$$|C_{12}| = (-1)^3 |M_{12}| = -1(-4) = 4$$
$$|C_{22}| = (-1)^4 |M_{22}| = -51$$
$$|C_{32}| = (-1)^5 |M_{32}| = -1(-80) = 80$$

11.29. Find (1) the cofactor matrix C and (2) the adjoint matrix Adj A for each of the following:

(a) $A = \begin{bmatrix} 7 & 12 \\ 4 & 3 \end{bmatrix}$

(1) $C = \begin{bmatrix} |C_{11}| & |C_{12}| \\ |C_{21}| & |C_{22}| \end{bmatrix} = \begin{bmatrix} |M_{11}| & -|M_{12}| \\ -|M_{21}| & |M_{22}| \end{bmatrix} = \begin{bmatrix} 3 & -4 \\ -12 & 7 \end{bmatrix}$ (2) Adj $A = C' = \begin{bmatrix} 3 & -12 \\ -4 & 7 \end{bmatrix}$

(b) $A = \begin{bmatrix} -2 & 5 \\ 13 & 6 \end{bmatrix}$

(1) $C = \begin{bmatrix} 6 & -13 \\ -5 & -2 \end{bmatrix}$ (2) Adj $A = \begin{bmatrix} 6 & -5 \\ -13 & -2 \end{bmatrix}$

(c) $A = \begin{bmatrix} 9 & -16 \\ -20 & 7 \end{bmatrix}$

(1) $C = \begin{bmatrix} 7 & 20 \\ 16 & 9 \end{bmatrix}$ (2)   Adj $A = \begin{bmatrix} 7 & 16 \\ 20 & 9 \end{bmatrix}$

(d) $A = \begin{bmatrix} 6 & 2 & 7 \\ 5 & 4 & 9 \\ 3 & 3 & 1 \end{bmatrix}$

(1) $C = \begin{bmatrix} |C_{11}| & |C_{12}| & |C_{13}| \\ |C_{21}| & |C_{22}| & |C_{23}| \\ |C_{31}| & |C_{32}| & |C_{33}| \end{bmatrix} = \begin{bmatrix} \begin{vmatrix} 4 & 9 \\ 3 & 1 \end{vmatrix} & -\begin{vmatrix} 5 & 9 \\ 3 & 1 \end{vmatrix} & \begin{vmatrix} 5 & 4 \\ 3 & 3 \end{vmatrix} \\ -\begin{vmatrix} 2 & 7 \\ 3 & 1 \end{vmatrix} & \begin{vmatrix} 6 & 7 \\ 3 & 1 \end{vmatrix} & -\begin{vmatrix} 6 & 2 \\ 3 & 3 \end{vmatrix} \\ \begin{vmatrix} 2 & 7 \\ 4 & 9 \end{vmatrix} & -\begin{vmatrix} 6 & 7 \\ 5 & 9 \end{vmatrix} & \begin{vmatrix} 6 & 2 \\ 5 & 4 \end{vmatrix} \end{bmatrix} = \begin{bmatrix} -23 & 22 & 3 \\ 19 & -15 & -12 \\ -10 & -19 & 14 \end{bmatrix}$

(2)   Adj $A = C' = \begin{bmatrix} -23 & 19 & -10 \\ 22 & -15 & -19 \\ 3 & -12 & 14 \end{bmatrix}$

(e) $A = \begin{bmatrix} 13 & -2 & 8 \\ -9 & 6 & -4 \\ -3 & 2 & -1 \end{bmatrix}$

(1) $C = \begin{bmatrix} \begin{vmatrix} 6 & -4 \\ 2 & -1 \end{vmatrix} & -\begin{vmatrix} -9 & -4 \\ -3 & -1 \end{vmatrix} & \begin{vmatrix} -9 & 6 \\ -3 & 2 \end{vmatrix} \\ -\begin{vmatrix} -2 & 8 \\ 2 & -1 \end{vmatrix} & \begin{vmatrix} 13 & 8 \\ -3 & -1 \end{vmatrix} & -\begin{vmatrix} 13 & -2 \\ -3 & 2 \end{vmatrix} \\ \begin{vmatrix} -2 & 8 \\ 6 & -4 \end{vmatrix} & -\begin{vmatrix} 13 & 8 \\ -9 & -4 \end{vmatrix} & \begin{vmatrix} 13 & -2 \\ -9 & 6 \end{vmatrix} \end{bmatrix} = \begin{bmatrix} 2 & 3 & 0 \\ 14 & 11 & -20 \\ -40 & -20 & 60 \end{bmatrix}$

(2)   Adj $A = C' = \begin{bmatrix} 2 & 14 & -40 \\ 3 & 11 & -20 \\ 0 & -20 & 60 \end{bmatrix}$

LAPLACE EXPANSION

11.30.   Use Laplace expansion to find the determinants for each of the following, using whatever row or column is easiest:

(a) $A = \begin{bmatrix} 15 & 7 & 9 \\ 2 & 5 & 6 \\ 9 & 0 & 12 \end{bmatrix}$

Expanding along the second column,

$$|A| = a_{12}|C_{12}| + a_{22}|C_{22}| + a_{32}|C_{32}| = 7(-1)\begin{vmatrix} 2 & 6 \\ 9 & 12 \end{vmatrix} + 5\begin{vmatrix} 15 & 9 \\ 9 & 12 \end{vmatrix} + 0$$

$$= -7(-30) + 5(99) = 705$$

(b) $A = \begin{bmatrix} 23 & 35 & 0 \\ 72 & 46 & 10 \\ 15 & 29 & 0 \end{bmatrix}$

Expanding along the third column,

$$|A| = a_{13}|C_{13}| + a_{23}|C_{23}| + a_{33}|C_{33}|$$

$$= 0 + 10(-1)\begin{vmatrix} 23 & 35 \\ 15 & 29 \end{vmatrix} + 0 = -10(142) = -1420$$

(c) $A = \begin{bmatrix} 12 & 98 & 15 \\ 0 & 25 & 0 \\ 21 & 84 & 19 \end{bmatrix}$

Expanding along the second row,

$$|A| = a_{21}|C_{21}| + a_{22}|C_{22}| + a_{23}|C_{23}| = 0 + 25\begin{vmatrix} 12 & 15 \\ 21 & 19 \end{vmatrix} + 0 = 25(-87) = -2175$$

(d) $A = \begin{bmatrix} 2 & 4 & 1 & 5 \\ 3 & 2 & 5 & 1 \\ 1 & 2 & 1 & 4 \\ 3 & 4 & 3 & 2 \end{bmatrix}$

Expanding along the first row,

$$|A| = a_{11}|C_{11}| + a_{12}|C_{12}| + a_{13}|C_{13}| + a_{14}|C_{14}|$$

$$= 2(-1)^{1+1}\begin{vmatrix} 2 & 5 & 1 \\ 2 & 1 & 4 \\ 4 & 3 & 2 \end{vmatrix} + 4(-1)^{1+2}\begin{vmatrix} 3 & 5 & 1 \\ 1 & 1 & 4 \\ 3 & 3 & 2 \end{vmatrix} + 1(-1)^{1+3}\begin{vmatrix} 3 & 2 & 1 \\ 1 & 2 & 4 \\ 3 & 4 & 2 \end{vmatrix} + 5(-1)^{1+4}\begin{vmatrix} 3 & 2 & 5 \\ 1 & 2 & 1 \\ 3 & 4 & 3 \end{vmatrix}$$

Then expanding each of the (3×3) subdeterminants along the first row,

$$|A| = 2\left[2\begin{vmatrix} 1 & 4 \\ 3 & 2 \end{vmatrix} - 5\begin{vmatrix} 2 & 4 \\ 4 & 2 \end{vmatrix} + 1\begin{vmatrix} 2 & 1 \\ 4 & 3 \end{vmatrix} \right] - 4\left[3\begin{vmatrix} 1 & 4 \\ 3 & 2 \end{vmatrix} - 5\begin{vmatrix} 1 & 4 \\ 3 & 2 \end{vmatrix} + 1\begin{vmatrix} 1 & 1 \\ 3 & 3 \end{vmatrix} \right]$$

$$+ 1\left[3\begin{vmatrix} 2 & 4 \\ 4 & 2 \end{vmatrix} - 2\begin{vmatrix} 1 & 4 \\ 3 & 2 \end{vmatrix} + 1\begin{vmatrix} 1 & 2 \\ 3 & 4 \end{vmatrix} \right] - 5\left[3\begin{vmatrix} 2 & 1 \\ 4 & 3 \end{vmatrix} - 2\begin{vmatrix} 1 & 1 \\ 3 & 3 \end{vmatrix} + 5\begin{vmatrix} 1 & 2 \\ 3 & 4 \end{vmatrix} \right]$$

$$= 2[2(-10) - 5(-12) + 1(2)] - 4[3(-10) - 5(-10) + 1(0)]$$

$$+ 1[3(-12) - 2(-10) + 1(-2)] - 5[3(2) - 2(0) + 5(-2)]$$

$$= 2(42) - 4(20) + 1(-18) - 5(-4) = 6$$

(e) $A = \begin{bmatrix} 5 & 0 & 1 & 3 \\ 4 & 2 & 6 & 0 \\ 3 & 0 & 1 & 5 \\ 0 & 1 & 4 & 2 \end{bmatrix}$

Expanding along the second column,

$$|A| = a_{12}|C_{12}| + a_{22}|C_{22}| + a_{32}|C_{32}| + a_{42}|C_{42}|$$

$$= 0 + 2(-1)^{2+2}\begin{vmatrix} 5 & 1 & 3 \\ 3 & 1 & 5 \\ 0 & 4 & 2 \end{vmatrix} + 0 + 1(-1)^{4+2}\begin{vmatrix} 5 & 1 & 3 \\ 4 & 6 & 0 \\ 3 & 1 & 5 \end{vmatrix}$$

Then substituting the values for the (3×3) subdeterminants,

$$|A| = 2(-60) + 1(88) = -32$$

(f) $A = \begin{bmatrix} 7 & 3 & 5 & 1 \\ 2 & 4 & 3 & 6 \\ 1 & 0 & 9 & 5 \\ 2 & 5 & 4 & 3 \end{bmatrix}$

Simplifying the matrix first by subtracting 7 times column$_4$ from column$_1$, 3 times column$_4$ from column$_2$, and 5 times column$_4$ from column$_3$,

$$A = \begin{bmatrix} 0 & 0 & 0 & 1 \\ -40 & -14 & -27 & 6 \\ -34 & -15 & -16 & 5 \\ -19 & -4 & -11 & 3 \end{bmatrix}$$

Then expanding along row$_1$,

$$|A| = a_{11}|C_{11}| + a_{12}|C_{12}| + a_{13}|C_{13}| + a_{14}|C_{14}| = 0 + 0 + 0 + 1(-1)^{1+4} \begin{vmatrix} -40 & -14 & -27 \\ -34 & -15 & -16 \\ -19 & -4 & -11 \end{vmatrix}$$

Substituting the value of the (3×3) determinant in parentheses,

$$|A| = -1(963) = -963$$

INVERTING A MATRIX

11.31. Find the inverse A^{-1} for each of the following matrices. Check your answer to part (a).

(a) $A = \begin{bmatrix} 24 & 15 \\ 8 & 7 \end{bmatrix}$

$$A^{-1} = \frac{1}{|A|} \text{Adj } A$$

Evaluating the determinant, $|A| = 24(7) - 8(15) = 48$

Then finding the cofactor matrix to get the adjoint,

$$C = \begin{bmatrix} 7 & -8 \\ -15 & 24 \end{bmatrix}$$

and $\text{Adj } A = C' = \begin{bmatrix} 7 & -15 \\ -8 & 24 \end{bmatrix}$

Thus, $A^{-1} = \frac{1}{48} \begin{bmatrix} 7 & -15 \\ -8 & 24 \end{bmatrix} = \begin{bmatrix} \frac{7}{48} & -\frac{5}{16} \\ -\frac{1}{6} & \frac{1}{2} \end{bmatrix}$ (11.5)

Checking to make sure $A^{-1}A = I$, and using the unreduced form of A^{-1} from (11.5) for easier computation,

$$A^{-1}A = \frac{1}{48} \begin{bmatrix} 7 & -15 \\ -8 & 24 \end{bmatrix} \begin{bmatrix} 24 & 15 \\ 8 & 7 \end{bmatrix} = \frac{1}{48} \begin{bmatrix} 7(24) - 15(8) & 7(15) - 15(7) \\ -8(24) + 24(8) & -8(15) + 24(7) \end{bmatrix} = \frac{1}{48} \begin{bmatrix} 48 & 0 \\ 0 & 48 \end{bmatrix} = \begin{bmatrix} 1 & 0 \\ 0 & 1 \end{bmatrix}$$

(b) $A = \begin{bmatrix} 7 & 9 \\ 6 & 12 \end{bmatrix}$

$$|A| = 7(12) - 6(9) = 30$$

The cofactor matrix is

$$C = \begin{bmatrix} 12 & -6 \\ -9 & 7 \end{bmatrix}$$

and $\text{Adj } A = C' = \begin{bmatrix} 12 & -9 \\ -6 & 7 \end{bmatrix}$

Thus, $A^{-1} = \frac{1}{30} \begin{bmatrix} 12 & -9 \\ -6 & 7 \end{bmatrix} = \begin{bmatrix} \frac{2}{5} & -\frac{3}{10} \\ -\frac{1}{5} & \frac{7}{30} \end{bmatrix}$

(c) $A = \begin{bmatrix} -7 & 16 \\ -9 & 13 \end{bmatrix}$

$$|A| = -7(13) - (-9)(16) = 53$$

$$C = \begin{bmatrix} 13 & 9 \\ -16 & -7 \end{bmatrix}$$

$$\text{Adj } A = C' = \begin{bmatrix} 13 & -16 \\ 9 & -7 \end{bmatrix}$$

$$A^{-1} = \frac{1}{53} \begin{bmatrix} 13 & -16 \\ 9 & -7 \end{bmatrix} = \begin{bmatrix} \frac{13}{53} & -\frac{16}{53} \\ \frac{9}{53} & -\frac{7}{53} \end{bmatrix}$$

(d) $A = \begin{bmatrix} 4 & 2 & 5 \\ 3 & 1 & 8 \\ 9 & 6 & 7 \end{bmatrix}$

$$|A| = 4(7 - 48) - 2(21 - 72) + 5(18 - 9) = -17$$

The cofactor matrix is

$$C = \begin{bmatrix} \begin{vmatrix} 1 & 8 \\ 6 & 7 \end{vmatrix} & -\begin{vmatrix} 3 & 8 \\ 9 & 7 \end{vmatrix} & \begin{vmatrix} 3 & 1 \\ 9 & 6 \end{vmatrix} \\ -\begin{vmatrix} 2 & 5 \\ 6 & 7 \end{vmatrix} & \begin{vmatrix} 4 & 5 \\ 9 & 7 \end{vmatrix} & -\begin{vmatrix} 4 & 2 \\ 9 & 6 \end{vmatrix} \\ \begin{vmatrix} 2 & 5 \\ 1 & 8 \end{vmatrix} & -\begin{vmatrix} 4 & 5 \\ 3 & 8 \end{vmatrix} & \begin{vmatrix} 4 & 2 \\ 3 & 1 \end{vmatrix} \end{bmatrix} = \begin{bmatrix} -41 & 51 & 9 \\ 16 & -17 & -6 \\ 11 & -17 & -2 \end{bmatrix}$$

and

$$\text{Adj } A = C' = \begin{bmatrix} -41 & 16 & 11 \\ 51 & -17 & -17 \\ 9 & -6 & -2 \end{bmatrix}$$

Thus,

$$A^{-1} = -\frac{1}{17} \begin{bmatrix} -41 & 16 & 11 \\ 51 & -17 & -17 \\ 9 & -6 & -2 \end{bmatrix} = \begin{bmatrix} \frac{41}{17} & -\frac{16}{17} & -\frac{11}{17} \\ -3 & 1 & 1 \\ -\frac{9}{17} & \frac{6}{17} & \frac{2}{17} \end{bmatrix}$$

(e) $A = \begin{bmatrix} 14 & 0 & 6 \\ 9 & 5 & 0 \\ 0 & 11 & 8 \end{bmatrix}$

$$|A| = 14(40) - 0 + 6(99) = 1154$$

The cofactor matrix is

$$C = \begin{bmatrix} 40 & -72 & 99 \\ 66 & 112 & -154 \\ -30 & 54 & 70 \end{bmatrix}$$

The adjoint is

$$\text{Adj } A = \begin{bmatrix} 40 & 66 & -30 \\ -72 & 112 & 54 \\ 99 & -154 & 70 \end{bmatrix}$$

Then,

$$A^{-1} = \frac{1}{1154} \begin{bmatrix} 40 & 66 & -30 \\ -72 & 112 & 54 \\ 99 & -154 & 70 \end{bmatrix} = \begin{bmatrix} \frac{20}{577} & \frac{33}{577} & -\frac{15}{577} \\ -\frac{36}{577} & \frac{56}{577} & \frac{27}{577} \\ \frac{99}{1154} & -\frac{77}{577} & \frac{35}{577} \end{bmatrix}$$

MATRIX INVERSION IN EQUATION SOLUTIONS

11.32. Use matrix inversion to solve the following systems of linear equations. Check your answers on your own by substituting into the original equations.

(a) $4x_1 + 3x_2 = 28$

       $2x_1 + 5x_2 = 42$

$$\begin{bmatrix} 4 & 3 \\ 2 & 5 \end{bmatrix} \begin{bmatrix} x_1 \\ x_2 \end{bmatrix} = \begin{bmatrix} 28 \\ 42 \end{bmatrix}$$

where from Section 11.8, $X = A^{-1}B$.   Find first the inverse of A, where $|A| = 4(5) - 2(3) = 14$. The cofactor matrix of A is

$$C = \begin{bmatrix} 5 & -2 \\ -3 & 4 \end{bmatrix}$$

and

$$\text{Adj } A = C' = \begin{bmatrix} 5 & -3 \\ -2 & 4 \end{bmatrix}$$

Thus,

$$A^{-1} = \frac{1}{14} \begin{bmatrix} 5 & -3 \\ -2 & 4 \end{bmatrix} = \begin{bmatrix} \frac{5}{14} & -\frac{3}{14} \\ -\frac{1}{7} & \frac{2}{7} \end{bmatrix}$$

Then substituting in $X = A^{-1}B$,

$$X = \begin{bmatrix} \frac{5}{14} & -\frac{3}{14} \\ -\frac{1}{7} & \frac{2}{7} \end{bmatrix}_{(2\times2)} \begin{bmatrix} 28 \\ 42 \end{bmatrix}_{(2\times1)} = \begin{bmatrix} 10 - 9 \\ -4 + 12 \end{bmatrix}_{(2\times1)} = \begin{bmatrix} 1 \\ 8 \end{bmatrix}_{(2\times1)}$$

Thus, $\bar{x}_1 = 1$ and $\bar{x}_2 = 8$.

(b) $6x_1 + 7x_2 = 56$

     $2x_1 + 3x_2 = 44$

$$\begin{bmatrix} 6 & 7 \\ 2 & 3 \end{bmatrix} \begin{bmatrix} x_1 \\ x_2 \end{bmatrix} = \begin{bmatrix} 56 \\ 44 \end{bmatrix}$$

where $|A| = 6(3) - 2(7) = 4$.

$$C = \begin{bmatrix} 3 & -2 \\ -7 & 6 \end{bmatrix} \qquad \text{Adj } A = C' = \begin{bmatrix} 3 & -7 \\ -2 & 6 \end{bmatrix}$$

and

$$A^{-1} = \frac{1}{4} \begin{bmatrix} 3 & -7 \\ -2 & 6 \end{bmatrix} = \begin{bmatrix} \frac{3}{4} & -\frac{7}{4} \\ -\frac{1}{2} & \frac{3}{2} \end{bmatrix}$$

Thus,

$$X = \begin{bmatrix} \frac{3}{4} & -\frac{7}{4} \\ -\frac{1}{2} & \frac{3}{2} \end{bmatrix}_{(2\times2)} \begin{bmatrix} 56 \\ 44 \end{bmatrix}_{(2\times1)} = \begin{bmatrix} 42 - 77 \\ -28 + 66 \end{bmatrix}_{(2\times1)} = \begin{bmatrix} -35 \\ 38 \end{bmatrix}_{(2\times1)}$$

and $\bar{x}_1 = -35$ and $\bar{x}_2 = 38$.

11.33. The equilibrium conditions for two related markets (pork and beef) are given by

$$18P_b - P_p = 87$$

$$-2P_b + 36P_p = 98$$

Find the equilibrium price for each market.

$$\begin{bmatrix} 18 & -1 \\ -2 & 36 \end{bmatrix} \begin{bmatrix} P_b \\ P_p \end{bmatrix} = \begin{bmatrix} 87 \\ 98 \end{bmatrix}$$

where $|A| = 18(36) - (-2)(-1) = 646$.

$$C = \begin{bmatrix} 36 & 2 \\ 1 & 18 \end{bmatrix} \qquad \text{Adj } A = \begin{bmatrix} 36 & 1 \\ 2 & 18 \end{bmatrix}$$

and

$$A^{-1} = \frac{1}{646}\begin{bmatrix} 36 & 1 \\ 2 & 18 \end{bmatrix} = \begin{bmatrix} \frac{18}{323} & \frac{1}{646} \\ \frac{1}{323} & \frac{9}{323} \end{bmatrix}$$

Thus,

$$X = \begin{bmatrix} \frac{18}{323} & \frac{1}{646} \\ \frac{1}{323} & \frac{9}{323} \end{bmatrix}\begin{bmatrix} 87 \\ 98 \end{bmatrix} = \begin{bmatrix} \frac{1615}{323} \\ \frac{969}{323} \end{bmatrix} = \begin{bmatrix} 5 \\ 3 \end{bmatrix}$$

and $\bar{P}_b = 5$ and $\bar{P}_p = 3$.

This is the same solution as that obtained by simultaneous equations in Problem 2.16. For practice try the inverse matrix solution for Problem 2.17.

11.34. The equilibrium condition for two substitute goods is given by

$$5P_1 - 2P_2 = 15$$
$$-P_1 + 8P_2 = 16$$

Find the equilibrium prices.

$$\begin{bmatrix} 5 & -2 \\ -1 & 8 \end{bmatrix}\begin{bmatrix} P_1 \\ P_2 \end{bmatrix} = \begin{bmatrix} 15 \\ 16 \end{bmatrix}$$

where $\quad |A| = 5(8) - (-1)(-2) = 38$.

$$C = \begin{bmatrix} 8 & 1 \\ 2 & 5 \end{bmatrix} \qquad \text{Adj } A = \begin{bmatrix} 8 & 2 \\ 1 & 5 \end{bmatrix}$$

and

$$A^{-1} = \frac{1}{38}\begin{bmatrix} 8 & 2 \\ 1 & 5 \end{bmatrix} = \begin{bmatrix} \frac{4}{19} & \frac{1}{19} \\ \frac{1}{38} & \frac{5}{38} \end{bmatrix}$$

Thus,

$$X = \begin{bmatrix} \frac{4}{19} & \frac{1}{19} \\ \frac{1}{38} & \frac{5}{38} \end{bmatrix}\begin{bmatrix} 15 \\ 16 \end{bmatrix} = \begin{bmatrix} \dfrac{60+16}{19} \\ \dfrac{15+80}{38} \end{bmatrix} = \begin{bmatrix} 4 \\ 2.5 \end{bmatrix}$$

and $\quad \bar{P}_1 = 4$ and $\bar{P}_2 = 2.5$.

11.35. Given the *IS* equation $\quad 0.3Y + 100i - 252 = 0 \quad$ and the *LM* equation
$$0.25Y - 200i - 176 = 0$$

Find the equilibrium level of income and rate of interest.

The *IS–LM* equations can be reduced to the form

$$0.3Y + 100i = 252$$
$$0.25Y - 200i = 176$$

and then expressed in matrix form where

$$A = \begin{bmatrix} 0.3 & 100 \\ 0.25 & -200 \end{bmatrix} \qquad X = \begin{bmatrix} Y \\ i \end{bmatrix} \qquad B = \begin{bmatrix} 252 \\ 176 \end{bmatrix}$$

Thus,

$$|A| = 0.3(-200) - 100(0.25) = -85$$

$$C = \begin{bmatrix} -200 & -0.25 \\ -100 & 0.3 \end{bmatrix}$$

$$\text{Adj } A = \begin{bmatrix} -200 & -100 \\ -0.25 & 0.3 \end{bmatrix}$$

and
$$A^{-1} = -\frac{1}{85}\begin{bmatrix} -200 & -100 \\ -0.25 & 0.3 \end{bmatrix} = \begin{bmatrix} \dfrac{40}{17} & \dfrac{20}{17} \\ \dfrac{0.05}{17} & -\dfrac{0.06}{17} \end{bmatrix}$$

Thus,
$$X = \begin{bmatrix} \dfrac{40}{17} & \dfrac{20}{17} \\ \dfrac{0.05}{17} & -\dfrac{0.06}{17} \end{bmatrix}\begin{bmatrix} 252 \\ 176 \end{bmatrix} = \begin{bmatrix} \dfrac{10,080 + 3520}{17} \\ \dfrac{12.6 - 10.56}{17} \end{bmatrix} = \begin{bmatrix} 800 \\ 0.12 \end{bmatrix}$$

In equilibrium $\bar{Y} = 800$ and $\bar{i} = 0.12$ as found in Problem 2.28 where simultaneous equations were used. On your own, practice with Problems 2.29–2.31.

11.36. Use matrix inversion to solve for the unknowns in the system of linear equations given below.

$$3x_1 + 5x_2 + x_3 = 36$$
$$x_1 + 2x_2 + 4x_3 = 42$$
$$4x_1 + 3x_2 + 2x_3 = 28$$

$$\begin{bmatrix} 3 & 5 & 1 \\ 1 & 2 & 4 \\ 4 & 3 & 2 \end{bmatrix}\begin{bmatrix} x_1 \\ x_2 \\ x_3 \end{bmatrix} = \begin{bmatrix} 36 \\ 42 \\ 28 \end{bmatrix}$$

where $|A| = 3(4-12) - 5(2-16) + 1(3-8) = 41$.

$$C = \begin{bmatrix} \begin{vmatrix} 2 & 4 \\ 3 & 2 \end{vmatrix} & -\begin{vmatrix} 1 & 4 \\ 4 & 2 \end{vmatrix} & \begin{vmatrix} 1 & 2 \\ 4 & 3 \end{vmatrix} \\ -\begin{vmatrix} 5 & 1 \\ 3 & 2 \end{vmatrix} & \begin{vmatrix} 3 & 1 \\ 4 & 2 \end{vmatrix} & -\begin{vmatrix} 3 & 5 \\ 4 & 3 \end{vmatrix} \\ \begin{vmatrix} 5 & 1 \\ 2 & 4 \end{vmatrix} & -\begin{vmatrix} 3 & 1 \\ 1 & 4 \end{vmatrix} & \begin{vmatrix} 3 & 5 \\ 1 & 2 \end{vmatrix} \end{bmatrix} = \begin{bmatrix} -8 & 14 & -5 \\ -7 & 2 & 11 \\ 18 & -11 & 1 \end{bmatrix}$$

$$\text{Adj } A = \begin{bmatrix} -8 & -7 & 18 \\ 14 & 2 & -11 \\ -5 & 11 & 1 \end{bmatrix}$$

and
$$A^{-1} = \frac{1}{41}\begin{bmatrix} -8 & -7 & 18 \\ 14 & 2 & -11 \\ -5 & 11 & 1 \end{bmatrix} = \begin{bmatrix} -\frac{8}{41} & -\frac{7}{41} & \frac{18}{41} \\ \frac{14}{41} & \frac{2}{41} & -\frac{11}{41} \\ -\frac{5}{41} & \frac{11}{41} & \frac{1}{41} \end{bmatrix}$$

Thus,
$$X = \begin{bmatrix} -\frac{8}{41} & -\frac{7}{41} & \frac{18}{41} \\ \frac{14}{41} & \frac{2}{41} & -\frac{11}{41} \\ -\frac{5}{41} & \frac{11}{41} & \frac{1}{41} \end{bmatrix}\begin{bmatrix} 36 \\ 42 \\ 28 \end{bmatrix} = \begin{bmatrix} \dfrac{-288 - 294 + 504}{41} \\ \dfrac{504 + 84 - 308}{41} \\ \dfrac{-180 + 462 + 28}{41} \end{bmatrix} = \begin{bmatrix} -1.902 \\ 6.829 \\ 7.561 \end{bmatrix} = \begin{bmatrix} x_1 \\ x_2 \\ x_3 \end{bmatrix}$$

11.37. Redo Problem 11.36, given

$$2x_1 + 4x_2 - 3x_3 = 12$$
$$3x_1 - 5x_2 + 2x_3 = 13$$
$$-x_1 + 3x_2 + 2x_3 = 17$$

$$\begin{bmatrix} 2 & 4 & -3 \\ 3 & -5 & 2 \\ -1 & 3 & 2 \end{bmatrix}\begin{bmatrix} x_1 \\ x_2 \\ x_3 \end{bmatrix} = \begin{bmatrix} 12 \\ 13 \\ 17 \end{bmatrix}$$

where $\quad |A| = 2(-16) - 4(8) - 3(4) = -76.$

$$C = \begin{bmatrix} \begin{vmatrix} -5 & 2 \\ 3 & 2 \end{vmatrix} & -\begin{vmatrix} 3 & 2 \\ -1 & 2 \end{vmatrix} & \begin{vmatrix} 3 & -5 \\ -1 & 3 \end{vmatrix} \\ -\begin{vmatrix} 4 & -3 \\ 3 & 2 \end{vmatrix} & \begin{vmatrix} 2 & -3 \\ -1 & 2 \end{vmatrix} & -\begin{vmatrix} 2 & 4 \\ -1 & 3 \end{vmatrix} \\ \begin{vmatrix} 4 & -3 \\ -5 & 2 \end{vmatrix} & -\begin{vmatrix} 2 & -3 \\ 3 & 2 \end{vmatrix} & \begin{vmatrix} 2 & 4 \\ 3 & -5 \end{vmatrix} \end{bmatrix} = \begin{bmatrix} -16 & -8 & 4 \\ -17 & 1 & -10 \\ -7 & -13 & -22 \end{bmatrix}$$

$$\text{Adj } A = \begin{bmatrix} -16 & -17 & -7 \\ -8 & 1 & -13 \\ 4 & -10 & -22 \end{bmatrix}$$

$$A^{-1} = -\frac{1}{76}\begin{bmatrix} -16 & -17 & -7 \\ -8 & 1 & -13 \\ 4 & -10 & -22 \end{bmatrix} = \begin{bmatrix} \frac{16}{76} & \frac{17}{76} & \frac{7}{76} \\ \frac{8}{76} & -\frac{1}{76} & \frac{13}{76} \\ -\frac{4}{76} & \frac{10}{76} & \frac{22}{76} \end{bmatrix}$$

where the common denominator 76 is deliberately kept to simplify later calculations.

Thus, $\quad X = \begin{bmatrix} \frac{16}{76} & \frac{17}{76} & \frac{7}{76} \\ \frac{8}{76} & -\frac{1}{76} & \frac{13}{76} \\ -\frac{4}{76} & \frac{10}{76} & \frac{22}{76} \end{bmatrix}\begin{bmatrix} 12 \\ 13 \\ 17 \end{bmatrix} = \begin{bmatrix} \dfrac{192 + 221 + 119}{76} \\ \dfrac{96 - 13 + 221}{76} \\ \dfrac{-48 + 130 + 374}{76} \end{bmatrix} = \begin{bmatrix} 7 \\ 4 \\ 6 \end{bmatrix} = \begin{bmatrix} x_1 \\ x_2 \\ x_3 \end{bmatrix}$

11.38. The equilibrium condition for three related markets is given by

$$\begin{aligned} 11P_1 - P_2 - P_3 &= 31 \\ -P_1 + 6P_2 - 2P_3 &= 26 \\ -P_1 - 2P_2 + 7P_3 &= 24 \end{aligned}$$

Find the equilibrium price for each market.

$$\begin{bmatrix} 11 & -1 & -1 \\ -1 & 6 & -2 \\ -1 & -2 & 7 \end{bmatrix}\begin{bmatrix} P_1 \\ P_2 \\ P_3 \end{bmatrix} = \begin{bmatrix} 31 \\ 26 \\ 24 \end{bmatrix}$$

where $\quad |A| = 11(38) + 1(-9) - 1(8) = 401.$

$$C = \begin{bmatrix} \begin{vmatrix} 6 & -2 \\ -2 & 7 \end{vmatrix} & -\begin{vmatrix} -1 & -2 \\ -1 & 7 \end{vmatrix} & \begin{vmatrix} -1 & 6 \\ -1 & -2 \end{vmatrix} \\ -\begin{vmatrix} -1 & -1 \\ -2 & 7 \end{vmatrix} & \begin{vmatrix} 11 & -1 \\ -1 & 7 \end{vmatrix} & -\begin{vmatrix} 11 & -1 \\ -1 & -2 \end{vmatrix} \\ \begin{vmatrix} -1 & -1 \\ 6 & -2 \end{vmatrix} & -\begin{vmatrix} 11 & -1 \\ -1 & -2 \end{vmatrix} & \begin{vmatrix} 11 & -1 \\ -1 & 6 \end{vmatrix} \end{bmatrix} = \begin{bmatrix} 38 & 9 & 8 \\ 9 & 76 & 23 \\ 8 & 23 & 65 \end{bmatrix}$$

$$\text{Adj } A = \begin{bmatrix} 38 & 9 & 8 \\ 9 & 76 & 23 \\ 8 & 23 & 65 \end{bmatrix}$$

$$A^{-1} = \frac{1}{401}\begin{bmatrix} 38 & 9 & 8 \\ 9 & 76 & 23 \\ 8 & 23 & 65 \end{bmatrix} = \begin{bmatrix} \frac{38}{401} & \frac{9}{401} & \frac{8}{401} \\ \frac{9}{401} & \frac{76}{401} & \frac{23}{401} \\ \frac{8}{401} & \frac{23}{401} & \frac{65}{401} \end{bmatrix}$$

$$X = \begin{bmatrix} \frac{38}{401} & \frac{9}{401} & \frac{8}{401} \\ \frac{9}{401} & \frac{76}{401} & \frac{23}{401} \\ \frac{8}{401} & \frac{23}{401} & \frac{65}{401} \end{bmatrix}\begin{bmatrix} 31 \\ 26 \\ 24 \end{bmatrix} = \begin{bmatrix} \dfrac{1178 + 234 + 192}{401} \\ \dfrac{279 + 1976 + 552}{401} \\ \dfrac{248 + 598 + 1560}{401} \end{bmatrix} = \begin{bmatrix} 4 \\ 7 \\ 6 \end{bmatrix}$$

See Problem 2.20 for the same solution with simultaneous equations.

11.39. Given $Y = C + I_0$, where $C = C_0 + bY$. Use matrix inversion to find the equilibrium level of Y and C.

The given equations can first be rearranged so that the endogenous variables C and Y, together with their coefficients $(-b)$, are on the left-hand side of the equation and the exogenous variables C_0 and I_0 are on the right.

$$Y - C = I_0$$
$$-bY + C = C_0$$

Thus,

$$\begin{bmatrix} 1 & -1 \\ -b & 1 \end{bmatrix}\begin{bmatrix} Y \\ C \end{bmatrix} = \begin{bmatrix} I_0 \\ C_0 \end{bmatrix}$$

The determinant of the coefficient matrix is $|A| = 1(1) + 1(-b) = 1 - b$. The cofactor matrix is

$$C = \begin{bmatrix} 1 & b \\ 1 & 1 \end{bmatrix}$$

$$\text{Adj } A = \begin{bmatrix} 1 & 1 \\ b & 1 \end{bmatrix}$$

and

$$A^{-1} = \frac{1}{1-b}\begin{bmatrix} 1 & 1 \\ b & 1 \end{bmatrix}$$

Letting $X = \begin{bmatrix} Y \\ C \end{bmatrix}$,

$$X = \frac{1}{1-b}\begin{bmatrix} 1 & 1 \\ b & 1 \end{bmatrix}\begin{bmatrix} I_0 \\ C_0 \end{bmatrix} = \frac{1}{1-b}\begin{bmatrix} I_0 + C_0 \\ bI_0 + C_0 \end{bmatrix}$$

Thus,

$$\bar{Y} = \frac{1}{1-b}(I_0 + C_0) \qquad \bar{C} = \frac{1}{1-b}(C_0 + bI_0)$$

Example 3 in Chapter 2 was solved for the equilibrium level of income without matrices.

CRAMER'S RULE

11.40. Use Cramer's rule to solve for the unknowns in each of the following:

(a) $2x_1 + 6x_2 = 22$

$-x_1 + 5x_2 = 53$

From Cramer's rule,

$$\bar{x}_i = \frac{|A_i|}{|A|}$$

where A_i is a special matrix formed by replacing the column of coefficients of x_i with the column of constants. Thus, from the original data,

$$\begin{bmatrix} 2 & 6 \\ -1 & 5 \end{bmatrix}\begin{bmatrix} x_1 \\ x_2 \end{bmatrix} = \begin{bmatrix} 22 \\ 53 \end{bmatrix}$$

where $|A| = 2(5) - (-1)(6) = 16$.

Replacing the first column of the coefficient matrix with the column of constants,

$$A_1 = \begin{bmatrix} 22 & 6 \\ 53 & 5 \end{bmatrix}$$

where $|A_1| = 22(5) - 53(6) = -208$.   Thus,

$$\bar{x}_1 = \frac{|A_1|}{|A|} = -\frac{208}{16} = -13$$

Replacing the second column of the coefficient matrix with the column of constants,

$$A_2 = \begin{bmatrix} 2 & 22 \\ -1 & 53 \end{bmatrix}$$

where $|A_2| = 2(53) - (-1)(22) = 128$.   Thus,

$$\bar{x}_2 = \frac{|A_2|}{|A|} = \frac{128}{16} = 8$$

(b) $5x_1 - 3x_2 = 28$
        $-2x_1 + 4x_2 = 14$

$$A = \begin{bmatrix} 5 & -3 \\ -2 & 4 \end{bmatrix}$$

where $|A| = 5(4) - (-3)(-2) = 14$

$$A_1 = \begin{bmatrix} 28 & -3 \\ 14 & 4 \end{bmatrix}$$

where $|A_1| = 28(4) - (-3)(14) = 154$.

$$A_2 = \begin{bmatrix} 5 & 28 \\ -2 & 14 \end{bmatrix}$$

where $|A_2| = 5(14) - 28(-2) = 126$.   Thus,

$$\bar{x}_1 = \frac{|A_1|}{|A|} = \frac{154}{14} = 11 \qquad \text{and} \qquad \bar{x}_2 = \frac{|A_2|}{|A|} = \frac{126}{14} = 9$$

(c) $7p_1 + 2p_2 = 60$
       $p_1 + 8p_2 = 78$

$$A = \begin{bmatrix} 7 & 2 \\ 1 & 8 \end{bmatrix}$$

where $|A| = 7(8) - 2(1) = 54$.

$$A_1 = \begin{bmatrix} 60 & 2 \\ 78 & 8 \end{bmatrix}$$

where $|A_1| = 60(8) - 2(78) = 324$.

$$A_2 = \begin{bmatrix} 7 & 60 \\ 1 & 78 \end{bmatrix}$$

where $|A_2| = 7(78) - 60(1) = 486$.

$$\bar{p}_1 = \frac{|A_1|}{|A|} = \frac{324}{54} = 6 \qquad \text{and} \qquad \bar{p}_2 = \frac{|A_2|}{|A|} = \frac{486}{54} = 9$$

(d) $18P_b - \quad P_p = 87$
       $-2P_b + 36P_p = 98$

$$A = \begin{bmatrix} 18 & -1 \\ -2 & 36 \end{bmatrix}$$

where $|A| = 18(36) - (-1)(-2) = 646$.

$$A_1 = \begin{bmatrix} 87 & -1 \\ 98 & 36 \end{bmatrix}$$

where $|A_1| = 87(36) + 1(98) = 3230.$

$$A_2 = \begin{bmatrix} 18 & 87 \\ -2 & 98 \end{bmatrix}$$

where $|A_2| = 18(98) - 87(-2) = 1938.$

$$\bar{P}_b = \frac{|A_1|}{|A|} = \frac{3230}{646} = 5 \qquad \text{and} \qquad \bar{P}_p = \frac{|A_2|}{|A|} = \frac{1938}{646} = 3$$

Compare the work involved in this method of solution with the work involved in Problems 2.16 and 11.33 where the same problem is treated first with simultaneous equations and then with matrix inversion.

11.41.   Redo Problem 11.40 for each of the following:

(a) $0.4\,Y + 150i = 209$

$0.1\,Y - 250i = \ \ 35$

$$A = \begin{bmatrix} 0.4 & 150 \\ 0.1 & -250 \end{bmatrix}$$

where $|A| = 0.4(-250) - 150(0.1) = -115.$

$$A_1 = \begin{bmatrix} 209 & 150 \\ 35 & -250 \end{bmatrix}$$

where $|A_1| = 209(-250) - 150(35) = -57{,}500.$

$$A_2 = \begin{bmatrix} 0.4 & 209 \\ 0.1 & 35 \end{bmatrix}$$

where $|A_2| = 0.4(35) - 209(0.1) = -6.9.$

$$\bar{Y} = \frac{|A_1|}{|A|} = \frac{-57{,}500}{-115} = 500 \qquad \text{and} \qquad \bar{i} = \frac{|A_2|}{|A|} = \frac{-6.9}{-115} = 0.06$$

Compare this method of solution with Problem 2.30.

(b) $5x_1 - 2x_2 + 3x_3 = 16$

$2x_1 + 3x_2 - 5x_3 = \ \ 2$

$4x_1 - 5x_2 + 6x_3 = \ \ 7$

$$|A| = \begin{vmatrix} 5 & -2 & 3 \\ 2 & 3 & -5 \\ 4 & -5 & 6 \end{vmatrix} = 5(18 - 25) + 2(12 + 20) + 3(-10 - 12) = -37$$

$$|A_1| = \begin{vmatrix} 16 & -2 & 3 \\ 2 & 3 & -5 \\ 7 & -5 & 6 \end{vmatrix} = 16(18 - 25) + 2(12 + 35) + 3(-10 - 21) = -111$$

$$|A_2| = \begin{vmatrix} 5 & 16 & 3 \\ 2 & 2 & -5 \\ 4 & 7 & 6 \end{vmatrix} = 5(12 + 35) - 16(12 + 20) + 3(14 - 8) = -259$$

$$|A_3| = \begin{vmatrix} 5 & -2 & 16 \\ 2 & 3 & 2 \\ 4 & -5 & 7 \end{vmatrix} = 5(21 + 10) + 2(14 - 8) + 16(-10 - 12) = -185$$

$$\bar{x}_1 = \frac{|A_1|}{|A|} = \frac{-111}{-37} = 3 \qquad \bar{x}_2 = \frac{|A_2|}{|A|} = \frac{-259}{-37} = 7 \qquad \bar{x}_3 = \frac{|A_3|}{|A|} = \frac{-185}{-37} = 5$$

(c) $5x_1 - 4x_2 \qquad = 10$

$\qquad 4x_2 - 5x_3 = -5$

$3x_1 \qquad - 2x_3 = 20$

$$|A| = \begin{vmatrix} 5 & -4 & 0 \\ 0 & 4 & -5 \\ 3 & 0 & -2 \end{vmatrix} = 5(-8) + 4(15) = 20$$

$$|A_1| = \begin{vmatrix} 10 & -4 & 0 \\ -5 & 4 & -5 \\ 20 & 0 & -2 \end{vmatrix} = 10(-8) + 4(110) = 360$$

$$|A_2| = \begin{vmatrix} 5 & 10 & 0 \\ 0 & -5 & -5 \\ 3 & 20 & -2 \end{vmatrix} = 5(110) - 10(15) = 400$$

$$|A_3| = \begin{vmatrix} 5 & -4 & 10 \\ 0 & 4 & -5 \\ 3 & 0 & 20 \end{vmatrix} = 5(80) + 3(-20) = 340$$

$$\bar{x}_1 = \frac{|A_1|}{|A|} = \frac{360}{20} = 18 \qquad \bar{x}_2 = \frac{|A_2|}{|A|} = \frac{400}{20} = 20 \qquad \bar{x}_3 = \frac{|A_3|}{|A|} = \frac{340}{20} = 17$$

(d) $2x_1 + 4x_2 - x_3 = 52$

$-x_1 + 5x_2 + 3x_3 = 72$

$3x_1 - 7x_2 + 2x_3 = 10$

$$|A| = \begin{vmatrix} 2 & 4 & -1 \\ -1 & 5 & 3 \\ 3 & -7 & 2 \end{vmatrix} = 2(31) - 4(-11) - 1(-8) = 114$$

$$|A_1| = \begin{vmatrix} 52 & 4 & -1 \\ 72 & 5 & 3 \\ 10 & -7 & 2 \end{vmatrix} = 52(31) - 4(114) - 1(-554) = 1710$$

$$|A_2| = \begin{vmatrix} 2 & 52 & -1 \\ -1 & 72 & 3 \\ 3 & 10 & 2 \end{vmatrix} = 2(114) - 52(-11) - 1(-226) = 1026$$

$$|A_3| = \begin{vmatrix} 2 & 4 & 52 \\ -1 & 5 & 72 \\ 3 & -7 & 10 \end{vmatrix} = 2(554) - 4(-226) + 52(-8) = 1596$$

$$\bar{x}_1 = \frac{|A_1|}{|A|} = \frac{1710}{114} = 15 \qquad \bar{x}_2 = \frac{|A_2|}{|A|} = \frac{1026}{114} = 9 \qquad \bar{x}_3 = \frac{|A_3|}{|A|} = \frac{1596}{114} = 14$$

(e) $11p_1 - p_2 - p_3 = 31$

$-p_1 + 6p_2 - 2p_3 = 26$

$-p_1 - 2p_2 + 7p_3 = 24$

$$|A| = \begin{vmatrix} 11 & -1 & -1 \\ -1 & 6 & -2 \\ -1 & -2 & 7 \end{vmatrix} = 11(38) + 1(-9) - 1(8) = 401$$

$$|A_1| = \begin{vmatrix} 31 & -1 & -1 \\ 26 & 6 & -2 \\ 24 & -2 & 7 \end{vmatrix} = 31(38) + 1(230) - 1(-196) = 1604$$

$$|A_2| = \begin{vmatrix} 11 & 31 & -1 \\ -1 & 26 & -2 \\ -1 & 24 & 7 \end{vmatrix} = 11(230) - 31(-9) - 1(2) = 2807$$

$$|A_3| = \begin{vmatrix} 11 & -1 & 31 \\ -1 & 6 & 26 \\ -1 & -2 & 24 \end{vmatrix} = 11(196) + 1(2) + 31(8) = 2406$$

Thus, $\bar{p}_1 = \dfrac{|A_1|}{|A|} = \dfrac{1604}{401} = 4$ $\bar{p}_2 = \dfrac{|A_2|}{|A|} = \dfrac{2807}{401} = 7$ $\bar{p}_3 = \dfrac{|A_3|}{|A|} = \dfrac{2406}{401} = 6$

Compare the work involved in this type of solution with the work involved in Problems 2.20 and 11.37.

11.42. The first-order conditions for constrained optimization in Example 7 of Chapter 6 were

$$\frac{\partial TC}{\partial x} = 16x - y + \lambda = 0$$

$$\frac{\partial TC}{\partial y} = 24y - x + \lambda = 0$$

$$\frac{\partial TC}{\partial \lambda} = x + y - 42 = 0$$

Use Cramer's rule to solve for x and y.

Rearranging the given equations,

$$16x - y + \lambda = 0$$
$$-x + 24y + \lambda = 0$$
$$x + y = 42$$

Setting them in matrix form,

$$\begin{bmatrix} 16 & -1 & 1 \\ -1 & 24 & 1 \\ 1 & 1 & 0 \end{bmatrix} \begin{bmatrix} x \\ y \\ \lambda \end{bmatrix} = \begin{bmatrix} 0 \\ 0 \\ 42 \end{bmatrix}$$

Thus, expanding along the third column, $|A| = 1(-1 - 24) - 1(16 + 1) = -42$.

$$A_1 = \begin{bmatrix} 0 & -1 & 1 \\ 0 & 24 & 1 \\ 42 & 1 & 0 \end{bmatrix}$$

Expanding along the first column, $|A_1| = 42(-1 - 24) = -1050$.

$$A_2 = \begin{bmatrix} 16 & 0 & 1 \\ -1 & 0 & 1 \\ 1 & 42 & 0 \end{bmatrix}$$

Expanding along the second column, $|A_2| = -42(16 + 1) = -714$.

$$A_3 = \begin{bmatrix} 16 & -1 & 0 \\ -1 & 24 & 0 \\ 1 & 1 & 42 \end{bmatrix}$$

Expanding along the third column, $|A_3| = 42(384 - 1) = 16,086$.   Thus,

$\bar{x} = \dfrac{|A_1|}{|A|} = \dfrac{-1050}{-42} = 25$ $\bar{y} = \dfrac{|A_2|}{|A|} = \dfrac{-714}{-42} = 17$ $\bar{\lambda} = \dfrac{|A_3|}{|A|} = \dfrac{16,086}{-42} = -383$

11.43. The first-order conditions for constrained utility maximization in Problem 6.43 were

$$Q_2 + 10\lambda \qquad = 0$$
$$Q_1 + 2\lambda \qquad = 0$$
$$10Q_1 + 2Q_2 - 240 = 0$$

Use Cramer's rule to solve for the unknowns.

$$\begin{vmatrix} 0 & 1 & 10 \\ 1 & 0 & 2 \\ 10 & 2 & 0 \end{vmatrix} \begin{vmatrix} Q_1 \\ Q_2 \\ \lambda \end{vmatrix} = \begin{vmatrix} 0 \\ 0 \\ 240 \end{vmatrix}$$

Thus, $|A| = -1(-20) + 10(2) = 40.$

$$|A_1| = \begin{vmatrix} 0 & 1 & 10 \\ 0 & 0 & 2 \\ 240 & 2 & 0 \end{vmatrix} = 240(2) = 480$$

$$|A_2| = \begin{vmatrix} 0 & 0 & 10 \\ 1 & 0 & 2 \\ 10 & 240 & 0 \end{vmatrix} = -240(-10) = 2400$$

$$|A_3| = \begin{vmatrix} 0 & 1 & 0 \\ 1 & 0 & 0 \\ 10 & 2 & 240 \end{vmatrix} = 240(-1) = -240$$

$$\bar{Q}_1 = \frac{|A_1|}{|A|} = \frac{480}{40} = 12 \qquad \bar{Q}_2 = \frac{|A_2|}{|A|} = \frac{2400}{40} = 60 \qquad \bar{\lambda} = \frac{|A_3|}{|A|} = -\frac{240}{40} = -6$$

11.44. Given

$$ax_1 + bx_2 = g \qquad\qquad (11.6)$$
$$cx_1 + dx_2 = h \qquad\qquad (11.7)$$

Prove Cramer's rule by showing

$$\bar{x}_1 = \frac{\begin{vmatrix} g & b \\ h & d \end{vmatrix}}{\begin{vmatrix} a & b \\ c & d \end{vmatrix}} = \frac{|A_1|}{|A|} \qquad \bar{x}_2 = \frac{\begin{vmatrix} a & g \\ c & h \end{vmatrix}}{\begin{vmatrix} a & b \\ c & d \end{vmatrix}} = \frac{|A_2|}{|A|}$$

Dividing (11.6) by b,

$$\frac{a}{b}x_1 + x_2 = \frac{g}{b} \qquad\qquad (11.8)$$

Multiplying (11.8) by d and subtracting (11.7)

$$\frac{ad}{b}x_1 + dx_2 = \frac{dg}{b}$$
$$-cx_1 - dx_2 = -h$$
$$\overline{\left(\frac{ad - cb}{b}\right)x_1 = \frac{dg - hb}{b}}$$

$$\bar{x}_1 = \frac{dg - hb}{ad - cb} = \frac{\begin{vmatrix} g & b \\ h & d \end{vmatrix}}{\begin{vmatrix} a & b \\ c & d \end{vmatrix}} = \frac{|A_1|}{|A|}$$

Similarly, dividing (*11.6*) by *a*, $x_1 + \dfrac{b}{a} x_2 = \dfrac{g}{a}$ (*11.9*)

Multiplying (*11.9*) by $-c$ and adding to (*11.7*)

$$-cx_1 - \frac{bc}{a} x_2 = -\frac{cg}{a}$$

$$cx_1 + dx_2 = h$$

$$\overline{\left(\frac{ad - bc}{a}\right) x_2 = \frac{ah - cg}{a}}$$

$$\bar{x}_2 = \frac{ah - cg}{ad - bc} = \frac{\begin{vmatrix} a & g \\ c & h \end{vmatrix}}{\begin{vmatrix} a & b \\ c & d \end{vmatrix}} = \frac{|A_2|}{|A|} \qquad \text{Q.E.D.}$$

GAUSSIAN METHOD FOR FINDING THE INVERSE

11.45. Use the Gaussian elimination method to find the inverse of the following matrix:

$$A = \begin{bmatrix} 7 & 9 \\ 6 & 12 \end{bmatrix}$$

Set up an augmented matrix with the identity matrix to the right. Then apply row operations until the original matrix is reduced to an identity matrix. The matrix on the right will then be the inverse A^{-1}. Thus,

$$A \,|\, B = \begin{bmatrix} 7 & 9 & | & 1 & 0 \\ 6 & 12 & | & 0 & 1 \end{bmatrix}$$

1*a*.   Multiply row$_1$ by $\frac{1}{7}$,

$$\begin{bmatrix} 1 & \frac{9}{7} & | & \frac{1}{7} & 0 \\ 6 & 12 & | & 0 & 1 \end{bmatrix}$$

1*b*.   Subtract 6 times row$_1$ from row$_2$,

$$\begin{bmatrix} 1 & \frac{9}{7} & | & \frac{1}{7} & 0 \\ 0 & \frac{30}{7} & | & -\frac{6}{7} & 1 \end{bmatrix}$$

2*a*.   Multiply row$_2$ by $\frac{7}{30}$,

$$\begin{bmatrix} 1 & \frac{9}{7} & | & \frac{1}{7} & 0 \\ 0 & 1 & | & -\frac{1}{5} & \frac{7}{30} \end{bmatrix}$$

2*b*.   Subtract $\frac{9}{7}$ times row$_2$ from row$_1$,

$$\begin{bmatrix} 1 & 0 & | & \frac{2}{5} & -\frac{3}{10} \\ 0 & 1 & | & -\frac{1}{5} & \frac{7}{30} \end{bmatrix}$$

Thus, $A^{-1} = \begin{bmatrix} \frac{2}{5} & -\frac{3}{10} \\ -\frac{1}{5} & \frac{7}{30} \end{bmatrix}$

as was found by the adjoint method in Problem 11.31(*b*).

11.46. Redo Problem 11.45, given

$$A = \begin{bmatrix} 4 & 2 & 5 \\ 3 & 1 & 8 \\ 9 & 6 & 7 \end{bmatrix}$$

$$A \mid B = \begin{bmatrix} 4 & 2 & 5 & 1 & 0 & 0 \\ 3 & 1 & 8 & 0 & 1 & 0 \\ 9 & 6 & 7 & 0 & 0 & 1 \end{bmatrix}$$

1. Multiply row$_1$ by $\frac{1}{4}$,

$$\begin{bmatrix} 1 & \frac{1}{2} & \frac{5}{4} & \frac{1}{4} & 0 & 0 \\ 3 & 1 & 8 & 0 & 1 & 0 \\ 9 & 6 & 7 & 0 & 0 & 1 \end{bmatrix}$$

2. Subtract 3 times row$_1$ from row$_2$ and 9 times row$_1$ from row$_3$,

$$\begin{bmatrix} 1 & \frac{1}{2} & \frac{5}{4} & \frac{1}{4} & 0 & 0 \\ 0 & -\frac{1}{2} & \frac{17}{4} & -\frac{3}{4} & 1 & 0 \\ 0 & \frac{3}{2} & -\frac{17}{4} & -\frac{9}{4} & 0 & 1 \end{bmatrix}$$

3. Multiply row$_2$ by -2,

$$\begin{bmatrix} 1 & \frac{1}{2} & \frac{5}{4} & \frac{1}{4} & 0 & 0 \\ 0 & 1 & -\frac{17}{2} & \frac{3}{2} & -2 & 0 \\ 0 & \frac{3}{2} & -\frac{17}{4} & -\frac{9}{4} & 0 & 1 \end{bmatrix}$$

4. Subtract $\frac{1}{2}$ row$_2$ from row$_1$ and $\frac{3}{2}$ row$_2$ from row$_3$,

$$\begin{bmatrix} 1 & 0 & \frac{11}{2} & -\frac{1}{2} & 1 & 0 \\ 0 & 1 & -\frac{17}{2} & \frac{3}{2} & -2 & 0 \\ 0 & 0 & \frac{17}{2} & -\frac{9}{2} & 3 & 1 \end{bmatrix}$$

5. Multiply row$_3$ by $\frac{2}{17}$,

$$\begin{bmatrix} 1 & 0 & \frac{11}{2} & -\frac{1}{2} & 1 & 0 \\ 0 & 1 & -\frac{17}{2} & \frac{3}{2} & -2 & 0 \\ 0 & 0 & 1 & -\frac{9}{17} & \frac{6}{17} & \frac{2}{17} \end{bmatrix}$$

6. Subtract $\frac{11}{2}$ times row$_3$ from row$_1$ and add $\frac{17}{2}$ times row$_3$ to row$_2$,

$$\begin{bmatrix} 1 & 0 & 0 & \frac{41}{17} & -\frac{16}{17} & -\frac{11}{17} \\ 0 & 1 & 0 & -3 & 1 & 1 \\ 0 & 0 & 1 & -\frac{9}{17} & \frac{6}{17} & \frac{2}{17} \end{bmatrix}$$

Thus,
$$A^{-1} = \begin{bmatrix} \frac{41}{17} & -\frac{16}{17} & -\frac{11}{17} \\ -3 & 1 & 1 \\ -\frac{9}{17} & \frac{6}{17} & \frac{2}{17} \end{bmatrix}$$

as was found by the adjoint method in Problem 11.31(d).

Chapter 12

Special Determinants and Matrices and Their Use in Economics

12.1 THE JACOBIAN

Section 11.1 showed how to test for linear dependence through the use of a simple determinant. In contrast, a *Jacobian determinant* permits testing for functional dependence, both linear *and* nonlinear. A Jacobian determinant $|J|$ is composed of all the first-order partial derivatives of a system of equations, arranged in ordered sequence. Given

$$y_1 = f_1(x_1, x_2, x_3)$$
$$y_2 = f_2(x_1, x_2, x_3)$$
$$y_3 = f_3(x_1, x_2, x_3)$$

$$|J| = \left| \frac{\partial y_1, \partial y_2, \partial y_3}{\partial x_1, \partial x_2, \partial x_3} \right| = \begin{vmatrix} \dfrac{\partial y_1}{\partial x_1} & \dfrac{\partial y_1}{\partial x_2} & \dfrac{\partial y_1}{\partial x_3} \\[2mm] \dfrac{\partial y_2}{\partial x_1} & \dfrac{\partial y_2}{\partial x_2} & \dfrac{\partial y_2}{\partial x_3} \\[2mm] \dfrac{\partial y_3}{\partial x_1} & \dfrac{\partial y_3}{\partial x_2} & \dfrac{\partial y_3}{\partial x_3} \end{vmatrix}$$

If $|J| = 0$, the equations are functionally dependent; if $|J| \neq 0$, the equations are functionally independent.

Example 1. Use of the Jacobian to test for functional dependence is demonstrated below, given

$$y_1 = 5x_1 + 3x_2$$
$$y_2 = 25x_1^2 + 30x_1x_2 + 9x_2^2$$

First, take the first-order partials,

$$\frac{\partial y_1}{\partial x_1} = 5 \qquad \frac{\partial y_1}{\partial x_2} = 3 \qquad \frac{\partial y_2}{\partial x_1} = 50x_1 + 30x_2 \qquad \frac{\partial y_2}{\partial x_2} = 30x_1 + 18x_2$$

Then set up the Jacobian,

$$|J| = \begin{vmatrix} 5 & 3 \\ 50x_1 + 30x_2 & 30x_1 + 18x_2 \end{vmatrix}$$

and evaluate,

$$|J| = 5(30x_1 + 18x_2) - 3(50x_1 + 30x_2) = 0$$

Since $|J| = 0$, there is functional dependence between the equations. In this, the simplest of cases, $(5x_1 + 3x_2)^2 = 25x_1^2 + 30x_1x_2 + 9x_2^2$.

12.2 THE HESSIAN

To optimize a multivariable function $z = f(x, y)$, given that the first-order condition $z_x = z_y = 0$ is met, two further conditions must be met:

238

(1)
$$z_{xx}, z_{yy} > 0 \qquad \text{for a minimum}$$
$$z_{xx}, z_{yy} < 0 \qquad \text{for a maximum}$$

(2)
$$z_{xx}z_{yy} > (z_{xy})^2$$

See Section 5.7. A convenient test for this second-order condition is the Hessian. A *Hessian* $|H|$ is a determinant composed of all the second-order partial derivatives, with the second-order direct partials on the principal diagonal and the second-order cross partials off the principal diagonal. Thus,

$$|H| = \begin{vmatrix} z_{xx} & z_{xy} \\ z_{yx} & z_{yy} \end{vmatrix}$$

where $z_{xy} = z_{yx}$. If the first element on the principal diagonal, the *first principal minor*, $|H_1| = z_{xx}$, is positive and the *second principal minor*,

$$|H_2| = \begin{vmatrix} z_{xx} & z_{xy} \\ z_{xy} & z_{yy} \end{vmatrix} = z_{xx}z_{yy} - (z_{xy})^2 > 0$$

the second-order conditions for a minimum are met. When $|H_1| > 0$ and $|H_2| > 0$, the Hessian is called *positive definite*. A positive definite Hessian fulfills the second-order conditions for a minimum.

If the first principal minor, $|H_1| = z_{xx} < 0$ and the second principal minor,

$$|H_2| = \begin{vmatrix} z_{xx} & z_{xy} \\ z_{xy} & z_{yy} \end{vmatrix} > 0$$

the second-order conditions for a maximum are met. When $|H_1| < 0$, $|H_2| > 0$, the Hessian is *negative definite*. A negative definite Hessian fulfills the second-order conditions for a maximum.

Example 2. In Example 14 of Chapter 5 it was determined that

$$z = 6x^2 - 9x - 3xy - 7y + 5y^2$$

is optimized at $\bar{x} = 1$, $\bar{y} = 1$. The second partials were $z_{xx} = 12$, $z_{yy} = 10$, and $z_{xy} = -3$. Using the Hessian to test the second-order conditions,

$$|H| = \begin{vmatrix} z_{xx} & z_{xy} \\ z_{yx} & z_{yy} \end{vmatrix} = \begin{vmatrix} 12 & -3 \\ -3 & 10 \end{vmatrix}$$

Taking the principal minors, $|H_1| = 12 > 0$ and

$$|H_2| = \begin{vmatrix} 12 & -3 \\ -3 & 10 \end{vmatrix} = 12(10) - (-3)(-3) = 111 > 0$$

With $|H_1| > 0$ and $|H_2| > 0$, the Hessian is positive definite and z is minimized at the critical values.

Example 3. Determinants may also be used to test for positive or negative definiteness of any quadratic form. The determinant of a quadratic form is also called a *discriminant* $|D|$. Given a simple quadratic form in two variables such as

$$z = 2x^2 + 5xy + 8y^2$$

to form the discriminant, place the coefficients of the squared variables on the principal diagonal and divide the coefficient of the unsquared variables equally between the two off-diagonal positions. Thus,

$$|D| = \begin{vmatrix} 2 & 2.5 \\ 2.5 & 8 \end{vmatrix}$$

Then, evaluate the principal minors as in the Hessian test.

$$|D_1| = 2 > 0 \qquad |D_2| = \begin{vmatrix} 2 & 2.5 \\ 2.5 & 8 \end{vmatrix} = 16 - 6.25 = 9.75 > 0$$

Thus, z is positive definite, meaning that it will be greater than zero for all nonzero values of x and y.

12.3 THIRD-ORDER HESSIANS

Given $y = f(x_1, x_2, x_3)$,   the third-order Hessian is

$$|H| = \begin{vmatrix} y_{11} & y_{12} & y_{13} \\ y_{21} & y_{22} & y_{23} \\ y_{31} & y_{32} & y_{33} \end{vmatrix}$$

where the elements are the various second-order partial derivatives of y:

$$y_{11} = \frac{\partial^2 y}{\partial x_1^2} \qquad y_{12} = \frac{\partial^2 y}{\partial x_1 \partial x_2} \qquad y_{23} = \frac{\partial^2 y}{\partial x_2 \partial x_3} \qquad \text{etc.}$$

Conditions for a relative minimum or maximum depend on the signs of the first, second, and third principal minors respectively.   If $|H_1| = y_{11} > 0$,

$$|H_2| = \begin{vmatrix} y_{11} & y_{12} \\ y_{21} & y_{22} \end{vmatrix} > 0 \qquad \text{and} \qquad |H_3| = |H| > 0$$

where $|H_3|$ is the *third principal minor*, $|H|$ is positive definite and fulfills the second-order conditions for a minimum.   If $|H_1| = y_{11} < 0$,

$$|H_2| = \begin{vmatrix} y_{11} & y_{12} \\ y_{21} & y_{22} \end{vmatrix} > 0 \qquad \text{and} \qquad |H_3| = |H| < 0$$

$|H|$ is negative definite and will fulfill the second-order condition for a maximum.   In short, if the principal minors are all positive, $|H|$ is positive definite and the second-order conditions for a relative minimum are met; if the principal minors alternate in sign between negative and positive, $|H|$ is negative definite and the second-order conditions for a relative maximum are met.

Example 4.   The function
$$y = -5x_1^2 + 10x_1 + x_1 x_3 - 2x_2^2 + 4x_2 + 2x_2 x_3 - 4x_3^2$$

is optimized as follows, using the Hessian to test the second-order conditions.

The first-order conditions are

$$\frac{\partial y}{\partial x_1} = y_1 = -10x_1 + 10 + x_3 = 0$$

$$\frac{\partial y}{\partial x_2} = y_2 = -4x_2 + 2x_3 + 4 = 0$$

$$\frac{\partial y}{\partial x_3} = y_3 = x_1 + 2x_2 - 8x_3 = 0$$

which can be expressed in matrix form as

$$\begin{bmatrix} -10 & 0 & 1 \\ 0 & -4 & 2 \\ 1 & 2 & -8 \end{bmatrix} \begin{bmatrix} x_1 \\ x_2 \\ x_3 \end{bmatrix} = \begin{bmatrix} -10 \\ -4 \\ 0 \end{bmatrix} \qquad (12.1)$$

Using Cramer's rule (see Section 11.9) and taking the different determinants, $|A| = -10(28) + 1(4) = -276 \neq 0$.   Since $|A|$ in this case is the Jacobian, and does not equal zero, the three equations are functionally independent.

$$|A_1| = -10(28) + 1(-8) = -288 \qquad |A_2| = -10(32) - (-10)(-2) + 1(4) = -336 \qquad |A_3| = -10(8) - 10(4) = -120$$

Thus, $\bar{x}_1 = \dfrac{|A_1|}{|A|} = \dfrac{-288}{-276} \cong 1.04 \qquad \bar{x}_2 = \dfrac{|A_2|}{|A|} = \dfrac{-336}{-276} \cong 1.22 \qquad \bar{x}_3 = \dfrac{|A_3|}{|A|} = \dfrac{-120}{-276} \cong 0.43$

Taking the second partials for the second-order condition,

$$\begin{array}{lll} y_{11} = -10 & y_{12} = 0 & y_{13} = 1 \\ y_{21} = 0 & y_{22} = -4 & y_{23} = 2 \\ y_{31} = 1 & y_{32} = 2 & y_{33} = -8 \end{array}$$

Thus,
$$|H| = \begin{vmatrix} -10 & 0 & 1 \\ 0 & -4 & 2 \\ 1 & 2 & -8 \end{vmatrix}$$

which has the same elements as the coefficient matrix in (12.1) since the first-order partials are all linear. Finally, applying the Hessian test, by checking the signs of the first, second, and third principal minors, respectively,

$$|H_1| = -10 < 0 \qquad |H_2| = \begin{vmatrix} -10 & 0 \\ 0 & -4 \end{vmatrix} = 40 > 0 \qquad |H_3| = |H| = |A| = -276 < 0$$

Since the principal minors alternate correctly in sign, the Hessian is negative definite and the function is maximized at $\bar{x}_1 = 1.04$, $\bar{x}_2 = 1.22$, and $\bar{x}_3 = 0.43$.

12.4 THE BORDERED HESSIAN FOR CONSTRAINED OPTIMIZATION

To optimize a function $f(x, y)$ subject to a constraint $g(x, y)$, Section 5.8 showed that a new function could be formed $F(x, y, \lambda) = f(x, y) + \lambda g(x, y)$ where the first-order conditions are $F_x = F_y = F_\lambda = 0$.

The second-order conditions can now be expressed in terms of a *bordered Hessian* $|\bar{H}|$, in either of two ways.

$$|\bar{H}| = \begin{vmatrix} F_{xx} & F_{xy} & g_x \\ F_{yx} & F_{yy} & g_y \\ g_x & g_y & 0 \end{vmatrix} \qquad \text{or} \qquad \begin{vmatrix} 0 & g_x & g_y \\ g_x & F_{xx} & F_{xy} \\ g_y & F_{yx} & F_{yy} \end{vmatrix}$$

which is simply the plain Hessian

$$\begin{vmatrix} F_{xx} & F_{xy} \\ F_{yx} & F_{yy} \end{vmatrix}$$

bordered by the first derivatives of the constraint with zero on the principal diagonal. The order of a *bordered principal minor* is determined by the order of the principal minor being bordered. Hence $|\bar{H}|$ above represents a second bordered principal minor $|\bar{H}_2|$, because the principal minor being bordered is (2×2).

For a function in n variables $f(x_1, x_2, \ldots, x_n)$, subject to $g(x_1, x_2, \ldots, x_n)$,

$$|\bar{H}| = \begin{vmatrix} F_{11} & F_{12} & \cdots & F_{1n} & g_1 \\ F_{21} & F_{22} & \cdots & F_{2n} & g_2 \\ \cdots & \cdots & \cdots & \cdots & \cdots \\ F_{n1} & F_{n2} & \cdots & F_{nn} & g_n \\ g_1 & g_2 & \cdots & g_n & 0 \end{vmatrix} \qquad \text{or} \qquad \begin{vmatrix} 0 & g_1 & g_2 & \cdots & g_n \\ g_1 & F_{11} & F_{12} & \cdots & F_{1n} \\ g_2 & F_{21} & F_{22} & \cdots & F_{2n} \\ \cdots & \cdots & \cdots & \cdots & \cdots \\ g_n & F_{n1} & F_{n2} & \cdots & F_{nn} \end{vmatrix}$$

where $|\bar{H}| = |\bar{H}_n|$, because of the $(n \times n)$ principal minor being bordered.

If $|\bar{H}_2|, |\bar{H}_3|, \ldots, |\bar{H}_n| < 0$, the bordered Hessian is positive definite, which is a sufficient condition for a minimum. Note that the test starts with $|\bar{H}_2|$, and *not* $|\bar{H}_1|$.

If $|\bar{H}_2| > 0$, $|\bar{H}_3| < 0$, $|\bar{H}_4| > 0$, etc., the bordered Hessian is negative definite, which is a sufficient condition for a maximum. If a given $|\bar{H}|$ meets the criteria, one is assured of a minimum or a maximum. Further tests beyond the scope of the present book are needed if the criteria are not met, since the given criteria represent sufficient conditions, and not necessary conditions.

Example 5. Refer to Example 16 in Chapter 5. The bordered Hessian can be used to check the second-order conditions of the optimized function and to determine if Z is maximized or minimized, as demonstrated below.

Since $Z_{xx} = 8$, $Z_{yy} = 12$, $Z_{xy} = Z_{yx} = 3$, and from the constraint, $g_x = 1$, $g_y = 1$,

$$|\bar{H}| = \begin{vmatrix} 8 & 3 & 1 \\ 3 & 12 & 1 \\ 1 & 1 & 0 \end{vmatrix}$$

Starting with the second principal minor $|\bar{H}_2|$,

$$|\bar{H}_2| = 8(-1) - 3(-1) + 1(3 - 12) = -14$$

With $|\bar{H}_2| < 0$, $|\bar{H}|$ is positive definite, which means that Z is at a minimum.

Example 6. The bordered Hessian is applied below to test the second-order condition of the generalized Cobb–Douglas production function maximized in Section 9.11.

Since $Q_{KK} = -0.24\,K^{-1.6}L^{0.5}$, $Q_{LL} = -0.25\,K^{0.4}L^{-1.5}$, $Q_{KL} = Q_{LK} = 0.2\,K^{-0.6}L^{-0.5}$, and from the constraint, $g_K = 3$, $g_L = 4$,

$$|\bar{H}| = \begin{vmatrix} -0.24\,K^{-1.6}L^{0.5} & 0.2\,K^{-0.6}L^{-0.5} & 3 \\ 0.2\,K^{-0.6}L^{-0.5} & -0.25\,K^{0.4}L^{-1.5} & 4 \\ 3 & 4 & 0 \end{vmatrix}$$

Starting with $|\bar{H}_2|$, and expanding along the third row,

$$|\bar{H}_2| = 3(0.8\,K^{-0.6}L^{-0.5} + 0.75\,K^{0.4}L^{-1.5}) - 4(-0.96\,K^{-1.6}L^{0.5} - 0.6\,K^{-0.6}L^{-0.5})$$

$$= 2.25\,K^{0.4}L^{-1.5} + 4.8\,K^{-0.6}L^{-0.5} + 3.84\,K^{-1.6}L^{0.5} = \frac{2.25\,K^{0.4}}{L^{1.5}} + \frac{4.8}{K^{0.6}L^{0.5}} + \frac{3.84\,L^{0.5}}{K^{1.6}} > 0$$

With $|\bar{H}_2| > 0$, $|\bar{H}|$ is negative definite and Q is maximized.

12.5   DERIVATION OF A MARSHALLIAN DEMAND FUNCTION

A Marshallian demand function expresses the amount of a good a consumer will buy as a function of commodity prices and available income. The Marshallian demand function is derived by means of utility maximization subject to a budgetary constraint. Given $u = Q_1 Q_2$ subject to $P_1 Q_1 + P_2 Q_2 = B$, where B = the budget or amount of income available, the Lagrangian function is

$$U = Q_1 Q_2 + \lambda(P_1 Q_1 + P_2 Q_2 - B)$$

Thus,

$$U_1 = Q_2 + \lambda P_1 = 0 \tag{12.2}$$

$$U_2 = Q_1 + \lambda P_2 = 0 \tag{12.3}$$

$$U_\lambda = P_1 Q_1 + P_2 Q_2 - B = 0 \tag{12.4}$$

Solving simultaneously, from (12.2) and (12.3),

$$\frac{-Q_2}{P_1} = \lambda = \frac{-Q_1}{P_2}$$

Thus,

$$\bar{Q}_2 = \frac{Q_1 P_1}{P_2} \qquad \bar{Q}_1 = \frac{Q_2 P_2}{P_1}$$

Substituting $Q_2 = Q_1 P_1 / P_2$ in (12.4),

$$P_1 Q_1 + \frac{P_2(Q_1 P_1)}{P_2} = B \qquad \bar{Q}_1 = \frac{B}{2P_1}$$

Similarly, substituting $Q_1 = Q_2 P_2 / P_1$ in (12.4),

$$\bar{Q}_2 = \frac{B}{2P_2}$$

These are the Marshallian demand functions for Q_1 and Q_2, maximizing the consumer's satisfaction subject to his income and commodity prices.

Then testing the second-order conditions, where $U_{11} = 0$, $U_{22} = 0$, $U_{12} = U_{21} = 1$, $g_1 = P_1$, and $g_2 = P_2$,

$$|\bar{H}| = \begin{vmatrix} 0 & 1 & P_1 \\ 1 & 0 & P_2 \\ P_1 & P_2 & 0 \end{vmatrix}$$

$$|\bar{H}_2| = -1(-P_1 P_2) + P_1(P_2) = 2P_1 P_2 > 0$$

With $|\bar{H}_2| > 0$, $|\bar{H}|$ is negative definite and U is maximized.

Example 7. Given $B = 250$, the demand function for Q_1 at $P_1 = 5$, 10, and 25 is derived as follows on the basis of the preceding discussion.

At $P_1 = 5$, $\qquad\qquad\qquad\qquad \bar{Q}_1 = \dfrac{250}{2(5)} = 25$

At $P_1 = 10$, $\qquad\qquad\qquad\qquad \bar{Q}_1 = \dfrac{250}{2(10)} = 12.5$

At $P_1 = 25$, $\qquad\qquad\qquad\qquad \bar{Q}_1 = \dfrac{250}{2(25)} = 5$

(Since in this simple model demand for each good depends in the same way on income and its own price, both demand functions will be identical. For more realistic functions see Problems 12.54–55.)

12.6 INPUT–OUTPUT ANALYSIS

In a modern economy where the production of one good requires the input of many other goods as *intermediate goods* in the production process (steel requires coal, iron ore, electricity, etc.), total demand x for product$_i$ will be the summation of all intermediate demand for the product plus the *final demand b* for the product arising from consumers, investors, the government, and exporters, as ultimate users. If a_{ij} is a *technical coefficient* expressing the value of input$_i$ required to produce one dollar's worth of product$_j$, the total demand for product$_i$ can be expressed as

$$x_i = a_{i1}x_1 + a_{i2}x_2 \cdots + a_{in}x_n + b_i$$

for $i = 1, 2, \ldots, n$. In matrix form this can be expressed as

$$X = AX + B \tag{12.5}$$

where $\qquad X = \begin{bmatrix} x_1 \\ x_2 \\ \vdots \\ x_n \end{bmatrix} \qquad A = \begin{bmatrix} a_{11} & a_{12} & \cdots & a_{1n} \\ a_{21} & a_{22} & \cdots & a_{2n} \\ \cdots\cdots\cdots\cdots\cdots\cdots\cdots \\ a_{n1} & a_{n2} & \cdots & a_{nn} \end{bmatrix} \qquad B = \begin{bmatrix} b_1 \\ b_2 \\ \vdots \\ b_n \end{bmatrix}$

and A is called the *matrix of technical coefficients*. To find the level of total output (intermediate and final) needed to satisfy final demand, we can solve for X in terms of the matrix of technical coefficients and the column vector of final demand, both of which are given. From (*12.5*),

$$X - AX = B$$
$$(I - A)X = B$$
$$X = (I - A)^{-1}B \tag{12.6}$$

Thus, for a three-sector economy

$$\begin{bmatrix} x_1 \\ x_2 \\ x_3 \end{bmatrix} = \begin{bmatrix} 1 - a_{11} & -a_{12} & -a_{13} \\ -a_{21} & 1 - a_{22} & -a_{23} \\ -a_{31} & -a_{32} & 1 - a_{33} \end{bmatrix}^{-1} \begin{bmatrix} b_1 \\ b_2 \\ b_3 \end{bmatrix}$$

where the $(I - A)$ matrix is called the *Leontief matrix*. In a complete input–output table, labor and capital would also be included as inputs, constituting value added by the firm. The vertical summation of elements along column$_j$ in such a model would equal one: the input cost of producing one unit or one dollar's worth of the commodity. See Problem 12.43.

Example 8.   Determine the total demand x for industries 1, 2, and 3, given the matrix of technical coefficients A and the final demand vector B.

$$A = \begin{bmatrix} 0.3 & 0.4 & 0.1 \\ 0.5 & 0.2 & 0.6 \\ 0.1 & 0.3 & 0.1 \end{bmatrix} \qquad B = \begin{bmatrix} 20 \\ 10 \\ 30 \end{bmatrix}$$

From (12.6), $X = (I - A)^{-1}B$,   where

$$(I - A) = \begin{bmatrix} 1 & 0 & 0 \\ 0 & 1 & 0 \\ 0 & 0 & 1 \end{bmatrix} - \begin{bmatrix} 0.3 & 0.4 & 0.1 \\ 0.5 & 0.2 & 0.6 \\ 0.1 & 0.3 & 0.1 \end{bmatrix} = \begin{bmatrix} 0.7 & -0.4 & -0.1 \\ -0.5 & 0.8 & -0.6 \\ -0.1 & -0.3 & 0.9 \end{bmatrix}$$

Taking the inverse,

$$(I - A)^{-1} = \frac{1}{0.151} \begin{bmatrix} 0.54 & 0.39 & 0.32 \\ 0.51 & 0.62 & 0.47 \\ 0.23 & 0.25 & 0.36 \end{bmatrix}$$

and substituting in (12.6),

$$X = \frac{1}{0.151} \begin{bmatrix} 0.54 & 0.39 & 0.32 \\ 0.51 & 0.62 & 0.47 \\ 0.23 & 0.25 & 0.36 \end{bmatrix} \begin{bmatrix} 20 \\ 10 \\ 30 \end{bmatrix} = \frac{1}{0.151} \begin{bmatrix} 24.3 \\ 30.5 \\ 17.9 \end{bmatrix} = \begin{bmatrix} 160.93 \\ 201.99 \\ 118.54 \end{bmatrix} = \begin{bmatrix} x_1 \\ x_2 \\ x_3 \end{bmatrix}$$

12.7   CHARACTERISTIC ROOTS AND VECTORS (EIGENVALUES, EIGENVECTORS)

To this point, the sign-definiteness of a Hessian and a quadratic form have been tested using the principal minors. Sign-definiteness can also be tested by using the characteristic roots of a matrix. Given a square matrix A, if it is possible to find a vector $V \neq 0$ and a scalar c such that

$$AV = cV \qquad\qquad (12.7)$$

the scalar c is called the *characteristic root*, *latent root*, or *eigenvalue*; and the vector is called the *characteristic vector*, *latent vector*, or *eigenvector*. Equation (12.7) can also be expressed

$$AV = cIV$$

which can be rearranged so that

$$AV - cIV = 0$$
$$(A - cI)V = 0 \qquad\qquad (12.8)$$

where $(A - cI)$ is called the *characteristic matrix* of A. Since by assumption, $V \neq 0$, the characteristic matrix $(A - cI)$ must be singular (see Problem 10.49) and thus its determinant must vanish. If $A = (3 \times 3)$ matrix, then

$$|A - cI| = \begin{vmatrix} a_{11} - c & a_{12} & a_{13} \\ a_{21} & a_{22} - c & a_{23} \\ a_{31} & a_{32} & a_{33} - c \end{vmatrix} = 0$$

With $|A - cI| = 0$ in (12.8), there will be an infinite number of solutions for V. To force a unique solution, the solution is *normalized* by requiring of the elements v_i of V, that $\Sigma v_i^2 = 1$, as shown in Example 10.

If

(1) all characteristic roots (c) are positive, A is positive definite.

(2) all c are negative, A is negative definite.

(3) all c are nonnegative and at least one $c = 0$, A is positive semidefinite.

(4) all c are nonpositive and at least one $c = 0$, A is negative semidefinite.

(5) some c are positive and some negative, A is indefinite.

Example 9.   Given

$$A = \begin{bmatrix} -6 & 3 \\ 3 & -6 \end{bmatrix}$$

To find the characteristic roots of A, the determinant of the characteristic matrix $(A - cI)$ must equal zero. Thus,

$$|A - cI| = \begin{vmatrix} -6 - c & 3 \\ 3 & -6 - c \end{vmatrix} = 0 \qquad (12.9)$$

$$(-6 - c)(-6 - c) - (3)(3) = 0$$

$$c^2 + 12c + 27 = 0 \qquad (c + 9)(c + 3) = 0$$

$$c_1 = -9 \qquad c_2 = -3$$

Testing for sign-definiteness, since both characteristic roots are negative, A is negative definite.

Example 10.   Continuing with Example 9, the first root $c_1 = -9$ is now used to find the characteristic vector. Substituting $c = -9$ in (12.9),

$$\begin{bmatrix} -6 - (-9) & 3 \\ 3 & -6 - (-9) \end{bmatrix} \begin{bmatrix} v_1 \\ v_2 \end{bmatrix} = 0$$

$$\begin{bmatrix} 3 & 3 \\ 3 & 3 \end{bmatrix} \begin{bmatrix} v_1 \\ v_2 \end{bmatrix} = 0 \qquad (12.10)$$

Since the coefficient matrix is linearly dependent, (12.10) is capable of an infinite number of solutions. The product of the matrices gives two equations which are identical:

$$3v_1 + 3v_2 = 0$$

Solving for v_2 in terms of v_1,

$$v_2 = -v_1 \qquad (12.11)$$

Then, normalizing the solution in (12.11) so that

$$v_1^2 + v_2^2 = 1 \qquad (12.12)$$

$v_2 = -v_1$ is substituted in (12.12), getting

$$v_1^2 + (-v_1)^2 = 1$$

Thus, $2v_1^2 = 1$, $v_1^2 = \frac{1}{2}$. Then taking the positive square root, $v_1 = \sqrt{\frac{1}{2}} = \sqrt{0.5}$. From (12.11), $v_2 = -v_1$. Thus, $v_2 = -\sqrt{0.5}$ and the first characteristic vector is

$$V_1 = \begin{bmatrix} \sqrt{0.5} \\ -\sqrt{0.5} \end{bmatrix}$$

When the second characteristic root $c_2 = -3$ is used,

$$\begin{bmatrix} -6 - (-3) & 3 \\ 3 & -6 - (-3) \end{bmatrix} \begin{bmatrix} v_1 \\ v_2 \end{bmatrix} = \begin{bmatrix} -3 & 3 \\ 3 & -3 \end{bmatrix} \begin{bmatrix} v_1 \\ v_2 \end{bmatrix} = 0$$

Multiplying the (2×2) matrix by the column vector,

$$-3v_1 + 3v_2 = 0$$
$$3v_1 - 3v_2 = 0$$

Thus, $v_1 = v_2$. Normalizing,

$$v_1^2 + v_2^2 = 1$$
$$(v_2)^2 + v_2^2 = 1$$
$$2v_2^2 = 1$$
$$v_2 = \sqrt{0.5} \qquad v_1 = \sqrt{0.5}$$

Thus,

$$V_2 = \begin{bmatrix} \sqrt{0.5} \\ \sqrt{0.5} \end{bmatrix}$$

12.8 TRANSFORMATION MATRIX

Having found the characteristic vectors, V_1 and V_2, a *transformation matrix* $T = [V_1 \quad V_2]$ can be found such that the product $T'AT$ will be a diagonal matrix with the characteristic roots as the diagonal elements. Thus for a (3×3) matrix,

$$T'AT = \begin{bmatrix} c_1 & 0 & 0 \\ 0 & c_2 & 0 \\ 0 & 0 & c_3 \end{bmatrix}$$

Example 11. Using the data from Examples 9 and 10, the transformation matrix T is

$$T = [V_1 \quad V_2] = \begin{bmatrix} \sqrt{0.5} & \sqrt{0.5} \\ -\sqrt{0.5} & \sqrt{0.5} \end{bmatrix} \qquad \text{and} \qquad T' = \begin{bmatrix} \sqrt{0.5} & -\sqrt{0.5} \\ \sqrt{0.5} & \sqrt{0.5} \end{bmatrix}$$

Thus,

$$T'AT = \begin{bmatrix} \sqrt{0.5} & -\sqrt{0.5} \\ \sqrt{0.5} & \sqrt{0.5} \end{bmatrix} \begin{bmatrix} -6 & 3 \\ 3 & -6 \end{bmatrix} \begin{bmatrix} \sqrt{0.5} & \sqrt{0.5} \\ -\sqrt{0.5} & \sqrt{0.5} \end{bmatrix}$$

where

$$T'A = \begin{bmatrix} -9\sqrt{0.5} & 9\sqrt{0.5} \\ -3\sqrt{0.5} & -3\sqrt{0.5} \end{bmatrix}$$

and

$$T'AT = \begin{bmatrix} -18(0.5) & 0 \\ 0 & -6(0.5) \end{bmatrix} = \begin{bmatrix} -9 & 0 \\ 0 & -3 \end{bmatrix} = \begin{bmatrix} c_1 & 0 \\ 0 & c_2 \end{bmatrix}$$

Solved Problems

THE JACOBIAN

12.1. Use the Jacobian to test for functional dependence in the following system of equations:

$$y_1 = 6x_1 + 4x_2$$
$$y_2 = 7x_1 + 9x_2$$

Taking the first-order partials to set up the Jacobian $|J|$,

$$\frac{\partial y_1}{\partial x_1} = 6 \qquad \frac{\partial y_1}{\partial x_2} = 4 \qquad \frac{\partial y_2}{\partial x_1} = 7 \qquad \frac{\partial y_2}{\partial x_2} = 9$$

Thus,

$$|J| = \begin{vmatrix} 6 & 4 \\ 7 & 9 \end{vmatrix} = 6(9) - 7(4) = 26$$

Since $|J| \neq 0$, there is no functional dependence. Notice that in a system of linear equations the Jacobian $|J|$ equals the determinant $|A|$ of the coefficient matrix, and all their elements are identical. See Section 11.1, where the determinant test for nonsingularity of a matrix is nothing more than an application of the Jacobian to a system of linear equations.

12.2. Redo Problem 12.1, given

$$y_1 = 3x_1 - 4x_2$$
$$y_2 = 9x_1^2 - 24x_1x_2 + 16x_2^2$$

The first-order partials are

$$\frac{\partial y_1}{\partial x_1} = 3 \qquad \frac{\partial y_1}{\partial x_2} = -4 \qquad \frac{\partial y_2}{\partial x_1} = 18x_1 - 24x_2 \qquad \frac{\partial y_2}{\partial x_2} = -24x_1 + 32x_2$$

Thus,
$$|J| = \begin{vmatrix} 3 & -4 \\ 18x_1 - 24x_2 & -24x_1 + 32x_2 \end{vmatrix} = 3(-24x_1 + 32x_2) + 4(18x_1 - 24x_2) = 0$$

There is functional dependence: $(3x_1 - 4x_2)^2 = 9x_1^2 - 24x_1x_2 + 16x_2^2$.

12.3. Redo Problem 12.1, given

$$y_1 = x_1^2 - 3x_2 + 5$$
$$y_2 = x_1^4 - 6x_1^2x_2 + 9x_2^2$$

$$\frac{\partial y_1}{\partial x_1} = 2x_1 \qquad \frac{\partial y_1}{\partial x_2} = -3 \qquad \frac{\partial y_2}{\partial x_1} = 4x_1^3 - 12x_1x_2 \qquad \frac{\partial y_2}{\partial x_2} = -6x_1^2 + 18x_2$$

$$|J| = \begin{vmatrix} 2x_1 & -3 \\ 4x_1^3 - 12x_1x_2 & -6x_1^2 + 18x_2 \end{vmatrix} = 2x_1(-6x_1^2 + 18x_2) + 3(4x_1^3 - 12x_1x_2) = 0$$

There is functional dependence: $y_2 = (y_1 - 5)^2$, where

$$y_1 - 5 = x_1^2 - 3x_2 + 5 - 5 = x_1^2 - 3x_2$$

and
$$(x_1^2 - 3x_2)^2 = x_1^4 - 6x_1^2x_2 + 9x^2$$

12.4. Test for functional dependence in each of the following by means of the Jacobian.

(a) $y_1 = 4x_1 - x_2$
$y_2 = 16x_1^2 + 8x_1x_2 + x_2^2$

$$|J| = \begin{vmatrix} 4 & -1 \\ 32x_1 + 8x_2 & 8x_1 + 2x_2 \end{vmatrix} = 4(8x_1 + 2x_2) + 1(32x_1 + 8x_2) = 64x_1 + 16x_2 \neq 0$$

The equations are functionally independent.

(b) $y_1 = 1.5x_1^2 + 12x_1x_2 + 24x_2^2$
$y_2 = 2x_1 + 8x_2$

$$|J| = \begin{vmatrix} 3x_1 + 12x_2 & 12x_1 + 48x_2 \\ 2 & 8 \end{vmatrix} = 8(3x_1 + 12x_2) - 2(12x_1 + 48x_2) = 0$$

There is functional dependence between the equations.

(c) $y_1 = 4x_1^2 + 3x_2 + 9$
$y_2 = 16x_1^4 + 24x_1^2x_2 + 9x_2^2 + 12$

$$|J| = \begin{vmatrix} 8x_1 & 3 \\ 64x_1^3 + 48x_1x_2 & 24x_1^2 + 18x_2 \end{vmatrix} = 8x_1(24x_1^2 + 18x_2) - 3(64x_1^3 + 48x_1x_2) = 0$$

The equations are functionally dependent.

DISCRIMINANTS AND SIGN-DEFINITENESS OF QUADRATIC FUNCTIONS

12.5. Use discriminants to determine whether each of the following quadratic functions is positive or negative definite.

(a) $y = -3x_1^2 + 4x_1x_2 - 4x_2^2$

Since the coefficients of the squared terms are placed on the principal diagonal and the coefficient of the nonsquared term x_1x_2 is divided evenly between the a_{12} and a_{21} positions, in this case,

$$|D| = \begin{vmatrix} -3 & 2 \\ 2 & -4 \end{vmatrix}$$

where $\quad |D_1| = -3 < 0 \qquad |D_2| = \begin{vmatrix} -3 & 2 \\ 2 & -4 \end{vmatrix} = (-3)(-4) - (2)(2) = 8 > 0$

With $|D_1| < 0$ and $|D_2| > 0$, y is negative definite and y will be negative for all nonzero values of x_1 and x_2.

(b) $y = 5x_1^2 - 2x_1x_2 + 7x_2^2$

The discriminant is $\qquad |D| = \begin{vmatrix} 5 & -1 \\ -1 & 7 \end{vmatrix}$

where $|D_1| = 5 > 0$ and $|D_2| = |D| = 5(7) - (-1)(-1) = 34 > 0$. With $|D_1| > 0$ and $|D_2| > 0$, y is positive definite and y will be positive for all nonzero values of x_1 and x_2.

12.6. Redo Problem 12.5 for $\quad y = 5x_1^2 - 6x_1x_2 + 3x_2^2 - 2x_2x_3 + 8x_3^2 - 3x_1x_3$.

For a quadratic form in three variables, the coefficients of the squared terms continue to go on the principal diagonal, while the coefficient of x_1x_3 is divided evenly between the a_{13} and a_{31} positions, the coefficient of x_2x_3 is divided between the a_{23} and a_{32} positions, etc. Thus,

$$|D| = \begin{vmatrix} 5 & -3 & -1.5 \\ -3 & 3 & -1 \\ -1.5 & -1 & 8 \end{vmatrix}$$

where $\qquad |D_1| = 5 > 0 \qquad |D_2| = \begin{vmatrix} 5 & -3 \\ -3 & 3 \end{vmatrix} = 6 > 0$

and $|D_3| = |D| = 5(23) + 3(-25.5) - 1.5(7.5) = 27.25 > 0$. Therefore, y is positive definite.

12.7. Use discriminants to determine the sign-definiteness of each of the following functions:

(a) $y = -2x_1^2 + 4x_1x_2 - 5x_2^2 + 2x_2x_3 - 3x_3^2 + 2x_1x_3$

$$|D| = \begin{vmatrix} -2 & 2 & 1 \\ 2 & -5 & 1 \\ 1 & 1 & -3 \end{vmatrix}$$

where $\qquad |D_1| = -2 < 0 \qquad |D_2| = \begin{vmatrix} -2 & 2 \\ 2 & -5 \end{vmatrix} = 6 > 0$

and $|D_3| = |D| = -2(14) - 2(-7) + 1(7) = -7 < 0$. y is negative definite.

(b) $y = -7x_1^2 - 2x_2^2 + 2x_2x_3 - 4x_3^2 - 6x_1x_3$

$$|D| = \begin{vmatrix} -7 & 0 & -3 \\ 0 & -2 & 1 \\ -3 & 1 & -4 \end{vmatrix}$$

where $\qquad |D_1| = -7 \qquad |D_2| = \begin{vmatrix} -7 & 0 \\ 0 & -2 \end{vmatrix} = 14$

and $|D_3| = |D| = -7(7) - 3(-6) = -31$. y is negative definite.

THE HESSIAN IN OPTIMIZATION PROBLEMS

12.8.   Optimize the following function, using (a) Cramer's rule for the first-order condition and   (b) the Hessian for the second-order condition.

$$y = 3x_1^2 - 5x_1 - x_1x_2 + 6x_2^2 - 4x_2 + 2x_2x_3 + 4x_3^2 + 2x_3 - 3x_1x_3$$

(a)   The first-order conditions are

$$y_1 = 6x_1 - 5 - x_2 - 3x_3 = 0$$

$$y_2 = -x_1 + 12x_2 - 4 + 2x_3 = 0 \tag{12.13}$$

$$y_3 = 2x_2 + 8x_3 + 2 - 3x_1 = 0$$

which in matrix form is
$$\begin{bmatrix} 6 & -1 & -3 \\ -1 & 12 & 2 \\ -3 & 2 & 8 \end{bmatrix} \begin{bmatrix} x_1 \\ x_2 \\ x_3 \end{bmatrix} = \begin{bmatrix} 5 \\ 4 \\ -2 \end{bmatrix}$$

Using Cramer's rule, $|A| = 6(92) + 1(-2) - 3(34) = 448$.   Since $|A|$ also equals $|J|$, the equations are functionally independent.

$$|A_1| = 5(92) + 1(36) - 3(32) = 400$$

$$|A_2| = 6(36) - 5(-2) - 3(14) = 184$$

$$|A_3| = 6(-32) + 1(14) + 5(34) = -8$$

Thus, $\bar{x}_1 = \dfrac{400}{448} \cong 0.89$ $\bar{x}_2 = \dfrac{184}{448} \cong 0.41$ $\bar{x}_3 = \dfrac{-8}{448} \cong -0.02$

(b)   Testing the second-order condition by taking the second-order partials of (12.13) to form the Hessian,

$$y_{11} = 6 \qquad y_{12} = -1 \qquad y_{13} = -3$$

$$y_{21} = -1 \qquad y_{22} = 12 \qquad y_{23} = 2$$

$$y_{31} = -3 \qquad y_{32} = 2 \qquad y_{33} = 8$$

Thus, $|H| = \begin{vmatrix} 6 & -1 & -3 \\ -1 & 12 & 2 \\ -3 & 2 & 8 \end{vmatrix}$

where $|H_1| = 6 > 0$ $|H_2| = \begin{vmatrix} 6 & -1 \\ -1 & 12 \end{vmatrix} = 71 > 0$

and $|H_3| = |H| = |A| = 448 > 0$.   With $|H|$ positive definite, y is minimized at the critical values.

12.9.   Redo Problem 12.8, given $y = -5x_1^2 + 10x_1 + x_1x_3 - 2x_2^2 + 4x_2 + 2x_2x_3 - 4x_3^2$.

(a)
$$y_1 = -10x_1 + 10 + x_3 = 0$$

$$y_2 = -4x_2 + 4 + 2x_3 = 0 \tag{12.14}$$

$$y_3 = x_1 + 2x_2 - 8x_3 = 0$$

In matrix form,
$$\begin{bmatrix} -10 & 0 & 1 \\ 0 & -4 & 2 \\ 1 & 2 & -8 \end{bmatrix} \begin{bmatrix} x_1 \\ x_2 \\ x_3 \end{bmatrix} = \begin{bmatrix} -10 \\ -4 \\ 0 \end{bmatrix}$$

Using Cramer's rule, $|A| = -10(28) + 1(4) = -276$

$$|A_1| = -10(28) + 1(-8) = -288$$

$$|A_2| = -10(32) + 10(-2) + 1(4) = -336$$

$$|A_3| = -10(8) - 10(4) = -120$$

Thus, $\bar{x}_1 = \dfrac{-288}{-276} \cong 1.04$ $\bar{x}_2 = \dfrac{-336}{-276} \cong 1.22$ $\bar{x}_3 = \dfrac{-120}{-276} \cong 0.43$

(b) Taking the second partials of (12.14) and forming the Hessian,

$$|H| = \begin{vmatrix} -10 & 0 & 1 \\ 0 & -4 & 2 \\ 1 & 2 & -8 \end{vmatrix}$$

where $|H_1| = -10 < 0$, $|H_2| = 40 > 0$, and $|H_3| = |A| = -276 < 0$. Thus, $|H|$ is negative definite and y is maximized.

12.10. A firm produces two goods in pure competition, and has the following total revenue and total cost functions:

$$TR = 15Q_1 + 18Q_2 \qquad TC = 2Q_1^2 + 2Q_1Q_2 + 3Q_2^2$$

The two goods are *technically related in production*, since the marginal cost of one is dependent on the level of output of the other (e.g. $\partial TC/\partial Q_1 = 4Q_1 + 2Q_2$). Maximize profits for the firm, using (a) Cramer's rule for the first-order condition and (b) the Hessian for the second-order condition.

(a) $$\Pi = TR - TC = 15Q_1 + 18Q_2 - 2Q_1^2 - 2Q_1Q_2 - 3Q_2^2$$

The first-order conditions are

$$\Pi_1 = 15 - 4Q_1 - 2Q_2 = 0$$
$$\Pi_2 = 18 - 2Q_1 - 6Q_2 = 0$$

In matrix form,

$$\begin{bmatrix} -4 & -2 \\ -2 & -6 \end{bmatrix} \begin{bmatrix} Q_1 \\ Q_2 \end{bmatrix} = \begin{bmatrix} -15 \\ -18 \end{bmatrix}$$

Solving by Cramer's rule,

$$|A| = 24 - 4 = 20 \qquad |A_1| = 90 - 36 = 54 \qquad |A_2| = 72 - 30 = 42$$

Thus, $$\bar{Q}_1 = \frac{54}{20} = 2.7 \qquad \bar{Q}_2 = \frac{42}{20} = 2.1$$

(b) Using the Hessian to test for the second-order condition,

$$|H| = \begin{vmatrix} -4 & -2 \\ -2 & -6 \end{vmatrix}$$

where $|H_1| = -4$ and $|H_2| = 20$. With $|H|$ negative definite, Π is maximized.

12.11. Using the techniques of Problem 12.10, maximize profits for the competitive firm whose goods are not technically related in production. The firm's total revenue and total cost functions are

$$TR = 7Q_1 + 9Q_2 \qquad TC = Q_1^2 + 2Q_1 + 5Q_2 + 2Q_2^2$$

(a) $$\Pi = 7Q_1 + 9Q_2 - Q_1^2 - 2Q_1 - 5Q_2 - 2Q_2^2$$

$$\Pi_1 = 7 - 2Q_1 - 2 = 0 \qquad \bar{Q}_1 = 2.5$$
$$\Pi_2 = 9 - 5 - 4Q_2 = 0 \qquad \bar{Q}_2 = 1$$

(b) $$|H| = \begin{vmatrix} -2 & 0 \\ 0 & -4 \end{vmatrix}$$

where $|H_1| = -2$ and $|H_2| = 8$. $|H|$ is negative definite and Π is maximized.

12.12. Maximize profits for a monopolistic firm producing two related goods

i.e. $P_1 = f(Q_1, Q_2)$

when the goods are substitutes and the demand and total cost functions are

$$P_1 = 80 - 5Q_1 - 2Q_2 \qquad P_2 = 50 - Q_1 - 3Q_2 \qquad TC = 3Q_1^2 + Q_1Q_2 + 2Q_2^2$$

Use (a) Cramer's rule and (b) the Hessian, as in Problem 12.10.

(a) $\Pi = TR - TC$, where $TR = P_1Q_1 + P_2Q_2$.

$$\Pi = (80 - 5Q_1 - 2Q_2)Q_1 + (50 - Q_1 - 3Q_2)Q_2 - (3Q_1^2 + Q_1Q_2 + 2Q_2^2)$$
$$= 80Q_1 + 50Q_2 - 4Q_1Q_2 - 8Q_1^2 - 5Q_2^2$$

$$\Pi_1 = 80 - 4Q_2 - 16Q_1 = 0 \qquad \Pi_2 = 50 - 4Q_1 - 10Q_2 = 0$$

In matrix form,
$$\begin{bmatrix} -16 & -4 \\ -4 & -10 \end{bmatrix} \begin{bmatrix} Q_1 \\ Q_2 \end{bmatrix} = \begin{bmatrix} -80 \\ -50 \end{bmatrix}$$

$$|A| = 160 - 16 = 144 \qquad |A_1| = 800 - 200 = 600 \qquad |A_2| = 800 - 320 = 480$$

and
$$\bar{Q}_1 = \frac{600}{144} \cong 4.17 \qquad \bar{Q}_2 = \frac{480}{144} \cong 3.33$$

(b)
$$|H| = \begin{vmatrix} -16 & -4 \\ -4 & -10 \end{vmatrix}$$

where $|H_1| = -16$ and $|H_2| = 144$. Π is maximized.

12.13. Maximize profits for a producer of two substitute goods, given

$$P_1 = 130 - 4Q_1 - Q_2 \qquad P_2 = 160 - 2Q_1 - 5Q_2 \qquad TC = 2Q_1^2 + 2Q_1Q_2 + 4Q_2^2$$

Use (a) Cramer's rule for the first-order condition and (b) the Hessian for the second-order condition.

(a)
$$\Pi = (130 - 4Q_1 - Q_2)Q_1 + (160 - 2Q_1 - 5Q_2)Q_2 - (2Q_1^2 + 2Q_1Q_2 + 4Q_2^2)$$
$$= 130Q_1 + 160Q_2 - 5Q_1Q_2 - 6Q_1^2 - 9Q_2^2$$

$$\Pi_1 = 130 - 5Q_2 - 12Q_1 = 0 \qquad \Pi_2 = 160 - 5Q_1 - 18Q_2 = 0$$

Thus,

$$\begin{bmatrix} -12 & -5 \\ -5 & -18 \end{bmatrix} \begin{bmatrix} Q_1 \\ Q_2 \end{bmatrix} = \begin{bmatrix} -130 \\ -160 \end{bmatrix}$$

$$|A| = 191$$

$$|A_1| = 1540 \qquad \bar{Q}_1 = \frac{1540}{191} \cong 8.06$$

$$|A_2| = 1270 \qquad \bar{Q}_2 = \frac{1270}{191} \cong 6.65$$

(b)
$$|H| = \begin{vmatrix} -12 & -5 \\ -5 & -18 \end{vmatrix}$$

$|H_1| = -12$ and $|H_2| = 191$. Π is maximized.

12.14. Redo Problem 12.13 for a monopolistic firm producing three related goods, when the demand functions and the cost function are

$$P_1 = 180 - 3Q_1 - Q_2 - 2Q_3 \qquad P_2 = 200 - Q_1 - 4Q_2 \qquad P_3 = 150 - Q_2 - 3Q_3$$
$$TC = Q_1^2 + Q_1Q_2 + Q_2^2 + Q_2Q_3 + Q_3^2$$

(a) $\quad \Pi = (180 - 3Q_1 - Q_2 - 2Q_3)Q_1 + (200 - Q_1 - 4Q_2)Q_2 + (150 - Q_2 - 3Q_3)Q_3$

$$- (Q_1^2 + Q_1Q_2 + Q_2^2 + Q_2Q_3 + Q_3^2)$$

$$= 180Q_1 + 200Q_2 + 150Q_3 - 3Q_1Q_2 - 2Q_2Q_3 - 2Q_1Q_3 - 4Q_1^2 - 5Q_2^2 - 4Q_3^2$$

$$\Pi_1 = 180 - 3Q_2 - 2Q_3 - 8Q_1 = 0 \qquad \Pi_2 = 200 - 3Q_1 - 2Q_3 - 10Q_2 = 0$$

$$\Pi_3 = 150 - 2Q_2 - 2Q_1 - 8Q_3 = 0$$

In matrix form,

$$\begin{bmatrix} -8 & -3 & -2 \\ -3 & -10 & -2 \\ -2 & -2 & -8 \end{bmatrix} \begin{bmatrix} Q_1 \\ Q_2 \\ Q_3 \end{bmatrix} = \begin{bmatrix} -180 \\ -200 \\ -150 \end{bmatrix}$$

$$|A| = -8(76) + 3(20) - 2(-14) = -520$$

$$|A_1| = -180(76) + 3(1300) - 2(-1100) = -7580$$

$$|A_2| = -8(1300) + 180(20) - 2(50) = -6900$$

$$|A_3| = -8(1100) + 3(50) - 180(-14) = -6130$$

Thus, $\quad \bar{Q}_1 = \dfrac{-7580}{-520} \cong 14.58 \qquad \bar{Q}_2 = \dfrac{-6900}{-520} \cong 13.27 \qquad \bar{Q}_3 = \dfrac{-6130}{-520} \cong 11.79$

(b)
$$|H| = \begin{vmatrix} -8 & -3 & -2 \\ -3 & -10 & -2 \\ -2 & -2 & -8 \end{vmatrix}$$

where $\quad |H_1| = -8, \quad |H_2| = 71, \quad$ and $\quad |H_3| = |H| = |A| = -520.$ $\quad \Pi$ is maximized.

12.15. Maximize profits as in Problem 12.14, given

$$P_1 = 70 - 2Q_1 - Q_2 - Q_3 \qquad P_2 = 120 - Q_1 - 4Q_2 - 2Q_3 \qquad P_3 = 90 - Q_1 - Q_2 - 3Q_3$$

$$TC = Q_1^2 + Q_1Q_2 + 2Q_2^2 + 2Q_2Q_3 + Q_3^2 + Q_1Q_3$$

(a) $\quad \Pi = 70Q_1 + 120Q_2 + 90Q_3 - 3Q_1Q_2 - 5Q_2Q_3 - 3Q_1Q_3 - 3Q_1^2 - 6Q_2^2 - 4Q_3^2$

$$\Pi_1 = 70 - 3Q_2 - 3Q_3 - 6Q_1 = 0 \qquad \Pi_2 = 120 - 3Q_1 - 5Q_3 - 12Q_2 = 0$$

$$\Pi_3 = 90 - 3Q_1 - 5Q_2 - 8Q_3 = 0$$

Thus,

$$\begin{bmatrix} -6 & -3 & -3 \\ -3 & -12 & -5 \\ -3 & -5 & -8 \end{bmatrix} \begin{bmatrix} Q_1 \\ Q_2 \\ Q_3 \end{bmatrix} = \begin{bmatrix} -70 \\ -120 \\ -90 \end{bmatrix}$$

$$|A| = -336$$

$$|A_1| = -2000 \qquad \bar{Q}_1 = \frac{-2000}{-336} \cong 5.95$$

$$|A_2| = -2160 \qquad \bar{Q}_2 = \frac{-2160}{-336} \cong 6.43$$

$$|A_3| = -1680 \qquad \bar{Q}_3 = \frac{-1680}{-336} = 5$$

(b)
$$|H| = \begin{vmatrix} -6 & -3 & -3 \\ -3 & -12 & -5 \\ -3 & -5 & -8 \end{vmatrix}$$

where $\quad |H_1| = -6, \quad |H_2| = 63, \quad$ and $\quad |H_3| = |H| = |A| = -336.$ $\quad \Pi$ is maximized.

12.16. Given that $Q = f(P)$, maximize profits by (a) finding the inverse function, $P = f(Q)$, (b) using Cramer's rule for the first-order condition, and (c) using the Hessian for the second-order condition. The demand functions and total cost function are

$$Q_1 = 100 - 3P_1 + 2P_2 \qquad Q_2 = 75 + 0.5P_1 - P_2 \qquad TC = Q_1^2 + 2Q_1Q_2 + Q_2^2$$

where Q_1 and Q_2 are substitute goods, as indicated by the opposite signs for P_1 and P_2 in each equation (i.e. an increase in P_2 will increase demand for Q_1 and an increase in P_1 will increase demand for Q_2).

(a) Since the markets are interrelated, the inverse functions must be found simultaneously. Rearranging the demand functions to get $P = f(Q)$, in order ultimately to maximize Π as a function of Q alone,

$$-3P_1 + 2P_2 = Q_1 - 100$$
$$0.5P_1 - P_2 = Q_2 - 75$$

In matrix form,

$$\begin{bmatrix} -3 & 2 \\ 0.5 & -1 \end{bmatrix} \begin{bmatrix} P_1 \\ P_2 \end{bmatrix} = \begin{bmatrix} Q_1 - 100 \\ Q_2 - 75 \end{bmatrix}$$

Using Cramer's rule,

$$|A| = 2$$

$$|A_1| = \begin{vmatrix} Q_1 - 100 & 2 \\ Q_2 - 75 & -1 \end{vmatrix} = -Q_1 + 100 - 2Q_2 + 150 = 250 - Q_1 - 2Q_2$$

$$P_1 = \frac{|A_1|}{|A|} = \frac{250 - Q_1 - 2Q_2}{2} = 125 - 0.5Q_1 - Q_2$$

$$|A_2| = \begin{vmatrix} -3 & Q_1 - 100 \\ 0.5 & Q_2 - 75 \end{vmatrix} = -3Q_2 + 225 - 0.5Q_1 + 50 = 275 - 0.5Q_1 - 3Q_2$$

$$P_2 = \frac{|A_2|}{|A|} = \frac{275 - 0.5Q_1 - 3Q_2}{2} = 137.5 - 0.25Q_1 - 1.5Q_2$$

(b)
$$\Pi = (125 - 0.5Q_1 - Q_2)Q_1 + (137.5 - 0.25Q_1 - 1.5Q_2)Q_2 - (Q_1^2 + 2Q_1Q_2 + Q_2^2)$$
$$= 125Q_1 + 137.5Q_2 - 3.25Q_1Q_2 - 1.5Q_1^2 - 2.5Q_2^2$$

$$\Pi_1 = 125 - 3.25Q_2 - 3Q_1 = 0 \qquad \Pi_2 = 137.5 - 3.25Q_1 - 5Q_2 = 0$$

Thus,

$$\begin{bmatrix} -3 & -3.25 \\ -3.25 & -5 \end{bmatrix} \begin{bmatrix} Q_1 \\ Q_2 \end{bmatrix} = \begin{bmatrix} -125 \\ -137.5 \end{bmatrix}$$

$$|A| = 4.4375$$

$$|A_1| = 178.125 \qquad \bar{Q}_1 = \frac{178.125}{4.4375} \cong 40.14$$

$$|A_2| = 6.25 \qquad \bar{Q}_2 = \frac{6.25}{4.4375} \cong 1.4$$

(c)
$$|H| = \begin{vmatrix} -3 & -3.25 \\ -3.25 & -5 \end{vmatrix}$$

$|H_1| = -3$, $|H_2| = |H| = |A| = 4.4375$, and Π is maximized.

12.17. Redo Problem 12.16 by maximizing profits for

$$Q_1 = 90 - 6P_1 - 2P_2 \qquad Q_2 = 80 - 2P_1 - 4P_2 \qquad TC = 2Q_1^2 + 3Q_1Q_2 + 2Q_2^2$$

where Q_1 and Q_2 are complements, as indicated by the same sign for P_1 and P_2 in each equation.

(a)   Converting the demand functions to functions of Q,

$$\begin{bmatrix} -6 & -2 \\ -2 & -4 \end{bmatrix} \begin{bmatrix} P_1 \\ P_2 \end{bmatrix} = \begin{bmatrix} Q_1 - 90 \\ Q_2 - 80 \end{bmatrix}$$

$$|A| = 20$$

$$|A_1| = \begin{vmatrix} Q_1 - 90 & -2 \\ Q_2 - 80 & -4 \end{vmatrix} = -4Q_1 + 360 + 2Q_2 - 160 = 200 - 4Q_1 + 2Q_2$$

$$P_1 = \frac{200 - 4Q_1 + 2Q_2}{20} = 10 - 0.2\,Q_1 + 0.1\,Q_2$$

$$|A_2| = \begin{vmatrix} -6 & Q_1 - 90 \\ -2 & Q_2 - 80 \end{vmatrix} = -6Q_2 + 480 + 2Q_1 - 180 = 300 - 6Q_2 + 2Q_1$$

$$P_2 = \frac{300 - 6Q_2 + 2Q_1}{20} = 15 - 0.3\,Q_2 + 0.1\,Q_1$$

(b) $$\Pi = (10 - 0.2\,Q_1 + 0.1\,Q_2)Q_1 + (15 - 0.3\,Q_2 - 0.1\,Q_1)Q_2 - (2Q_1^2 + 3Q_1Q_2 + 2Q_2^2)$$
$$= 10Q_1 + 15Q_2 - 2.8\,Q_1Q_2 - 2.2\,Q_1^2 - 2.3\,Q_2^2$$

$$\Pi_1 = 10 - 2.8\,Q_2 - 4.4\,Q_1 = 0 \qquad \Pi_2 = 15 - 2.8\,Q_1 - 4.6\,Q_2 = 0$$

Thus,

$$\begin{bmatrix} -4.4 & -2.8 \\ -2.8 & -4.6 \end{bmatrix} \begin{bmatrix} Q_1 \\ Q_2 \end{bmatrix} = \begin{bmatrix} -10 \\ -15 \end{bmatrix}$$

$$|A| = 12.4$$

$$|A_1| = 4 \qquad \bar{Q}_1 = \frac{4}{12.4} \cong 0.32$$

$$|A_2| = 38 \qquad \bar{Q}_2 = \frac{38}{12.4} \cong 3.06$$

(c) $$|H| = \begin{vmatrix} -4.4 & -2.8 \\ -2.8 & -4.6 \end{vmatrix}$$

$$|H_1| = -4.4, \quad |H_2| = |A| = 12.4, \quad \text{and } \Pi \text{ is maximized.}$$

12.18. Redo Problem 12.16, given

$$Q_1 = 150 - 3P_1 + P_2 + P_3 \qquad Q_2 = 180 + P_1 - 4P_2 + 2P_3 \qquad Q_3 = 200 + 2P_1 + P_2 - 5P_3$$

$$TC = Q_1^2 + Q_1Q_2 + 2Q_2^2 + Q_2Q_3 + Q_3^2 + Q_1Q_3$$

(a)   Finding the inverses of the demand functions

$$\begin{bmatrix} -3 & 1 & 1 \\ 1 & -4 & 2 \\ 2 & 1 & -5 \end{bmatrix} \begin{bmatrix} P_1 \\ P_2 \\ P_3 \end{bmatrix} = \begin{bmatrix} Q_1 - 150 \\ Q_2 - 180 \\ Q_3 - 200 \end{bmatrix}$$

$$|A| = -36$$

$$|A_1| = (Q_1 - 150)(20 - 2) - 1(-5Q_2 + 900 - 2Q_3 + 400) + 1(Q_2 - 180 + 4Q_3 - 800)$$
$$= -4980 + 18Q_1 + 6Q_2 + 6Q_3$$

$$P_1 = \frac{-4980 + 18Q_1 + 6Q_2 + 6Q_3}{-36} = 138.33 - 0.5\,Q_1 - 0.17\,Q_2 - 0.17\,Q_3$$

$$|A_2| = -3(-5Q_2 + 900 - 2Q_3 + 400) - (Q_1 - 150)(-5 - 4) + 1(Q_3 - 200 - 2Q_2 + 360)$$
$$= -5090 + 9Q_1 + 13Q_2 + 7Q_3$$

$$P_2 = \frac{-5090 + 9Q_1 + 13Q_2 + 7Q_3}{-36} = 141.39 - 0.25\,Q_1 - 0.36\,Q_2 - 0.19\,Q_3$$

$$|A_3| = -3(-4Q_3 + 800 - Q_2 + 180) - 1(Q_3 - 200 - 2Q_2 + 360) + (Q_1 - 150)(1 + 8)$$

$$= -4450 + 9Q_1 + 5Q_2 + 11Q_3$$

$$P_3 = \frac{-4450 + 9Q_1 + 5Q_2 + 11Q_3}{-36} = 123.61 - 0.25Q_1 - 0.14Q_2 - 0.31Q_3$$

(b)
$$\Pi = P_1Q_1 + P_2Q_2 + P_3Q_3 - TC$$

$$= 138.33Q_1 + 141.39Q_2 + 123.61Q_3 - 1.42Q_1Q_2$$

$$- 1.33Q_2Q_3 - 1.42Q_1Q_3 - 1.5Q_1^2 - 2.36Q_2^2 - 1.31Q_3^2$$

$$\Pi_1 = 138.33 - 1.42Q_2 - 1.42Q_3 - 3Q_1 = 0$$

$$\Pi_2 = 141.39 - 1.42Q_1 - 1.33Q_3 - 4.72Q_2 = 0$$

$$\Pi_3 = 123.61 - 1.33Q_2 - 1.42Q_1 - 2.62Q_3 = 0$$

Thus,

$$\begin{bmatrix} -3 & -1.42 & -1.42 \\ -1.42 & -4.72 & -1.33 \\ -1.42 & -1.33 & -2.62 \end{bmatrix} \begin{bmatrix} Q_1 \\ Q_2 \\ Q_3 \end{bmatrix} = \begin{bmatrix} -138.33 \\ -141.39 \\ -123.61 \end{bmatrix}$$

$$|A| = -22.37$$

$$|A_1| = -612.27 \qquad \bar{Q}_1 = \frac{-612.27}{-22.37} \cong 27.37$$

$$|A_2| = -329.14 \qquad \bar{Q}_2 = \frac{-329.14}{-22.37} \cong 14.71$$

$$|A_3| = -556.64 \qquad \bar{Q}_3 = \frac{-556.64}{-22.37} \cong 24.88$$

(c)
$$|H_1| = \begin{vmatrix} -3 & -1.42 & -1.42 \\ -1.42 & -4.72 & -1.33 \\ -1.42 & -1.33 & -2.62 \end{vmatrix}$$

$|H_1| = -3$, $|H_2| = 12.14$, and $|H_3| = |A| = -22.37$. Π is maximized.

PRICE DISCRIMINATION AND ELASTICITY OF DEMAND

Note: While the parameters of the problems in this section are kept unrealistically low for easier computation, the economic significance is not affected.

12.19. A telephone company has isolated three distinct demands for its service:

Weekdays:	$Q_1 = 90 - 0.5P_1$	
Holidays:	$Q_2 = 35 - 0.25P_2$	(12.15)
Nights:	$Q_3 = 30 - 0.2P_3$	

$TC = 25 + 20Q$ where $Q = Q_1 + Q_2 + Q_3$.

Show that as a discriminating monopolist, this company will maximize profits by charging the highest price in the market where the price elasticity $|\epsilon|$ of demand is lowest, by finding (a) the profit-maximizing level of output, (b) the profit-maximizing price, and (c) the price elasticity of demand in each market. Use Cramer's rule for solving simultaneous equations and the Hessian for second-order conditions.

(a)   From (12.15),

$$P_1 = 180 - 2Q_1 \qquad P_2 = 140 - 4Q_2 \qquad P_3 = 150 - 5Q_3 \qquad (12.16)$$

Thus,

$$\Pi = (180 - 2Q_1)Q_1 + (140 - 4Q_2)Q_2 + (150 - 5Q_3)Q_3 - (25 + 20Q_1 + 20Q_2 + 20Q_3)$$

$$= 160Q_1 - 2Q_1^2 + 120Q_2 - 4Q_2^2 + 130Q_3 - 5Q_3^2 - 25$$

$$\Pi_1 = 160 - 4Q_1 = 0 \qquad \bar{Q}_1 = 40 \qquad \Pi_2 = 120 - 8Q_2 = 0 \qquad \bar{Q}_2 = 15$$

$$\Pi_3 = 130 - 10Q_3 = 0 \qquad \bar{Q}_3 = 13 \tag{12.17}$$

Taking the second partials of (12.17) and forming the Hessian to test for the second-order condition,

$$|H| = \begin{vmatrix} -4 & 0 & 0 \\ 0 & -8 & 0 \\ 0 & 0 & -10 \end{vmatrix}$$

$|H_1| = -4$, $|H_2| = 32$, and $|H_3| = -320$. Π is maximized.

(b) Substituting the critical values in (12.16),

$$\bar{P}_1 = 180 - 2(40) = 100 \qquad \bar{P}_2 = 140 - 4(15) = 80 \qquad \bar{P}_3 = 150 - 5(13) = 85$$

(c)
$$\epsilon_i = \frac{dQ_i}{dP_i} \frac{P_i}{Q_i}$$

Taking the derivatives of (12.15) and using the equilibrium prices and quantities,

$$\epsilon_1 = -0.5\tfrac{100}{40} = -1.25 \qquad \epsilon_2 = -0.25\tfrac{80}{15} = -1.33 \qquad \epsilon_3 = -0.2\tfrac{85}{13} = -1.31$$

For profit maximization, market$_1$ is charged the highest price ($P_1 = 100$) because elasticity $|\epsilon|$ is lowest ($|\epsilon_1| = |-1.25|$); market$_2$ is charged the lowest price ($P_2 = 80$) because elasticity $|\epsilon|$ is highest ($|\epsilon_2| = |-1.33|$).

12.20. Redo Problem 12.19 for an airline which has isolated three distinct demands for air-flight services, as follows:

Day service:
$$Q_1 = 12 - \tfrac{1}{12}P_1$$

Night coach:
$$Q_2 = 11 - \tfrac{1}{10}P_2 \tag{12.18}$$

Standby:
$$Q_3 = 13 - \tfrac{1}{8}P_3$$

$$TC = 40 + 10Q + 0.5Q^2 \tag{12.19}$$

where $Q = Q_1 + Q_2 + Q_3$.

(a) From (12.18), $P_1 = 144 - 12Q_1$ $P_2 = 110 - 10Q_2$ $P_3 = 104 - 8Q_3$ $\tag{12.20}$

$$\Pi = (144 - 12Q_1)Q_1 + (110 - 10Q_2)Q_2 + (104 - 8Q_3)Q_3 - TC$$

Substituting $Q = Q_1 + Q_2 + Q_3$ in (12.19),

$$TC = 0.5Q_1^2 + Q_1Q_2 + 10Q_1 + 0.5Q_2^2 + Q_2Q_3 + 10Q_2 + 0.5Q_3^2 + Q_1Q_3 + 10Q_3 + 40$$

Thus,

$$\Pi = -12.5Q_1^2 + 134Q_1 - Q_1Q_2 - 10.5Q_2^2 + 100Q_2 - Q_2Q_3 - 8.5Q_3^2 + 94Q_3 - Q_1Q_3 - 40$$

$$\Pi_1 = -25Q_1 + 134 - Q_2 - Q_3 = 0 \qquad \Pi_2 = -Q_1 - 21Q_2 + 100 - Q_3 = 0$$

$$\Pi_3 = -17Q_3 + 94 - Q_2 - Q_1 = 0 \tag{12.21}$$

Thus,

$$\begin{bmatrix} -25 & -1 & -1 \\ -1 & -21 & -1 \\ -1 & -1 & -17 \end{bmatrix} \begin{bmatrix} Q_1 \\ Q_2 \\ Q_3 \end{bmatrix} = \begin{bmatrix} -134 \\ -100 \\ -94 \end{bmatrix}$$

$$|A| = -8864$$

$$|A_1| = -44,224 \qquad \bar{Q}_1 = \frac{-44,224}{-8864} \cong 4.99$$

$$|A_2| = -38,000 \qquad \bar{Q}_2 = \frac{-38,000}{-8864} \cong 4.29$$

$$|A_3| = -44,176 \qquad \bar{Q}_3 = \frac{-44,176}{-8864} \cong 4.98$$

Taking the second partials of (12.21) to form the Hessian,

$$|H| = \begin{vmatrix} -25 & -1 & -1 \\ -1 & -21 & -1 \\ -1 & -1 & -17 \end{vmatrix}$$

$|H_1| = -25$, $|H_2| = 524$, and $|H_3| = |A| = -8864$. Π is maximized.

(b) Substituting the critical values in (12.20), $\bar{P}_1 = 84.12$, $\bar{P}_2 = 67.10$, and $\bar{P}_3 = 64.16$.

(c)
$$\epsilon_i = \frac{dQ_i}{dP_i} \frac{P_i}{Q_i}$$

Thus,

$$\epsilon_1 = \frac{-1}{12}\left(\frac{84.12}{4.99}\right) \cong -1.40 \qquad \epsilon_2 = \frac{-1}{10}\left(\frac{67.10}{4.29}\right) \cong -1.56 \qquad \epsilon_3 = -\frac{1}{8}\left(\frac{64.16}{4.98}\right) \cong -1.61$$

The airline maximizes profit by charging the highest price in the market where $|\epsilon|$ is lowest.

12.21. A university club can distinguish three separate demands for membership:

Student membership:	$Q_1 = 46.67 - \frac{1}{6}P_1$
Junior membership:	$Q_2 = 72.86 - \frac{1}{7}P_2$
Senior membership:	$Q_3 = 80 - \frac{1}{8}P_3$

$$\text{TC} = Q^2 + 30Q + 75 \tag{12.23}$$

where $Q = Q_1 + Q_2 + Q_3$.

Redo Problem 12.19 for this club, using the $MR = MC$ approach.

(a) From (12.22),

$$P_1 = 280 - 6Q_1 \qquad P_2 = 510 - 7Q_2 \qquad P_3 = 640 - 8Q_3 \tag{12.24}$$

With $TR = PQ$,

$$TR_1 = 280Q_1 - 6Q_1^2 \qquad TR_2 = 510Q_2 - 7Q_2^2 \qquad TR_3 = 640Q_3 - 8Q_3^2 \tag{12.25}$$

Taking the derivatives of (12.25) and (12.23) to get marginal revenue and marginal cost (see Problem 4.13),

$$MR_1 = 280 - 12Q_1 \qquad MR_2 = 510 - 14Q_2 \qquad MR_3 = 640 - 16Q_3 \tag{12.26}$$

$$MC = 30 + 2Q \tag{12.27}$$

Substituting $Q = Q_1 + Q_2 + Q_3$ in (12.27),

$$MC = 30 + 2Q_1 + 2Q_2 + 2Q_3 \tag{12.27a}$$

Equating MR and MC in each market in order to maximize profits,

$$280 - 12Q_1 = 30 + 2Q_1 + 2Q_2 + 2Q_3$$
$$510 - 14Q_2 = 30 + 2Q_1 + 2Q_2 + 2Q_3$$
$$640 - 16Q_3 = 30 + 2Q_1 + 2Q_2 + 2Q_3$$

Simplifying,

$$250 - 14Q_1 - 2Q_2 - 2Q_3 = 0$$
$$480 - 2Q_1 - 16Q_2 - 2Q_3 = 0 \tag{12.28}$$
$$610 - 2Q_1 - 2Q_2 - 18Q_3 = 0$$

In matrix form,

$$\begin{bmatrix} -14 & -2 & -2 \\ -2 & -16 & -2 \\ -2 & -2 & -18 \end{bmatrix} \begin{bmatrix} Q_1 \\ Q_2 \\ Q_3 \end{bmatrix} = \begin{bmatrix} -250 \\ -480 \\ -610 \end{bmatrix}$$

$$|A| = -3856$$

$$|A_1| = -38,560 \qquad \bar{Q}_1 = \frac{-38,560}{-3856} = 10$$

$$|A_2| = -96,400 \qquad \bar{Q}_2 = \frac{-96,400}{-3856} = 25$$

$$|A_3| = -115,680 \qquad \bar{Q}_3 = \frac{-115,680}{-3856} = 30$$

To test for the second-order condition, we can take the second partials of (12.28) because (12.28) was derived by subtracting MC from MR. This is equivalent to the first partials of the profit function since

$$\frac{d\Pi}{dQ} = \frac{d\text{TR}}{dQ} - \frac{d\text{TC}}{dQ} = \text{MR} - \text{MC}$$

Thus,
$$|H| = \begin{vmatrix} -14 & -2 & -2 \\ -2 & -16 & -2 \\ -2 & -2 & -18 \end{vmatrix}$$

$|H_1| = -14$, $|H_2| = 220$, and $|H_3| = |A| = -3856$. Π is maximized.

(b) Substituting the critical values in (12.24), $\bar{P}_1 = 220$, $\bar{P}_2 = 335$, and $\bar{P}_3 = 400$.

(c) $\epsilon_1 = -\frac{1}{6}\left(\frac{220}{10}\right) \cong -3.67$ $\epsilon_2 = -\frac{1}{7}\left(\frac{335}{25}\right) \cong -1.91$ $\epsilon_3 = -\frac{1}{8}\left(\frac{400}{30}\right) \cong -1.67$

12.22.   It can be demonstrated that

$$\text{MR} = P\left(1 - \frac{1}{|\epsilon|}\right)$$

Check the answer for market$_1$ in Problem 12.21.

$$\text{MR}_1 = 220\left(1 - \frac{1}{3.67}\right) \cong 160$$

In comparison, by substituting $\bar{Q}_1 = 10$ in (12.26), $\text{MR}_1 = 280 - 12(10) = 160$.
On your own, check your answers for MR_2 and MR_3.

THE BORDERED HESSIAN IN CONSTRAINED OPTIMIZATION

12.23.   Maximize utility $u = 2xy$ subject to a budget constraint equal to $3x + 4y = 90$ by (a) finding the critical values and (b) using the bordered Hessian $|\bar{H}|$ to test the second-order condition.

(a) The Lagrangian function is $U = 2xy + \lambda(3x + 4y - 90)$

The first-order conditions are

$$U_x = 2y + 3\lambda = 0 \qquad U_y = 2x + 4\lambda = 0 \qquad U_\lambda = 3x + 4y - 90 = 0$$

In matrix form,

$$\begin{bmatrix} 0 & 2 & 3 \\ 2 & 0 & 4 \\ 3 & 4 & 0 \end{bmatrix} \begin{bmatrix} x \\ y \\ \lambda \end{bmatrix} = \begin{bmatrix} 0 \\ 0 \\ 90 \end{bmatrix} \qquad\qquad (12.29)$$

Solving by Cramer's rule, $|A| = 48$, $|A_1| = 720$, $|A_2| = 540$, and $|A_3| = -360$. Thus, $\bar{x} = 15$, $\bar{y} = 11.25$, and $\bar{\lambda} = -7.5$.

(b) Taking the second partials of U with respect to x and y, and the first partials of the constraint with respect to x and y to form the bordered Hessian,

$$U_{xx} = 0 \qquad U_{yy} = 0 \qquad U_{xy} = 2 = U_{yx} \qquad c_x = 3 \qquad c_y = 4$$

From Section 12.4,

$$|\bar{H}| = \begin{vmatrix} 0 & 2 & 3 \\ 2 & 0 & 4 \\ 3 & 4 & 0 \end{vmatrix} \qquad \text{or} \qquad |\bar{H}| = \begin{vmatrix} 0 & 3 & 4 \\ 3 & 0 & 2 \\ 4 & 2 & 0 \end{vmatrix}$$

$$|\bar{H}_2| = |\bar{H}| = -2(-12) + 3(8) = 48 > 0 \qquad |\bar{H}_2| = |\bar{H}| = -3(-8) + 4(6) = 48 > 0$$

The bordered Hessian can be set up in either of the above forms without affecting the value of the principal minor. Notice, however, that if the objective function is bilinear or quadratic and the constraint is linear, the bordered Hessian on the left is identical to the coefficient matrix A in (12.29). This reduces calculation time since $|\bar{H}|$ is evidently equal to $|A|$. With $|\bar{H}| = |A| > 0$, from the rules of Section 12.4 $|\bar{H}|$ is negative definite, and U is maximized.

12.24. Maximize utility $u = xy + x$ subject to the budget constraint $6x + 2y = 110$, by using the techniques of Problem 12.23.

(a)
$$U = xy + x + \lambda(6x + 2y - 110)$$

$$U_x = y + 1 + 6\lambda = 0 \qquad U_y = x + 2\lambda = 0 \qquad U_\lambda = 6x + 2y - 110 = 0$$

In matrix form,

$$\begin{bmatrix} 0 & 1 & 6 \\ 1 & 0 & 2 \\ 6 & 2 & 0 \end{bmatrix} \begin{bmatrix} x \\ y \\ \lambda \end{bmatrix} = \begin{bmatrix} -1 \\ 0 \\ 110 \end{bmatrix}$$

Solving by Cramer's rule, $\bar{x} = 9\frac{1}{3}$, $\bar{y} = 27$, and $\bar{\lambda} = -4\frac{2}{3}$.

(b) Since $U_{xx} = 0$, $U_{yy} = 0$, $U_{xy} = 1 = U_{yx}$, $c_x = 6$, and $c_y = 2$,

$$|\bar{H}| = \begin{vmatrix} 0 & 1 & 6 \\ 1 & 0 & 2 \\ 6 & 2 & 0 \end{vmatrix} \qquad |\bar{H}_2| = |\bar{H}| = |A| = 24$$

With $|\bar{H}_2| > 0$, $|\bar{H}|$ is negative definite, and U is maximized.

12.25. Minimize a firm's total costs $c = 45x^2 + 90xy + 90y^2$ when the firm has to meet a production quota (g) equal to $2x + 3y = 60$ by (a) finding the critical values and (b) using the bordered Hessian to test the second-order conditions.

(a)
$$C = 45x^2 + 90xy + 90y^2 + \lambda(2x + 3y - 60)$$

$$C_x = 90x + 90y + 2\lambda = 0 \qquad C_y = 90x + 180y + 3\lambda = 0 \qquad C_\lambda = 2x + 3y - 60 = 0$$

In matrix form,

$$\begin{bmatrix} 90 & 90 & 2 \\ 90 & 180 & 3 \\ 2 & 3 & 0 \end{bmatrix} \begin{bmatrix} x \\ y \\ \lambda \end{bmatrix} = \begin{bmatrix} 0 \\ 0 \\ 60 \end{bmatrix}$$

Solving by Cramer's rule, $\bar{x} = 12$, $\bar{y} = 12$, and $\bar{\lambda} = -1080$.

(b) Since $C_{xx} = 90$, $C_{yy} = 180$, $C_{xy} = 90 = C_{yx}$, $g_x = 2$, and $g_y = 3$,

$$|\bar{H}| = \begin{vmatrix} 90 & 90 & 2 \\ 90 & 180 & 3 \\ 2 & 3 & 0 \end{vmatrix}$$

$|\bar{H}_2| = -450$. With $|\bar{H}_2| < 0$, $|\bar{H}|$ is positive definite and C is minimized.

12.26. Minimize a firm's costs $c = 3x^2 + 5xy + 6y^2$ when the firm must meet a production quota of $5x + 7y = 800$, using the techniques of Problem 12.25.

(a)
$$C = 3x^2 + 5xy + 6y^2 + \lambda(5x + 7y - 800)$$

$$C_x = 6x + 5y + 5\lambda = 0 \qquad C_y = 5x + 12y + 7\lambda = 0 \qquad C_\lambda = 5x + 7y - 800 = 0$$

Solving simultaneously, $\bar{x} = 81.97$, $\bar{y} = 55.74$, and $\bar{\lambda} = -154.1$.

(b) With $C_{xx} = 6$, $C_{yy} = 12$, $C_{xy} = 5 = C_{yx}$, $g_x = 5$, and $g_y = 7$,

$$|\bar{H}| = \begin{vmatrix} 6 & 5 & 5 \\ 5 & 12 & 7 \\ 5 & 7 & 0 \end{vmatrix}$$

$|\bar{H}_2| = 5(35 - 60) - 7(42 - 25) = -244$. Thus, $|\bar{H}|$ is positive definite and C is minimized.

12.27. Redo Problem 12.25 by maximizing utility $u = x^{0.5}y^{0.3}$ subject to the budget constraint $10x + 3y = 140$.

(a)
$$U = x^{0.5}y^{0.3} + \lambda(10x + 3y - 140)$$

$$U_x = 0.5x^{-0.5}y^{0.3} + 10\lambda = 0 \qquad U_y = 0.3x^{0.5}y^{-0.7} + 3\lambda = 0 \qquad U\lambda = 10x + 3y - 140 = 0$$

Solving simultaneously, as shown in Section 9.11, $\bar{x} = 8.75$, $\bar{y} = 17.5$, and $\bar{\lambda} = -0.04$.

(b) With $U_{xx} = -0.25x^{-1.5}y^{0.3}$, $U_{yy} = -0.21x^{0.5}y^{-1.7}$, $U_{xy} = U_{yx} = 0.15x^{-0.5}y^{-0.7}$, $g_x = 10$, and $g_y = 3$,

$$|\bar{H}| = \begin{vmatrix} -0.25x^{-1.5}y^{0.3} & 0.15x^{-0.5}y^{-0.7} & 10 \\ 0.15x^{-0.5}y^{-0.7} & -0.21x^{0.5}y^{-1.7} & 3 \\ 10 & 3 & 0 \end{vmatrix}$$

Expanding along the third column,

$$|\bar{H}_2| = 10(0.45x^{-0.5}y^{-0.7} + 2.1x^{0.5}y^{-1.7}) - 3(-0.75x^{-1.5}y^{0.3} - 1.5x^{-0.5}y^{-0.7})$$
$$= 21x^{0.5}y^{-1.7} + 9x^{-0.5}y^{-0.7} + 2.25x^{-1.5}y^{0.3} > 0$$

since x and $y > 0$, and a positive number x raised to a negative power $(-n)$ equals $1/x^n$, which is also positive. With $|\bar{H}_2| > 0$, $|\bar{H}|$ is negative definite and U is maximized.

12.28. Maximize utility $u = x^{0.25}y^{0.4}$ subject to the budget constraint $2x + 8y = 104$, as in Problem 12.27.

(a)
$$U = x^{0.25}y^{0.4} + \lambda(2x + 8y - 104)$$

$$U_x = 0.25x^{-0.75}y^{0.4} + 2\lambda = 0 \qquad U_y = 0.4x^{0.25}y^{-0.6} + 8\lambda = 0 \qquad U_\lambda = 2x + 8y - 104 = 0$$

Solving simultaneously, $\bar{x} = 20$, $\bar{y} = 8$, and $\bar{\lambda} = -0.03$.

(b)
$$|\bar{H}| = \begin{vmatrix} -0.1875x^{-1.75}y^{0.4} & 0.1x^{-0.75}y^{-0.6} & 2 \\ 0.1x^{-0.75}y^{-0.6} & -0.24x^{0.25}y^{-1.6} & 8 \\ 2 & 8 & 0 \end{vmatrix}$$

Expanding along the third row,

$$|\bar{H}_2| = 2(0.8x^{-0.75}y^{-0.6} + 0.48x^{0.25}y^{-1.6}) - 8(-1.5x^{-1.75}y^{0.4} - 0.2x^{-0.75}y^{-0.6})$$
$$= 0.96x^{0.25}y^{-1.6} + 3.2x^{-0.75}y^{-0.6} + 12x^{-1.75}y^{0.4} > 0$$

Thus, $|\bar{H}|$ is negative definite, and U is maximized.

12.29. A monopolistic producer of two substitute goods faces the demand functions

$$x = 80 - 4P_x + 2P_y \qquad y = 110 + 2P_x - 6P_y$$

His total cost function is $TC = 0.5x^2 + xy + y^2$. What is the profit-maximizing level of output if a production quota requires $3x + 4y = 350$?

(a) Converting x and y from functions of P to $P = f(x, y)$, as in Problem 12.16,

$$\begin{bmatrix} -4 & 2 \\ 2 & -6 \end{bmatrix} \begin{bmatrix} P_x \\ P_y \end{bmatrix} = \begin{bmatrix} x - 80 \\ y - 110 \end{bmatrix}$$

By Cramer's rule,

$$P_x = 35 - 0.3x - 0.1y \qquad P_y = 30 - 0.1x - 0.2y$$

Thus, $\Pi = P_x x + P_y y - TC = 35x + 30y - 1.2xy - 0.8x^2 - 1.2y^2$

and the Lagrangian expression is

$$\Pi = 35x + 30y - 1.2xy - 0.8x^2 - 1.2y^2 + \lambda(3x + 4y - 350)$$

$$\Pi_x = 35 - 1.2y - 1.6x + 3\lambda = 0$$

$$\Pi_y = 30 - 1.2x - 2.4y + 4\lambda = 0$$

$$\Pi_\lambda = 3x + 4y - 350 = 0$$

Solving simultaneously, $\bar{x} = 56.52$, $\bar{y} = 45.11$, and $\bar{\lambda} = 36.52$. (Here the firm will suffer a loss by fulfilling its quota. Hence $\bar{\lambda}$ is positive. An increase in the quota will lead to a decrease in Π or a bigger loss, and a decrease in the quota will lead to an increase in Π or a smaller loss. See Section 5.9.)

(b)
$$|\bar{H}| = \begin{vmatrix} -1.6 & -1.2 & 3 \\ -1.2 & -2.4 & 4 \\ 3 & 4 & 0 \end{vmatrix}$$

$|\bar{H}_2| = 18.4$. Thus, $|\bar{H}|$ is negative definite and Π is maximized, i.e. losses are kept to a minimum.

12.30. Minimize costs $c = 3x + 4y$ subject to the constraint $2xy = 337.5$, using the techniques of Problem 12.25(a) and (b). (c) Discuss the relationship between this solution and that for Problem 12.23.

(a)
$$C = 3x + 4y + \lambda(2xy - 337.5)$$

$$C_x = 3 + 2\lambda y = 0 \qquad \lambda = -\frac{1.5}{y} \qquad\qquad (12.30)$$

$$C_y = 4 + 2\lambda x = 0 \qquad \lambda = -\frac{2}{x} \qquad\qquad (12.31)$$

$$C_\lambda = 2xy - 337.5 = 0 \qquad\qquad (12.32)$$

Equating λ's in (12.30) and (12.31),

$$-\frac{1.5}{y} = -\frac{2}{x}$$

$$y = 0.75x$$

Substituting in (12.32),

$$2x(0.75x) = 337.5$$

$$1.5x^2 = 337.5$$

$$x^2 = 225 \qquad \bar{x} = 15$$

Thus, $\bar{y} = 11.25$ and $\bar{\lambda} = -0.133$.

(b) Since $C_{xx} = 0$, $C_{yy} = 0$, $C_{xy} = C_{yx} = 2\lambda$, and from the constraint, $g_x = 2y$, and $g_y = 2x$,

$$|\bar{H}| = \begin{vmatrix} 0 & 2\lambda & 2y \\ 2\lambda & 0 & 2x \\ 2y & 2x & 0 \end{vmatrix}$$

$|\bar{H}_2| = -2\lambda(-4xy) + 2y(4x\lambda) = 16xy\lambda$. With $\bar{x}, \bar{y} > 0$ and $\bar{\lambda} < 0$, $|\bar{H}_2| < 0$. Hence $|\bar{H}|$ is positive definite and C is minimized.

(c) This problem and Problem 12.23 are the same, except that the objective functions and constraints are reversed. In Problem 12.23, the objective function $u = 2xy$ was maximized subject to the constraint $3x + 4y = 90$; in this problem the objective function $c = 3x + 4y$ was minimized subject to the constraint $2xy = 337.5$. Therefore, one may maximize utility subject to a budget constraint *or* minimize the cost of achieving a given level of utility.

12.31. Minimize the cost of 434 units of production for a firm when $Q = 10K^{0.7}L^{0.1}$ and $P_K = 28$, $P_L = 10$ by (a) finding the critical values and (b) using the bordered Hessian. (c) Check the answer with that of Problem 9.38.

(a) The objective function is $c = 28K + 10L$ and the constraint is $10K^{0.7}L^{0.1} = 434$. Thus, $C = 28K + 10L + \lambda(10K^{0.7}L^{0.1} - 434)$.

$$C_K = 28 + 7\lambda K^{-0.3}L^{0.1} = 0 \qquad \lambda = -4K^{0.3}L^{-0.1} \qquad (12.33)$$
$$C_L = 10 + \lambda K^{0.7}L^{-0.9} = 0 \qquad \lambda = -10K^{-0.7}L^{0.9} \qquad (12.34)$$
$$C_\lambda = 10K^{0.7}L^{0.1} - 434 = 0 \qquad\qquad\qquad (12.35)$$

Equating λ's in (12.33) and (12.34),

$$-4K^{0.3}L^{-0.1} = -10K^{-0.7}L^{0.9} \qquad K = 2.5L$$

Substituting in (12.35) and using logs privately for powers and roots,

$$10(2.5)^{0.7}(L)^{0.7}L^{0.1} = 434 \qquad 19L^{0.8} = 434$$

$$\bar{L} = (22.8)^{1/0.8} = (22.8)^{1.25} \cong 50$$

Thus, $\bar{K} = 125$ and $\bar{\lambda} = -11.5$.

(b) Since $C_{KK} = -2.1\lambda K^{-1.3}L^{0.1}$, $C_{LL} = -0.9\lambda K^{0.7}L^{-1.9}$, $C_{KL} = C_{LK} = 0.7\lambda K^{-0.3}L^{-0.9}$, and from the constraint $g_K = 7K^{-0.3}L^{0.1}$ and $g_L = K^{0.7}L^{-0.9}$,

$$|\bar{H}| = \begin{vmatrix} -2.1\lambda K^{-1.3}L^{0.1} & 0.7\lambda K^{-0.3}L^{-0.9} & 7K^{-0.3}L^{0.1} \\ 0.7\lambda K^{-0.3}L^{-0.9} & -0.9\lambda K^{0.7}L^{-1.9} & K^{0.7}L^{-0.9} \\ 7K^{-0.3}L^{0.1} & K^{0.7}L^{-0.9} & 0 \end{vmatrix}$$

Expanding along the third row,

$$|\bar{H}_2| = 7K^{-0.3}L^{0.1}(0.7\lambda K^{0.4}L^{-1.8} + 6.3\lambda K^{0.4}L^{-1.8}) - K^{0.7}L^{-0.9}(-2.1\lambda K^{-0.6}L^{-0.8} - 4.9K^{-0.6}L^{-0.8})$$
$$= 49\lambda K^{0.1}L^{-1.7} + 7\lambda K^{0.1}L^{-1.7} = 56\lambda K^{0.1}L^{-1.7}$$

With $K, L > 0$, $\lambda < 0$, and $|\bar{H}_2| < 0$, $|\bar{H}|$ is positive definite and C is minimized.

(c) The answers are identical with those in Problem 9.38, but note the difference in work involved when the linear function is selected as the objective function and not the constraint. See also the bordered Hessian for Problem 9.38 calculated in Problem 12.32(c).

12.32. Use the bordered Hessian to check the second-order condition for (a) Example 7 in Chapter 6, (b) Problem 9.37, and (c) Problem 9.38.

(a)
$$|\bar{H}| = \begin{vmatrix} 16 & -1 & 1 \\ -1 & 24 & 1 \\ 1 & 1 & 0 \end{vmatrix}$$

$|\bar{H}_2| = 1(-1 - 24) - 1(16 + 1) = -42$. With $|\bar{H}_2| < 0$, $|\bar{H}|$ is positive definite and C is minimized.

(b)
$$|\bar{H}| = \begin{vmatrix} -0.21K^{-1.7}L^{0.5} & 0.15K^{-0.7}L^{-0.5} & 6 \\ 0.15K^{-0.7}L^{-0.5} & -0.25K^{0.3}L^{-1.5} & 2 \\ 6 & 2 & 0 \end{vmatrix}$$

$$|\bar{H}_2| = 6(0.30K^{-0.7}L^{-0.5} + 1.5K^{0.3}L^{-1.5}) - 2(-0.42K^{-1.7}L^{0.5} - 0.9K^{-0.7}L^{-0.5})$$
$$= 9K^{0.3}L^{-1.5} + 3.6K^{-0.7}L^{-0.5} + 0.84K^{-1.7}L^{0.5} > 0$$

With $|\bar{H}_2| > 0$, $|\bar{H}|$ is negative definite and Q is maximized.

$$(c) \qquad |\bar{H}| = \begin{vmatrix} -2.1K^{-1.3}L^{0.1} & 0.7K^{-0.3}L^{-0.9} & 28 \\ 0.7K^{-0.3}L^{-0.9} & -0.9K^{0.7}L^{-1.9} & 10 \\ 28 & 10 & 0 \end{vmatrix}$$

$$|\bar{H}_2| = 28(7K^{-0.3}L^{-0.9} + 25.2K^{0.7}L^{-1.9}) - 10(-21K^{-1.3}L^{0.1} - 19.6K^{-0.3}L^{-0.9})$$
$$= 705.6K^{0.7}L^{-1.9} + 392K^{-0.3}L^{-0.9} + 210K^{-1.3}L^{0.1} > 0$$

With $|\bar{H}_2| > 0$, $|\bar{H}|$ is negative definite and Q is maximized.

INPUT–OUTPUT ANALYSIS

12.33. Determine the total demand for industries 1, 2, and 3, given the matrix of technical coefficients A and the final demand vector B below.

Output Industry
1   2   3

$$A = \begin{bmatrix} 0.2 & 0.3 & 0.2 \\ 0.4 & 0.1 & 0.3 \\ 0.3 & 0.5 & 0.2 \end{bmatrix} \begin{matrix} 1 \\ 2 \\ 3 \end{matrix} \quad \begin{matrix} \text{Input} \\ \text{Industry} \end{matrix} \qquad B = \begin{bmatrix} 150 \\ 200 \\ 210 \end{bmatrix}$$

From (12.6), the total demand vector is $X = (I - A)^{-1}B$, where

$$(I - A) = \begin{bmatrix} 0.8 & -0.3 & -0.2 \\ -0.4 & 0.9 & -0.3 \\ -0.3 & -0.5 & 0.8 \end{bmatrix}$$

Taking the inverse of $(I - A)$,

$$(I - A)^{-1} = \frac{1}{0.239}\begin{bmatrix} 0.57 & 0.34 & 0.27 \\ 0.41 & 0.58 & 0.32 \\ 0.47 & 0.49 & 0.60 \end{bmatrix}$$

Substituting in $X = (I - A)^{-1}B$,

$$X = \frac{1}{0.239}\begin{bmatrix} 0.57 & 0.34 & 0.27 \\ 0.41 & 0.58 & 0.32 \\ 0.47 & 0.49 & 0.60 \end{bmatrix}\begin{bmatrix} 150 \\ 200 \\ 210 \end{bmatrix} = \frac{1}{0.239}\begin{bmatrix} 210.2 \\ 244.7 \\ 294.5 \end{bmatrix} = \begin{bmatrix} 879.50 \\ 1023.85 \\ 1232.22 \end{bmatrix} = \begin{bmatrix} x_1 \\ x_2 \\ x_3 \end{bmatrix}$$

12.34. Determine the new level of total demand X_2 for Problem 12.33 if final demand increases by 40 in industry 1, 20 in industry 2, and 25 in industry 3.

$$\Delta X = (I - A)^{-1}\Delta B$$

$$\Delta X = \frac{1}{0.239}\begin{bmatrix} 0.57 & 0.34 & 0.27 \\ 0.41 & 0.58 & 0.32 \\ 0.47 & 0.49 & 0.60 \end{bmatrix}\begin{bmatrix} 40 \\ 20 \\ 25 \end{bmatrix} = \frac{1}{0.239}\begin{bmatrix} 36.35 \\ 36.00 \\ 43.60 \end{bmatrix} = \begin{bmatrix} 152.09 \\ 150.63 \\ 182.43 \end{bmatrix}$$

$$X_2 = X_1 + \Delta X = \begin{bmatrix} 879.50 \\ 1023.85 \\ 1232.22 \end{bmatrix} + \begin{bmatrix} 152.09 \\ 150.63 \\ 182.43 \end{bmatrix} = \begin{bmatrix} 1031.09 \\ 1174.48 \\ 1414.65 \end{bmatrix}$$

12.35. Determine the total demand for industries 1, 2, and 3, given the matrix of technical coefficients A and the final demand vector B below.

Output Industry
1   2   3

$$A = \begin{bmatrix} 0.4 & 0.3 & 0.1 \\ 0.2 & 0.2 & 0.3 \\ 0.2 & 0.4 & 0.2 \end{bmatrix} \begin{matrix} 1 \\ 2 \\ 3 \end{matrix} \quad \begin{matrix} \text{Input} \\ \text{Industry} \end{matrix} \qquad B = \begin{bmatrix} 140 \\ 220 \\ 180 \end{bmatrix}$$

$$X = (I - A)^{-1}B$$

where

$$(I - A) = \begin{bmatrix} 0.6 & -0.3 & -0.1 \\ -0.2 & 0.8 & -0.3 \\ -0.2 & -0.4 & 0.8 \end{bmatrix}$$

and the inverse

$$(I - A)^{-1} = \frac{1}{0.222} \begin{bmatrix} 0.52 & 0.28 & 0.17 \\ 0.22 & 0.46 & 0.20 \\ 0.24 & 0.30 & 0.42 \end{bmatrix}$$

Thus,

$$X = \frac{1}{0.222} \begin{bmatrix} 0.52 & 0.28 & 0.17 \\ 0.22 & 0.46 & 0.20 \\ 0.24 & 0.30 & 0.42 \end{bmatrix} \begin{bmatrix} 140 \\ 220 \\ 180 \end{bmatrix} = \begin{bmatrix} 743.24 \\ 756.76 \\ 789.19 \end{bmatrix} = \begin{bmatrix} x_1 \\ x_2 \\ x_3 \end{bmatrix}$$

12.36. Determine the new total demand X_2 if final demand increases by 30 for industry 1 and decreases by 15 and 35 for industries 2 and 3, respectively, in Problem 12.35.

$$\Delta X = (I - A)^{-1}\Delta B$$

$$\Delta X = \frac{1}{0.222} \begin{bmatrix} 0.52 & 0.28 & 0.17 \\ 0.22 & 0.46 & 0.20 \\ 0.24 & 0.30 & 0.42 \end{bmatrix} \begin{bmatrix} 30 \\ -15 \\ -35 \end{bmatrix} = \frac{1}{0.222} \begin{bmatrix} 5.45 \\ -7.30 \\ -12.00 \end{bmatrix} = \begin{bmatrix} 24.55 \\ -32.88 \\ -54.05 \end{bmatrix}$$

$$X_2 = X_1 + \Delta X = \begin{bmatrix} 743.24 \\ 756.76 \\ 789.19 \end{bmatrix} + \begin{bmatrix} 24.55 \\ -32.88 \\ -54.05 \end{bmatrix} = \begin{bmatrix} 767.79 \\ 723.88 \\ 735.14 \end{bmatrix}$$

12.37. Given the Interindustry Transaction Demand Table in millions of dollars below, find the matrix of technical coefficients.

	Sector of Destination				Final Demand	Total Demand
Sector of Origin	Steel	Coal	Iron	Auto		
Steel	80	20	110	230	160	600
Coal	200	50	90	120	140	600
Iron	220	110	30	40	0	400
Auto	60	140	160	240	400	1000
Value added	40	280	10	370		
Gross production	600	600	400	1000		

The technical coefficient a_{ij} expresses the number of units or dollars of input$_i$ required to produce one unit or one dollar of product$_j$. Thus a_{11} = the percentage of steel in one dollar of steel, a_{21} = the percentage of coal in one dollar of steel, a_{31} = the percentage of iron in one dollar of steel, and a_{41} = the percentage of autos in one dollar of steel. To find the technical coefficients simply divide every element in each column by the value of gross production at the bottom of the column omitting value added. Thus,

$$A = \begin{bmatrix} \frac{80}{600} & \frac{20}{600} & \frac{110}{400} & \frac{230}{1000} \\ \frac{200}{600} & \frac{50}{600} & \frac{90}{400} & \frac{120}{1000} \\ \frac{220}{600} & \frac{110}{600} & \frac{30}{400} & \frac{40}{1000} \\ \frac{60}{600} & \frac{140}{600} & \frac{160}{400} & \frac{240}{1000} \end{bmatrix} = \begin{bmatrix} 0.133 & 0.033 & 0.275 & 0.23 \\ 0.333 & 0.083 & 0.225 & 0.12 \\ 0.367 & 0.183 & 0.075 & 0.04 \\ 0.10 & 0.233 & 0.40 & 0.24 \end{bmatrix}$$

12.38. Check the matrix of technical coefficients (A) in Problem 12.37.

To check matrix A, multiply it by the column vector of total demand (X). The product should equal the intermediate demand which is total demand (X) − final demand (B). Allow for slight errors due to rounding.

$$AX = \begin{bmatrix} 0.133 & 0.033 & 0.275 & 0.23 \\ 0.333 & 0.083 & 0.225 & 0.12 \\ 0.367 & 0.183 & 0.075 & 0.04 \\ 0.10 & 0.233 & 0.40 & 0.24 \end{bmatrix} \begin{bmatrix} 600 \\ 600 \\ 400 \\ 1000 \end{bmatrix} = \begin{bmatrix} 439.6 \\ 459.6 \\ 400 \\ 599.8 \end{bmatrix}$$

$$X - B = \begin{bmatrix} 600 \\ 600 \\ 400 \\ 1000 \end{bmatrix} - \begin{bmatrix} 160 \\ 140 \\ 0 \\ 400 \end{bmatrix} = \begin{bmatrix} 440 \\ 460 \\ 400 \\ 600 \end{bmatrix}$$

12.39. Given the Interindustry Transaction Demand Table below, (a) find the matrix of technical coefficients. (b) Check your answer.

Sector of Origin	Sector of Destination			Final Demand	Total Demand
	1	2	3		
1	20	60	10	50	140
2	50	10	80	10	150
3	40	30	20	40	130
Value added	30	50	20		
Gross production	140	150	130		

(a)
$$A = \begin{bmatrix} \frac{20}{140} & \frac{60}{150} & \frac{10}{130} \\ \frac{50}{140} & \frac{10}{150} & \frac{80}{130} \\ \frac{40}{140} & \frac{30}{150} & \frac{20}{130} \end{bmatrix} = \begin{bmatrix} 0.143 & 0.4 & 0.077 \\ 0.357 & 0.067 & 0.615 \\ 0.286 & 0.2 & 0.154 \end{bmatrix}$$

(b)
$$AX = \begin{bmatrix} 0.143 & 0.4 & 0.077 \\ 0.357 & 0.067 & 0.615 \\ 0.286 & 0.2 & 0.154 \end{bmatrix} \begin{bmatrix} 140 \\ 150 \\ 130 \end{bmatrix} = \begin{bmatrix} 90 \\ 140 \\ 90 \end{bmatrix}$$

$$X - B = \begin{bmatrix} 140 \\ 150 \\ 130 \end{bmatrix} - \begin{bmatrix} 50 \\ 10 \\ 40 \end{bmatrix} = \begin{bmatrix} 90 \\ 140 \\ 90 \end{bmatrix}$$

12.40. Find the new level of total demand in Problem 12.39 if in year 2 final demand is 70 in industry 1, 25 in industry 2, and 50 in industry 3.

$$X = (I - A)^{-1}B$$

where $(I - A) = \begin{bmatrix} 0.857 & -0.4 & -0.077 \\ -0.357 & 0.933 & -0.615 \\ -0.286 & -0.2 & 0.846 \end{bmatrix}$ and $(I - A)^{-1} = \frac{1}{0.354} \begin{bmatrix} 0.666 & 0.354 & 0.318 \\ 0.478 & 0.703 & 0.555 \\ 0.338 & 0.286 & 0.657 \end{bmatrix}$

Thus,

$$X = \frac{1}{0.354} \begin{bmatrix} 0.666 & 0.354 & 0.318 \\ 0.478 & 0.703 & 0.555 \\ 0.338 & 0.286 & 0.657 \end{bmatrix} \begin{bmatrix} 70 \\ 25 \\ 50 \end{bmatrix} = \frac{1}{0.354} \begin{bmatrix} 71.37 \\ 78.79 \\ 63.66 \end{bmatrix} = \begin{bmatrix} 201.61 \\ 222.57 \\ 179.83 \end{bmatrix}$$

12.41. Having found the inverse of $(I - A)$, use it to check the accuracy of the matrix of coefficients derived in Problem 12.39, i.e. check to see if $(I - A)^{-1}B = X$.

$$(I - A)^{-1}B = \frac{1}{0.354}\begin{bmatrix} 0.666 & 0.354 & 0.318 \\ 0.478 & 0.703 & 0.555 \\ 0.338 & 0.286 & 0.657 \end{bmatrix}\begin{bmatrix} 50 \\ 10 \\ 40 \end{bmatrix} = \frac{1}{0.354}\begin{bmatrix} 49.56 \\ 53.13 \\ 46.04 \end{bmatrix} = \begin{bmatrix} 140 \\ 150 \\ 130 \end{bmatrix}$$

12.42. Assume in Problem 12.39 that value added is composed entirely of the primary input labor. How much labor would be necessary to obtain the final demand (a) in Problem 12.39? (b) In Problem 12.40? (c) If the amount of labor available in the economy is 100, is the output mix feasible?

(a) To get the technical coefficient of labor a_{Lj} in Problem 12.39, simply divide the value added in each column by the gross production. Thus, $a_{L1} = \frac{30}{140} = 0.214$, $a_{L2} = \frac{50}{150} = 0.333$, and $a_{L3} = \frac{20}{130} = 0.154$. The amount of labor needed to meet the final demand will then equal the row of technical coefficients for labor times the column vector of total demand, since labor must also be used to produce the intermediate products. Thus,

$$L_1 = [0.214 \quad 0.333 \quad 0.154]\begin{bmatrix} 140 \\ 150 \\ 130 \end{bmatrix} = 99.93$$

(b)
$$L_2 = [0.214 \quad 0.333 \quad 0.154]\begin{bmatrix} 201.61 \\ 222.57 \\ 179.83 \end{bmatrix} = 144.95$$

(c) Final demand in Problem 12.39 is feasible since $99.93 < 100$. Final demand in Problem 12.40 is not feasible since society does not have sufficient labor resources to produce it.

12.43. Check the accuracy of the technical coefficients found in Problem 12.42.

Having found the technical coefficients of labor for Problem 12.39, where value added was due totally to labor inputs, the accuracy of the technical coefficients can easily be checked. Since each dollar of output must be completely accounted for in terms of inputs, simply add up each column of technical coefficients to be sure it equals one.

	1	2	3
1	0.143	0.4	0.077
2	0.357	0.067	0.615
3	0.286	0.2	0.154
Value added (labor)	0.214	0.333	0.154
	1.000	1.000	1.000

EIGENVALUES, EIGENVECTORS

12.44. Use eigenvalues (characteristic roots, latent roots) to determine sign-definiteness for

$$A = \begin{bmatrix} 10 & 3 \\ 3 & 4 \end{bmatrix}$$

To find the characteristic roots of A, the determinant of the characteristic matrix $(A - cI)$ must equal zero. Thus,

$$|A - cI| = \begin{vmatrix} 10 - c & 3 \\ 3 & 4 - c \end{vmatrix} = 0$$

$$40 + c^2 - 14c - 9 = 0 \qquad c^2 - 14c + 31 = 0$$

Using the quadratic formula,

$$c = \frac{14 \pm \sqrt{196 - 4(31)}}{2} = \frac{14 \pm 8.485}{2}$$

$$c_1 = 11.2425 \qquad c_2 = 2.7575$$

With both characteristic roots positive, A is positive definite.

12.45. Redo Problem 12.44, given

$$A = \begin{bmatrix} -4 & -2 \\ -2 & -6 \end{bmatrix}$$

$$|A - cI| = \begin{vmatrix} -4 - c & -2 \\ -2 & -6 - c \end{vmatrix} = 0$$

$$24 + c^2 + 10c - 4 = 0 \qquad c^2 + 10c + 20 = 0$$

$$c = \frac{-10 \pm \sqrt{100 - 4(20)}}{2} = \frac{-10 \pm 4.4721}{2}$$

$$c_1 = \frac{-5.5279}{2} = -2.764 \qquad c_2 = \frac{-14.4721}{2} = -7.236$$

With both characteristic roots negative, A is negative definite.

12.46. Redo Problem 12.44, given

$$A = \begin{bmatrix} 6 & 2 \\ 2 & 2 \end{bmatrix}$$

$$|A - cI| = \begin{vmatrix} 6 - c & 2 \\ 2 & 2 - c \end{vmatrix} = 0$$

$$12 + c^2 - 8c - 4 = 0 \qquad c^2 - 8c + 8 = 0$$

$$c = \frac{8 \pm \sqrt{64 - 4(8)}}{2} = \frac{8 \pm 5.66}{2}$$

$$c_1 = 1.17 \qquad c_2 = 6.83$$

A is positive definite.

12.47. Redo Problem 12.44, given

$$A = \begin{bmatrix} 4 & 6 & 3 \\ 0 & 2 & 5 \\ 0 & 1 & 3 \end{bmatrix}$$

$$|A - cI| = \begin{vmatrix} 4 - c & 6 & 3 \\ 0 & 2 - c & 5 \\ 0 & 1 & 3 - c \end{vmatrix} = 0$$

Expanding along the first column,

$$|A - cI| = (4 - c)[(2 - c)(3 - c) - 5] = 0 \qquad\qquad (12.36)$$

$$-c^3 + 9c^2 - 21c + 4 = 0 \qquad\qquad (12.37)$$

To solve for (*12.37*) we may use a standard formula for finding cube roots or note that (*12.37*) will equal zero if in (*12.36*)

$$4 - c = 0 \qquad \text{or} \qquad (2 - c)(3 - c) - 5 = 0$$

Thus, the characteristic roots are

$$4 - c = 0 \qquad (2 - c)(3 - c) - 5 = 0$$
$$c_1 = 4 \qquad c^2 - 5c + 1 = 0$$
$$c = \frac{5 \pm \sqrt{25 - 4}}{2} = \frac{5 \pm 4.58}{2}$$
$$c_2 = 4.79 \qquad c_3 = 0.21$$

With all three characteristic roots positive, A is positive definite.

12.48. Redo Problem 12.44, given

$$A = \begin{bmatrix} 6 & 1 & 0 \\ 13 & 4 & 0 \\ 5 & 1 & 9 \end{bmatrix}$$

$$|A - cI| = \begin{vmatrix} 6 - c & 1 & 0 \\ 13 & 4 - c & 0 \\ 5 & 1 & 9 - c \end{vmatrix} = 0$$

Expanding along the third column,

$$|A - cI| = (9 - c)[(6 - c)(4 - c) - 13] = 0 \qquad (12.38)$$
$$-c^3 + 19c^2 - 101c + 99 = 0 \qquad (12.39)$$

which will equal zero, if in (12.38)

$$9 - c = 0 \qquad \text{or} \qquad (6 - c)(4 - c) - 13 = 0$$

Thus, $\qquad\qquad c_1 = 9 \qquad\qquad c^2 - 10c + 11 = 0$

$$c = \frac{10 \pm \sqrt{100 - 4(11)}}{2} = \frac{10 \pm 7.48}{2}$$
$$c_2 = 8.74 \qquad c_3 = 1.26$$

With all latent roots positive, A is positive definite.

12.49. Redo Problem 12.44, given

$$A = \begin{bmatrix} -5 & 1 & 2 \\ 0 & -2 & 0 \\ 4 & 2 & -3 \end{bmatrix}$$

$$|A - cI| = \begin{vmatrix} -5 - c & 1 & 2 \\ 0 & -2 - c & 0 \\ 4 & 2 & -3 - c \end{vmatrix} = 0$$

Expanding along the second row,

$$|A - cI| = (-2 - c)[(-5 - c)(-3 - c) - 8] = 0$$

Thus, $\qquad\qquad -2 - c = 0 \qquad \text{or} \qquad (-5 - c)(-3 - c) - 8 = 0$
$$c_1 = -2 \qquad\qquad c^2 + 8c + 7 = 0$$
$$(c + 7)(c + 1) = 0$$
$$c_2 = -7 \qquad c_3 = -1$$

With all latent roots negative, A is negative definite.

12.50. Given $\qquad\qquad\qquad A = \begin{bmatrix} 6 & 6 \\ 6 & -3 \end{bmatrix}$

Find (a) the characteristic roots and (b) the characteristic vectors. (c) Check the characteristic vectors with the transformation matrix, showing

$$T'AT = \begin{bmatrix} c_1 & 0 \\ 0 & c_2 \end{bmatrix}$$

(a)

$$|A - cI| = \begin{vmatrix} 6-c & 6 \\ 6 & -3-c \end{vmatrix} = 0$$

$$-18 + c^2 - 3c - 36 = 0$$

$$c^2 - 3c - 54 = 0$$

$$(c-9)(c+6) = 0$$

$$c_1 = 9 \qquad c_2 = -6$$

With one root positive and the other negative, A is indefinite.

(b) Using $c_1 = 9$ for the first characteristic vector V_1,

$$\begin{bmatrix} 6-9 & 6 \\ 6 & -3-9 \end{bmatrix}\begin{bmatrix} v_1 \\ v_2 \end{bmatrix} = \begin{bmatrix} -3 & 6 \\ 6 & -12 \end{bmatrix}\begin{bmatrix} v_1 \\ v_2 \end{bmatrix} = 0$$

$$v_1 = 2v_2$$

Normalizing, as in Example 10,

$$(2v_2)^2 + v_2^2 = 1$$

$$5v_2^2 = 1$$

$$v_2 = \sqrt{0.2} \qquad v_1 = 2v_2 = 2\sqrt{0.2}$$

Thus,

$$V_1 = \begin{bmatrix} 2\sqrt{0.2} \\ \sqrt{0.2} \end{bmatrix}$$

Using $c_2 = -6$ for the second characteristic vector,

$$\begin{bmatrix} 6-(-6) & 6 \\ 6 & -3-(-6) \end{bmatrix}\begin{bmatrix} v_1 \\ v_2 \end{bmatrix} = \begin{bmatrix} 12 & 6 \\ 6 & 3 \end{bmatrix}\begin{bmatrix} v_1 \\ v_2 \end{bmatrix} = 0$$

$$v_2 = -2v_1$$

Normalizing,

$$v_1^2 + (-2v_1)^2 = 1$$

$$5v_1^2 = 1$$

$$v_1 = \sqrt{0.2} \qquad v_2 = -2v_1 = -2\sqrt{0.2}$$

Thus,

$$V_2 = \begin{bmatrix} \sqrt{0.2} \\ -2\sqrt{0.2} \end{bmatrix}$$

(c)

$$T = [V_1 \quad V_2] = \begin{bmatrix} 2\sqrt{0.2} & \sqrt{0.2} \\ \sqrt{0.2} & -2\sqrt{0.2} \end{bmatrix}$$

Thus,

$$T'AT = \begin{bmatrix} 2\sqrt{0.2} & \sqrt{0.2} \\ \sqrt{0.2} & -2\sqrt{0.2} \end{bmatrix}\begin{bmatrix} 6 & 6 \\ 6 & -3 \end{bmatrix}\begin{bmatrix} 2\sqrt{0.2} & \sqrt{0.2} \\ \sqrt{0.2} & -2\sqrt{0.2} \end{bmatrix}$$

where

$$T'A = \begin{bmatrix} 18\sqrt{0.2} & 9\sqrt{0.2} \\ -6\sqrt{0.2} & 12\sqrt{0.2} \end{bmatrix}$$

and

$$T'AT = \begin{bmatrix} 45(0.2) & 0 \\ 0 & -30(0.2) \end{bmatrix} = \begin{bmatrix} 9 & 0 \\ 0 & -6 \end{bmatrix} = \begin{bmatrix} c_1 & 0 \\ 0 & c_2 \end{bmatrix}$$

12.51. Redo Problem 12.50, given $A = \begin{bmatrix} 6 & 3 \\ 3 & -2 \end{bmatrix}$

(a)
$$|A - cI| = \begin{vmatrix} 6-c & 3 \\ 3 & -2-c \end{vmatrix} = 0$$

$$c^2 - 4c - 21 = 0$$

$$c_1 = 7 \qquad c_2 = -3$$

With $c_1 > 0$ and $c_2 < 0$, A is indefinite.

(b) Using $c_1 = 7$ to form the first characteristic vector,

$$\begin{bmatrix} 6-7 & 3 \\ 3 & -2-7 \end{bmatrix} \begin{bmatrix} v_1 \\ v_2 \end{bmatrix} = \begin{bmatrix} -1 & 3 \\ 3 & -9 \end{bmatrix} \begin{bmatrix} v_1 \\ v_2 \end{bmatrix} = 0$$

$$v_1 = 3v_2$$

Normalizing,
$$(3v_2)^2 + v_2^2 = 1$$

$$9v_2^2 + v_2^2 = 1$$

$$10v_2^2 = 1$$

$$v_2 = \sqrt{0.1} \qquad \text{and} \qquad v_1 = 3v_2 = 3\sqrt{0.1}$$

Thus,
$$V_1 = \begin{bmatrix} 3\sqrt{0.1} \\ \sqrt{0.1} \end{bmatrix}$$

Using $c_2 = -3$,

$$\begin{bmatrix} 6-(-3) & 3 \\ 3 & -2-(-3) \end{bmatrix} \begin{bmatrix} v_1 \\ v_2 \end{bmatrix} = \begin{bmatrix} 9 & 3 \\ 3 & 1 \end{bmatrix} \begin{bmatrix} v_1 \\ v_2 \end{bmatrix} = 0$$

$$v_2 = -3v_1$$

Normalizing,
$$v_1^2 + (-3v_1)^2 = 1$$

$$10v_1^2 = 1$$

$$v_1 = \sqrt{0.1} \qquad \text{and} \qquad v_2 = -3v_1 = -3\sqrt{0.1}$$

Thus,
$$V_2 = \begin{bmatrix} \sqrt{0.1} \\ -3\sqrt{0.1} \end{bmatrix}$$

(c) Checking,
$$T'AT = \begin{bmatrix} 3\sqrt{0.1} & \sqrt{0.1} \\ \sqrt{0.1} & -3\sqrt{0.1} \end{bmatrix} \begin{bmatrix} 6 & 3 \\ 3 & -2 \end{bmatrix} \begin{bmatrix} 3\sqrt{0.1} & \sqrt{0.1} \\ \sqrt{0.1} & -3\sqrt{0.1} \end{bmatrix}$$

where
$$T'A = \begin{bmatrix} 21\sqrt{0.1} & 7\sqrt{0.1} \\ -3\sqrt{0.1} & 9\sqrt{0.1} \end{bmatrix}$$

and
$$T'AT = \begin{bmatrix} 21\sqrt{0.1} & 7\sqrt{0.1} \\ -3\sqrt{0.1} & 9\sqrt{0.1} \end{bmatrix} \begin{bmatrix} 3\sqrt{0.1} & \sqrt{0.1} \\ \sqrt{0.1} & -3\sqrt{0.1} \end{bmatrix} = \begin{bmatrix} 7 & 0 \\ 0 & -3 \end{bmatrix} = \begin{bmatrix} c_1 & 0 \\ 0 & c_2 \end{bmatrix}$$

12.52. Using the data from (a) Problem 12.50 and (b) Problem 12.51, prove that characteristic vectors are *orthonormal*, i.e. $V_i' V_i = 1$.

(a)
$$V_1' V_1 = [2\sqrt{0.2} \quad \sqrt{0.2}] \begin{bmatrix} 2\sqrt{0.2} \\ \sqrt{0.2} \end{bmatrix} = 4(0.2) + 0.2 = 1$$

$$V_2' V_2 = [\sqrt{0.2} \quad -2\sqrt{0.2}] \begin{bmatrix} \sqrt{0.2} \\ -2\sqrt{0.2} \end{bmatrix} = 0.2 + 4(0.2) = 1$$

(b)
$$V_1' V_1 = [3\sqrt{0.1} \quad \sqrt{0.1}] \begin{bmatrix} 3\sqrt{0.1} \\ \sqrt{0.1} \end{bmatrix} = 9(0.1) + 0.1 = 1$$

$$V_2' V_2 = [\sqrt{0.1} \quad -3\sqrt{0.1}] \begin{bmatrix} \sqrt{0.1} \\ -3\sqrt{0.1} \end{bmatrix} = 0.1 + 9(0.1) = 1$$

12.53. From Problem 12.52, prove that characteristic vectors are *orthogonal*, i.e. $V_i'V_j = 0$.

(a)
$$V_1'V_2 = [2\sqrt{0.2} \quad \sqrt{0.2}]\begin{bmatrix} \sqrt{0.2} \\ -2\sqrt{0.2} \end{bmatrix} = 2(0.2) - 2(0.2) = 0$$

(b)
$$V_1'V_2 = [3\sqrt{0.1} \quad \sqrt{0.1}]\begin{bmatrix} \sqrt{0.1} \\ -3\sqrt{0.1} \end{bmatrix} = 3(0.1) - 3(0.1) = 0$$

CONSTRUCTION OF DEMAND FUNCTIONS

12.54. Given the utility function and budget constraint

$$u = 3x + xy + 2y \qquad P_x x + P_y y = B$$

(a) Construct the Marshallian demand function.

(b) Estimate the demand for x at $P_x = 2, 4$,   when $B = 60$, $P_y = 4$.

(c) Estimate the demand for y at $P_y = 2, 4$,   when $B = 60$, $P_x = 4$.

(a) Forming the Lagrangian expression and taking the first partials,

$$U = xy + 3x + 2y + \lambda(P_x x + P_y y - B)$$

$$U_x = y + 3 + \lambda P_x = 0 \qquad U_y = x + 2 + \lambda P_y = 0 \qquad U_\lambda = P_x x + P_y y - B = 0$$

In matrix form,

$$\begin{bmatrix} 0 & 1 & P_x \\ 1 & 0 & P_y \\ P_x & P_y & 0 \end{bmatrix}\begin{bmatrix} x \\ y \\ \lambda \end{bmatrix} = \begin{bmatrix} -3 \\ -2 \\ B \end{bmatrix}$$

Using Cramer's rule, $|A| = -1(-P_x P_y) + P_x(P_y) = 2P_x P_y$.   Expanding along the third column here and below,

$$|A_1| = \begin{vmatrix} -3 & 1 & P_x \\ -2 & 0 & P_y \\ B & P_y & 0 \end{vmatrix} = P_x(-2P_y) - P_y(-3P_y - B)$$

$$\bar{x} = \frac{|A_1|}{|A|} = \frac{-2P_x P_y + 3P_y^2 + P_y B}{2P_x P_y} = \frac{B - 2P_x + 3P_y}{2P_x}$$

$$|A_2| = \begin{vmatrix} 0 & -3 & P_x \\ 1 & -2 & P_y \\ P_x & B & 0 \end{vmatrix} = P_x(B + 2P_x) - P_y(3P_x)$$

$$\bar{y} = \frac{|A_2|}{|A|} = \frac{BP_x + 2P_x^2 - 3P_x P_y}{2P_x P_y} = \frac{B + 2P_x - 3P_y}{2P_y}$$

Testing the second-order condition,

$$|\bar{H}| = \begin{vmatrix} 0 & 1 & P_x \\ 1 & 0 & P_y \\ P_x & P_y & 0 \end{vmatrix} = |A| = 2P_x P_y > 0$$

Thus $|\bar{H}|$ is negative definite and U is maximized.

(b) Given $B = 60$, $P_y = 4$,   and having found

$$x = \frac{B - 2P_x + 3P_y}{2P_x}$$

At $P_x = 2$,
$$x = \frac{60 - 2(2) + 3(4)}{2(2)} = \frac{68}{4} = 17$$

At $P_x = 4$,
$$x = \frac{60 - 2(4) + 3(4)}{2(4)} = \frac{64}{8} = 8$$

(c) At $B = 60$, $P_x = 4$,

$$y = \frac{B + 2P_x - 3P_y}{2P_y}$$

At $P_y = 2$,
$$y = \frac{60 + 2(4) - 3(2)}{2(2)} = \frac{62}{4} = 15.5$$

At $P_y = 4$,
$$y = \frac{60 + 2(4) - 3(4)}{2(4)} = \frac{56}{8} = 7$$

12.55. (a) Derive the Marshallian demand function given

$$u = 2x + 2xy + 5y \qquad P_x x + P_y y = B$$

(b) Estimate the demand for x and y when $B = 100$, $P_x = 2$, and $P_y = 10$.

(a)
$$U = 2xy + 2x + 5y + \lambda(P_x x + P_y y - B)$$
$$U_x = 2y + 2 + \lambda P_x = 0 \qquad U_y = 2x + 5 + \lambda P_y = 0 \qquad U_\lambda = P_x x + P_y y - B = 0$$

In matrix form,

$$\begin{bmatrix} 0 & 2 & P_x \\ 2 & 0 & P_y \\ P_x & P_y & 0 \end{bmatrix} \begin{bmatrix} x \\ y \\ \lambda \end{bmatrix} = \begin{bmatrix} -2 \\ -5 \\ B \end{bmatrix}$$

Solving by Cramer's rule, $|A| = -2(-P_x P_y) + P_x(2P_y) = 4P_x P_y$. Expanding along the third column,

$$|A_1| = P_x(-5P_y) - P_y(-2P_y - 2B)$$
$$\bar{x} = \frac{|A_1|}{|A|} = \frac{-5P_x P_y + 2P_y^2 + 2P_y B}{4P_x P_y} = \frac{2B - 5P_x + 2P_y}{4P_x}$$
$$|A_2| = P_x(2B + 5P_x) - P_y(2P_x)$$
$$\bar{y} = \frac{|A_2|}{|A|} = \frac{2P_x B + 5P_x^2 - 2P_x P_y}{4P_x P_y} = \frac{2B + 5P_x - 2P_y}{4P_y}$$

Testing the second-order condition,

$$|\bar{H}| = \begin{vmatrix} 0 & 2 & P_x \\ 2 & 0 & P_y \\ P_x & P_y & 0 \end{vmatrix} = |A| = 4P_x P_y > 0$$

$|\bar{H}|$ is negative definite and U is maximized.

(b) At $B = 100$, $P_x = 2$, and $P_y = 10$,

$$\bar{x} = \frac{2(100) - 5(2) + 2(10)}{4(2)} = 26.25 \qquad \bar{y} = \frac{2(100) + 5(2) - 2(10)}{4(10)} = 4.75$$

Chapter 13

Linear Programming: A Graphic Approach

13.1 GRAPHIC SOLUTIONS

The objective of linear programming is to determine the optimal allocation of scarce resources among competing products or activities. Economic situations frequently call for optimizing a function subject to several inequality constraints. For optimization subject to a single inequality constraint, the Lagrangian method (see Section 6.7) is relatively simple. When more than one inequality constraint is involved, linear programming is easier. If the constraints, however numerous, are limited to two variables, the easiest solution is the graphic approach. The graphic approach for maximization and minimization is demonstrated in Examples 1 and 2, respectively.

Example 1. A manufacturer produces tables (x_1) and desks (x_2). Each table requires 2.5 hours for assembling (A), 3 hours for buffing (B), and 1 hour for crating (C). Each desk requires 1 hour for assembling, 3 hours for buffing, and 2 hours for crating. The firm can use no more than 20 hours for assembling, 30 hours for buffing, and 16 hours for crating each week. Its profit margin is \$3 per table and \$4 per desk.

The graphic approach is used below to find the output mix that will maximize the firm's weekly profits. It is demonstrated in four easy steps.

1. Express the data as equations or inequalities. The function to be optimized, the *objective function*, becomes

$$\Pi = 3x_1 + 4x_2 \qquad (13.1)$$

subject to the constraints,

Constraint from A: $\qquad\qquad 2.5x_1 + x_2 \leq 20$

Constraint from B: $\qquad\qquad 3x_1 + 3x_2 \leq 30$

Constraint from C: $\qquad\qquad x_1 + 2x_2 \leq 16$

Nonnegativity constraint: $\qquad\qquad x_1, x_2 \geq 0$

The first three inequalities are *technical constraints* determined by the state of technology and the availability of inputs; the fourth is a *nonnegativity constraint* imposed on every problem to preclude negative (hence unacceptable) values from the solution.

2. Treat the three inequality constraints as equations, solve each one for x_2 in terms of x_1, and graph. Thus,

From A, $\qquad\qquad x_2 = 20 - 2.5x_1$

From B, $\qquad\qquad x_2 = 10 - x_1$

From C, $\qquad\qquad x_2 = 8 - 0.5x_1$

The graph of the original "less than or equal to" inequality will include all the points *on the line and to the left of it*. See Fig. 13-1(*a*). The nonnegativity constraints, $x_1, x_2 \geq 0$, are represented by the vertical and horizontal axes, respectively. The shaded area is called the *feasible region*. It contains all the points that satisfy all three constraints plus the nonnegativity constraints. x_1 and x_2 are called *decision* or *structural variables*.

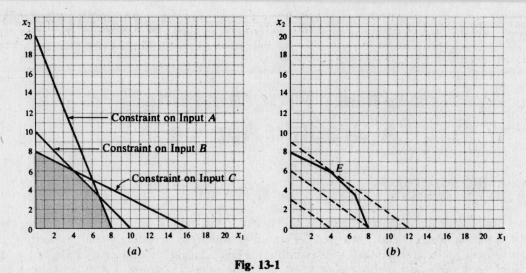

Fig. 13-1

3. To find the optimal solution within the feasible region, if it exists, graph the objective function as a series of isoprofit lines.   From (13.1),

$$x_2 = \frac{\Pi}{4} - \frac{3}{4}x_1$$

Thus, the isoprofit line has a slope of $-\frac{3}{4}$.   Drawing a series of (dashed) isoprofit lines allowing for larger and larger profits, we find the isoprofit line representing the largest possible profit touches the feasible region at E, where $\bar{x}_1 = 4$ and $\bar{x}_2 = 6$.   See Fig. 13-1(b).   Substituting in (13.1), $\bar{\Pi} = 3(4) + 4(6) = 36$.

4. Profit is maximized at the intersection of two constraints, called an *extreme point*.

13.2   THE EXTREME POINT THEOREM

The *extreme point theorem* states that if an optimal feasible value of the objective function exists, it will be found at one of the extreme (or corner) points of the boundary.   Notice that there are ten extreme points: (0,20), (0,10), (6,5), (10,0), (16,0), (0,8), (4,6), (7,3), (8,0), and (0,0) in Fig. 13-1(a), the last being the intersection of the nonnegativity constraints.   All are called *basic solutions*, but only the last five are basic *feasible* solutions since they violate none of the constraints.   Ordinarily only one of the basic feasible solutions will be optimal.   At (7,3), for instance, $\Pi = 3(7) + 4(3) = 31$,   which is lower than $\Pi = 36$ above.

Example 2.   A farmer wants to see that his herd gets the minimum daily requirement of three basic nutrients A, B, and C.   Daily requirements are 14 for A, 12 for B, and 18 for C.   Product y_1 has two units of A, and one unit each of B and C; product y_2 has one unit each of A and B, and three units of C.   The cost of y_1 is \$2 and the cost of y_2 is \$4.   The graphic method is used below to determine the least-cost combination of y_1 and y_2 that will fulfill all minimum requirements.   Following the procedure used in Example 1,

1. The objective function to be minimized is

$$c = 2y_1 + 4y_2 \qquad (13.2)$$

subject to the constraints

Constraint from A: $2y_1 + y_2 \geqslant 14$

Constraint from B: $y_1 + y_2 \geqslant 12$

Constraint from C: $y_1 + 3y_2 \geqslant 18$

Nonnegativity constraint: $y_1, y_2 \geqslant 0$

where the technical constraints read $\geqslant$ since minimum requirements must be fulfilled but may be exceeded.

2. Treat the inequalities as equations, solve each one for y_2 in terms of y_1, and graph. The graph of the original "greater than or equal to" inequality will include all the points *on the line and to the right of it*. See Fig. 13-2(*a*). The shaded area is the feasible region containing all the points that satisfy all three requirements plus the nonnegativity constraint.

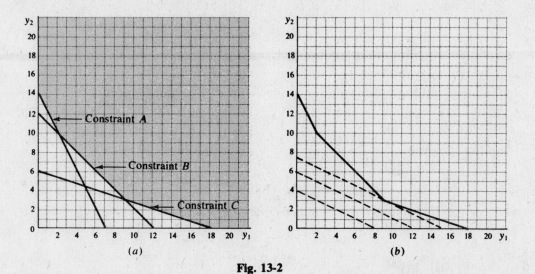

Fig. 13-2

3. To find the optimal solution, graph the objective function as a series of (dashed) isocost lines. From (*13.2*),

$$y_2 = \frac{c}{4} - \frac{1}{2} y_1$$

The lowest isocost line that will touch the feasible region is tangent at $\bar{y}_1 = 9$ and $\bar{y}_2 = 3$ in Fig. 13-2(*b*). Thus, $\bar{c} = 2(9) + 4(3) = 30$, which represents a cost lower than at any other feasible extreme point. For example, at (2,10), $c = 2(2) + 4(10) = 44$. [For minimization problems, (0,0) is not in the feasible region.]

13.3 SLACK AND SURPLUS VARIABLES

Problems involving more than two variables are beyond the scope of the two-dimensional graphic approach presented in the preceding sections. Because equations are needed, the system of linear inequalities must be converted to a system of linear equations. This is done by incorporating a separate slack or surplus variable (s_i) into each inequality (the ith constraint) in the system. See Example 3.

A "less than or equal to" inequality such as $5x_1 + 3x_2 \leq 30$ can be converted to an equation by *adding a slack variable* $s \geq 0$, such that $5x_1 + 3x_2 + s = 30$. If $5x_1 + 3x_2 = 30$, the slack variable $s = 0$. If $5x_1 + 3x_2 < 30$, s is a positive value equal to the difference between $5x_1 + 3x_2$ and 30.

A "greater than or equal to" inequality such as $4x_1 + 7x_2 \geq 60$ is converted to an equation by *subtracting a surplus variable* $s \geq 0$, such that $4x_1 + 7x_2 - s = 60$. If $4x_1 + 7x_2 = 60$, the surplus variable $s = 0$. If $4x_1 + 7x_2 > 60$, s is a positive value equal to the difference between $4x_1 + 7x_2$ and 60.

Example 3. Since the technical constraints in Example 1 all involve "less than or equal to" inequalities, slack variables are added, as follows:

$$2.5x_1 + x_2 + s_1 = 20 \qquad 3x_1 + 3x_2 + s_2 = 30 \qquad x_1 + 2x_2 + s_3 = 16$$

Expressed in matrix form,

$$\begin{bmatrix} 2.5 & 1 & 1 & 0 & 0 \\ 3 & 3 & 0 & 1 & 0 \\ 1 & 2 & 0 & 0 & 1 \end{bmatrix} \begin{bmatrix} x_1 \\ x_2 \\ s_1 \\ s_2 \\ s_3 \end{bmatrix} = \begin{bmatrix} 20 \\ 30 \\ 16 \end{bmatrix}$$

In contrast, the constraints in Example 2 are all "greater than or equal to." Hence surplus variables are subtracted.

$$2y_1 + y_2 - s_1 = 14 \qquad y_1 + y_2 - s_2 = 12 \qquad y_1 + 3y_2 - s_3 = 18$$

In matrix form,

$$\begin{bmatrix} 2 & 1 & -1 & 0 & 0 \\ 1 & 1 & 0 & -1 & 0 \\ 1 & 3 & 0 & 0 & -1 \end{bmatrix} \begin{bmatrix} y_1 \\ y_2 \\ s_1 \\ s_2 \\ s_3 \end{bmatrix} = \begin{bmatrix} 14 \\ 12 \\ 18 \end{bmatrix}$$

13.4 THE BASIS THEOREM

For a system of m consistent equations and n variables, where $n > m$, there will be an infinite number of solutions. But the number of extreme points is finite. The *basis theorem* states that for a system of m equations and n variables, where $n > m$, a solution in which at least $n - m$ variables equal zero is an extreme point. Thus by setting $n - m$ variables equal to zero and solving the m equations for the remaining m variables, an extreme point, or basic solution, can be found. The number of basic solutions is given by the formula

$$\frac{n!}{m!(n-m)!}$$

where $n!$ reads n *factorial*. See Example 4.

Example 4. Reducing the inequalities to equations in Example 3 left three equations and five variables. The calculations to determine (1) the number of variables that must be set equal to zero to find a basic solution and (2) the number of basic solutions that exist, are demonstrated below.

1. Since there are 3 equations and 5 variables, and $n - m$ variables must equal zero for a basic solution, $5 - 3$ or 2 variables must equal zero for a basic solution or extreme point.

2. Using the formula for the number of basic solutions, $n!/[m!(n-m)!]$ and substituting the given parameters,

$$\frac{5!}{3!(2)!}$$

where $5! = 5(4)(3)(2)(1)$. Thus,

$$\frac{5(4)(3)(2)(1)}{3(2)(1)(2)(1)} = 10$$

Example 5. Some basic solutions can be read directly from matrices without any algebraic manipulation. Refer to Example 3.

In the first matrix, setting $x_1 = 0$ and $x_2 = 0$ leaves an identity matrix for s_1, s_2, s_3. Thus, $s_1 = 20$, $s_2 = 30$, and $s_3 = 16$ is a basic solution which can be read directly from the matrix.

In the second matrix, setting $y_1 = 0$ and $y_2 = 0$ leaves a negative identity matrix for s_1, s_2, s_3. Thus, $s_1 = -14$, $s_2 = -12$, and $s_3 = -18$ is a basic solution. Note, however, that it is not a basic *feasible* solution since it violates the nonnegativity constraint.

Solved Problems

MATHEMATICAL EXPRESSION OF ECONOMIC PROBLEMS

13.1. A specialty steel manufacturer produces two types of steel (g_1 and g_2). Type 1 requires 2 hours of melting, 4 hours of rolling, and 10 hours of cutting. Type 2 requires 5 hours of melting, 1 hour of rolling, and 5 hours of cutting. Forty hours are available for melting, 20 for rolling, and 60 for cutting. The profit margin for type 1 is 24; for type 2 it is 8. Reduce the data to the equations and inequalities necessary to determine the output mix that will maximize profits.

Maximize $$\Pi = 24g_1 + 8g_2$$

subject to

$$2g_1 + 5g_2 \leq 40 \quad \text{melting constraint}$$
$$4g_1 + g_2 \leq 20 \quad \text{rolling constraint}$$
$$10g_1 + 5g_2 \leq 60 \quad \text{cutting constraint}$$
$$g_1, g_2 \geq 0$$

For a graphic solution, see Problem 13.9.

13.2. A manufacturer of pebbles for patios produces two different kinds: coarse (x_1) and fine (x_2). The coarse pebbles require 2 hours of crushing, 5 hours of sifting, and 8 hours of drying. The fine pebbles require 6 hours of crushing, 3 hours of sifting, and 2 hours of drying. The profit margin for the coarse pebbles is 40; for the fine pebbles it is 50. The manufacturer has available 36 hours for crushing, 30 hours for sifting, and 40 hours for drying.

   Determine the profit-maximizing output mix by reducing this data to equations and inequalities.

Maximize $$\Pi = 40x_1 + 50x_2$$

subject to

$$2x_1 + 6x_2 \leq 36 \quad \text{crushing constraint}$$
$$5x_1 + 3x_2 \leq 30 \quad \text{sifting constraint}$$
$$8x_1 + 2x_2 \leq 40 \quad \text{drying constraint}$$
$$x_1, x_2 \geq 0$$

For a graphic solution, see Problem 13.10.

13.3. A toy manufacturer makes two games: Bong (g_1) and Zong (g_2). The profit margin on Bong is 30; the profit margin on Zong is 20. Bong takes 6 hours of processing, 4 hours of assembly, and 5 hours of packaging. Zong takes 3 hours of processing, 6 hours of assembly, and 5 hours of packaging. If 54 hours are available for processing, 48 hours for assembling, and 50 hours for packaging, what is the profit-maximizing output mix in terms of equations and inequalities?

Maximize $$\Pi = 30g_1 + 20g_2$$

subject to

$$6g_1 + 3g_2 \leq 54 \quad \text{processing constraint}$$
$$4g_1 + 6g_2 \leq 48 \quad \text{assembling constraint}$$
$$5g_1 + 5g_2 \leq 50 \quad \text{packaging constraint}$$
$$g_1, g_2 \geq 0$$

13.4. A stereo manufacturer makes three types of stereos: standard (y_1), quality (y_2), and deluxe (y_3). His profit margin from each is 15, 20, and 24, respectively. The standard model requires 3 hours for wiring and 1 hour for encasing. The quality model requires 1 hour for wiring and 5 hours for encasing. The deluxe model requires 3 hours for wiring and 2 hours for encasing. If 120 hours are available for wiring and 60 hours for encasing, express the output mix that will maximize profits as equations and inequalities.

Maximize $\quad\quad\quad\quad\quad\quad\quad\quad\Pi = 15y_1 + 20y_2 + 24y_3$

subject to $\quad\quad\quad\quad\quad 3y_1 + y_2 + 3y_3 \leqslant 120 \quad\quad$ wiring constraint

$\quad\quad\quad\quad\quad\quad\quad\quad y_1 + 5y_2 + 2y_3 \leqslant 60 \quad\quad$ encasing constraint

$\quad\quad\quad\quad\quad\quad\quad\quad\quad\quad y_1, y_2, y_3 \geqslant 0$

13.5. A furniture manufacturer makes three types of end tables: provincial (x_1), contemporary (x_2), and modern (x_3). The provincial model requires 2 hours for sanding and 3 hours for staining. Its profit margin is 36. The contemporary model requires 2 hours for sanding and 2 hours for staining. Its profit margin is 28. The modern model requires 4 hours for sanding and 1 hour for staining, while contributing a profit margin of 32. How should production be allocated to maximize profits if 60 hours are available for sanding and 80 hours for staining?

Maximize $\quad\quad\quad\quad\quad\quad\quad\quad\Pi = 36x_1 + 28x_2 + 32x_3$

subject to $\quad\quad\quad\quad\quad 2x_1 + 2x_2 + 4x_3 \leqslant 60 \quad\quad$ sanding constraint

$\quad\quad\quad\quad\quad\quad\quad\quad 3x_1 + 2x_2 + x_3 \leqslant 80 \quad\quad$ staining constraint

$\quad\quad\quad\quad\quad\quad\quad\quad\quad\quad x_1, x_2, x_3 \geqslant 0$

13.6. A horticulturist wishes to mix fertilizer that will provide a minimum of 15 units of potash, 20 units of nitrates, and 24 units of phosphates. Brand 1 provides 3 units of potash, 1 unit of nitrates, and 3 units of phosphates; it costs \$120. Brand 2 provides 1 unit of potash, 5 units of nitrates, and 2 units of phosphates; it costs \$60. Express the least-cost combination of fertilizers that will meet the desired specifications as equations and inequalities.

Minimize $\quad\quad\quad\quad\quad\quad\quad\quad c = 120x_1 + 60x_2$

subject to $\quad\quad\quad\quad\quad 3x_1 + x_2 \geqslant 15 \quad\quad$ potash requirement

$\quad\quad\quad\quad\quad\quad\quad\quad x_1 + 5x_2 \geqslant 20 \quad\quad$ nitrate requirement

$\quad\quad\quad\quad\quad\quad\quad\quad 3x_1 + 2x_2 \geqslant 24 \quad\quad$ phosphate requirement

$\quad\quad\quad\quad\quad\quad\quad\quad\quad\quad x_1, x_2 \geqslant 0$

For a graphic solution, see Problem 13.14.

13.7. A health enthusiast wishes to have a minimum of 36 units of vitamin A each day, 28 units of vitamin C, and 32 units of vitamin D. Brand 1 costs \$3 and supplies 2 units of vitamin A, 2 units of vitamin C, and 8 units of vitamin D. Brand 2 costs \$4 and supplies 3 units of vitamin A, 2 units of vitamin C, and 2 units of vitamin D. In terms of equations and inequalities, what is the least-cost combination guaranteeing daily requirements?

Minimize $\quad\quad\quad\quad\quad\quad\quad\quad c = 3y_1 + 4y_2$

subject to $\quad\quad\quad\quad\quad 2y_1 + 3y_2 \geqslant 36 \quad\quad$ vitamin A requirement

$\quad\quad\quad\quad\quad\quad\quad\quad 2y_1 + 2y_2 \geqslant 28 \quad\quad$ vitamin C requirement

$\quad\quad\quad\quad\quad\quad\quad\quad 8y_1 + 2y_2 \geqslant 32 \quad\quad$ vitamin D requirement

$\quad\quad\quad\quad\quad\quad\quad\quad\quad\quad y_1, y_2 \geqslant 0$

For a graphic solution, see Problem 13.15.

13.8. Hank Burdue makes sure his chickens get at least 24 units of iron and 8 units of vitamins each day. Corn (x_1) provides 2 units of iron and 5 units of vitamins. Bone meal (x_2) provides 4 units of iron and 1 unit of vitamins. Millet (x_3) provides 2 units of iron and 1 unit of vitamins. How should the feeds be mixed to provide least-cost satisfaction of daily requirements if feed costs are \$40, \$20, and \$60, respectively.

Minimize $\quad\quad\quad\quad\quad\quad\quad\quad c = 40x_1 + 20x_2 + 60x_3$

subject to $\quad\quad\quad\quad\quad 2x_1 + 4x_2 + 2x_3 \geqslant 24 \quad\quad$ iron requirement

$\quad\quad\quad\quad\quad\quad\quad\quad 5x_1 + x_2 + x_3 \geqslant 8 \quad\quad$ vitamin requirement

$\quad\quad\quad\quad\quad\quad\quad\quad\quad\quad x_1, x_2, x_3 \geqslant 0$

GRAPHING THE SOLUTION

13.9.   Using the data below,

(1) graph the inequality constraints after solving each for g_2 in terms of g_1.

(2) Regraph and darken in the feasible region.

(3) Compute the slope of the objective function.   Set a ruler with this slope, move it to the point of contact with the objective function, and construct a dashed line.

(4) Read the critical values for g_1 and g_2 at the point of contact, and evaluate the objective function at these values.

From Problem 13.1,

Maximize $\Pi = 24g_1 + 8g_2$

subject to $2g_1 + 5g_2 \leqslant 40$ constraint 1

$4g_1 + g_2 \leqslant 20$ constraint 2

$10g_1 + 5g_2 \leqslant 60$ constraint 3

$g_1, g_2 \geqslant 0$

The inequality constraints should be graphed as shown in Fig. 13-3(a). For constraint 1, from $g_2 = 8 - \frac{2}{5}g_1$, when $g_1 = 0$, $g_2 = 8$; when $g_2 = 0$, $g_1 = 20$. Note that the nonnegativity constraints merely limit analysis to the first quadrant.

The feasible region is graphed in Fig. 13-3(b). From the objective function, $g_2 = \Pi/8 - 3g_1$; slope $= -3$. At the point of contact, $\bar{g}_1 = 4$ and $\bar{g}_2 = 4$. Thus, $\bar{\Pi} = 24(4) + 8(4) = 128$.

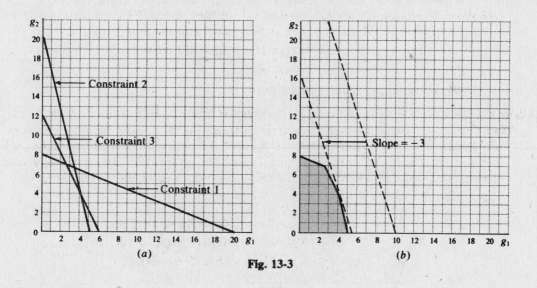

Fig. 13-3

13.10.   Redo Problem 13.9, using the following data derived in Problem 13.2:

Maximize $\Pi = 40x_1 + 50x_2$

subject to $2x_1 + 6x_2 \leqslant 36$ constraint 1

$5x_1 + 3x_2 \leqslant 30$ constraint 2

$8x_1 + 2x_2 \leqslant 40$ constraint 3

$x_1, x_2 \geqslant 0$

See Fig. 13-4(a) for the graphed constraints; Fig. 13-4(b) for the feasible region.

From the objective function, $x_2 = \Pi/50 - \frac{4}{5}x_1$; slope $= -\frac{4}{5}$. In Fig. 13-4(b), $\bar{x}_1 = 3$ and $\bar{x}_2 = 5$. Thus, $\bar{\Pi} = 40(3) + 50(5) = 370$.

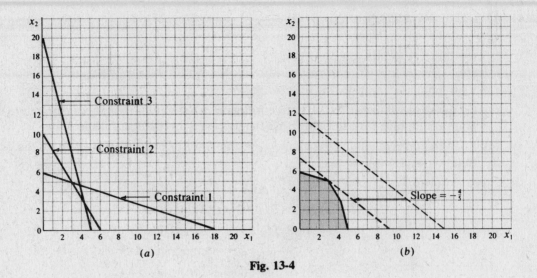

Fig. 13-4

13.11. Redo Problem 13.9 for the following data:

Maximize $$\Pi = 5x_1 + 3x_2$$

subject to $6x_1 + 2x_2 \leqslant 36$ constraint 1 $2x_1 + 4x_2 \leqslant 28$ constraint 3

   $5x_1 + 5x_2 \leqslant 40$ constraint 2 $x_1, x_2 \geqslant 0$

The inequalities are graphed in Fig. 13-5(a); the feasible region in Fig. 13-5(b).

From the objective function, $x_2 = \Pi/3 - \frac{5}{3}x_1$;   slope $= -\frac{5}{3}$.   In Fig. 13-5(b), $\bar{x}_1 = 5$ and $\bar{x}_2 = 3$.
Thus, $\bar{\bar{\Pi}} = 5(5) + 3(3) = 34$.

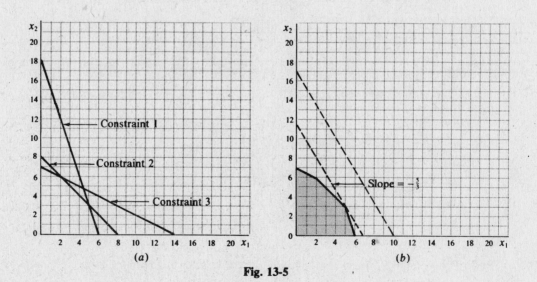

Fig. 13-5

13.12. Redo Problem 13.9, given the data below:

Maximize $$\Pi = 40y_1 + 30y_2$$

subject to $5y_1 + 2y_2 \leqslant 30$ constraint 1 $y_2 \leqslant 6$ constraint 3

   $2y_1 + 4y_2 \leqslant 28$ constraint 2 $y_1, y_2 \geqslant 0$

See Fig. 13-6(a) for the graphed constraints; Fig. 13-6(b) for the feasible region. From the critical values, $\bar{y}_1 = 4$, $\bar{y}_2 = 5$, and $\bar{\Pi} = 40(4) + 30(5) = 310$.

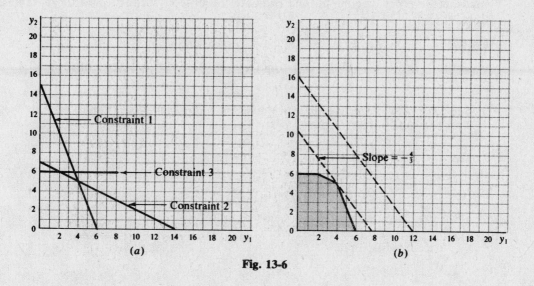

Fig. 13-6

13.13.   Redo Problem 13.9, given the following data:

Maximize $\Pi = 20x_1 + 10x_2$

subject to $4x_1 + 3x_2 \leqslant 48$ constraint 1 $x_1 \leqslant 9$ constraint 3

$3x_1 + 5x_2 \leqslant 60$ constraint 2 $x_1, x_2 \geqslant 0$

See Fig. 13.7.

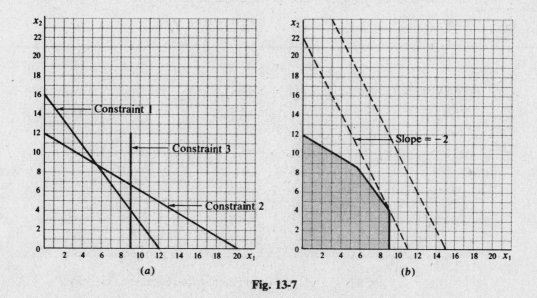

Fig. 13-7

From the critical values, $\bar{x}_1 = 9$, $\bar{x}_2 = 4$, and $\bar{\Pi} = 20(9) + 10(4) = 220$.

13.14. Using the data provided, (1) graph the inequality constraints after solving each for x_2 in terms of x_1. (2) Regraph and darken in the feasible region. (3) Compute the slope of the objective function, and construct a dashed line as in Problem 13.9. (4) Read the critical values at the point of contact, and evaluate the objective function at these values. From Problem 13.6,

Minimize $$c = 120x_1 + 60x_2$$

subject to $3x_1 + x_2 \geqslant 15$ constraint 1 $3x_1 + 2x_2 \geqslant 24$ constraint 3

$x_1 + 5x_2 \geqslant 20$ constraint 2 $x_1, x_2 \geqslant 0$

See Fig. 13-8. From the objective function, $x_2 = c/60 - 2x_1$; slope $= -2$. In Fig. 13-8(b), $\bar{x}_1 = 2$, $\bar{x}_2 = 9$, and $\bar{c} = 120(2) + 60(9) = 780$.

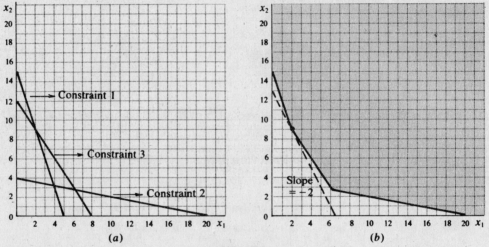

Fig. 13-8

13.15. Redo Problem 13.14, using the data derived in Problem 13.7.

Minimize $$c = 3y_1 + 4y_2$$

subject to $2y_1 + 3y_2 \geqslant 36$ constraint 1 $8y_1 + 2y_2 \geqslant 32$ constraint 3

$2y_1 + 2y_2 \geqslant 28$ constraint 2 $y_1, y_2 \geqslant 0$

See Fig. 13-9. From Fig. 13-9(b), $\bar{y}_1 = 6$ and $\bar{y}_2 = 8$; therefore, $\bar{c} = 3(6) + 4(8) = 50$.

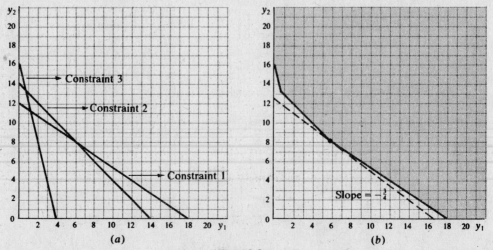

Fig. 13-9

13.16. Redo Problem 13.14, using the following data:

Minimize $$c = 30x_1 + 50x_2$$

subject to $6x_1 + 2x_2 \geqslant 30$ constraint 1 $5x_1 + 10x_2 \geqslant 60$ constraint 3

$3x_1 + 2x_2 \geqslant 24$ constraint 2 $x_1, x_2 \geqslant 0$

The constraints are graphed in Fig. 13-10(a); the feasible region in Fig. 13-10(b). In Fig. 13-10(b), the slope $= -\frac{3}{5}$; $\bar{x}_1 = 6$ and $\bar{x}_2 = 3$.   Thus, $\bar{c} = 30(6) + 50(3) = 330$.

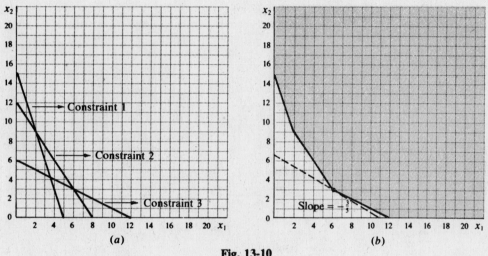

(a)   (b)

Fig. 13-10

13.17. Redo Problem 13.14, given the data below:

Minimize $$c = 4g_1 + 5g_2$$

subject to $4g_1 + 2g_2 \geqslant 28$ constraint 1 $g_2 \geqslant 4$ constraint 3

$2g_1 + 3g_2 \geqslant 30$ constraint 2 $g_1, g_2 \geqslant 0$

See Fig. 13-11.   In Fig. 13-11(b),   the slope $= -\frac{4}{5}$, $\bar{g}_1 = 3$,   and $\bar{g}_2 = 8$; $\bar{c} = 4(3) + 5(8) = 52$.

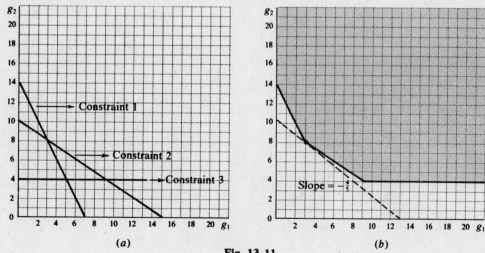

(a)   (b)

Fig. 13-11

13.18.   Redo Problem 13.14, using the following data:

Minimize $\qquad\qquad\qquad\qquad c = 2x_1 + 8x_2$

subject to $\quad\ 4x_1 + 4x_2 \geqslant 32 \quad$ constraint 1 $\qquad \bar{x}_1 \geqslant 2 \quad$ constraint 3

$\qquad\qquad\ \ x_1 + 5x_2 \geqslant 20 \quad$ constraint 2 $\qquad x_1, x_2 \geqslant 0$

See Fig. 13-12.

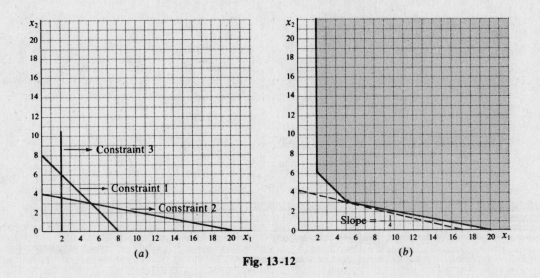

(a) $\qquad\qquad\qquad\qquad\qquad\qquad$ (b)

Fig. 13-12

From Fig. 13-12(b),   the slope $= -\frac{1}{4}$, $\bar{x}_1 = 5$, and $\bar{x}_2 = 3$.   Thus, $\bar{c} = 2(5) + 8(3) = 34$.

MULTIPLE OPTIMAL SOLUTIONS

13.19.   Redo Problem 13.14, given the following data:

Minimize $\qquad\qquad\qquad\qquad c = 4x_1 + 2x_2$

subject to $\quad\ 4x_1 + x_2 \geqslant 20 \quad$ constraint 1 $\qquad x_1 + 6x_2 \geqslant 18 \quad$ constraint 3

$\qquad\qquad\ \ 2x_1 + x_2 \geqslant 14 \quad$ constraint 2 $\qquad x_1, x_2 \geqslant 0$

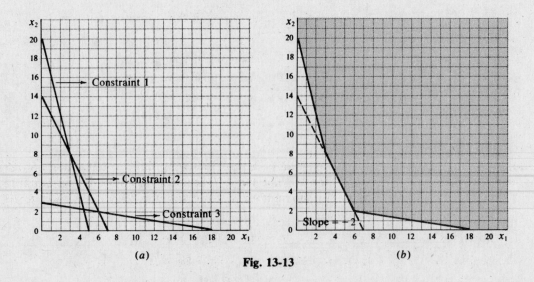

(a) $\qquad\qquad\qquad\qquad\qquad\qquad$ (b)

Fig. 13-13

In Fig. 13-13, with the isocost line tangent to the second constraint, there is no *unique* optimal feasible solution. Any point on the line between (3,8) and (6,2) will minimize the objective function subject to the constraints. Multiple optimal solutions occur whenever there is linear dependence between the objective function and one of the constraints. In this case, the objective function and constraint 2 are linearly dependent because one can be expressed as a multiple of the other. Notice that multiple optimal solutions do not contradict the extreme point theorem since the extreme points (3,8) and (6,2) are also included in the optimal solutions, to wit, $c = 4(3) + 2(8) = 28$ or $c = 4(6) + 2(2) = 28$.

SLACK AND SURPLUS VARIABLES

13.20. (*a*) Convert the inequality constraints in the following data to equations by adding slack variables or subtracting surplus variables, and (*b*) express the equations in matrix form.

Maximize
$$\Pi = 24y_1 + 8y_2$$

subject to
$$2y_1 + 5y_2 \leqslant 40 \qquad 10y_1 + 5y_2 \leqslant 60$$
$$4y_1 + y_2 \leqslant 20 \qquad y_1, y_2 \geqslant 0$$

(*a*) For "less than or equal to" inequalities, add slack variables. Thus,

$$2y_1 + 5y_2 + s_1 = 40 \qquad 4y_1 + y_2 + s_2 = 20 \qquad 10y_1 + 5y_2 + s_3 = 60$$

(*b*)
$$\begin{bmatrix} 2 & 5 & 1 & 0 & 0 \\ 4 & 1 & 0 & 1 & 0 \\ 10 & 5 & 0 & 0 & 1 \end{bmatrix} \begin{bmatrix} y_1 \\ y_2 \\ s_1 \\ s_2 \\ s_3 \end{bmatrix} = \begin{bmatrix} 40 \\ 20 \\ 60 \end{bmatrix}$$

13.21. Redo Problem 13.20 for the following:

Minimize
$$c = 60x_1 + 80x_2$$

subject to
$$2x_1 + 3x_2 \geqslant 36 \qquad 8x_1 + 2x_2 \geqslant 32$$
$$2x_1 + 2x_2 \geqslant 28 \qquad x_1, x_2 \geqslant 0$$

(*a*) For "greater than or equal to" inequalities, subtract surplus variables.

$$2x_1 + 3x_2 - s_1 = 36 \qquad 2x_1 + 2x_2 - s_2 = 28 \qquad 8x_1 + 2x_2 - s_3 = 32$$

(*b*)
$$\begin{bmatrix} 2 & 3 & -1 & 0 & 0 \\ 2 & 2 & 0 & -1 & 0 \\ 8 & 2 & 0 & 0 & -1 \end{bmatrix} \begin{bmatrix} x_1 \\ x_2 \\ s_1 \\ s_2 \\ s_3 \end{bmatrix} = \begin{bmatrix} 36 \\ 28 \\ 32 \end{bmatrix}$$

13.22. (*a*) Reduce the inequality constraints of the following data to equations and express in matrix form. Determine (*b*) the number of variables that must be set equal to zero to find a basic solution and (*c*) the number of basic solutions that exist. (*d*) Read the first basic solution from the matrix.

Minimize
$$c = 54g_1 + 48g_2 + 50g_3$$

subject to
$$6g_1 + 4g_2 + 5g_3 \geqslant 30 \qquad 3g_1 + 6g_2 + 5g_3 \geqslant 20 \qquad g_1, g_2, g_3 \geqslant 0$$

(a)
$$6g_1 + 4g_2 + 5g_3 - s_1 = 30$$
$$3g_1 + 6g_2 + 5g_3 - s_2 = 20$$

$$\begin{bmatrix} 6 & 4 & 5 & -1 & 0 \\ 3 & 6 & 5 & 0 & -1 \end{bmatrix} \begin{bmatrix} g_1 \\ g_2 \\ g_3 \\ s_1 \\ s_2 \end{bmatrix} = \begin{bmatrix} 30 \\ 20 \end{bmatrix}$$

(b) Since there are 2 equations and 5 variables, $n - m = 5 - 2 = 3$ variables must be set equal to zero for a basic solution.

(c) The number of solutions is

$$\frac{n!}{m!(n-m)!} = \frac{5!}{2!(3!)} = \frac{5(4)(3)(2)(1)}{2(1)(3)(2)(1)} = 10$$

(d) Setting $g_1 = g_2 = g_3 = 0$, the first basic solution is $\bar{s}_1 = -30$ and $\bar{s}_2 = -20$. Since both are negative, they would fail to constitute a basic *feasible* solution.

Chapter 14

Linear Programming: The Simplex Algorithm

14.1 SIMPLEX ALGORITHM: MAXIMIZATION

An *algorithm* is a set of rules or a systematic procedure for finding the solution to a problem. The *simplex algorithm* is a method (or computational procedure) for determining basic feasible solutions to a system of equations and testing the solutions for optimality. Since at least $n - m$ variables must equal zero for a basic solution, $n - m$ variables are set equal to zero in each step of the procedure, and a basic solution is found by solving the m equations for the remaining m variables. The algorithm moves from one basic feasible solution to another, always improving upon the previous solution, until the optimal solution is reached. Those variables set equal to zero at a particular step are called *not in the basis*, or *not in the solution*. Those not set equal to zero are called *in the basis*, *in the solution*, or, more simply, *basic variables*. The simplex method is demonstrated in Example 1 for maximization and in Example 3 for minimization.

Example 1. The simplex algorithm is used as follows to maximize profits, given

$$\Pi = 5x_1 + 3x_2$$

subject to the constraints,

$$6x_1 + 2x_2 \leq 36 \qquad 2x_1 + 4x_2 \leq 28$$
$$5x_1 + 5x_2 \leq 40 \qquad x_1, x_2 \geq 0$$

1. *The Initial Simplex Tableau (or Table)*

   i. Convert the inequalities to equations by adding slack variables.

   $$6x_1 + 2x_2 + s_1 = 36$$
   $$5x_1 + 5x_2 + s_2 = 40 \qquad\qquad (14.1)$$
   $$2x_1 + 4x_2 + s_3 = 28$$

   ii. Express the constraint equations in matrix form.

   $$\begin{bmatrix} 6 & 2 & 1 & 0 & 0 \\ 5 & 5 & 0 & 1 & 0 \\ 2 & 4 & 0 & 0 & 1 \end{bmatrix} \begin{bmatrix} x_1 \\ x_2 \\ s_1 \\ s_2 \\ s_3 \end{bmatrix} = \begin{bmatrix} 36 \\ 40 \\ 28 \end{bmatrix}$$

   iii. Set up an initial simplex tableau composed of the coefficient matrix of the constraint equations and the column vector of constants set above a row of *indicators* which are the negatives of the coefficients of the objective function and a zero coefficient for each slack variable. The constant column entry of the last row is also zero, corresponding to the value of the objective function at the origin (when $x_1 = x_2 = 0$).

Initial Simplex Tableau:

x_1	x_2	s_1	s_2	s_3	Constant
⑥	2	1	0	0	36
5	5	0	1	0	40
2	4	0	0	1	28
−5	−3	0	0	0	0

↑ Indicators

iv. The first basic feasible solution can be read from the initial simplex tableau. Setting $x_1 = 0$ and $x_2 = 0$, as in Chapter 13, Example 5, $s_1 = 36$, $s_2 = 40$, and $s_3 = 28$. At the first basic feasible solution, the objective function has a value of zero.

2. *The Pivot Element and a Change of Basis*

To increase the value of the objective function, a new basic solution is examined. To move to a new basic feasible solution, a new variable must be introduced into the basis and one of the variables formerly in the basis must be excluded. The process of selecting the variable to be included and the variable to be excluded is called *change of basis*.

i. The negative indicator with the largest absolute value determines the variable to enter the basis. Since −5 in the first (or x_1) column is the negative indicator with the largest absolute value, x_1 is brought into the basis. The x_1 column becomes the *pivot column* and is denoted by an arrow.

ii. The variable to be eliminated is determined by the smallest *displacement ratio*. Displacement ratios are found by dividing the elements of the constant column by the elements of the pivot column. The row with the smallest displacement ratio (i.e. the *pivot row*), ignoring ratios less than or equal to 0, determines the variable to leave the basis. Since $\frac{36}{6}$ provides the smallest ratio ($\frac{36}{6} < \frac{40}{5} < \frac{28}{2}$), row$_1$ is the pivot row. Since the unit vector with 1 in the first row appears under the column for s_1, s_1 leaves the basis. The *pivot element* is ⑥, the element at the intersection of the column of the variable entering the basis and the row associated with the variable leaving the basis (i.e. the element at the intersection of the pivot row and column).

3. *Pivoting*

Pivoting is the process of solving the m equations in terms of the m variables presently in the basis. Since only one new variable enters the basis at each step of the process, and the previous step always involves an identity matrix, pivoting simply involves converting the pivot element to 1 and all the other elements in the pivot column to zero, as in the Gaussian elimination method (see Section 10.12), as follows:

i. Multiply the pivot row by the reciprocal of the pivot element. In this case, multiply row$_1$ by $\frac{1}{6}$.

x_1	x_2	s_1	s_2	s_3	Constant
1	$\frac{1}{3}$	$\frac{1}{6}$	0	0	6
5	5	0	1	0	40
2	4	0	0	1	28
−5	−3	0	0	0	0

ii. Having reduced the pivot element to 1, clear the pivot column. Here subtract 5 times row$_1$ from row$_2$, 2 times row$_1$ from row$_3$, and add 5 times row$_1$ to row$_4$. This gives the second tableau.

Second Tableau:

x_1	x_2	s_1	s_2	s_3	Constant
1	$\frac{1}{3}$	$\frac{1}{6}$	0	0	6
0	$\frac{10}{3}$	$-\frac{5}{6}$	1	0	10
0	$\frac{10}{3}$	$-\frac{1}{3}$	0	1	16
0	$-\frac{4}{3}$	$\frac{5}{6}$	0	0	30

↑

The second basic feasible solution can be read directly from the second tableau. Setting $x_2 = 0$ and $s_1 = 0$, we are left with an identity matrix which gives $x_1 = 6$, $s_2 = 10$, and $s_3 = 16$. The last element in the last row (in this case, 30) is the value of the objective function at the second basic feasible solution.

4. *Optimization*

The objective function is maximized when there are no negative indicators in the last row. Changing the basis and pivoting continue according to the rules above until this is achieved. Since $-\frac{4}{3}$ in the second column is the only negative indicator, x_2 is introduced into the basis; column$_2$ becomes the pivot column. Dividing the constant column by the pivot column shows that the smallest ratio is in the second row. Thus, $\frac{10}{3}$ becomes the new pivot element. Since the unit vector with 1 in the second row is under s_2, s_2 will leave the basis. To pivot,

i. Multiply row$_2$ by $\frac{3}{10}$.

x_1	x_2	s_1	s_2	s_3	Constant
1	$\frac{1}{3}$	$\frac{1}{6}$	0	0	6
0	1	$-\frac{1}{4}$	$\frac{3}{10}$	0	3
0	$\frac{10}{3}$	$-\frac{1}{3}$	0	1	16
0	$-\frac{4}{3}$	$\frac{5}{6}$	0	0	30

ii. Then, subtract $\frac{1}{3}$ times row$_2$ from row$_1$, $\frac{10}{3}$ times row$_2$ from row$_3$, and add $\frac{4}{3}$ times row$_2$ to row$_4$, deriving the third tableau.

Third Tableau:

x_1	x_2	s_1	s_2	s_3	Constant
1	0	$\frac{1}{4}$	$-\frac{1}{10}$	0	5
0	1	$-\frac{1}{4}$	$\frac{3}{10}$	0	3
0	0	$\frac{1}{2}$	-1	1	6
0	0	$\frac{1}{2}$	$\frac{2}{5}$	0	34

The third basic feasible solution can be read directly from the tableau. With $s_1 = 0$ and $s_2 = 0$, $x_1 = 5$, $x_2 = 3$, and $s_3 = 6$. Since there are no negative indicators left in the last row, this is the optimal solution. The last element in the last row indicates that at $\bar{x}_1 = 5$, $\bar{x}_2 = 3$, $\bar{s}_1 = 0$, $\bar{s}_2 = 0$, and $\bar{s}_3 = 6$,   the objective function reaches a maximum at $\bar{\Pi} = 34$. With $\bar{s}_1 = 0$ and $\bar{s}_2 = 0$, from (*14.1*) there is no slack in the first two constraints and the first two inputs are all used up. With $\bar{s}_3 = 6$, however, 6 units of the third input remain unused. For a graphical representation, see Problem 13.11.

14.2 MARGINAL VALUE OR SHADOW PRICING

The value of the indicator under each slack variable in the final tableau expresses the marginal value or *shadow price* of the input associated with the variable, i.e. how much the objective function would change as a result of a one-unit increase in the input. Thus, in Example 1, profits would increase by $\frac{1}{2}$ unit or 50¢ for a one-unit change in the constant value of constraint 1; by $\frac{2}{5}$ or 40¢ for a one-unit increase in the constant value of constraint 2; and by 0 for a one-unit increase in the constant value of constraint 3. Since constraint 3 has a positive slack variable, it is not fully utilized in the optimal solution and its marginal value is zero (i.e. the addition of still another unit would add nothing to the profit function). The optimal value of the objective function will always equal the sum of the marginal value of each input times the amount available of each input.

Example 2. The answer to Example 1 can be checked by (1) substituting the critical values in both the objective function and the constraint equations in (*14.1*) and (2) evaluating the sum of the marginal values of the resources. All conditions must be satisfied for an optimum. Let A, B, C symbolize the constants in constraints 1, 2, 3.

1.
$$\Pi = 5x_1 + 3x_2 \qquad\qquad 5x_1 + 5x_2 + s_2 = 40$$
$$= 5(5) + 3(3) = 34 \qquad 5(5) + 5(3) + 0 = 40$$
$$6x_1 + 2x_2 + s_1 = 36 \qquad 2x_1 + 4x_2 + s_3 = 28$$
$$6(5) + 2(3) + 0 = 36 \qquad 2(5) + 4(3) + 6 = 28$$

2.
$$\Pi = MP_A(A) + MP_B(B) + MC_C(C) = \tfrac{1}{2}(36) + \tfrac{2}{5}(40) + 0(28) = 34$$

14.3 SIMPLEX ALGORITHM: MINIMIZATION

When the simplex algorithm is used to find a minimal value, the negative values generated by the surplus variables present a special problem. See Example 3. It is frequently easier to solve minimization problems by using the dual, which is treated in Chapter 15.   The reader, therefore, may prefer to read Chapter 15 first.

Example 3.   The simplex algorithm is used below to minimize costs.   The data is from Example 2 in Chapter 13, with x now used for y, where $c = 2x_1 + 4x_2$,   subject to the nutritional constraints

$$2x_1 + x_2 \geq 14 \qquad x_1 + 3x_2 \geq 18$$
$$x_1 + x_2 \geq 12 \qquad x_1, x_2 \geq 0$$

1. *The Initial Simplex Tableau* (*slightly modified*)

   i. Convert the inequalities to equations by subtracting surplus variables.

$$2x_1 + x_2 - s_1 = 14$$
$$x_1 + x_2 - s_2 = 12$$
$$x_1 + 3x_2 - s_3 = 18$$

   ii. Express the constraint equations in matrix form.

$$\begin{bmatrix} 2 & 1 & -1 & 0 & 0 \\ 1 & 1 & 0 & -1 & 0 \\ 1 & 3 & 0 & 0 & -1 \end{bmatrix} \begin{bmatrix} x_1 \\ x_2 \\ s_1 \\ s_2 \\ s_3 \end{bmatrix} = \begin{bmatrix} 14 \\ 12 \\ 18 \end{bmatrix}$$

   From the matrix it is clear that if $x_1 = 0$ and $x_2 = 0$,   as in the initial simplex tableau for maximization, the basic solution will not be feasible since $s_1 = -14$, $s_2 = -12$, $s_3 = -18$ and negative values are nonfeasible.   To overcome the problem, artificial variables must be introduced.

   iii. Add artificial variables.   An *artificial variable* ($A_i \geq 0$) is a dummy variable added for the specific purpose of generating an initial basic feasible solution.   It has no economic meaning.   A separate artificial variable is added for each original "greater than or equal to" inequality.   Thus,

$$\begin{bmatrix} 2 & 1 & -1 & 0 & 0 & 1 & 0 & 0 \\ 1 & 1 & 0 & -1 & 0 & 0 & 1 & 0 \\ 1 & 3 & 0 & 0 & -1 & 0 & 0 & 1 \end{bmatrix} \begin{bmatrix} x_1 \\ x_2 \\ s_1 \\ s_2 \\ s_3 \\ A_1 \\ A_2 \\ A_3 \end{bmatrix} = \begin{bmatrix} 14 \\ 12 \\ 18 \end{bmatrix} \qquad (14.2)$$

2. *The Initial Simplex Tableau Adapted for Minimization*

   i. Prepare the initial simplex tableau by setting the matrix of coefficients and the column vector of constants in (*14.2*) above a row of indicators which are the negatives of the coefficients of the objective function.   The objective function has zero coefficients for the surplus variables and M coefficients for the artificial variables, where M is an impossibly large number to insure that A will be excluded from the optimal solution.

x_1	x_2	s_1	s_2	s_3	A_1	A_2	A_3	Constant
2	1	-1	0	0	1	0	0	14
1	1	0	-1	0	0	1	0	12
1	3	0	0	-1	0	0	1	18
-2	-4	0	0	0	$-M$	$-M$	$-M$	

Indicators

ii. Then remove the M's from the columns of artificial variables by adding M times $(\text{row}_1 + \text{row}_2 + \text{row}_3)$ to row_4. This gives the initial tableau.

Initial Tableau:	x_1	x_2	s_1	s_2	s_3	A_1	A_2	A_3	Constant
	2	1	-1	0	0	1	0	0	14
	1	1	0	-1	0	0	1	0	12
	1	③	0	0	-1	0	0	1	18
	$4M-2$	$5M-4$	$-M$	$-M$	$-M$	0	0	0	$44M$
		↑							

The first basic feasible solution can be read directly from the initial tableau. Letting $x_1 = x_2 = s_1 = s_2 = s_3 = 0$, the first basic feasible solution is $A_1 = 14$, $A_2 = 12$, $A_3 = 18$, and the objective function is $44M$, an impossibly large number. To reduce costs, seek a change of basis.

3. The Pivot Element

i. For minimization, the largest positive indicator determines the pivot column and the variable to enter the basis. Since the last entry of the bottom row, $44M$, is not an indicator, $5M-4$ is the largest positive indicator. Thus, x_2 enters the basis and the x_2 column becomes the pivot column, as indicated by the arrow.

ii. The pivot row and the variable to leave the basis are determined by the smallest ratio resulting from division of the elements of the constant column by the elements of the pivot column, exactly as for maximization problems. Since $\frac{18}{3} = 6$ is the smallest resulting ratio, row_3 becomes the pivot row. A_3 leaves the basis since the unit vector with 1 in the third row is associated with A_3. The pivot element at the intersection of the pivot column and pivot row is ③.

4. Pivoting

i. Reduce the pivot element to 1 by multiplying row_3 by $\frac{1}{3}$.

2	1	-1	0	0	1	0	0	14
1	1	0	-1	0	0	1	0	12
$\frac{1}{3}$	1	0	0	$-\frac{1}{3}$	0	0	$\frac{1}{3}$	6
$4M-2$	$5M-4$	$-M$	$-M$	$-M$	0	0	0	$44M$

ii. Clear the pivot column by subtracting row_3 from row_1 and row_2, and $(5M-4)$ times row_3 from row_4.

Second Tableau:	x_1	x_2	s_1	s_2	s_3	A_1	A_2	A_3	Constant
	$\frac{5}{3}$	0	-1	0	$\frac{1}{3}$	1	0	$-\frac{1}{3}$	8
	$\frac{2}{3}$	0	0	-1	$\frac{1}{3}$	0	1	$-\frac{1}{3}$	6
	$\frac{1}{3}$	1	0	0	$-\frac{1}{3}$	0	0	$\frac{1}{3}$	6
	$\frac{7M-2}{3}$	0	$-M$	$-M$	$\frac{2M-4}{3}$	0	0	$\frac{-5M+4}{3}$	$14M+24$
	↑								

5. Reiteration

As long as a positive indicator remains, the process continues. The new pivot column becomes column_1; the new pivot row is row_1. Thus, x_1 enters the basis and A_1 leaves the basis. The pivot element is $\frac{5}{3}$.

i. Multiply row_1 by $\frac{3}{5}$.

1	0	$-\frac{3}{5}$	0	$\frac{1}{5}$	$\frac{3}{5}$	0	$-\frac{1}{5}$	$\frac{24}{5}$
$\frac{2}{3}$	0	0	-1	$\frac{1}{3}$	0	1	$-\frac{1}{3}$	6
$\frac{1}{3}$	1	0	0	$-\frac{1}{3}$	0	0	$\frac{1}{3}$	6
$\frac{7M-2}{3}$	0	$-M$	$-M$	$\frac{2M-4}{3}$	0	0	$\frac{-5M+4}{3}$	$14M+24$

  ii. Clear column$_1$ by subtracting $\frac{2}{3}$ row$_1$ from row$_2$, $\frac{1}{3}$ row$_1$ from row$_3$, and $[(7M-2)/3]$ row$_1$ from row$_4$, deriving the third tableau.

Third Tableau:

x_1	x_2	s_1	s_2	s_3	A_1	A_2	A_3	Constant
1	0	$-\frac{3}{5}$	0	$\frac{1}{5}$	$\frac{3}{5}$	0	$-\frac{1}{5}$	$\frac{24}{5}$
0	0	$\textcircled{\frac{2}{5}}$	-1	$\frac{1}{5}$	$-\frac{2}{5}$	1	$-\frac{1}{5}$	$\frac{14}{5}$
0	1	$\frac{1}{5}$	0	$-\frac{2}{5}$	$-\frac{1}{5}$	0	$\frac{2}{5}$	$\frac{22}{5}$
0	0	$\frac{2M-2}{5}$	$-M$	$\frac{M-6}{5}$	$\frac{-7M+2}{5}$	0	$\frac{-6M+6}{5}$	$\frac{14M+136}{5}$

$\uparrow$

6. Fourth Pivot

  i. Multiply row$_2$ by $\frac{5}{2}$.

1	0	$-\frac{3}{5}$	0	$\frac{1}{5}$	$\frac{3}{5}$	0	$-\frac{1}{5}$	$\frac{24}{5}$
0	0	1	$-\frac{5}{2}$	$\frac{1}{2}$	-1	$\frac{5}{2}$	$-\frac{1}{2}$	7
0	1	$\frac{1}{5}$	0	$-\frac{2}{5}$	$-\frac{1}{5}$	0	$\frac{2}{5}$	$\frac{22}{5}$
0	0	$\frac{2M-2}{5}$	$-M$	$\frac{M-6}{5}$	$\frac{-7M+2}{5}$	0	$\frac{-6M+6}{5}$	$\frac{14M+136}{5}$

  ii. Add $\frac{3}{5}$ row$_2$ to row$_1$, and subtract $\frac{1}{5}$ row$_2$ from row$_3$ and $[(2M-2)/5]$ row$_2$ from row$_4$.

Fourth Tableau:

x_1	x_2	s_1	s_2	s_3	A_1	A_2	A_3	Constant
1	0	0	$-\frac{3}{2}$	$\frac{1}{2}$	0	$\frac{3}{2}$	$-\frac{1}{2}$	9
0	0	1	$-\frac{5}{2}$	$\frac{1}{2}$	-1	$\frac{5}{2}$	$-\frac{1}{2}$	7
0	1	0	$\frac{1}{2}$	$-\frac{1}{2}$	0	$-\frac{1}{2}$	$\frac{1}{2}$	3
0	0	0	-1	-1	$-M$	$-M+1$	$-M+1$	30

     With all indicators negative, an optimal feasible solution has been reached. Isolating the identity matrix, and noting that the unit vectors for x_2 and s_1 are reversed, the optimal feasible solution is read directly from the fourth tableau: $\bar{x}_1 = 9$, $\bar{x}_2 = 3$, $\bar{s}_1 = 7$, $\bar{s}_2 = 0$, and $\bar{s}_3 = 0$. The value of the objective function is indicated by the last element of the last row, where $\bar{c} = 30$.

Several points are worth noticing:

1. With $\bar{s}_2 = \bar{s}_3 = 0$, the second and third requirements are exactly fulfilled. There is no surplus. With $\bar{s}_1 = 7$, the first requirement is overfulfilled by 7 units.

2. The absolute value of the indicators for the surplus variables gives the marginal value or shadow price of the constraint. With the indicator for s_1 equal to zero, a unit reduction in the first nutritional requirement would not reduce costs. However, a unit reduction in the second or third nutritional requirement would reduce costs by \$1, since the absolute value of the indicators for s_2 and s_3 is 1. As in the case of marginal value, total costs will equal the sum of the different requirements times their respective shadow prices.

3. The indicators of the artificial variables are all negative in the final tableau. This must always be true for an optimal solution.

4. The coefficient elements of the surplus variables (s_1, s_2, s_3) always equal the negative of the coefficient elements of their corresponding artificial variables (A_1, A_2, A_3). This must be true in each successive tableau and can be helpful in picking up mathematical errors.

5. An artificial variable will never appear in the basis of the final tableau if an optimal *feasible* solution has been reached.

     For a dual solution to the same problem, see Examples 4 and 5 in Chapter 15.

Example 4. The answer to Example 3 can be checked by (1) substituting the critical values in both the objective function and constraint equations, and (2) evaluating the sum of the marginal cost of resources. Let A, B, C symbolize the constants in constraints 1, 2, 3.

1. $c = 2x_1 + 4x_2$ $x_1 + x_2 - s_2 = 12$
      $= 2(9) + 4(3) = 30$ $9 + 3 - 0 = 12$
      $2x_1 + x_2 - s_1 = 14$ $x_1 + 3x_2 - s_3 = 18$
      $2(9) + 3 - 7 = 14$ $9 + 3(3) - 0 = 18$

2. $c = MC_A(A) + MC_B(B) + MC_C(C) = 0(14) + 1(12) + 1(18) = 30$

Solved Problems

MAXIMIZATION

14.1. Use the simplex algorithm to solve the following system of equations and inequalities. Determine the shadow prices of the inputs (or requirements) of the constraints.

Maximize $\qquad\qquad\qquad \Pi = 3y_1 + 4y_2$

subject to $\qquad\qquad 2.5\, y_1 + y_2 \leqslant 20 \qquad y_1 + 2y_2 \leqslant 16$

$\qquad\qquad\qquad\quad 3y_1 + 3y_2 \leqslant 30 \qquad y_1, y_2 \geqslant 0$

1. Construct the initial simplex tableau.

    i. Add slack variables to the constraints to make them equations.

    $\qquad 2.5\, y_1 + y_2 + s_1 = 20 \qquad 3y_1 + 3y_2 + s_2 = 30 \qquad y_1 + 2y_2 + s_3 = 16$

    ii. Express the equations in matrix form.

$$\begin{bmatrix} 2.5 & 1 & 1 & 0 & 0 \\ 3 & 3 & 0 & 1 & 0 \\ 1 & 2 & 0 & 0 & 1 \end{bmatrix} \begin{bmatrix} y_1 \\ y_2 \\ s_1 \\ s_2 \\ s_3 \end{bmatrix} = \begin{bmatrix} 20 \\ 30 \\ 16 \end{bmatrix}$$

    iii. Form the initial simplex tableau composed of the coefficient matrix of the constraint equations and the column vector of constants set above a row of indicators which are the negatives of the coefficients of the objective function with zero coefficients for the slack variables.

Initial Tableau:

y_1	y_2	s_1	s_2	s_3	Constant
$\frac{5}{2}$	1	1	0	0	20
3	3	0	1	0	30
1	②	0	0	1	16
−3	−4	0	0	0	0

Setting $y_1 = y_2 = 0$, the first basic feasible solution is $s_1 = 20$, $s_2 = 30$, and $s_3 = 16$. At the first basic feasible solution, $\Pi = 0$.

2. Change the basis. The negative indicator with the largest absolute value (arrow) determines the pivot column. The smallest displacement ratio arising from the division of the elements of the constant column by the elements of the pivot column determines the pivot row. Thus, ② becomes the pivot element, the element at the intersection of the pivot row and pivot column.

3. Pivot.

i. Convert the pivot element to 1 by multiplying row_3 by $\frac{1}{2}$.

$$
\begin{array}{ccccc|c}
\frac{5}{2} & 1 & 1 & 0 & 0 & 20 \\
3 & 3 & 0 & 1 & 0 & 30 \\
\frac{1}{2} & 1 & 0 & 0 & \frac{1}{2} & 8 \\
\hline
-3 & -4 & 0 & 0 & 0 & 0
\end{array}
$$

ii. Clear the pivot column by subtracting row_3 from row_1, 3 times row_3 from row_2, and adding 4 times row_3 to row_4.

Second Tableau:

	y_1	y_2	s_1	s_2	s_3	Constant
	2	0	1	0	$-\frac{1}{2}$	12
	③⃝ ($\frac{3}{2}$)	0	0	1	$-\frac{3}{2}$	6
	$\frac{1}{2}$	1	0	0	$\frac{1}{2}$	8
	-1	0	0	0	2	32

$\uparrow$

4. Change the basis and pivot again. $Column_1$ is the pivot column, row_2 the pivot row, and $\frac{3}{2}$ the pivot element.

i. Multiply row_2 by $\frac{2}{3}$.

$$
\begin{array}{ccccc|c}
2 & 0 & 1 & 0 & -\frac{1}{2} & 12 \\
1 & 0 & 0 & \frac{2}{3} & -1 & 4 \\
\frac{1}{2} & 1 & 0 & 0 & \frac{1}{2} & 8 \\
\hline
-1 & 0 & 0 & 0 & 2 & 32
\end{array}
$$

ii. Clear the pivot column by subtracting 2 times row_2 from row_1, $\frac{1}{2}$ times row_2 from row_3, and adding row_2 to row_4.

Final Tableau:

	y_1	y_2	s_1	s_2	s_3	Constant
	0	0	1	$-\frac{4}{3}$	$\frac{3}{2}$	4
	1	0	0	$\frac{2}{3}$	-1	4
	0	1	0	$-\frac{1}{3}$	1	6
	0	0	0	$\frac{2}{3}$	1	36

Since there are no negative indicators left, the final tableau has been reached. Correcting for the fact that the unit vectors of the identity matrix are out of order, $\bar{y}_1 = 4$, $\bar{y}_2 = 6$, $\bar{s}_1 = 4$, $\bar{s}_2 = 0$, $\bar{s}_3 = 0$, and $\bar{\Pi} = 36$. See Example 1 in Chapter 13 where x was used in place of y. The shadow prices of the inputs are 0, $\frac{2}{3}$, and 1, respectively.

14.2. Redo Problem 14.1 for the equation and inequalities specified below:

Maximize $$\Pi = 30x_1 + 24x_2 + 60x_3$$

subject to $6x_1 + 3x_2 + 5x_3 \leqslant 30$ $2x_1 + 2x_2 + 10x_3 \leqslant 50$ $x_1, x_2, x_3 \geqslant 0$

First, add the slack variables and express the constraint equations in matrix form.

$$6x_1 + 3x_2 + 5x_3 + s_1 = 30 \qquad 2x_1 + 2x_2 + 10x_3 + s_2 = 50$$

$$
\begin{bmatrix} 6 & 3 & 5 & 1 & 0 \\ 2 & 2 & 10 & 0 & 1 \end{bmatrix}
\begin{bmatrix} x_1 \\ x_2 \\ x_3 \\ s_1 \\ s_2 \end{bmatrix}
= \begin{bmatrix} 30 \\ 50 \end{bmatrix}
$$

Then, set up the initial tableau.

Initial Tableau:

x_1	x_2	x_3	s_1	s_2	Constant
6	3	⑤	1	0	30
2	2	⑩	0	1	50
-30	-24	-60	0	0	0

↑

Then, change the basis and pivot, as follows: (1) Multiply row$_2$ by $\frac{1}{10}$.

6	3	5	1	0	30
$\frac{1}{5}$	$\frac{1}{5}$	1	0	$\frac{1}{10}$	5
-30	-24	-60	0	0	0

(2) Clear the pivot column by subtracting 5 times row$_2$ from row$_1$ and adding 60 times row$_2$ to row$_3$.

Second Tableau:

x_1	x_2	x_3	s_1	s_2	Constant
⑤	2	0	1	$-\frac{1}{2}$	5
$\frac{1}{5}$	$\frac{1}{5}$	1	0	$\frac{1}{10}$	5
-18	-12	0	0	6	300

↑

Change the basis and pivot again, as follows: (1) Multiply row$_1$ by $\frac{1}{5}$.

1	$\frac{2}{5}$	0	$\frac{1}{5}$	$-\frac{1}{10}$	1
$\frac{1}{5}$	$\frac{1}{5}$	1	0	$\frac{1}{10}$	5
-18	-12	0	0	6	300

(2) Clear the pivot column by subtracting $\frac{1}{5}$ row$_1$ from row$_2$ and adding 18 times row$_1$ to row$_3$.

Third Tableau:

x_1	x_2	x_3	s_1	s_2	Constant
1	②/⑤	0	$\frac{1}{5}$	$-\frac{1}{10}$	1
0	$\frac{3}{25}$	1	$-\frac{1}{25}$	$\frac{3}{25}$	$\frac{24}{5}$
0	$-\frac{24}{5}$	0	$\frac{18}{5}$	$\frac{21}{5}$	318

↑

Pivot a third time. Note that x_1, which was brought into the basis by the second pivot, leaves the basis on the third pivot. It is possible for a variable to enter and leave; but note that optimal value of the objective function continues to increase.   (1) Multiply row$_1$ by $\frac{5}{2}$.

$\frac{5}{2}$	1	0	$\frac{1}{2}$	$-\frac{1}{4}$	$\frac{5}{2}$
0	$\frac{3}{25}$	1	$-\frac{1}{25}$	$\frac{3}{25}$	$\frac{24}{5}$
0	$-\frac{24}{5}$	0	$\frac{18}{5}$	$\frac{21}{5}$	318

(2) Subtract $\frac{3}{25}$ row$_1$ from row$_2$ and add $\frac{24}{5}$ row$_1$ to row$_3$.

Final Tableau:

x_1	x_2	x_3	s_1	s_2	Constant
$\frac{5}{2}$	1	0	$\frac{1}{2}$	$-\frac{1}{4}$	$\frac{5}{2}$
$-\frac{3}{10}$	0	1	$-\frac{1}{10}$	$\frac{3}{20}$	$\frac{9}{2}$
12	0	0	6	3	330

In this case, $\bar{x}_1 = 0$, $\bar{x}_2 = 2.5$, $\bar{x}_3 = 4.5$, $\bar{s}_1 = 0$, $\bar{s}_2 = 0$, and $\bar{\Pi} = 330$. The shadow price of the first input is 6; of the second, 3.

14.3. Redo Problem 14.1 for the data given below:

Maximize $\qquad\qquad\qquad\qquad \Pi = 60g_1 + 100g_2$

subject to $\qquad\qquad 4g_1 + 5g_2 \le 40 \qquad\qquad 2g_1 + 6g_2 \le 42$

$\qquad\qquad\qquad\qquad 6g_1 + 3g_2 \le 42 \qquad\qquad\qquad g_1, g_2 \ge 0$

1. Set up the initial tableau.

    Initial Tableau:

g_1	g_2	s_1	s_2	s_3	Constant
4	5	1	0	0	40
6	3	0	1	0	42
2	⑥	0	0	1	42
-60	-100	0	0	0	0

    $\qquad\qquad\qquad\qquad\qquad\quad \uparrow$

2. Change the basis and pivot.

    i. Multiply row$_3$ by $\frac{1}{6}$.

4	5	1	0	0	40
6	3	0	1	0	42
$\frac{1}{3}$	1	0	0	$\frac{1}{6}$	7
-60	-100	0	0	0	0

    ii. Clear the pivot column by subtracting 5 times row$_3$ from row$_1$, 3 times row$_3$ from row$_2$, and adding 100 times row$_3$ to row$_4$.

    Second Tableau:

g_1	g_2	s_1	s_2	s_3	Constant
⑦⁄₃	0	1	0	$-\frac{5}{6}$	5
5	0	0	1	$-\frac{1}{2}$	21
$\frac{1}{3}$	1	0	0	$\frac{1}{6}$	7
$-\frac{80}{3}$	0	0	0	$\frac{50}{3}$	700

    $\quad \uparrow$

3. Change the basis and pivot again.

    i. Multiply row$_1$ by $\frac{3}{7}$.

1	0	$\frac{3}{7}$	0	$-\frac{5}{14}$	$\frac{15}{7}$
5	0	0	1	$-\frac{1}{2}$	21
$\frac{1}{3}$	1	0	0	$\frac{1}{6}$	7
$-\frac{80}{3}$	0	0	0	$\frac{50}{3}$	700

    ii. Clear the pivot column by subtracting 5 times row$_1$ from row$_2$, $\frac{1}{3}$ times row$_1$ from row$_3$, and adding $\frac{80}{3}$ row$_1$ to row$_4$.

    Final Tableau:

g_1	g_2	s_1	s_2	s_3	Constant
1	0	$\frac{3}{7}$	0	$-\frac{5}{14}$	$\frac{15}{7}$
0	0	$-\frac{15}{7}$	1	$\frac{9}{7}$	$\frac{72}{7}$
0	1	$-\frac{1}{7}$	0	$\frac{4}{14}$	$\frac{44}{7}$
0	0	$\frac{80}{7}$	0	$\frac{50}{7}$	$\frac{5300}{7}$

Noting the position of the unit vectors in the identity matrix portion of the tableau,

$$\bar{g}_1 = \tfrac{15}{7} = 2.14 \qquad \bar{s}_1 = 0 \qquad \bar{s}_3 = 0$$

$$\bar{g}_2 = \tfrac{44}{7} = 6.29 \qquad \bar{s}_2 = \tfrac{72}{7} = 10.29 \qquad \bar{\Pi} = \tfrac{5300}{7} = 757.14$$

The shadow prices of the inputs are 11.43, 0, and 7.14, respectively.

MINIMIZATION

14.4. Use the simplex algorithm to solve the equation and inequalities given below. Determine the shadow price of each constraint requirement.

Minimize $\qquad c = 60x_1 + 80x_2$

subject to $\qquad 2x_1 + 3x_2 \geqslant 36 \qquad\qquad 8x_1 + 2x_2 \geqslant 32$

$\qquad\qquad\qquad 2x_1 + 2x_2 \geqslant 28 \qquad\qquad x_1, x_2 \geqslant 0$

1. Convert the inequalities to equations by subtracting surplus variables, and express in matrix form.

$$2x_1 + 3x_2 - s_1 = 36 \qquad 2x_1 + 2x_2 - s_2 = 28 \qquad 8x_1 + 2x_2 - s_3 = 32$$

$$\begin{bmatrix} 2 & 3 & -1 & 0 & 0 \\ 2 & 2 & 0 & -1 & 0 \\ 8 & 2 & 0 & 0 & -1 \end{bmatrix} \begin{bmatrix} x_1 \\ x_2 \\ s_1 \\ s_2 \\ s_3 \end{bmatrix} = \begin{bmatrix} 36 \\ 28 \\ 32 \end{bmatrix}$$

Since the first basic solution will be nonfeasible, add artificial variables.

$$\begin{bmatrix} 2 & 3 & -1 & 0 & 0 & 1 & 0 & 0 \\ 2 & 2 & 0 & -1 & 0 & 0 & 1 & 0 \\ 8 & 2 & 0 & 0 & -1 & 0 & 0 & 1 \end{bmatrix} \begin{bmatrix} x_1 \\ x_2 \\ s_1 \\ s_2 \\ s_3 \\ A_1 \\ A_2 \\ A_3 \end{bmatrix} = \begin{bmatrix} 36 \\ 28 \\ 32 \end{bmatrix}$$

2. Prepare for the initial tableau by setting the coefficient matrix and the column vector of constants over the negatives of the coefficients of the objective function which has zero coefficients for the surplus variables and artificially large coefficients (M) for the artificial variables.

x_1	x_2	s_1	s_2	s_3	A_1	A_2	A_3	Constant
2	3	−1	0	0	1	0	0	36
2	2	0	−1	0	0	1	0	28
8	2	0	0	−1	0	0	1	32
−60	−80	0	0	0	−M	−M.	−M	

Clear the artificial variable columns of M by adding M times (row$_1$ + row$_2$ + row$_3$) to row$_4$ to obtain the initial tableau.

Initial Tableau:

x_1	x_2	s_1	s_2	s_3	A_1	A_2	A_3	Constant
2	3	−1	0	0	1	0	0	36
2	2	0	−1	0	0	1	0	28
⑧	2	0	0	−1	0	0	1	32
$12M-60$	$7M-80$	−M	−M	−M	0	0	0	$96M$

3. Choose the pivot element and pivot. Since $12M - 60$ is the largest positive indicator and $\frac{32}{8}$ is the smallest displacement ratio, 8 is the pivot element.

i. Multiply row$_3$ by $\frac{1}{8}$.

2	3	-1	0	0	1	0	0	36
2	2	0	-1	0	0	1	0	28
1	$\frac{1}{4}$	0	0	$-\frac{1}{8}$	0	0	$\frac{1}{8}$	4
$12M-60$	$7M-80$	$-M$	$-M$	$-M$	0	0	0	$96M$

ii. Subtract 2 times row$_3$ from row$_1$, 2 times row$_3$ from row$_2$, and $(12M-60)$ times row$_3$ from row$_4$.

Second Tableau:	x_1	x_2	s_1	s_2	s_3	A_1	A_2	A_3	Constant
	0	$\frac{5}{2}$	-1	0	$\frac{1}{4}$	1	0	$-\frac{1}{4}$	28
	0	$\frac{3}{2}$	0	-1	$\frac{1}{4}$	0	1	$-\frac{1}{4}$	20
	1	$\frac{1}{4}$	0	0	$-\frac{1}{8}$	0	0	$\frac{1}{8}$	4
	0	$4M-65$	$-M$	$-M$	$\frac{M-15}{2}$	0	0	$\frac{-3M+15}{2}$	$48M+240$
		$\uparrow$							

4. Pivot again.

i. Multiply row$_1$ by $\frac{2}{5}$.

0	1	$-\frac{2}{5}$	0	$\frac{1}{10}$	$\frac{2}{5}$	0	$-\frac{1}{10}$	$\frac{56}{5}$
0	$\frac{3}{2}$	0	-1	$\frac{1}{4}$	0	1	$-\frac{1}{4}$	20
1	$\frac{1}{4}$	0	0	$-\frac{1}{8}$	0	0	$\frac{1}{8}$	4
0	$4M-65$	$-M$	$-M$	$\frac{M-15}{2}$	0	0	$\frac{-3M+15}{2}$	$48M+240$

ii. Subtract $\frac{3}{2}$ row$_1$ from row$_2$, $\frac{1}{4}$ row$_1$ from row$_3$, and $(4M-65)$ row$_1$ from row$_4$.

Third Tableau:	x_1	x_2	s_1	s_2	s_3	A_1	A_2	A_3	Constant
	0	1	$-\frac{2}{5}$	0	$\frac{1}{10}$	$\frac{2}{5}$	0	$-\frac{1}{10}$	$\frac{56}{5}$
	0	0	$\frac{3}{5}$	-1	$\frac{1}{10}$	$-\frac{3}{5}$	1	$-\frac{1}{10}$	$\frac{16}{5}$
	1	0	$\frac{1}{10}$	0	$-\frac{3}{20}$	$-\frac{1}{10}$	0	$\frac{3}{20}$	$\frac{6}{5}$
	0	0	$\frac{3M}{5}-26$	$-M$	$\frac{M}{10}-1$	$\frac{-8M}{5}+26$	0	$\frac{-11M}{10}+1$	$\frac{16M}{5}+968$
			$\uparrow$						

5. Pivot a third time. Recalling that negative elements cannot be used in the denominator of the displacement ratio, $\frac{3}{5}$ is the new pivot element.

i. Multiply row$_2$ by $\frac{5}{3}$.

0	1	$-\frac{2}{5}$	0	$\frac{1}{10}$	$\frac{2}{5}$	0	$-\frac{1}{10}$	$\frac{56}{5}$
0	0	1	$-\frac{5}{3}$	$\frac{1}{6}$	-1	$\frac{5}{3}$	$-\frac{1}{6}$	$\frac{16}{3}$
1	0	$\frac{1}{10}$	0	$-\frac{3}{20}$	$-\frac{1}{10}$	0	$\frac{3}{20}$	$\frac{6}{5}$
0	0	$\frac{3M}{5}-26$	$-M$	$\frac{M}{10}-1$	$\frac{-8M}{5}+26$	0	$\frac{-11M}{10}+1$	$\frac{16M}{5}+968$

ii. Add $\frac{2}{5}$ times row$_2$ to row$_1$ and subtract $\frac{1}{10}$ times row$_2$ from row$_3$ and $[(3M/5)-26]$ times row$_2$ from row$_4$.

Fourth Tableau:	x_1	x_2	s_1	s_2	s_3	A_1	A_2	A_3	Constant
	0	1	0	$-\frac{2}{3}$	$\frac{1}{6}$	0	$\frac{2}{3}$	$-\frac{1}{6}$	$\frac{40}{3}$
	0	0	1	$-\frac{5}{3}$	$\frac{1}{6}$	-1	$\frac{5}{3}$	$-\frac{1}{6}$	$\frac{16}{3}$
	1	0	0	$\frac{1}{6}$	$-\frac{1}{6}$	0	$-\frac{1}{6}$	$\frac{1}{6}$	$\frac{2}{3}$
	0	0	0	$-\frac{130}{3}$	$\frac{10}{3}$	$-M$	$-M+\frac{130}{3}$	$-M-\frac{10}{3}$	$\frac{3320}{3}$
					$\uparrow$				

6. Pivot a fourth time.

    i. Multiply row$_2$ by 6.

$$
\begin{array}{ccccccccc|c}
0 & 1 & 0 & -\frac{2}{3} & \frac{1}{6} & 0 & & \frac{2}{3} & -\frac{1}{6} & \frac{40}{3} \\
0 & 0 & 6 & -10 & 1 & -6 & & 10 & -1 & 32 \\
1 & 0 & 0 & \frac{1}{6} & -\frac{1}{6} & 0 & & -\frac{1}{6} & \frac{1}{6} & \frac{2}{3} \\
\hline
0 & 0 & 0 & -\frac{130}{3} & \frac{10}{3} & -M & -M+\frac{130}{3} & -M-\frac{10}{3} & & \frac{3320}{3}
\end{array}
$$

    ii. Subtract $\frac{1}{6}$ times row$_2$ from row$_1$, add $\frac{1}{6}$ times row$_2$ to row$_3$, and subtract $\frac{10}{3}$ times row$_2$ from row$_4$.

Final Tableau:

x_1	x_2	s_1	s_2	s_3	A_1	A_2	A_3	Constant
0	1	-1	1	0	1	-1	0	8
0	0	6	-10	1	-6	10	-1	32
1	0	1	$-\frac{3}{2}$	0	-1	$\frac{3}{2}$	0	6
0	0	-20	-10	0	$-M+20$	$-M+10$	$-M$	1000

Noting the order of the unit vectors, $\bar{x}_1 = 6$, $\bar{x}_2 = 8$, $\bar{s}_1 = \bar{s}_2 = 0$, $\bar{s}_3 = 32$, and $\bar{c} = 1000$. The shadow prices of the constraint requirements are 20, 10, and 0, respectively.

14.5.   Redo Problem 14.4 for the data specified below:

Minimize $c = 36x_1 + 40x_2 + 28x_3$

subject to $6x_1 + 5x_2 + 2x_3 \geqslant 5$ $2x_1 + 5x_2 + 4x_3 \geqslant 3$ $x_1, x_2, x_3 \geqslant 0$

1. Convert the constraint inequalities to equations by subtracting surplus variables and add the necessary artificial variables.

$$6x_1 + 5x_2 + 2x_3 - s_1 + A_1 = 5 \qquad 2x_1 + 5x_2 + 4x_3 - s_2 + A_2 = 3$$

2. Prepare for the initial tableau.

x_1	x_2	x_3	s_1	s_2	A_1	A_2	Constant
6	5	2	-1	0	1	0	5
2	5	4	0	-1	0	1	3
-36	-40	-28	0	0	$-M$	$-M$	

Clear the artificial variable columns to obtain the initial tableau.

Initial Tableau:

x_1	x_2	x_3	s_1	s_2	A_1	A_2	Constant
6	5	2	-1	0	1	0	5
2	⑤	4	0	-1	0	1	3
$8M-36$	$10M-40$	$6M-28$	$-M$	$-M$	0	0	$8M$

3. Pivot by multiplying row$_2$ by $\frac{1}{5}$. Having reduced the pivot element to 1, subtract 5 times row$_2$ from row$_1$, and $(10M-40)$ times row$_2$ from row$_3$.

Second Tableau:

x_1	x_2	x_3	s_1	s_2	A_1	A_2	Constant
④	0	-2	-1	1	1	-1	2
$\frac{2}{5}$	1	$\frac{4}{5}$	0	$-\frac{1}{5}$	0	$\frac{1}{5}$	$\frac{3}{5}$
$4M-20$	0	$-2M+4$	$-M$	$M-8$	0	$-2M+8$	$2M+24$

4. Pivot again. Multiply row_1 by $\frac{1}{4}$. Then having reduced the pivot element to 1, subtract $\frac{2}{3}$ times row_1 from row_2, and $(4M - 20)$ times row_1 from row_3.

Final Tableau:

x_1	x_2	x_3	s_1	s_2	A_1	A_2	Constant
1	0	$-\frac{1}{2}$	$-\frac{1}{4}$	$\frac{1}{4}$	$\frac{1}{4}$	$-\frac{1}{4}$	$\frac{1}{2}$
0	1	1	$\frac{1}{10}$	$-\frac{3}{10}$	$-\frac{1}{10}$	$\frac{3}{10}$	$\frac{2}{5}$
0	0	-6	-5	-3	$-M+5$	$-M+3$	34

Thus, $\bar{x}_1 = \frac{1}{2}$, $\bar{x}_2 = \frac{2}{3}$, $\bar{x}_3 = 0$, $\bar{s}_1 = 0$, $\bar{s}_2 = 0$, and $\bar{c} = 34$. With $\bar{s}_1 = \bar{s}_2 = 0$, the constraints are exactly fulfilled and there is no surplus. The shadow prices of the constraint requirements are 5 and 3, respectively.

14.6. Redo Problem 14.4 for the following data:

Minimize $\qquad\qquad c = 20y_1 + 30y_2 + 16y_3$

subject to $\qquad 2.5y_1 + 3y_2 + y_3 \geqslant 3 \qquad y_1 + 3y_2 + 2y_3 \geqslant 4 \qquad y_1, y_2, y_3 \geqslant 0$

1. Set up the initial tableau.

Initial Tableau:

y_1	y_2	y_3	s_1	s_2	A_1	A_2	Constant
$\frac{5}{2}$	③	1	-1	0	1	0	3
1	3	2	0	-1	0	1	4
$\frac{7M}{2}-20$	$6M-30$	$3M-16$	$-M$	$-M$	0	0	$7M$

$\qquad\qquad\qquad\qquad\uparrow$

2. Pivot.

y_1	y_2	y_3	s_1	s_2	A_1	A_2	Constant
$\frac{5}{6}$	1	$\frac{1}{3}$	$-\frac{1}{3}$	0	$\frac{1}{3}$	0	1
$-\frac{3}{2}$	0	①	1	-1	-1	1	1
$\frac{-3M}{2}+5$	0	$M-6$	$M-10$	$-M$	$-2M+10$	0	$M+30$

$\qquad\qquad\qquad\qquad\qquad\uparrow$

3. Pivot again.

y_1	y_2	y_3	s_1	s_2	A_1	A_2	Constant
$\frac{4}{3}$	1	0	$-\frac{2}{3}$	$\frac{1}{3}$	$\frac{2}{3}$	$-\frac{1}{3}$	$\frac{2}{3}$
$-\frac{3}{2}$	0	1	1	-1	-1	1	1
-4	0	0	-4	-6	$-M+4$	$-M+6$	36

Thus, $\bar{y}_1 = 0$, $\bar{y}_2 = \frac{2}{3}$, $\bar{y}_3 = 1$, $\bar{s}_1 = 0$, $\bar{s}_2 = 0$, and $\bar{c} = 36$. The shadow prices of the constraint requirements are 4 and 6, respectively.

MULTIPLE OPTIMAL SOLUTIONS

14.7. Use the simplex algorithm to solve the following equation and inequalities:

Minimize $\qquad\qquad c = 4x_1 + 2x_2$

subject to $\qquad\qquad 4x_1 + x_2 \geqslant 20 \qquad x_1 + 6x_2 \geqslant 18$

$\qquad\qquad\qquad\qquad 2x_1 + x_2 \geqslant 14 \qquad\quad x_1, x_2 \geqslant 0$

1. Set up the initial tableau.

Initial Tableau:

x_1	x_2	s_1	s_2	s_3	A_1	A_2	A_3	Constant
4	1	-1	0	0	1	0	0	20
2	1	0	-1	0	0	1	0	14
1	⑥	0	0	-1	0	0	1	18
$7M-4$	$8M-2$	$-M$	$-M$	$-M$	0	0	0	$52M$

$\uparrow$

2. Pivot. Multiply row$_3$ by $\frac{1}{6}$. Having reduced the pivot element to 1, subtract row$_3$ from row$_1$ and from row$_2$, and $(8M-2)$ times row$_3$ from row$_4$, deriving the second tableau.

Second Tableau:

x_1	x_2	s_1	s_2	s_3	A_1	A_2	A_3	Constant
$\frac{23}{6}$	0	-1	0	$\frac{1}{6}$	1	0	$-\frac{1}{6}$	17
$\frac{11}{6}$	0	0	-1	$\frac{1}{6}$	0	1	$-\frac{1}{6}$	11
$\frac{1}{6}$	1	0	0	$-\frac{1}{6}$	0	0	$\frac{1}{6}$	3
$\frac{17M-11}{3}$	0	$-M$	$-M$	$\frac{M-1}{3}$	0	0	$\frac{-4M+1}{3}$	$28M+6$

$\uparrow$

3. Pivot again. Multiply row$_1$ by $\frac{6}{23}$. Then subtract $\frac{11}{6}$ times row$_1$ from row$_2$, $\frac{1}{6}$ times row$_1$ from row$_3$, and $[(17M-11)/3]$ times row$_1$ from row$_4$.

Third Tableau:

x_1	x_2	s_1	s_2	s_3	A_1	A_2	A_3	Constant
1	0	$-\frac{6}{23}$	0	$\frac{1}{23}$	$\frac{6}{23}$	0	$-\frac{1}{23}$	$\frac{102}{23}$
0	0	⑪⁄₂₃	-1	$\frac{2}{23}$	$-\frac{11}{23}$	1	$-\frac{2}{23}$	$\frac{66}{23}$
0	1	$\frac{1}{23}$	0	$-\frac{4}{23}$	$-\frac{1}{23}$	0	$\frac{4}{23}$	$\frac{52}{23}$
0	0	$\frac{11M-22}{23}$	$-M$	$\frac{2M-4}{23}$	$\frac{-34M+22}{23}$	0	$\frac{-25M+4}{23}$	$\frac{66M+512}{23}$

$\uparrow$

4. Pivot a third time. Multiply row$_2$ by $\frac{23}{11}$. Then add $\frac{6}{23}$ times row$_2$ to row$_1$, subtract $\frac{1}{23}$ times row$_2$ from row$_3$, and $[(11M-22)/23]$ times row$_2$ from row$_4$.

Final Tableau:

x_1	x_2	s_1	s_2	s_3	A_1	A_2	A_3	Constant
1	0	0	$-\frac{6}{11}$	$\frac{1}{11}$	0	$\frac{6}{11}$	$-\frac{1}{11}$	6
0	0	1	$-\frac{23}{11}$	$\frac{2}{11}$	-1	$\frac{23}{11}$	$-\frac{2}{11}$	6
0	1	0	$\frac{1}{11}$	$-\frac{2}{11}$	0	$-\frac{1}{11}$	$\frac{2}{11}$	2
0	0	0	-2	0	$-M$	$-M+2$	$-M$	28

From the final tableau, $\bar{x}_1 = 6$, $\bar{x}_2 = 2$, $\bar{s}_1 = 6$, $\bar{s}_2 = 0$, $\bar{s}_3 = 0$, and $\bar{c} = 28$. But s_3, which is not in the final basis, has a zero indicator. This means that the variable s_3 can be included in the basis without affecting the value of the objective function. Since the objective function is already at an optimum, it follows that there must be more than one optimal solution. Whenever a variable not in the basis has a zero indicator, the objective function must have multiple optimal solutions. For a graphic solution to this problem, see Problem 13.19.

Chapter 15

Linear Programming: The Dual

15.1 THE DUAL

Every maximization (minimization) problem in linear programming has a corresponding minimization (maximization) problem. The original problem is called the *primal*; the corresponding problem is called the *dual*. The relationship between the two can best be expressed through the use of the parameters they share in common. [For similar properties in Lagrangian functions, see Problems 12.30(c) and 12.31(c).]

Example 1. Given an original or primal problem,

Maximize

$$\Pi = g_1 x_1 + g_2 x_2 + g_3 x_3$$

subject to

$$a_{11} x_1 + a_{12} x_2 + a_{13} x_3 \leqslant b_1$$

$$a_{21} x_1 + a_{22} x_2 + a_{23} x_3 \leqslant b_2$$

$$a_{31} x_1 + a_{32} x_2 + a_{33} x_3 \leqslant b_3$$

$$x_1, x_2, x_3 \geqslant 0$$

the related dual problem is

Minimize

$$c = b_1 z_1 + b_2 z_2 + b_3 z_3$$

subject to

$$a_{11} z_1 + a_{21} z_2 + a_{31} z_3 \geqslant g_1$$

$$a_{12} z_1 + a_{22} z_2 + a_{32} z_3 \geqslant g_2$$

$$a_{13} z_1 + a_{23} z_2 + a_{33} z_3 \geqslant g_3$$

$$z_1, z_2, z_3 \geqslant 0$$

15.2 RULES OF TRANSFORMATION TO OBTAIN THE DUAL

In the formulation of a dual from a primal problem,

1. The direction of optimization is reversed. Maximization in the primal becomes minimization in the dual and vice versa.

2. The inequality signs of the technical constraints are reversed, but the nonnegativity restraint on decision variables is always maintained.

3. The rows of the coefficient matrix of the constraints in the primal are transposed into columns for the coefficient matrix of constraints in the dual.

4. The row vector of coefficients in the objective function in the primal is transposed into a column vector of constants for the dual constraints.

5. The column vector of constants from the primal constraints is transposed into a row vector of coefficients for the objective function in the dual.

6. Primal decision variables (x_j) are replaced by dual decision variables (z_i).

302

Example 2. The dual of the linear programming problem,

Maximize $\Pi = 5x_1 + 3x_2$

subject to
$$6x_1 + 2x_2 \leqslant 36$$
$$5x_1 + 5x_2 \leqslant 40$$
$$2x_1 + 4x_2 \leqslant 28 \qquad x_1, x_2 \geqslant 0$$

is

Minimize $c = 36z_1 + 40z_2 + 28z_3$

subject to $\quad 6z_1 + 5z_2 + 2z_3 \geqslant 5 \qquad 2z_1 + 5z_2 + 4z_3 \geqslant 3 \qquad z_1, z_2, z_3 \geqslant 0$

Example 3. The dual of the linear programming problem,

Minimize $c = 20z_1 + 30z_2 + 16z_3$

subject to $\quad 2.5z_1 + 3z_2 + z_3 \geqslant 3$

$$z_1 + 3z_2 + 2z_3 \geqslant 4 \qquad z_1, z_2, z_3 \geqslant 0$$

is

Maximize $\Pi = 3x_1 + 4x_2$

subject to $\quad 2.5x_1 + x_2 \leqslant 20 \qquad x_1 + 2x_2 \leqslant 16$

$$3x_1 + 3x_2 \leqslant 30 \qquad x_1, x_2 \geqslant 0$$

Note that if the dual of the dual were taken here or in the examples above, the corresponding primal would be obtained.

15.3 THE DUAL THEOREMS

Two dual theorems are of extreme importance for linear programming. They state

1. The optimal value of the primal objective function always equals the optimal value of the dual objective function, provided an optimal feasible solution exists.

2. If in the optimal feasible solution

    i. a decision variable in the primal program has a nonzero value, the corresponding slack (or surplus) variable in the dual program must have an optimal value of zero.

    ii. a slack (or surplus) variable in the primal has a nonzero value, the corresponding decision variable in the dual program must have an optimal value of zero.

Example 4. Given the following linear programming problem,

Maximize: $\Pi = 14x_1 + 12x_2 + 18x_3$

subject to
$$2x_1 + x_2 + x_3 \leqslant 2$$
$$x_1 + x_2 + 3x_3 \leqslant 4 \qquad x_1, x_2, x_3 \geqslant 0$$

The dual theorems are used as follows to find the optimal value of (1) the primal objective function and (2) the primal decision variables. The dual program is

Minimize $c = 2z_1 + 4z_2$

subject to
$$2z_1 + z_2 \geqslant 14$$
$$z_1 + z_2 \geqslant 12$$
$$z_1 + 3z_2 \geqslant 18 \qquad z_1, z_2 \geqslant 0$$

1. The optimal values of the dual program were found graphically in Chapter 13, Example 2: $\bar{z}_1 = 9$, $\bar{z}_2 = 3$, and $\bar{c} = 30$. With the optimal value of the dual equal to 30, it is clear from the first dual theorem that $\bar{\Pi}$ must also equal 30.

2. To find the optimal values of the primal decision variables, convert the inequality constraints to equations by adding slack variables to the primal (I) and subtracting surplus variables from the dual (II). To distinguish the slack variables of the primal from the surplus variables of the dual, s_i is used for the primal and t_i for the dual.

$$\text{I.} \quad 2x_1 + x_2 + x_3 + s_1 = 2$$
$$x_1 + x_2 + 3x_3 + s_2 = 4 \tag{15.1}$$

$$\text{II.} \quad 2z_1 + z_2 - t_1 = 14$$
$$z_1 + z_2 - t_2 = 12 \tag{15.2}$$
$$z_1 + 3z_2 - t_3 = 18$$

Substitute $\bar{z}_1 = 9$, $\bar{z}_2 = 3$ in (15.2) to find $\bar{t}_1$, $\bar{t}_2$, $\bar{t}_3$ as follows:

$$2(9) + 3 - t_1 = 14 \qquad \bar{t}_1 = 7$$
$$9 + 3 - t_2 = 12 \qquad \bar{t}_2 = 0$$
$$9 + 3(3) - t_3 = 18 \qquad \bar{t}_3 = 0$$

With the surplus variables ($\bar{t}_2$, $\bar{t}_3$) for the second and third dual constraints equal to zero, according to the second dual theorem, the corresponding primal decision variables ($\bar{x}_2, \bar{x}_3$) must be non-zero. With $\bar{t}_1 \neq 0$, the corresponding decision variable $\bar{x}_1$ must equal zero. Therefore $\bar{x}_1 = 0$.

The second dual theorem also states that if the optimal dual decision variables ($\bar{z}_1, \bar{z}_2$) do not equal zero in the dual, the corresponding primal slack variables ($\bar{s}_1, \bar{s}_2$) in the primary must equal zero. Substituting $\bar{s}_1 = \bar{s}_2 = 0$ in (15.1), and recalling that $\bar{x}_1 = 0$, (15.1) reduces to

$$x_2 + x_3 = 2 \qquad x_2 + 3x_3 = 4$$

Solving simultaneously by Cramer's rule, $\bar{x}_2 = 1$ and $\bar{x}_3 = 1$. Thus the optimal decision variables are $\bar{x}_1 = 0$, $\bar{x}_2 = 1$, and $\bar{x}_3 = 1$, which can easily be checked by substitution into the objective function: $\Pi = 14(0) + 12(1) + 18(1) = 30$.

Example 5. The dual in Example 4 was solved as a primal in Chapter 14, Example 3. Converting x_i to z_i and s_i to t_i for the dual form, the final tableau reads

Final Tableau:

z_1	z_2	t_1	t_2	t_3	A_1	A_2	A_3	Constant
1	0	0	$-\frac{3}{2}$	$\frac{1}{2}$	0	$\frac{3}{2}$	$-\frac{1}{2}$	9
0	0	1	$-\frac{5}{2}$	$\frac{1}{2}$	-1	$\frac{5}{2}$	$-\frac{1}{2}$	7
0	1	0	$\frac{1}{2}$	$-\frac{1}{2}$	0	$-\frac{1}{2}$	$\frac{1}{2}$	3
0	0	0	-1	-1	$-M$	$-M+1$	$-M+1$	30

The final tableau of the dual can be used to determine the optimal values of (1) the primal objective function and (2) the primal decision variables.

1. The optimal value of the primal objective function, just as the optimal value for the dual objective function, is indicated by the last element of the last row: 30.

2. The optimal values for the primal decision variables can also be read directly from the dual tableau. They are given by the absolute values of the indicators in the columns under the corresponding dual surplus variables. Since t_1 is the surplus variable for the first dual constraint and it corresponds to x_1 in the primal, $\bar{x}_1 = 0$. Since t_2 is the dual surplus variable for the second constraint and it corresponds to x_2 in the primal, $\bar{x}_2 = 1$. Similarly, $\bar{x}_3 = 1$. The dual indicators whose absolute values give the optimal values of the primal decision variables are boxed. The indicators in the artificial variable columns have no economic meaning.

15.4 ADVANTAGES OF THE DUAL

From the relationship between the primal and dual, as outlined above, it is clear that the optimal value of the objective function can be found through either the primal or dual. Because of the complementary relationship between decision variables in one program and slack (or surplus) variables in the other, solution of one program provides full solution of the other. This is beneficial because

1. It enables minimization problems to be solved in terms of maximization, which is frequently easier.

2. For primal problems with three decision variables, the dual reduces the program to two decision variables (see Example 3), which can then be graphed.

Example 6. The dual is used below to find the optimal values of the minimization problem in Example 3.

The dual of the minimization problem in Example 3 is graphed in Chapter 13, Example 1, where $\bar{z}_1 = 4$, $\bar{z}_2 = 6$, and $\bar{\Pi} = 36$. Costs for the primal problem in Example 3 are minimized at $\bar{c} = 36$. Using the techniques in Example 4, $\bar{x}_1 = 0$, $\bar{x}_2 = \frac{2}{3}$, and $\bar{x}_3 = 1$. For similar solutions, see Problems 15.1–15.4. For solution by the simplex algorithm, see Problem 15.8.

15.5 SHADOW PRICES IN THE DUAL

When using the dual to solve the primal, the marginal value or shadow price of the ith resource in the primal is given directly by the corresponding decision variable in the objective function of the dual. Thus, z_i in the dual gives the shadow price of the ith resource in the primal. The optimal value of the objective function will always equal the sum of resources times their respective shadow prices. In terms of the parameters of Example 1,

$$\Pi = \sum_{i=1}^{3} b_i z_i = b_1 z_1 + b_2 z_2 + b_3 z_3 \tag{15.3}$$

Example 7. The final tableau for the dual in Example 5 is used to determine the shadow prices of the primal resources in Example 4, as follows: Correcting for the order of unit vectors in the identity-matrix portion of the final dual tableau, $\bar{z}_1 = 9$ and $\bar{z}_2 = 3$. Since z_1 and z_2 are the dual decision variables corresponding to the two resources in the primal constraints, the shadow price of the first resource is 9; the shadow price of the second resource is 3.

These shadow prices can be used to determine the optimal value of the primal objective function. From the primal constraints in Example 4, there are 2 units of the first resource and 4 units of the second. Multiplying the available resources by their shadow prices and adding the products, $\Pi = 2(9) + 4(3) = 30$. Compare.

15.6 SHADOW PRICES AND THE LAGRANGIAN MULTIPLIER

Shadow prices serve the same function as Lagrangian multipliers (see Section 5.9). They estimate the change in the objective function arising from a small change in the constraint. This is easily demonstrated by taking the partial derivatives of (15.3) with respect to the constraints b_1, b_2, and b_3:

$$\frac{\partial \Pi}{\partial b_1} = z_1 \qquad \frac{\partial \Pi}{\partial b_2} = z_2 \qquad \frac{\partial \Pi}{\partial b_3} = z_3 \tag{15.4}$$

From (15.4) it is clear that for a one-unit change in the constraints b_1, b_2, or b_3, the objective function will change by z_1, z_2, or z_3, respectively.

Solved Problems

SOLVING THE PRIMAL THROUGH THE DUAL

15.1. For the following primal problem, (a) formulate the dual. (b) Solve the dual graphically. Then use the dual solution to find the optimal values of (c) the primal objective function and (d) the primal decision variables.

$$\text{Minimize} \quad c = 40x_1 + 20x_2 + 60x_3$$

$$\text{subject to} \quad 2x_1 + 4x_2 + 10x_3 \geq 24$$

$$5x_1 + x_2 + 5x_3 \geq 8 \qquad x_1, x_2, x_3 \geq 0$$

(a) The dual is

$$\text{Maximize} \quad \Pi = 24z_1 + 8z_2$$

$$\text{subject to} \quad 2z_1 + 5z_2 \leq 40$$

$$4z_1 + z_2 \leq 20$$

$$10z_1 + 5z_2 \leq 60 \qquad z_1, z_2 \geq 0$$

(b) The dual was solved graphically as a primal in Problem 13.9. Converting x_i to z_i, $\bar{z}_1 = 4$, $\bar{z}_2 = 4$, and $\bar{\Pi} = 128$.

(c) With $\bar{\Pi} = 128$, $\bar{c} = 128$.

(d) To find the primal decision variables (x_1, x_2, x_3) from the dual decision variables (z_1, z_2), first convert the primal (I) and dual (II) inequalities to equations.

$$\text{I.} \quad 2x_1 + 4x_2 + 10x_3 - s_1 = 24 \qquad \text{II.} \quad 2z_1 + 5z_2 + t_1 = 40$$

$$5x_1 + x_2 + 5x_3 - s_2 = 8 \qquad\qquad 4z_1 + z_2 + t_2 = 20$$

$$10z_1 + 5z_2 + t_3 = 60$$

Then substitute $\bar{z}_1 = \bar{z}_2 = 4$ into the dual constraint equations to solve for the slack variables.

$$2(4) + 5(4) + t_1 = 40 \qquad \bar{t}_1 = 12$$

$$4(4) + 4 + t_2 = 20 \qquad \bar{t}_2 = 0$$

$$10(4) + 5(4) + t_3 = 60 \qquad \bar{t}_3 = 0$$

With $\bar{t}_1 \neq 0$, the corresponding primal decision variable $\bar{x}_1$ must equal zero. With $\bar{t}_2 = \bar{t}_3 = 0$, $\bar{x}_2, \bar{x}_3 \neq 0$.

Since the optimal values of the dual decision variables (z_1, z_2) do not equal zero, the corresponding primal surplus variables (s_1, s_2) must equal zero. Incorporating the knowledge that $\bar{x}_1 = \bar{s}_1 = \bar{s}_2 = 0$ into the primal constraint equations,

$$2(0) + 4x_2 + 10x_3 - 0 = 24 \qquad 5(0) + x_2 + 5x_3 - 0 = 8$$

Solved simultaneously, $\bar{x}_2 = 4$ and $\bar{x}_3 = 0.8$. Thus the primal decision variables are $\bar{x}_1 = 0$, $\bar{x}_2 = 4$, and $\bar{x}_3 = 0.8$.

15.2. Redo Problem 15.1 for the following primal problem:

$$\text{Minimize} \quad c = 36x_1 + 30x_2 + 40x_3$$

$$\text{subject to} \quad 2x_1 + 5x_2 + 8x_3 \geq 40$$

$$6x_1 + 3x_2 + 2x_3 \geq 50 \qquad x_1, x_2, x_3 \geq 0$$

(a) Maximize

$$\Pi = 40z_1 + 50z_2$$

$$\text{subject to} \quad 2z_1 + 6z_2 \leq 36$$

$$5z_1 + 3z_2 \leq 30$$

$$8z_1 + 2z_2 \leq 40 \qquad z_1, z_2 \geq 0$$

(b) The equivalent of the dual was solved graphically in Problem 13.10: $\bar{z}_1 = 3$, $\bar{z}_2 = 5$, and $\bar{\Pi} = 370$.

(c) With $\bar{\Pi} = 370$, $\bar{c} = 370$.

(d)   I. $2x_1 + 5x_2 + 8x_3 - s_1 = 40$ II. $2z_1 + 6z_2 + t_1 = 36$

$6x_1 + 3x_2 + 2x_3 - s_2 = 50$ $5z_1 + 3z_2 + t_2 = 30$

$8z_1 + 2z_2 + t_3 = 40$

Substituting $\bar{z}_1 = 3$ and $\bar{z}_2 = 5$ in II,

$$2(3) + 6(5) + t_1 = 36 \qquad \bar{t}_1 = 0$$
$$5(3) + 3(5) + t_2 = 30 \qquad \bar{t}_2 = 0$$
$$8(3) + 2(5) + t_3 = 40 \qquad \bar{t}_3 = 6$$

With $\bar{t}_1 = \bar{t}_2 = 0$, $\bar{x}_1, \bar{x}_2 \neq 0$. Since $\bar{t}_3 \neq 0$, $\bar{x}_3 = 0$. With $\bar{z}_1, \bar{z}_2 \neq 0$, $\bar{s}_1 = \bar{s}_2 = 0$. Substituting in I,

$$2x_1 + 5x_2 + 8(0) - 0 = 40 \qquad 6x_1 + 3x_2 + 2(0) - 0 = 50$$

Thus, $\bar{x}_1 = 5.42$, $\bar{x}_2 = 5.83$, and $\bar{x}_3 = 0$.

15.3. Redo Problem 15.1, given the following linear programming problem:

Maximize $\qquad\qquad\qquad \Pi = 15x_1 + 20x_2 + 24x_3$

subject to $\qquad\qquad 3x_1 + x_2 + 3x_3 \leq 120$

$x_1 + 5x_2 + 2x_3 \leq 60 \qquad x_1, x_2, x_3 \geq 0$

(a) Minimize $\qquad\qquad\qquad c = 120z_1 + 60z_2$

subject to $\qquad\qquad 3z_1 + z_2 \geq 15$

$z_1 + 5z_2 \geq 20$

$3z_1 + 2z_2 \geq 24 \qquad z_1, z_2 \geq 0$

(b) The equivalent of the dual was solved in Problem 13.14: $\bar{z}_1 = 2$, $\bar{z}_2 = 9$, and $\bar{c} = 780$.

(c) With $\bar{c} = 780$, $\bar{\Pi} = 780$.

(d)   I. $3x_1 + x_2 + 3x_3 + s_1 = 120$ II. $3z_1 + z_2 - t_1 = 15$

$x_1 + 5x_2 + 2x_3 + s_2 = 60$ $z_1 + 5z_2 - t_2 = 20$

$3z_1 + 2z_2 - t_3 = 24$

Substituting $\bar{z}_1 = 2$ and $\bar{z}_2 = 9$ in II,

$$3(2) + 9 - t_1 = 15 \qquad \bar{t}_1 = 0$$
$$2 + 5(9) - t_2 = 20 \qquad \bar{t}_2 = 27$$
$$3(2) + 2(9) - t_3 = 24 \qquad \bar{t}_3 = 0$$

With $\bar{t}_1 = \bar{t}_3 = 0$, $\bar{x}_1, \bar{x}_3 \neq 0$. Since $\bar{t}_2 \neq 0$, $\bar{x} = 0$. With $\bar{z}_1, \bar{z}_2 \neq 0$, $\bar{s}_1 = \bar{s}_2 = 0$. Substituting in I,

$$3x_1 + 0 + 3x_3 + 0 = 120 \qquad x_1 + 5(0) + 2x_3 + 0 = 60$$

Thus, $\bar{x}_1 = 20$, $\bar{x}_2 = 0$, and $\bar{x}_3 = 20$.

15.4. Redo Problem 15.1, given the linear programming problem below:

Maximize $\qquad\qquad\qquad \Pi = 36x_1 + 28x_2 + 32x_3$

subject to $\qquad\qquad 2x_1 + 2x_2 + 8x_3 \leq 3$

$3x_1 + 2x_2 + 2x_3 \leq 4 \qquad x_1, x_2, x_3 \geq 0$

(a) Minimize
$$c = 3z_1 + 4z_2$$

subject to
$$2z_1 + 3z_2 \geq 36$$
$$2z_1 + 2z_2 \geq 28$$
$$8z_1 + 2z_2 \geq 32 \qquad z_1, z_2 \geq 0$$

(b) The equivalent of the dual was solved in Problem 13.15: $\bar{z}_1 = 6$, $\bar{z}_2 = 8$, and $\bar{c} = 50$.

(c) With $\bar{c} = 50$, $\bar{\Pi} = 50$.

(d)

I. $2x_1 + 2x_2 + 8x_3 + s_1 = 3$ II. $2z_1 + 3z_2 - t_1 = 36$
    $3x_1 + 2x_2 + 2x_3 + s_2 = 4$ $2z_1 + 2z_2 - t_2 = 28$
                                            $8z_1 + 2z_2 - t_3 = 32$

Substituting $\bar{z}_1 = 6$ and $\bar{z}_2 = 8$ in II,

$$2(6) + 3(8) - t_1 = 36 \qquad \bar{t}_1 = 0$$
$$2(6) + 2(8) - t_2 = 28 \qquad \bar{t}_2 = 0$$
$$8(6) + 2(8) - t_3 = 32 \qquad \bar{t}_3 = 32$$

With $\bar{t}_1 = \bar{t}_2 = 0$, $\bar{x}_1, \bar{x}_2 \neq 0$; $\bar{x}_3 = 0$ since $\bar{t}_3 \neq 0$. With $\bar{z}_1, \bar{z}_2 \neq 0$, $\bar{s}_1 = \bar{s}_2 = 0$. Substituting in I,

$$2x_1 + 2x_2 + 8(0) + 0 = 3 \qquad 3x_1 + 2x_2 + 2(0) + 0 = 4$$

Thus, $\bar{x}_1 = 1$, $\bar{x}_2 = \frac{1}{2}$, and $\bar{x}_3 = 0$.

15.5. Use the duals in Problems 15.1–15.4 to determine the shadow prices or marginal values (MV) of the resources in the primal constraints. Use A and B for the resources in constraints 1 and 2, respectively.

The shadow prices of resources A and B in the primal constraints are given by the optimal values of the dual decision variables z_1 and z_2. Thus,

For Problem 15.1, $MV_A = \bar{z}_1 = 4$ and $MV_B = \bar{z}_2 = 4$.

For Problem 15.2, $MV_A = \bar{z}_1 = 3$ and $MV_B = \bar{z}_2 = 5$.

For Problem 15.3, $MV_A = \bar{z}_1 = 2$ and $MV_B = \bar{z}_2 = 9$.

For Problem 15.4, $MV_A = \bar{z}_1 = 6$ and $MV_B = \bar{z}_2 = 8$.

SIMPLEX ALGORITHM AND THE DUAL

15.6. For the following problem, (a) formulate the dual and (b) solve it using the simplex method. (c) Use the final dual tableau to determine the optimal values of the primal objective function and decision variables.

Maximize
$$\Pi = 5x_1 + 3x_2$$

subject to
$$6x_1 + 2x_2 \leq 36$$
$$5x_1 + 5x_2 \leq 40$$
$$2x_1 + 4x_2 \leq 28 \qquad x_1, x_2 \geq 0$$

(a) Minimize
$$c = 36z_1 + 40z_2 + 28z_3$$

subject to
$$6z_1 + 5z_2 + 2z_3 \geq 5$$
$$2z_1 + 5z_2 + 4z_3 \geq 3 \qquad z_1, z_2, z_3 \geq 0$$

(b) The dual was solved as a primal in Problem 14.5. Converting x_i to z_i and s_i to t_i, the final tableau reads

Final Tableau:

z_1	z_2	z_3	t_1	t_2	A_1	A_2	Constant
1	0	$-\frac{1}{2}$	$-\frac{1}{4}$	$\frac{1}{4}$	$\frac{1}{4}$	$-\frac{1}{4}$	$\frac{1}{2}$
0	1	1	$\frac{1}{10}$	$-\frac{3}{10}$	$-\frac{1}{10}$	$\frac{3}{10}$	$\frac{2}{5}$
0	0	-6	$\boxed{-5}$	-3	$-M+5$	$-M+3$	34

(c) The absolute value of the indicators under the dual surplus variables t_1 and t_2 in the final tableau gives the optimal values of the primal decision variables x_1 and x_2. Thus, $\bar{x}_1 = 5$, $\bar{x}_2 = 3$, and $\bar{\Pi} = 34$. Check this answer with Example 1 in Chapter 14, where the primal was solved directly.

15.7. Redo Problem 15.6 for the following problem:

Minimize $\qquad\qquad\qquad c = 30x_1 + 50x_2$

subject to $\qquad\qquad 6x_1 + 2x_2 \geqslant 30$

$\qquad\qquad\qquad\qquad 3x_1 + 2x_2 \geqslant 24$

$\qquad\qquad\qquad\qquad 5x_1 + 10x_2 \geqslant 60 \qquad x_1, x_2 \geqslant 0$

(a) Maximize $\qquad\qquad\qquad \Pi = 30z_1 + 24z_2 + 60z_3$

subject to $\qquad\qquad 6z_1 + 3z_2 + 5z_3 \leqslant 30$

$\qquad\qquad\qquad\qquad 2z_1 + 2z_2 + 10z_3 \leqslant 50 \qquad z_1, z_2, z_3 \geqslant 0$

(b) The dual was solved as a primal in Problem 14.2. Making the necessary adjustments for variable notation, the final tableau is

Final Tableau:

z_1	z_2	z_3	t_1	t_2	Constant
$\frac{5}{2}$	1	0	$\frac{1}{2}$	$-\frac{1}{4}$	$\frac{5}{2}$
$-\frac{3}{10}$	0	1	$-\frac{1}{10}$	$\frac{3}{20}$	$\frac{9}{2}$
12	0	0	6	3	330

(c) Thus, $\bar{x}_1 = 6$, $\bar{x}_2 = 3$, and $\bar{c} = 330$. See Problem 13.16, where the primal was solved graphically.

15.8. Redo Problem 15.6 for the following linear programming problem:

Minimize $\qquad\qquad\qquad c = 20x_1 + 30x_2 + 16x_3$

subject to $\qquad\qquad 2.5x_1 + 3x_2 + x_3 \geqslant 3$

$\qquad\qquad\qquad\qquad x_1 + 3x_2 + 2x_3 \geqslant 4 \qquad x_1, x_2, x_3 \geqslant 0$

(a) Maximize $\qquad\qquad\qquad \Pi = 3z_1 + 4z_2$

subject to $\qquad\qquad 2.5z_1 + z_2 \leqslant 20$

$\qquad\qquad\qquad\qquad 3z_1 + 3z_2 \leqslant 30$

$\qquad\qquad\qquad\qquad z_1 + 2z_2 \leqslant 16 \qquad z_1, z_2 \geqslant 0$

(b) The dual was solved as a primal in Problem 14.1. Making the necessary adjustments to accommodate dual notation, the final tableau reads

Final Tableau:

z_1	z_2	t_1	t_2	t_3	Constant
0	0	1	$-\frac{4}{3}$	$\frac{3}{2}$	4
1	0	0	$\frac{2}{3}$	-1	4
0	1	0	$-\frac{1}{3}$	1	6
0	0	0	$\frac{2}{3}$	1	36

(c) Thus, $\bar{x}_1 = 0$, $\bar{x}_2 = \frac{2}{3}$, $\bar{x}_3 = 1$, and $\bar{c} = 36$. See Example 6 for an earlier approach to this problem.

15.9. Redo Problem 15.6 for the following problem:

Maximize $\qquad\qquad\qquad \Pi = 36x_1 + 28x_2 + 32x_3$

subject to $\qquad\qquad 2x_1 + 2x_2 + 8x_3 \leqslant 60$

$\qquad\qquad\qquad\qquad 3x_1 + 2x_2 + 2x_3 \leqslant 80 \qquad x_1, x_2, x_3 \geqslant 0$

(a) Minimize $c = 60z_1 + 80z_2$

subject to $2z_1 + 3z_2 \geqslant 36$

$2z_1 + 2z_2 \geqslant 28$

$8z_1 + 2z_2 \geqslant 32$ $z_1, z_2 \geqslant 0$

(b) The dual was solved as a primal in Problem 14.4. The adjusted final tableau reads

Final Tableau:	z_1	z_2	t_1	t_2	t_3	A_1	A_2	A_3	Constant
	0	1	-1	1	0	1	-1	0	8
	0	0	6	-10	1	-6	10	-1	32
	1	0	1	$-\frac{3}{2}$	0	-1	$\frac{3}{2}$	0	6
	0	0	-20	-10	0	$-M+20$	$-M+10$	$-M$	1000

(c) Thus, $\bar{x}_1 = 20$, $\bar{x}_2 = 10$, $\bar{x}_3 = 0$, and $\bar{\bar{\Pi}} = 1000$.

DEGENERACY

15.10. A linear program is said to *degenerate* if any of the variables *in the basis* assumes a value of zero. In effect, it means that there is linear dependence between column vectors, precluding a unique optimal solution. For the following problem, (a) formulate the dual, (b) solve it by the simplex method, and (c) determine the optimal primal values.

Minimize $c = 4x_1 + 2x_2$ (15.5)

subject to $4x_1 + x_2 \geqslant 20$

$2x_1 + x_2 \geqslant 14$

$x_1 + 6x_2 \geqslant 18$ $x_1, x_2 \geqslant 0$

(a) Maximize $\Pi = 20z_1 + 14z_2 + 18z_3$ (15.6)

subject to $4z_1 + 2z_2 + z_3 \leqslant 4$

$z_1 + z_2 + 6z_3 \leqslant 2$ $z_1, z_2, z_3 \geqslant 0$

(b) Express the constraints as equations in matrix form.

$$\begin{bmatrix} 4 & 2 & 1 & 1 & 0 \\ 1 & 1 & 6 & 0 & 1 \end{bmatrix} \begin{bmatrix} z_1 \\ z_2 \\ z_3 \\ t_1 \\ t_2 \end{bmatrix} = \begin{bmatrix} 4 \\ 2 \end{bmatrix}$$ (15.7)

Set up the initial tableau.

Initial Tableau:	z_1	z_2	z_3	t_1	t_2	Constant
	④	2	1	1	0	4
	1	1	6	0	1	2
	-20	-14	-18	0	0	0

Pivot by first multiplying row₁ by $\frac{1}{4}$, then subtracting row₁ from row₂, and adding 20 times row₁ to row₃.

Second Tableau:

z_1	z_2	z_3	t_1	t_2	Constant
1	$\frac{1}{2}$	$\frac{1}{4}$	$\frac{1}{4}$	0	1
0	$\frac{1}{2}$	$\left(\frac{23}{4}\right)$	$-\frac{1}{4}$	1	1
0	-4	-13	5	0	20

Pivot again. Multiply row$_2$ by $\frac{4}{23}$; then subtract $\frac{1}{4}$ times row$_2$ from row$_1$, and add 13 times row$_2$ to row$_3$.

Third Tableau:

z_1	z_2	z_3	t_1	t_2	Constant
1	$\left(\frac{11}{23}\right)$	0	$\frac{6}{23}$	$-\frac{1}{23}$	$\frac{22}{23}$
0	$\left(\frac{2}{23}\right)$	1	$-\frac{1}{23}$	$\frac{4}{23}$	$\frac{4}{23}$
0	$-\frac{66}{23}$	0	$\frac{102}{23}$	$\frac{52}{23}$	$\frac{512}{23}$

Pivot a third time. Here the displacement ratios are equal:

$$\frac{22}{23}\left(\frac{23}{11}\right) = 2 = \frac{4}{23}\left(\frac{23}{2}\right)$$

When two or more displacement ratios are equal, the linear program will degenerate, i.e. not all the variables in the basis will assume nonzero values. In the event of equal displacement ratios, either row in which they occur may be selected as the pivot row, but the one which will help form an identity matrix to the left of the tableau is often most useful. Here, selecting $\frac{2}{23}$ as the pivot element will generate an identity matrix in the first two columns. Then, multiply row$_2$ by $\frac{23}{2}$; subtract $\frac{11}{23}$ times row$_2$ from row$_1$, and add $\frac{66}{23}$ times row$_2$ to row$_3$.

Final Tableau:

z_1	z_2	z_3	t_1	t_2	Constant
1	0	$-\frac{11}{2}$	$\frac{1}{2}$	-1	0
0	1	$\frac{23}{2}$	$-\frac{1}{2}$	2	2
0	0	33	$\boxed{3 \qquad 8}$		28

The final tableau indicates that $\bar{z}_1 = 0$, $\bar{z}_2 = 2$, $\bar{z}_3 = 0$, $\bar{t}_1 = 0$, $\bar{t}_2 = 0$, and $\bar{\Pi} = 28$, which checks with the initial dual program in (15.6):

$$\Pi = 20(0) + 14(2) + 18(0) = 28$$

Converting to the primal, it indicates that $\bar{x}_1 = 3$, $\bar{x}_2 = 8$, and $\bar{c} = 28$, which also checks with (15.5): $c = 4(3) + 2(8) = 28$.

But, since one of the variables *in the basis* of the final tableau has a zero value, there is linear dependence and multiple optimal solutions exist. Note the linear dependence between column 2 of the coefficient matrix and the column vector of constants in (15.7). See Problem 14.7 where the primal was solved directly, where $\bar{x}_1 = 6$, $\bar{x}_2 = 2$, and $\bar{c} = 28$; this also checks with (15.5). For a graphic solution, see Problem 13.19.

Chapter 16

Integral Calculus:
The Indefinite Integral

16.1 INTEGRATION

Chapters 3 to 6 were devoted to differential calculus, which measures the rate of change of functions. Frequently in economics it is necessary to reverse the process of differentiation and find the function $F(x)$ whose rate of change [i.e. derivative $f(x)$] has been given. This is called *integration*. The function $F(x)$ is termed an *integral* or *antiderivative* of the function $f(x)$.

Example 1. The integral of a function $f(x)$ is expressed mathematically as

$$\int f(x)\, dx = F(x) + c$$

Here the left-hand side of the equation is read "the integral of f of x with respect to x." The symbol $\int$ is an *integral sign*, $f(x)$ is the *integrand*, c is the *constant of integration*, and $F(x) + c$ is an *indefinite integral*, so-called because, as a function of x, which is here unspecified, it can assume many values.

16.2 RULES OF INTEGRATION

The following rules of integration are obtained by reversing the corresponding rules of differentiation. Their accuracy is easily checked, since the derivative of the integral must equal the integrand. Each rule is illustrated in Example 2. The important role of the constant of integration c is demonstrated in Example 3.

Rule 1. The integral of a constant k is

$$\int k\, dx = kx + c$$

Rule 2. The integral of 1, written simply as dx, not $1\,dx$, is

$$\int dx = x + c$$

Rule 3. The integral of a power function x^n, where $n \neq -1$, is given by the *power rule*:

$$\int x^n\, dx = \frac{1}{n+1} x^{n+1} + c \qquad n \neq -1$$

Rule 4. The integral of x^{-1} (or $1/x$) is

$$\int x^{-1}\, dx = \ln x + c \qquad x > 0$$

The condition $x > 0$ is added because only positive numbers have logarithms. For negative numbers,

$$\int x^{-1}\, dx = \ln |x| + c \qquad x \neq 0$$

Rule 5. The integral of an exponential function is

$$\int a^{kx} \, dx = \frac{a^{kx}}{k \ln a} + c$$

Rule 6. The integral of a natural exponential function is

$$\int e^{kx} \, dx = \frac{e^{kx}}{k} + c \qquad \text{since} \quad \ln e = 1$$

Rule 7. The integral of a constant times a function equals the constant times the integral of the function.

$$\int kf(x) \, dx = k \int f(x) \, dx$$

Rule 8. The integral of the sum or difference of two or more functions equals the sum or difference of their integrals.

$$\int [f(x) + g(x)] \, dx = \int f(x) \, dx + \int g(x) \, dx$$

Rule 9. The integral of the negative of a function equals the negative of the integral of that function.

$$\int -f(x) \, dx = - \int f(x) \, dx$$

Example 2. The rules of integration are illustrated below. Check each answer on your own by making sure that the derivative of the integral equals the integrand.

$$(i) \quad \int 3 \, dx = 3x + c \qquad\qquad \text{(Rule 1)}$$

$$(ii) \quad \int x^2 \, dx = \frac{1}{2+1} x^{2+1} + c = \frac{1}{3} x^3 + c \qquad \text{(Rule 3)}$$

$$(iii) \quad \int 5x^4 \, dx = 5 \int x^4 \, dx \qquad\qquad \text{(Rule 7)}$$

$$= 5 \left(\frac{1}{5} x^5 + c_1 \right) \qquad\qquad \text{(Rule 3)}$$

$$= x^5 + c$$

where c_1 and c are arbitrary constants and $5c_1 = c$. Since c is an arbitrary constant, it can be ignored in the preliminary calculation and included only in the final solution.

$$(iv) \quad \int (3x^3 - x + 1) \, dx = 3 \int x^3 \, dx - \int x \, dx + \int dx \qquad \text{(Rules 7, 8, and 9)}$$

$$= 3 \left(\frac{1}{4} x^4 \right) - \frac{1}{2} x^2 + x + c \qquad \text{(Rules 2 and 3)}$$

$$= \frac{3}{4} x^4 - \frac{1}{2} x^2 + x + c$$

$$(v) \quad \int 3x^{-1} \, dx = 3 \int x^{-1} \, dx \qquad\qquad \text{(Rule 7)}$$

$$= 3 \ln x + c \qquad\qquad \text{(Rule 4)}$$

$$(vi) \quad \int 2^{3x} \, dx = \frac{2^{3x}}{3 \ln 2} + c \qquad\qquad \text{(Rule 5)}$$

$$(vii) \quad \int 9e^{-3x} \, dx = \frac{9e^{-3x}}{-3} + c \qquad\qquad \text{(Rule 6)}$$

$$= -3e^{-3x} + c$$

Example 3. Functions which differ only by a constant have the same derivative. The function $F(x) = 2x + k$ has the same derivative, $f(x) = 2$, for any infinite number of possible values for k. If the process is reversed, it is clear that $\int 2\, dx$ must be the antiderivative or indefinite integral for an infinite number of functions differing from each other only by a constant. The constant of integration c thus serves to represent the value of any constant which was part of the primitive function but precluded from the derivative by the rules of differentiation.

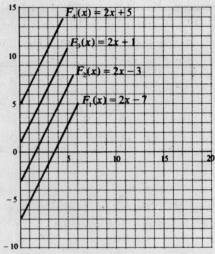

Fig. 16-1

The graph of an indefinite integral $\int f(x)\, dx = F(x) + c$, where c is unspecified, is a family of curves parallel in the sense that the slope of the tangent to any of them at x is $f(x)$. Specifying c specifies the curve; changing c shifts the curve. This is illustrated in Fig. 16-1 for the indefinite integral $\int 2\, dx = 2x + c$ where $c = -7$, -3, 1, and 5, respectively. If $c = 0$, the curve begins at the origin.

16.3 INITIAL CONDITIONS AND BOUNDARY CONDITIONS

In many problems an *initial condition* ($y = y_0$ when $x = 0$) or a *boundary condition* ($y = y_0$ when $x = x_0$) is given which uniquely determines the constant of integration. By permitting a unique determination of c, the initial or boundary condition singles out a specific curve from the family of curves illustrated in Example 3.

Example 4. Given the boundary condition $y = 11$ when $x = 3$, the integral $y = \int 2\, dx$ is evaluated as follows:

$$y = \int 2\, dx = 2x + c$$

Substituting $y = 11$ when $x = 3$,

$$11 = 2(3) + c \qquad c = 5$$

Therefore, $y = 2x + 5$. Note that even though c is specified, $\int 2\, dx$ remains an *indefinite* integral because x is unspecified. Thus, the integral $2x + 5$ can assume an infinite number of possible values.

16.4 INTEGRATION BY SUBSTITUTION

Integration of a product or quotient of two differentiable functions of x, such as

$$\int 12x^2(x^3 + 2)\, dx$$

cannot be done directly using the simple rules above. However, if the integrand can be expressed as a *constant* multiple of another function u and its derivative du/dx, integration by substitution is possible. By expressing the integrand $f(x)$ as a function of u and its derivative du/dx, and integrating with respect to x,

$$\int f(x)\, dx = \int \left(u\, \frac{du}{dx}\right) dx$$

Canceling dx's,

$$\int f(x)\, dx = \int u\, du = F(u) + c$$

The substitution method is the counterpart of the chain rule in differential calculus.

Example 5.   The substitution method is used below to determine the integral $\int 12x^2(x^3+2)\,dx$. Check the answer on your own, noticing how the chain rule is used.

1. Be sure that the integrand can be expressed as a constant multiple of u and du/dx. For u, pick the function in which the independent variable is raised to the higher power. Letting $u = x^3 + 2$, therefore, $du/dx = 3x^2$. Solving for dx, $dx = du/3x^2$. Then, substituting $u = x^3 + 2$ and $dx = du/3x^2$ in the original integrand,

$$\int 12x^2(x^3+2)\,dx = \int 12x^2 u\,\frac{du}{3x^2} = \int 4u\,du = 4\int u\,du \qquad \text{a constant multiple of } u$$

2. Integrate, using Rule 3, and ignoring c in the initial calculation.

$$4\int u\,du = 4\left(\frac{1}{2}u^2\right) = 2u^2 + c$$

3. Substitute $u = x^3 + 2$. Thus,

$$\int 12x^2(x^3+2)\,dx = 2u^2 + c = 2(x^3+2)^2 + c$$

See also Problems 16.7–16.18.

Example 6.   Determine the integral $\int 4x(x+1)^3\,dx$.
    Let $u = x + 1$. Then $du/dx = 1$ and $dx = du/1 = du$. Substitute $u = x + 1$ and $dx = du$ in the original integrand.

$$\int 4x(x+1)^3\,dx = \int 4xu^3\,du = 4\int xu^3\,du$$

Since x is a *variable* multiple which cannot be factored out, the original integrand cannot be transformed into a *constant* multiple of $u\,du/dx$. Hence the substitution method is ineffectual. Integration by parts is necessary (see Section 16.5).

16.5 INTEGRATION BY PARTS

    If an integrand is a product or quotient of differentiable functions of x and cannot be expressed as a constant multiple of $u\,du/dx$, integration by parts is frequently useful. The method is derived by reversing the process of differentiating a product.   If from the product rule in Section 3.4,

$$\frac{d}{dx}[f(x)g(x)] = f(x)g'(x) + g(x)f'(x)$$

taking the integral of the derivative gives

$$f(x)g(x) = \int f(x)g'(x)\,dx + \int g(x)f'(x)\,dx$$

Then solving for the first integral on the right-hand side,

$$\int f(x)g'(x)\,dx = f(x)g(x) - \int g(x)f'(x)\,dx \qquad\qquad (16.1)$$

For more complicated functions, *integration tables* are generally used.   Integration tables provide formulas for the integrals of as many as 500 different functions, and can be found in mathematical handbooks.

Example 7.   Integration by parts is used below to determine $\int 4x(x+1)^3\,dx$.

1. Separate the integrand into two parts amenable to the formula in (16.1). Let $f(x) = 4x$ and $g'(x) = (x+1)^3$. If $f(x) = 4x$, then $f'(x) = 4$. And if $g'(x) = (x+1)^3$, $g(x) = \int (x+1)^3\,dx$, which can be integrated using the power rule (Rule 3):

$$g(x) = \tfrac{1}{4}(x+1)^4 + c$$

where c can be omitted until the final stage.

2. Substitute the values for $f(x)$, $g(x)$, and $f'(x)$, in (16.1); and note that $g'(x)$ is not used in the formula.

$$\int 4x(x+1)^3\,dx = f(x)g(x) - \int g(x)f'(x)\,dx$$

$$= 4x\left[\frac{1}{4}(x+1)^4\right] - \int \frac{1}{4}(x+1)^4 4\,dx = x(x+1)^4 - \int (x+1)^4\,dx$$

3. Use Rule 3 to determine the remaining integral.

$$\int 4x(x+1)^3\,dx = x(x+1)^4 - \frac{1}{5}(x+1)^5 + c$$

Example 8. The integral $\int 2xe^x\,dx$ is determined as follows:
Let $f(x) = 2x$, $f'(x) = 2$, $g'(x) = e^x$, and $g(x) = \int e^x\,dx = e^x$. Substituting in (16.1),

$$\int 2xe^x\,dx = f(x)g(x) - \int g(x)f'(x)\,dx$$

$$= 2xe^x - \int e^x 2\,dx = 2xe^x - 2\int e^x\,dx$$

Applying Rule 6,

$$\int 2xe^x\,dx = 2xe^x - 2e^x + c = 2e^x(x-1) + c$$

16.6 ECONOMIC APPLICATIONS

Net investment I is defined as the rate of change in capital stock formation K over time t. If the process of capital formation is continuous over time, $I(t) = dK(t)/dt = K'(t)$. From the rate of investment, the level of capital stock can be estimated. Capital stock is the integral with respect to time of net investment:

$$K_t = \int I(t)\,dt = K(t) + c = K(t) + K_0$$

where c = the initial capital stock K_0.

Similarly, the integral can be used to estimate total cost from marginal cost. Since marginal cost is the change in total cost from an incremental change in output, $MC = dTC/dQ$, and only variable costs change with the level of output,

$$TC = \int MC\,dQ = VC + c = VC + FC$$

since c = the fixed or initial cost FC. Economic analysis which traces the time path of variables or attempts to determine whether variables will converge toward equilibrium over time is called *dynamics*. For similar applications, see Problems 16.25–16.35.

Example 9. The rate of net investment is given by $I(t) = 140t^{3/4}$ and the initial stock of capital at $t = 0$ is 150. Determining the function for capital K, the time path $K(t)$,

$$K = \int 140t^{3/4}\,dt = 140\int t^{3/4}\,dt$$

By the power rule,

$$K = 140(\tfrac{4}{7}t^{7/4}) + c = 80t^{7/4} + c$$

But $c = K_0 = 150$. Therefore, $K = 80t^{7/4} + 150$.

Solved Problems

INDEFINITE INTEGRALS

16.1   Determine the following integrals.   Check the answers on your own by making sure that the derivative of the integral equals the integrand.

(a) $\int 3.5\, dx$

$$\int 3.5\, dx = 3.5x + c \qquad \text{(Rule 1)}$$

(b) $\int -\frac{1}{2}\, dx$

$$\int -\frac{1}{2}\, dx = -\int \frac{1}{2}\, dx = -\frac{1}{2}x + c \qquad \text{(Rule 9)}$$

(c) $\int dx$

$$\int dx = x + c \qquad \text{(Rule 2)}$$

(d) $\int x^5\, dx$

$$\int x^5\, dx = \frac{1}{6}x^6 + c \qquad \text{(Rule 3)}$$

(e) $\int 4x^3\, dx$

$$\int 4x^3\, dx = 4\int x^3\, dx \qquad \text{(Rule 7)}$$
$$= 4(\tfrac{1}{4}x^4) + c = x^4 + c \qquad \text{(Rule 3)}$$

(f) $\int x^{2/3}\, dx$

$$\int x^{2/3}\, dx = \frac{3}{5}x^{5/3} + c \qquad \text{(Rule 3)}$$

(g) $\int x^{-1/5}\, dx$

$$\int x^{-1/5}\, dx = \frac{5}{4}x^{4/5} + c \qquad \text{(Rule 3)}$$

(h) $\int 4x^{-2}\, dx$

$$\int 4x^{-2}\, dx = -4x^{-1} + c \qquad \text{(Rule 3)}$$

(i) $\int x^{-5/2}\, dx$

$$\int x^{-5/2}\, dx = -\frac{2}{3}x^{-3/2} + c \qquad \text{(Rule 3)}$$

16.2.   Redo Problem 16.1 for each of the following:

(a) $\displaystyle\int \frac{dx}{x}$

$$\int \frac{dx}{x} = \int \frac{1}{x}\, dx = \ln x + c \qquad \text{(Rule 4)}$$

(b) $\displaystyle\int 5x^{-1}\, dx$

$$\int 5x^{-1}\, dx = 5 \ln x + c \qquad \text{(Rules 7 \& 4)}$$

(c) $\displaystyle\int \frac{1}{3x}\, dx$

$$\int \frac{1}{3x}\, dx = \frac{1}{3}\int \frac{1}{x}\, dx = \frac{1}{3}\ln x + c \qquad \text{(Rules 7 \& 4)}$$

(d) $\displaystyle\int \sqrt{x}\, dx$

$$\int \sqrt{x}\, dx = \int x^{1/2}\, dx = \frac{2}{3}x^{3/2} + c \qquad \text{(Rule 3)}$$

(e) $\displaystyle\int \frac{dx}{x^4}$

$$\int \frac{dx}{x^4} = \int x^{-4}\, dx = -\frac{1}{3}x^{-3} + c \qquad \text{(Rule 3)}$$

(f) $\displaystyle\int \frac{dx}{\sqrt[3]{x}}$

$$\int \frac{dx}{\sqrt[3]{x}} = \int x^{-1/3}\, dx = \frac{3}{2}x^{2/3} + c \qquad \text{(Rule 3)}$$

(g) $\displaystyle\int (5x^3 + 2x^2 + 3x)\, dx$

$$\int (5x^3 + 2x^2 + 3x)\, dx = 5\int x^3\, dx + 2\int x^2\, dx + 3\int x\, dx \qquad \text{(Rules 7 \& 8)}$$

$$= 5\left(\frac{1}{4}x^4\right) + 2\left(\frac{1}{3}x^3\right) + 3\left(\frac{1}{2}x^2\right) + c \qquad \text{(Rule 3)}$$

$$= \tfrac{5}{4}x^4 + \tfrac{2}{3}x^3 + \tfrac{3}{2}x^2 + c$$

(h) $\displaystyle\int (2x^6 - 3x^4)\, dx$

$$\int (2x^6 - 3x^4)\, dx = \frac{2}{7}x^7 - \frac{3}{5}x^5 + c \qquad \text{(Rules 3, 7, 8, \& 9)}$$

16.3.   Find the integral for $y = \int (x^{1/2} + 3x^{-1/2})\, dx$, given the initial condition $y = 0$ when $x = 0$.

$$y = \int (x^{1/2} + 3x^{-1/2})\, dx = \frac{2}{3}x^{3/2} + 6x^{1/2} + c$$

Substituting the initial condition $y = 0$ when $x = 0$ above, $c = 0$. Hence, $y = \tfrac{2}{3}x^{3/2} + 6x^{1/2}$.

16.4. Find the integral for $y = \int (2x^5 - 3x^{-1/4})\, dx$, given the initial condition $y = 6$ when $x = 0$.

$$y = \int (2x^5 - 3x^{-1/4})\, dx = \frac{1}{3}x^6 - 4x^{3/4} + c$$

Substituting $y = 6$ and $x = 0$, $c = 6$. Thus, $y = \frac{1}{3}x^6 - 4x^{3/4} + 6$.

16.5. Find the integral for $y = \int (10x^4 - 3)\, dx$, given the boundary condition $y = 21$ when $x = 1$.

$$y = \int (10x^4 - 3)\, dx = 2x^5 - 3x + c$$

Substituting $y = 21$ and $x = 1$, $\quad 21 = 2(1)^5 - 3(1) + c \qquad c = 22$
$$y = 2x^5 - 3x + 22$$

16.6. Redo Problem 16.1 for each of the following:

(a) $\displaystyle \int 2^{4x}\, dx$

(b) $\displaystyle \int 8^x\, dx$

$$\int 2^{4x}\, dx = \frac{2^{4x}}{4\ln 2} + c \qquad \text{(Rule 5)}$$

$$\int 8^x\, dx = \frac{8^x}{\ln 8} + c$$

(c) $\displaystyle \int e^{5x}\, dx$

(d) $\displaystyle \int 16e^{-4x}\, dx$

$$\int e^{5x}\, dx = \frac{e^{5x}}{5} + c \qquad \text{(Rule 6)}$$
$$= \tfrac{1}{5}e^{5x} + c$$

$$\int 16e^{-4x}\, dx = \frac{16e^{-4x}}{-4} + c = -4e^{-4x} + c$$

(e) $\displaystyle \int (6e^{3x} - 8e^{-2x})\, dx$

$$\int (6e^{3x} - 8e^{-2x})\, dx = \frac{6e^{3x}}{3} - \frac{8e^{-2x}}{-2} + c = 2e^{3x} + 4e^{-2x} + c$$

INTEGRATION BY SUBSTITUTION

16.7. Determine the following integral, using the substitution method. Check the answer on your own. Given $\int 10x(x^2 + 3)^4\, dx$.

Let $u = x^2 + 3$. Then $du/dx = 2x$ and $dx = du/2x$. Substituting in the original integrand to reduce it to a function of $u\, du/dx$,

$$\int 10x(x^2 + 3)^4\, dx = \int 10xu^4 \frac{du}{2x} = 5\int u^4\, du$$

Integrating by the power rule, $\qquad 5\int u^4\, du = 5\left(\frac{1}{5}u^5\right) = u^5 + c$

Substituting $u = x^2 + 3$, $\int 10x(x^2 + 3)^4\, dx = u^5 + c = (x^2 + 3)^5 + c$

16.8. Redo Problem 16.7, given $\int x^4(2x^5 - 5)^4\, dx$.

Let $u = 2x^5 - 5$, $du/dx = 10x^4$, and $dx = du/10x^4$. Substituting in the original integrand,

$$\int x^4(2x^5 - 5)^4\, dx = \int x^4 u^4 \frac{du}{10x^4} = \frac{1}{10}\int u^4\, du$$

Integrating, $\qquad \frac{1}{10}\int u^4\, du = \frac{1}{10}\left(\frac{1}{5}u^5\right) = \frac{1}{50}u^5 + c$

Substituting, $\qquad \int x^4(2x^5 - 5)^4\, dx = \frac{1}{50}u^5 + c = \frac{1}{50}(2x^5 - 5)^5 + c$

16.9. Redo Problem 16.7, given $\int (x-9)^{7/4}\,dx$.

Let $u = x - 9$. Then $du/dx = 1$ and $dx = du$. Substituting,

$$\int (x-9)^{7/4}\,dx = \int u^{7/4}\,du$$

Integrating,

$$\int u^{7/4}\,du = \frac{4}{11}u^{11/4} + c$$

Substituting,

$$\int (x-9)^{7/4}\,dx = \frac{4}{11}(x-9)^{11/4} + c$$

Whenever $du/dx = 1$, the power rule can be used immediately for integration by substitution.

16.10. Redo Problem 16.7, given $\int (6x-11)^{-5}\,dx$.

Let $u = 6x - 11$. Then $du/dx = 6$ and $dx = du/6$. Substituting,

$$\int (6x-11)^{-5}\,dx = \int u^{-5}\frac{du}{6} = \frac{1}{6}\int u^{-5}\,du$$

Integrating,

$$\frac{1}{6}\int u^{-5}\,du = \frac{1}{6}\left(\frac{1}{-4}u^{-4}\right) = -\frac{1}{24}u^{-4} + c$$

Substituting,

$$\int (6x-11)^{-5}\,dx = -\frac{1}{24}(6x-11)^{-4} + c$$

Notice that here $du/dx = 6 \neq 1$, and the power rule cannot be used directly.

16.11. Redo Problem 16.7, given

$$\int \frac{x^2}{(4x^3+7)^2}\,dx$$

$$\int \frac{x^2}{(4x^3+7)^2}\,dx = \int x^2(4x^3+7)^{-2}\,dx$$

Let $u = 4x^3 + 7$, $du/dx = 12x^2$, and $dx = du/12x^2$. Substituting,

$$\int x^2 u^{-2}\frac{du}{12x^2} = \frac{1}{12}\int u^{-2}\,du$$

Integrating,

$$\frac{1}{12}\int u^{-2}\,du = -\frac{1}{12}u^{-1} + c$$

Substituting,

$$\int \frac{x^2}{(4x^3+7)^2}\,dx = -\frac{1}{12(4x^3+7)} + c$$

16.12. Redo Problem 16.7, given

$$\int \frac{6x^2+4x+10}{(x^3+x^2+5x)^3}\,dx$$

Let $u = x^3 + x^2 + 5x$. Then $du/dx = 3x^2 + 2x + 5$ and $dx = du/(3x^2+2x+5)$. Substituting,

$$\int (6x^2+4x+10)u^{-3}\frac{du}{3x^2+2x+5} = 2\int u^{-3}\,du$$

Integrating,

$$2\int u^{-3}\,du = -u^{-2} + c$$

Substituting,

$$\int \frac{6x^2+4x+10}{(x^3+x^2+5x)^3}\,dx = -\frac{1}{(x^3+x^2+5x)^2} + c$$

16.13. Redo Problem 16.7, given

$$\int \frac{dx}{9x-5}$$

$$\int \frac{dx}{9x-5} = \int (9x-5)^{-1}\, dx$$

Let $u = 9x - 5$, $du/dx = 9$, and $dx = du/9$. Substituting,

$$\int u^{-1} \frac{du}{9} = \frac{1}{9} \int u^{-1}\, du$$

Integrating with Rule 4, $\frac{1}{9}\int u^{-1}\, du = \frac{1}{9}\ln|u| + c$. Since u may be ≥ 0, and only positive numbers have logs, always use the absolute value of u. See Rule 4. Substituting,

$$\int \frac{dx}{9x-5} = \frac{1}{9}\ln|9x-5| + c$$

16.14. Redo Problem 16.7, given

$$\int \frac{3x^2+2}{4x^3+8x}\, dx$$

Let $u = 4x^3 + 8x$, $du/dx = 12x^2 + 8$, and $dx = du/(12x^2+8)$. Substituting,

$$\int (3x^2+2)u^{-1} \frac{du}{12x^2+8} = \frac{1}{4}\int u^{-1}\, du$$

Integrating,

$$\frac{1}{4}\int u^{-1}\, du = \frac{1}{4}\ln|u| + c$$

Substituting,

$$\int \frac{3x^2+2}{4x^3+8x}\, dx = \frac{1}{4}\ln|4x^3+8x| + c$$

16.15. Use the substitution method to find the integral for $\int x^3 e^{x^4}\, dx$. Check your answer.

Let $u = x^4$. Then $du/dx = 4x^3$ and $dx = du/4x^3$. Substituting, and noting that u is now an exponent,

$$\int x^3 e^u \frac{du}{4x^3} = \frac{1}{4}\int e^u\, du$$

Integrating with Rule 6,

$$\frac{1}{4}\int e^u\, du = \frac{1}{4}e^u + c$$

Substituting,

$$\int x^3 e^{x^4}\, dx = \frac{1}{4}e^{x^4} + c$$

16.16. Redo Problem 16.15, given $\int 24xe^{3x^2}\, dx$.

Let $u = 3x^2$, $du/dx = 6x$, and $dx = du/6x$. Substituting,

$$\int 24xe^u \frac{du}{6x} = 4\int e^u\, du$$

Integrating,

$$4\int e^u\, du = 4e^u + c$$

Substituting,

$$\int 24xe^{3x^2}\, dx = 4e^{3x^2} + c$$

16.17. Redo Problem 16.15, given $\int 14e^{2x+7}\,dx$.

Let $u = 2x + 7$; then $du/dx = 2$ and $dx = du/2$. Substituting,

$$\int 14e^u \frac{du}{2} = 7 \int e^u\,du = 7e^u + c$$

Substituting, $\int 14e^{2x+7}\,dx = 7e^{2x+7} + c$

16.18. Redo Problem 16.15, given $\int 5xe^{5x^2+3}\,dx$.

Let $u = 5x^2 + 3$, $du/dx = 10x$, and $dx = du/10x$. Substituting,

$$\int 5xe^u \frac{du}{10x} = \frac{1}{2} \int e^u\,du$$

Integrating, $\frac{1}{2} \int e^u\,du = \frac{1}{2}e^u + c$

Substituting, $\int 5xe^{5x^2+3}\,dx = \frac{1}{2}e^{5x^2+3} + c$

INTEGRATION BY PARTS

16.19. Use integration by parts to evaluate the following integral. Keep in the habit of checking your answers. Given $\int 15x(x+4)^{3/2}\,dx$.

Let $f(x) = 15x$, then $f'(x) = 15$. Let $g'(x) = (x+4)^{3/2}$, then $g(x) = \int (x+4)^{3/2}\,dx = \frac{2}{5}(x+4)^{5/2}$. Substituting in (16.1),

$$\int 15x(x+4)^{3/2}\,dx = f(x)g(x) - \int g(x)f'(x)\,dx$$

$$= 15x\left[\frac{2}{5}(x+4)^{5/2}\right] - \int \frac{2}{5}(x+4)^{5/2}15\,dx = 6x(x+4)^{5/2} - 6\int (x+4)^{5/2}\,dx$$

Evaluating the remaining integral,

$$\int 15x(x+4)^{3/2}\,dx = 6x(x+4)^{5/2} - \frac{12}{7}(x+4)^{7/2} + c$$

16.20. Redo Problem 16.19, given

$$\int \frac{2x}{(x-8)^3}\,dx$$

Let $f(x) = 2x$, $f'(x) = 2$, and $g'(x) = (x-8)^{-3}$, then $g(x) = \int(x-8)^{-3}\,dx = -\frac{1}{2}(x-8)^{-2}$. Substituting in (16.1),

$$\int \frac{2x}{(x-8)^3}\,dx = 2x\left[-\frac{1}{2}(x-8)^{-2}\right] - \int -\frac{1}{2}(x-8)^{-2}2\,dx = -x(x-8)^{-2} + \int (x-8)^{-2}\,dx$$

Integrating for the last time,

$$\int \frac{2x}{(x-8)^3}\,dx = -x(x-8)^{-2} - (x-8)^{-1} + c$$

16.21. Redo Problem 16.19, given

$$\int \frac{5x}{(x-1)^2}\,dx$$

Let $f(x) = 5x$, $f'(x) = 5$, and $g'(x) = (x-1)^{-2}$; then $g(x) = \int (x-1)^{-2}\, dx = -(x-1)^{-1}$. Substituting in (16.1),

$$\int \frac{5x}{(x-1)^2}\, dx = 5x[-(x-1)^{-1}] - \int -(x-1)^{-1}5\, dx = -5x(x-1)^{-1} + 5\int (x-1)^{-1}\, dx$$

Integrating again, $$\int \frac{5x}{(x-1)^2}\, dx = -5x(x-1)^{-1} + 5\ln|x-1| + c$$

16.22. Redo Problem 16.19, given $\int 6xe^{x+7}\, dx$.

Let $f(x) = 6x$, $f'(x) = 6$, $g'(x) = e^{x+7}$, and $g(x) = \int e^{x+7}\, dx = e^{x+7}$. Using formula (16.1),

$$\int 6xe^{x+7}\, dx = 6xe^{x+7} - \int e^{x+7}6\, dx = 6xe^{x+7} - 6\int e^{x+7}\, dx$$

Integrating again,

$$\int 6xe^{x+7}\, dx = 6xe^{x+7} - 6e^{x+7} + c$$

16.23. Use integration by parts to evaluate $\int 16xe^{-(x+9)}\, dx$.

Let $f(x) = 16x$, $f'(x) = 16$, $g'(x) = e^{-(x+9)}$, and $g(x) = \int e^{-(x+9)}\, dx = -e^{-(x+9)}$. Using (16.1)

$$\int 16xe^{-(x+9)}\, dx = -16xe^{-(x+9)} - \int -e^{-(x+9)}16\, dx = -16xe^{-(x+9)} + 16\int e^{-(x+9)}\, dx$$

Integrating once more,

$$\int 16xe^{-(x+9)}\, dx = -16xe^{-(x+9)} - 16e^{-(x+9)} + c$$

16.24. Redo Problem 16.23, given $\int x^2 e^{2x}\, dx$.

Let $f(x) = x^2$, $f'(x) = 2x$, $g'(x) = e^{2x}$, and $g(x) = \int e^{2x}\, dx = \frac{1}{2}e^{2x}$. Substituting in (16.1),

$$\int x^2 e^{2x}\, dx = x^2\left(\frac{1}{2}e^{2x}\right) - \int \frac{1}{2}e^{2x}(2x)\, dx = \frac{1}{2}x^2 e^{2x} - \int xe^{2x}\, dx \qquad (16.2)$$

Using parts again for the remaining integral, $f(x) = x$, $f'(x) = 1$, $g'(x) = e^{2x}$, and $g(x) = \int e^{2x}\, dx = \frac{1}{2}e^{2x}$. Using (16.1),

$$\int xe^{2x}\, dx = x\left(\frac{1}{2}e^{2x}\right) - \int \frac{1}{2}e^{2x}\, dx = \frac{1}{2}xe^{2x} - \frac{1}{2}\left(\frac{1}{2}e^{2x}\right)$$

Finally, substituting in (16.2),

$$\int x^2 e^{2x}\, dx = \frac{1}{2}x^2 e^{2x} - \frac{1}{2}xe^{2x} + \frac{1}{4}e^{2x} + c$$

ECONOMIC APPLICATIONS

16.25. The rate of net investment is $I = 40t^{3/5}$ and capital stock at $t = 0$ is 75. Find the capital function K.

$$K = \int I\, dt = \int 40t^{3/5}\, dt = 40\left(\frac{5}{8}t^{8/5}\right) + c = 25t^{8/5} + c$$

Substituting $t = 0$ and $K = 75$,

$$75 = 0 + c \qquad c = 75$$

Thus, $K = 25t^{8/5} + 75$.

16.26. The rate of net investment is $I = 60t^{1/3}$ and capital stock at $t = 1$ is 85. Find K.

$$K = \int 60t^{1/3}\, dt = 45t^{4/3} + c$$

At $t = 1$ and $K = 85$,

$$85 = 45(1) + c \qquad c = 40$$

Thus, $K = 45t^{4/3} + 40$.

16.27. Marginal cost is given by $MC = dTC/dQ = 25 + 30Q - 9Q^2$. Fixed cost is 55. Find the (a) total cost, (b) average cost, and (c) variable cost functions.

(a)
$$TC = \int MC\, dQ = \int (25 + 30Q - 9Q^2)\, dQ = 25Q + 15Q^2 - 3Q^3 + c$$

With FC = 55, at $Q = 0$, TC = FC = 55. Thus, c = FC = 55 and TC = $25Q + 15Q^2 - 3Q^3 + 55$.

(b)
$$AC = \frac{TC}{Q} = 25 + 15Q - 3Q^2 + \frac{55}{Q}$$

(c)
$$VC = TC - FC = 25Q + 15Q^2 - 3Q^3$$

16.28. Given $MC = dTC/dQ = 32 + 18Q - 12Q^2$, FC = 43. Find the (a) TC, (b) AC, and (c) VC functions.

(a)
$$TC = \int MC\, dQ = \int (32 + 18Q - 12Q^2)\, dQ = 32Q + 9Q^2 - 4Q^3 + c$$

At $Q = 0$, TC = FC = 43, TC = $32Q + 9Q^2 - 4Q^3 + 43$.

(b)
$$AC = \frac{TC}{Q} = 32 + 9Q - 4Q^2 + \frac{43}{Q}$$

(c)
$$VC = TC - FC = 32Q + 9Q^2 - 4Q^3$$

16.29. Marginal revenue is given by $MR = dTR/dQ = 60 - 2Q - 2Q^2$. Find (a) the TR function and (b) the demand function $P = f(Q)$.

(a)
$$TR = \int MR\, dQ = \int (60 - 2Q - 2Q^2)\, dQ = 60Q - Q^2 - \frac{2}{3}Q^3 + c$$

At $Q = 0$, TR = 0. Therefore $c = 0$. Thus, TR = $60Q - Q^2 - \frac{2}{3}Q^3$.

(b) TR = PQ. Therefore, $P = TR/Q$, which is the same as saying that the demand function and the average revenue function are identical. Thus, $P = AR = TR/Q = 60 - Q - \frac{2}{3}Q^2$.

16.30. Find (a) the total revenue function and (b) the demand function, given

$$MR = 84 - 4Q - Q^2.$$

(a)
$$TR = \int MR\, dQ = \int (84 - 4Q - Q^2)\, dQ = 84Q - 2Q^2 - \frac{1}{3}Q^3 + c$$

At $Q = 0$, TR = 0. Therefore $c = 0$. Thus, TR = $84Q - 2Q^2 - \frac{1}{3}Q^3$.

(b)
$$P = AR = \frac{TR}{Q} = 84 - 2Q - \frac{1}{3}Q^2$$

16.31. With $C = f(Y)$,   the marginal propensity to consume is given by $MPC = dC/dY = f'(Y)$. If the $MPC = 0.8$ and consumption is 40 when income is zero, find the consumption function.

$$C = \int f'(Y)\, dY = \int 0.8\, dY = 0.8\, Y + c$$

At $Y = 0$, $C = 40$.   Thus, $c = 40$ and $C = 0.8\, Y + 40$.

16.32. Given $dC/dY = 0.6 + 0.1/\sqrt[3]{Y} = MPC$ and $C = 45$ when $Y = 0$.   Find the consumption function.

$$C = \int \left(0.6 + \frac{0.1}{\sqrt[3]{Y}}\right) dY = \int (0.6 + 0.1\, Y^{-1/3})\, dY = 0.6\, Y + 0.15\, Y^{2/3} + c$$

At $Y = 0$, $C = 45$.   Thus, $C = 0.6\, Y + 0.15\, Y^{2/3} + 45$.

16.33. The marginal propensity to save is given by $dS/dY = 0.5 - 0.2\, Y^{-1/2}$.   There is dissaving of 3.5 when income is 25, i.e. $S = -3.5$ when $Y = 25$.   Find the savings function.

$$S = \int (0.5 - 0.2\, Y^{-1/2})\, dY = 0.5\, Y - 0.4\, Y^{1/2} + c$$

At $Y = 25$, $S = -3.5$.

$$-3.5 = 0.5(25) - 0.4(\sqrt{25}) + c \qquad c = -14$$

Thus, $S = 0.5\, Y - 0.4\, Y^{1/2} - 14$.

16.34. Given $MC = dTC/dQ = 12e^{0.5Q}$ and $FC = 36$.   Find the total cost.

$$TC = \int 12e^{0.5Q}\, dQ = 12\frac{1}{0.5}e^{0.5Q} + c = 24e^{0.5Q} + c$$

With $FC = 36$, $TC = 36$ when $Q = 0$.   Substituting, $36 = 24e^{0.5(0)} + c$.   Since $e^0 = 1$, $36 = 24 + c$, and $c = 12$.   Thus, $TC = 24e^{0.5Q} + 12$.   Notice that c does not always equal FC.

16.35. Given $MC = 16e^{0.4Q}$ and $FC = 100$.   Find TC.

$$TC = \int 16e^{0.4Q}\, dQ = 16\left(\frac{1}{0.4}\right)e^{0.4Q} + c = 40e^{0.4Q} + c$$

At $Q = 0$, $TC = 100$.

$$100 = 40e^0 + c \qquad c = 60$$

Thus, $TC = 40e^{0.4Q} + 60$.

Chapter 17

Integral Calculus:
The Definite Integral

17.1 AREA UNDER A CURVE

There is no geometrical formula for the area under an irregularly shaped curve, such as $y = f(x)$ between $x = a$ and $x = b$ in Fig. 17-1(a). If the interval $[a,b]$ is divided into n subintervals $[x_1,x_2]$, $[x_2,x_3]$, etc., and rectangles are constructed such that the height of each is equal to the smallest value of the function in the subinterval, as in Fig. 17-1(b), the sum of the areas of the rectangles $\sum_{i=1}^{n} f(x_i)\,\Delta x_i$ will approximate, but underestimate, the actual area under the curve. The smaller the subintervals (the smaller the Δx_i), the more rectangles are created and the closer the combined area of the rectangles $\sum_{i=1}^{n} f(x_i)\,\Delta x_i$ approaches the actual area under the curve. If the number of subintervals is increased so that $n \to \infty$, each subinterval becomes infinitesimal ($\Delta x_i = dx_i = dx$) and the area of the curve A can be expressed mathematically as

$$A = \lim_{n \to \infty} \sum_{i=1}^{n} f(x_i)\,\Delta x_i = \int_{a}^{b} f(x)\,dx$$

where the integral symbol $\int$ replaces Σ because Σ properly represents the sum of a finite number of terms.

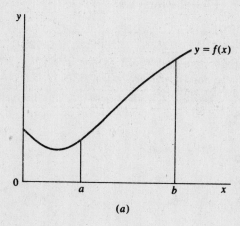
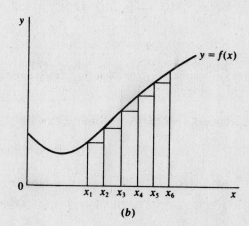

Fig. 17-1

17.2 THE DEFINITE INTEGRAL

The definite integral of a continuous function $f(x)$ over the interval a to b ($a < b$) is expressed mathematically as $\int_{a}^{b} f(x)\,dx$ which reads "the integral from a to b of f of x dx." a is termed the *lower limit* of integration, b the *upper limit* of integration. Limit in this context means the value of the variable at the given end of its range. Unlike the indefinite integral, which is a function of a variable with no specified value and hence possesses no definite numerical value, the *definite integral* of $f(x)$ with x ranging from a to b has a numerical value which can be calculated from the indefinite integral by using the fundamental theorem of calculus. See Section 17.3.

17.3 THE FUNDAMENTAL THEOREM OF CALCULUS

The *fundamental theorem of calculus* states that the numerical value of the definite integral of the continuous function $f(x)$ over the interval from a to b is given by the indefinite integral $F(x) + c$ evaluated at the upper limit of integration b, minus the same indefinite integral $F(x) + c$ evaluated at the lower limit of integration a.   Since c is common to both, the constant of integration is eliminated in subtraction.   Expressed mathematically,

$$\int_a^b f(x)\,dx = F(x)\,\Big|_a^b = F(b) - F(a)$$

where the symbol $|_a^b$, $]_a^b$, or $[\cdots]_a^b$ indicates that b and a are to be substituted successively for x.

Example 1.   The definite integrals given below

$$(1)\quad \int_1^4 10x\,dx \qquad (2)\quad \int_1^3 (4x^3 + 6x)\,dx$$

are evaluated as follows:

(1)

$$\int_1^4 10x\,dx = 5x^2\,\Big|_1^4 = 5(4)^2 - 5(1)^2 = 75$$

(2)

$$\int_1^3 (4x^3 + 6x)\,dx = [x^4 + 3x^2]_1^3 = [(3)^4 + 3(3)^2] - [(1)^4 + 3(1)^2] = 108 - 4 = 104$$

Example 2.   The definite integral is used below to determine the area under the curve in Fig. 17-2 over the interval 0 to 20 as follows:

$$A = \int_0^{20} \frac{1}{2}x\,dx = \frac{1}{4}x^2\,\Big|_0^{20}$$

$$= \frac{1}{4}(20)^2 - \frac{1}{4}(0)^2 = 100$$

The answer can be checked by using the geometrical formula $A = \frac{1}{2}xy$:

$$A = \frac{1}{2}xy = \frac{1}{2}(20)(10) = 100 \qquad \text{Compare}$$

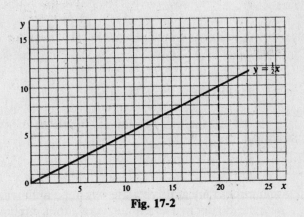

Fig. 17-2

17.4 PROPERTIES OF DEFINITE INTEGRALS

1. Reversing the order of the limits changes the sign of the definite integral.

$$\int_a^b f(x)\,dx = -\int_b^a f(x)\,dx \tag{17.1}$$

2. If the upper limit of integration equals the lower limit of integration, the value of the definite integral is zero.

$$\int_a^a f(x)\,dx = F(a) - F(a) = 0 \tag{17.2}$$

3. The definite integral can be expressed as the sum of component subintegrals.

$$\int_a^c f(x)\,dx = \int_a^b f(x)\,dx + \int_b^c f(x)\,dx \qquad a \le b \le c \tag{17.3}$$

Example 3. To illustrate the properties presented above, the following definite integrals are evaluated.

1. $\displaystyle\int_1^3 2x^3\,dx = -\int_3^1 2x^3\,dx$

$$\int_1^3 2x^3\,dx = \frac{1}{2}x^4\bigg|_1^3 = \frac{1}{2}(3)^4 - \frac{1}{2}(1)^4 = 40$$

Checking this answer,

$$\int_3^1 2x^3\,dx = \frac{1}{2}x^4\bigg|_3^1 = \frac{1}{2}(1)^4 - \frac{1}{2}(3)^4 = -40$$

2. $\displaystyle\int_5^5 (2x+3)\,dx = 0$

Checking this answer,

$$\int_5^5 (2x+3)\,dx = [x^2 + 3x]_5^5 = [(5)^2 + 3(5)] - [(5)^2 + 3(5)] = 0$$

3. $\displaystyle\int_0^4 6x\,dx = \int_0^3 6x\,dx + \int_3^4 6x\,dx$

$$\int_0^4 6x\,dx = 3x^2\bigg|_0^4 = 3(4)^2 - 3(0)^2 = 48$$

$$\int_0^3 6x\,dx = 3x^2\bigg|_0^3 = 3(3)^2 - 3(0)^2 = 27$$

$$\int_3^4 6x\,dx = 3x^2\bigg|_3^4 = 3(4)^2 - 3(3)^2 = 21$$

Checking this answer, $\qquad\qquad 48 = 27 + 21$

17.5 IMPROPER INTEGRALS

A definite integral with infinity for either an upper or lower limit of integration is called an *improper integral*.

$$\int_a^\infty f(x)\,dx \qquad\text{and}\qquad \int_{-\infty}^b f(x)\,dx$$

are improper integrals because ∞ is not a number and cannot be substituted for x in $F(x)$. However, they can be defined as the limits of other integrals, as shown below.

$$\int_a^\infty f(x)\,dx \equiv \lim_{b\to\infty}\int_a^b f(x)\,dx \qquad\text{and}\qquad \int_{-\infty}^b f(x)\,dx \equiv \lim_{a\to-\infty}\int_a^b f(x)\,dx$$

If the limit in either case exists, the improper integral is said to *converge*, and the integral has a definite value. If the limit does not exist, the improper integral *diverges* and is meaningless.

Example 4. The improper integrals given below

$$(1)\quad \int_1^\infty 3x^{-2}\,dx \qquad (2)\quad \int_1^\infty \frac{5}{x}\,dx$$

are evaluated as follows:

(1)
$$\int_1^\infty 3x^{-2}\,dx = \lim_{b\to\infty}\int_1^b 3x^{-2}\,dx = \lim_{b\to\infty}\left[\frac{-3}{x}\right]_1^b = \lim_{b\to\infty}\left[\frac{-3}{b} - \frac{(-3)}{1}\right] = \lim_{b\to\infty}\left[\frac{-3}{b} + 3\right] = 3$$

because $-3/b \to 0$ as $b \to \infty$. Hence the improper integral is convergent and equal to 3. For simplicity, the limit notation is sometimes omitted.

(2)
$$\int_1^\infty \frac{5}{x}\,dx = \lim_{b\to\infty}\int_1^b \frac{5}{x}\,dx = [5\ln|x|]_1^b = 5\ln|b| - 5\ln|1| = 5\ln|b|$$

since $\ln|1| = 0$. As $b \to \infty$, $5\ln|b| \to \infty$. The improper integral diverges and has no definite value.

Example 5.   Integrals with finite limits of integration can also be improper if within the interval of integration the integrand becomes infinite.   Such integrals also call for the use of limits.   For example, the integral $\int_0^{27} x^{-2/3}\,dx$ is improper because as x approaches 0 from the right $(x \to 0^+)$, $x^{-2/3} \to \infty$.   Evaluated,

$$\int_0^{27} x^{-2/3}\,dx = \lim_{a \to 0}\int_a^{27} x^{-2/3}\,dx = 3x^{1/3}\ \Big]_a^{27} = 3\sqrt[3]{27} - 3\sqrt[3]{a} = 9 - 3\sqrt[3]{a}$$

As $a \to 0^+$,   the integral converges to 9.   See Problems 17.20–17.21.

17.6   PRESENT VALUE OF CASH FLOWS

In Section 8.3, the present value of a sum of money to be received in the future, when interest is compounded continuously, was given by $P = Se^{-rt}$.   The present value of a *stream of future income* (money to be received *each year* for n years), therefore, is given by the integral

$$P_n = \int_0^n Se^{-rt}\,dt = S\int_0^n e^{-rt}\,dt = S\left[-\frac{1}{r}e^{-rt}\right]_0^n = -\frac{S}{r}\left[e^{-rt}\right]_0^n$$

$$= -\frac{S}{r}(e^{-rn} - e^{-r(0)}) = -\frac{S}{r}(e^{-rn} - 1)$$

$$= \frac{S}{r}(1 - e^{-rn}) \tag{17.4}$$

Notice the similarity to the formula in Section 8.4 for the present value of a future stream of income under conditions of annual compounding.

Example 6.   The present value of \$1000 to be paid each year for 3 years when the interest rate is 5% compounded continuously is calculated below using (17.4).

$$P_n = \frac{1000}{0.05}[1 - e^{-(0.05)(3)}] = 20{,}000(1 - e^{-0.15}) = 20{,}000(1 - 0.8607) = \$2786$$

17.7   CONSUMERS' AND PRODUCERS' SURPLUS

A demand function $P_1 = f_1(Q)$,   as in Fig. 17-3(a), represents the different prices consumers are willing to pay for different quantities of a good.   If equilibrium in the market is at (Q_0, P_0), then the consumers who would be willing to pay more than P_0 benefit.   Total benefit to consumers is represented by the shaded area and is called *consumers' surplus*.   Mathematically,

$$\text{Consumers' surplus} = \int_0^{Q_0} f_1(Q)\,dQ - Q_0 P_0 \tag{17.5}$$

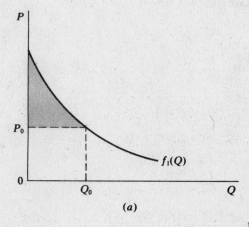 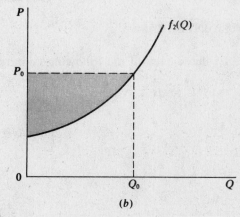

(a)   (b)

Fig. 17-3

A supply function $P_2 = f_2(Q)$, as in Fig. 17-3(b), represents the prices at which different quantities of a good will be supplied. If market equilibrium occurs at (Q_0, P_0), the producers who would supply at a lower price than P_0 benefit. Total gain to producers is called *producers' surplus* and is designated by the shaded area. Mathematically,

$$\text{Producers' surplus} = Q_0 P_0 - \int_0^{Q_0} f_2(Q) \, dQ \qquad (17.6)$$

Example 7. Given the demand function $P = 42 - 5Q - Q^2$. Assuming that the equilibrium price is 6, the consumers' surplus is evaluated as follows:

At $P_0 = 6$,
$$42 - 5Q - Q^2 = 6$$
$$36 - 5Q - Q^2 = 0$$
$$(Q + 9)(-Q + 4) = 0$$

$Q_0 = 4$, because $Q = -9$ is not feasible. Substituting in (17.5),

$$\text{Consumers' surplus} = \int_0^4 (42 - 5Q - Q^2) \, dQ - (4)(6)$$
$$= \left[42Q - 2.5Q^2 - \frac{1}{3}Q^3 \right]_0^4 - 24$$
$$= (168 - 40 - 21\tfrac{1}{3}) - (0) - 24 = 82\tfrac{2}{3}$$

17.8   THE DEFINITE INTEGRAL AND PROBABILITY

The probability P that an event will occur can be measured by the corresponding area under a probability density function. A *probability density* or *frequency function* is a continuous function $f(x)$ such that:

1. $f(x) \geq 0$.   Or, probability cannot be negative.
2. $\int_{-\infty}^{\infty} f(x) \, dx = 1$.   Or, the probability of the event occurring over the entire range of x is 1.
3. $P(a < x < b) = \int_a^b f(x) \, dx$.   Or, the probability of the value of x falling within the interval $[a,b]$ is the value of the definite integral from a to b.

Example 8. The time in minutes between cars passing on a highway is given by the frequency function $f(t) = 2e^{-2t}$ for $t \geq 0$. The probability of a car passing in 0.25 minutes is calculated as follows:

$$P = \int_0^{0.25} 2e^{-2t} \, dt = -e^{-2t} \Big|_0^{0.25} = (-e^{-0.5}) - (-e^0) = -0.606531 + 1 = 0.393469$$

Solved Problems

DEFINITE INTEGRALS

17.1.   Evaluate each of the following definite integrals:

(a) $\displaystyle \int_0^6 5x \, dx$

$$\int_0^6 5x \, dx = 2.5x^2 \Big|_0^6 = 2.5(6)^2 - 2.5(0)^2 = 90$$

(b) $\displaystyle \int_1^{10} 3x^2 \, dx$

$$\int_1^{10} 3x^2 \, dx = x^3 \Big|_1^{10} = (10)^3 - (1)^3 = 999$$

(c) $\displaystyle\int_1^{64} x^{-2/3}\, dx$

$$\int_1^{64} x^{-2/3}\, dx = 3x^{1/3}\,\Big|_1^{64} = 3\sqrt[3]{64} - 3\sqrt[3]{1} = 9$$

(d) $\displaystyle\int_1^3 (x^3 + x + 6)\, dx$

$$\int_1^3 (x^3 + x + 6)\, dx = \tfrac{1}{4}x^4 + \tfrac{1}{2}x^2 + 6x\,\Big|_1^3 = [\tfrac{1}{4}(3)^4 + \tfrac{1}{2}(3)^2 + 6(3)] - [\tfrac{1}{4}(1)^4 + \tfrac{1}{2}(1)^2 + 6(1)] = 36$$

(e) $\displaystyle\int_1^4 (x^{-1/2} + 3x^{1/2})\, dx$

$$\int_1^4 (x^{-1/2} + 3x^{1/2})\, dx = 2x^{1/2} + 2x^{3/2}\,\Big|_1^4 = (2\sqrt{4} + 2\sqrt{4^3}) - (2\sqrt{1} + 2\sqrt{1^3}) = 16$$

(f) $\displaystyle\int_0^3 4e^{2x}\, dx$

$$\int_0^3 4e^{2x}\, dx = 2e^{2x}\,\Big|_0^3 = 2[e^{2(3)} - e^{2(0)}]$$

$$= 2(403.4 - 1) = 804.8 \qquad \text{from Appendix III}$$

(g) $\displaystyle\int_0^{10} 2e^{-2x}\, dx$

$$\int_0^{10} 2e^{-2x}\, dx = -e^{-2x}\,\Big|_0^{10} = -e^{-2(10)} - (-e^{-2(0)}) = -e^{-20} + e^0 = 1$$

SUBSTITUTION METHOD

17.2. Use the substitution method to integrate the following definite integral:

$$\int_0^3 8x(2x^2 + 3)\, dx$$

Let $u = 2x^2 + 3$. Then $du/dx = 4x$ and $dx = du/4x$. Ignore the limits of integration for the moment and treat the integral as an indefinite integral. Substituting in the original integrand,

$$\int 8x(2x^2 + 3)\, dx = \int 8xu\,\frac{du}{4x} = 2\int u\, du$$

Integrating with respect to u,

$$2\int u\, du = 2\left(\frac{u^2}{2}\right) + c = u^2 + c \qquad (17.7)$$

Finally, by substituting $u = 2x^2 + 3$ in (17.7) and recalling that c will drop out in the integration, the definite integral can be written in terms of x, incorporating the original limits:

$$\int_0^3 8x(2x^2 + 3)\, dx = (2x^2 + 3)^2\,\Big|_0^3 = [2(3)^2 + 3]^2 - [2(0)^2 + 3]^2 = 441 - 9 = 432$$

Because in the original substitution, $u \neq x$ but $2x^2 + 3$, the limits of integration in terms of x will differ from the limits of integration in terms of u. The limits can be expressed in terms of u, if so desired. Since we have set $u = 2x^2 + 3$ and x ranges from 0 to 3, the limits in terms of u are $u = 2(3)^2 + 3 = 21$ and $u = 2(0)^2 + 3 = 3$. Using these limits with the integral expressed in terms of u, as in (17.7),

$$2\int_3^{21} u\, du = u^2\,\Big|_3^{21} = 441 - 9 = 432 \qquad \text{Check.}$$

17.3. Redo Problem 17.2, given $\int_1^2 x^2(x^3-5)^2\,dx$.

Let $u = x^3 - 5$, $du/dx = 3x^2$, and $dx = du/3x^2$. Substituting independently of the limits,

$$\int x^2(x^3-5)^2\,dx = \int x^2 u^2 \frac{du}{3x^2} = \frac{1}{3}\int u^2\,du$$

Integrating with respect to u and ignoring the constant,

$$\frac{1}{3}\int u^2\,du = \frac{1}{3}\left[\frac{1}{3}u^3\right] = \frac{1}{9}u^3$$

Substituting $u = x^3 - 5$ and incorporating the limits for x,

$$\int_1^2 x^2(x^3-5)^2\,dx = \left[\frac{1}{9}(x^3-5)^3\right]_1^2$$

$$= \frac{1}{9}[(2)^3-5]^3 - \frac{1}{9}[(1)^3-5]^3 = \frac{1}{9}(27) - \frac{1}{9}(-64) = 10.11$$

Since $u = x^3 - 5$ and the limits for x are $x = 1$ and $x = 2$, by substitution the limits for u are $u = (1)^3 - 5 = -4$ and $u = (2)^3 - 5 = 3$. Incorporating these limits for the integral with respect to u,

$$\frac{1}{3}\int_{-4}^3 u^2\,du = \left[\frac{1}{9}u^3\right]_{-4}^3 = \frac{1}{9}(3)^3 - \frac{1}{9}(-4)^3 = 10.11 \qquad \text{Check}$$

17.4. Redo Problem 17.2, given

$$\int_0^2 \frac{3x^2}{(x^3+1)^2}\,dx$$

Let $u = x^3 + 1$. Then $du/dx = 3x^2$ and $dx = du/3x^2$. Substituting,

$$\int \frac{3x^2}{(x^3+1)^2}\,dx = \int 3x^2 u^{-2}\frac{du}{3x^2} = \int u^{-2}\,du$$

Integrating with respect to u and ignoring the constant,

$$\int u^{-2}\,du = -u^{-1}$$

Substituting $u = x^3 + 1$ with the original limits,

$$\int_0^2 \frac{3x^2}{(x^3+1)^2}\,dx = -(x^3+1)^{-1}\Big|_0^2 = \left(\frac{-1}{2^3+1}\right) - \left(\frac{-1}{0^3+1}\right) = -\frac{1}{9} + 1 = \frac{8}{9}$$

With $u = x^3 + 1$, and the limits of x from 0 to 2, the limits of u are $u = (0)^3 + 1 = 1$ and $u = (2)^3 + 1 = 9$. Thus,

$$\int_1^9 u^{-2}\,du = -u^{-1}\Big|_1^9 = \left(-\frac{1}{9}\right) - \left(-\frac{1}{1}\right) = \frac{8}{9} \qquad \text{Check}$$

17.5. Integrate the following definite integral by means of the substitution method:

$$\int_0^3 \frac{6x}{x^2+1}\,dx$$

Let $u = x^2 + 1$, $du/dx = 2x$, and $dx = du/2x$. Substituting,

$$\int \frac{6x}{x^2+1}\,dx = \int 6xu^{-1}\frac{du}{2x} = 3\int u^{-1}\,du$$

Integrating with respect to u,

$$3\int u^{-1}\,du = 3\ln u$$

Substituting $u = x^2 + 1$,

$$\int_0^3 \frac{6x}{x^2+1}\, dx = 3 \ln |x^2 + 1| \,\Big|_0^3$$

$$= 3 \ln |3^2 + 1| - 3 \ln |0^2 + 1| = 3 \ln 10 - 3 \ln 1$$

Since $\ln 1 = 0$, $= 3 \ln 10 = 6.9078$

The limits of u are $u = (0)^2 + 1 = 1$ and $u = (3)^2 + 1 = 10$.   Integrating with respect to u,

$$3\int_1^{10} u^{-1}\, du = 3 \ln u \,\Big|_1^{10} = 3 \ln 10 - 3 \ln 1 = 3 \ln 10 = 6.9078 \qquad \text{Compare}$$

17.6. Redo Problem 17.5, given $\int_1^2 4xe^{x^2+2}\, dx$.

Let $u = x^2 + 2$.   Then $du/dx = 2x$ and $dx = du/2x$.   Substituting,

$$\int 4xe^{x^2+2}\, dx = \int 4xe^u \frac{du}{2x} = 2\int e^u\, du$$

Integrating with respect to u and ignoring the constant,

$$2\int e^u\, du = 2e^u$$

Substituting $u = x^2 + 2$,

$$\int_1^2 4xe^{x^2+2}\, dx = 2e^{x^2+2} \,\Big|_1^2 = 2(e^{(2)^2+2} - e^{(1)^2+2}) = 2(e^6 - e^3)$$

$$= 2(403.4 - 20.09) = 766.62 \qquad \text{using Appendix III}$$

With $u = x^2 + 2$,   the limits of u are $u = (1)^2 + 2 = 3$ and $u = (2)^2 + 2 = 6$.

$$2\int_3^6 e^u\, du = 2e^u \,\Big|_3^6 = 2(e^6 - e^3) = 766.62 \qquad \text{Compare}$$

17.7. Redo Problem 17.5, given $\int_0^1 3x^2 e^{2x^3+1}\, dx$.

Let $u = 2x^3 + 1$, $du/dx = 6x^2$, and $dx = du/6x^2$.   Substituting,

$$\int 3x^2 e^{2x^3+1}\, dx = \int 3x^2 e^u \frac{du}{6x^2} = \frac{1}{2}\int e^u\, du$$

Integrating with respect to u,

$$\frac{1}{2}\int e^u\, du = \frac{1}{2}e^u$$

Substituting $u = 2x^3 + 1$,

$$\int_0^1 3x^2 e^{2x^3+1}\, dx = \frac{1}{2}e^{2x^3+1} \,\Big|_0^1 = \frac{1}{2}(e^3 - e^1) = \frac{1}{2}(20.09 - 2.718) = 8.68$$

With $u = 2x^3 + 1$,   the limits of u are $u = 2(0)^3 + 1 = 1$ and $u = 2(1)^3 + 1 = 3$.   Thus

$$\frac{1}{2}\int_1^3 e^u\, du = \frac{1}{2}e^u \,\Big|_1^3 = \frac{1}{2}(e^3 - e^1) = 8.68 \qquad \text{Compare}$$

INTEGRATION BY PARTS

17.8. Integrate the following definite integral, using the method of integration by parts:

$$\int_2^5 \frac{3x}{(x+1)^2}\, dx$$

Let $f(x) = 3x$; then $f'(x) = 3$. Let $g'(x) = (x + 1)^{-2}$; then $g(x) = \int (x + 1)^{-2} dx = -(x + 1)^{-1}$. Substituting in (16.1),

$$\int \frac{3x}{(x + 1)^2} dx = 3x[-(x + 1)^{-1}] - \int -(x + 1)^{-1}3\, dx$$

$$= -3x(x + 1)^{-1} + 3 \int (x + 1)^{-1}\, dx$$

Integrating again and ignoring the constant,

$$\int \frac{3x}{(x + 1)^2} dx = -3x(x + 1)^{-1} + 3 \ln |x + 1|$$

Applying the limits,

$$\int_2^5 \frac{3x}{(x + 1)^2} dx = [-3x(x + 1)^{-1} + 3 \ln |x + 1|]_2^5$$

$$= \left[-\frac{3(5)}{5 + 1} + 3 \ln |5 + 1| \right] - \left[-\frac{3(2)}{2 + 1} + 3 \ln |2 + 1| \right]$$

$$= -\tfrac{5}{2} + 3 \ln 6 + 2 - 3 \ln 3$$

$$= 3(\ln 6 - \ln 3) - \tfrac{1}{2} = 3(1.7918 - 1.0986) - 0.5 = 1.5796$$

17.9.   Redo Problem 17.8, given

$$\int_1^3 \frac{4x}{(x + 2)^3} dx$$

Let $f(x) = 4x$, $f'(x) = 4$, $g'(x) = (x + 2)^{-3}$, and $g(x) = \int (x + 2)^{-3} dx = -\tfrac{1}{2}(x + 2)^{-2}$. Substituting in (16.1),

$$\int \frac{4x}{(x + 2)^3} dx = 4x\left[-\frac{1}{2}(x + 2)^{-2} \right] - \int -\frac{1}{2}(x + 2)^{-2}4\, dx$$

$$= -2x(x + 2)^{-2} + 2 \int (x + 2)^{-2}\, dx$$

Integrating,

$$\int \frac{4x}{(x + 2)^3} dx = -2x(x + 2)^{-2} - 2(x + 2)^{-1}$$

Applying the limits,

$$\int_1^3 \frac{4x}{(x + 2)^3} dx = [-2x(x + 2)^{-2} - 2(x + 2)^{-1}]_1^3$$

$$= [-2(3)(3 + 2)^{-2} - 2(3 + 2)^{-1}] - [-2(1)(1 + 2)^{-2} - 2(1 + 2)^{-1}]$$

$$= -\tfrac{6}{25} - \tfrac{2}{5} + \tfrac{2}{9} + \tfrac{2}{3} = \tfrac{56}{225}$$

17.10.   Redo Problem 17.8, given $\int_1^3 5xe^{x+2}\, dx$.

Let $f(x) = 5x$, $f'(x) = 5$, $g'(x) = e^{x+2}$, and $g(x) = \int e^{x+2} dx = e^{x+2}$. Applying (16.1),

$$\int 5xe^{x+2}\, dx = 5xe^{x+2} - \int e^{x+2}5\, dx = 5xe^{x+2} - 5 \int e^{x+2}\, dx$$

Integrating,

$$\int 5xe^{x+2}\, dx = 5xe^{x+2} - 5e^{x+2}$$

Applying the limits,

$$\int_1^3 5xe^{x+2}\, dx = [5xe^{x+2} - 5e^{x+2}]_1^3 = (15e^5 - 5e^5) - (5e^3 - 5e^3) = 10e^5 = 10(148.4) = 1484$$

PROPERTIES OF DEFINITE INTEGRALS

17.11. Show $\int_{-4}^{4} (8x^3 + 9x^2)\, dx = \int_{-4}^{0} (8x^3 + 9x^2)\, dx + \int_{0}^{4} (8x^3 + 9x^2)\, dx$.

$$\int_{-4}^{4} (8x^3 + 9x^2)\, dx = 2x^4 + 3x^3 \Big|_{-4}^{4} = 704 - 320 = 384$$

$$\int_{-4}^{0} (8x^3 + 9x^2)\, dx = 2x^4 + 3x^3 \Big|_{-4}^{0} = 0 - 320 = -320$$

$$\int_{0}^{4} (8x^3 + 9x^2)\, dx = 2x^4 + 3x^3 \Big|_{0}^{4} = 704 - 0 = 704$$

Checking this answer, $-320 + 704 = 384$

17.12. Show $\int_{0}^{16} (x^{-1/2} + 3x)\, dx = \int_{0}^{4} (x^{-1/2} + 3x)\, dx + \int_{4}^{9} (x^{-1/2} + 3x)\, dx + \int_{9}^{16} (x^{-1/2} + 3x)\, dx$.

$$\int_{0}^{16} (x^{-1/2} + 3x)\, dx = 2x^{1/2} + 1.5x^2 \Big|_{0}^{16} = 392 - 0 = 392$$

$$\int_{0}^{4} (x^{-1/2} + 3x)\, dx = 2x^{1/2} + 1.5x^2 \Big|_{0}^{4} = 28 - 0 = 28$$

$$\int_{4}^{9} (x^{-1/2} + 3x)\, dx = 2x^{1/2} + 1.5x^2 \Big|_{4}^{9} = 127.5 - 28 = 99.5$$

$$\int_{9}^{16} (x^{-1/2} + 3x)\, dx = 2x^{1/2} + 1.5x^2 \Big|_{9}^{16} = 392 - 127.5 = 264.5$$

Checking this answer, $28 + 99.5 + 264.5 = 392$

17.13. Show

$$\int_{0}^{3} \frac{6x}{x^2 + 1}\, dx = \int_{0}^{1} \frac{6x}{x^2 + 1}\, dx + \int_{1}^{2} \frac{6x}{x^2 + 1}\, dx + \int_{2}^{3} \frac{6x}{x^2 + 1}\, dx$$

From Problem 17.5,

$$\int_{0}^{3} \frac{6x}{x^2 + 1}\, dx = 3 \ln |x^2 + 1| \Big|_{0}^{3} = 3 \ln 10$$

$$\int_{0}^{1} \frac{6x}{x^2 + 1}\, dx = 3 \ln |x^2 + 1| \Big|_{0}^{1} = 3 \ln 2 - 0 = 3 \ln 2$$

$$\int_{1}^{2} \frac{6x}{x^2 + 1}\, dx = 3 \ln |x^2 + 1| \Big|_{1}^{2} = 3 \ln 5 - 3 \ln 2$$

$$\int_{2}^{3} \frac{6x}{x^2 + 1}\, dx = 3 \ln |x^2 + 1| \Big|_{2}^{3} = 3 \ln 10 - 3 \ln 5$$

Checking this answer, $3 \ln 2 + 3 \ln 5 - 3 \ln 2 + 3 \ln 10 - 3 \ln 5 = 3 \ln 10$

17.14. Show $\int_{1}^{3} 5xe^{x+2}\, dx = \int_{1}^{2} 5xe^{x+2}\, dx + \int_{2}^{3} 5xe^{x+2}\, dx$.

From Problem 17.10,

$$\int_{1}^{3} 5xe^{x+2}\, dx = [5xe^{x+2} - 5e^{x+2}]_{1}^{3} = 10e^5$$

$$\int_{1}^{2} 5xe^{x+2}\, dx = [5xe^{x+2} - 5e^{x+2}]_{1}^{2} = (10e^4 - 5e^4) - (5e^3 - 5e^3) = 5e^4$$

$$\int_{2}^{3} 5xe^{x+2}\, dx = [5xe^{x+2} - 5e^{x+2}]_{2}^{3} = (15e^5 - 5e^5) - (10e^4 - 5e^4) = 10e^5 - 5e^4$$

Checking this answer, $5e^4 + 10e^5 - 5e^4 = 10e^5$

IMPROPER INTEGRALS AND CONVERGENCE

17.15. (*a*) Specify why the integral given below is improper and (*b*) test for convergence. Evaluate where possible.

$$\int_1^\infty \frac{2x}{(x^2+1)^2}\, dx$$

(*a*) This is an example of an improper integral because the upper limit of integration is infinite.

(*b*)
$$\int_1^\infty \frac{2x}{(x^2+1)^2}\, dx = \lim_{b\to\infty} \int_1^b \frac{2x}{(x^2+1)^2}\, dx$$

Let $u = x^2 + 1$, $du/dx = 2x$, and $dx = du/2x$. Substituting,

$$\int \frac{2x}{(x^2+1)^2}\, dx = \int 2xu^{-2}\frac{du}{2x} = \int u^{-2}\, du$$

Integrating with respect to u and ignoring the constant,

$$\int u^{-2}\, du = -u^{-1}$$

Substituting $u = x^2 + 1$ and incorporating the limits of x,

$$\int_1^\infty \frac{2x}{(x^2+1)^2}\, dx = \lim_{b\to\infty} \int_1^b \frac{2x}{(x^2+1)^2}\, dx = -(x^2+1)^{-1}\Big|_1^b$$

$$= \frac{-1}{b^2+1} + \frac{1}{(1)^2+1} = \frac{1}{2} - \frac{1}{b^2+1}$$

As $b\to\infty$, $1/(b^2+1)\to 0$. The integral converges and has a value of $\frac{1}{2}$.

17.16. Redo Problem 17.15, given

$$\int_1^\infty \frac{dx}{x+7}$$

(*a*) This is an improper integral because one of its limits of integration is infinite.

(*b*)
$$\int_1^\infty \frac{dx}{x+7} = \lim_{b\to\infty} \int_1^b \frac{dx}{x+7} = \ln|x+7|\Big|_1^b$$

$$= \ln|b+7| - \ln|1+7|$$

As $b\to\infty$, $\ln|b+7|\to\infty$. The integral diverges and is meaningless.

17.17. Redo Problem 17.15, given $\int_{-\infty}^0 e^{3x}\, dx$.

(*a*) The lower limit is infinite.

(*b*)
$$\int_{-\infty}^0 e^{3x}\, dx = \lim_{a\to-\infty} \int_a^0 e^{3x}\, dx = \frac{1}{3}e^{3x}\Big|_a^0$$

$$= \frac{1}{3}e^{3(0)} - \frac{1}{3}e^{3a} = \frac{1}{3} - \frac{1}{3}e^{3a}$$

As $a\to-\infty$, $\frac{1}{3}e^{3a}\to 0$. The integral converges and has a value of $\frac{1}{3}$.

17.18. (*a*) Specify why the integral given below is improper and (*b*) test for convergence. Evaluate where possible.

$$\int_{-\infty}^0 (5-x)^{-2}\, dx$$

(a)   The lower limit is infinite.

(b)
$$\int_{-\infty}^{0} (5-x)^{-2}\, dx = \lim_{a \to -\infty} \int_{a}^{0} (5-x)^{-2}\, dx$$

Let $u = 5 - x$, $du/dx = -1$, and $dx = -du$.   Substituting,

$$\int (5-x)^{-2}\, dx = \int u^{-2}(-du) = -\int u^{-2}\, du$$

Integrating with respect to u,

$$-\int u^{-2}\, du = u^{-1}$$

Substituting $u = 5 - x$,   and incorporating the limits of x,

$$\int_{-\infty}^{0} (5-x)^{-2}\, dx = \lim_{a \to -\infty} \int_{a}^{0} (5-x)^{-2}\, dx = (5-x)^{-1} \Big|_{a}^{0}$$

$$= \frac{1}{5-0} - \frac{1}{5-a} = \frac{1}{5} - \frac{1}{5-a}$$

As $a \to -\infty$, $1/(5-a) \to 0$.   The integral converges and equals $\frac{1}{5}$.

17.19.   Redo Problem 17.18, given $\int_{-\infty}^{0} 2xe^{x}\, dx$.

(a)   The lower limit is infinite.

(b)
$$\int_{-\infty}^{0} 2xe^{x}\, dx = \lim_{a \to -\infty} \int_{a}^{0} 2xe^{x}\, dx$$

Using integration by parts, let $f(x) = 2x$, $f'(x) = 2$, $g'(x) = e^{x}$, and $g(x) = \int e^{x}\, dx = e^{x}$.   Substituting in (16.1),

$$\int 2xe^{x}\, dx = 2xe^{x} - \int e^{x}2\, dx$$

Integrating once again,

$$\int 2xe^{x}\, dx = 2xe^{x} - 2e^{x}$$

Incorporating the limits,

$$\int_{-\infty}^{0} 2xe^{x}\, dx = \lim_{a \to -\infty} \int_{a}^{0} 2xe^{x}\, dx = 2xe^{x} - 2e^{x} \Big|_{a}^{0}$$

$$= [2(0)e^{0} - 2e^{0}] - [2ae^{a} - 2e^{a}]$$

$$= -2 - 2ae^{a} + 2e^{a}   \text{since}   e^{0} = 1$$

As $a \to -\infty$, $e^{a} \to 0$.   Therefore the integral converges and has a value of -2.

17.20.   Redo Problem 17.18, given

$$\int_{0}^{6} \frac{dx}{x-6}$$

(a)   This is also an improper integral because, as x approaches 6 from the left $(x \to 6^{-})$, the integrand $\to -\infty$.

(b)
$$\int_{0}^{6} \frac{dx}{x-6} = \lim_{b \to 6} \int_{0}^{b} \frac{dx}{x-6} = \ln|x-6| \Big|_{0}^{b}$$

$$= \ln|b-6| - \ln|0-6|$$

As $b \to 6^{-}$, $|b-6| \to 0$ and $\ln 0$ is undefined.   Therefore, the integral diverges and is meaningless.

17.21. Redo Problem 17.18, given $\int_0^8 (8-x)^{-1/2}\,dx$.

(a) As $x \to 8^-$, the integrand approaches infinity.

(b)
$$\int_0^8 (8-x)^{-1/2}\,dx = \lim_{b \to 8} \int_0^b (8-x)^{-1/2}\,dx = -2(8-x)^{1/2}\Big|_0^b \quad \text{(see Problem 17.18)}$$
$$= (-2\sqrt{8-b}) - (-2\sqrt{8-0}) = 2\sqrt{8} - 2\sqrt{8-b}$$

As $b \to 8^-$, $-2\sqrt{8-b} \to 0$. The integral converges and has a value of $2\sqrt{8} = 4\sqrt{2}$.

CONSUMERS' AND PRODUCERS' SURPLUS

17.22. Given the demand function $P = 45 - 0.5Q$, find the consumers' surplus CS when $P_0 = 32.5$ and $Q_0 = 25$.

Using (17.5),
$$CS = \int_0^{25} (45 - 0.5Q)\,dQ - (32.5)(25) = [45Q - 0.25Q^2]_0^{25} - 812.5$$
$$= [45(25) - 0.25(25)^2] - [0] - 812.5 = 156.25$$

17.23. Given the supply function $P = (Q+3)^2$, find the producers' surplus PS at $P_0 = 81$ and $Q_0 = 6$.

From (17.6),
$$PS = (81)(6) - \int_0^6 (Q+3)^2\,dQ = 486 - \left[\frac{1}{3}(Q+3)^3\right]_0^6$$
$$= 486 - \left[\frac{1}{3}(6+3)^3 - \frac{1}{3}(0+3)^3\right] = 252$$

17.24. Given the demand function $P_d = 25 - Q^2$ and the supply function $P_s = 2Q + 1$. Assuming pure competition, find (a) the consumers' surplus and (b) the producers' surplus.

For market equilibrium, $s = d$. Thus,
$$2Q + 1 = 25 - Q^2 \qquad Q^2 + 2Q - 24 = 0$$
$$(Q+6)(Q-4) = 0 \qquad Q_0 = 4 \qquad P_0 = 9$$

since Q_0 cannot equal -6.

(a)
$$CS = \int_0^4 (25 - Q^2)\,dQ - (9)(4) = \left[25Q - \frac{1}{3}Q^3\right]_0^4 - 36$$
$$= \left[25(4) - \frac{1}{3}(4)^3\right] - [0] - 36 = 42.67$$

(b)
$$PS = (9)(4) - \int_0^4 (2Q+1)\,dQ$$
$$= 36 - [Q^2 + Q]_0^4 = 16$$

17.25. Given the demand function $P_d = 113 - Q^2$ and the supply function $P_s = (Q+1)^2$ under pure competition, find (a) CS and (b) PS.

Multiplying the supply function out and equating supply and demand,
$$Q^2 + 2Q + 1 = 113 - Q^2 \qquad 2(Q^2 + Q - 56) = 0$$
$$(Q+8)(Q-7) = 0 \qquad Q_0 = 7 \qquad P_0 = 64$$

(a) $$CS = \int_0^7 (113 - Q^2)\, dQ - (64)(7) = \left[113Q - \frac{1}{3}Q^3\right]_0^7 - 448 = 228.67$$

(b) $$PS = (64)(7) - \int_0^7 (Q+1)^2\, dQ = 448 - \left[\frac{1}{3}(Q+1)^3\right]_0^7 = 448 - (170.67 - 0.33) = 277.67$$

17.26. Under a monopoly the quantity sold and market price are determined by the demand function. If the demand function for a profit-maximizing monopolist is $P = 274 - Q^2$ and $MC = 4 + 3Q$, find the consumers' surplus.

Given $P = 274 - Q^2$,

$$TR = PQ = (274 - Q^2)Q = 274Q - Q^3$$

and $$MR = \frac{dTR}{dQ} = 274 - 3Q^2$$

The monopolist maximizes profit at $MR = MC$. Thus,

$$274 - 3Q^2 = 4 + 3Q \qquad 3(Q^2 + Q - 90) = 0$$
$$(Q + 10)(Q - 9) = 0 \qquad Q_0 = 9 \qquad P_0 = 193$$

and $$CS = \int_0^9 (274 - Q^2)\, dQ - (193)(9) = \left[274Q - \frac{1}{3}Q^3\right]_0^9 - 1737 = 486$$

FREQUENCY FUNCTIONS AND PROBABILITY

17.27. The probability in minutes of being waited on in a large chain restaurant is given by the frequency function $f(t) = \frac{4}{81}t^3$ for $0 \leq t \leq 3$. What is the probability of being waited on between 1 and 2 minutes?

$$P = \int_1^2 \frac{4}{81}t^3\, dt = \frac{1}{81}t^4 \Big|_1^2 = \frac{1}{81}(16) - \frac{1}{81}(1) = 0.1852$$

17.28. The proportion of assignments completed within a given day is described by the probability density function $f(x) = 12(x^2 - x^3)\, dx$ for $0 \leq x \leq 1$. What is the probability that (a) 50 percent or less of the assignments will be completed within the day, and (b) 50 percent or more will be completed?

(a) $$P = \int_0^{0.5} 12(x^2 - x^3)\, dx = 12\left[\frac{x^3}{3} - \frac{x^4}{4}\right]_0^{0.5}$$
$$= 12\left[\left(\frac{0.125}{3} - \frac{0.0625}{4}\right) - 0\right] = 0.3125$$

(b) $$P = \int_{0.5}^1 12(x^2 - x^3)\, dx = 12\left[\frac{x^3}{3} - \frac{x^4}{4}\right]_{0.5}^1$$
$$= 12\left[\left(\frac{1}{3} - \frac{1}{4}\right) - \left(\frac{0.125}{3} - \frac{0.0625}{4}\right)\right] = 0.6875$$

As expected, $P_a + P_b = 0.3125 + 0.6875 = 1$.

OTHER ECONOMIC APPLICATIONS

17.29. Given $I(t) = 9t^{1/2}$, find the level of capital formation in (a) 8 years and (b) for the fifth through the eighth year (interval [4,8]).

(a) $$K = \int_0^8 9t^{1/2}\, dt = 6t^{3/2} \Big|_0^8 = 6(8)^{3/2} - 0 = 96\sqrt{2} = 135.76$$

(b) $$K = \int_4^8 9t^{1/2}\, dt = 6t^{3/2} \Big|_4^8 = 6(8)^{3/2} - 6(4)^{3/2} = 135.76 - 48 = 87.76$$

Chapter 18

Differential Equations

18.1 DEFINITIONS AND CONCEPTS

Differential equations are equations involving derivatives (or differentials).   They express rates of change of continuous functions over time.   The objective in working with differential equations is to find a function, without derivative or differential, which satisfies the differential equation.   Such a function is called the *solution* or *integral* of the equation.

The *order* of a differential equation is the order of the highest derivative in the equation.   The *degree* of a differential equation is the highest power to which the derivative of the highest order is raised.   See Example 1.

Example 1.   Determining the order and degree of differential equations is illustrated below.

1. $\dfrac{dy}{dx} = 2x + 6$.   First order, first degree.

2. $\left(\dfrac{dy}{dx}\right)^4 - 5x^5 = 0$.   First order, fourth degree.

3. $\dfrac{d^2y}{dx^2} + \left(\dfrac{dy}{dx}\right)^3 + x^2 = 0$.   Second order, first degree.

4. $\left(\dfrac{d^2y}{dx^2}\right)^7 + \left(\dfrac{d^3y}{dx^3}\right)^5 = 75y$.   Third order, fifth degree.

Example 2.   Given the differential equation $f''(y) = 7$,   by successive integration,

$$f'(y) = \int 7\, dx = 7x + c_1$$

and

$$f(y) = \int (7x + c_1)\, dx = 3.5x^2 + c_1 x + c_2$$

which is called a *general solution* since c_1 and c_2 are not specified.

18.2 GENERAL FORMULA FOR FIRST-ORDER LINEAR DIFFERENTIAL EQUATIONS

For a first-order *linear* differential equation, dy/dt and y must be no higher than the first degree and no product $y(dy/dt)$ may occur.   For such an equation,

$$\frac{dy}{dt} + vy = z$$

where v and z may be constants or functions of time, the formula for a *general solution* is

$$y(t) = e^{-\int v\, dt}\left(A + \int z e^{\int v\, dt}\, dt\right) \tag{18.1}$$

where A is an arbitrary constant.   If an initial condition is given, A can be specified, in which case a *definite solution* is possible.   A solution is composed of two parts. $e^{-\int v\, dt}A$ is called the *complementary function*; $e^{-\int v\, dt}\int z e^{\int v\, dt}\, dt$ is called the *particular integral*.   The particular integral

y_p equals the *intertemporal equilibrium level* of $y(t)$; the complementary function y_c represents the *deviation from the equilibrium*. For $y(t)$ to be *dynamically stable*, y_c must approach zero as t approaches infinity (i.e. k in e^{kt} must be negative). The solution of a differential equation can always be checked by differentiation.

Example 3. The general solution for the differential equation $\dfrac{dy}{dt} + 4y = 12$ is calculated as follows. Since $v = 4$ and $z = 12$, substituting in (*18.1*) gives

$$y(t) = e^{-\int 4\,dt}\left(A + \int 12e^{\int 4\,dt}\,dt\right)$$

From Section 16.2, $\int 4\,dt = 4t + c$. When using (*18.1*), c is always ignored and subsumed under A. Thus,

$$y(t) = e^{-4t}\left(A + \int 12e^{4t}\,dt\right) \tag{18.2}$$

Integrating the remaining integral, $\int 12e^{4t}\,dt = 3e^{4t} + c$. Ignoring the constant again and substituting in (*18.2*),

$$y(t) = e^{-4t}(A + 3e^{4t}) = Ae^{-4t} + 3 \tag{18.3}$$

since $e^{-4t}e^{4t} = e^0 = 1$. As $t \to \infty$, $y_c = Ae^{-4t} \to 0$ and $y(t)$ approaches $y_p = 3$, the intertemporal equilibrium level. $y(t)$ is dynamically stable.

To check the general solution, first take the derivative of (*18.3*),

$$\frac{dy}{dt} = -4Ae^{-4t}$$

From the original problem,

$$\frac{dy}{dt} + 4y = 12 \qquad \frac{dy}{dt} = 12 - 4y$$

Substituting $y = Ae^{-4t} + 3$ from (*18.3*),

$$\frac{dy}{dt} = 12 - 4(Ae^{-4t} + 3) = -4Ae^{-4t} \qquad \text{Compare}$$

Example 4. Given $\dfrac{dy}{dt} + 3t^2y = t^2$ where $v = 3t^2$ and $z = t^2$. To find the general solution, first substitute in (*18.1*),

$$y(t) = e^{-\int 3t^2\,dt}\left(A + \int t^2 e^{\int 3t^2\,dt}\,dt\right) \tag{18.4}$$

Integrating the exponents, $\int 3t^2\,dt = t^3$. Substituting in (*18.4*),

$$y(t) = e^{-t^3}\left(A + \int t^2 e^{t^3}\,dt\right) \tag{18.5}$$

Integrating the remaining integral in (*18.5*) calls for the substitution method. Letting $u = t^3$, $du/dt = 3t^2$, and $dt = du/3t^2$,

$$\int t^2 e^{t^3}\,dt = \int t^2 e^u \frac{du}{3t^2} = \frac{1}{3}\int e^u\,du = \frac{1}{3}e^u = \frac{1}{3}e^{t^3}$$

Finally, substituting in (*18.5*),

$$y(t) = e^{-t^3}(A + \tfrac{1}{3}e^{t^3}) = Ae^{-t^3} + \tfrac{1}{3} \tag{18.6}$$

As $t \to \infty$, $y_c = Ae^{-t^3} \to 0$ and $y(t)$ approaches $\tfrac{1}{3}$. The equilibrium is dynamically stable.

Differentiating (*18.6*) to check the general solution, $dy/dt = -3t^2Ae^{-t^3}$. From the original problem,

$$\frac{dy}{dt} + 3t^2y = t^2 \qquad \frac{dy}{dt} = t^2 - 3t^2y$$

Substituting y from (*18.6*),

$$\frac{dy}{dt} = t^2 - 3t^2(Ae^{-t^3} + \tfrac{1}{3}) = -3t^2Ae^{-t^3} \qquad \text{Compare}$$

Example 5. Suppose that $y(0) = 1$ in Example 4. The definite solution is calculated as follows: From (18.6), $y = Ae^{-t^3} + \frac{1}{3}$. At $t = 0$, $y(0) = 1$. Hence, $1 = A + \frac{1}{3}$ since $e^0 = 1$, and $A = \frac{2}{3}$. Substituting $A = \frac{2}{3}$ in (18.6), the definite solution is $y = \frac{2}{3}e^{-t^3} + \frac{1}{3}$.

18.3 EXACT DIFFERENTIAL EQUATIONS

If for a function of two variables $F(y,t)$, $M = \partial F / \partial y$ and $N = \partial F / \partial t$, then the total differential is

$$dF(y,t) = M \, dy + N \, dt \tag{18.7}$$

Since M and N are partial derivatives, this is called a *partial differential equation*. If the differential is set equal to zero, so that $M \, dy + N \, dt = 0$, it is called an *exact differential equation* because the left side exactly equals the differential of the primitive function $F(y,t)$. For an exact differential equation, $\partial M / \partial t$ must equal $\partial N / \partial y$, i.e. $\partial^2 F / \partial y \partial t = \partial^2 F / \partial t \partial y$.

Solution of an exact differential equation calls for successive integration with respect to one variable at a time while the other is held constant. (This is called *partial integration*, and is the inverse of partial differentiation.) See Example 6.

Example 6. To solve the exact nonlinear differential equation

$$(6yt + 9y^2) \, dy + (3y^2 + 8t) \, dt = 0 \tag{18.8}$$

1. Test to see if it is an exact differential equation. Here $M = 6yt + 9y^2$ and $N = 3y^2 + 8t$. Thus, $\partial M / \partial t = 6y$ and $\partial N / \partial y = 6y$. If $\partial M / \partial t \neq \partial N / \partial y$, it is not an exact differential equation.

2. Since $M = \partial F / \partial y$ is a partial derivative, integrate M partially with respect to y and add a new function $Z(t)$ for any additive terms of t which would have been eliminated by the original differentiation with respect to y.   Note that ∂y replaces dy in partial integration.

$$F(y,t) = \int (6yt + 9y^2) \partial y + Z(t) = 3y^2 t + 3y^3 + Z(t) \tag{18.9}$$

This gives the original function except for the unknown additive terms of t, $Z(t)$.

3. Differentiate (18.9) with respect to t to find $\partial F / \partial t$ (earlier called N).   Thus,

$$\frac{\partial F}{\partial t} = 3y^2 + Z'(t) \tag{18.10}$$

Since $\partial F / \partial t = N$ and from (18.8) $N = 3y^2 + 8t$, substitute $\partial F / \partial t = 3y^2 + 8t$ in (18.10).

$$3y^2 + 8t = 3y^2 + Z'(t) \qquad Z'(t) = 8t$$

4. Next integrate $Z'(t)$ with respect to t to find the missing t terms.

$$Z(t) = \int Z'(t) \, dt = \int 8t \, dt = 4t^2 \tag{18.11}$$

5. Substitute (18.11) in (18.9), and add a constant of integration.

$$F(y,t) = 3y^2 t + 3y^3 + 4t^2 + c$$

This is easily checked by differentiation.

18.4 INTEGRATING FACTORS

Not all differential equations are exact. However, some can be made exact by means of an *integrating factor*. This is a multiplier which permits the equation to be integrated.

Example 7. Testing the nonlinear differential equation, $5yt \, dy + (5y^2 + 8t) \, dt = 0$, reveals that it is not exact. With $M = 5yt$ and $N = 5y^2 + 8t$, $\partial M / \partial t = 5y \neq \partial N / \partial y = 10y$. Multiplying by an integrating factor of t, however, makes it exact: $5yt^2 \, dy + (5y^2 t + 8t^2) \, dt = 0$. Now $\partial M / \partial t = 10yt = \partial N / \partial y$, and the equation can be solved by the procedure outlined above. See Problem 18.22.

To check the answer to a problem in which an integrating factor was used, take the total differential of the answer and then divide by the integrating factor.

18.5 RULES FOR THE INTEGRATING FACTOR

Two rules will help to find the integrating factor for a nonlinear first-order differential equation, if such a factor exists.   Assuming $\partial M/\partial t \neq \partial N/\partial y$,

Rule 1.   If $\dfrac{1}{N}\left[\dfrac{\partial M}{\partial t} - \dfrac{\partial N}{\partial y}\right] = f(y)$ alone, then $e^{\int f(y)\,dy}$ is an integrating factor.

Rule 2.   If $\dfrac{1}{M}\left[\dfrac{\partial N}{\partial y} - \dfrac{\partial M}{\partial t}\right] = g(t)$ alone, then $e^{\int g(t)\,dt}$ is an integrating factor.

Example 8.   To illustrate the rules above, find the integrating factor given in Example 7, where

$$5yt\,dy + (5y^2 + 8t)\,dt = 0 \qquad M = 5yt \qquad N = 5y^2 + 8t \qquad \partial M/\partial t = 5y \neq \partial N/\partial y = 10y$$

Applying Rule 1,

$$\frac{1}{5y^2 + 8t}(5y - 10y) = \frac{-5y}{5y^2 + 8t}$$

which is not a function of y alone and will not supply an integrating factor for the equation.   Applying Rule 2,

$$\frac{1}{5yt}(10y - 5y) = \frac{5y}{5yt} = \frac{1}{t}$$

which is a function of t alone.   The integrating factor, therefore, is $e^{\int (1/t)\,dt} = e^{\ln t} = t$.

18.6 SEPARATION OF VARIABLES

Solution of nonlinear first-order, first-degree differential equations is complex.   (A first-order, first-degree differential equation is one in which the highest derivative is the first derivative dy/dt and that derivative is not raised to a power higher than one.   It is *nonlinear* if it contains a product of y and dy/dt, or y raised to a power higher than one.)   If the equation is exact or can be rendered exact by an integrating factor, the procedure outlined in Example 6 can be used.   If, however, the equation can be written in the form of *separated variables* such that $M(y)\,dy + N(t)\,dt = 0$ where M and N respectively are functions of y and t alone, the equation can be solved by ordinary integration.

Example 9.   The following calculations illustrate the separation of variables to solve the nonlinear differential equation

$$\frac{dy}{dt} = y^2 t \tag{18.12}$$

First, rearranging terms, $dy/y^2 = t\,dt$.   Thus, $M = 1/y^2$ and $N = t$.   Integrating both sides,

$$\int y^{-2}\,dy = \int t\,dt$$

$$-y^{-1} + c_1 = \frac{t^2}{2} + c_2$$

$$-\frac{1}{y} = \frac{t^2 + 2c_2 - 2c_1}{2}$$

Letting $c = 2c_2 - 2c_1$,

$$y = \frac{-2}{t^2 + c} \tag{18.13}$$

Since the constant of integration is arbitrary until it is evaluated to obtain a particular solution, it will be treated generally and not specifically in the initial steps of the solution. e^c and $\ln c$ can also be used to express the constant.

This solution can be checked as follows: Taking the derivative of $y = -2(t^2 + c)^{-1}$ by the chain rule,

$$\frac{dy}{dt} = (-1)(-2)(t^2 + c)^{-2}(2t) = \frac{4t}{(t^2 + c)^2}$$

From (18.12), $dy/dt = y^2 t$. Substituting into (18.12) from (18.13),

$$\frac{dy}{dt} = \left(\frac{-2}{t^2 + c}\right)^2 t = \frac{4t}{(t^2 + c)^2} \qquad \text{Compare}$$

Example 10. Given: the nonlinear differential equation

$$t^2 \, dy + y^3 \, dt = 0 \qquad\qquad (18.14)$$

where $M \neq f(y)$ and $N \neq f(t)$. But multiplying (18.14) by $(1/t^2 y^3)$ to separate the variables gives

$$\frac{1}{y^3} \, dy + \frac{1}{t^2} \, dt = 0 \qquad\qquad (18.14a)$$

Integrating the separated variables,

$$\int y^{-3} \, dy + \int t^{-2} \, dt = -\frac{1}{2} y^{-2} - t^{-1} + c$$

and

$$F(y,t) = -\tfrac{1}{2} y^{-2} - t^{-1} + c$$

For complicated functions, the answer is frequently left in this form. It can be checked by differentiating and comparing with ($18.14a$), which can be reduced to (18.14) through multiplication by $y^3 t^2$. For other forms in which an answer can be expressed, see Problems 18.20–18.22 and 18.29–18.31.

18.7 BERNOULLI EQUATIONS

A *Bernoulli equation* is a nonlinear differential equation in the specific form

$$\frac{dy}{dt} + ay = by^n \qquad\qquad (18.15)$$

where a and b are constants or functions of t, $n \neq 0$ and $n \neq 1$. By letting $w = y^{1-n}$, Equation (18.15) can be transformed into a linear equation of the form

$$\frac{dw}{dt} + (1 - n)aw = (1 - n)b \qquad\qquad (18.15a)$$

which can be solved by (18.1) with $v = (1 - n)a$ and $z = (1 - n)b$. See Problem 18.48.

Example 11. The Bernoulli equation, $\dfrac{dy}{dt} - y = ty^2$ is solved below.

Here $n = 2$, so $w = y^{1-2} = y^{-1}$; $a = -1$, $b = t$; and $(1 - n) = -1$. Substituting in ($18.15a$),

$$\frac{dw}{dt} + w = -t$$

Using (18.1) with $v = 1$ and $z = -t$,

$$w(t) = e^{-\int 1 \, dt}\left(A + \int -te^{\int 1 \, dt} \, dt\right) = e^{-t}\left(A + \int -te^t \, dt\right)$$

By parts,

$$w(t) = e^{-t}(A - te^t + e^t) = Ae^{-t} - t + 1$$

Since $w(t) = y(t)^{-1}$,

$$y(t) = (Ae^{-t} - t + 1)^{-1}$$

18.8 ECONOMIC APPLICATIONS

Differential equations serve many functions in economics. They are used to determine the conditions for dynamic stability in microeconomic models of market equilibria and to trace the time path of growth under various conditions in macroeconomics. Given the growth rate of a function, differential equations enable the economist to find the function whose growth is described; from point elasticity, they enable him to estimate the demand function (see Example 12 and Problems 18.39–18.50). In Section 16.6 they were used to estimate capital functions from investment functions and total cost and total revenue functions from marginal cost and marginal revenue functions.

Example 12. Given the demand function $Q_d = c + bP$ and the supply function $Q_s = g + hP$, the equilibrium price is

$$\bar{P} = \frac{c-g}{h-b} \tag{18.16}$$

Assume that the rate of change of price in the market (dP/dt) is a positive linear function of *excess demand* ($Q_d - Q_s$) such that

$$\frac{dP}{dt} = m(Q_d - Q_s) \quad m = \text{a constant} > 0 \tag{18.17}$$

the conditions for dynamic price stability in the market [i.e. under what conditions $P(t)$ will converge to $\bar{P}$ as $t \to \infty$] can be calculated as shown below.

Substituting the given parameters for Q_d and Q_s in (18.17),

$$\frac{dP}{dt} = m[(c + bP) - (g + hP)] = m(c + bP - g - hP)$$

Rearranging to fit the general format of Section 18.2, $\dfrac{dP}{dt} + m(h-b)P = m(c-g)$. Letting $v = m(h-b)$ and $z = m(c-g)$, and using (18.1),

$$P(t) = e^{-\int v\,dt}\left(A + \int z e^{\int v\,dt}\,dt\right) = e^{-vt}\left(A + \int z e^{vt}\,dt\right)$$

$$= e^{-vt}\left(A + \frac{z e^{vt}}{v}\right) = A e^{-vt} + \frac{z}{v} \, . \tag{18.18}$$

At $t = 0$, $P(0) = A + z/v$ and $A = P(0) - z/v$.

Substituting in (18.18),

$$P(t) = \left[P(0) - \frac{z}{v}\right]e^{-vt} + \frac{z}{v}$$

Finally, replacing $v = m(h-b)$ and $z = m(c-g)$,

$$P(t) = \left[P(0) - \frac{c-g}{h-b}\right]e^{-m(h-b)t} + \frac{c-g}{h-b}$$

and making use of (18.16), the time path is

$$P(t) = [P(0) - \bar{P}]e^{-m(h-b)t} + \bar{P} \tag{18.19}$$

Since $P(0)$, $\bar{P}$, $m > 0$, the first term on the right-hand side will converge toward zero as $t \to \infty$, and thus $P(t)$ will converge toward $\bar{P}$, only if $h - b > 0$. For normal cases where demand is negatively sloped ($b < 0$) and supply is positively sloped ($h > 0$), the dynamic stability condition is assured. Markets with positively sloped demand functions or negatively sloped supply functions will also be dynamically stable as long as $h > b$.

Solved Problems

ORDER AND DEGREE

18.1. Specify the order and degree of each of the following differential equations:

(a) $\dfrac{d^2y}{dx^2} + \left(\dfrac{dy}{dx}\right)^3 = 12x$ 　　　　　(d) $\left(\dfrac{d^2y}{dx^2}\right)^3 + \dfrac{d^4y}{dx^4} - 75y = 0$

(b) $\dfrac{dy}{dx} = 3x^2$ 　　　　　(e) $\dfrac{d^3y}{dx^3} + x^2y\left(\dfrac{d^2y}{dx^2}\right) - 4y^4 = 0$

(c) $\left(\dfrac{d^3y}{dx^3}\right)^4 + \left(\dfrac{d^2y}{dx^2}\right)^6 = 4 - y$

(a) Second order, first degree 　(b) First order, first degree 　(c) Third order, fourth degree
(d) Fourth order, first degree 　(e) Third order, first degree

FIRST-ORDER, FIRST-DEGREE LINEAR DIFFERENTIAL EQUATIONS

18.2 (a) Use the formula for a general solution to solve the following equation. (b) Check your answer.

$$\frac{dy}{dt} + 5y = 0 \tag{18.20}$$

(a) Here $v = 5$ and $z = 0$. Substituting in (18.1),

$$y(t) = e^{-\int 5\,dt}\left(A + \int 0 e^{\int 5\,dt}\,dt\right)$$

Integrating the exponents, $\int 5\,dt = 5t + c$, where c can be ignored because it is subsumed under A. Thus, $y(t) = e^{-5t}(A + \int 0\,dt)$. $\int 0\,dt = k$, a constant, which can also be subsumed under A. Hence,

$$y(t) = e^{-5t}(A) = Ae^{-5t} \tag{18.21}$$

(b) Taking the derivative of (18.21), $dy/dt = -5Ae^{-5t}$. From (18.20), $dy/dt = -5y$. Substituting y from (18.21),

$$\frac{dy}{dt} = -5(Ae^{-5t}) = -5Ae^{-5t} \qquad \text{Compare}$$

18.3. Redo Problem 18.2, given

$$\frac{dy}{dt} = 3y \qquad y(0) = 2 \tag{18.22}$$

(a) Rearranging to obtain the general format,

$$\frac{dy}{dt} - 3y = 0$$

Here $v = -3$ and $z = 0$. Substituting in (18.1),

$$y(t) = e^{-\int -3\,dt}\left(A + \int 0 e^{\int -3\,dt}\,dt\right)$$

Substituting $\int -3\,dt = -3t$, $y(t) = e^{3t}(A + \int 0\,dt) = Ae^{3t}$. At $t = 0$, $y = 2$. Thus, $2 = Ae^{3(0)}$, $A = 2$. Substituting,

$$y(t) = 2e^{3t} \tag{18.23}$$

(b) Taking the derivative of (18.23), $dy/dt = 6e^{3t}$. From (18.22), $dy/dt = 3y$. Substituting y from (18.23), $dy/dt = 3(2e^{3t}) = 6e^{3t}$. Compare.

18.4.   Redo Problem 18.2, given

$$\frac{dy}{dt} = 15 \qquad\qquad (18.24)$$

(a) Here $v = 0$ and $z = 15$.   Thus,

$$y(t) = e^{-\int 0\,dt}\left(A + \int 15 e^{\int 0\,dt}\,dt\right)$$

where $\int 0\,dt = k$, a constant. Substituting, and recalling that e^k is also a constant,

$$y(t) = e^{-k}\left(A + \int 15 e^{k}\,dt\right)$$
$$= e^{-k}(A + 15te^{k}) = Ae^{-k} + 15t = 15t + A \qquad\qquad (18.25)$$

where A is an arbitrary constant equal to Ae^{-k} or simply c.   Whenever the derivative is equal to a constant, simply integrate as in Example 2.

(b) Taking the derivative of (18.25), $dy/dt = 15$.   From (18.24), $dy/dt = 15$.   Compare.

18.5.   Redo Problem 18.2, given

$$\frac{dy}{dt} - 6y = 18 \qquad\qquad (18.26)$$

(a) Here $v = -6$, $z = 18$, and $\int -6\,dt = -6t$.   Substituting in (18.1),

$$y(t) = e^{6t}\left(A + \int 18 e^{-6t}\,dt\right)$$

where $\int 18 e^{-6t}\,dt = -3e^{-6t}$. Thus,

$$y(t) = e^{6t}(A - 3e^{-6t}) = Ae^{6t} - 3 \qquad\qquad (18.27)$$

(b) Taking the derivative of (18.27), $dy/dt = 6Ae^{6t}$.   From (18.26), $dy/dt = 18 + 6y$.   Substituting y from (18.27), $dy/dt = 18 + 6(Ae^{6t} - 3) = 6Ae^{6t}$.   Compare.

18.6.   Redo Problem 18.2, given

$$\frac{dy}{dt} + 4y = -20 \qquad\qquad y(0) = 10 \qquad\qquad (18.28)$$

(a) Here $v = 4$, $z = -20$, and $\int 4\,dt = 4t$.   Thus,

$$y(t) = e^{-4t}\left(A + \int -20 e^{4t}\,dt\right)$$

where $\int -20 e^{4t}\,dt = -5e^{4t}$.   Substituting, $y(t) = e^{-4t}(A - 5e^{4t}) = Ae^{-4t} - 5$.   At $t = 0$, $y = 10$.   Thus, $10 = Ae^{-4(0)} - 5$, and $A = 15$.   Substituting,

$$y(t) = 15e^{-4t} - 5 = 5(3e^{-4t} - 1) \qquad\qquad (18.29)$$

(b) The derivative of (18.29) is $dy/dt = -60e^{-4t}$.   From (18.28), $dy/dt = -20 - 4y$.   Substituting from (18.29) for y, $dy/dt = -20 - 4(15e^{-4t} - 5) = -60e^{-4t}$.   Compare.

18.7.   Redo Problem 18.2, given

$$\frac{dy}{dt} + 4ty = 6t \qquad\qquad (18.30)$$

(a) $v = 4t$, $z = 6t$, and $\int 4t\,dt = 2t^2$.   Thus,

$$y(t) = e^{-2t^2}\left(A + \int 6te^{2t^2}\,dt\right) \qquad\qquad (18.31)$$

Using the substitution method for the remaining integral, let $u = 2t^2$, $du/dt = 4t$, and $dt = du/4t$. Thus,

$$\int 6te^{2t^2} dt = \int 6te^u \frac{du}{4t} = 1.5 \int e^u du = 1.5 e^{2t^2}$$

Substituting back in (18.31),

$$y(t) = e^{-2t^2}(A + 1.5 e^{2t^2}) = Ae^{-2t^2} + 1.5 \qquad\qquad (18.32)$$

(b) The derivative of (18.32) is $dy/dt = -4tAe^{-2t^2}$. From (18.30), $dy/dt = 6t - 4ty$. Substituting from (18.32), $dy/dt = 6t - 4t(Ae^{-2t^2} + 1.5) = -4tAe^{-2t^2}$. Compare.

18.8. (a) Solve the equation below using the formula for a general solution. (b) Check your answer.

$$2\frac{dy}{dt} - 2t^2 y = 9t^2 \qquad\qquad y(0) = -2.5 \qquad\qquad (18.33)$$

(a) Dividing through by 2, $dy/dt - t^2 y = 4.5 t^2$. Thus, $v = -t^2$, $z = 4.5 t^2$, and $\int -t^2 dt = -\frac{1}{3}t^3$. Substituting,

$$y(t) = e^{(1/3)t^3}\left(A + \int 4.5 t^2 e^{-(1/3)t^3} dt\right) \qquad\qquad (18.34)$$

Let $u = -\frac{1}{3}t^3$, $du/dt = -t^2$, and $dt = -du/t^2$. Thus,

$$\int 4.5 t^2 e^{-(1/3)t^3} dt = \int 4.5 t^2 e^u \frac{du}{-t^2} = -4.5 \int e^u du = -4.5 e^{-(1/3)t^3}$$

Substituting in (18.34),

$$y(t) = e^{(1/3)t^3}(A - 4.5 e^{-(1/3)t^3}) = Ae^{(1/3)t^3} - 4.5$$

At $t = 0$, $-2.5 = A - 4.5$; $A = 2$. Thus,

$$y(t) = 2e^{(1/3)t^3} - 4.5 \qquad\qquad (18.35)$$

(b) Taking the derivative of (18.35), $dy/dt = 2t^2 e^{(1/3)t^3}$. From (18.33), $dy/dt = 4.5 t^2 + t^2 y$. Substituting from (18.35), $dy/dt = 4.5t^2 + t^2(2e^{(1/3)t^3} - 4.5) = 2t^2 e^{(1/3)t^3}$. Compare.

18.9. Redo Problem 18.8, given

$$\frac{dy}{dt} - 2ty = e^{t^2} \qquad\qquad (18.36)$$

(a) $v = -2t$, $z = e^{t^2}$, and $\int -2t\, dt = -t^2$. Thus,

$$y(t) = e^{t^2}\left(A + \int e^{t^2} e^{-t^2} dt\right) = e^{t^2}\left(A + \int e^0 dt\right)$$

where $e^0 = 1$ and $\int 1\, dt = t$. Substituting back,

$$y(t) = e^{t^2}(A + t) \qquad\qquad (18.37)$$

(b) The derivative of (18.37), by the product rule, is $dy/dt = 2te^{t^2}(A + t) + e^{t^2}(1) = 2tAe^{t^2} + 2t^2 e^{t^2} + e^{t^2}$. From (18.36), $dy/dt = e^{t^2} + 2ty$. Substituting from (18.37),

$$\frac{dy}{dt} = e^{t^2} + 2t[e^{t^2}(A + t)] = e^{t^2} + 2tAe^{t^2} + 2t^2 e^{t^2}. \qquad \text{Compare}$$

18.10. Redo Problem 18.8, given

$$\frac{dy}{dt} + 3y = 6t \qquad\qquad y(0) = \frac{1}{3} \qquad\qquad (18.38)$$

(a) $v = 3$, $z = 6t$, and $\int 3\, dt = 3t$. Then,

$$y(t) = e^{-3t}\left(A + \int 6te^{3t} dt\right) \qquad\qquad (18.39)$$

Using integration by parts for the remaining integral, let $f(t) = 6t$, then $f'(t) = 6$; let $g'(t) = e^{3t}$, then $g(t) = \int e^{3t} \, dt = \frac{1}{3}e^{3t}$. Substituting in (16.1),

$$\int 6te^{3t} \, dt = 6t\left(\frac{1}{3}e^{3t}\right) - \int \frac{1}{3}e^{3t}6 \, dt$$

$$= 2te^{3t} - 2\int e^{3t} \, dt = 2te^{3t} - \frac{2}{3}e^{3t}$$

Substituting back in (18.39),

$$y(t) = e^{-3t}(A + 2te^{3t} - \tfrac{2}{3}e^{3t}) = Ae^{-3t} + 2t - \tfrac{2}{3}$$

At $t = 0$, $\frac{1}{3} = Ae^{-3(0)} + 2(0) - \frac{2}{3}$; $A = 1$. Thus,

$$y(t) = e^{-3t} + 2t - \tfrac{2}{3} \tag{18.40}$$

(b) Taking the derivative of (18.40), $dy/dt = -3e^{-3t} + 2$. From (18.38), $dy/dt = 6t - 3y$. Substituting (18.40) directly above, $dy/dt = 6t - 3(e^{-3t} + 2t - \frac{2}{3}) = -3e^{-3t} + 2$. Compare.

18.11. Redo Problem 18.8, given

$$\frac{dy}{dt} - \frac{y}{t} = 0 \qquad y(3) = 12 \tag{18.41}$$

(a) $v = -1/t$, $z = 0$, and $\int -(1/t) \, dt = -\ln t$. Thus,

$$y(t) = e^{\ln t}\left(A + \int 0 \, dt\right) = At$$

since $e^{\ln t} = t$. At $t = 3$, $12 = A(3)$; $A = 4$. Thus,

$$y(t) = 4t \tag{18.42}$$

(b) The derivative of (18.42) is $dy/dt = 4$. From (18.41), $dy/dt = y/t$. Substituting from (18.42), $dy/dt = 4t/t = 4$. Compare.

18.12. Redo Problem 18.8, given

$$\frac{dy}{dt} = -y \qquad y(3) = 20 \tag{18.43}$$

(a) With rearranging, $dy/dt + y = 0$. Therefore, $v = 1$, $z = 0$, and $\int 1 \, dt = t$. Thus,

$$y(t) = e^{-t}\left(A + \int 0 \, dt\right) = Ae^{-t}$$

At $t = 3$, $20 = Ae^{-3}$. From Appendix III, $20 = A(0.05)$; $A = 400$. Thus,

$$y(t) = 400e^{-t} \tag{18.44}$$

(b) Taking the derivative of (18.44), $dy/dt = -400e^{-t}$. From (18.43), $dy/dt = -y$. Substituting from (18.44), $dy/dt = -(400e^{-t}) = -400e^{-t}$. Compare.

EXACT DIFFERENTIAL EQUATIONS

18.13. Solve the following exact differential equation. Check the answer on your own.

$$(4y + 8t^2) \, dy + (16yt - 3) \, dt = 0$$

As outlined in Example 6,

1. Check to see if it is an exact differential equation. Letting $M = (4y + 8t^2)$ and $N = (16yt - 3)$, $\partial M/\partial t = 16t = \partial N/\partial y$. Compare.

2. Integrate M partially with respect to y and add $Z(t)$ to get $F(y,t)$.

$$F(y,t) = \int (4y + 8t^2) \, \partial y + Z(t) = 2y^2 + 8t^2y + Z(t) \tag{18.45}$$

3. Differentiate $F(y,t)$ partially with respect to t and equate with N above.

$$\frac{\partial F}{\partial t} = 16ty + Z'(t)$$

But $\partial F/\partial t = N = 16yt - 3$,   so

$$16ty + Z'(t) = 16yt - 3 \qquad Z'(t) = -3$$

4. Integrate $Z'(t)$ with respect to t to get $Z(t)$.

$$Z(t) = \int Z'(t)\, dt = \int -3\, dt = -3t \qquad\qquad (18.46)$$

5. Substitute (18.46) in (18.45) and add a constant of integration.

$$F(y,t) = 2y^2 + 8t^2 y - 3t + c$$

18.14. Redo Problem 18.13, given $(12y + 7t + 6)\, dy + (7y + 4t - 9)\, dt = 0$.

1. $\partial M/\partial t = 7 = \partial N/\partial y$.   Check.

2. $$F(y,t) = \int (12y + 7t + 6)\, \partial y + Z(t) = 6y^2 + 7yt + 6y + Z(t)$$

3. $\partial F/\partial t = 7y + Z'(t)$.   But $\partial F/\partial t = N = 7y + 4t - 9$,   so
$$7y + Z'(t) = 7y + 4t - 9 \qquad Z'(t) = 4t - 9$$

4. $$Z(t) = \int (4t - 9)\, dt = 2t^2 - 9t$$

5. $$F(y,t) = 6y^2 + 7yt + 6y + 2t^2 - 9t + c$$

18.15. Redo Problem 18.13, given $(12y^2 t^2 + 10y)\, dy + (8y^3 t)\, dt = 0$.

1. $\partial M/\partial t = 24y^2 t = \partial N/\partial y$.   Check.

2. $$F(y,t) = \int (12y^2 t^2 + 10y)\, \partial y + Z(t) = 4y^3 t^2 + 5y^2 + Z(t)$$

3. $\partial F/\partial t = 8y^3 t + Z'(t)$.   But $N = 8y^3 t$, so
$$8y^3 t = 8y^3 t + Z'(t) \qquad Z'(t) = 0$$

4. $Z(t) = \int 0\, dt = k$,   which will be subsumed under c.

5. $$F(y,t) = 4y^3 t^2 + 5y^2 + c$$

18.16. Redo Problem 18.13, given $8tyy' = -(3t^2 + 4y^2)$.

By rearranging,

$$8ty\, dy = -(3t^2 + 4y^2)\, dt \qquad 8ty\, dy + (3t^2 + 4y^2)\, dt = 0$$

1. $\partial M/\partial t = 8y = \partial N/\partial y$.   Check.

2. $$F(y,t) = \int 8ty\, \partial y + Z(t) = 4ty^2 + Z(t)$$

3. $\partial F/\partial t = 4y^2 + Z'(t)$.   But $\partial F/\partial t = N = 3t^2 + 4y^2$,   so
$$4y^2 + Z'(t) = 3t^2 + 4y^2 \qquad Z'(t) = 3t^2$$

4. $$Z(t) = \int 3t^2\, dt = t^3$$

5. $$F(y,t) = t^3 + 4ty^2 + c$$

18.17. Redo Problem 18.13, given $60ty^2y' = -(12t^3 + 20y^3)$.

By rearranging, $60ty^2\,dy + (12t^3 + 20y^3)\,dt = 0$

1. $\partial M/\partial t = 60y^2 = \partial N/\partial y$.   Check.

2. $$F(y,t) = \int 60ty^2\,\partial y + Z(t) = 20ty^3 + Z(t)$$

3. $\partial F/\partial t = 20y^3 + Z'(t)$.   But $\partial F/\partial t = N = 12t^3 + 20y^3$,   so
$$20y^3 + Z'(t) = 12t^3 + 20y^3 \qquad Z'(t) = 12t^3$$

4. $$Z(t) = \int 12t^3\,dt = 3t^4$$

5. $$F(y,t) = 3t^4 + 20ty^3 + c$$

INTEGRATING FACTORS

18.18. Use the integrating factors provided in parentheses to solve the following differential equation.   Check the answer on your own (remember to divide by the integrating factor after taking the total differential of the answer).

$$6t\,dy + 12y\,dt = 0 \qquad (t)$$

1. $\partial M/\partial t = 6 \neq \partial N/\partial y = 12$.   But multiplying by the integrating factor t,
$$6t^2\,dy + 12yt\,dt = 0$$
where $\partial M/\partial t = 12t = \partial N/\partial y$.   Continuing with the new function,

2. $$F(y,t) = \int 6t^2\,\partial y + Z(t) = 6t^2y + Z(t)$$

3. $\partial F/\partial t = 12ty + Z'(t)$.   But $\partial F/\partial t = N = 12ty$,   so $Z'(t) = 0$.
4. $Z(t) = \int 0\,dt = k$,   which will be subsumed under the c below.
5. $$F(y,t) = 6t^2y + c$$

18.19. Redo Problem 18.18, given
$$t^2\,dy + 3yt\,dt = 0 \qquad (t)$$

1. $\partial M/\partial t = 2t \neq \partial N/\partial y = 3t$.   But multiplying by t,
$$t^3\,dy + 3yt^2\,dt = 0$$
where $\partial M/\partial t = 3t^2 = \partial N/\partial y$.   Compare.

2. $$F(y,t) = \int t^3\,\partial y + Z(t) = t^3y + Z(t)$$

3. $\partial F/\partial t = 3t^2y + Z'(t)$.   But $\partial F/\partial t = N = 3t^2y$,   so $Z'(t) = 0$ and $F(y,t) = t^3y + c$.

18.20. Redo Problem 18.18, given
$$\frac{dy}{dt} = \frac{y}{t} \qquad \left(\frac{1}{ty}\right)$$

Rearranging, $t\,dy = y\,dt \qquad t\,dy - y\,dt = 0$

1. $\partial M/\partial t = 1 \neq \partial N/\partial y = -1$.   Multiplying by $(1/ty)$,
$$\frac{dy}{y} - \frac{dt}{t} = 0$$
where $\partial M/\partial t = 0 = \partial N/\partial y$,   since neither function contains the variable with respect to which it is being partially differentiated.   Compare.

2. $$F(y,t) = \int \frac{1}{y}\, \partial y + Z(t) = \ln y + Z(t)$$

3. $\partial F/\partial t = Z'(t)$.   But $\partial F/\partial t = N = -(1/t)$,   so $Z'(t) = -1/t$.

4. $$Z(t) = \int -\frac{1}{t}\, dt = -\ln t$$

5. $F(y,t) = \ln y - \ln t + c$ which can be expressed in different ways.   Since c is an arbitrary constant, we can write $\ln y - \ln t = c$.   Making use of the laws of logs (Section 7.8), $\ln y - \ln t = \ln(y/t)$.   Thus, $\ln(y/t) = c$.   Finally, expressing each side of the equation as exponents of e, and recalling that $e^{\ln x} = x$,

$$e^{(\ln y/t)} = e^c$$

$$\frac{y}{t} = e^c \qquad \text{or} \qquad y = te^c$$

For other treatments of c, see Problems 18.29–18.35.

18.21. Redo Problem 18.18, given

$$4t\, dy + (16y - t^2)\, dt = 0 \qquad (t^3)$$

1. $\partial M/\partial t = 4 \neq \partial N/\partial y = 16$.   Multiplying by t^3, $4t^4\, dy + (16t^3 y - t^5)\, dt = 0$ where $\partial M/\partial t = 16t^3 = \partial N/\partial y$.   Compare.

2. $$F(y,t) = \int 4t^4\, \partial y + Z(t) = 4t^4 y + Z(t)$$

3. $\partial F/\partial t = 16t^3 y + Z'(t)$.   But $\partial F/\partial t = N = 16t^3 y - t^5$,   so

$$16t^3 y + Z'(t) = 16t^3 y - t^5 \qquad Z'(t) = -t^5$$

4. $$Z(t) = \int -t^5\, dt = -\frac{1}{6}t^6$$

5. $$F(y,t) = 4t^4 y - \frac{1}{6}t^6 + c = 24t^4 y - t^6 + c$$

or

$$24t^4 y - t^6 = c$$

18.22. Redo Problem 18.18, given

$$5yt\, dy + (5y^2 + 8t)\, dt = 0 \qquad (t)$$

1. $\partial M/\partial t = 5y \neq \partial N/\partial y = 10y$.   Multiplying by t, as in Example 7, $5yt^2\, dy + (5y^2 t + 8t^2)\, dt = 0$ where $\partial M/\partial t = 10yt = \partial N/\partial y$.

2. $$F(y,t) = \int 5yt^2\, \partial y + Z(t) = 2.5\, y^2 t^2 + Z(t)$$

3. $\partial F/\partial t = 5y^2 t + Z'(t)$.   But $\partial F/\partial t = N = 5y^2 t + 8t^2$,   so

$$5y^2 t + Z'(t) = 5y^2 t + 8t^2 \qquad Z'(t) = 8t^2$$

4. $$Z(t) = \int 8t^2\, dt = \tfrac{8}{3}t^3$$

5. $$F(y,t) = 2.5\, y^2 t^2 + \tfrac{8}{3}t^3 + c = 7.5\, y^2 t^2 + 8t^3 + c$$

FINDING THE INTEGRATING FACTOR

18.23. (a) Find the integrating factor for the differential equation given below, and   (b) solve the equation, using the five steps from Section 18.3.

$$(7y + 4t^2)\, dy + 4ty\, dt = 0 \tag{18.47}$$

(a) $\partial M/\partial t = 8t \neq \partial N/\partial y = 4t$. Applying Rule 1 from Section 18.5, since $M = 7y + 4t^2$ and $N = 4ty$,

$$\frac{1}{4ty}(8t - 4t) = \frac{4t}{4ty} = \frac{1}{y} = f(y) \qquad \text{alone}$$

Thus the integrating factor is

$$e^{\int (1/y)\,dy} = e^{\ln y} = y$$

(b) Multiplying (18.47) by the integrating factor y, $(7y^2 + 4yt^2)\,dy + 4ty^2\,dt = 0$.

1. $\partial M/\partial t = 8yt = \partial N/\partial y$. Thus,

2. $$F(y,t) = \int (7y^2 + 4yt^2)\partial y + Z(t) = \tfrac{7}{3}y^3 + 2y^2t^2 + Z(t)$$

3. $$\frac{\partial F}{\partial t} = 4y^2t + Z'(t)$$

4. $\partial F/\partial t = N = 4y^2t$,   so $Z'(t) = 0$ and $Z(t)$ is a constant. Thus,

5. $$F(y,t) = \tfrac{7}{3}y^3 + 2y^2t^2 + c = 7y^3 + 6y^2t^2 + c$$

18.24. Redo Problem 18.23, given

$$y^3t\,dy + \tfrac{1}{2}y^4\,dt = 0 \tag{18.48}$$

(a) $\partial M/\partial t = y^3 \neq \partial N/\partial y = 2y^3$. Applying Rule 1,

$$\frac{1}{(1/2)y^4}(y^3 - 2y^3) = \frac{2}{y^4}(-y^3) = -\frac{2}{y} = f(y) \qquad \text{alone}$$

Thus, $$e^{\int -2y^{-1}\,dy} = e^{-2\ln y} = e^{\ln y^{-2}} = y^{-2}$$

(b) Multiplying (18.48) by y^{-2}, $yt\,dy + \tfrac{1}{2}y^2\,dt = 0$.

1. $\partial M/\partial t = y = \partial N/\partial y$. Thus,

2. $$F(y,t) = \int yt\,\partial y + Z(t) = \tfrac{1}{2}y^2t + Z(t)$$

3. $$\frac{\partial F}{\partial t} = \tfrac{1}{2}y^2 + Z'(t)$$

4. $\partial F/\partial t = N = \tfrac{1}{2}y^2$,   so $Z'(t) = 0$,   and $Z(t)$ is a constant. Thus,

5. $$F(y,t) = \tfrac{1}{2}y^2t + c$$

18.25. Redo Problem 18.23, given

$$4t\,dy + (16y - t^2)\,dt = 0 \tag{18.49}$$

(a) $M = 4t$, $N = 16y - t^2$, and $\partial M/\partial t = 4 \neq \partial N/\partial y = 16$. Applying Rule 1,

$$\frac{1}{16y - t^2}(4 - 16) = \frac{-12}{16y - t^2} \neq f(y) \qquad \text{alone}$$

Applying Rule 2,

$$\frac{1}{4t}(16 - 4) = \frac{3}{t} = g(t) \qquad \text{alone}$$

Thus, $$e^{\int 3t^{-1}\,dt} = e^{3\ln t} = e^{\ln t^3} = t^3$$

(b) Multiplying (18.49) by t^3, $4t^4\,dy + (16yt^3 - t^5)\,dt = 0$ which was solved in Problem 18.21.

18.26. Redo Problem 18.23, given

$$t^2\,dy + 3yt\,dt = 0 \tag{18.50}$$

(a) Here $M = t^2$, $N = 3yt$, and $\partial M/\partial t = 2t \neq \partial N/\partial y = 3t$. Applying Rule 1,

$$\frac{1}{3yt}(2t - 3t) = \frac{-t}{3yt} = \frac{-1}{3y} = f(y) \qquad \text{alone}$$

Thus,
$$e^{\int (-1/3y)\, dy} = e^{-(1/3)\ln y} = e^{\ln y^{-1/3}} = y^{-1/3}$$

Consequently, $y^{-1/3}$ is an integrating factor for the equation, although in Problem 18.19, t was given as an integrating factor. Let us check $y^{-1/3}$ first.

(b) Multiplying (18.50) by $y^{-1/3}$, $t^2 y^{-1/3}\, dy + 3ty^{2/3}\, dt = 0$.

1. $\partial M/\partial t = 2ty^{-1/3} = \partial N/\partial y$. Check. Thus,

2. $$F(y,t) = \int t^2 y^{-1/3}\, \partial y + Z(t) = 1.5\, t^2 y^{2/3} + Z(t)$$

3. $$\frac{\partial F}{\partial t} = 3ty^{2/3} + Z'(t)$$

4. $\partial F/\partial t = N = 3ty^{2/3}$, so $Z'(t) = 0$ and $Z(t)$ is a constant. Hence,

5. $$F_1(y,t) = 1.5\, t^2 y^{2/3} + c \qquad\qquad\qquad (18.51)$$

Here F_1 is used to distinguish this function from the function F_2 below.

18.27. Test to see if t is a possible integrating factor in Problem 18.26.

Applying Rule 2 to the original equation,

$$\frac{1}{t^2}(3t - 2t) = \frac{t}{t^2} = \frac{1}{t}$$

Thus,
$$e^{\int (1/t)\, dt} = e^{\ln t} = t$$

Hence t is also a possible integrating factor, as demonstrated in Problem 18.19, where the solution was $F_2(y,t) = t^3 y + c$. This differs from (18.51) but is equally correct, as you can check on your own.

18.28. Redo Problem 18.23, given
$$(y - t)\, dy - dt = 0 \qquad\qquad\qquad (18.52)$$

(a) $M = y - t$, $N = -1$, and $\partial M/\partial t = -1 \neq \partial N/\partial y = 0$. Applying Rule 1,

$$\frac{1}{-1}(-1 - 0) = 1 = f(y) \qquad \text{alone}$$

Thus, $e^{\int 1\, dy} = e^y$

(b) Multiplying (18.52) by e^y,
$$(y - t)e^y\, dy - e^y\, dt = 0 \qquad\qquad\qquad (18.53)$$

1. $\partial M/\partial t = -e^y = \partial N/\partial y$. Thus,

2. $$F(y,t) = \int (y - t)e^y\, \partial y + Z(t) \qquad\qquad\qquad (18.54)$$

which requires integration by parts. Let

$$f(y) = y - t \qquad f'(y) = 1 \qquad g'(y) = e^y \qquad g(y) = \int e^y\, dy = e^y$$

Substituting in (16.1),

$$\int (y - t)e^y\, \partial y = (y - t)e^y - \int e^y 1\, dy = (y - t)e^y - e^y$$

Substituting in (18.45), $F(y,t) = (y - t)e^y - e^y + Z(t)$.

3. $$\frac{\partial F}{\partial t} = -e^y + Z'(t)$$

4. $\partial F/\partial t = N = -e^y$ in (18.53), so $Z'(t) = 0$ and $Z(t)$ is a constant. Thus,

5. $$F(y,t) = (y - t)e^y - e^y + c \qquad \text{or} \qquad (y - 1)e^y - te^y + c$$

SEPARATION OF VARIABLES

18.29. Solve the following differential equation using the procedure for separating variables described in Section 18.6.

$$\frac{dy}{dt} = \frac{-5t}{y}$$

Separating the variables,

$$y\,dy = -5t\,dt \qquad y\,dy + 5t\,dt = 0$$

Integrating each term separately,

$$\frac{y^2}{2} + \frac{5t^2}{2} = c_1$$

$$y^2 + 5t^2 = 2c_1$$

Letting $c = 2c_1$,

$$y^2 + 5t^2 = c$$

18.30. Redo Problem 18.29, given

(a) $\dfrac{dy}{dt} = \dfrac{t^5}{y^4}$
 (b) $t^2\,dy - y^2\,dt = 0$

$$y^4\,dy - t^5\,dt = 0$$

$$\frac{dy}{y^2} - \frac{dt}{t^2} = 0$$

Integrating,
$$\frac{y^5}{5} - \frac{t^6}{6} = c_1$$

Integrating,
$$-\frac{1}{y} + \frac{1}{t} = c$$

$$6y^5 - 5t^6 = 30c_1$$

$$y - t = cty$$

Letting $c = 30c_1$,
$$6y^5 - 5t^6 = c$$

18.31. Redo Problem 18.29, given $t\,dy + y\,dt = 0$.

$$\frac{dy}{y} + \frac{dt}{t} = 0$$

Integrating,
$$\ln y + \ln t = \ln c \qquad \text{(an arbitrary constant)}$$

By the rule of logs,
$$\ln yt = \ln c \qquad yt = c$$

18.32. Redo Problem 18.29, given $(t + 5)\,dy - (y + 9)\,dt = 0$.

$$\frac{dy}{y + 9} - \frac{dt}{t + 5} = 0$$

Integrating,
$$\ln(y + 9) - \ln(t + 5) = \ln c$$

By the rule of logs,
$$\ln \frac{y + 9}{t + 5} = \ln c$$

$$\frac{y + 9}{t + 5} = c \qquad \text{or} \qquad y + 9 = c(t + 5)$$

18.33. Using the procedure for separating variables, solve the differential equation $dy = 3t^2 y\,dt$.

$$\frac{dy}{y} - 3t^2\,dt = 0$$

Integrating,
$$\ln y - t^3 = \ln c$$

Expressing each side of the equation as an exponent of e,

$$e^{\ln y - t^3} = e^{\ln c}$$

$$e^{\ln y} e^{-t^3} = e^{\ln c}$$

$$ye^{-t^3} = c$$

$$y = ce^{t^3}$$

18.34. Redo Problem 18.33, given $y^2(t^3 + 1)\, dy + t^2(y^3 - 5)\, dt = 0$.

$$\frac{y^2}{(y^3 - 5)}\, dy + \frac{t^2}{(t^3 + 1)}\, dt = 0$$

Integrating by substitution,

$$\tfrac{1}{3} \ln (y^3 - 5) + \tfrac{1}{3} \ln (t^3 + 1) = \ln c$$

$$\ln [(y^3 - 5)(t^3 + 1)] = \ln c \qquad (y^3 - 5)(t^3 + 1) = c$$

18.35. Redo Problem 18.33, given

$$3\, dy + \frac{t}{t^2 - 1}\, dt = 0$$

Integrating, $\qquad\qquad 3y + \tfrac{1}{2} \ln (t^2 - 1) = c$

Setting the left-hand side as an exponent of e and ignoring c, because, as an arbitrary constant, it can be expressed equally well as c or e^c,

$$e^{3y + (1/2) \ln (t^2 - 1)} = c$$

$$e^{3y} e^{\ln (t^2 - 1)^{1/2}} = c \qquad e^{3y} (t^2 - 1)^{1/2} = c$$

BERNOULLI EQUATIONS

18.36. Solve the following Bernoulli equation.

$$\frac{dy}{dt} + y = ty^3$$

Using the method outlined in Section 18.7, here $n = 3$, $w = y^{1-3} = y^{-2}$, $a = 1$, $b = t$, and $(1 - n) = -2$. Substituting in (18.15a),

$$\frac{dw}{dt} - 2w = -2t$$

Using (18.1) with $v = -2$ and $z = -2t$,

$$w(t) = e^{-\int -2\, dt}\left(A + \int -2te^{\int -2\, dt}\, dt\right) = e^{2t}\left(A + \int -2te^{-2t}\, dt\right)$$

By parts, $\qquad\qquad w(t) = e^{2t}(A + te^{-2t} + \tfrac{1}{2}e^{-2t}) = Ae^{2t} + t + \tfrac{1}{2}$

Since $w = y^{-2}$, $\;y = w^{-1/2}$. Thus, $\qquad y = (Ae^{2t} + t + \tfrac{1}{2})^{-1/2}$

18.37. Redo Problem 18.36, given

$$\frac{dy}{dt} + \frac{y}{t} = y^4$$

Here $n = 4$, $w = y^{1-4} = y^{-3}$, $a = 1/t$, $b = 1$, and $(1 - n) = -3$. Substituting in (18.15a),

$$\frac{dw}{dt} - \frac{3w}{t} = -3$$

Using (18.1) with $v = -3/t$ and $z = -3$,

$$w(t) = e^{-\int -(3/t)\, dt}\left(A + \int -3e^{\int -(3/t)\, dt}\, dt\right)$$

$$= e^{3 \ln t}\left(A + \int -3e^{-3 \ln t}\, dt\right) = t^3\left(A + \int -3t^{-3}\, dt\right)$$

$$= t^3(A + 1.5 t^{-2}) = At^3 + 1.5 t$$

Since $w(t) = y(t)^{-3}$, $\qquad\qquad y(t) = w(t)^{-1/3} = (At^3 + 1.5 t)^{-1/3}$

18.38. Redo Problem 18.36, given

$$\frac{dy}{dt} + \frac{1}{2}y = \frac{1}{2}(t+1)y^3$$

Here $n = 3$, $w = y^{1-3} = y^{-2}$, $a = \frac{1}{2}$, $b = \frac{1}{2}(t+1)$, and $(1-n) = -2$. Substituting in (18.15a),

$$\frac{dw}{dt} - w = -(t+1)$$

Using (18.1) with $v = -1$ and $z = -(t+1)$,

$$w(t) = e^{-\int -1\,dt}\left(A + \int -(t+1)e^{\int -1\,dt}\,dt\right) = e^{t}\left(A - \int (t+1)e^{-t}\,dt\right)$$

$$= e^{t}[A + (t+1)e^{-t} + e^{-t}] = Ae^{t} + t + 1 + 1 = Ae^{t} + t + 2$$

Since $w = y^{-2}$, $y = w^{-1/2} = (Ae^{t} + t + 2)^{-1/2}$

USE OF DIFFERENTIAL EQUATIONS IN ECONOMICS

18.39. Find the demand function $Q = f(P)$ if point elasticity, ϵ, is -1 for all $P > 0$.

$$\epsilon = \frac{dQ}{dP}\frac{P}{Q} = -1 \qquad \frac{dQ}{dP} = -\frac{Q}{P}$$

Separating the variables,

$$\frac{dQ}{Q} + \frac{dP}{P} = 0$$

Integrating, $\ln Q + \ln P = \ln c$

$$QP = c \qquad Q = \frac{c}{P}$$

18.40. Find the demand function $Q = f(P)$ if $\epsilon = -k$, a constant.

$$\epsilon = \frac{dQ}{dP}\frac{P}{Q} = -k \qquad \frac{dQ}{dP} = -\frac{kQ}{P}$$

Separating the variables,

$$\frac{dQ}{Q} + \frac{k}{P}\,dP = 0$$

$$\ln Q + k\ln P = c$$

$$QP^{k} = c \qquad Q = cP^{-k}$$

18.41. Find the demand function $Q = f(P)$ if $\epsilon = -(5P + 2P^2)/Q$ and $Q = 500$ when $P = 10$.

$$\epsilon = \frac{dQ}{dP}\frac{P}{Q} = \frac{-(5P + 2P^2)}{Q}$$

$$\frac{dQ}{dP} = \frac{-(5P + 2P^2)}{Q}\frac{Q}{P} = -(5 + 2P)$$

Separating the variables,

$$dQ + (5 + 2P)\,dP = 0$$

Integrating, $Q + 5P + P^2 = c \qquad Q = -P^2 - 5P + c$

At $P = 10$ and $Q = 500$,

$$500 = -100 - 50 + c \qquad c = 650$$

Thus, $Q = 650 - 5P - P^2$.   See Example 6 in Chapter 4.

18.42. Derive the formula P for the total value of an initial sum of money $P(0)$ set out for t years at interest rate i, when i is compounded continuously.

If i is compounded continuously,

$$\frac{dP}{dt} = iP$$

Separating the variables,

$$\frac{dP}{P} - i\,dt = 0$$

Integrating,

$$\ln P - it = c$$

Setting the left-hand side as an exponent of e,

$$e^{\ln P - it} = c$$
$$Pe^{-it} = c \qquad P = ce^{it}$$

At $t = 0$, $P = P(0)$. Thus $P(0) = ce^0$, $c = P(0)$, and $P = P(0)e^{it}$.

18.43. Determine the stability conditions for a two-sector income determination model in which $\hat{C}$, $\hat{I}$, $\hat{Y}$ are deviations of consumption, investment, and income, respectively, from their equilibrium values C_e, I_e, Y_e. That is, $\hat{C} = C(t) - C_e$, etc., where $\hat{C}$ is read C hat; income changes at a rate proportional to excess demand $(C + I - Y)$; and

$$\hat{C}(t) = g\hat{Y}(t) \qquad \hat{I}(t) = b\hat{Y}(t) \qquad \frac{d\hat{Y}(t)}{dt} = a(\hat{C} + \hat{I} - \hat{Y}) \qquad 0 < a,b,g < 1$$

Substituting the first two equations in the third,

$$\frac{d\hat{Y}}{dt} = a(g + b - 1)\hat{Y}$$

Separating the variables and then integrating,

$$\frac{d\hat{Y}}{\hat{Y}} = a(g + b - 1)\,dt$$
$$\ln \hat{Y} = a(g + b - 1)t + c$$
$$e^{\ln \hat{Y}} = e^{a(g+b-1)t+c}$$

Letting the constant $e^c = c$,

$$\hat{Y} = ce^{a(g+b-1)t}$$

At $t = 0$, $\hat{Y} = Y(0) - Y_e = c$. Substituting above, $\hat{Y} = [Y(0) - Y_e]e^{a(g+b-1)t}$. Since $\hat{Y} = Y(t) - Y_e$, $Y(t) = Y_e + \hat{Y}$. Thus,

$$Y(t) = Y_e + [Y(0) - Y_e]e^{a(g+b-1)t}$$

As $t \to \infty$, $Y(t) \to Y_e$ only if $g + b < 1$. The sum of the marginal propensity to consume g and the marginal propensity to invest b must be less than one.

18.44. In Example 12 we found $P(t) = [P(0) - \bar{P}]e^{-m(h-b)t} + \bar{P}$. (a) Explain the time path if (1) the initial price $P(0) = \bar{P}$, (2) $P(0) > \bar{P}$, and (3) $P(0) < \bar{P}$. (b) Graph your findings.

(a) (1) If the initial price equals the equilibrium price, $P(0) = \bar{P}$, the first term on the right disappears and $P(t) = \bar{P}$. The time path is a horizontal line and adjustment is immediate. See Fig. 18.1.

   (2) If $P(0) > \bar{P}$, the first term on the right is positive. Thus $P(t) > \bar{P}$ and $P(t)$ approaches $\bar{P}$ from above as $t \to \infty$ and the first term on the right $\to 0$.

   (3) If $P(0) < \bar{P}$, the first term on the right is negative. $P(t) < \bar{P}$ and approaches it from below as $t \to \infty$ and the first term $\to 0$.

(b) See Fig. 18-1.

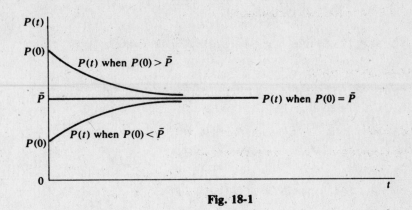

Fig. 18-1

18.45. A change in the rate of investment will affect both aggregate demand and the productive capability of an economy. The Domar model seeks to find the time path along which an economy can grow while maintaining full utilization of its productive capacity. If the marginal propensity to save (s) and the marginal capital/output ratio (k) are constant, find the investment function needed for the desired growth.

The change in aggregate demand is equal to the change in investment times the multiplier $1/s$,

$$\frac{dY}{dt} = \frac{1}{s}\frac{dI}{dt} \qquad (18.55)$$

The change in productive capacity is equal to the change in the capital stock times the reciprocal of the marginal capital/output ratio,

$$\frac{dQ}{dt} = \frac{1}{k}\frac{dK}{dt} = \frac{1}{k}I \qquad \text{since} \qquad \frac{dK}{dt} = I \qquad (18.56)$$

Equating (18.55) and (18.56) for fully utilized capacity,

$$\frac{1}{s}\frac{dI}{dt} = \frac{1}{k}I \qquad \frac{1}{s}dI = \frac{1}{k}I\,dt$$

Separating the variables,

$$\frac{dI}{I} - \frac{s}{k}\,dt = 0$$

Integrating,

$$\ln I - \frac{s}{k}t = c$$

$$Ie^{-(s/k)t} = c \qquad I = ce^{(s/k)t}$$

At $t = 0$, $I(0) = c$, and $I = I(0)e^{(s/k)t}$.

Investment must grow at a constant rate determined by s/k: the savings rate divided by the capital/output ratio.

18.46. The Solow model examines equilibrium growth paths with full employment of both capital and labor. Based on the assumptions that

1. Output is a linearly homogeneous function of capital and labor exhibiting constant returns to scale,

$$Y = f(K,L) \qquad (18.57)$$

2. A constant proportion s of output is saved and invested,

$$\frac{dK}{dt} \equiv \dot{K} = sY \tag{18.58}$$

3. The supply of labor is growing at a constant rate r,

$$L = L_0 e^{rt} \tag{18.59}$$

derive the differential equation in terms of the single variable, K/L, which serves as the basis of the model.

Substituting Y from (18.57) in (18.58),

$$\frac{dK}{dt} = sf(K,L) \tag{18.60}$$

Substituting L from (18.59) in (18.60),

$$\frac{dK}{dt} = sf(K,L_0 e^{rt}) \tag{18.61}$$

This is the time path capital formation (dK/dt) must follow for full employment of a growing labor force. Preparing to convert to a function of K/L, let $z = K/L$, then $K = zL$. Making use of (18.59),

$$K = zL_0 e^{rt} \tag{18.62}$$

Taking the derivative of (18.62), and using the product rule since z is a function of t,

$$\frac{dK}{dt} = z(rL_0 e^{rt}) + (L_0 e^{rt})\frac{dz}{dt} = \left(zr + \frac{dz}{dt}\right)L_0 e^{rt} \tag{18.63}$$

Equating (18.61) and (18.63),

$$sf(K,L_0 e^{rt}) = \left(zr + \frac{dz}{dt}\right)L_0 e^{rt} \tag{18.64}$$

Since the left-hand side of (18.64) is a linearly homogeneous production function, we may divide both inputs by $L_0 e^{rt}$ and multiply the function itself by $L_0 e^{rt}$ without changing its value. Thus,

$$sf(K,L_0 e^{rt}) = sL_0 e^{rt} f\left(\frac{K}{L_0 e^{rt}}, 1\right) \tag{18.65}$$

Substituting (18.65) in (18.64) and dividing both sides by $L_0 e^{rt}$,

$$sf\left(\frac{K}{L_0 e^{rt}}, 1\right) = zr + \frac{dz}{dt} \tag{18.66}$$

Finally, substituting z for $K/L_0 e^{rt}$ and subtracting zr from both sides,

$$\frac{dz}{dt} = sf(z,1) - zr \tag{18.67}$$

which is a differential equation in terms of the single variable z and two parameters r and s, where $z = K/L$, $r =$ the rate of growth of the labor force, and $s =$ the savings rate.

18.47. Suppose that the production function in (18.57) is further specified to be a strict Cobb–Douglas production function. Find the growth path of the capital/labor ratio that will provide full employment of all resources, i.e. solve the differential equation in (18.67), given the new conditions.

A strict Cobb–Douglas function has the form $Y = K^\alpha L^{1-\alpha} = L(K/L)^\alpha$ since $L^{1-\alpha} = L/L^\alpha$. Substituting $z = K/L$,

$$Y = Lz^\alpha \tag{18.68}$$

In the previously unspecified linearly homogeneous production function (*18.57*), $Y = f(K,L)$. Dividing the inputs by L and multiplying the function by L, as in (*18.65*), will leave the value of the function unaltered. Thus,

$$Y = f(K,L) = Lf\left(\frac{K}{L},1\right) = Lf(z,1) \qquad (18.69)$$

Equating Y in (*18.68*) and (*18.69*), since we now assume a strict Cobb–Douglas function,

$$Lz^{\alpha} = Lf(z,1)$$
$$z^{\alpha} = f(z,1) \qquad (18.70)$$

Substituting (*18.70*) in (*18.67*) gives

$$\frac{dz}{dt} = sz^{\alpha} - zr \qquad \frac{dz}{dt} + rz = sz^{\alpha} \qquad (18.71)$$

which is a Bernoulli equation, where $n = \alpha$, so $w = z^{1-\alpha}$, $a = r$, and $b = s$. Substituting in (*18.15a*),

$$\frac{dw}{dt} + (1 - \alpha)rw = (1 - \alpha)s$$

Using (*18.1*) where $v = (1 - \alpha)r$ and $z = (1 - \alpha)s$,

$$w(t) = e^{-\int (1-\alpha)r\,dt}\left(A + \int (1-\alpha)se^{\int (1-\alpha)r\,dt}\,dt\right)$$

$$= e^{-(1-\alpha)rt}\left(A + \int (1-\alpha)se^{(1-\alpha)rt}\,dt\right)$$

$$= e^{-(1-\alpha)rt}\left[A + \frac{(1-\alpha)s}{(1-\alpha)r}e^{(1-\alpha)rt}\right] = Ae^{-(1-\alpha)rt} + \frac{s}{r}.$$

At $t = 0$, $w(0) = A + s/r$ and $A = w(0) - s/r$. Thus,

$$w(t) = \left[w(0) - \frac{s}{r}\right]e^{-(1-\alpha)rt} + \frac{s}{r}$$

Since $w(t) = z^{1-\alpha}$, $\qquad z^{1-\alpha} = \left[z[0]^{1-\alpha} - \frac{s}{r}\right]e^{-(1-\alpha)rt} + \frac{s}{r}$

With $0 < \alpha < 1$ and $(1 - \alpha)$ and $r > 0$, as $t \to \infty$, $z^{1-\alpha} \to s/r$; and $z \to (s/r)^{1/(1-\alpha)}$. z, the capital/labor ratio, approaches $(s/r)^{1/(1-\alpha)}$ as its equilibrium value. In the Solow model the equilibrium level of the capital/labor ratio varies directly with the rate of savings (s) and inversely with the rate of growth of the supply of labor (r).

18.48. Prove that by letting $w = y^{1-n}$, a Bernoulli equation in the form

$$\frac{dy}{dt} + ay = by^{n} \qquad (18.72)$$

can be transformed into the linear differential equation

$$\frac{dw}{dt} + (1 - n)aw = (1 - n)b \qquad (18.73)$$

Dividing (*18.72*) by y^{n},

$$y^{-n}\frac{dy}{dt} + ay^{1-n} = b \qquad (18.74)$$

Letting $w = y^{1-n}$ and taking the derivative to facilitate substitution in (*18.74*),

$$\frac{dw}{dt} = \frac{dw}{dy}\frac{dy}{dt}$$

$$= (1-n)y^{-n}\frac{dy}{dt} \qquad y^{-n}\frac{dy}{dt} = \frac{1}{1-n}\frac{dw}{dt} \qquad (18.75)$$

Substituting (18.75) and $w = y^{1-n}$ in (18.74), and multiplying by $(1 - n)$,

$$\frac{dw}{dt} + (1 - n)aw = (1 - n)b \qquad \text{Q.E.D.} \qquad (18.76)$$

18.49. Assume that the demand for money is for transaction purposes only. Thus,

$$M_d = kP(t)Q \qquad (18.77)$$

where k is constant, P is the price level, and Q is real output. Assume $M_s = M$ and is exogenously determined by monetary authorities. If inflation or the rate of change of prices is proportional to excess demand for goods in society and, from Walras' law, an excess demand for goods is the same thing as an excess supply of money, so that

$$\frac{dP(t)}{dt} = b(M_s - M_d) \qquad (18.78)$$

find the stability conditions, when real output (Q) is constant.

Substituting (18.77) in (18.78),

$$\frac{dP(t)}{dt} = bM_s - bkP(t)Q \qquad (18.79)$$

If we let

$$\hat{P} = P(t) - P_e \qquad (18.80)$$

where $\hat{P}$ is the deviation of prices from the equilibrium price level P_e, then taking the derivative of (18.80),

$$\frac{d\hat{P}}{dt} = \frac{dP(t)}{dt} - \frac{dP_e}{dt}$$

But in equilibrium, $dP_e/dt = 0$. Hence,

$$\frac{d\hat{P}}{dt} = \frac{dP(t)}{dt} \qquad (18.81)$$

Substituting in (18.79),

$$\frac{d\hat{P}}{dt} = bM_s - bkP(t)Q \qquad (18.82)$$

In equilibrium, $M_s = M_d = kP_eQ$. Hence $M_s - kP_eQ = 0$ and $b(M_s - kP_eQ) = 0$. Subtracting this from (18.82),

$$\frac{d\hat{P}}{dt} = bM_s - bkP(t)Q - bM_s + bkP_eQ = -bkQ[P(t) - P_e] = -bkQ\hat{P} \qquad (18.83)$$

which is a differential equation. Separating the variables,

$$\frac{d\hat{P}}{\hat{P}} = -bkQ \, dt$$

Integrating, $\ln \hat{P} = -kbQt + c$, $\hat{P} = Ae^{-bkQt}$, where $e^c = A$.

Since $b, k, Q > 0$, $\hat{P} \to 0$ as $t \to \infty$, and the system is stable. To find the time path $P(t)$ from $\hat{P}$, see the conclusion of Problem 18.42, where $Y(t)$ was derived from $\hat{Y}$.

18.50. If the expectation of inflation is a positive function of the present rate of inflation

$$\left[\frac{dP(t)}{dt}\right]_E = h \frac{dP(t)}{dt} \qquad (18.84)$$

and the expectation of inflation reduces people's desire to hold money, so that

$$M_d = kP(t)Q - g\left[\frac{dP(t)}{dt}\right]_E \qquad (18.85)$$

check the stability conditions, assuming that the rate of inflation is proportional to the excess supply of money as in (18.78).

Substituting (18.84) in (18.85),

$$M_d = kP(t)Q - gh\,\frac{dP(t)}{dt} \qquad (18.86)$$

Substituting (18.86) in (18.78),

$$\frac{dP(t)}{dt} = bM_s - b\left[kP(t)Q - gh\,\frac{dP(t)}{dt}\right]$$

By a process similar to the steps involving (18.80) to (18.83),

$$\frac{d\hat{P}}{dt} = bM_s - bkP(t)Q + bgh\,\frac{dP(t)}{dt} - bM_s + bkP_eQ = -bkQ\hat{P} + bgh\,\frac{dP(t)}{dt} \qquad (18.87)$$

Substituting (18.81) for $dP(t)/dt$ in (18.87),

$$\frac{d\hat{P}}{dt} = -bkQ\hat{P} + bgh\,\frac{d\hat{P}}{dt} = \frac{-bkQ\hat{P}}{1 - bgh}$$

Separating the variables,

$$\frac{d\hat{P}}{\hat{P}} = \frac{-bkQ}{1 - bgh}\,dt$$

Integrating, $\ln \hat{P} = -bkQt/(1 - bgh)$

$$\hat{P} = Ae^{-bkQt/(1-bgh)}$$

Since $b, k, Q > 0$, $\hat{P} \to 0$ as $t \to \infty$, if $bgh < 1$. Hence even if h is greater than one, meaning people expect inflation to accelerate, the economy need not be unstable, as long as b and g are sufficiently small.

Chapter 19

Difference Equations

19.1 DEFINITIONS AND CONCEPTS

A *difference equation* expresses a relationship between a dependent variable and a lagged independent variable (or variables) which changes at discrete intervals of time, e.g. $I_t = f(Y_{t-1})$, where I and Y are measured at the end of each year. The *order* of a difference equation is determined by the greatest number of periods lagged. A *first-order* difference equation expresses a time lag of one period; a *second-order*, two periods, etc. The change in y as t changes from t to $t+1$ is called the *first difference of y*. It is written

$$\frac{\Delta y}{\Delta t} = \Delta y_t = y_{t+1} - y_t \qquad (19.1)$$

where Δ is an operator replacing d/dt used to measure continuous change in differential equations. The *solution* of a difference equation defines y for every value of t and does not contain a difference expression.

Example 1. Each of the following is a difference equation of the order indicated.

$$I_t = a(Y_{t-1} - Y_{t-2}) \qquad \text{Order 2}$$
$$Q_s = a + bP_{t-1} \qquad \text{Order 1}$$
$$y_{t+3} - 9y_{t+2} + 2y_{t+1} + 6y_t = 8 \qquad \text{Order 3}$$
$$\Delta y_t = 5y_t \qquad \text{Order 1}$$

Substituting from (*19.1*) for Δy_t above,

$$y_{t+1} - y_t = 5y_t \qquad y_{t+1} = 6y_t \qquad \text{Order 1}$$

Example 2. Given that the initial value of y is y_0, in the difference equation

$$y_{t+1} = by_t \qquad (19.2)$$

a solution is found as follows. By successive substitutions of $t = 0, 1, 2, 3$, etc. in (*19.2*),

$$y_1 = by_0 \qquad\qquad y_3 = by_2 = b(b^2 y_0) = b^3 y_0$$
$$y_2 = by_1 = b(by_0) = b^2 y_0 \qquad\qquad y_4 = by_3 = b(b^3 y_0) = b^4 y_0$$

Thus, for any period t,

$$y_t = b^t y_0$$

This method is called the *iterative method*. Since y_0 is a constant, notice the crucial role b plays in determining values for y as t changes.

19.2 GENERAL FORMULA FOR FIRST-ORDER LINEAR DIFFERENCE EQUATIONS

Given a first-order difference equation which is *linear* (i.e., the dependent variable does not appear raised to a power higher than one or as a cross-product),

$$y_t = by_{t-1} + a \qquad (19.3)$$

364

where b and a are constants, the general formula for a *definite solution* is

$$y_t = \left(y_0 - \frac{a}{1-b}\right)b^t + \frac{a}{1-b} \quad \text{when} \quad b \neq 1 \tag{19.4}$$

$$y_t = y_0 + at \quad \text{when} \quad b = 1 \tag{19.4a}$$

If no initial condition is given, an arbitrary constant A is used for $[y_0 - a/(1-b)]$ in (*19.4*) and for y_0 in (*19.4a*). This is called a *general solution*.

Example 3. Given the difference equation, $y_t = -7y_{t-1} + 16$ and $y_0 = 5$. In the equation, $b = -7$ and $a = 16$. Since $b \neq 1$, it is solved using (*19.4*), as follows:

$$y_t = \left(5 - \frac{16}{1+7}\right)(-7)^t + \frac{16}{1+7} = 3(-7)^t + 2 \tag{19.5}$$

To check the answer, substitute $t = 0$ and $t = 1$ in (*19.5*).

$$y_0 = 3(-7)^0 + 2 = 5 \quad \text{since } (-7)^0 = 1$$
$$y_1 = 3(-7)^1 + 2 = -19$$

Substituting $y_1 = -19$ for y_t and $y_0 = 5$ for y_{t-1} in the original equation,

$$-19 = -7(5) + 16 = -35 + 16 \quad \text{Compare}$$

19.3 STABILITY CONDITIONS

Equation (*19.4*) can be expressed in the general form

$$y_t = Ab^t + c \tag{19.6}$$

where $A = [y_0 - a/(1-b)]$ and $c = a/(1-b)$. Ab^t is called the *complementary function*; c the *particular solution*. The particular solution expresses the *intertemporal equilibrium level of* y; the complementary function represents the *deviations from that equilibrium*. (*19.6*) will be dynamically stable, therefore, only if the complementary function $Ab^t \to 0$, as $t \to \infty$. All depends on the base b. Assuming $A = 1$ and $c = 0$ for the moment, the exponential expression b^t will generate seven different time paths depending on the value of b, as illustrated in Example 4. As seen there, if $|b| > 1$, the time path will explode and move farther and farther away from equilibrium; if $|b| < 1$, the time path will be damped and move toward equilibrium. If $b < 0$, the time path will oscillate between positive and negative values; if $b > 0$, the time path will be nonoscillating. If $A \neq 1$, the value of the multiplicative constant will scale up or down the magnitude of b^t, but will not change the basic pattern of movement. If $A = -1$, a mirror image of the time path of b^t with respect to the horizontal axis will be produced. If $c \neq 0$, the vertical intercept of the graph is affected, and the graph shifts up or down accordingly.

Example 4. In the equation $y_t = b^t$, b can range from $-\infty$ to ∞. Seven different time paths can be generated, each of which is explained below and graphed in Fig. 19-1.

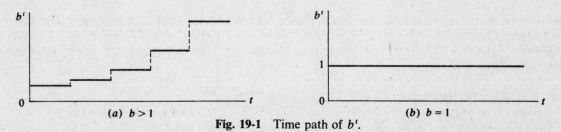

Fig. 19-1 Time path of b^t.

1. If $b > 1$, b^t increases at an increasing rate as t increases, thus moving farther and farther away from the horizontal axis. This is illustrated in Fig. 19-1(*a*), which is a step function representing changes at discrete intervals of time, not a continuous function. Assume $b = 3$. Then as t goes from 0 to 4, $b^t = 1, 3, 9, 27, 81$.

2. If $b = 1$, $b^t = 1$ for all values of t. This is represented by a horizontal line in Fig. 19-1(*b*).

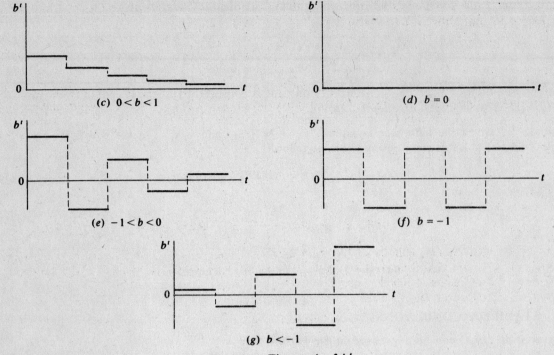

Fig. 19-1 Time path of b^t.

3. If $0 < b < 1$, b is a positive fraction and b^t decreases as t increases, drawing closer and closer to the horizontal axis, but always remaining positive, as illustrated in Fig. 19-1(c). Assume $b = \frac{1}{3}$. Then as t goes from 0 to 4, $b^t = 1, \frac{1}{3}, \frac{1}{9}, \frac{1}{27}, \frac{1}{81}$.

4. If $b = 0$, $b^t = 0$ for all values of t. See Fig. 19-1(d).

5. If $-1 < b < 0$, b is a negative fraction; b^t will alternate in sign and draw closer and closer to the horizontal axis as t increases. See Fig. 19-1(e). Assume $b = -\frac{1}{3}$. Then as t goes from 0 to 4, $b^t = 1, -\frac{1}{3}, \frac{1}{9}, -\frac{1}{27}, \frac{1}{81}$.

6. If $b = -1$, b^t oscillates between $+1$ and -1. See Fig. 19-1(f).

7. If $b < -1$, b^t will oscillate and move farther and farther away from the horizontal axis, as illustrated in Fig. 19-1(g). Assume $b = -3$. Then $b^t = 1, -3, 9, -27, 81$, as t goes from 0 to 4.

In short, if

$|b| > 1$	the time path explodes
$|b| < 1$	the time path converges
$b > 0$	the time path is nonoscillating
$b < 0$	the time path oscillates

Example 5. In the equation, $y_t = 6(-\frac{1}{4})^t + 6$, since $b = -\frac{1}{4} < 0$, the time path oscillates. Since $|b| < 1$, the time path converges.

When $y_t = 5(6)^t + 9$ and $b = 6 > 0$, there is no oscillation. With $|b| > 1$, the time path explodes.

19.4 LAGGED INCOME DETERMINATION MODEL

In the simple income determination model of Section 2.3 there were no lags. Now assume that consumption is a function of the previous period's income, so that

$$C_t = C_0 + cY_{t-1} \qquad Y_t = C_t + I_t$$

where $I_t = I_0$. Thus, $Y_t = C_0 + cY_{t-1} + I_0$. Rearranging terms to conform with (19.3),

$$Y_t = cY_{t-1} + C_0 + I_0 \tag{19.7}$$

where $b = c$ and $a = C_0 + I_0$. Substituting these values in (19.4) since the marginal propensity to consume c cannot equal 1, and assuming $Y_t = Y_0$ at $t = 0$,

$$Y_t = \left(Y_0 - \frac{C_0 + I_0}{1 - c}\right)(c)^t + \frac{C_0 + I_0}{1 - c} \qquad (19.8)$$

The stability of the time path thus depends on c. Since $0 < \text{MPC} < 1$, $|c| < 1$ and the time path will converge. Since $c > 0$, there will be no oscillations. The equilibrium is stable and as $t \to \infty$, $Y_t \to (C_0 + I_0)/(1 - c)$, which is the intertemporal equilibrium level of income.

Example 6. Given $Y_t = C_t + I_t$, $C_t = 200 + 0.9 Y_{t-1}$, $I_t = 100$, and $Y_0 = 4500$. Solving for Y_t,

$$Y_t = 200 + 0.9 Y_{t-1} + 100 = 0.9 Y_{t-1} + 300 \qquad (19.9)$$

Using (19.4),

$$Y_t = \left(4500 - \frac{300}{1 - 0.9}\right)(0.9)^t + \frac{300}{1 - 0.9} = 1500(0.9)^t + 3000 \qquad (19.10)$$

With $|0.9| < 1$, the time path converges; with $0.9 > 0$, there is no oscillation. Thus, Y_t is dynamically stable. As $t \to \infty$, the first term on the right-hand side goes to zero and Y_t approaches the intertemporal equilibrium level of income: $300/(1 - 0.9) = 3000$.

To check this answer, let $t = 0$ and $t = 1$ in (19.10). Thus,

$$Y_0 = 1500(0.9)^0 + 3000 = 4500$$

$$Y_1 = 1500(0.9)^1 + 3000 = 4350$$

Substituting $Y_1 = 4350$ for Y_t and $Y_0 = 4500$ for Y_{t-1} in (19.9),

$$4350 - 0.9(4500) = 300$$

$$4350 - 4050 = 300 \qquad \text{Compare}$$

19.5 THE COBWEB MODEL

For many products, such as agricultural commodities, which are planted a year before marketing, current supply depends on last year's price. This poses interesting stability questions. If

$$Q_{dt} = c + bP_t \qquad \text{and} \qquad Q_{st} = g + hP_{t-1}$$

in equilibrium,

$$c + bP_t = g + hP_{t-1} \qquad (19.11)$$

$$bP_t = hP_{t-1} + (g - c) \qquad (19.12)$$

Dividing (19.12) by b to conform to (19.3),

$$P_t = \frac{h}{b} P_{t-1} + \frac{g - c}{b}$$

Since $b < 0$ and $h > 0$ under normal demand and supply conditions, $h/b \neq 1$. Using (19.4),

$$P_t = \left[P_0 - \frac{(g - c)/b}{1 - (h/b)}\right]\left(\frac{h}{b}\right)^t + \frac{(g - c)/b}{1 - (h/b)}$$

$$= \left(P_0 - \frac{g - c}{b - h}\right)\left(\frac{h}{b}\right)^t + \frac{g - c}{b - h} \qquad (19.13)$$

When the model is in equilibrium, $P_t = P_{t-1}$. Substituting P_e for P_t and P_{t-1} in (19.11)

$$P_e = \frac{g - c}{b - h} \qquad (19.13a)$$

Substituting in (19.13),

$$P_t = (P_0 - P_e)(h/b)^t + P_e$$

With an ordinary negative demand function and positive supply function, $b < 0$ and $h > 0$. Therefore, $h/b < 0$ and the time path will oscillate.

If $|h| > |b|$, $|h/b| > 1$, and the time path P_t explodes.

If $|h| = |b|$, $h/b = -1$, and the time path oscillates uniformly.

If $|h| < |b|$, $|h/b| < 1$, the time path converges, and P_t approaches P_e.

In short, for stability the supply curve must be flatter than the demand curve.

Example 7. Given $Q_{dt} = 86 - 0.8 P_t$ and $Q_{st} = -10 + 0.2 P_{t-1}$ the market price P_t for any time period and the equilibrium price P_e can be found as follows. Equating demand and supply,

$$86 - 0.8 P_t = -10 + 0.2 P_{t-1} \qquad -0.8 P_t = 0.2 P_{t-1} - 96$$

Dividing through by -0.8 to conform to (19.3), $P_t = -0.25 P_{t-1} + 120$. Using (19.4),

$$P_t = \left(P_0 - \frac{120}{1 + 0.25} \right)(-0.25)^t + \frac{120}{1 + 0.25} = (P_0 - 96)(-0.25)^t + 96$$

which can be checked by substituting the appropriate values in (19.13). From $(19.13a)$, $P_e = (-10 - 86)/(-0.8 - 0.2) = (-96)/(-1) = 96$.

With the base $b = -0.25$, which is negative and less than 1, the time path oscillates and converges. The equilibrium is stable and P_t will converge to $P_e = 96$, as $t \to \infty$.

19.6   THE HARROD MODEL

The Harrod model attempts to explain the dynamics of growth in the economy. It assumes

$$S_t = s Y_t$$

where s is a constant equal to both the MPS and APS. It also assumes the *acceleration principle*, i.e. investment is proportional to the rate of change of national income over time.

$$I_t = a(Y_t - Y_{t-1})$$

where a is a constant equal to both the marginal and average capital-output ratios. In equilibrium, $I_t = S_t$. Therefore,

$$a(Y_t - Y_{t-1}) = s Y_t \qquad (a - s) Y_t = a Y_{t-1}$$

Dividing through by $(a - s)$ to conform to (19.3), $Y_t = [a/(a - s)] Y_{t-1}$. Using (19.4) since $a/(a - s) \neq 1$,

$$Y_t = (Y_0 - 0) \left(\frac{a}{a - s} \right)^t + 0 = \left(\frac{a}{a - s} \right)^t Y_0 \qquad (19.14)$$

The stability of the time path thus depends on $a/(a - s)$. Since $a =$ the capital-output ratio, which is normally larger than 1, and since $s =$ MPS which is larger than zero and less than one, the base $a/(a - s)$ will be larger than zero and usually larger than one. Y_t is explosive, therefore, but nonoscillating. Income will expand indefinitely, which means it has no bounds.

Example 8. The *warranted rate of growth* (i.e., the path the economy must follow to have equilibrium between saving and investment each year) can be found as follows in the Harrod model.

From (19.14) Y_t increases indefinitely. Income in one period is $a/(a - s)$ times the income of the previous period.

$$Y_1 = \left(\frac{a}{a - s} \right) Y_0 \qquad (19.15)$$

The rate of growth (G) between the periods is defined as

$$G = \frac{Y_1 - Y_0}{Y_0}$$

Substituting from (19.15),

$$G = \frac{[a/(a-s)]Y_0 - Y_0}{Y_0} = \frac{[a/(a-s) - 1]Y_0}{Y_0}$$

$$= \frac{a}{a-s} - 1 = \frac{a}{a-s} - \frac{a-s}{a-s} = \frac{s}{a-s}$$

The warranted rate of growth, therefore, is

$$G_w = \frac{s}{a-s} \qquad (19.16)$$

Example 9. Assume that the marginal propensity to save in the Harrod model above is 0.12 and the capital-output ratio is 2.12. To find Y_t from (19.14),

$$Y_t = \left[\frac{2.12}{2.12 - 0.12}\right]^t Y_0 = (1.06)^t Y_0$$

The warranted rate of growth, from (19.16), is

$$G_w = \frac{0.12}{2.12 - 0.12} = \frac{0.12}{2} = 0.06$$

Solved Problems

USE OF GENERAL FORMULA FOR FIRST-ORDER LINEAR DIFFERENCE EQUATIONS

19.1. (a) Solve the difference equation given below, (b) check your answer using $t = 0$ and $t = 1$, and (c) comment on the nature of the time path.

$$y_t = 6y_{t-1}$$

(a) Here $b = 6$ and $a = 0$. Using (19.4) for all cases in which $b \neq 1$,

$$y_t = (y_0 - 0)(6)^t + 0 = y_0(6)^t = A(6)^t \qquad (19.17)$$

where A, as a more generally used unspecified constant, replaces y_0.

(b) Estimating (19.17) at $t = 0$ and $t = 1$,

$$y_0 = A(6)^0 = A \qquad y_1 = A(6) = 6A$$

Substituting $y_0 = A$ for y_{t-1} and $y_1 = 6A$ for y_t in the original problem, $6A = 6(A)$. Compare.

(c) With the base $b = 6$ in (19.17) positive and greater than 1, i.e. $b > 0$ and $|b| > 1$, the time path is nonoscillating and explosive.

19.2. Redo Problem 19.1 for $y_t = \frac{1}{8}y_{t-1}$.

(a) Using (19.4),

$$y_t = (y_0 - 0)(\tfrac{1}{8})^t + 0 = y_0(\tfrac{1}{8})^t = A(\tfrac{1}{8})^t$$

(b) At $t = 0$, $y_0 = A(\tfrac{1}{8})^0 = A$. At $t = 1$, $y_1 = A(\tfrac{1}{8}) = \tfrac{1}{8}A$. Substituting $y_0 = A$ for y_{t-1} and $y_1 = \tfrac{1}{8}A$ for y_t in the original equation, $\tfrac{1}{8}A = \tfrac{1}{8}(A)$. Compare.

(c) With $b = \tfrac{1}{8}$, $b > 0$ and $|b| < 1$. The time path is nonoscillating and converging.

19.3. Redo Problem 19.1, given $y_t = -\frac{1}{4}y_{t-1} + 60$ and $y_0 = 8$.

(a)

$$y_t = \left(8 - \frac{60}{1 + 1/4}\right)\left(-\frac{1}{4}\right)^t + \frac{60}{1 + 1/4} = -40(-\tfrac{1}{4})^t + 48$$

(b) At $t = 0$, $y_0 = -40(-\frac{1}{4})^0 + 48 = 8$. At $t = 1$, $y_1 = -40(-\frac{1}{4}) + 48 = 58$. Substituting in the original equation, $58 = -\frac{1}{4}(8) + 60 = 58$. Compare.

(c) With $b = -\frac{1}{4}$, $b < 0$ and $|b| < 1$. The time path oscillates and converges.

19.4. Redo Problem 19.1, given $x_t + 3x_{t-1} + 8 = 0$ and $x_0 = 16$.

(a) Rearranging to conform with (19.3),

$$x_t = -3x_{t-1} - 8$$

Thus, $b = -3$ and $a = -8$. Substituting in (19.4),

$$x_t = \left(16 + \frac{8}{1+3}\right)(-3)^t - \frac{8}{1+3} = 18(-3)^t - 2$$

(b) At $t = 0$, $x_0 = 18(-3)^0 - 2 = 16$. At $t = 1$, $x_1 = 18(-3) - 2 = -56$. Substituting in the original, $-56 + 3(16) + 8 = 0$. Compare.

(c) With $b = -3$, $b < 0$ and $|b| > 1$. The time path oscillates and explodes.

19.5. Redo Problem 19.1, given $y_t - y_{t-1} = 17$.

(a) Rearranging, $y_t = y_{t-1} + 17$. Here $b = 1$. Using (19.4a), therefore, $y_t = y_0 + 17t = A + 17t$.

(b) At $t = 0$, $y_0 = A$. At $t = 1$, $y_1 = A + 17$. Substituting in the original, $(A + 17) - (A) = 17$. Compare.

(c) Here $b = 1$. Thus $b > 0$ and y_t will not oscillate. But with $|b| = 1$, $1 \nless |b| \nless 1$. This presents a special case. With $a \neq 0$, unless $y_0 = A = 0$, the time path is *divergent* because the complementary function A does not approach 0 as $t \to \infty$. Thus, y_t approaches $A + at$, and not the particular solution, at, itself. For $b = 1$ and $a = 0$, see Problem 19.17.

19.6. Redo Problem 19.1, given $g_t = g_{t-1} - 25$ and $g_0 = 40$.

(a) Using (19.4a), $g_t = 40 - 25t$.

(b) At $t = 0$, $g_0 = 40$. At $t = 1$, $g_t = 15$. Substituting in the original, $15 = 40 - 25$. Compare.

(c) With $b = 1$, $a \neq 0$ and $A = g_0 \neq 0$. The time path is nonoscillatory and divergent.

19.7. Redo Problem 19.1, given $2y_t = y_{t-1} - 18$.

(a) Dividing through by 2 to conform to (19.3), and then using (19.4),

$$y_t = \frac{1}{2}y_{t-1} - 9 = \left(y_0 + \frac{9}{1 - 1/2}\right)\left(\frac{1}{2}\right)^t - \frac{9}{1 - 1/2} = A\left(\frac{1}{2}\right)^t - 18$$

where A is an arbitrary constant for $(y_0 + 18)$.

(b) At $t = 0$, $y_0 = A - 18$. At $t = 1$, $y_1 = \frac{1}{2}A - 18$. Substituting in the original, $2(\frac{1}{2}A - 18) = (A - 18) - 18$; $A - 36 = A - 36$. Compare.

(c) With $b = \frac{1}{2}$, $b > 0$ and $|b| < 1$. y_t is nonoscillating and convergent.

19.8. (a) Solve the following difference equation, (b) check the answer using $t = 0$ and $t = 1$, and (c) comment on the nature of the time path.

$$5y_t + 2y_{t-1} - 140 = 0 \qquad y_0 = 30$$

(a) Dividing by 5, rearranging terms, and using (19.4),

$$y_t = -0.4y_{t-1} + 28 = \left(30 - \frac{28}{1 + 0.4}\right)(-0.4)^t + \frac{28}{1 + 0.4} = 10(-0.4)^t + 20$$

(b) At $t = 0$, $y_0 = 30$. At $t = 1$, $y_1 = 16$. Substituting in the original, $5(16) + 2(30) - 140 = 0$. Compare.

(c) With $b = -0.4$, $b < 0$ and $|b| < 1$. y_t oscillates and converges.

19.9. Redo Problem 19.8, given $x_{t+1} = 4x_t - 36$.

(a) Shifting the time periods back one period to conform with (*19.3*), $x_t = 4x_{t-1} - 36$. Using (*19.4*) and allowing A to replace $[x_0 - a/(1-b)]$ as in Problem 19.7,

$$x_t = A(4)^t - 36/(1-4) = A(4)^t + 12$$

(b) At $t = 0$, $x_0 = A + 12$. At $t = 1$, $x_1 = 4A + 12$. Substituting $x_1 = 4A + 12$ for x_{t+1} and $x_0 = A + 12$ for x_t in the original equation, $4A + 12 = 4(A + 12) - 36$; $4A + 12 = 4A + 12$. Compare.

(c) With $b = 4$, $b > 0$ and $|b| > 1$. x_t does not oscillate but it explodes.

19.10. Redo Problem 19.8, given $y_{t+5} + 2y_{t+4} + 57 = 0$ and $y_0 = 11$.

(a) Moving the time periods back 5 periods, rearranging terms, and using (*19.4*),

$$y_t = -2y_{t-1} - 57 = \left(11 + \frac{57}{1+2}\right)(-2)^t - \frac{57}{1+2} = 30(-2)^t - 19$$

(b) At $t = 0$, $y_0 = 11$. At $t = 1$, $y_1 = -79$. Substituting y_1 for y_{t+5} and y_0 for y_{t+4} in the original equation, $-79 + 2(11) + 57 = 0$. Compare.

(c) With $b = -2$, $b < 0$ and $|b| > 1$. y_t oscillates and explodes.

19.11. Redo Problem 19.8, given $8y_{t-2} - 2y_{t-3} = 120$ and $y_0 = 28$.

(a) Divide through by 8, shift the time periods ahead by 2, and rearrange terms.

$$y_t = \frac{1}{4}y_{t-1} + 15 = \left(28 - \frac{15}{1-1/4}\right)\left(\frac{1}{4}\right)^t + \frac{15}{1-1/4} = 8\left(\frac{1}{4}\right)^t + 20$$

(b) At $t = 0$, $y_0 = 28$. At $t = 1$, $y_1 = 22$. Substitute y_1 for y_{t-2} and y_0 for y_{t-3}.

$$8(22) - 2(28) = 120; \quad 120 = 120 \qquad \text{Compare}$$

(c) With $b = \frac{1}{4}$, $b > 0$ and $|b| < 1$. y_t is nonoscillating and convergent.

19.12. Redo Problem 19.8, given $\Delta g_t = 14$.

(a) Substituting (*19.1*) for Δg_t,

$$g_{t+1} - g_t = 14 \qquad\qquad\qquad (19.18)$$

Set the time periods back 1 and rearrange terms.

$$g_t = g_{t-1} + 14$$

Using (*19.4a*), $g_t = g_0 + 14t = A + 14t$.

(b) At $t = 0$, $g_0 = A$. At $t = 1$, $g_1 = A + 14$. Substituting g_1 for g_{t+1} and g_0 for g_t in (*19.18*), $(A + 14) = (A) + 14$. Compare.

(c) With $b = 1$, g_t is nonoscillatory. If $A \neq 0$, g_t is divergent.

19.13. Redo Problem 19.8, given $\Delta y_t = y_t + 13$ and $y_0 = 45$.

(a) Substituting from (*19.1*), moving the time periods back 1, and rearranging terms,

$$y_t = 2y_{t-1} + 13 \qquad\qquad\qquad (19.19)$$

Using (*19.4*), $$y_t = \left(45 - \frac{13}{1-2}\right)(2)^t + \frac{13}{1-2} = 58(2)^t - 13$$

(b) At $t = 0$, $y_0 = 45$. At $t = 1$, $y_1 = 103$. Substituting in (*19.19*), $103 = 2(45) + 13$; $103 = 103$. Compare.

(c) With $b = 2$, $b > 0$ and $|b| > 1$. y_t is nonoscillatory and explosive.

LAGGED INCOME DETERMINATION MODELS

19.14. Given the data below, (a) find the time path of national income Y_t, (b) check your answer, using $t = 0$ and $t = 1$, and (c) comment on the stability of the time path.

$$C_t = 90 + 0.8\, Y_{t-1} \qquad I_t = 50 \qquad Y_0 = 1200$$

(a) In equilibrium, $Y_t = C_t + I_t$. Thus,

$$Y_t = 90 + 0.8\, Y_{t-1} + 50 = 0.8\, Y_{t-1} + 140 \qquad\qquad (19.20)$$

Using (19.4), $\qquad Y_t = \left(1200 - \dfrac{140}{1-0.8}\right)(0.8)^t + \dfrac{140}{1-0.8} = 500(0.8)^t + 700$

(b) $Y_0 = 1200$; $Y_1 = 1100$. Substituting in (19.20),

$$1100 = 0.8(1200) + 140; \quad 1100 = 1100 \quad \text{Compare}$$

(c) With $b = 0.8$, $b > 0$ and $|b| < 1$. The time path Y_t is nonoscillating and convergent. Y_t converges to the equilibrium level of income 700.

19.15. Redo Problem 19.14, given $C_t = 200 + 0.75\, Y_{t-1}$, $I_t = 50 + 0.15\, Y_{t-1}$, and $Y_0 = 3000$.

(a) $\qquad\qquad Y_t = 200 + 0.75\, Y_{t-1} + 50 + 0.15\, Y_{t-1} = 0.9\, Y_{t-1} + 250$

Using (19.4), $\qquad Y_t = \left(3000 - \dfrac{250}{1-0.9}\right)(0.9)^t + \dfrac{250}{1-0.9} = 500(0.9)^t + 2500$

(b) $Y_0 = 3000$; $Y_1 = 2950$. Substituting above, $2950 = 0.9(3000) + 250$; $2950 = 2950$. Compare.

(c) With $b = 0.9$, the time path Y_t is nonoscillatory and converges toward 2500.

19.16. Redo Problem 19.14, given $C_t = 300 + 0.87\, Y_{t-1}$, $I_t = 150 + 0.13\, Y_{t-1}$, and $Y_0 = 6000$.

(a) $\qquad\qquad Y_t = 300 + 0.87\, Y_{t-1} + 150 + 0.13\, Y_{t-1} = Y_{t-1} + 450 \qquad\qquad (19.21)$

Using $(19.4a)$, $Y_t = 6000 + 450t$.

(b) $Y_0 = 6000$; $Y_1 = 6450$. Substituting in (19.21) above, $6450 = 6000 + 450$. Compare.

(c) With $b = 1$ and $A \neq 0$, the time path Y_t is nonoscillatory but divergent. See Problem 19.5.

19.17. Redo Problem 19.14, given $C_t = 0.92\, Y_{t-1}$, $I_t = 0.08\, Y_{t-1}$, and $Y_0 = 4000$.

(a) $\qquad\qquad Y_t = 0.92\, Y_{t-1} + 0.08\, Y_{t-1} = Y_{t-1}$

Using $(19.4a)$, $Y_t = 4000 + 0 = 4000$.

(b) $\qquad\qquad\qquad\qquad Y_0 = 4000 = Y_1$

(c) When $b = 1$ and $a = 0$, Y_t is a stationary path.

19.18. Redo Problem 19.14, given $C_t = 400 + 0.6\, Y_t + 0.35\, Y_{t-1}$, $I_t = 240 + 0.15\, Y_{t-1}$, and $Y_0 = 7000$.

(a) $\qquad Y_t = 400 + 0.6\, Y_t + 0.35\, Y_{t-1} + 240 + 0.15\, Y_{t-1} \qquad 0.4\, Y_t = 0.5\, Y_{t-1} + 640$

Divide through by 0.4 and then use (19.4).

$$Y_t = 1.25\, Y_{t-1} + 1600 = \left(7000 - \dfrac{1600}{1-1.25}\right)(1.25)^t + \dfrac{1600}{1-1.25} = 13{,}400(1.25)^t - 6400$$

(b) $Y = 7000$; $Y_1 = 10{,}350$. Substituting in the initial equation,

$$10{,}350 = 400 + 0.6(10{,}350) + 0.35(7000) + 240 + 0.15(7000) = 10{,}350 \quad \text{Compare}$$

(c) With $b = 1.25$, the time path Y_t is nonoscillatory and explosive.

19.19. Redo Problem 19.14, given $C_t = 300 + 0.5\, Y_t + 0.4\, Y_{t-1}$, $I_t = 200 + 0.2\, Y_{t-1}$, and $Y_0 = 6500$.

(a) $Y_t = 300 + 0.5\, Y_t + 0.4\, Y_{t-1} + 200 + 0.2\, Y_{t-1}$ $0.5\, Y_t = 0.6\, Y_{t-1} + 500$

Dividing through by 0.5 and then using (19.4),

$$Y_t = 1.2\, Y_{t-1} + 1000 = \left(6500 - \frac{1000}{1 - 1.2}\right)(1.2)^t + \frac{1000}{1 - 1.2} = 11{,}500(1.2)^t - 5000$$

(b) $Y_0 = 6500$; $Y_1 = 8800$.   Substituting in the initial equation,

$$8800 = 300 + 0.5(8800) + 0.4(6500) + 200 + 0.2(6500) = 8800 \quad \text{Compare}$$

(c) With $b = 1.2$, Y_t is nonoscillatory and explosive.

19.20. Redo Problem 19.14, given $C_t = 200 + 0.5\, Y_t$, $I_t = 3(Y_t - Y_{t-1})$, and $Y_0 = 10{,}000$.

(a) $Y_t = 200 + 0.5\, Y_t + 3(Y_t - Y_{t-1})$ $-2.5\, Y_t = -3\, Y_{t-1} + 200$

Dividing through by -2.5 and then using (19.4),

$$Y_t = 1.2\, Y_{t-1} - 80 = \left(10{,}000 + \frac{80}{1 - 1.2}\right)(1.2)^t - \frac{80}{1 - 1.2} = 9600(1.2)^t + 400$$

(b) $Y_0 = 10{,}000$; $Y_1 = 11{,}920$.   Substituting in the initial equation,

$$11{,}920 = 200 + 0.5(11{,}920) + 3(11{,}920 - 10{,}000) = 11{,}920 \quad \text{Compare}$$

(c) With $b = 1.2$,   the time path Y_t explodes but does not oscillate.

THE COBWEB MODEL

19.21. For the data given below, determine   (a) the market price P_t in any time period,   (b) the equilibrium price P_e, and   (c) the stability of the time path.

$$Q_{dt} = 180 - 0.75\, P_t \qquad Q_{st} = -30 + 0.3\, P_{t-1} \qquad P_0 = 220$$

(a) Equating demand and supply,

$$180 - 0.75\, P_t = -30 + 0.3\, P_{t-1} \tag{19.21}$$
$$-0.75\, P_t = 0.3\, P_{t-1} - 210$$

Dividing through by -0.75 and using (19.4),

$$P_t = -0.4\, P_{t-1} + 280 = \left(220 - \frac{280}{1 + 0.4}\right)(-0.4)^t + \frac{280}{1 + 0.4} = 20(-0.4)^t + 200 \tag{19.22}$$

(b) If the market is in equilibrium, $P_t = P_{t-1}$.   Substituting P_e for P_t and P_{t-1} in (19.21),

$$180 - 0.75\, P_e = -30 + 0.3\, P_e \qquad P_e = 200$$

which is the second term on the right-hand side of (19.22).

(c) With $b = -0.4$,   the time path P_t will oscillate and converge.

19.22. Check the answer to Problem 19.21(a), using $t = 0$ and $t = 1$.

From (19.22), $P_0 = 20(-0.4)^0 + 200 = 220$ and $P_1 = 20(-0.4) + 200 = 192$.   Substituting P_1 for P_t and P_0 for P_{t-1} in (19.21),

$$180 - 0.75(192) = -30 + 0.3(220)$$
$$36 = 36$$

19.23. Redo Problem 19.21, given $Q_{dt} = 160 - 0.8\,P_t$, $Q_{st} = -20 + 0.4\,P_{t-1}$, and $P_0 = 153$.

(a)
$$160 - 0.8\,P_t = -20 + 0.4\,P_{t-1} \qquad (19.23)$$
$$-0.8\,P_t = 0.4\,P_{t-1} - 180$$

Dividing through by -0.8 and using (19.4),

$$P_t = -0.5\,P_{t-1} + 225 = \left(153 - \frac{225}{1+0.5}\right)(-0.5)^t + \frac{225}{1+0.5} = 3(-0.5)^t + 150 \qquad (19.24)$$

(b) As shown in Problem 19.21(b), $P_e = 150$. See also Section 19.5.

(c) With $b = -0.5$, P_t oscillates and converges toward 150.

19.24. Check the answer to Problem 19.23(a) using $t = 0$ and $t = 1$.

From (19.24), $P_0 = 3(-0.5)^0 + 150 = 153$ and $P_1 = 3(-0.5) + 150 = 148.5$. Substituting in (19.23),

$$160 - 0.8(148.5) = -20 + 0.4(153)$$
$$41.2 = 41.2 \qquad \text{Compare}$$

19.25. Redo Problem 19.21, given $Q_{dt} = 220 - 0.4\,P_t$, $Q_{st} = -30 + 0.6\,P_{t-1}$, and $P_0 = 254$.

(a)
$$220 - 0.4\,P_t = -30 + 0.6\,P_{t-1}$$
$$-0.4\,P_t = 0.6\,P_{t-1} - 250$$

Dividing through by -0.4 and then using (19.4),

$$P_t = -1.5\,P_{t-1} + 625 = \left(254 - \frac{625}{1+1.5}\right)(-1.5)^t + \frac{625}{1+1.5} = 4(-1.5)^t + 250$$

(b)
$$P_e = 250$$

(c) With $b = -1.5$, P_t oscillates and explodes.

THE HARROD GROWTH MODEL

19.26. For the following data, find (a) the level of income Y_t for any period and (b) the warranted rate of growth.

$$I_t = 2.66(Y_t - Y_{t-1}) \qquad S_t = 0.16\,Y_t \qquad Y_0 = 9000$$

(a) In equilibrium,

$$2.66(Y_t - Y_{t-1}) = 0.16\,Y_t \qquad 2.5\,Y_t = 2.66\,Y_{t-1}$$

Dividing through by 2.5 and then using (19.4),

$$Y_t = 1.064\,Y_{t-1} = (9000 - 0)(1.064)^t + 0 = 9000(1.064)^t$$

(b) From (19.16), $G_w = 0.16/(2.66 - 0.16) = 0.064$.

19.27. Redo Problem 19.26, given $I_t = 4.2(Y_t - Y_{t-1})$, $S_t = 0.2\,Y_t$, and $Y_0 = 5600$.

(a)
$$4.2(Y_t - Y_{t-1}) = 0.2\,Y_t$$
$$4\,Y_t = 4.2\,Y_{t-1}$$
$$Y_t = 1.05\,Y_{t-1}$$

Using (19.4), $Y_t = 5600(1.05)^t$.

(b)
$$G_w = \frac{0.2}{4.2 - 0.2} = 0.05$$

OTHER ECONOMIC APPLICATIONS

19.28. Derive the formula for the value P_t of an initial amount of money P_0 deposited at i interest for t years when compounded annually.

When interest is compounded annually,

$$P_{t+1} = P_t + iP_t = (1+i)P_t$$

Moving the time periods back one to conform with (19.3),

$$P_t = (1+i)P_{t-1}$$

Using (19.4) since $i \neq 0$, $\qquad P_t = (P_0 + 0)(1+i)^t + 0 = P_0(1+i)^t$

19.29. Assume that $\quad Q_{dt} = c + zP_t, \; Q_{st} = g + hP_t,$ and

$$P_{t+1} = P_t - a(Q_{st} - Q_{dt}) \qquad\qquad (19.25)$$

i.e. price is no longer determined by a market-clearing mechanism but by the level of inventory $(Q_{st} - Q_{dt})$. Assume, too, that $\;a > 0\;$ since a buildup in inventory $(Q_{st} > Q_{dt})$ will tend to reduce price, and a depletion of inventory $(Q_{st} < Q_{dt})$ will cause prices to rise. (*a*) Find the price P_t for any period and (*b*) comment on the stability conditions of the time path.

(*a*) Substituting Q_{st} and Q_{dt} in (19.25),

$$P_{t+1} = P_t - a(g + hP_t - c - zP_t)$$
$$= [1 - a(h - z)]P_t - a(g - c) = [1 + a(z - h)]P_t - a(g - c)$$

Shifting the time periods back one to conform to (19.3) and using (19.4),

$$P_t = \left[P_0 + \frac{a(g-c)}{1 - [1 + a(z-h)]} \right][1 + a(z-h)]^t - \frac{a(g-c)}{1 - [1 + a(z-h)]}$$
$$= \left(P_0 - \frac{g-c}{z-h} \right)[1 + a(z-h)]^t + \frac{g-c}{z-h} \qquad\qquad (19.26)$$

Substituting as in (19.13a), $\qquad P_t = (P_0 - P_e)[1 + a(z-h)]^t + P_e \qquad\qquad (19.27)$

(*b*) The stability of the time path depends on $\;b = 1 + a(z - h)$. Since $\;a > 0\;$ and under normal conditions $\;z < 0$ and $h > 0$, $\;a(z-h) < 0$. Thus,

If $\;0 < |a(z-h)| < 1, \quad 0 < b < 1$. $\;P_t$ converges and is nonoscillatory.

If $\;a(z-h) = -1, \quad b = 0$. $\;P_t$ remains in equilibrium $(P_t = P_0)$.

If $\;-2 < a(z-h) < -1, \quad -1 < b < 0$. $\;P_t$ converges with oscillation.

If $\;a(z-h) = -2, \quad b = -1$. Uniform oscillation takes place.

If $\;a(z-h) < -2, \quad b < -1$. $\;P_t$ oscillates and explodes.

19.30. Given the following data, (*a*) find the price P_t for any time period, (*b*) check the answer using $\;t = 0$ and $t = 1$, and (*c*) comment on the stability conditions.

$$Q_{dt} = 120 - 0.5 P_t \qquad Q_{st} = -30 + 0.3 P_t \qquad P_{t+1} = P_t - 0.2(Q_{st} - Q_{dt}) \qquad P_0 = 200$$

(*a*) Substituting, $\qquad P_{t+1} = P_t - 0.2(-30 + 0.3 P_t - 120 + 0.5 P_t) = 0.84 P_t + 30$

Shifting time periods back one and using (19.4),

$$P_t = 0.84 P_{t-1} + 30 = \left(200 - \frac{30}{1 - 0.84} \right)(0.84)^t + \frac{30}{1 - 0.84} = 12.5(0.84)^t + 187.5$$

(*b*) $P_0 = 200$; $P_1 = 198$. Substituting in the first equation of the solution, $198 = 200 - 0.2[-30 + 0.3(200) - 120 + 0.5(200)] = 198$. Compare.

(*c*) With $\;b = 0.84$, $\;P_t$ converges without oscillation toward 187.5.

Chapter 20

Second-Order Differential Equations and Difference Equations

20.1 SECOND-ORDER DIFFERENTIAL EQUATIONS

Second-order differential equations require separate solution for the complementary function y_c and the particular integral y_p. The general solution is the sum of the two: $y(t) = y_c + y_p$. Given the second-order linear differential equation

$$y''(t) + b_1 y'(t) + b_2 y(t) = a \qquad (20.1)$$

where b_1, b_2, and a are constants, the particular integral will be

$$y_p = \frac{a}{b_2} \qquad b_2 \neq 0 \qquad (20.2)$$

$$y_p = \frac{a}{b_1} t \qquad b_2 = 0 \quad b_1 \neq 0 \qquad (20.2a)$$

$$y_p = \frac{a}{2} t^2 \qquad b_1 = b_2 = 0 \qquad (20.2b)$$

The complementary function is

$$y_c = y_1 + y_2 \qquad (20.3)$$

where

$$y_1 = A_1 e^{r_1 t} \qquad (20.3a)$$

$$y_2 = A_2 e^{r_2 t} \qquad (20.3b)$$

and

$$r_1, r_2 = \frac{-b_1 \pm \sqrt{b_1^2 - 4b_2}}{2} \qquad (20.4)$$

Here, A_1, A_2 are arbitrary constants, and $b_1^2 \neq 4b_2$. r_1 and r_2 are referred to as *characteristic roots*, and (20.4) is the solution to the *characteristic* or *auxiliary equation*: $r^2 + b_1 r + b_2 = 0$.

Example 1. The particular integral for each of the following equations

$$(1) \quad y''(t) - 5y'(t) + 4y(t) = 2 \qquad (2) \quad y''(t) + 3y'(t) = 12 \qquad (3) \quad y''(t) = 16$$

is found as shown below.

For (1), using (20.2), $\qquad\qquad\qquad\quad y_p = \frac{2}{4} = \frac{1}{2}$ $\qquad\qquad\qquad\qquad\qquad$ (20.5)

For (2), using (20.2a), $\qquad\qquad\qquad y_p = \frac{12}{3} t = 4t$ $\qquad\qquad\qquad\qquad\quad$ (20.5a)

For (3), using (20.2b), $\qquad\qquad\qquad y_p = \frac{16}{2} t^2 = 8t^2$ $\qquad\qquad\qquad\qquad\quad$ (20.5b)

Example 2. The complementary functions for equations (1) and (2) in Example 1 are calculated below. Equation (3) will be treated in Example 9.

For (1), from (20.4),

$$r_1, r_2 = \frac{+5 \pm \sqrt{(-5)^2 - 4(4)}}{2} = \frac{5 \pm 3}{2} = 1, 4$$

Substituting in (20.3a) and (20.3b), and finally in (20.3),

$$y_c = A_1 e^t + A_2 e^{4t} \tag{20.6}$$

For (2),
$$r_1, r_2 = \frac{-3 \pm \sqrt{(3)^2 - 4(0)}}{2} = \frac{-3 \pm 3}{2} = 0, -3$$

Thus,
$$y_c = A_1 e^0 + A_2 e^{-3t} = A_1 + A_2 e^{-3t} \tag{20.6a}$$

Example 3. The general solution of a differential equation is composed of the complementary function and the particular integral (Section 18.2), i.e. $y(t) = y_c + y_p$. As applied to the equations in Example 1,

For (1), from (20.6) and (20.5), $y(t) = A_1 e^t + A_2 e^{4t} + \frac{1}{2}$ (20.7)

For (2), from (20.6a) and (20.5a), $y(t) = A_1 + A_2 e^{-3t} + 4t$ (20.7a)

Example 4. The definite solution for (1) in Example 3 is calculated below. Assume $y(0) = 5\frac{1}{2}$ and $y'(0) = 11$.

From (20.7),

$$y(t) = A_1 e^t + A_2 e^{4t} + \frac{1}{2} \tag{20.8}$$

Thus,
$$y'(t) = A_1 e^t + 4A_2 e^{4t} \tag{20.8a}$$

Evaluating (20.8) and (20.8a) at $t = 0$, and setting $y(0) = 5\frac{1}{2}$ and $y'(0) = 11$ from the initial conditions,

$$y(0) = A_1 e^0 + A_2 e^{4(0)} + \frac{1}{2} = 5\frac{1}{2} \quad \text{thus} \quad A_1 + A_2 = 5$$
$$y'(0) = A_1 e^0 + 4A_2 e^{4(0)} = 11 \quad \text{thus} \quad A_1 + 4A_2 = 11$$

Solving simultaneously, $A_1 = 3$ and $A_2 = 2$. Substituting in (20.7),

$$y(t) = 3e^t + 2e^{4t} + \frac{1}{2} \tag{20.9}$$

To check this solution, from (20.9),

$$y(t) = 3e^t + 2e^{4t} + \frac{1}{2}$$

Thus,
$$y'(t) = 3e^t + 8e^{4t} \qquad y''(t) = 3e^t + 32e^{4t}$$

Substituting in the original equation [(1) in Example 1],

$$(3e^t + 32e^{4t}) - 5(3e^t + 8e^{4t}) + 4(3e^t + 2e^{4t} + \tfrac{1}{2}) = 2 \qquad \text{Compare}$$

20.2 SECOND-ORDER DIFFERENCE EQUATIONS

The general solution of a second-order difference equation is composed of a complementary function and a particular solution: $y(t) = y_c + y_p$. Given the second-order linear difference equation

$$y_t + b_1 y_{t-1} + b_2 y_{t-2} = a \tag{20.10}$$

where b_1, b_2, and a are constants, the particular solution is

$$y_p = \frac{a}{1 + b_1 + b_2} \qquad b_1 + b_2 \neq -1 \tag{20.11}$$

$$y_p = \frac{a}{2 + b_1} t \qquad b_1 + b_2 = -1 \quad b_1 \neq -2 \tag{20.11a}$$

$$y_p = \frac{a}{2} t^2 \qquad b_1 + b_2 = -1 \quad b_1 = -2 \tag{20.11b}$$

The complementary function is

$$y_c = A_1 r_1^t + A_2 r_2^t \tag{20.12}$$

where A_1 and A_2 are arbitrary constants and the characteristic roots r_1 and r_2 are found using (20.4), assuming $b_1^2 \neq 4b_2$.

Example 5.   The particular solution for each of the following equations

$$(1) \quad y_t - 10y_{t-1} + 16y_{t-2} = 14 \qquad (2) \quad y_t - 6y_{t-1} + 5y_{t-2} = 12 \qquad (3) \quad y_t - 2y_{t-1} + y_{t-2} = 8$$

is found as shown below.

For (1), using (20.11),

$$y_p = \frac{14}{1 - 10 + 16} = 2 \tag{20.13}$$

For (2), using (20.11a),

$$y_p = \frac{12}{2 - 6}t = -3t \tag{20.13a}$$

For (3), using (20.11b),

$$y_p = \tfrac{8}{2}t^2 = 4t^2 \tag{20.13b}$$

Example 6.   From Example 5, the complementary functions for (1) and (2) are calculated below.   For (3), see Example 9.

For (1), using (20.4), and then substituting in (20.12),

$$r_1, r_2 = \frac{10 \pm \sqrt{100 - 4(16)}}{2} = \frac{10 \pm 6}{2} = 2, 8$$

Thus,

$$y_c = A_1(2)^t + A_2(8)^t \tag{20.14}$$

For (2),

$$r_1, r_2 = \frac{6 \pm \sqrt{36 - 4(5)}}{2} = \frac{6 \pm 4}{2} = 1, 5$$

Thus,

$$y_c = A_1(1)^t + A_2(5)^t = A_1 + A_2(5)^t \tag{20.14a}$$

Example 7.   The general solutions for (1) and (2) from Example 5 are calculated below.

For (1), $y(t) = y_c + y_p$.   From (20.14) and (20.13),

$$y(t) = A_1(2)^t + A_2(8)^t + 2 \tag{20.15}$$

For (2), from (20.14a) and (20.13a),

$$y(t) = A_1 + A_2(5)^t - 3t \tag{20.15a}$$

Example 8.   Given $y(0) = 10$ and $y(1) = 36$,   the definite solution for (1) in Example 7 is calculated as follows: Letting $t = 0$ and $t = 1$ successively in (20.15),

$$y(0) = A_1(2)^0 + A_2(8)^0 + 2 = A_1 + A_2 + 2 \qquad y(1) = A_1(2) + A_2(8) + 2 = 2A_1 + 8A_2 + 2$$

Setting $y(0) = 10$ and $y(1) = 36$ from the initial conditions,

$$A_1 + A_2 + 2 = 10$$
$$2A_1 + 8A_2 + 2 = 36$$

Solving simultaneously, $A_1 = 5$ and $A_2 = 3$.   Finally, substituting in (20.15),

$$y(t) = 5(2)^t + 3(8)^t + 2 \tag{20.16}$$

This answer is checked by evaluating (20.16) at $t = 0$, $t = 1$, and $t = 2$,

$$y(0) = 5 + 3 + 2 = 10 \qquad y(1) = 10 + 24 + 2 = 36 \qquad y(2) = 20 + 192 + 2 = 214$$

Substituting $y(2)$ for y_t, $y(1)$ for y_{t-1}, and $y(0)$ for y_{t-2} in $y_t - 10y_{t-1} + 16y_{t-2} = 14$ of Equation (1) in Example 5, $214 - 10(36) + 16(10) = 14$.   Compare.

20.3   CHARACTERISTIC ROOTS

A characteristic equation can have three different types of roots.

1.   *Distinct real roots.* If $b_1^2 > 4b_2$,   the square root in (20.4) will be a real number and r_1 and r_2 will be distinct real numbers as in (20.6) and (20.6a).

2.   *Repeated real roots.* If $b_1^2 = 4b_2$,   the square root in (20.4) will vanish and r_1 and r_2 will equal the same real number.   In the case of repeated real roots, the formulas for y_c in (20.3) and (20.12) must be changed to

$$y_c = A_1 e^{rt} + A_2 t e^{rt} \tag{20.17}$$
$$y_c = A_1 r^t + A_2 t r^t \tag{20.18}$$

3. *Complex roots.* If $b_1^2 < 4b_2$, (20.4) contains the square root of a negative number, which is called an *imaginary number*. In this case r_1 and r_2 are complex numbers. A *complex number* contains a real part and an imaginary part; for example, $(12 + i)$ where $i = \sqrt{-1}$.

(As a simple test to check your answers when using (20.4), $r_1 + r_2$ must equal $-b_1$; $r_1 \times r_2$ must equal b_2.)

Example 9. The complementary function for Equation (3) in Example 1, where $y''(t) = 16$, is found as follows: From (20.4),

$$r_1, r_2 = \frac{0 \pm \sqrt{0 - 4(0)}}{2} = 0$$

Using (20.17) since $r_1 = r_2 = 0$, which is a case of repeated real roots, $y_c = A_1 e^0 + A_2 t e^0 = A_1 + A_2 t$.

In Equation (3) of Example 5, $y_t - 2y_{t-1} + y_{t-2} = 8$. Solving for the complementary function, from (20.4),

$$r_1, r_2 = \frac{2 \pm \sqrt{4 - 4(1)}}{2} = \frac{2 \pm 0}{2} = 1$$

Using (20.18) because $r_1 = r_2 = 1$, $y_c = A_1(1)^t + A_2 t(1)^t = A_1 + A_2 t$.

20.4 CONJUGATE COMPLEX NUMBERS

If $b_1^2 < 4b_2$ in (20.4), factoring out $\sqrt{-1}$ gives

$$r_1, r_2 = \frac{-b_1 \pm \sqrt{-1}\sqrt{4b_2 - b_1^2}}{2} = \frac{-b_1 \pm i\sqrt{4b_2 - b_1^2}}{2}$$

Put more succinctly,

$$r_1, r_2 = g \pm hi \qquad (20.19)$$

where

$$g = -\tfrac{1}{2}b_1 \quad \text{and} \quad h = \tfrac{1}{2}\sqrt{4b_2 - b_1^2}$$

$g \pm hi$ are called *conjugate* complex numbers because they always appear together. Substituting (20.19) in (20.3) and (20.12) to find y_c for cases of complex roots,

$$y_c = A_1 e^{(g+hi)t} + A_2 e^{(g-hi)t} = e^{gt}(A_1 e^{hit} + A_2 e^{-hit}) \qquad (20.20)$$

$$y_c = A_1(g + hi)^t + A_2(g - hi)^t \qquad (20.21)$$

Example 10. The complementary function for $y''(t) + 2y'(t) + 5y(t) = 18$ is calculated as shown below. Using (20.19) since $b_1^2 < 4b_2$,

$$g = -\tfrac{1}{2}(2) = -1 \qquad h = \tfrac{1}{2}\sqrt{4(5) - (2)^2} = \tfrac{1}{2}(4) = 2$$

Thus, $r_1, r_2 = -1 \pm 2i$. Substituting in (20.20), $y_c = e^{-t}(A_1 e^{2it} + A_2 e^{-2it})$.

20.5 TRIGONOMETRIC FUNCTIONS

Trigonometric functions are often used in connection with complex numbers. Given the angle θ in Fig. 20-1, which is at the center of a circle of radius k and measured counterclockwise, the trigonometric functions of θ are

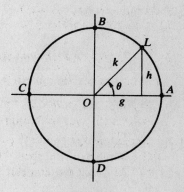

Fig. 20-1

$$\text{sine (sin) } \theta = \frac{h}{k} \qquad \text{cosine (cos) } \theta = \frac{g}{k}$$

$$\text{tangent (tan) } \theta = \frac{h}{g} \qquad \text{cotangent (cot) } \theta = \frac{g}{h}$$

$$\text{secant (sec) } \theta = \frac{k}{g} \qquad \text{cosecant (csc) } \theta = \frac{k}{h}$$

The signs of the trigonometric functions in each of the four quadrants are

$$\frac{+\ |\ +}{-\ |\ -} \qquad \frac{-\ |\ +}{-\ |\ +} \qquad \frac{-\ |\ +}{+\ |\ -}$$

sin, csc   cos, sec   tan, cot

The angle θ is frequently measured in *radians*. Since there are 2π radians in a circle, $1° = \pi/180$ radians. Thus $360° = 2\pi$ radians, $180° = \pi$ radians, $90° = \pi/2$ radians, and $45° = \pi/4$ radians.

Example 11. If the radius OL in Fig. 20-1 starts at A and moves counterclockwise 360°, $\sin \theta = h/k$ goes from 0 at A, to 1 at B, to 0 at C, to -1 at D, and back to 0 at A. Cosine $\theta = g/k$ goes from 1 at A, to 0 at B, to -1 at C, to 0 at D, and back to 1 at A. This is summarized in Table 1 and graphed in Fig. 20-2. Notice that both functions are *periodic* with a *period* of 2π (i.e. they repeat themselves every 360° or 2π radians). Both have an *amplitude* of fluctuation of 1 and differ only in *phase* or location of their peaks.

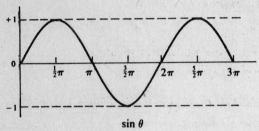
sin θ

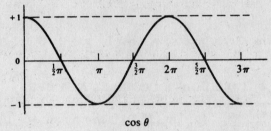
cos θ

Fig. 20-2

Table 1

Degrees	0	90	180	270	360
Radians	0	$\frac{\pi}{2}$	π	$\frac{3}{2}\pi$	2π
$\sin \theta$	0	1	0	-1	0
$\cos \theta$	1	0	-1	0	1

20.6 DERIVATIVES OF TRIGONOMETRIC FUNCTIONS

Given that u is a differentiable function of x,

(1) $\dfrac{d}{dx}(\sin u) = \cos u \dfrac{du}{dx}$ (4) $\dfrac{d}{dx}(\cot u) = -\csc^2 u \dfrac{du}{dx}$

(2) $\dfrac{d}{dx}(\cos u) = -\sin u \dfrac{du}{dx}$ (5) $\dfrac{d}{dx}(\sec u) = \sec u \tan u \dfrac{du}{dx}$

(3) $\dfrac{d}{dx}(\tan u) = \sec^2 u \dfrac{du}{dx}$ (6) $\dfrac{d}{dx}(\csc u) = -\csc u \cot u \dfrac{du}{dx}$

Example 12. The derivatives for the trigonometric functions given below

(1) $y = \sin(3x^2 + 6)$ (2) $y = 4\cos 2x$ (3) $y = (1 + \tan x)^2$

are calculated as follows:

(1) $\dfrac{dy}{dx} = 6x \cos(3x^2 + 6)$ (2) $\dfrac{dy}{dx} = -8 \sin 2x$ (3) $\dfrac{dy}{dx} = 2(1 + \tan x)(\sec^2 x) = 2\sec^2 x(1 + \tan x)$

20.7 TRANSFORMATION OF IMAGINARY AND COMPLEX NUMBERS

Three rules are helpful in transforming imaginary and complex numbers into trigonometric functions.

1. g and h, which are *cartesian coordinates* in Fig. 20-1, can be expressed in terms of θ and k, which are called *polar coordinates*, by the simple formula

$$g = k \cos \theta \qquad h = k \sin \theta \qquad k > 0$$

Thus for the conjugate complex number $(g \pm hi)$,

$$g \pm hi = k \cos \theta \pm ik \sin \theta = k(\cos \theta \pm i \sin \theta) \qquad (20.22)$$

2. By what are called *Euler relations*,

$$\epsilon^{\pm i\theta} = \cos \theta \pm i \sin \theta \qquad (20.23)$$

Thus, by substituting (20.23) in (20.22) we can also express $(g \pm hi)$ as

$$g \pm hi = ke^{\pm i\theta} \qquad (20.23a)$$

3. From $(20.23a)$, raising a conjugate complex number to the nth power means

$$(g \pm hi)^n = (ke^{\pm i\theta})^n = k^n e^{\pm in\theta} \qquad (20.24)$$

Or, by making use of (20.23) and noting that $n\theta$ replaces θ, we have *De Moivre's theorem*:

$$(g \pm hi)^n = k^n(\cos n\theta \pm i \sin n\theta) \qquad (20.25)$$

Example 13. The value of the imaginary exponential function $e^{2i\pi}$ is found as follows. Using (20.23), where $\theta = 2\pi$,

$$e^{2i\pi} = \cos 2\pi + i \sin 2\pi$$

From Table 1, $\cos 2\pi = 1$ and $\sin 2\pi = 0$. Thus, $e^{2i\pi} = 1 + i(0) = 1$.

Example 14. The imaginary exponential expressions in (20.20) and (20.21) are transformed into trigonometric functions as shown below.

From (20.20), $y_c = e^{gt}(A_1 e^{hit} + A_2 e^{-hit})$. Using (20.23) where $\theta = ht$,

$$y_c = e^{gt}[A_1(\cos ht + i \sin ht) + A_2(\cos ht - i \sin ht)]$$
$$= e^{gt}[(A_1 + A_2) \cos ht + (A_1 - A_2)i \sin ht]$$
$$= e^{gt}(B_1 \cos ht + B_2 \sin ht) \qquad (20.26)$$

where $B_1 = A_1 + A_2$ and $B_2 = (A_1 - A_2)i$.

From (20.21), $y_c = A_1(g + hi)^t + A_2(g - hi)^t$. Using (20.25) and substituting t for n,

$$y_c = A_1 k^t(\cos t\theta + i \sin t\theta) + A_2 k^t(\cos t\theta - i \sin t\theta)$$
$$= k^t[(A_1 + A_2) \cos t\theta + (A_1 - A_2)i \sin t\theta]$$
$$= k^t(B_1 \cos t\theta + B_2 \sin t\theta) \qquad (20.27)$$

where $B_1 = A_1 + A_2$ and $B_2 = (A_1 - A_2)i$.

Example 15. The time paths of (20.26) and (20.27) are evaluated as follows: Examining each term in (20.26),

1. $(B_1 \cos ht)$ is a cosine function of t, as in Fig. 20-2, with period $2\pi/h$ instead of 2π, and amplitude of the multiplicative constant B_1 instead of 1.

2. $(B_2 \sin ht)$ is likewise a sine function of t with period $2\pi/h$ and amplitude of B_2.

3. With the first two terms constantly fluctuating, stability depends on e^{gt}:

   If $g > 0$, e^{gt} gets increasingly larger as t increases. This increases the amplitude and leads to explosive fluctuations of y_c, precluding convergence.

If $g = 0$, $e^{gt} = 1$ and y_c displays uniform fluctuations determined by the sine and cosine functions. This also precludes convergence.

If $g < 0$, e^{gt} approaches zero as t increases. This diminishes the amplitude, produces damped fluctuations, and leads to convergence. See Fig. 20-3.

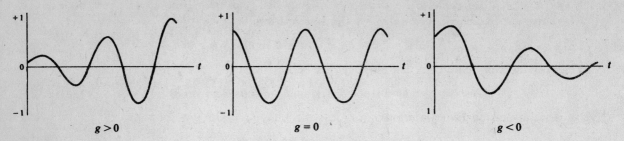

Fig. 20-3 Time path of $y_c(t)$.

Since (20.27) concerns a difference equation in which t can only change at discrete intervals, y_c is a step function rather than a continuous function (see Fig. 19-1). Like (20.26), it will fluctuate, and stability will depend on k^t. If $|k| < 1$, y_c will converge. See Problems 20.8–20.11, 20.18–20.20, and 20.31–20.35.

20.8 STABILITY CONDITIONS

For a second-order linear differential equation with distinct or repeated real roots, both roots must be negative for convergence. If one of the roots is positive, the exponential term with the positive root approaches infinity as t approaches infinity, thereby precluding convergence. See Problems 20.8–20.11. In the case of complex roots, g in e^{gt} of (20.26) must be negative, as illustrated in Example 15.

For a second-order linear difference equation with distinct or repeated real roots, the root with the largest absolute value is called the *dominant root* because it dominates the time path. For convergence, the absolute value of the dominant root must be less than one. See Problems 20.18–20.20. In the case of complex roots, the absolute value of k in (20.27) must be less than one, as explained in Example 15.

Solved Problems

SECOND-ORDER LINEAR DIFFERENTIAL EQUATIONS

Distinct Real Roots

20.1. For the following equation, find (a) the particular integral y_p, (b) the complementary function y_c, and (c) the general solution $y(t)$.

$$y''(t) + 9y'(t) + 14y(t) = 7$$

(a) Using (20.2), $y_p = \frac{7}{14} = \frac{1}{2}$.

(b) Using (20.4),

$$r_1, r_2 = \frac{-9 \pm \sqrt{81 - 4(14)}}{2} = \frac{-9 \pm 5}{2} = -2, -7$$

Substituting in (20.3), $y_c = A_1 e^{-2t} + A_2 e^{-7t}$.

(c) $y(t) = y_c + y_p = A_1 e^{-2t} + A_2 e^{-7t} + \frac{1}{2}$ (20.28)

20.2.   Redo Problem 20.1, given $y''(t) - 12y'(t) + 20y(t) = -100.$

(a)   From (20.2), $y_p = -\dfrac{100}{20} = -5.$

(b)   From (20.4),

$$r_1, r_2 = \frac{12 \pm \sqrt{144 - 4(20)}}{2} = \frac{12 \pm 8}{2} = 2, 10$$

Thus, $y_c = A_1 e^{2t} + A_2 e^{10t}.$

(c) $$y(t) = y_c + y_p = A_1 e^{2t} + A_2 e^{10t} - 5 \qquad (20.29)$$

20.3.   Redo Problem 20.1, given $y''(t) - 4y'(t) - 5y(t) = 35.$

(a)   From (20.2), $y_p = \dfrac{35}{-5} = -7.$

(b)   From (20.4)

$$r_1, r_2 = \frac{4 \pm \sqrt{16 - 4(-5)}}{2} = \frac{4 \pm 6}{2} = 5, -1$$

Thus, $y_c = A_1 e^{5t} + A_2 e^{-t}.$

(c) $$y(t) = A_1 e^{5t} + A_2 e^{-t} - 7 \qquad (20.30)$$

20.4.   Redo Problem 20.1, given $y''(t) + 7y'(t) = 28.$

(a)   Using (20.2a), $y_p = \frac{28}{7}t = 4t.$

(b)   From (20.4),

$$r_1, r_2 = \frac{-7 \pm \sqrt{49 - 4(0)}}{2} = \frac{-7 \pm 7}{2} = 0, -7$$

Thus, $y_c = A_1 e^{(0)t} + A_2 e^{-7t} = A_1 + A_2 e^{-7t}.$

(c) $$y(t) = A_1 + A_2 e^{-7t} + 4t \qquad (20.31)$$

20.5.   Redo Problem 20.1, given $y''(t) - \frac{1}{2}y'(t) = 13.$

(a)   From (20.2a), $y_p = \dfrac{13}{-1/2}t = -26t.$

(b) $$r_1, r_2 = \frac{1/2 \pm \sqrt{1/4 - 4(0)}}{2} = \frac{1/2 \pm 1/2}{2} = 0, \tfrac{1}{2}$$

Thus, $y_c = A_1 + A_2 e^{(1/2)t}.$

(c) $$y(t) = A_1 + A_2 e^{(1/2)t} - 26t \qquad (20.32)$$

Repeated Real Roots

20.6.   Find   (a) the particular integral y_p,   (b) the complementary function y_c, and   (c) the general solution $y(t)$, given $y''(t) - 12y'(t) + 36y(t) = 108.$

(a) $$y_p = \tfrac{108}{36} = 3$$

(b) $$r_1, r_2 = \frac{12 \pm \sqrt{144 - 4(36)}}{2} = \frac{12 \pm 0}{2} = 6$$

Using (20.17) since $r_1 = r_2 = 6$, $y_c = A_1 e^{6t} + A_2 t e^{6t}.$

(c) $$y(t) = A_1 e^{6t} + A_2 t e^{6t} + 3 \qquad (20.33)$$

20.7.   Redo Problem 20.6, given $y''(t) + y'(t) + \frac{1}{4}y(t) = 9$.

$$y_p = \frac{9}{1/4} = 36$$

(b) $$r_1, r_2 = \frac{-1 \pm \sqrt{1 - 4(1/4)}}{2} = \frac{-1 \pm 0}{2} = -\frac{1}{2}$$

Using (20.17) since $r_1 = r_2 = -\frac{1}{2}$, $y_c = A_1 e^{-(1/2)t} + A_2 t e^{-(1/2)t}$.

(c) $$y(t) = A_1 e^{-(1/2)t} + A_2 t e^{-(1/2)t} + 36 \qquad (20.34)$$

DEFINITE SOLUTIONS AND STABILITY CONDITIONS

20.8.   Find   (a) the definite solution for the following equation,   (b) check your answer, and (c) comment on the dynamic stability of the time path, given $y''(t) + 9y'(t) + 14y(t) = 7$, $y(0) = -2\frac{1}{2}$, and $y'(0) = 31$.

(a)   From (20.28),

$$y(t) = A_1 e^{-2t} + A_2 e^{-7t} + \frac{1}{2} \qquad (20.35)$$

Thus, $$y'(t) = -2A_1 e^{-2t} - 7A_2 e^{-7t} \qquad (20.35a)$$

Evaluating (20.35) and (20.35a) at $t = 0$,

$$y(0) = A_1 + A_2 + \frac{1}{2} \qquad y'(0) = -2A_1 - 7A_2$$

Setting $y(0) = -2\frac{1}{2}$ and $y'(0) = 31$ from the initial conditions,

$$A_1 + A_2 + \frac{1}{2} = -2\frac{1}{2}$$
$$-2A_1 - 7A_2 = 31$$

Solving simultaneously, $A_1 = 2$ and $A_2 = -5$,   which when substituted in (20.35) gives

$$y(t) = 2e^{-2t} - 5e^{-7t} + \frac{1}{2} \qquad (20.36)$$

(b)   From (20.36), $y(t) = 2e^{-2t} - 5e^{-7t} + \frac{1}{2}$.   Thus,

$$y'(t) = -4e^{-2t} + 35e^{-7t} \qquad y''(t) = 8e^{-2t} - 245e^{-7t}$$

Substituting these values in the original problem, where $y'' + 9y'(t) + 14y(t) = 7$

$$8e^{-2t} - 245e^{-7t} + 9(-4e^{-2t} + 35e^{-7t}) + 14(2e^{-2t} - 5e^{-7t} + \frac{1}{2}) = 7 \quad \text{Compare}$$

(c)   With both characteristic roots negative, (20.36) will approach $\frac{1}{2}$ as $t \to \infty$. Therefore $y(t)$ is convergent.   Any time both characteristic roots are negative, the time path will converge.

20.9.   Redo Problem 20.8, given $y''(t) - 4y'(t) - 5y(t) = 35$, $y(0) = 5$, and $y'(0) = 6$.

(a)   From (20.30),

$$y(t) = A_1 e^{5t} + A_2 e^{-t} - 7 \qquad (20.37)$$

Thus, $$y'(t) = 5A_1 e^{5t} - A_2 e^{-t} \qquad (20.37a)$$

Evaluating (20.37) and (20.37a) at $t = 0$ and setting them equal to the initial conditions where $y(0) = 5$ and $y'(0) = 6$,

$$y(0) = A_1 + A_2 - 7 = 5 \qquad \text{thus} \qquad A_1 + A_2 = 12$$
$$y'(0) = 5A_1 - A_2 = 6$$

Solving simultaneously, $A_1 = 3$ and $A_2 = 9$,   which when substituted in (20.37) gives

$$y(t) = 3e^{5t} + 9e^{-t} - 7 \qquad (20.38)$$

(b) From (20.38), $y(t) = 3e^{5t} + 9e^{-t} - 7$. Thus, $y'(t) = 15e^{5t} - 9e^{-t}$ and $y''(t) = 75e^{5t} + 9e^{-t}$. Substituting these values in the original problem, where $y''(t) - 4y'(t) - 5y(t) = 35$,

$$75e^{5t} + 9e^{-t} - 4(15e^{5t} - 9e^{-t}) - 5(3e^{5t} + 9e^{-t} - 7) = 35 \quad \text{Compare}$$

(c) With one characteristic root positive and the other negative, the time path is divergent. The positive root dominates the negative root independently of their relative absolute values because as $t \to \infty$, the positive root $\to \infty$ and the negative root $\to 0$.

20.10. Redo Problem 20.8, given $y''(t) - \frac{1}{2}y'(t) = 13$, $y(0) = 17$, and $y'(0) = -19\frac{1}{2}$.

(a) From (20.32),

$$y(t) = A_1 + A_2 e^{(1/2)t} - 26t \tag{20.39}$$

Thus,
$$y'(t) = \tfrac{1}{2}A_2 e^{(1/2)t} - 26 \tag{20.39a}$$

Evaluating (20.39) and ($20.39a$) at $t = 0$ and setting them equal to the initial conditions,

$$y(0) = A_1 + A_2 = 17$$
$$y'(0) = \tfrac{1}{2}A_2 - 26 = -19\tfrac{1}{2} \qquad A_2 = 13$$

With $A_2 = 13$, $A_1 = 4$. Substituting in (20.39) and rearranging terms,

$$y(t) = 13e^{(1/2)t} - 26t + 4 \tag{20.40}$$

(b) From (20.40), $y(t) = 13e^{(1/2)t} - 26t + 4$. Thus,

$$y'(t) = 6.5\, e^{(1/2)t} - 26 \qquad y''(t) = 3.25\, e^{(1/2)t}$$

Substituting these values in the original equation,

$$3.25\, e^{(1/2)t} - \tfrac{1}{2}(6.5\, e^{(1/2)t} - 26) = 13 \quad \text{Compare}$$

(c) With both characteristic roots positive, the time path will diverge.

20.11. Redo Problem 20.8, given $y''(t) + y'(t) + \frac{1}{4}y(t) = 9$, $y(0) = 30$, and $y'(0) = 15$.

(a) From (20.34),

$$y(t) = A_1 e^{-(1/2)t} + A_2 t e^{-(1/2)t} + 36 \tag{20.41}$$

Using the product rule for the derivative of the second term,

$$y'(t) = -\tfrac{1}{2}A_1 e^{-(1/2)t} - \tfrac{1}{2}A_2 t e^{-(1/2)t} + A_2 e^{-(1/2)t} \tag{20.41a}$$

Evaluating (20.41) and ($20.41a$) at $t = 0$ and equating to the initial conditions,

$$y(0) = A_1 + 36 = 30 \qquad A_1 = -6$$
$$y'(0) = -\tfrac{1}{2}A_1 + A_2 = 15$$

With $A_1 = -6$, $A_2 = 12$. Substituting in (20.41),

$$y(t) = 12t e^{-(1/2)t} - 6e^{-(1/2)t} + 36 \tag{20.42}$$

(b) From (20.42), $y(t) = 12t e^{-(1/2)t} - 6e^{-(1/2)t} + 36$. By the product rule,

$$y'(t) = -6t e^{-(1/2)t} + 12 e^{-(1/2)t} + 3 e^{-(1/2)t}$$
$$y''(t) = 3t e^{-(1/2)t} - 6e^{-(1/2)t} - 6e^{-(1/2)t} - 1.5\, e^{-(1/2)t} = 3t e^{-(1/2)t} - 13.5\, e^{-(1/2)t}$$

Substituting in the original equation,

$$(3t e^{-(1/2)t} - 13.5\, e^{-(1/2)t}) + (-6t e^{-(1/2)t} + 15 e^{-(1/2)t}) + \tfrac{1}{4}(12t e^{-(1/2)t} - 6e^{-(1/2)t} + 36) = 9 \quad \text{Compare}$$

(c) With the repeated characteristic roots negative, the time path will converge since te^{rt} follows basically the same time path as e^{rt}.

SECOND-ORDER LINEAR DIFFERENCE EQUATIONS

Distinct Real Roots

20.12. Find (a) the particular solution, (b) the complementary function, and (c) the general solution, given $y_t + 7y_{t-1} + 6y_{t-2} = 42$.

(a) From (20.11), $$y_p = 42/(1 + 7 + 6) = 3$$

(b) From (20.4), $$r_1, r_2 = \frac{-7 \pm \sqrt{49 - 4(6)}}{2} = \frac{-7 \pm 5}{2} = -1, -6$$

From (20.12), $$y_c = A_1(-1)^t + A_2(-6)^t$$

(c) $$y(t) = y_c + y_p = A_1(-1)^t + A_2(-6)^t + 3 \qquad (20.43)$$

20.13. Redo Problem 20.12, given $y_t + 12y_{t-1} + 11y_{t-2} = 6$.

(a) From (20.11), $$y_p = 6/(1 + 12 + 11) = \tfrac{1}{4}$$

(b) $$r_1, r_2 = \frac{-12 \pm \sqrt{144 - 4(11)}}{2} = \frac{-12 \pm 10}{2} = -1, -11$$

Thus, $$y_c = A_1(-1)^t + A_2(-11)^t$$

(c) $$y(t) = A_1(-1)^t + A_2(-11)^t + \tfrac{1}{4} \qquad (20.44)$$

20.14. Redo Problem 20.12, given $y_{t+2} - 11y_{t+1} + 10y_t = 27$.

(a) Shifting the time periods back two to conform with (20.10), $y_t - 11y_{t-1} + 10y_{t-2} = 27$. Then, from (20.11a),
$$y_p = \frac{27}{2 - 11} t = -3t$$

(b) $$r_1, r_2 = \frac{11 \pm \sqrt{121 - 4(10)}}{2} = \frac{11 \pm 9}{2} = 1, 10$$

$$y_c = A_1 + A_2(10)^t$$

(c) $$y(t) = A_1 + A_2(10)^t - 3t \qquad (20.45)$$

20.15. Redo Problem 20.12, given $y_t + 7y_{t-1} - 8y_{t-2} = 45$.

(a) From (20.11a), $$y_p = \frac{45}{2 + 7} t = 5t$$

(b) $$r_1, r_2 = \frac{-7 \pm \sqrt{49 - 4(-8)}}{2} = \frac{-7 \pm 9}{2} = 1, -8$$

$$y_c = A_1 + A_2(-8)^t$$

(c) $$y(t) = A_1 + A_2(-8)^t + 5t \qquad (20.46)$$

Repeated Real Roots

20.16. Redo Problem 20.12, given $y_t - 10y_{t-1} + 25y_{t-2} = 8$.

(a) $$y_p = \frac{8}{1 - 10 + 25} = \frac{1}{2}$$

(b) $$r_1, r_2 = \frac{10 \pm \sqrt{100 - 4(25)}}{2} = \frac{10 \pm 0}{2} = 5$$

Using (20.18) because $r_1 = r_2 = 5$, $y_c = A_1(5)^t + A_2 t(5)^t$.

(c) $$y(t) = A_1(5)^t + A_2 t(5)^t + \tfrac{1}{2} \qquad (20.47)$$

20.17. Redo Problem 20.12, given $y_t + 14y_{t-1} + 49y_{t-2} = 128$.

(a)
$$y_p = \frac{128}{1 + 14 + 49} = 2$$

(b)
$$r_1, r_2 = \frac{-14 \pm \sqrt{196 - 4(49)}}{2} = \frac{-14 \pm 0}{2} = -7$$

From (20.18), $y_c = A_1(-7)^t + A_2 t(-7)^t$.

(c)
$$y(t) = A_1(-7)^t + A_2 t(-7)^t + 2 \qquad\qquad (20.48)$$

DEFINITE SOLUTIONS AND STABILITY CONDITIONS

20.18. (a) Find the definite solution, (b) check the answer, and (c) comment on dynamic stability, given $y_t + 7y_{t-1} + 6y_{t-2} = 42$, $y(0) = 16$, and $y(1) = -35$.

(a) From (20.43),
$$y(t) = A_1(-1)^t + A_2(-6)^t + 3 \qquad\qquad (20.49)$$

Letting $t = 0$ and $t = 1$ successively in (20.49) and making use of the initial conditions,

$$y(0) = A_1 + A_2 + 3 = 16 \qquad y(1) = -A_1 - 6A_2 + 3 = -35$$

Solving simultaneously, $A_1 = 8$ and $A_2 = 5$.   Substituting in (20.49),

$$y(t) = 8(-1)^t + 5(-6)^t + 3 \qquad\qquad (20.50)$$

(b) Evaluating (20.50) at $t = 0$, $t = 1$, and $t = 2$ to check this answer,

$$y(0) = 8 + 5 + 3 = 16 \qquad y(1) = -8 - 30 + 3 = -35 \qquad y(2) = 8 + 180 + 3 = 191$$

Substituting in the initial equation with

$$y(2) = y_t \qquad y(1) = y_{t-1} \qquad y(0) = y_{t-2} \qquad 191 + 7(-35) + 6(16) = 42 \quad \text{Compare}$$

(c) The characteristic roots are -1 and -6.   The characteristic root with the largest absolute value is called the *dominant root* because it dominates the time path.   For convergence, the absolute value of the dominant root must be less than 1.   Since $|-6| > |-1|$ and $|-6| > 1$,   the time path is divergent.

20.19. (a) Find the definite solution and   (b) comment on dynamic stability given

$$y_{t+2} - 11y_{t+1} + 10y_t = 27 \qquad y(0) = 2 \qquad y(1) = 53$$

(a) From (20.45),
$$y(t) = A_1 + A_2(10)^t - 3t \qquad\qquad (20.51)$$

Letting $t = 0$ and $t = 1$,   and using the initial conditions,

$$y(0) = A_1 + A_2 = 2 \qquad y(1) = A_1 + 10A_2 - 3 = 53$$

Solving simultaneously, $A_1 = -4$ and $A_2 = 6$.   Substituting in (20.51),

$$y(t) = 6(10)^t - 3t - 4$$

(b) The time path is divergent because the dominant root 10 is greater than 1.

20.20. Redo Problem 20.19, given $y_t - 10y_{t-1} + 25y_{t-2} = 8$, $y(0) = 1$, and $y(1) = 5$.

(a) From (20.47),
$$y(t) = A_1(5)^t + A_2 t(5)^t + \tfrac{1}{2} \qquad\qquad (20.52)$$

Letting $t = 0$ and $t = 1$,   and using the initial conditions,

$$y(0) = A_1 + \tfrac{1}{2} = 1 \qquad A_1 = \tfrac{1}{2}$$
$$y(1) = 5A_1 + 5A_2 + \tfrac{1}{2} = 5$$

With $A_1 = \tfrac{1}{2}$, $A_2 = \tfrac{2}{5}$.   Substituting in (20.52),

$$y(t) = \tfrac{1}{2}(5)^t + \tfrac{2}{5}t(5)^t + \tfrac{1}{2} \qquad\qquad (20.53)$$

(b) Convergence in the case of repeated real roots likewise depends on $|r| < 1$ since the effect of r^t dominates the effect of t in the second term $A_2 t r^t$. Here with $r = 5 > 1$, the time path is divergent.

DERIVATIVES OF TRIGONOMETRIC FUNCTIONS

20.21. Find the first-order derivative for each of the following trigonometric functions. Note that they are also called *circular functions* or *sinusoidal functions*.

(a) $y = \sin 7x$ (b) $y = \cos(5x + 2)$

$\qquad dy/dx = 7 \cos 7x$ $dy/dx = -5 \sin(5x + 2)$

(c) $y = \tan 11x$ (d) $y = \csc(8x + 3)$

$\qquad dy/dx = 11 \sec^2 11x$ $dy/dx = -8[\csc(8x + 3) \cot(8x + 3)]$

(e) $y = \sin(3 - x^2)$ (f) $y = \sin(5 - x)^2$

$\qquad dy/dx = -2x \cos(3 - x^2)$ $dy/dx = -2(5 - x) \cos(5 - x)^2$ (Chain Rule)

20.22. Redo Problem 20.21, given $y = x^2 \tan x$.

By the product rule, $dy/dx = x^2(\sec^2 x) + \tan x(2x) = x^2 \sec^2 x + 2x \tan x$.

20.23. Redo Problem 20.21, given $y = x^3 \sin x$.

$$\frac{dy}{dx} = x^3(\cos x) + \sin x(3x^2) = x^3 \cos x + 3x^2 \sin x$$

20.24. Redo Problem 20.21, given $y = (1 + \cos x)^2$.

By the chain rule, $dy/dx = 2(1 + \cos x)(-\sin x) = -2 \sin x(1 + \cos x)$.

20.25. Redo Problem 20.21, given $y = (\sin x + \cos x)^2$.

$$\frac{dy}{dx} = 2(\sin x + \cos x)(\cos x - \sin x) = 2(\cos^2 x - \sin^2 x)$$

20.26. Redo Problem 20.21, given $y = \sin^2 5x$, where $\sin^2 5x = (\sin 5x)^2$.

By the chain rule, $dy/dx = 2 \sin 5x \cos 5x (5) = 10 \sin 5x \cos 5x$.

20.27. Redo Problem 20.21, given $y = \csc^2 12x$.

$$\frac{dy}{dx} = 2 \csc 12x[-\csc 12x \cot 12x (12)] = -24 \csc^2 12x \cot 12x$$

COMPLEX ROOTS IN SECOND-ORDER DIFFERENTIAL EQUATIONS

20.28. Find (a) the particular integral, (b) the complementary function, and (c) the general solution, given the second-order linear differential equation $y''(t) + 2y'(t) + 10y(t) = 80$.

(a) From (20.2), $y_p = \frac{80}{10} = 8$

(b) Using (20.19) since $b_1^2 < 4b_2$, i.e. $(2)^2 < 4(10)$,

$$g = -\tfrac{1}{2}(2) = -1 \qquad h = \tfrac{1}{2}\sqrt{4(10) - (2)^2} = 3$$

Thus, $r_1, r_2 = -1 \pm 3i$. Substituting g and h in (20.26),

$$y_c = e^{-t}(B_1 \cos 3t + B_2 \sin 3t)$$

(c) $y(t) = y_c + y_p = e^{-t}(B_1 \cos 3t + B_2 \sin 3t) + 8$ (20.54)

20.29. Redo Problem 20.28, given $y''(t) - 6y'(t) + 25y(t) = 150$.

(a)
$$y_p = \tfrac{150}{25} = 6$$

(b) From (20.19), $g = -\tfrac{1}{2}(-6) = 3$ and $h = \tfrac{1}{2}\sqrt{4(25) - (-6)^2} = 4$. Substituting in (20.26),
$$y_c = e^{3t}(B_1 \cos 4t + B_2 \sin 4t)$$

(c)
$$y(t) = e^{3t}(B_1 \cos 4t + B_2 \sin 4t) + 6 \tag{20.55}$$

20.30. Redo Problem 20.28, given $y''(t) + 4y'(t) + 40y(t) = 10$.

(a)
$$y_p = \tfrac{10}{40} = \tfrac{1}{4}$$

(b) From (20.19), $g = -2$ and $h = \tfrac{1}{2}\sqrt{160 - 16} = 6$. Thus, $y_c = e^{-2t}(B_1 \cos 6t + B_2 \sin 6t)$.

(c)
$$y(t) = e^{-2t}(B_1 \cos 6t + B_2 \sin 6t) + \tfrac{1}{4} \tag{20.56}$$

20.31. (a) Find the definite solution for the following data. (b) Comment on the dynamic stability.
$$y''(t) + 2y'(t) + 10y(t) = 80 \qquad y(0) = 10 \qquad y'(0) = 13$$

(a) From (20.54),
$$y(t) = e^{-t}(B_1 \cos 3t + B_2 \sin 3t) + 8 \tag{20.57}$$

By the product rule,
$$y'(t) = e^{-t}(-3B_1 \sin 3t + 3B_2 \cos 3t) + (B_1 \cos 3t + B_2 \sin 3t)(-e^{-t})$$
$$= e^{-t}(3B_2 \cos 3t - 3B_1 \sin 3t) - e^{-t}(B_1 \cos 3t + B_2 \sin 3t) \tag{20.57a}$$

Evaluating (20.57) and (20.57a) at $t = 0$ and equating them to the initial conditions,
$$y(0) = e^0(B_1 \cos 0 + B_2 \sin 0) + 8 = 10$$

From Table 1 (see page 380), $\cos 0 = 1$ and $\sin 0 = 0$. Thus,
$$y(0) = B_1 + 0 + 8 = 10 \qquad B_1 = 2$$

Similarly, $y'(0) = e^0(3B_2 \cos 0 - 3B_1 \sin 0) - e^0(B_1 \cos 0 + B_2 \sin 0) = 13$.
$$y'(0) = 3B_2 - 0 - B_1 = 13$$

Since $B_1 = 2$ from above, $B_2 = 5$. Finally, substituting in (20.57),
$$y(t) = e^{-t}(2 \cos 3t + 5 \sin 3t) + 8$$

(b) With $g = -1$, the time path converges, as it does in Fig. 20-3 (see Example 15).

20.32. Redo Problem 20.31, given $y''(t) - 6y'(t) + 25y(t) = 150$, $y(0) = 13$, and $y'(0) = 25$.

(a) From (20.55),
$$y(t) = e^{3t}(B_1 \cos 4t + B_2 \sin 4t) + 6 \tag{20.58}$$

Thus,
$$y'(t) = e^{3t}(-4B_1 \sin 4t + 4B_2 \cos 4t) + 3e^{3t}(B_1 \cos 4t + B_2 \sin 4t) \tag{20.58a}$$

Evaluating (20.58) and (20.58a) at $t = 0$ and equating them to the initial conditions,
$$y(0) = e^0(B_1 \cos 0 + B_2 \sin 0) + 6 = 13$$
$$y(0) = B_1 + 0 + 6 = 13 \qquad B_1 = 7$$

and $y'(0) = e^0(-4B_1 \sin 0 + 4B_2 \cos 0) + 3e^0(B_1 \cos 0 + B_2 \sin 0)$.
$$y'(0) = 4B_2 + 3B_1 = 25 \qquad B_2 = 1$$

Substituting in (20.58), $y(t) = e^{3t}(7 \cos 4t + \sin 4t) + 6$.

(b) With $g = 3$, the time path is divergent.

20.33. Redo Problem 20.31, given $y''(t) + 4y'(t) + 40y(t) = 10$, $y(0) = \tfrac{1}{2}$, and $y'(0) = 2\tfrac{1}{2}$.

(a) From (20.56),
$$y(t) = e^{-2t}(B_1 \cos 6t + B_2 \sin 6t) + \tfrac{1}{4} \tag{20.59}$$

Thus,
$$y'(t) = e^{-2t}(-6B_1 \sin 6t + 6B_2 \cos 6t) - 2e^{-2t}(B_1 \cos 6t + B_2 \sin 6t) \tag{20.59a}$$

Evaluating (20.59) and $(20.59a)$ at $t = 0$ and equating them to the initial conditions,

$$y(0) = B_1 + \tfrac{1}{4} = \tfrac{1}{2} \qquad\qquad B_1 = \tfrac{1}{4}$$
$$y'(0) = 6B_2 - 2B_1 = 2\tfrac{1}{2} \qquad\qquad B_2 = \tfrac{1}{2}$$

Thus, $y(t) = e^{-2t}(\tfrac{1}{4}\cos 6t + \tfrac{1}{2}\sin 6t) + \tfrac{1}{4} = \tfrac{1}{4}e^{-2t}(\cos 6t + 2\sin 6t) + \tfrac{1}{4}.$

(b)   With $g = -2$, the time path is convergent.

COMPLEX ROOTS IN SECOND-ORDER DIFFERENCE EQUATIONS

20.34.   Find (a) the particular solution, (b) the complementary function, (c) the general solution, (d) the definite solution, and (e) comment on the dynamic stability of the following second-order linear difference equation:

$$y_t + 4y_{t-2} = 15 \qquad y(0) = 12 \qquad y(1) = 11$$

(a)   From (20.11), $y_p = 15/(1 + 0 + 4) = 3$

(b)   From (20.19), $g = -\tfrac{1}{2}(0) = 0$ and $h = \tfrac{1}{2}\sqrt{4(4) - 0} = 2$.   For second-order difference equations we now need k and θ.   Applying the Pythagorean theorem to Fig. 20-1,

$$k^2 = g^2 + h^2 \qquad k = \sqrt{g^2 + h^2}$$

Substituting with the parameters of (20.19) for greater generality,

$$k = \sqrt{\frac{b_1^2 + 4b_2 - b_1^2}{4}} = \sqrt{b_2} \qquad\qquad (20.60)$$

Thus, $k = \sqrt{4} = 2$.   From the definitions of Section 20.5,

$$\sin\theta = \frac{h}{k} \qquad \cos\theta = \frac{g}{k} \qquad\qquad (20.61)$$

Substituting the values from the present problem,

$$\sin\theta = \tfrac{2}{2} = 1 \qquad\qquad \cos\theta = \tfrac{0}{2} = 0$$

From Table 1 (page 380), the angle with $\sin\theta = 1$ and $\cos\theta = 0$ is $\pi/2$.   Thus, $\theta = \pi/2$. Substituting in (20.27),

$$y_c = 2^t\left[B_1\cos\left(\frac{\pi}{2}t\right) + B_2\sin\left(\frac{\pi}{2}t\right)\right]$$

(c) $$y(t) = 2^t\left[B_1\cos\left(\frac{\pi}{2}t\right) + B_2\sin\left(\frac{\pi}{2}t\right)\right] + 3 \qquad\qquad (20.62)$$

(d)   Using Table 1 to evaluate (20.62) at $t = 0$ and $t = 1$ from the initial conditions,

$$y(0) = (B_1 + 0) + 3 = 12 \qquad B_1 = 9$$
$$y(1) = 2(0 + B_2) + 3 = 11 \qquad B_2 = 4$$

Thus, $y(t) = 2^t\{9\cos[(\pi/2)t] + 4\sin[(\pi/2)t]\} + 3$

(e)   With $k = 2$, the time path is divergent, as explained in Example 15.

20.35.   Redo Problem 20.34, given $y_t + 2y_{t-2} = 24$, $y(0) = 11$, and $y(1) = 18$.

(a)   From (20.11), $y_p = 24/(1 + 0 + 2) = 8$

(b)   From (20.60), $k = \sqrt{b_2} = \sqrt{2}$.   From (20.19)

$$g = -\tfrac{1}{2}(0) = 0 \qquad\qquad h = \tfrac{1}{2}\sqrt{4(2) - 0} = \sqrt{2}$$

From (20.61), $\sin\theta = \dfrac{\sqrt{2}}{\sqrt{2}} = 1 \qquad\qquad \cos\theta = 0$

From Table 1, $\theta = \pi/2$. Substituting in (20.27),

$$y_c = (\sqrt{2})^t \left[B_1 \cos\left(\frac{\pi}{2}t\right) + B_2 \sin\left(\frac{\pi}{2}t\right) \right]$$

(c) $$y(t) = (\sqrt{2})^t \left[B_1 \cos\left(\frac{\pi}{2}t\right) + B_2 \sin\left(\frac{\pi}{2}t\right) \right] + 8 \qquad (20.63)$$

(d) $$y(0) = B_1 + 8 = 11 \qquad B_1 = 3$$
$$y(1) = \sqrt{2}B_2 + 8 = 18 \qquad B_2 = 7.07$$

Thus, $$y(t) = (\sqrt{2})^t\{3\cos[(\pi/2)t] + 7.07\sin[(\pi/2)t]\} + 8$$

(e) With $k = \sqrt{2} > 1$, the time path is divergent.

ECONOMIC APPLICATIONS

20.36. In many markets supply and demand are influenced by current prices and price trends (i.e. whether prices are rising or falling, and whether they are rising or falling at an increasing or decreasing rate). The economist, therefore, needs to know the current price $P(t)$, the first derivative $dP(t)/dt$, and the second derivative $d^2P(t)/dt^2$. Assume

$$Q_s = c_1 + w_1 P + u_1 P' + v_1 P'' \qquad Q_d = c_2 + w_2 P + u_2 P' + v_2 P'' \qquad (20.64)$$

Comment on the dynamic stability of the market if price clears the market at each point in time.

In equilibrium, $Q_s = Q_d$. Therefore,

$$c_1 + w_1 P + u_1 P' + v_1 P'' = c_2 + w_2 P + u_2 P' + v_2 P''$$
$$(v_1 - v_2)P'' + (u_1 - u_2)P' + (w_1 - w_2)P = -(c_1 - c_2)$$

Letting $v = v_1 - v_2$, $u = u_1 - u_2$, $w = w_1 - w_2$, $c = c_1 - c_2$,   and dividing through by v to conform to (20.1),

$$P'' + \frac{u}{v}P' + \frac{w}{v}P = -\frac{c}{v} \qquad (20.65)$$

Using (20.2) to find the particular integral, which will be the intertemporal equilibrium price $\bar{P}$,

$$\bar{P} = P_p = \frac{-(c/v)}{w/v} = -\frac{c}{w}$$

Since $c = c_1 - c_2$ and $w = w_1 - w_2$ where under ordinary supply conditions, $c_1 < 0$, $w_1 > 0$, and under ordinary demand conditions, $c_2 > 0$, $w_2 < 0$, $-c/w > 0$, as is necessary for $\bar{P}$. Using (20.4) to find the characteristic roots for the complementary function,

$$r_1, r_2 = \frac{-(u/v) \pm \sqrt{(u/v)^2 - 4(w/v)}}{2} \qquad (20.66)$$

which can assume three different types of solutions, depending on the specification of w, u, and v:

1. If $(u/v)^2 > 4(w/v)$, r_1, r_2 will be *distinct real roots* solvable in terms of (20.66); and $P(t) = A_1 e^{r_1 t} + A_2 e^{r_2 t} - c/w$.

2. If $(u/v)^2 = 4(w/v)$, r_1, r_2 will be *repeated real roots*. Thus, (20.66) reduces to $-(u/v)/2$ or $-(u/2v)$. Then from (20.17), $P(t) = A_1 e^{-(u/2v)t} + A_2 t e^{-(u/2v)t} - c/w$.

3. If $(u/v)^2 < 4(w/v)$, r_1, r_2 will be *complex roots* and from (20.26), $P(t) = e^{gt}(B_1 \cos ht + B_2 \sin ht) - c/w$, where from (20.19), $g = -u/2v$ and $h = \frac{1}{2}\sqrt{4(w/v) - (u/v)^2}$.

Specification of w, u, v depends on expectations. If people are bothered by inflationary psychology and expect prices to keep rising, u_2 in (20.64) will be positive; if they expect prices to ultimately fall and hold off buying because of that expectation, u_2 will be negative, and so forth.

20.37. In a model similar to Samuelson's interaction model between the multiplier and the accelerator, assume

$$Y_t = C_t + I_t + G_t \tag{20.67}$$

$$C_t = C_0 + cY_{t-1} \tag{20.68}$$

$$I_t = I_0 + w(C_t - C_{t-1}) \tag{20.69}$$

where $0 < c < 1$, $w > 0$, and $G_t = G_0$.   (a) Find the time path $Y(t)$ of national income and   (b) comment on the stability conditions.

(a)   Substituting (20.68) in (20.69),

$$I_t = I_0 + cw(Y_{t-1} - Y_{t-2}) \tag{20.70}$$

Substituting $G_t = G_0$, (20.70), and (20.68) into (20.67), and then rearranging to conform with (20.10),

$$Y_t = C_0 + cY_{t-1} + I_0 + cw(Y_{t-1} - Y_{t-2}) + G_0$$

$$Y_t - c(1+w)Y_{t-1} + cwY_{t-2} = C_0 + I_0 + G_0 \tag{20.71}$$

Using (20.11) for the particular solution,

$$Y_p = \frac{C_0 + I_0 + G_0}{1 - c(1+w) + cw} = \frac{C_0 + I_0 + G_0}{1 - c}$$

which is the intertemporal equilibrium level of income $\bar{Y}$.   Using (20.4) to find the characteristic roots for the complementary function,

$$r_1, r_2 = \frac{c(1+w) \pm \sqrt{[-c(1+w)]^2 - 4cw}}{2} \tag{20.72}$$

which can assume three different types of solutions depending on the values assigned to c and w:

1.   If $c^2(1+w)^2 > 4cw$, or equivalently, if $c(1+w)^2 > 4w$, r_1, r_2 will be *distinct real roots* solvable in terms of (20.72) and,

$$Y(t) = A_1 r_1^t + A_2 r_2^t + \frac{C_0 + I_0 + G_0}{1 - c}$$

2.   If $c(1+w)^2 = 4w$, r_1, r_2 will be *repeated real roots*, and from (20.72) and (20.18),

$$Y(t) = A_1 [\tfrac{1}{2}c(1+w)]^t + A_2 t [\tfrac{1}{2}c(1+w)]^t + \frac{C_0 + I_0 + G_0}{1 - c}$$

3.   If $c(1+w)^2 < 4w$, r_1, r_2 will be *complex roots*; from (20.27),

$$Y(t) = k^t (B_1 \cos t\theta + B_2 \sin t\theta) + \frac{C_0 + I_0 + G_0}{1 - c}$$

where from (20.60), $k = \sqrt{cw}$,   and from (20.61) θ must be such that

$$\sin \theta = \frac{h}{k} \qquad \cos \theta = \frac{g}{k}$$

where from (20.19), $g = \tfrac{1}{2}c(1+w)$ and $h = \tfrac{1}{2}\sqrt{4cw - c^2(1+w)^2}$.

(b)   For stability in the model under all possible initial conditions, the necessary and sufficient conditions are   (1) $c < 1$ and (2) $cw < 1$.   Since $c = \text{MPC}$ with respect to the previous year's income, c will be less than 1; for $cw < 1$,   the product of the MPC and the marginal capital-output ratio must also be less than 1.   If the characteristic roots are conjugate complex, the time path will oscillate.

Four-Place Common Logarithms

N	0	1	2	3	4	5	6	7	8	9
10	0000	0043	0086	0128	0170	0212	0253	0294	0334	0374
11	0414	0453	0492	0531	0569	0607	0645	0682	0719	0755
12	0792	0828	0864	0899	0934	0969	1004	1038	1072	1106
13	1139	1173	1206	1239	1271	1303	1335	1367	1399	1430
14	1461	1492	1523	1553	1584	1614	1644	1673	1703	1732
15	1761	1790	1818	1847	1875	1903	1931	1959	1987	2014
16	2041	2068	2095	2122	2148	2175	2201	2227	2253	2279
17	2304	2330	2355	2380	2405	2430	2455	2480	2504	2529
18	2553	2577	2601	2625	2648	2672	2695	2718	2742	2765
19	2788	2810	2833	2856	2878	2900	2923	2945	2967	2989
20	3010	3032	3054	3075	3096	3118	3139	3160	3181	3201
21	3222	3243	3263	3284	3304	3324	3345	3365	3385	3404
22	3424	3444	3464	3483	3502	3522	3541	3560	3579	3598
23	3617	3636	3655	3674	3692	3711	3729	3747	3766	3784
24	3802	3820	3838	3856	3874	3892	3909	3927	3945	3962
25	3979	3997	4014	4031	4048	4065	4082	4099	4116	4133
26	4150	4166	4183	4200	4216	4232	4249	4265	4281	4298
27	4314	4330	4346	4362	4378	4393	4409	4425	4440	4456
28	4472	4487	4502	4518	4533	4548	4564	4579	4594	4609
29	4624	4639	4654	4669	4683	4698	4713	4728	4742	4757
30	4771	4786	4800	4814	4829	4843	4857	4871	4886	4900
31	4914	4928	4942	4955	4969	4983	4997	5011	5024	5038
32	5051	5065	5079	5092	5105	5119	5132	5145	5159	5172
33	5185	5198	5211	5224	5237	5250	5263	5276	5289	5302
34	5315	5328	5340	5353	5366	5378	5391	5403	5416	5428
35	5441	5453	5465	5478	5490	5502	5514	5527	5539	5551
36	5563	5575	5587	5599	5611	5623	5635	5647	5658	5670
37	5682	5694	5705	5717	5729	5740	5752	5763	5775	5786
38	5798	5809	5821	5832	5843	5855	5866	5877	5888	5899
39	5911	5922	5933	5944	5955	5966	5977	5988	5999	6010
40	6021	6031	6042	6053	6064	6075	6085	6096	6107	6117
41	6128	6138	6149	6160	6170	6180	6191	6201	6212	6222
42	6232	6243	6253	6263	6274	6284	6294	6304	6314	6325
43	6335	6345	6355	6365	6375	6385	6395	6405	6415	6425
44	6435	6444	6454	6464	6474	6484	6493	6503	6513	6522
45	6532	6542	6551	6561	6571	6580	6590	6599	6609	6618
46	6628	6637	6646	6656	6665	6675	6684	6693	6702	6712
47	6721	6730	6739	6749	6758	6767	6776	6785	6794	6803
48	6812	6821	6830	6839	6848	6857	6866	6875	6884	6893
49	6902	6911	6920	6928	6937	6946	6955	6964	6972	6981
50	6990	6998	7007	7016	7024	7033	7042	7050	7059	7067
51	7076	7084	7093	7101	7110	7118	7126	7135	7143	7152
52	7160	7168	7177	7185	7193	7202	7210	7218	7226	7235
53	7243	7251	7259	7267	7275	7284	7292	7300	7308	7316
54	7324	7332	7340	7348	7356	7364	7372	7380	7388	7396
N	0	1	2	3	4	5	6	7	8	9

From Murray R. Spiegel, *Mathematical Handbook of Formulas and Tables*, Schaum's Outline Series, McGraw-Hill Book Co., 1968.

Four-Place Common Logarithms (Continued)

N	0	1	2	3	4	5	6	7	8	9
55	7404	7412	7419	7427	7435	7443	7451	7459	7466	7474
56	7482	7490	7497	7505	7513	7520	7528	7536	7543	7551
57	7559	7566	7574	7582	7589	7597	7604	7612	7619	7627
58	7634	7642	7649	7657	7664	7672	7679	7686	7694	7701
59	7709	7716	7723	7731	7738	7745	7752	7760	7767	7774
60	7782	7789	7796	7803	7810	7818	7825	7832	7839	7846
61	7853	7860	7868	7875	7882	7889	7896	7903	7910	7917
62	7924	7931	7938	7945	7952	7959	7966	7973	7980	7987
63	7993	8000	8007	8014	8021	8028	8035	8041	8048	8055
64	8062	8069	8075	8082	8089	8096	8102	8109	8116	8122
65	8129	8136	8142	8149	8156	8162	8169	8176	8182	8189
66	8195	8202	8209	8215	8222	8228	8235	8241	8248	8254
67	8261	8267	8274	8280	8287	8293	8299	8306	8312	8319
68	8325	8331	8338	8344	8351	8357	8363	8370	8376	8382
69	8388	8395	8401	8407	8414	8420	8426	8432	8439	8445
70	8451	8457	8463	8470	8476	8482	8488	8494	8500	8506
71	8513	8519	8525	8531	8537	8543	8549	8555	8561	8567
72	8573	8579	8585	8591	8597	8603	8609	8615	8621	8627
73	8633	8639	8645	8651	8657	8663	8669	8675	8681	8686
74	8692	8698	8704	8710	8716	8722	8727	8733	8739	8745
75	8751	8756	8762	8768	8774	8779	8785	8791	8797	8802
76	8808	8814	8820	8825	8831	8837	8842	8848	8854	8859
77	8865	8871	8876	8882	8887	8893	8899	8904	8910	8915
78	8921	8927	8932	8938	8943	8949	8954	8960	8965	8971
79	8976	8982	8987	8993	8998	9004	9009	9015	9020	9025
80	9031	9036	9042	9047	9053	9058	9063	9069	9074	9079
81	9085	9090	9096	9101	9106	9112	9117	9122	9128	9133
82	9138	9143	9149	9154	9159	9165	9170	9175	9180	9186
83	9191	9196	9201	9206	9212	9217	9222	9227	9232	9238
84	9243	9248	9253	9258	9263	9269	9274	9279	9284	9289
85	9294	9299	9304	9309	9315	9320	9325	9330	9335	9340
86	9345	9350	9355	9360	9365	9370	9375	9380	9385	9390
87	9395	9400	9405	9410	9415	9420	9425	9430	9435	9440
88	9445	9450	9455	9460	9465	9469	9474	9479	9484	9489
89	9494	9499	9504	9509	9513	9518	9523	9528	9533	9538
90	9542	9547	9552	9557	9562	9566	9571	9576	9581	9586
91	9590	9595	9600	9605	9609	9614	9619	9624	9628	9633
92	9638	9643	9647	9652	9657	9661	9666	9671	9675	9680
93	9685	9689	9694	9699	9703	9708	9713	9717	9722	9727
94	9731	9736	9741	9745	9750	9754	9759	9763	9768	9773
95	9777	9782	9786	9791	9795	9800	9805	9809	9814	9818
96	9823	9827	9832	9836	9841	9845	9850	9854	9859	9863
97	9868	9872	9877	9881	9886	9890	9894	9899	9903	9908
98	9912	9917	9921	9926	9930	9934	9939	9943	9948	9952
99	9956	9961	9965	9969	9974	9978	9983	9987	9991	9996
N	0	1	2	3	4	5	6	7	8	9

Appendix II

Natural or Naperian Logarithms
0.000–0.499

N	0	1	2	3	4	5	6	7	8	9
0.00	−∞	−6 .90776	−6 .21461	−5 .80914	−5 .52146	−5 .29832	−5 .11600	−4 .96185	−4 .82831	−4 .71053
.01	−4.60517	.50986	.42285	.34281	.26870	.19971	.13517	.07454	.01738	*.96332
.02	−3.91202	.86323	.81671	.77226	.72970	.68888	.64966	.61192	.57555	.54046
.03	.50656	.47377	.44202	.41125	.38139	.35241	.32424	.29684	.27017	.24419
.04	.21888	.19418	.17009	.14656	.12357	.10109	.07911	.05761	.03655	.01593
.05	−2.99573	.97593	.95651	.93746	.91877	.90042	.88240	.86470	.84731	.83022
.06	.81341	.79688	.78062	.76462	.74887	.73337	.71810	.70306	.68825	.67365
.07	.65926	.64508	.63109	.61730	.60369	.59027	.57702	.56395	.55105	.53831
.08	.52573	.51331	.50104	.48891	.47694	.46510	.45341	.44185	.43042	.41912
.09	.40795	.39690	.38597	.37516	.36446	.35388	.34341	.33304	.32279	.31264
0.10	−2.30259	.29263	.28278	.27303	.26336	.25379	.24432	.23493	.22562	.21641
.11	.20727	.19823	.18926	.18037	.17156	.16282	.15417	.14558	.13707	.12863
.12	.12026	.11196	.10373	.09557	.08747	.07944	.07147	.06357	.05573	.04794
.13	.04022	.03256	.02495	.01741	.00992	.00248	*.99510	*.98777	*.98050	*.97328
.14	−1.96611	.95900	.95193	.94491	.93794	.93102	.92415	.91732	.91054	.90381
.15	.89712	.89048	.88387	.87732	.87080	.86433	.85790	.85151	.84516	.83885
.16	.83258	.82635	.82016	.81401	.80789	.80181	.79577	.78976	.78379	.77786
.17	.77196	.76609	.76026	.75446	.74870	.74297	.73727	.73161	.72597	.72037
.18	.71480	.70926	.70375	.69827	.69282	.68740	.68201	.67665	.67131	.66601
.19	.66073	.65548	.65026	.64507	.63990	.63476	.62964	.62455	.61949	.61445
0.20	−1.60944	.60445	.59949	.59455	.58964	.58475	.57988	.57504	.57022	.56542
.21	.56065	.55590	.55117	.54646	.54178	.53712	.53248	.52786	.52326	.51868
.22	.51413	.50959	.50508	.50058	.49611	.49165	.48722	.48281	.47841	.47403
.23	.46968	.46534	.46102	.45672	.45243	.44817	.44392	.43970	.43548	.43129
.24	.42712	.42296	.41882	.41469	.41059	.40650	.40242	.39837	.39433	.39030
.25	.38629	.38230	.37833	.37437	.37042	.36649	.36258	.35868	.35480	.35093
.26	.34707	.34323	.33941	.33560	.33181	.32803	.32426	.32051	.31677	.31304
.27	.30933	.30564	.30195	.29828	.29463	.29098	.28735	.28374	.28013	.27654
.28	.27297	.26940	.26585	.26231	.25878	.25527	.25176	.24827	.24479	.24133
.29	.23787	.23443	.23100	.22758	.22418	.22078	.21740	.21402	.21066	.20731
0.30	−1.20397	.20065	.19733	.19402	.19073	.18744	.18417	.18091	.17766	.17441
.31	.17118	.16796	.16475	.16155	.15836	.15518	.15201	.14885	.14570	.14256
.32	.13943	.13631	.13320	.13010	.12701	.12393	.12086	.11780	.11474	.11170
.33	.10866	.10564	.10262	.09961	.09661	.09362	.09064	.08767	.08471	.08176
.34	.07881	.07587	.07294	.07002	.06711	.06421	.06132	.05843	.05555	.05268
.35	−1.04982	.04697	.04412	.04129	.03846	.03564	.03282	.03002	.02722	.02443
.36	.02165	.01888	.01611	.01335	.01060	.00786	.00512	.00239	*.99967	*.99696
.37	−0.99425	.99155	.98886	.98618	.98350	.98083	.97817	.97551	.97286	.97022
.38	.96758	.96496	.96233	.95972	.95711	.95451	.95192	.94933	.94675	.94418
.39	.94161	.93905	.93649	.93395	.93140	.92887	.92634	.92382	.92130	.91879
0.40	−0.91629	.91379	.91130	.90882	.90634	.90387	.90140	.89894	.89649	.89404
.41	.89160	.88916	.88673	.88431	.88189	.87948	.87707	.87467	.87227	.86988
.42	.86750	.86512	.86275	.86038	.85802	.85567	.85332	.85097	.84863	.84630
.43	.84397	.84165	.83933	.83702	.83471	.83241	.83011	.82782	.82554	.82326
.44	.82098	.81871	.81645	.81419	.81193	.80968	.80744	.80520	.80296	.80073
.45	.79851	.79629	.79407	.79186	.78966	.78746	.78526	.78307	.78089	.77871
.46	.77653	.77436	.77219	.77003	.76787	.76572	.76357	.76143	.75929	.75715
.47	.75502	.75290	.75078	.74866	.74655	.74444	.74234	.74024	.73814	.73605
.48	.73397	.73189	.72981	.72774	.72567	.72361	.72155	.71949	.71744	.71539
.49	.71335	.71131	.70928	.70725	.70522	.70320	.70118	.69917	.69716	.69515
N	0	1	2	3	4	5	6	7	8	9

Reprinted with permission from William H. Berger, *Standard Mathematical Tables*, 25th ed., © 1978. The Chemical Rubber Co., CRC Press, Inc.

Natural or Naperian Logarithms (Continued)
0.500–0.999

N	0	1	2	3	4	5	6	7	8	9
0.50	−0.69315	.69115	.68916	.68717	.68518	.68320	.68122	.67924	.67727	.67531
.51	.67334	.67139	.66943	.66748	.66553	.66359	.66165	.65971	.65778	.65585
.52	.65393	.65201	.65009	.64817	.64626	.64436	.64245	.64055	.63866	.63677
.53	.63488	.63299	.63111	.62923	.62736	.62549	.62362	.62176	.61990	.61804
.54	.61619	.61434	.61249	.61065	.60881	.60697	.60514	.60331	.60148	.59966
.55	.59784	.59602	.59421	.59240	.59059	.58879	.58699	.58519	.58340	.58161
.56	.57982	.57803	.57625	.57448	.57270	.57093	.56916	.56740	.56563	.56387
.57	.56212	.56037	.55862	.55687	.55513	.55339	.55165	.54991	.54818	.54645
.58	.54473	.54300	.54128	.53957	.53785	.53614	.53444	.53273	.53103	.52933
.59	.52763	.52594	.52425	.52256	.52088	.51919	.51751	.51584	.51416	.51249
0.60	−0.51083	.50916	.50750	.50584	.50418	.50253	.50088	.49923	.49758	.49594
.61	.49430	.49266	.49102	.48939	.48776	.48613	.48451	.48289	.48127	.47965
.62	.47804	.47642	.47482	.47321	.47160	.47000	.46840	.46681	.46522	.46362
.63	.46204	.46045	.45887	.45728	.45571	.45413	.45256	.45099	.44942	.44785
.64	.44629	.44473	.44317	.44161	.44006	.43850	.43696	.43541	.43386	.43232
.65	.43078	.42925	.42771	.42618	.42465	.42312	.42159	.42007	.41855	.41703
.66	.41552	.41400	.41249	.41098	.40947	.40797	.40647	.40497	.40347	.40197
.67	.40048	.39899	.39750	.39601	.39453	.39304	.39156	.39008	.38861	.38713
.68	.38566	.38419	.38273	.38126	.37980	.37834	.37688	.37542	.37397	.37251
.69	.37106	.36962	.36817	.36673	.36528	.36384	.36241	.36097	.35954	.35810
0.70	−0.35667	.35525	.35382	.35240	.35098	.34956	.34814	.34672	.34531	.34390
.71	.34249	.34108	.33968	.33827	.33687	.33547	.33408	.33268	.33129	.32989
.72	.32850	.32712	.32573	.32435	.32296	.32158	.32021	.31883	.31745	.31608
.73	.31471	.31334	.31197	.31061	.30925	.30788	.30653	.30517	.30381	.30246
.74	.30111	.29975	.29841	.29706	.29571	.29437	.29303	.29169	.29035	.28902
.75	.28768	.28635	.28502	.28369	.28236	.28104	.27971	.27839	.27707	.27575
.76	.27444	.27312	.27181	.27050	.26919	.26788	.26657	.26527	.26397	.26266
.77	.26136	.26007	.25877	.25748	.25618	.25489	.25360	.25231	.25103	.24974
.78	.24846	.24718	.24590	.24462	.24335	.24207	.24080	.23953	.23826	.23699
.79	.23572	.23446	.23319	.23193	.23067	.22941	.22816	.22690	.22565	.22439
0.80	−0.22314	.22189	.22065	.21940	.21816	.21691	.21567	.21433	.21319	.21196
.81	.21072	.20949	.20825	.20702	.20579	.20457	.20334	.20212	.20089	.19967
.82	.19845	.19723	.19601	.19480	.19358	.19237	.19116	.18995	.18874	.18754
.83	.18633	.18513	.18392	.18272	.18152	.18032	.17913	.17793	.17674	.17554
.84	.17435	.17316	.17198	.17079	.16960	.16842	.16724	.16605	.16487	.16370
.85	−0.16252	.16134	.16017	.15900	.15782	.15665	.15548	.15432	.15315	.15199
.86	.15082	.14966	.14850	.14734	.14618	.14503	.14387	.14272	.14156	.14041
.87	.13926	.13811	.13697	.13582	.13467	.13353	.13239	.13125	.13011	.12897
.88	.12783	.12670	.12556	.12443	.12330	.12217	.12104	.11991	.11878	.11766
.89	.11653	.11541	.11429	.11317	.11205	.11093	.10981	.10870	.10759	.10647
0.90	−0.10536	.10425	.10314	.10203	.10093	.09982	.09872	.09761	.09651	.09541
.91	.09431	.09321	.09212	.09102	.08992	.08883	.08774	.08665	.08556	.08447
.92	.08338	.08230	.08121	.08013	.07904	.07796	.07688	.07580	.07472	.07365
.93	.07257	.07150	.07042	.06935	.06828	.06721	.06614	.06507	.06401	.06294
.94	.06188	.06081	.05975	.05869	.05763	.05657	.05551	.05446	.05340	.05235
.95	.05129	.05024	.04919	.04814	.04709	.04604	.04500	.04395	.04291	.04186
.96	.04082	.03978	.03874	.03770	.03666	.03563	.03459	.03356	.03252	.03149
.97	.03046	.02943	.02840	.02737	.02634	.02532	.02429	.02327	.02225	.02122
.98	.02020	.01918	.01816	.01715	.01613	.01511	.01410	.01309	.01207	.01106
.99	.01005	.00904	.00803	.00702	.00602	.00501	.00401	.00300	.00200	.00100
N	0	1	2	3	4	5	6	7	8	9

Natural or Naperian Logarithms (Continued)
1.00–4.99

N	0	1	2	3	4	5	6	7	8	9
1.0	0.00000	.00995	.01980	.02956	.03922	.04879	.05827	.06766	.07696	.08618
.1	.09531	.10436	.11333	.12222	.13103	.13976	.14842	.15700	.16551	.17395
.2	.18232	.19062	.19885	.20701	.21511	.22314	.23111	.23902	.24686	.25464
.3	.26236	.27003	.27763	.28518	.29267	.30010	.30748	.31481	.32208	.32930
.4	.33647	.34359	.35066	.35767	.36464	.37156	.37844	.38526	.39204	.39878
.5	.40547	.41211	.41871	.42527	.43178	.43825	.44469	.45108	.45742	.46373
.6	.47000	.47623	.48243	.48858	.49470	.50078	.50682	.51282	.51879	.52473
.7	.53063	.53649	.54232	.54812	.55389	.55962	.56531	.57098	.57661	.58222
.8	.58779	.59333	.59884	.60432	.60977	.61519	.62058	.62594	.63127	.63658
.9	.64185	.64710	.65233	.65752	.66269	.66783	.67294	.67803	.68310	.68813
2.0	0.69315	.69813	.70310	.70804	.71295	.71784	.72271	.72755	.73237	.73716
.1	.74194	.74669	.75142	.75612	.76081	.76547	.77011	.77473	.77932	.78390
.2	.78846	.79299	.79751	.80200	.80648	.81093	.81536	.81978	.82418	.82855
.3	.83291	.83725	.84157	.84587	.85015	.85442	.85866	.86289	.86710	.87129
.4	.87547	.87963	.88377	.88789	.89200	.89609	.90016	.90422	.90826	.91228
.5	.91629	.92028	.92426	.92822	.93216	.93609	.94001	.94391	.94779	.95166
.6	.95551	.95935	.96317	.96698	.97078	.97456	.97833	.98208	.98582	.98954
.7	.99325	.99695	*.00063	*.00430	*.00796	*.01160	*.01523	*.01885	*.02245	*.02604
.8	1.02962	.03318	.03674	.04028	.04380	.04732	.05082	.05431	.05779	.06126
.9	.06471	.06815	.07158	.07500	.07841	.08181	.08519	.08856	.09192	.09527
3.0	1.09861	.10194	.10526	.10856	.11186	.11514	.11841	.12168	.12493	.12817
.1	.13140	.13462	.13783	.14103	.14422	.14740	.15057	.15373	.15688	.16002
.2	.16315	.16627	.16938	.17248	.17557	.17865	.18173	.18479	.18784	.19089
.3	.19392	.19695	.19996	.20297	.20597	.20896	.21194	.21491	.21788	.22083
.4	.22378	.22671	.22964	.23256	.23547	.23837	.24127	.24415	.24703	.24990
.5	.25276	.25562	.25846	.26130	.26413	.26695	.26976	.27257	.27536	.27815
.6	.28093	.28371	.28647	.28923	.29198	.29473	.29746	.30019	.30291	.30563
.7	.30833	.31103	.31372	.31641	.31909	.32176	.32442	.32708	.32972	.33237
.8	.33500	.33763	.34025	.34286	.34547	.34807	.35067	.35325	.35584	.35841
.9	.36098	.36354	.36609	.36864	.37118	.37372	.37624	.37877	.38128	.38379
4.0	1.38629	.38879	.39128	.39377	.39624	.39872	.40118	.40364	.40610	.40854
.1	.41099	.41342	.41585	.41828	.42070	.42311	.42552	.42792	.43031	.43270
.2	.43508	.43746	.43984	.44220	.44456	.44692	.44927	.45161	.45395	.45629
.3	.45862	.46094	.46326	.46557	.46787	.47018	.47247	.47476	.47705	.47933
.4	.48160	.48387	.48614	.48840	.49065	.49290	.49515	.49739	.49962	.50185
.5	.50408	.50630	.50851	.51072	.51293	.51513	.51732	.51951	.52170	.52388
.6	.52606	.52823	.53039	.53256	.53471	.53687	.53902	.54116	.54330	.54543
.7	.54756	.54969	.55181	.55393	.55604	.55814	.56025	.56235	.56444	.56653
.8	.56862	.57070	.57277	.57485	.57691	.57898	.58104	.58309	.58515	.58719
.9	.58924	.59127	.59331	.59534	.59737	.59939	.60141	.60342	.60543	.60744
N	0	1	2	3	4	5	6	7	8	9

Natural or Naperian Logarithms (Continued)

5.00–9.99

N	0	1	2	3	4	5	6	7	8	9
5.0	1.60944	.61144	.61343	.61542	.61741	.61939	.62137	.62334	.62531	.62728
.1	.62924	.63120	.63315	.63511	.63705	.63900	.64094	.64287	.64481	.64673
.2	.64866	.65058	.65250	.65441	.65632	.65823	.66013	.66203	.66393	.66582
.3	.66771	.66959	.67147	.67335	.67523	.67710	.67896	.68083	.68269	.68455
.4	.68640	.68825	.69010	.69194	.69378	.69562	.69745	.69928	.70111	.70293
.5	.70475	.70656	.70838	.71019	.71199	.71380	.71560	.71740	.71919	.72098
.6	.72277	.72455	.72633	.72811	.72988	.73166	.73342	.73519	.73695	.73871
.7	.74047	.74222	.74397	.74572	.74746	.74920	.75094	.75267	.75440	.75613
.8	.75786	.75958	.76130	.76302	.76473	.76644	.76815	.76985	.77156	.77326
.9	.77495	.77665	.77834	.78002	.78171	.78339	.78507	.78675	.78842	.79009
6.0	1.79176	.79342	.79509	.79675	.79840	.80006	.80171	.80336	.80500	.80665
.1	.80829	.80993	.81156	.81319	.81482	.81645	.81808	.81970	.82132	.82294
.2	.82455	.82616	.82777	.82938	.83098	.83258	.83418	.83578	.83737	.83896
.3	.84055	.84214	.84372	.84530	.84688	.84845	.85003	.85160	.85317	.85473
.4	.85630	.85786	.85942	.86097	.86253	.86408	.86563	.86718	.86872	.87026
.5	.87180	.87334	.87487	.87641	.87794	.87947	.88099	.88251	.88403	.88555
.6	.88707	.88858	.89010	.89160	.89311	.89462	.89612	.89762	.89912	.90061
.7	.90211	.90360	.90509	.90658	.90806	.90954	.91102	.91250	.91398	.91545
.8	.91692	.91839	.91986	.92132	.92279	.92425	.92571	.92716	.92862	.93007
.9	.93152	.93297	.93442	.93586	.93730	.93874	.94018	.94162	.94305	.94448
7.0	1.94591	.94734	.94876	.95019	.95161	.95303	.95445	.95586	.95727	.95869
.1	.96009	.96150	.96291	.96431	.96571	.96711	.96851	.96991	.97130	.97269
.2	.97408	.97547	.97685	.97824	.97962	.98100	.98238	.98376	.98513	.98650
.3	.98787	.98924	.99061	.99198	.99334	.99470	.99606	.99742	.99877	*.00013
.4	2.00148	.00283	.00418	.00553	.00687	.00821	.00956	.01089	.01223	.01357
.5	.01490	.01624	.01757	.01890	.02022	.02155	.02287	.02419	.02551	.02683
.6	.02815	.02946	.03078	.03209	.03340	.03471	.03601	.03732	.03862	.03992
.7	.04122	.04252	.04381	.04511	.04640	.04769	.04898	.05027	.05156	.05284
.8	.05412	.05540	.05668	.05796	.05924	.06051	.06179	.06306	.06433	.06560
.9	.06686	.06813	.06939	.07065	.07191	.07317	.07443	.07568	.07694	.07819
8.0	2.07944	.08069	.08194	.08318	.08443	.08567	.08691	.08815	.08939	.09063
.1	.09186	.09310	.09433	.09556	.09679	.09802	.09924	.10047	.10169	.10291
.2	.10413	.10535	.10657	.10779	.10900	.11021	.11142	.11263	.11384	.11505
.3	.11626	.11746	.11866	.11986	.12106	.12226	.12346	.12465	.12585	.12704
.4	.12823	.12942	.13061	.13180	.13298	.13417	.13535	.13653	.13771	.13889
.5	.14007	.14124	.14242	.14359	.14476	.14593	.14710	.14827	.14943	.15060
.6	.15176	.15292	.15409	.15524	.15640	.15756	.15871	.15987	.16102	.16217
.7	.16332	.16447	.16562	.16677	.16791	.16905	.17020	.17134	.17248	.17361
.8	.17475	.17589	.17702	.17816	.17929	.18042	.18155	.18267	.18380	.18493
.9	.18605	.18717	.18830	.18942	.19054	.19165	.19277	.19389	.19500	.19611
9.0	2.19722	.19834	.19944	.20055	.20166	.20276	.20387	.20497	.20607	.20717
.1	.20827	.20937	.21047	.21157	.21266	.21375	.21485	.21594	.21703	.21812
.2	.21920	.22029	.22138	.22246	.22354	.22462	.22570	.22678	.22786	.22894
.3	.23001	.23109	.23216	.23324	.23431	.23538	.23645	.23751	.23858	.23965
.4	.24071	.24177	.24284	.24390	.24496	.24601	.24707	.24813	.24918	.25024
.5	.25129	.25234	.25339	.25444	.25549	.25654	.25759	.25863	.25968	.26072
.6	.26176	.26280	.26384	.26488	.26592	.26696	.26799	.26903	.27006	.27109
.7	.27213	.27316	.27419	.27521	.27624	.27727	.27829	.27932	.28034	.28136
.8	.28238	.28340	.28442	.28544	.28646	.28747	.28849	.28950	.29051	.29152
.9	.29253	.29354	.29455	.29556	.29657	.29757	.29858	.29958	.30058	.30158
N	0	1	2	3	4	5	6	7	8	9

Natural or Naperian Logarithms (Continued)
0–499

N	0	1	2	3	4	5	6	7	8	9
0	−∞	0.0000	0.69315	1.09861	.38629	.60944	.79176	.94591	*.07944	*.19722
1	2.30259	.39790	.48491	.56495	.63906	.70805	.77259	.83321	.89037	.94444
2	.99573	*.04452	*.09104	*.13549	*.17805	*.21888	*.25810	*.29584	*.33220	*.36730
3	3.40120	.43399	.46574	.49651	.52636	.55535	.58352	.61092	.63759	.66356
4	.68888	.71357	.73767	.76120	.78419	.80666	.82864	.85015	.87120	.89182
5	.91202	.93183	.95124	.97029	.98898	*.00733	*02535	*.04305	*.06044	*.07754
6	4.09434	.11087	.12713	.14313	.15888	.17439	.18965	.20469	.21951	.23411
7	.24850	.26268	.27667	.29046	.30407	.31749	.33073	.34381	.35671	.36945
8	.38203	.39445	.40672	.41884	.43082	.44265	.45435	.46591	.47734	.48864
9	.49981	.51086	.52179	.53260	.54329	.55388	.56435	.57471	.58497	.59512
10	4.60517	.61512	.62497	.63473	.64439	.65396	.66344	.67283	.68213	.69135
11	.70048	.70953	.71850	.72739	.73620	.74493	.75359	.76217	.77068	.77912
12	.78749	.79579	.80402	.81218	.82028	.82831	.83628	.84419	.85203	.85981
13	.86753	.87520	.88280	.89035	.89784	.90527	.91265	.91998	.92725	.93447
14	.94164	.94876	.95583	.96284	.96981	.97673	.98361	.99043	.99721	*.00395
15	5.01064	.01728	.02388	.03044	.03695	.04343	.04986	.05625	.06260	.06890
16	.07517	.08140	.08760	.09375	.09987	.10595	.11199	.11799	.12396	.12990
17	.13580	.14166	.14749	.15329	.15906	.16479	.17048	.17615	.18178	.18739
18	.19296	.19850	.20401	.20949	.21494	.22036	.22575	.23111	.23644	.24175
19	.24702	.25227	.25750	.26269	.26786	.27300	.27811	.28320	.28827	.29330
20	5.29832	.30330	.30827	.31321	.31812	.32301	.32788	.33272	.33754	.34233
21	.34711	.35186	.35659	.36129	.36598	.37064	.37528	.37990	.38450	.38907
22	.39363	.39816	.40268	.40717	.41165	.41610	.42053	.42495	.42935	.43372
23	.43808	.44242	.44674	.45104	.45532	.45959	.46383	.46806	.47227	.47646
24	.48064	.48480	.48894	.49306	.49717	.50126	.50533	.50939	.51343	.51745
25	.52146	.52545	.52943	.53339	.53733	.54126	.54518	.54908	.55296	.55683
26	.56068	.56452	.56834	.57215	.57595	.57973	.58350	.58725	.59099	.59471
27	.59842	.60212	.60580	.60947	.61313	.61677	.62040	.62402	.62762	.63121
28	.63479	.63835	.64191	.64545	.64897	.65249	.65599	.65948	.66296	.66643
29	.66988	.67332	.67675	.68017	.68358	.68698	.69036	.69373	.69709	.70044
30	5.70378	.70711	.71043	.71373	.71703	.72031	.72359	.72685	.73010	.73334
31	.73657	.73979	.74300	.74620	.74939	.75257	.75574	.75890	.76205	.76519
32	.76832	.77144	.77455	.77765	.78074	.78383	.78690	.78996	.79301	.79606
33	.79909	.80212	.80513	.80814	.81114	.81413	.81711	.82008	.82305	.82600
34	.82895	.83188	.83481	.83773	.84064	.84354	.84644	.84932	.85220	.85507
35	.85793	.86079	.86363	.86647	.86930	.87212	.87493	.87774	.88053	.88332
36	.88610	.88888	.89164	.89440	.89715	.89990	.90263	.90536	.90808	.91080
37	.91350	.91620	.91889	.92158	.92426	.92693	.92959	.93225	.93489	.93754
38	.94017	.94280	.94542	.94803	.95064	.95324	.95584	.95842	.86101	.96358
39	.96615	.96871	.97126	.97381	.97635	.97889	.98141	.98394	.98645	.98896
40	5.99146	.99396	.99645	.99894	*.00141	*.00389	*.00635	*.00881	*.01127	*.01372
41	6.01616	.01859	.02102	.02345	.02587	.02828	.03069	.03309	.03548	.03787
42	.04025	.04263	.04501	.04737	.04973	.05209	.05444	.05678	.05912	.06146
43	.06379	.06611	.06843	.07074	.07304	.07535	.07764	.07993	.08222	.08450
44	.08677	.08904	.09131	.09357	.09582	.09807	.10032	.10256	.10479	.10702
45	.10925	.11147	.11368	.11589	.11810	.12030	.12249	.12468	.12687	.12905
46	.13123	.13340	.13556	.13773	.13988	.14204	.14419	.14633	.14847	.15060
47	.15273	.15486	.15698	.15910	.16121	.16331	.16542	.16752	.16961	.17170
48	.17379	.17587	.17794	.18002	.18208	.18415	.18621	.18826	.19032	.19236
49	.19441	.19644	.19848	.20051	.20254	.20456	.20658	.20859	.21060	.21261
N	0	1	2	3	4	5	6	7	8	9

Natural or Naperian Logarithms (Continued)
500–999

N	0	1	2	3	4	5	6	7	8	9
50	6.21461	.21661	.21860	.22059	.22258	.22456	.22654	.22851	.23048	.23245
51	.23441	.23637	.23832	.24028	.24222	.24417	.24611	.24804	.24998	.25190
52	.25383	.25575	.25767	.25958	.26149	.26340	.26530	.26720	.26910	.27099
53	.27288	.27476	.27664	.27852	.28040	.28227	.28413	.28600	.28786	.28972
54	.29157	.29342	.29527	.29711	.29895	.30079	.30262	.30445	.30628	.30810
55	.30992	.31173	.31355	.31536	.31716	.31897	.32077	.32257	.32436	.32615
56	.32794	.32972	.33150	.33328	.33505	.33683	.33859	.34036	.34212	.34388
57	.34564	.34739	.34914	.35089	.35263	.35437	.35611	.35784	.35957	.36130
58	.36303	.36475	.36647	.36819	.36990	.37161	.37332	.37502	.37673	.37843
59	.38012	.38182	.38351	.38519	.38688	.38856	.39024	.39192	.39359	.39526
60	6.39693	.39859	.40026	.40192	.40357	.40523	.40688	.40853	.41017	.41182
61	.41346	.41510	.41673	.41836	.41999	.42162	.42325	.42487	.42649	.42811
62	.42972	.43133	.43294	.43455	.43615	.43775	.43935	.44095	.44254	.44413
63	.44572	.44731	.44889	.45047	.45205	.45362	.45520	.45677	.45834	.45990
64	.46147	.46303	.46459	.46614	.46770	.46925	.47080	.47235	.47389	.47543
65	.47697	.47851	.48004	.48158	.48311	.48464	.48616	.48768	.48920	.49072
66	.49224	.49375	.49527	.49677	.49828	.49979	.50129	.50279	.50429	.50578
67	.50728	.50877	.51026	.51175	.51323	.51471	.51619	.51767	.51915	.52062
68	.52209	.52356	.52503	.52649	.52796	.52942	.53088	.53233	.53379	.53524
69	.53669	.53814	.53959	.54103	.54247	.54391	.54535	.54679	.54822	.54965
70	6.55108	.55251	.55393	.55536	.55678	.55820	.55962	.56103	.56244	.56386
71	.56526	.56667	.56808	.56948	.57088	.57228	.57368	.57508	.57647	.57786
72	.57925	.58064	.58203	.58341	.58479	.58617	.58755	.58893	.59030	.59167
73	.59304	.59441	.59578	.59715	.59851	.59987	.60123	.60259	.60394	.60530
74	.60665	.60800	.60935	.61070	.61204	.61338	.61473	.61607	.61740	.61874
75	.62007	.62141	.62274	.62407	.62539	.62672	.62804	.62936	.63068	.63200
76	.63332	.63463	.63595	.63726	.63857	.63988	.64118	.64249	.64379	.64509
77	.64639	.64769	.64898	.65028	.65157	.65286	.65415	.65544	.65673	.65801
78	.65929	.66058	.66185	.66313	.66441	.66568	.66696	.66823	.66950	.67077
79	.67203	.67330	.67456	.67582	.67708	.67834	.67960	.68085	.68211	.68336
80	6.68461	.68586	.68711	.68835	.68960	.69084	.69208	.69332	.69456	.69580
81	.69703	.69827	.69950	.70073	.70196	.70319	.70441	.70564	.70686	.70808
82	.70930	.71052	.71174	.71296	.71417	.71538	.71659	.71780	.71901	.72022
83	.72143	.72263	.72383	.72503	.72623	.72743	.72863	.72982	.73102	.73221
84	.73340	.73459	.73578	.73697	.73815	.73934	.74052	.74170	.74288	.74406
85	.74524	.74641	.74759	.74876	.74993	.75110	.75227	.75344	.75460	.75577
86	.75693	.75809	.75926	.76041	.76157	.76273	.76388	.76504	.76619	.76734
87	.76849	.76964	.77079	.77194	.77308	.77422	.77537	.77651	.77765	.77878
88	.77992	.78106	.78219	.78333	.78446	.78559	.78672	.78784	.78897	.79010
89	.79122	.79234	.79347	.79459	.79571	.79682	.79794	.79906	.80017	.80128
90	6.80239	.80351	.80461	.80572	.80683	.80793	.80904	.81014	.81124	.81235
91	.81344	.81454	.81564	.81674	.81783	.81892	.82002	.82111	.82220	.82329
92	.82437	.82546	.82655	.82763	.82871	.82979	.83087	.83195	.83303	.83411
93	.83518	.83626	.83733	.83841	.83948	.84055	.84162	.84268	.84375	.84482
94	.84588	.84694	.84801	.84907	.85013	.85118	.85224	.85330	.85435	.85541
95	.85646	.85751	.85857	.85961	.86066	.86171	.86276	.86380	.86485	.86589
96	.86693	.86797	.86901	.87005	.87109	.87213	.87316	.87420	.87523	.87626
97	.87730	.87833	.87936	.88038	.88141	.88244	.88346	.88449	.88551	.88653
98	.88755	.88857	.88959	.89061	.89163	.89264	.89366	.89467	.89568	.89669
99	.89770	.89871	.89972	.90073	.90174	.90274	.90375	.90475	.90575	.90675
N	0	1	2	3	4	5	6	7	8	9

Exponential Functions

x	e^x	e^{-x}	x	e^x	e^{-x}
0.00	1.0000	1.000000	0.50	1.6487	0.606531
0.01	1.0101	0.990050	0.51	1.6653	.600496
0.02	1.0202	.980199	0.52	1.6820	.594521
0.03	1.0305	.970446	0.53	1.6989	.588605
0.04	1.0408	.960789	0.54	1.7160	.582748
0.05	1.0513	0.951229	0.55	1.7333	0.576950
0.06	1.0618	.941765	0.56	1.7507	.571209
0.07	1.0725	.932394	0.57	1.7683	.565525
0.08	1.0833	.923116	0.58	1.7860	.559898
0.09	1.0942	.913931	0.59	1.8040	.554327
0.10	1.1052	0.904837	0.60	1.8221	0.548812
0.11	1.1163	.895834	0.61	1.8404	.543351
0.12	1.1275	.886920	0.62	1.8589	.537944
0.13	1.1388	.878095	0.63	1.8776	.532592
0.14	1.1503	.869358	0.64	1.8965	.527292
0.15	1.1618	0.860708	0.65	1.9155	0.522046
0.16	1.1735	.852114	0.66	1.9348	.516851
0.17	1.1853	.843665	0.67	1.9542	.511709
0.18	1.1972	.835270	0.68	1.9739	.506617
0.19	1.2092	.826959	0.69	1.9937	.501576
0.20	1.2214	0.818731	0.70	2.0138	0.496585
0.21	1.2337	.810584	0.71	2.0340	.491644
0.22	1.2461	.802519	0.72	2.0544	.486752
0.23	1.2586	.794534	0.73	2.0751	.481909
0.24	1.2712	.786628	0.74	2.0959	.477114
0.25	1.2840	0.778801	0.75	2.1170	0.472367
0.26	1.2969	.771052	0.76	2.1383	.467666
0.27	1.3100	.763379	0.77	2.1598	.463013
0.28	1.3231	.755784	0.78	2.1815	.458406
0.29	1.3364	.748264	0.79	2.2034	.453845
0.30	1.3499	0.740818	0.80	2.2255	0.449329
0.31	1.3634	.733447	0.81	2.2479	.444858
0.32	1.3771	.726149	0.82	2.2705	.440432
0.33	1.3910	.718924	0.83	2.2933	.436049
0.34	1.4049	.711770	0.84	2.3164	.431711
0.35	1.4191	0.704688	0.85	2.3396	0.427415
0.36	1.4333	.697676	0.86	2.3632	.423162
0.37	1.4477	.690734	0.87	2.3869	.418952
0.38	1.4623	.683861	0.88	2.4109	.414783
0.39	1.4770	.677057	0.89	2.4351	.410656
0.40	1.4918	0.670320	0.90	2.4596	0.406570
0.41	1.5068	.663650	0.91	2.4843	.402524
0.42	1.5220	.657047	0.92	2.5093	.398519
0.43	1.5373	.650509	0.93	2.5345	.394554
0.44	1.5527	.644036	0.94	2.5600	.390628
0.45	1.5683	0.637628	0.95	2.5857	0.386741
0.46	1.5841	.631284	0.96	2.6117	.382893
0.47	1.6000	.625002	0.97	2.6379	.379083
0.48	1.6161	.618783	0.98	2.6645	.375311
0.49	1.6323	.612626	0.99	2.6912	.371577
0.50	1.6487	0.606531	1.00	2.7183	0.367870
x	e^x	e^{-x}	x	e^x	e^{-x}

Reprinted with permission from William H. Berger, *Standard Mathematical Tables*, 25th ed., © 1978. The Chemical Rubber Co., CRC Press, Inc.

APPENDIX III

Exponential Functions (Continued)

x	e^x	e^{-x}	x	e^x	e^{-x}
1.0	2.7183	0.3679	5.5	244.69	0.0041
1.1	3.0042	0.3329	5.6	270.43	0.0037
1.2	3.3201	0.3012	5.7	298.87	0.0033
1.3	3.6693	0.2725	5.8	330.30	0.0030
1.4	4.0552	0.2466	5.9	365.04	0.0027
1.5	4.4817	0.2231	6.0	403.43	0.0025
1.6	4.9530	0.2019	6.1	445.86	0.0022
1.7	5.4739	0.1827	6.2	492.75	0.0020
1.8	6.0496	0.1653	6.3	544.57	0.0018
1.9	6.6859	0.1496	6.4	601.85	0.0017
2.0	7.3891	0.1353	6.5	665.14	0.0015
2.1	8.1662	0.1225	6.6	735.10	0.0014
2.2	9.0250	0.1108	6.7	812.41	0.0012
2.3	9.9742	0.1003	6.8	897.85	0.0011
2.4	11.023	0.0907	6.9	992.27	0.0010
2.5	12.182	0.0821	7.0	1,096.6	0.00091
2.6	13.464	0.0743	7.1	1,212.0	0.00083
2.7	14.880	0.0672	7.2	1,339.4	0.00075
2.8	16.445	0.0608	7.3	1,480.3	0.00068
2.9	18.174	0.0550	7.4	1,636.0	0.00061
3.0	20.086	0.0498	7.5	1,808.0	0.00055
3.1	22.198	0.0450	7.6	1,998.2	0.00050
3.2	24.533	0.0408	7.7	2,208.3	0.00045
3.3	27.113	0.0369	7.8	2,440.6	0.00041
3.4	29.964	0.0334	7.9	2,697.3	0.00037
3.5	33.115	0.0302	8.0	2,981.0	0.00034
3.6	36.598	0.0273	8.1	3,294.5	0.00030
3.7	40.447	0.0248	8.2	3,641.0	0.00027
3.8	44.701	0.0224	8.3	4,023.9	0.00025
3.9	49.402	0.0202	8.4	4,447.1	0.00022
4.0	54.598	0.0183	8.5	4,914.8	0.00020
4.1	60.340	0.0166	8.6	5,431.7	0.00018
4.2	66.686	0.0150	8.7	6,002.9	0.00017
4.3	73.700	0.0136	8.8	6,634.2	0.00015
4.4	81.451	0.0123	8.9	7,332.0	0.00014
4.5	90.017	0.0111	9.0	8,103.1	0.00012
4.6	99.484	0.0101	9.1	8,955.3	0.00011
4.7	109.95	0.0091	9.2	9,897.1	0.00010
4.8	121.51	0.0082	9.3	10,938	0.00009
4.9	134.29	0.0074	9.4	12,088	0.00008
5.0	148.41	0.0067	9.5	13,360	0.00007
5.1	164.02	0.0061	9.6	14,765	0.00007
5.2	181.27	0.0055	9.7	16,318	0.00006
5.3	200.34	0.0050	9.8	18,034	0.00006
5.4	221.41	0.0045	9.9	19,930	0.00005
x	e^x	e^{-x}	x	e^x	e^{-x}

Index

The letter *p* following a page number refers to a Problem.

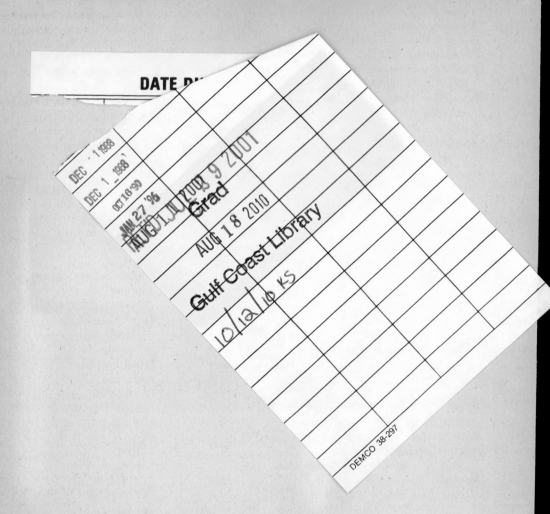
Catalog

If you are interested in a list of SCHAUM'S
OUTLINE SERIES send your name
and address, requesting your free catalog, to:

SCHAUM'S OUTLINE SERIES, Dept. C
McGRAW-HILL BOOK COMPANY
1221 Avenue of Americas
New York, N.Y. 10020